Scared to Death

From BSE to Global Warming – How Scares Are Costing Us the Earth

CHRISTOPHER BOOKER AND
RICHARD NORTH

continuum

Continuum UK
The Tower Building
11 York Road
London SE1 7NX

Continuum US
80 Maiden Lane
Suite 704
New York, NY 10038

www.continuumbooks.com

First published 2007

Reprinted 2007, 2008

British Library Cataloguing-in-Publication Data
A catalogue record for this book is available from the British Library.

ISBN 0–8264–8614–2
978–0–8264–8614–1

Typeset by YHT Ltd, London
Printed and bound by The Cromwell Press, Trowbridge, Wiltshire.

This book is dedicated to all those scientists and campaigners who, amid the madness of our age of 'scares', have kept a sense of proportion and fought for the truth to prevail.

.

Contents

Part Two: General Scares

Acknowledgements

For various forms of help along the way we would like to thank:
Nicholas Booker; Professor John Bridle; Nigel Calder; Laura
Conway-Gordon; Georgina Downs; Dr John Etherington; Jan van
Ginderachter; Dr John Hoskins; John Hoyte; Dr Peter Hunt;
Angela Kelly; the Countess of Mar; Bob Larbey; Linda Lazarides;
Tristan Loraine; Susan Michaelis; Alan Monckton; Michael
O'Connell; Owen Paterson MP; Keith Pulman; Margaret Reichlin;
Liz Sigmund; Paul Smith; Ross Teperek and Lord Tyler.

Much of this book is based on a mass of scientific data and in
many cases it has been important to show the sources of that data.
Where notes refer only to scientific papers or other publications,
they are numbered and have been collected at the end of each
chapter. More general footnotes, marked with a * are shown at the
bottom of the page.

Extract from T.S. Eliot's 'The Hollow Men' reproduced with
kind permission from Faber and Faber.

Athough we are particularly grateful for technical help and
advice given by various experts, the responsibility for everything
which appears in the text is, naturally, our own.

Introduction

In the night, imagining some fear,
how easy is a bush supposed a bear.
                    A Midsummer Night's Dream, Act V, Scene 1

In the past twenty years, Western society in general and Britain in particular has been in the grip of a remarkable and very dangerous psychological phenomenon. Again and again since the 1980s we have seen the rise of some great fear, centred on a mysterious new threat to human health and wellbeing. As a result, we are told, large numbers of people will suffer or die.

Salmonella in eggs; listeria in cheese; BSE in beef; dioxins in poultry; the 'Millennium Bug'; DDT; nitrate in water; vitamin B6; 'Satanic' child abuse; lead in petrol and computers; passive smoking; asbestos; SARS; Asian bird flu – the list is seemingly endless.

Indeed, we are currently in the grip of the greatest such fear of all: that of a warming of the world's climate which, we are officially told, could well put an end to much of civilized life as we know it.

The price we have paid for such panics has been immense; most notably the colossal financial costs arising from the means society has chosen to defend itself from these threats. Yet, again and again, we have seen how it eventually emerged that the fear was largely or wholly misplaced. The threat of disaster came to be seen as having been no more than what we call a 'scare'.

The purpose of this book is to show how there has been a common pattern behind each of these scares – one that has been strikingly consistent.

Each was based on what appeared at the time to be scientific evidence that was widely accepted. Each has inspired obsessive coverage by the media. Each has then provoked a massive response from politicians and officials, imposing new laws that inflicted enormous economic and social damage. But eventually the scientific reasoning on which the panic was based has been found to be fundamentally flawed. Either the scare originated in some genuine threat that had then become wildly exaggerated, or the danger was found never to have existed at all.

By now, however, the damage has been done. The costs have amounted in some cases to billions, even hundreds of billions, of pounds, imposing an enormous hidden drain on the economy. Yet almost all of this money has been spent, it turns out, to no purpose.

What does it say about the psychology of our time that such an extraordinary thing can happen, not just once but again and again?

When we examine the pattern behind these scares we find further elements which each has in common.

- The source of the supposed danger must be something universal, to which almost anyone in the population might be exposed, such as eggs or beef, asbestos or climate change.
- The nature of the danger it poses must be novel, a threat that has never appeared in this form before.
- While the scientific basis for the scare must seem plausible, the threat must also contain a powerful element of uncertainty. It must in some way be ill-defined, maximizing the opportunity for alarmist speculation as to the damage it might cause.
- Society's response to the threat must be disproportionate. It is this more than anything which defines a true 'scare'; that, even where the threat is not wholly imaginary, the response to it is eventually seen to have been out of all proportion to its reality.

In the unfolding of any scare, we then see how two competing forces are at work. On one hand, there are the 'pushers': those whose interest is to promote the scare and to talk it up, such as scientists for whom it provides the promise of winning public attention or further funding. On the other there are the 'blockers': those whose interest is to downplay it, such as an industry it threatens to damage, or a government under pressure to be seen to be taking action.

In each of the scares we examine, we shall see how these two groups line up in opposition to each other. What decides whether or not a scare is going to take off is whether pressure from the 'pushers' can override resistance from the 'blockers'.

Two professions that play a particularly crucial part in the unleashing of a scare are the politicians and the media. Politicians can be either blockers or pushers. Initially, as we saw in the case of BSE in Britain, it may be very much in the interest of a government to downplay or deny a threat. But it may just as well serve a politician's interest to go along with a scare, posing as a champion of the public interest, as we saw with Edwina Currie and salmonella. Certainly the most dangerous moment in any scare comes when the pushers carry the day and the politicians and their officials unleash their regulatory response, since it is then that the real damage is caused.

The media also include both pushers and blockers. On one hand, there are few things most newspaper or television editors relish more than the chance to take part in a full-blown scare drama, devoting acres of newsprint and hours of airtime to the possibility that some sinister threat, which could cause huge numbers of people to die, is on the way. In this their closest collaborators are those scientists for whom the lure of publicity or the need to justify funding have come to overrule their scientific objectivity.

On the other hand, there has invariably been a minority of scientists and commentators, better informed or just more naturally sceptical, who are anxious to point out that those pushing the scare are misreading or distorting the evidence. They try to point out that the whole thing has been exaggerated beyond any relation to the facts.

For the time being, however, it is the scaremongers who generally win the day. There is little the sceptics can do to counter the scare until the hysteria has run its course. And usually, when the evidence emerges to show that this hysteria had been baseless, it attracts very much less notice than the scare itself had done when it was raging at its height.

*   *   *

The story told in this book divides into two parts. Part One, centred chiefly on events in Britain in the 1980s and 1990s, is devoted to food scares, such as those over 'salmonella in eggs', and

BSE. We begin with these examples, not just because it was with them that the modern 'scare phenomenon' became familiar to those of us living in Britain, but also because they provide a useful introduction to the pattern that was to shape the later scares, described in the rest of this book.

Part Two describes the more conspicuous of these other, more general scares, the economic and social costs of which have been far greater than those resulting from the food scares. Some of the most damaging have originated in the USA, culminating in what threatens to become the most destructive scare of them all: the fear of 'global warming'.

As the book's authors, we originally came to recognize the pattern behind this phenomenon through our direct involvement in several of the scares we describe. In 1988, for instance, at the time of the salmonella scare associated with the names of Mrs Currie and Professor Richard Lacey, Dr North was working with Lacey as a food safety consultant. He then became drawn into the centre of the crisis when acting as an expert adviser to the small egg-producers, who were the chief victims of the regulatory onslaught that followed.*

In 1992 our professional collaboration began when, for more than a year, we were able to expose in the *Sunday* and *Daily Telegraph* the most damaging consequence of the food scares of the late 1980s. This was the 'hygiene blitz' inflicted on Britain's food businesses in 1992 and 1993 by environmental health officers (or EHOs). As a former EHO himself, North's experience proved invaluable in showing how this overreaction was a case of a group of officials misusing their power and going seriously off the rails.

North also came to play a role in the aftermath of several other food scares, as when, in Britain's longest-ever food poisoning trial, involving listeria and Lanark Blue cheese, he masterminded the case for the defence, which was eventually victorious. He was later involved in two more significant dramas involving *E. coli* in meat and cheese, which highlighted just how long the damage done by the hysteria over food poisoning continued.

Although we were not so directly involved in the BSE scare, which came to a head in 1996, our extensive coverage of this story

---

* When Richard North was a direct participant in the events described in this book, his part in them will be reported in the third-person.

in the *Sunday Telegraph*, and elsewhere, was marked out by the fact that, almost alone in the media at that time, we questioned the central scientific assumptions on which the scare was based. In this, history was to prove our scepticism right. But the cost of this panic, greater than that of any other food scare, ran into many billions of pounds.

The last food scare described in Part One is that which exploded in Belgium in 1999 over the discovery of 'deadly dioxins' in poultry. Here we were able to report for the first time the inside story behind a bizarre outbreak of mass-hysteria, which inflicted a cost of more than a billion pounds on the Belgian economy, brought down the Belgian government and revolutionized European Union food law.

In the longer second part of the book we widen out the picture, to look at some of the more prominent and damaging scares of recent years. This begins with a prologue giving a brief account of an example everyone can recall: the amazingly costly panic, which broke out in the late 1990s, over the 'Millennium Bug'.

The scene is set for Part Two with four brief case histories, beginning with a chapter on what was arguably the first of all the truly modern scares, centred on the pesticide DDT. The belief that this was not only harmful to wildlife but also caused cancer in human beings was a misconception which, rather than saving life, may have ended up costing the lives of millions.

The next chapter varies the usual pattern slightly by reconstructing a hysteria that spread to Britain from America in the late 1980s and early 1990s, centred on the belief that large numbers of children were being subjected to ritual or 'satanic' sexual abuse. Although several such episodes were widely publicized, such as those in Nottingham, Rochdale and Orkney, the chapter ends with a further example, as harrowing as any, which at the time we were alone in the national press to report.

The pattern is again varied with a chapter looking at how the British government became carried away in the 1990s by the idea that speeding motorists were the main cause of road accidents and that, by concentrating all its efforts on enforcing speed limits, the accident rate would be cut. Based on faulty analysis and distorted statistics, the evidence suggests that this shift of policy ended up costing more lives than it saved.

We then return to the more familiar pattern, with four chapters analysing some of the most influential scares of all, each of which has had a profound and continuing effect on our modern world.

The first, originating in a series of flawed scientific studies in the USA, was that which resulted in the banning of various uses of lead, first in petrol, then in electronic and electrical equipment. The cost of these bans was to run into hundreds of billions of pounds.

A second chapter analyses the manipulation of science that lay behind the campaign to outlaw 'environmental tobacco smoke' or 'passive smoking'.

A third describes the astronomically expensive confusion that arose over the dangers of different forms of asbestos. This was a scare that again originated in flawed science, in both America and Europe. But it was then actively promoted by various interests – such as compensation lawyers and the asbestos removal industry – which stood to profit from perpetuating the confusion, again at immense cost to the general public.

Finally, our narrative comes to a climax with a lengthy analysis of what threatens to become easily the greatest and most costly scare of them all, the worldwide political response to the fear of global warming. Unlike most of the examples described earlier in the book, this one is still in full swing; so all-pervasive that many readers may respond with hostility to the idea that it should be described as a 'scare' at all. But at least it is undeniable that our civilization has only just begun to pay the immense price this fear is imposing on us; from drastic curbs on economic activity to the covering of unspoiled landscapes with forests of giant wind turbines. And even those who are still persuaded by the thesis of man-made global warming may find it salutary to see this story set in the more general perspective of a study of scares in general. Looked at in this light, far too much of the scientific reasoning used to promote the fear of climate change, and the political response to it, becomes uncomfortably familiar.

Before moving on to the epilogue, we include one more chapter that at first might seem oddly out of place in this narrative because it describes an episode that was not a scare. But for this very reason it has shed its own light on the 'scare phenomenon'. This is the story of the damage done to the health of many thousands of people by organophosphorus chemicals, or 'OPs'. Unlike any other example in the book, this was a genuine public health disaster, which was never properly brought to light because such a determined effort was made by politicians and officials to cover it up. They prevented it from becoming a 'scare' because it resulted from a catastrophic failure in the government's own system for protecting the public from the dangers of toxic chemicals.

The book concludes with an epilogue reflecting on some of the wider lessons which can be drawn from the part played by the scare phenomenon in our modern world. The basic psychology behind the scare dynamic, we argue, is nothing new. In history we can see how similar waves of irrationality have frequently swept through societies in the past, from millennial fears of some fast-approaching apocalypse to the terror inspired by a particular social group, such as the great 'witch craze' which held western Europe in its grip through much of the sixteenth and seventeenth centuries.

Viewed in retrospect, few aspects of the behaviour of our ancestors arouse in us more puzzlement than their readiness to fall for such overwrought visions of threat and disaster. How, we ask, could people in past ages have been so credulous? Yet it is a remarkable fact, as this book shows, that no period in history has been more easily prey to such imaginary 'scares' than our own.

What does it tell us about the state of mind of our modern society that it should so continually fall victim to these bouts of collective hysteria? Is there any way we can learn to protect ourselves better from the horrifying damage they bring in their wake?

Certainly a precondition of that must be that we should learn to recognize the scare phenomenon for what it is: a form of human irrationality which almost invariably takes on the same recognizable pattern. We must learn to understand that the scare dynamic obeys certain identifiable rules, and is, therefore, itself susceptible to scientific study. To suggest the foundations for that study is the purpose of this book.

Part One
The Food Scares

Prologue to Part One

In 2005 the world's media became increasingly transfixed by a mysterious new disease – 'Asian bird flu'.

It was a long-familiar fact that certain strains of influenza could be deadly to human beings. The 'Spanish flu' epidemic of 1918–19, for instance, had killed between 20 and 40 million people; more than the death toll of World War One.

Already in Asia, people were dying from what the media had come to call the 'deadly H5N1 strain' of the bird flu virus. In Asian domestic poultry flocks, it was estimated, more than a billion birds might already be infected. And now, it seemed, spread by migrating wild birds, the lethal virus was fanning out across the globe.

This was hailed by the World Health Organization (WHO) as 'the greatest single health challenge' to mankind, greater than HIV/AIDS or malaria. A severe pandemic, it was estimated, could wipe out two percent of the global economy. In Britain, the government's chief medical officer, Sir Liam Donaldson, claimed that such a pandemic was now 'a biological inevitability' – 'no longer a matter of "if" but "when"'.[1]

By the end of the summer of that year, with the approach of the autumn migration season for geese, ducks and swans, media interest rose to fever pitch, particularly when the first cases of H5N1 were found on the edge of Europe. Night after night, television journalists were filmed stumbling in white suits through obscure villages in Turkey and Romania where bird corpses had been found with H5N1 confirmed as the cause of death.

On 30 September David Nabarro, the senior official in charge of co-ordinating the WHO's worldwide response to bird flu, hit the headlines by warning that a pandemic could now occur at any time, and that the number of resulting deaths could be anything up to '150 million people'. 'It's like a combination of global warming and HIV/Aids,' he told the BBC. Although a WHO 'media spokesman' quickly pointed out that this was not an official WHO view, Mr Nabarro insisted that he stood by his claim.

Informed observers noted that there appeared to be a good deal of scientific confusion behind all these excitable reports. For a start, H5N1 was not so much a single flu virus as a whole family of viruses, or sub-types, only three of which had been associated with human deaths. The total number of fatalities so far associated with H5N1 over a ten-year period had been only 67, all in eastern Asia, and all these victims had been in physical contact with domestic poultry.

Furthermore, for the disease to reach epidemic, let alone pandemic, levels in the human population, it would have to go through a very significant transformation. The bird flu virus on its own might occasionally manage to infect a human contact. But for this then to be passed on from human to human was a wholly different matter. This would require a switch of components between one of the viral sub-types which were pathogenic in poultry and a sub-type of some quite different human flu strain, in such a way as to combine the pathogenicity of the one with the human infectivity of the other.

Even to identify which sub-types of H5N1 might be pathogenic to humans required a further refinement of DNA analysis, to show which 'clade' (or genetic grouping) they belonged to. And the chances of all this happening so as to produce a new strain of bird flu capable of setting off a human epidemic were so infinitesimally remote that they could scarcely be estimated, even at many billions to one.

Then, on 22 October 2005, it was announced in London by the Department for the Environment, Food and Rural Affairs (Defra) that the first case of H5N1 bird flu had been reported in Britain. A South American parrot, part of a consignment imported from Surinam, had been found dead in a quarantine unit in Essex (as chance had it, right next to the abattoir where the Pan-Asian strain of foot-and-mouth disease had first been spotted in Britain in 2001).

Three days later, on 25 October, the MPs on the House of Commons Agriculture Committee were summoned to Defra headquarters for an emergency briefing. The seniority of the officials on the Defra team, headed by the government's chief vet Debby Reynolds, indicated how seriously the issue was being taken. Also present, apart from Ms Reynolds' deputy, were the department's chief scientific adviser, Professor Howard Dalton, and its top civil servant, the acting permanent secretary.

The meeting began with an admission that the H5N1 virus had been found not just in one parrot but two, kept in quarantine with a consignment of mynah birds from Taiwan. But since samples taken from the birds had been muddled together, it was not clear to Defra which birds had been the original source of the infection.*

After this unpromising start, Owen Paterson MP, a Tory frontbench spokesman, tried to establish a few basic facts. Which clade of the H5N1 family of viruses, he wanted to know, had been found in the birds? This was highly relevant because only three clades had so far been linked to human deaths (none in Taiwan).[2]

Although Paterson asked his question three times, Defra's embarrassed experts conspicuously went out of their way to ignore it. Not only were they unsure of which birds were infected, or where they had come from, but when it came to the most crucial evidence of all, identifying the clade, it seemed they did not even understand why such a question might be relevant. Yet these were the people in charge of Britain's response to what looked to be fast spiralling into a worldwide health scare of historic and hugely damaging proportions.

Watching these bizarre events unfolding in 2005, observers might have cast their minds back nine years, to the day when a statement to the House of Commons by the then Secretary of State for Health had set off what was to become the greatest and most costly of all Britain's food scares.

This was Stephen Dorrell's admission, on 20 March 1996, that there might be some connection between the mysterious and terrible disease recently identified as 'new variant CJD' (Creutzfeldt-Jakob Disease) and the epidemic of 'mad cow disease' or BSE

* When this was later made public, the Taiwanese health authorities were outraged. When they checked out the farm that exported the mynah birds, not a trace of infection was found. This 'dead parrot sketch' only descended further into farce when Defra finally admitted that the infection had probably originated not with the mynah birds but with a consignment of Taiwanese mesia finches.

(bovine spongiform encephalopathy), which over the previous decade had been sweeping through Britain's dairy herds.

Relying on a briefing from the government's top advisers, the Spongiform Encephalopathy Advisory Committee (SEAC), Dorrell referred to the recently identified cases of vCJD, and went on to say that, while there was no 'scientific proof' of a link, 'the most likely explanation at present is that those cases are linked to exposure to BSE'.

Rarely can a mere 16 words have had such explosive political and financial consequences. For several years speculation had been rife as to whether BSE could in some way be passed on to humans, but until now this had always been categorically denied. The very fact that the government was now prepared to admit the possibility of such a link was enough to trigger off hysteria.

As one European Union country after another rushed to ban imports of British beef, Britain's media vied with each other to see who could come up with the most horrific scenario for what the future might now hold.

On *Newsnight*, Jeremy Paxman put it to Dr John Pattison, the chairman of SEAC, that the number of deaths from vCJD might rise as high as 500,000. Dr Pattison agreed that this was not impossible. The following Sunday even this was outbid by the *Observer*, which devoted a whole page to an apocalyptic vision of the future, based on the views of Professor Richard Lacey, the microbiologist who had earlier played a leading role in stoking up public alarm during earlier food scares over salmonella in eggs, and listeria.

The *Observer* conjured up a picture of how Britain might look in 20 years' time. By 2016, it predicted, vCJD caught from eating BSE-infected beef in the late twentieth century would be killing half a million Britons every year. National Euthanasia Clinics would be on overtime, 'struggling to help 500 people a week to a dignified death before brain disease robs them of reason and self-control'. Britain would long have been a nation in quarantine, totally shunned by the outside world. The Channel Tunnel would have been blocked off by 'five miles of French concrete'. The health service would have collapsed under 'the strain of caring for more than two million CJD victims'. The entire 'fabric of the nation' would be disintegrating.

Such, said the *Observer*, were the expert predictions of a

scientist 'once reviled by the establishment' but 'now proven right and whose views last week took on a disturbing new authority'.

Yet what was astonishing about Dorrell's statement was not just that there was not a scrap of firm scientific evidence to justify it (even Dorrell himself had conceded there was 'no evidence of a direct link' and talked only of 'the most likely explanation'), but, in fact, such evidence as did exist pointed in precisely the opposite direction. BSE had been appearing in British cattle herds for well over a decade. The meat from some 750,000 animals of the right age to contract the disease had got into the human food chain, most of it in the years before 1989. This meant that, if there was any connection between CJD and BSE-infected beef, the incidence of vCJD should now be rapidly rising.

In fact the incidence of CJD of all kinds was at the time going down. To the original ten cases of 'new variant CJD' on which SEAC had based its predictions, only two more new cases had been added in the previous six months. On epidemiological grounds alone, it already seemed improbable that there was any link at all between vCJD and beef.

Yet, once unleashed, the political and media hysteria surrounding BSE knew no bounds. The EU imposed a total ban on exports of British beef to anywhere in the world. It was even solemnly proposed that every dairy cow in Britain should be slaughtered.

As a political compromise it was agreed that every animal over 30 months old, once it had reached the end of its useful life, should be sent up in smoke, even though not a single scientist had suggested that this was necessary. This scheme alone was to cost taxpayers £3.7 billion, quite apart from the wider damage inflicted by an avalanche of BSE-related regulations on Britain's farming economy, which would cost billions more.

Yet in May 1997, only fourteen months after predicting that the number of deaths from vCJD could eventually rise to 500,000, Dr Pattison confessed that his epidemic was not going to take place after all. The scientist who more than anyone else had engineered the BSE scare admitted that a continuing decline in the incidence of vCJD deaths now indicated that the final figure might 'end up at around 200'.[3]

This extraordinary climbdown attracted virtually no notice from the media. The vast regulatory apparatus erected in response to the scare all remained in place. Millions of healthy cattle would continue to be destroyed for years to come, at immense cost to the taxpayers. Only in 2006 did the EU finally lift the last of its restrictions on British beef exports – by which time the incidence of vCJD had fallen to near zero.

It had long been clear that the greatest food scare of them all had been just that: a scare, the apocalypse that never happened.

Yet, in March 2006, when the tenth anniversary of Dorrell's statement arrived, not one of those newspapers or television programmes which had done so much to stoke up the mass hysteria of 1996 bothered to record the fact. For the media, the great BSE/CJD panic of just ten years before had become the great unmentionable; the equivalent of one of Orwell's 'unpersons'.

How had Britain become the kind of society where such a thing could happen? To answer that question we have to go back to the 1980s. For it was during that decade that, in both Britain and America, the conditions that were about to unleash the modern scare phenomenon in its most extreme form were gradually coming together.

Notes

1. Revill, Jo, *Everything You Need To Know About Bird Flu* (London, Rodale, 2005), pp. 16, 127.
2. *Sunday Telegraph*, 30 October 2005.
3. 'We got it badly wrong over BSE admits top scientist', *Sunday Telegraph*, 8 June 1997.

1

Countdown to an Explosion

How Scares Became a Disaster Waiting to Happen, 1981–8

Between the idea
And the reality ...
Falls the Shadow

T. S. Eliot, 'The Hollow Men'

The modern 'scare phenomenon', as we shall see later in this book, really began to develop in the USA in the 1970s. But it first attained its full virulence in Mrs Thatcher's Britain of the 1980s. During those years we can see coming together all the conditions that would lead to the succession of food scares that were to make headlines for a decade. These in turn established the pattern for those later, more general scares which, in the years ahead, were to become infinitely more damaging.

As it happens, however, the first major scare to command national attention in Britain in the '80s related not to food but to sex.

At the beginning of the decade, word came from across the Atlantic that a number of gay men had been inexplicably dying in the USA from rare illnesses. In 1981 the first British victim died at the Brompton Hospital in London. In 1982, when the mystery condition was officially named Acquired Immune Deficiency Syndrome, or AIDS, the number of cases in America reached 1,000, with seven more victims recorded in the UK.[1]

In 1983, as the number of UK victims rose to 17, it became apparent that the condition also affected other groups, such as drug addicts using infected needles and haemophiliacs receiving infected blood. In August 'Scottish health experts' were reported as warning that the Edinburgh Festival could become 'a breeding ground for the spread of the mystery disease'. By the end of 1984 there had been 108 cases of AIDS in the UK, with 46 deaths.

In February 1985 the Royal College of Nursing predicted that, if present trends continued, the number of cases in the UK would have risen to a million by 1991. Parents removed their children from school when they learned that a fellow pupil was an AIDS-infected haemophiliac. Passengers on the *QE2* cut their holiday cruise short when it was discovered that a passenger on board had AIDS. By the end of the year, when the number of AIDS cases reported worldwide reached 20,303, including 275 in Britain, the Secretary of State for Health, Norman Fowler, had pledged the Government to spending a further £7.2 million on AIDS, including £2.5 million for a public health education campaign.

In 1986, when it was internationally agreed that the virus giving rise to AIDS should be called Human Immunodeficiency Virus (HIV), the British Government launched its first awareness campaign, 'Don't Aid AIDS', with full-page advertisements in national newspapers. Tabloid newspapers were denounced for their lurid coverage of the disease, under such headlines as 'The March of the Gay Plague' and 'Monster In Our Midst'.

In February 1987, the crescendo of publicity reached its peak. Under the direction of a junior health minister, Mrs Edwina Currie, the Government circulated to every one of the 23 million households in the country a leaflet bearing the slogan 'AIDS – Don't Die Of Ignorance'. Night after night it paid for melodramatic television commercials showing a crumbling tombstone or a mighty iceberg, only partly visible above the water, conveying the message that AIDS posed a deadly, hidden threat to almost everyone in the nation.

Yet from that time on, although the world became increasingly aware of the immense tragedy unfolding in Africa, where it was estimated that by 2005 20 million people had died of AIDS, public awareness of AIDS in the UK was never to be so intense again. By 2005 the total number of cases recorded in Britain had reached 20,099, of whom 13,386 had died.

No one can deny that AIDS was and is a genuine and horrifying disease. But the blizzard of publicity it excited in the 1980s gave it several of those key characteristics of a 'scare' that in later years were to become so familiar. Because it was so new and mysterious, it was a completely unknown quantity. And when it became apparent that not only gays but also other groups in society could be infected, there seemed for a while to be no limit to the devastation it might eventually cause, as was reflected in those apocalyptic visions conjured up on television for weeks on end by Mrs Currie and the Government's own Department of Health.

Even at the time there were many who felt that the Government's response to the threat was disproportionate.* In hindsight, there can be little doubt that the obsessive attention paid to AIDS in the mid-1980s not only qualifies it as the first of the 'scares' that are the theme of this book. It also provides us with a first revealing glimpse of just how twitchy the mood of those times was becoming.

Enter Food Poisoning

The fear naturally aroused by the sudden appearance of a deadly epidemic is as old as mankind. But such were the advances of modern science that, in the decades after World War Two, this ancient threat seemed, at least in the developed West, to have receded below the horizon.

In Britain, the last such epidemic to win national publicity was the outbreak of typhoid, which in 1964 all but shut off the Scottish city of Aberdeen. But even this was eventually traced to infected corned beef imported from South America, so that it was really an epidemic caused by food poisoning. In this sense, in the absence of any more dramatic mass outbreaks of infectious disease, it was less a survival from the past than a portent of what was to come.

What initially set the scene for the food scares that were to explode through the headlines from the late 1980s onwards was the inescapable fact that, in the preceding decade, reported food poisoning in Britain had suddenly begun to rise with dramatic speed. In the early 1970s, the average number of cases a year was

---

* In February 1987 a West Country village postman, who had been delivering the Government's 'Don't Die Of Ignorance' leaflet to every house in the parish, said that he had just driven a mile up a snow-covered farm track and back, for no other purpose than to present a copy to an aged farmer and his wife. 'I am not sure', he observed, 'that it was wholly necessary for the Government to warn a married couple in their 80s of the dangers of unprotected anal sex.'

little over 8,000. By 1982 this had shot up to 13,000, and was still hurtling upwards.

The causes of this poisoning were, of course, the various foodborne bacteria that can play havoc with human health, and since three of these in particular were to play a significant part in the later story, they may be given a brief introduction.

The most prominent culprit in the rise of food poisoning in the late 1970s and 1980s was salmonella. Although commonly found in poultry, cows, pigs, pets and wild animals, it includes more than 2,000 different strains, only relatively few of which are normally associated with human food poisoning. Because they can be killed off in various ways, as by cooking or exposure to the acid in vinegar, they usually only become dangerous where the handling of food is careless, either because it has been insufficiently cooked, or where it is infected by cross-contamination, then left in conditions which allow the bacteria to multiply.

Once in the human body, salmonella multiplies rapidly, causing within 8–36 hours symptoms of the illness known as salmonellosis, most typically diarrhoea, stomach pains and fever. Usually, within a day or two, the victim recovers. But in rare or extreme cases, particularly those affecting the elderly, young children or people already weakened by illness, poisoning can lead to death.

A second much less familiar form of bacteria later to become famous was *Listeria monocytogenes*. Although commonly found in soil, vegetation, animals, the human gut and even cheese, most strains are not pathogenic and it causes illness very much less often than salmonella. But where it does pose a danger to human health, by attacking the nervous system, it is also more deadly, particularly to pregnant mothers, infants and the elderly. Until the 1980s no obvious connection had been made between listeriosis and food. In 1981, however, although not noticed at the time in Britain, a serious outbreak in Nova Scotia was traced to contaminated coleslaw, involving more than 40 victims. This had resulted in five spontaneous abortions, four stillbirths and the deaths of six infants. Two years later another foodborne outbreak in a Massachusetts hospital struck down 49 patients, of whom 14 died.

Another new bacterial threat first appeared in America in 1982, when 50 people fell seriously ill after eating beefburgers from a branch of McDonald's. The cause was identified as *E. coli* O157:H7. *Escherichia coli* in general is abundantly found in the intestines of all animals, including humans. Of hundreds of strains, again most are non-pathogenic and serve a useful purpose in suppressing other harmful bacteria. But the new O157:H7 strain, first reported in 1977, generated powerful toxins, which can do severe damage to the intestinal lining and kidneys, and is potentially lethal.

Such were the three main agents of food poisoning, which were to play a key part in the story about to unfold.

In the front line of Britain's defences against these threats were two groups of public health officials. At national level, as part of what was still known as the Department of Health and Social Security (DHSS), was the Public Health Laboratory Service (PHLS). Originally set up in World War Two to cope with the epidemics that were expected to follow mass bombing, its main role subsequently switched to food poisoning. Based in Colindale, north London, with a nationwide network of 52 laboratories, the PHLS in 1977 set up a new unit, the Communicable Disease Surveillance Centre (CDSC) to collate national food poisoning figures, and to carry out 'epidemiological investigation and control of communicable disease'.

At a lower, local level, the task of carrying out hygiene inspections and investigating food poisoning incidents lay with a nationwide network of environmental health inspectors (EHOs), employed by local authorities.*

Faced by the explosion of food poisoning that began in the 1970s, however, the officials came up against a peculiar problem. An alarming feature of the rise was the high proportion of cases, nearly 50 per cent, being recorded in hospitals operated by the National Health Service. Yet here the hands of the public health officials were tied. Government buildings such as NHS hospitals were notionally Crown property. Under a 300-year-old legal 'loophole' this gave them 'Crown Immunity'. They were considered 'above the law', immune from prosecution.

The frustration of public health officials at this anomaly had

---

* EHOs were descended from the local authority 'sanitary inspectors', set up by mid-nineteenth century reforms designed to tackle sanitation problems in Britain's cities. In the 1950s they became 'public health inspectors'. They originally operated under a local Medical Officer of Health, until this office was abolished by the local government reform of 1974. Health inspectors became 'environmental health officers' in the 1970s.

first come to a head in 1973, when a serious outbreak of salmonella poisoning was reported at Leytonstone House Hospital in east London. Sixty patients were infected by Christmas turkey, two of whom died. It emerged that hygiene practices in the hospital kitchens were notoriously lax. But because of Crown Immunity, the EHOs were powerless to intervene. Their professional association therefore decided to highlight the problem by conducting a nationwide survey of hygiene practice in hospital kitchens.

Although the process whereby the report on this study was eventually to emerge was tortuous – the DHSS sought drastically to censor it* – its findings were alarming. Hygiene standards in hospital kitchens, unsupervised by EHOs, were low and declining. From that time on, many EHOs were convinced they must campaign to end the loophole of Crown Immunity: a battle that in due course was to have unforeseen and significant consequences.

In August 1984 an even more serious salmonella outbreak occurred at a large Yorkshire psychiatric hospital, Stanley Royd. By 7 September the death toll had risen to 19, and the final number of those made ill by salmonellosis included some 355 patients and 106 staff. A team from the PHLS, called in to assist with the investigation in London, headed by Dr Bernard Rowe, was initially refused access by the hospital authorities, under Crown Immunity. But, having gained access, Dr Rowe, using a technique known as 'plasmid typing', eventually established that the cause of the outbreak was roast beef, cross-contaminated by salmonella-infected chicken.

The Labour Opposition's social services spokesman called for a public inquiry, blaming the outbreak on Government spending cuts. Labour's front-bench health spokesman Frank Dobson joined in, calling also for an end to Crown Immunity. While the inquiry

---

* Dr North was at this time an EHO in Leeds and, as media spokesman for his colleagues, was due to be interviewed on the report by BBC television. When he borrowed a copy from a senior colleague, it soon emerged that its contents were wholly different from the public version issued to the BBC, which maintained that conditions in hospital kitchens were improving. The full version was damning in its criticisms, but these had been sanitized out of the public version, thanks to pressure, it emerged, from the DHSS. Because North had recent alarming experience of hospital kitchens, he issued a press release based on the original, critical version. For this breach of professional discipline he was suspended from his post.

was taking place in 1985, a health service union, the GMB, backed by the Institution of Environmental Health Officers (IEHO), claimed that Crown Immunity for hospitals was the chief cause of the national rise in food poisoning and should be scrapped.

When this led to a Granada Television *World In Action* documentary team, including Richard North, gaining access to three hospitals with concealed cameras, the evidence they uncovered was appalling. A junior Government health minister Barney Hayhoe, interviewed for the programme (due to be broadcast later to coincide with publication of the report of the Stanley Royd inquiry), he could only claim, without evidence, that since then conditions in hospital kitchens had 'improved'. As for the removal of Crown Immunity, the Government would only 'consider' it.

Fired with campaigning zeal, the IEHO now called not just for an end to Crown Immunity, but for the registration of all food premises; compulsory training courses for everyone working with food (conducted for a fee by EHOs); and new powers to close down food businesses by serving a 'prohibition notice'. All this would require a major new food safety Act.

Equally fired up was Dr Bernard Rowe who, fresh from his successful investigation at Stanley Royd, was put in charge of a powerful new unit at the PHLS, the Department of Enteric Pathogens. Part of its role was to type and collect isolates of salmonella from all over the country, giving him a unique overview of national trends in salmonella poisoning. As he told *The Times* on his appointment, 'food poisoning is not a success story'. He tellingly added, 'every bovine and chicken in the country has salmonella sitting in its bowels which, with inadequate refrigeration, thawing and cooking will reach us'.

The IEHO now issued a new report on hospital kitchens, concluding that not one of 1,000 kitchens inspected fully met accepted hygiene standards. Conditions in 97 of these were so 'appalling' that, if they were in the private sector, they would have been prosecuted or closed. Asked again whether he would end Crown Immunity, Hayhoe, the minister, again gave only an equivocal reply, saying the issue was 'complicated'.[2]

By now the media were on the attack, reporting new examples of poor hygiene under such headlines as 'The Scandal of Our Filthy Hospitals'.[3] Hayhoe was confronted by an angry delegation of

Labour MPs, senior trade union officials, EHOs, local councillors and nurses, demanding an end to Crown Immunity.

Yet more food poisoning outbreaks hit the headlines, including hospitals in Preston, Mansfield, Edinburgh and Southall. When Dr Rowe was called in to investigate the discovery of salmonella in a well-known brand of baby milk, this eventually led to its production plant in Cumbria being closed, costing the owners, Glaxo, more than £40 million.

In January 1986, when the report of the Stanley Royd inquiry finally appeared, finding that hygiene conditions in the hospital had been 'appalling', the media had a field day. Granada broadcast its *World In Action* documentary. The *Sunday Times* reported that 'a team of leading scientists', including Dr Rowe and his PHLS colleague Dr Richard Gilbert, were launching a 'national probe' into food poisoning, following a '45 per cent rise' in the three years since 1982. Dr Gilbert said his research had shown that the main carriers of infection were poultry and meat, and that '79 per cent of frozen chicken' was contaminated with salmonella.

A month later, after a backbench Tory MP, Richard Shepherd, had tabled a Bill to end Crown Immunity, Norman Fowler, as Secretary of State for Health, promised Parliament that it would go. This so embarrassed his junior minister Barney Hayhoe that he decided he had no alternative but to resign.

The Crown Immunity of NHS hospital kitchens was finally ended on 10 November, but not before *The Times* had reported that, in the six years between 1979 and 1985, there had been 211 outbreaks of food poisoning in hospitals, affecting 3,969 people, of whom 279 had died. The following year the *British Medical Journal* was to publish updated figures, showing that between 1978 and 1987 the total number of salmonella outbreaks reported had been 522. Of these, 248, no less than 48 per cent, had been in hospitals.

Hayhoe's successor as junior health minister, appointed on 10 September 1986, was a combative, ambitious 39-year-old, Mrs Edwina Currie.

Enter BSE

Meanwhile, elsewhere on the battlefield, another portent had appeared. Just before Christmas in 1984, a Hampshire vet, David

Bee, had been called to Pitsham Farm in Sussex, where farmer Peter Stent was puzzled by the behaviour of one his dairy cows. 'She's lost weight, was looking unwell and her back was up in the air', he said. Bee was baffled. When he examined the cow twice more in the next two months, it had developed a shaking head. On 11 February 1985 it died, by which time other cows in the herd were showing the same condition, which Bee found 'really spooky'.[4]

Two months later, in April, another vet, Colin Whitaker, inspected a dairy cow at Plurenden Manor Farm near Ashford. It was unsteady on its feet and seemed aggressive. Although he could not identify the cause, in July the animal was put down. Again, other cows in the herd began displaying the same condition.

In September 1985, when a tenth cow fell ill in Stent's herd at Pitsham, he took it directly to the Central Veterinary Laboratory (CVL) in Weybridge, a department of the Ministry of Agriculture, Fisheries and Food (MAFF). When a pathologist examined the cow's brain under a microscope, she saw tiny holes or vacuoles, a feature hitherto seen only in the brains of sheep affected by the disease specific to sheep known as scrapie. A colleague agreed that it looked like a case of 'bovine scrapie'. When Bee received a report on his cow, its condition was described as 'spongiform encephalopathy', which meant nothing to him. But the CVL's verdict was that the cause was probably some 'toxic poisoning'.

By February 1986 a sixth cow had died at Plurenden Manor Farm, and Whitaker also sent specimens to the CVL. Five similar cases had already been referred to the CVL, and soon others were being reported from Somerset, Dyfed, Devon and Hampshire. Not until November 1986, after Whitaker's specimens had been sent to the specialist Neuropathology Unit at Western General Hospital, Edinburgh, was a definite diagnosis arrived at. The new disease was confirmed as a form of 'cattle scrapie' and given the official title of bovine spongiform encephalopathy, or BSE.

At this stage, no one had even considered the possibility that the new disease might be transmissible to humans. Not a word about it had yet reached the media.

The focus of attention was still on more conventional forms of food poisoning (not to mention the 'AIDS scare' now approaching its height) – and on the aftermath to the change of ministers at the Department of Health.

Enter Currie and Lacey

One of Currie's first tasks when she took up her new job on 10 September 1986 was to consider how much it was going to cost to upgrade NHS hospital kitchens, following the exposure of how lax their hygiene standards had become and the end of Crown Immunity.

The big idea her officials came up with was 'cook-chill'. Instead of spending a fortune on every kitchen, why not reorganize NHS catering round a number of central production units, where food could be prepared on an industrial scale, chilled and then distributed to hospitals in refrigerated trucks for reheating? By reducing the number of catering staff, this could provide large savings.

This provoked angry opposition from the health service unions: not just because of the threat to their members' jobs, but because they saw it as a 'Trojan horse' for Mrs Thatcher's privatization of the health service. They commissioned a report on cook-chill from the London Food Commission (LFC), a pressure group set up in 1985 with £1 million from the Greater London Council, under its maverick left-wing leader Ken Livingstone.

The LFC's membership was chiefly confined to trade unions, local authorities, consumer groups and other organizations sympathetic to the aggressive campaigning stance of its director Tim Lang, deeply suspicious of the food industry in all its guises. Predictably its report on cook-chill, carried out by Julie Sheppard, was damning, identifying various practical flaws.[5]

Thanks to increasing demands on the health service, the Department of Health was now looking for possible cuts in all directions, and the unions were not alone in fearing the consequences. The PHLS too had been threatened with a severe reduction in its funding, which would force it to close some of its network of laboratories.

The IEHO weighed in by protesting that the timing of this would be disastrous. Not only was the PHLS having to cope with the explosion in food poisoning; it was also at the forefront of the battle against AIDS, then at the height of its media exposure. For the time being, the threat to PHLS funding receded.

But the attention of senior members of the PHLS was also becoming focused on another problem. At a symposium in Stratford-upon-Avon in January 1987, Dr Richard Gilbert raised the question of listeria.[6] The epidemiology of listeriosis, he suggested, might be changing. The disease appeared to be 'more frequently foodborne'. Because *Listeria monocytogenes* had the ability, very unusual in bacteria, 'to grow at low temperatures, to proliferate and to outgrow competing organisms', this might be due to the increasing use of refrigeration.

Not long afterwards his PHLS colleague Dr Jim McLauchlin was to write in a learned journal: 'it is some 50 years since it was first suggested that *L. monocytogenes* may be transmitted to humans via food'. Experiments, he suggested, now seemed to confirm that the growth and spread of listeria could make it 'an ideal candidate for transmission through food', particularly where this had been refrigerated.[7] Unwittingly, the PHLS's new line of thinking was to play right into the hands of the opponents of cook-chill.

In fact this political battle had now found a focus, as chance had it, at Stanley Royd Hospital, designated by Yorkshire health authorities as the site of one of six central cook-chill units to produce food for distribution to all the 160 hospitals in Yorkshire. The spotless new kitchens were ready, but health union members, on advice from the LFC, refused to operate them on 'hygiene grounds'.

Following the Stanley Royd report, health authorities had been told to appoint 'infection control officers', whose responsibilities should include hygiene. The Wakefield authority, responsible for Stanley Royd, appointed a professor of microbiology from nearby Leeds University, Richard Lacey.

Originally a medical doctor, Lacey, now aged 46, had no background in food hygiene or food poisoning. His speciality was resistance to antibiotics and drugs. But having accepted the new post on an honorary basis, he talked to the unions, read Sheppard's LFC report and, even though he had never seen a cook-chill kitchen, decided to oppose the new system on principle.

In May 1987, at a conference called by Wakefield in a bid to resolve the impasse, Lacey denounced cook-chill as 'microbiologically unsound and nutritionally unsafe'. It was 'totally unacceptable as a catering system', in Wakefield or anywhere else. His outspoken comments continued to be quoted in the local and national press for some time. One of the central figures in the food scare dramas of the next ten years had stepped onto the stage.

Increasingly beleaguered, as the leading proponent of cook-chill, Currie could only respond by insisting that it was a 'well-established catering system' and that, providing the DHSS guidelines issued in 1980 were followed, it was 'microbiologically and nutritionally sound'.[8]

Two months later it was clear that Lacey thought he had found the scientific underpinning he had been seeking for his opposition to cook-chill. The reason why he was 'deeply suspicious of this potentially fatal cooking technique', he said, was that certain pathogenic organisms were actually encouraged by the low temperatures used in cook-chill. Although he did not yet name listeria, he described the symptoms of the disease caused by it.[9]

What made this highly significant was that the DHSS guidelines, on which Currie was relying to defend her cook-chill policy, had been designed primarily to prevent the spread of salmonella, which below 10°C cannot multiply. *Listeria monocytogenes*, on the other hand, thrives at lower temperatures, making the guidelines irrelevant.

Furthermore, it was becoming clear that the incidence of listeriosis was rising rapidly, for reasons no one had yet explained. In the early 1980s, its incidence had been fairly static, at 20–40 cases a year. But in the mid-80s it started rising, by 1986 to 107, and by 1987 to 259, seven times the average for 1967–77. And the average fatality rate was as high as 30 per cent.

As the profile of this increase was compatible with the early stages of an epidemic, Lacey quickly recruited what he now called 'the new food poisoning' to his campaign, to exploit the gap in the DHSS's defences. And at this very time, as chance had it, the DHSS learned that the Swiss government had withdrawn from the market a famous soft cheese, Vacherin Mont d'Or, because it had been linked to listeriosis.

When news of the Swiss outbreak made British headlines, the DHSS, on 24 November 1987 issued a formal warning to the public not to eat Vacherin Mont d'Or. The *Guardian* claimed, somewhat excitably, 'Cheese is linked to 60 deaths'.* Behind the scenes the DHSS was seriously concerned. So far the major

---

* The true figure of listeriosis deaths attributed to Swiss Vacherin Mont d'Or since 1983 was 31.

listeriosis outbreaks had been across the Atlantic, but Switzerland was much nearer home.

The DHSS's Chief Medical Officer, Donald Acheson, set up a listeriosis working group, including senior members of the PHLS. On 17 December it recommended that more extensive epidemiological surveys should be carried out, and 'more information made available about the way soft cheeses are made'. Because of the particular vulnerability of pregnant mothers, the Department wrote to the Royal College of Obstetricians and Gynaecologists, asking whether pregnant mothers should be warned to avoid soft cheese, advice which the College put to its members on 1 February 1988.

On 16 February 1988, the *Daily Express* reported that goat's cheese had been blamed for a London woman contracting meningitis. This was confirmed two days later by a *Times* report that the PHLS had isolated large counts of *Listeria monocytogenes* from the cheese found in the woman's home. A week later Dr Gilbert and a PHLS colleague published in *The Lancet* the results of a study they had carried out in response to Acheson's working group, headed 'Listeriosis and Food Borne Transmission'. Their researches had found listeria in soft cheese from four countries, including Britain and France. Of 100 chickens bought from retailers, listeria had been found in 60.

There no longer seemed any doubt that listeria was foodborne, unusually impervious to refrigeration and highly dangerous – and that its incidence was now rising so rapidly that a serious epidemic could not be ruled out.

Enter Eggs

The PHLS, meanwhile, felt still under threat. On 19 May 1987, the *Guardian* reported that a firm of management consultants had been asked to advise on how £350 million a year could be saved on 'pathology services', and had focused on the PHLS. The Secretary of State for Health, the report went on, was 'understood to have vetoed a proposal to privatise the laboratories', but 'only for the time being'.

An understandable response from the PHLS itself was to emphasize the importance and urgency of its work, at a time when its resources were already overstretched by the explosion in food poisoning and the panic over AIDS. No one expressed this more volubly than Dr Rowe, who had recently told a private seminar of EHOs at Leeds University that the rise in salmonella poisoning, his particular concern, represented 'an epidemic of unprecedented proportions'.*

In August 1987, relying on his own salmonella database rather than that of the Communicable Disease Surveillance Centre, Rowe took the unusual step of releasing to the media the very latest figures available, relating to 1985 and 1986. The 1986 figure showed an increase of 3,000 on the previous year, or 25 per cent. And he was now forming his own theory as to where much of the increase was coming from. On 8 November, under the headline 'Eggs blamed for increase in food bugs', the *Sunday Times* reported Rowe's view that there had been a marked rise in 'the number of domestic cases caused by egg products infected with salmonella'.

The main culprit, Rowe believed at this stage, was liquid eggs used in cooking, which had become contaminated by a flaw in the pasteurization process. This might well be linked with the high percentage of chickens that were contaminated with salmonella: in particular a strain which had lately become particularly prominent in poultry, *Salmonella enteritidis*.**

On 5 January 1988, Rowe set up a special PHLS sub-committee on *S. enteritidis* (quickly dubbed the 'egg committee') to look into the sharp rise in the number of poisoning incidents with which this strain was associated. Its first meeting heard evidence that the most likely explanation for the rise, beginning in the early 1980s, was that *enteritidis* had been introduced to Britain by human carriers

---

* Rowe also claimed at the same time, in an interview with the mass-circulation magazine *Woman* (7 February 1987), that 'for every reported case of food poisoning, about 100 people suffer acute stomach aches caused by salmonella poisoning without recognising it'. In other words, he was suggesting that the true food poisoning figures might be 100 times larger than those reported.
** The term *enteritidis* had first been coined as long ago as 1881, even before the naming of *Salmonella* itself, to distinguish bacteria which cause gastro-enteritis from those which caused typhoid (the so-called *typhi* strains). In the early twentieth century, as knowledge of *salmonella* strains became more sophisticated, *enteritidis* was reserved for a specific strain, even though this itself was to become subdivided into 'phage types'.

returning from abroad (some 30 per cent of the initial cases were associated with people coming to Britain from Spain and Portugal).

But what Rowe was determined to pursue was the link with eggs. A consultant epidemiologist, Dr John Cowden, was sent to Hull to search out incidents involving pasteurized egg products. He could only report back that they were 'disappointingly rare'.[10]

On 27 February, however, James O'Brien, a vet, published a report in the *Veterinary Record* making two observations about the prevalence of *enteritidis* in broiler flocks – birds bred for meat – which aroused considerable interest. The first was this organism had the peculiar property in some birds to cause an enlargement of the heart sac, which became filled with an almost pure liquid culture of billions of *enteritidis*. This meant the birds could become so heavily infected that they posed an abnormal risk of cross-contamination. O'Brien's other finding was that *enteritidis* in broiler flocks could be 'vertically transmitted' by hens to their chicks, via their eggs. Might the same not be possible in laying flocks, thus infecting table eggs?

Five weeks later, this provocative idea seemed to be reinforced by a US paper on a salmonella incident involving 'shell eggs', which was given prominent coverage in Britain.* The US researchers claimed that the poisoning appeared to have originated from salmonella *inside* the eggs themselves.

Following O'Brien's earlier report, this suggestion that salmonella could occur inside the egg led Rowe to speculate that it might be fresh eggs, rather than pasteurized, which were the cause of his 'epidemic of unprecedented proportions'. He immediately set about looking for evidence, sending an instruction to MAFF's State Veterinary Service (SVS) on 29 April that all *enteritidis* incidents must be investigated.

That same day an *enteritidis* outbreak was reported following a 'Bridge and Pâté Party' to raise funds for the Conservative Party at Ottringham in East Yorkshire. Many of those present had fallen ill,

---

* Under the headline 'It's No Yolk', the *Today* newspaper, for instance, reported on 16 April that 'Britain's favourite breakfast – the egg – is not all it's cracked up to be. Egg heads in America say it could be a killer'. A *Times* report (same day) was headlined 'US scare threatens soft-boiled eggs'.

after eating a variety of pâtés and desserts, including ice cream made from raw eggs.*

The initial suspicion was that the cause of the outbreak was chicken liver pâté, supplied from a Lincoln plant where birds had been found infected with *enteritidis*. But when Dr Cowden from the PHLS arrived on 10 May to investigate, he seemed already sure that the cause must be eggs, as he indicated to the official who met him at the station and to the event's organizer.[11] Despite later admitting that it was 'impossible to prove epidemiologically' that eggs were the cause of the outbreak, Rowe viewed the discovery of *enteritidis* in dead chickens at the farm that supplied the eggs used to make the ice cream as a major breakthrough. Although no live birds on the farm were found infected, and three of the food poisoning victims had not eaten the ice cream, the official finding on the outbreak was, unequivocally, that it was due to eggs.

Over the next few weeks further incidents followed a similar pattern. EHOs investigating an *enteritidis* outbreak at the Gatwick Hilton hotel claimed that all the foods involved had been based on the same batch of home-made mayonnaise, even though the infection had first been noted the day before the mayonnaise had been made. Nevertheless the outbreak was classified as 'egg associated'.

A much-publicized outbreak involving mayonnaise in the House of Lords was also officially described as 'egg associated', even though the salmonella strain involved was not *enteritidis* but *typhimurium* DT49. Food poisoning traced to mayonnaise from a sandwich bar near St Mary's Hospital, Paddington, was again recorded as 'egg associated', even though sampling of 500 eggs showed no sign of infection and the kitchen where the mayonnaise was made was not inspected. A hospital outbreak in Holyhead classified as 'egg associated' was blamed on Scotch eggs, even though the eggs had been hard-boiled, more than enough to kill off any salmonella, and several of the victims had not eaten them.

By the midsummer of 1988, Rowe's belief that eggs might in themselves be a source of infection had become so much the ruling orthodoxy within the PHLS that they were now being blamed for almost any outbreak of salmonella poisoning, even when this

---

* All the food poisoning cases described in this and the paragraphs following were subjected to a full independent investigation by Dr North.

defied all the evidence. Certainly this idea had seized the imaginations of journalists, who were now devoting ever more excitable attention to the great 'food poisoning epidemic'. As the *Evening Standard* put it, reporting on a 'leaked' (and, as it turned out, inaccurate) preview of the official report on the House of Lords outbreak:

> *boiled egg eaters are in for a shock. Their Lordships will be warned that the risk of a disease like salmonella cannot be entirely discounted until an egg has been bubbled for eight minutes – rock hard in short.*

At least one official body remained, so far, impervious to all this excitement. As yet unconvinced by Rowe's egg theory, the DHSS called on the PHLS only to arrange for further research, 'to confirm or not the "hypothesis" of contamination by vertical transmission (i.e. internal infection of eggs)'.

In what was privately minuted as a 'defensive briefing', issued to coincide with the publication of the Lords report, the DHSS was prepared to admit that 'in a limited number of recent incidents of salmonella poisoning, raw egg has been implicated as the vehicle of infection'. It listed precautions that should be taken to minimize 'any risk', such as keeping eggs refrigerated. But, the Department concluded, 'we have no reason to advise at the moment that any additional precautions are needed in the cooking of eggs'.

For the moment the DHSS was holding the line.

'Another plague from Egypt'

In April 1987, following the identification of BSE by the Neuropathology Unit in Edinburgh, MAFF's chief epidemiologist, John Wilesmith, began an intensive programme of studies across 200 farms, without publicity, to discover just how widespread incidence of the new disease had become.

In July 1987 a conference of the British Cattle Veterinary Association in Nottingham heard a paper by Colin Whitaker, the Kent vet whose specimens from sick cattle had led to their disease being classified as bovine spongiform encephalopathy. Also in the audience was David Bee, who recognized what Whitaker and his co-author, Carl Johnson, were describing as the same condition he had identified in cows in Sussex.

Such were MAFF's sensitivities that the two authors were asked to remove any reference in their paper to a 'scrapie-like condition'. Nevertheless they noted the resemblances between BSE and encephalopathies (brain diseases) recorded in other species, such as sheep and goats. 'In man', they added, 'there is Kuru and Creutzfeldt-Jakob Disease'.

Kuru was a disease identified in cannibalistic New Guinea tribes, who were supposed to have contracted it by eating human tissue. CJD, a rare and invariably fatal form of dementia, usually affecting people from the age of 60 onwards and characterized by 'sponge-like holes' in the brain, had first been reported by two German scientists in the early 1920s and given its name in 1922.

When the discovery of BSE was first publicly reported in October 1987, by the *Veterinary Record*, this was picked up by the BBC and one or two newspapers as 'a potentially threatening cattle disease'. By 15 December, Wilesmith had completed his epidemiological studies – having discovered more than 100 cases – and concluded that 'the only viable hypothesis' was that cows had contracted the disease from 'infected ruminant feed containing meat and bonemeal'. This attracted little attention, although *The Times* reported two weeks later that the veterinary profession was 'baffled', quoting Dr Tony Andrews, a senior lecturer at the Royal Veterinary College, as suggesting that the disease 'may well have been latent for years'.

On 3 March 1988, however, MAFF passed a file on BSE to Donald Acheson, the Chief Medical Officer at the DHSS. The number of cases reported had now risen to 500. Acheson read the dossier with alarm, noting in his diary 'we have another plague from Egypt'. After giving the matter considerable thought, at the beginning of April he called Sir Richard Southwood, the Vice-Chancellor of Oxford University, with whom he had served on the Royal Commission on Environmental Pollution.

Acheson told his old colleague 'in great confidence' that there was 'this potentially very serious disease', and asked him to set up a committee to examine its 'implications for human health'. 'Why me?' Southwood later recalled asking. Acheson had replied 'because it is an ecological food problem and because I know you are an independent chap'.

Even before Southwood had assembled his committee, MAFF was already consulting with the rendering industry, the firms responsible for boiling down animal remains to provide feed, about a possible ban on using meat and bonemeal in feed for cattle and sheep. On 5 June, shortly after Mrs Thatcher's 1987 election victory, MAFF's Chief Vet, Keith Meldrum, decided that he must brief the new team of agriculture ministers on the potential threat posed by BSE.

On 14 June two newspapers picked up on a paper in the *Veterinary Record*. The *Guardian* noted the relationship between BSE, scrapie and CJD. The *Independent*, under the headline 'Mystery organism that could poison meat', asked whether people could be 'in danger of catching a fatal illness from eating contaminated beef and lamb'. 'The fear is', the article went on, that 'we could be eating contaminated brain tissue from sheep and cattle which could trigger an epidemic of the Creutzfeldt-Jakob type'.

The same day MAFF issued its BSE Order 1988, making BSE a 'notifiable disease' and imposing a temporary ban on 'the sale, supply or use of animal proteins for feeding to ruminants'. It was the start of what was to become a torrent of BSE legislation.

On 20 June the four members of the Southwood committee held their first meeting. Wilesmith from MAFF was present, and they were also given a MAFF briefing paper which suggested that 'thousands/millions' of people could be at risk from the mysterious new disease. But, because of its likely long incubation period, it might be ten years before the disease showed up in the human population.

Southwood later told the BBC, 'I think our mood was very serious. We felt that we could here be on the edge of something which could have enormous implications'. When Wilesmith explained that cattle 'showing the symptoms of BSE' were entering the human food chain, Southwood later recalled, 'we were all horrified'.

The next day Southwood wrote to MAFF's permanent secretary – also faxing a copy to underline the urgency of his committee's concern – asking that BSE-affected cattle should be removed from the food chain and destroyed, with compensation to be paid to their owners (this was to be put into effect just seven weeks later, on 8 August, by the BSE (Amendment) Order and the BSE Compensation Order).

On 27 June the Southwood Committee published an interim

report. It carefully concealed its concerns behind a bland statement that 'the risk of transmission of BSE to humans appears remote and it is unlikely that BSE will have any implications for human health'.

This soothing reassurance was highlighted in a joint DHSS/ MAFF press release the same day. But in fact the report went on, 'if our assessments of these likelihoods are incorrect, the implications would be extremely serious ... with the long incubation period of spongiform encephalopathies in humans, it may be a decade or more before complete reassurances can be given'.

This potentially explosive qualification was omitted from the official press release. The BBC and newspapers such as the *Guardian* ('BSE presents no health hazard') reported the press release version without checking the text of the report itself.

As on salmonella in eggs, the DHSS and MAFF – as 'blockers' – were managing to hold the line.

The Pressure Rises

On 23 July 1988 Mrs Thatcher reshuffled her Cabinet. The DHSS was split into two separate departments. Appointed as the first Secretary of State for the new Department of Health (DH) was Kenneth Clarke, with David Mellor as his minister of state. The only minister to remain in place, as Parliamentary Under-Secretary, was Edwina Currie.

They were about to be kept very busy. After the succession of scare stories that had made headlines in the first half of the year – salmonella in eggs, Peperami and bean sprouts, listeria in cheese, BSE – new scares were coming virtually every day. The 'pushers' were on the warpath.

Inevitably to the fore was Professor Lacey, still pursuing his crusade on listeria and cook-chill. In *The Lancet* on 2 July he and two Leeds University colleagues, Dr Stephen Dealler and Dr Kevin Kerr, had reported on tests they carried out on chilled meals sold to be re-heated, produced by a process similar to cook-chill in hospitals. *Today* headlined the story 'Peril in your TV dinner', announcing that Lacey and his colleagues had found 'killer bacteria' (*Listeria monocytogenes*) in a quarter of the meals they had bought from leading supermarkets. The *Daily Telegraph* similarly claimed 'Deadly bacteria found in a quarter of frozen meals'.

The *Guardian* went still further. Under the headline 'Food

poison deaths are covered up', it quoted Lacey's claim that the DHSS was trying to hide 150 deaths a year 'caused by bacteria in pre-cooked microwave meals'. The DHSS defensively pointed out 'there have been no UK deaths from listeriosis and there is no evidence that any of the 259 cases last year were caused by food'.

For the *Daily Mail* on 2 July excitement centred on the news that a French baby-food firm Milupa had withdrawn its products from supermarkets after finding salmonella in a pack at its French factory. To *Today*, this was inevitably 'Killer bug in baby food'.

The *British Medical Journal* the same day noted that food poisoning cases in the first five months of 1988 had increased by 37 per cent over the same period in 1987.

It was now the turn of the Consumer Association to get in on the act, with a report in the July edition of *Which?* magazine declaring that cooked meats bought from five supermarkets and 15 small shops had contained *E. coli*. This was picked up by *Today* ('Killer bug of cooked meat in summer salads'), *The Times* ('Shops sell dangerous meat') and James Erlichman in the *Guardian*, who reported that hygiene standards in all the small shops 'appeared poor' and that *E. coli* was 'associated with faecal contamination'.

On 11 July Erlichman was back to 'BSE: a cow disease to beef about'. Cattle rearers were 'suspected of covering up a fatal bovine brain disease which may trigger a similar condition in man'. He cited a warning from the *BMJ* that BSE, CJD and Kuru 'are all related and may be transmitted from species to species by dietary means'.

Five days later Erlichman was among many journalists who reported on a press conference staged by Tim Lang's London Food Commission, at which Lacey repeated his charge that the Government was 'covering up deaths'. Lang himself had protested that it was wrong 'to blame the victims of food poisoning. Who put the salmonella in their food in the first place? The Government must get out of bed with the food industry and ensure that improved hygiene regulations are adopted and obeyed'.

From the same conference, the *Independent* quoted the LFC (described as an 'independent watchdog') as warning that 'from the farmyard to the kitchen, Britain lags behind its European partners in safety standards for food production'. *The Grocer* headlined Lang's claim that 'Britain has the sick food of Europe'. What won notice from *The Times,* under the heading 'Food poisoning at record levels', was Lacey's attack on farming minister John Gummer for 'playing down the risk of listeria' (the paper described Lacey as 'a leading member of a government advisory committee', because he had served briefly on the Veterinary Products Committee which advises on animal pesticides).

On 17 July the *Sunday Times* called in veteran cookery writer Egon Ronay to sum it all up. He argued that 'our food is being polluted, our animals manipulated, our natural farming methods artificially thwarted'. The LFC, he said, was quite right to focus attention on 'the ways in which our food is adulterated'. On 21 July Australia became the first country in the world to ban imports of beef from Britain because of BSE.

In mid-July food poisoning outbreaks occurred simultaneously in three hospitals in Birmingham. Although few details were made public, health officials believed the most likely source was food distributed from a central cook-chill unit. This prompted the *New Scientist* (21 July) to publish an article headed 'Hospital caterers could cause listeriosis epidemic'. Even-handedly, it cited both Lacey's claim that cook-chill was mainly responsible for the rise in listeriosis, and the DHSS's response that this had not led to any UK deaths. It also quoted the DHSS describing Lacey as suffering from 'listeria hysteria'.

On 29 July, the now-renamed Department of Health decided to issue its own warning to NHS hospitals. In all recipes involving fresh eggs, catering managers were advised to substitute pasteurized egg. When this letter was leaked, revealing such a significant ministerial U-turn, media coverage was surprisingly muted.

Three weeks later, when a cook-chill unit at Manchester Airport was hit by a succession of salmonella outbreaks, ascribed by EHOs to eggs, this further provoked the DH, on 26 August, into issuing its first ever public warning on eggs. *Today* predictably shouted across its front-page 'Killer in your egg – poison bug warning from health chiefs'. The public, its report began, had been advised 'not to eat raw eggs because they can kill ... a strain of deadly salmonella bacterium which affects chickens has now been found in eggs'. Elsewhere, however, media coverage of the DH's announcement was still surprisingly low key.

In September the PHLS, which had launched the whole 'salmonella in eggs' thesis on its way, published a technical summary of the year's food poisoning outbreaks associated with raw eggs.

Despite its assiduous countrywide trawling for examples, all the PHLS could come up with was 19 outbreaks, involving 409 people. Eleven of the 19 had been in Crown premises – eight hospitals, two prisons and the House of Lords. It scarcely sounded like the basis for a major national epidemic.[12]

Few could have guessed that the eruption of Britain's first full-blown food scare was now just three months away.

The Fuse Is Lit

As the autumn of 1988 began there were three possible candidates for such a major scare: salmonella and eggs, listeria and BSE. Each had its 'pushers' in the scientific community, urged on by sections of the media.

Still to the fore on eggs was the PHLS, the head of whose Communicable Disease Surveillance Centre claimed in the *BMJ* that a particular feature of the '20,000 cases of food poisoning caused by salmonella' in 1988 had been those associated with 'the consumption of raw hen's eggs or foods containing raw egg'.[13]

Still to the fore on listeria was Professor Lacey who, in a full-page *Observer* feature headed 'Food poison plague hits Britain', was now claiming that listeriosis was responsible not for 150 but '300 deaths each year'.[14]

On BSE, with the number of cases now having reached 850, the running was chiefly being made by the journalists themselves, as in an *Independent* article which reported on cattle being burned in a Cornish quarry 'because they are suffering from a strange new disease which could possibly be transmitted to humans'.[15]

At the end of October, Lacey learned that a local Yorkshire woman had miscarried after contracting listeriosis. He rushed to her home and found a pre-cooked chicken portion in her dustbin, from which he recovered listeria bacteria. When he alerted the media this won him extensive press coverage. But, to his frustration, television showed no interest. The episode left him no nearer than ever to what was still his main goal, the banning of cook-chill. Indeed, soon afterwards, when the DH published new guidelines on cook-chill, it became clear that Lacey's advice had been ignored.[16]

On 15 November, MAFF received further advice from the Southwood Committee on BSE. Milk from infected cows should be destroyed. The ban on feeding cattle with meat and bonemeal, initially only temporary, should be made permanent. This prompted the *Guardian* to pick up a report in the *Veterinary Record* that experiments on injecting BSE-infected tissue into mouse brains had resulted in the mice showing all the symptoms of BSE. 'If BSE can be transmitted to other species,' the *Guardian* writer suggested, 'the possibility of a jump to humans is not absurd.'[17]

On 21 November, after considerable battles behind the scenes, the DH issued a press release attempting to backtrack on its late-summer alarm over eggs by reassuring the public that the problem of possible infection should be kept in perspective (the British Egg Industry Council, BEIC, had recently pointed out that 30 million eggs were eaten in Britain every day, and that the chances of eating an infected egg were no more than 'one in 200 million').

In advance of this announcement, Lacey was excited to receive his first call from a national television programme, the BBC's *Watchdog*. At last, he hoped, he could use it to publicize his views on listeria and cook-chill. But this was not what the BBC was after. They wanted his views on eggs, about which he knew nothing. He nevertheless agreed to appear, alongside Tim Lang of the LFC, and together they pursued a well-worn theme, claiming that the government had been conspiring to 'cover up' the growing 'egg peril' from the public. Significantly, however, they directed the blame for this 'cover up' at MAFF rather than the Department of Health. Both 'experts' advised against eating raw eggs.*

Despite the DH's new bid to downplay the egg scare, the media were following the BBC's lead in talking it up. The London *Evening Standard* reported an IEHO warning to the public not to eat lightly boiled eggs.[18] According to the *Western Daily Press*, egg sales in the West Country were slumping 'after the disclosure that some egg yolks have been contaminated with a strain of salmonella'. It quoted the LFC calling for 'a complete boycott of eggs'.[19]

---

* So unfamiliar was Lacey with the subject of eggs that, earlier in the day, in a conversation with North, he had railed against the 'Department of Health conspiracy' to cover up the dangers of eggs. North explained that this was hardly compatible with the DH's press release on 26 August, of which Lacey knew nothing. This accounted for his readiness on television that evening to switch the blame from the DH to MAFF (personal information).

The *Evening Standard* followed up by reporting that 'one of the West End's best-known restaurants', the *Neal Street* in Covent Garden, had decided 'to alter its egg-based sauces because of the risk of food poisoning highlighted by environmental health officers'.[20] The *Daily Telegraph* reported that the Women's Institute had changed its cake recipes, advising members not to use raw egg white in icing.[21] Under the headline 'Doctor says shoppers should boycott eggs to force action on the salmonella scare', the *Daily Mail* gave further publicity to the views of Tim Lang (failing to explain that he was not a medical doctor).[22] Rather less widely noticed was Lang's interview with *The Grocer* next day, in which he admitted that eggs were really only 'a low risk food' and that he was only using this controversy to illustrate 'general problems in the food trade'.[23]

On 29 November BSE was briefly back in the news, thanks to an intervention in the House of Commons by the maverick Labour MP Dennis Skinner. When agriculture ministers were being quizzed about what one parliamentary sketch-writer called a disease which 'turns cows' brains into sponge and makes them appear drunk', Skinner asked whether humans could catch it. His suggestion that one victim might be Nigel Lawson, the Chancellor of the Exchequer, roused MPs to 'roars of laughter'.

The real story now, however, was salmonella, with new 'egg stories' appearing every day. These were boosted, on 2 December, by an article in *The Lancet*, inspired by the PHLS, reporting on four 'egg associated' food poisoning outbreaks in Wales. This prompted the *Independent* to conclude that 'all eggs, including intact clean eggs, should be regarded as possibly infected. Raw egg consumption may therefore be unsafe'.

On Saturday 3 December articles on the dangers of salmonella and eggs were given prominence in *The Times*, the *Independent*, the *Daily Mail*, the *Daily Telegraph* and *Today*, among many other papers. Most were triggered off by the news that Plymouth Health Authority had told 25 local hospitals to switch from using fresh to pasteurized eggs ('Hospitals ban eggs over fears of deadly salmonella', as the *Mail* put it).

In truth there should have been nothing particularly newsworthy about this instruction. It merely echoed what the DH had told hospital caterers four months earlier. Nevertheless it was given further headline prominence on ITN's lunchtime news. The powder keg had been primed. All it needed, on what was otherwise a slow news day, was a spark. At five o'clock that evening it came.

ITN had decided to extend its lunchtime coverage of the Plymouth story, using extracts from a long interview recorded earlier in the day with the junior health minister Edwina Currie. Standing on a council estate in Chellaston, in her Derbyshire constituency, she was asked how the public should respond to the general concern over eggs.

'We do warn people now', she began, 'that most of the egg production in this country is now, sadly, infected with salmonella.'

Such were the 20 words by which Currie triggered off Britain's first fully-fledged food scare – and for which she was about to become one of the best-known politicians in the country.

Notes

1. All facts and figures in this passage come from the website of the AIDS charity Avert, www.avert.org.
2. *Daily Telegraph*, 24 September 1985.
3. *Daily Express*, 7 October 1985.
4. There is no single source for this narrative. It is assembled from a number of contemporary newspaper reports, including an article by Roger Highfield, *Daily Telegraph* Science Editor ('The woman who discovered BSE', 9 February 1997); published evidence from the BSE Inquiry (The Phillips Report, Vol. 3); and from details obtained from inspection of the Inquiry archives. Since the details are largely uncontroversial, we have not referenced comprehensively.
5. Julie Sheppard, 'The big chill: a report on the implications of cook-chill catering for the public services' (London: London Food Commission, 1987).
6. Symposium organized by the Campden Food Preservation Research Association, Stratford-upon-Avon, 19–21 January 1987.
7. J. McLauchlin, '*Listeria monocytogenes*: recent advances of the taxonomy and epidemiology of listeriosis in humans', *Journal of Applied Microbiology*, 63 (1987), 1–11.
8. *Caterer and Hotelkeeper*, September 1987.
9. Interview with Lacey, *Sunday Post*, 8 November 1987.
10. *S. enteritidis* sub-committee, Public Health Laboratory Service (PHLS). Minutes of meeting, 23 March 1988 (unpublished).
11. Personal testimony from the two witnesses.
12. *Communicable Disease Report*, PHLS, September 1988.
13. *British Medical Journal,* 17 September 1988.

14. *Observer*, 9 October 1988.
15. *Independent*, 1 October 1988.
16. For example: 'Official line unchanged on cook-chill dangers', *Guardian*, 10 November 1988.
17. *Guardian*, 15 November 1988.
18. *Evening Standard*, 23 November 1988.
19. *Western Daily Press*, 23 November 1988.
20. *Evening Standard*, 24 November 1988.
21. *Daily Telegraph*, 25 November 1988.
22. *Daily Mail*, 25 November 1988.
23. *The Grocer*, 26 November 1988.

2

'Killer Eggs'

The Great Salmonella Scare, 1988–9

> *We do warn people now that most of the egg production in this country is now, sadly, infected with salmonella.*
> Edwina Currie, *ITN News*, 3 December 1988

Considering the colossal damage it was to cause, two features of Mrs Currie's televised statement on that December Saturday were distinctly odd. The first was that her 'bombshell' seems to have been deliberately planned. The other was that she hadn't the faintest idea what she was talking about.

In her subsequent book *Life Lines*,[1] Currie wrote that she knew she was going to have to raise the issue of salmonella and eggs 'sooner or later'. 'But if I was going to raise the profile of this important topic,' she went on, 'it was not going to be on a radio phone in Norwich, but properly, nationally.'

The timing of her statement, to coincide with the news of Plymouth Health Authority's instruction to local hospitals not to use fresh eggs, was not accidental. The order was issued on advice from Dr Peter Wilkinson, head of the Plymouth PHLS. He was well known to Currie, as one of her chief advisers and defenders on cook-chill. What made this even odder was that the order was only repeating the instruction sent by the DH to all hospitals on August 26. Why should a local health authority issue a press release to the national media to announce an instruction already four months old (a sharp-eyed journalist might have asked the health authority why it had not complied with the order when it was originally issued)? And why, no sooner was it made public, did Currie let it be known that she was available in Derbyshire for a television interview?

The obvious inference from Currie's peculiar but careful

wording was that the majority of egg-laying chickens were infected with salmonella, which could then be passed on through their eggs. In both respects this was untrue. It was not the egg-layers but most frozen broiler chickens that had been found to be contaminated with salmonella, as the PHLS pointed out as early as 1986. Was it possible that Currie had (as many journalists were to do subsequently) confused chickens bred for meat with those kept to lay eggs?

More specifically, however, almost everything Currie knew about salmonella and eggs had come from her chief adviser on the issue, Dr Bernard Rowe of the PHLS, who since early summer had been pushing strongly his theory about the link between salmonella and eggs. It was he who had become convinced that eggs could be infected from the inside by 'vertical transmission'. And it was he who had issued the general instruction that all investigations of salmonella outbreaks, whether by the PHLS or by EHOs, should keep a close eye out for any links with eggs.

Yet about this in turn two things were remarkable. First, there was no real evidence to support Rowe's theory that eggs in themselves could be the source of salmonella poisoning. Only once had a scientific paper identified a case of salmonella as possibly originating inside an egg, and even this was argued as only a hypothesis.[2] Second, what above all characterized the outbreaks of food poisoning associated with eggs in the previous few months was the way in which the investigators had been so focused on eggs as their possible cause that they had shut their minds to any other possibility, most notably that of cross-contamination from another source.

It was highly relevant, for instance, that many of the recent salmonella outbreaks, such as those centred on the House of Lords, the Gatwick Hilton and the Paddington sandwich bar, had involved mayonnaise. Salmonella is killed off by acid, and the traditional method of making mayonnaise uses enough vinegar or lemon juice to ensure this. But the recent fashion in the 1980s for making mayonnaise blander by reducing its vinegar content, associated with *nouvelle cuisine* and sandwich fillings, had created ideal conditions in which salmonella introduced by cross-contamination from some other source could proliferate.

A subsequent expert inquiry into 19 of the outbreaks officially classed in previous months as 'egg associated' showed that in almost every case the investigation had not been carried out in a thorough fashion; that alternative sources of infection had not been properly considered; and that the blame had been placed on eggs only because this was what was expected from those responsible for the investigation.

In other words, when Currie made her statement, it derived largely from the advice of one man with a theory that had no proper scientific foundation, supported by investigations that were almost wholly unreliable.

Admittedly, much of this had yet to come to light. But what anyone might have noticed was that, despite the tireless efforts of Rowe's investigators, the total number of salmonella outbreaks so far officially linked to eggs in 1988 (of a total of 385 food-associated outbreaks for the year) had amounted to a mere 26.

Yet it was on this astonishingly flimsy basis that Currie had now launched Britain's first major food scare.

Phase One: The 'Nine Day Wonder'

Broadcast early on a Saturday evening, Currie's comment was too late for Sunday's newspapers to rise fully to the occasion. But already clear from those that did run the story were the main battle lines of the row, which was to dominate media attention for days to come.

First was a contemptuous response from the Ministry of Agriculture, Fisheries and Food. As Currie was aware, the minister of agriculture, John MacGregor, was out of the country, taking part in international trade talks in Canada. Under the rules, he was the only MAFF minister permitted to respond to a comment by a minister from another department. But this did not prevent MAFF indicating its anger. Emphasizing that the number of outbreaks so far associated with eggs in 1988 was only 26, a spokesman dismissed Currie's statement as 'highly irresponsible'.[3]

This revealed an unprecedented rift between the two ministries responsible for food safety. The hygiene regulation of farmers and other primary food producers, such as the egg and poultry industries, was the responsibility of MAFF. The DH was responsible for the rest of the food chain, including the 500,000 shops, restaurants and other businesses that sold food directly to the public. By pointing the finger at egg producers, Currie had stepped over that official dividing line.

Similarly affronted were the egg producers themselves. The British Egg Industry Council (BEIC), representing 300 or so large egg producers, called Currie's statement 'factually incorrect and highly irresponsible'. Representing thousands of smaller egg producers, a spokesman for UKEP (United Kingdom Egg Producers) was equally dismissive: 'Mrs Currie's comments are totally unfounded. She obviously knows nothing about the matter.'[4]

On the other side of the argument, only the *Sunday Times* had tracked down the man more than anyone else responsible for the scare. It quoted Rowe of the PHLS as saying that the DH and the PHLS were now considering the 'mass slaughter of infected birds' in Britain's laying flocks. This would be a 'massive job which could take 20 to 30 weeks'.

By Monday morning, 5 December, the story had exploded all over the newspaper front pages. MAFF was reported as 'extremely angry', describing Currie's comments as 'completely exaggerated'. UKEP claimed that 'half the small family firms will go out of business'. There were calls for Currie to be sacked, one from a Tory MP. Even the health ministry itself, clearly unprepared for the storm, weakly explained that all she had meant was that 'most chicken flocks throughout the country had been found to carry salmonella strains – not most eggs'.

But Currie had her supporters. Inevitably Lacey weighed in, described as a 'Government scientific adviser', proposing that 'the only option is to destroy all the country's 50 million-odd laying birds'.[5] Bob Tanner, head of the IEHO, claimed on the lunchtime *ITN News* that the problem of eggs was 'very serious', having already caused 'significantly more' than 10,000 poisoning cases in 1988.

That afternoon, the House of Commons staged an emergency debate, from which Currie was conspicuously absent. Her boss Kenneth Clarke, as secretary of state for health, attempted to calm things down by claiming, somewhat provocatively, that 'most eggs are fine'. But he also referred to '46 cases' of egg-related poisonings. This was inevitably picked up by the *Guardian*'s Erlichman, and others, as representing a dramatic rise over the previously stated 26, indicating that the figures must be hurtling upwards. Only later did it emerge that the reason for the increase was merely that Rowe had spent the weekend ringing EHOs all over the country asking for reports of new 'egg cases'. This was the sole explanation for the apparent rise.

What was to become a marked feature of media coverage of the story was the strategy favoured by television news programmes whereby spokesmen for the two sides of the 'debate' could be pitted against each other, without any journalistic attempt to evaluate the validity of their respective claims. This put the scare's 'pushers', led by Lacey, Lang of the LFC, and the IEHO's Tanner, in the driving seat, able to set the terms of the argument by talking up the threat to an almost unlimited degree. This immediately made spokesmen for the industry, with less media savvy, look awkward and defensive. On that Monday's *Newsnight*, for instance, Lacey's claim that eggs were now killing one person every week and Lang's that one in every 100,000 eggs was infected with what he called 'enterititis' (pronouncing it as 'ent-terry-tight-is'), left the two spokesmen from the BEIC and the National Farmers' Union floundering.

On Tuesday 6 December, media coverage became, if anything, even more frenzied (the still reasonably sober *Daily Telegraph*, for instance, ran no fewer than 11 separate stories on the 'eggs crisis', plus an editorial and two cartoons). A new factor in the story was that now egg sales were collapsing. As the *Sun* put it 'a poison scare panic swept Britain yesterday ... sales in supermarkets slumped by 15 percent ... and wholesale orders for hospitals and schools were slashed by 42 percent'. The *Star* reported that farmers were planning to sue Currie for £10 million, but told its readers that 'there are 1.5 million cases of salmonella poisoning in Britain every year, so the problem is hardly trivial'. The *Daily Express* front page reported that supermarkets were 'dumping hundreds of thousands of eggs', as 'housewives panicked', but went on to quote Lacey, Tanner and Acheson, the DH's Chief Medical Officer, to suggest that their alarm was not unjustified.

Later in the day Currie broke her silence with a press conference and an interview for the BBC. She had 'no regrets' about her statement, and her 'best information' was that there had been '20,000 cases of salmonella poisoning' in the year up to October. 'My assessment is that 10,000 cases have been caused by chicken and eggs' (her source for this, as usual, was Rowe, who on the same day announced 'new figures' showing that in the first ten months of the year 10,738 salmonella cases had been attributed to 'eggs and poultry').

Currie's 'defiant' interview made big headlines on 7 December, with the *Daily Telegraph* reporting the claim by Lacey, now described as a 'public health expert', that Britain was suffering from 'a massive epidemic of salmonella poisoning relating to eggs and poultry'. Salmonella, he said, had got into the internal organs of the 'hens and you cannot tell which ones are infected without killing them first ... it's a very big epidemic'.

Only *The Times* reported on its front page that the Prime Minister, Mrs Thatcher, had read a report on eggs by the Chief Medical Officer and 'immediately afterwards' had 'enjoyed' scrambled eggs for lunch. A longer report inside was headlined 'If you won't eat your words, I suppose I'll have to'.

By the end of the week, as coverage finally began to flag, it was beginning to look as though the great egg scare might be a classic 'nine day wonder', once defined as 'three days' amazement, three days' discussion of details and three days of subsidence'. After all, there was scarcely the trail of bodies, mass funerals, and horror stories of victims and anguished relatives, which might have been expected, to sustain all this talk of 'killer eggs' (although *Today* had done its best with a huge front-page headline 'Fried egg nearly killed my son', over the tale of a 10-year-old South London boy who it alleged had 'almost died' from salmonella poisoning after dining on fried eggs and sausages).

On 10 December, the *Sunday Times* did its best to keep interest alive with a lengthy feature, 'Cracking the Egg Mystery', drawing heavily on the views of Rowe and Lacey. It quoted a report by Rowe to the joint DH/MAFF and egg industry working group claiming that, to establish the true number of salmonella poisoning cases, taking account of all those which had not been reported, the reported figure should be multiplied by 100. 'This implies', said Rowe, 'that there may be up to 2 million salmonella infections per year in England and Wales', of which '1 million relate to poultry'. Rowe's 'multiplier' had not the remotest basis in fact; but it enabled him to suggest that the salmonella 'epidemic' was on a far greater scale than anyone had previously realized.*

* It had been known for a long time that the published figures for food poisoning were much lower than its actual incidence, because so many

Professor Lacey, according to the *Sunday Times*, 'appears to have the only theory' as to why salmonella poisoning was on the rise. This was because *enteritidis*, 'unlike other strains of salmonella', had adapted itself to live 'symbiotically' in the internal organs of chickens, rather than 'parasitically'. This meant that the chickens could 'carry it without showing any signs of illness' and 'most important, it can be present in egg yolks' without being detectible.

The *Observer*, on the other hand, reported that the egg industry had tested 8,000 eggs from 200 farms without finding salmonella in any of them, a finding Lacey was again quickly on hand to dismiss as worthless. The paper did also, however, persuade John MacGregor, the agriculture minister now returned from Canada, to give his first public pronouncement on the crisis. Currie, he said, was 'simply wrong'. 'We should go on eating eggs in exactly the same way as before.' In an editorial, the *Observer* summed up: 'If the Department of Health had deliberately wanted to confuse the public over eggs, they could not have done a better job than they did last week.'

Elsewhere, it was reported that '10 million chickens' were to be slaughtered, as the result of a '70 percent drop in sales'.[6] On Thursday 15 December, it was reported that the Department of Health and the Ministry of Agriculture were jointly to spend £500,000 on advertisements in every national and regional newspaper, designed 'to restore public faith in eggs'.

It might have seemed the worst of the scare was over. In fact it had only just begun.

Phase Two: The Tide Turns Against the Egg Men

The government's advertisements, designed to win back public confidence in eggs, began to appear on 16 December. They

cases remain unreported. The idea of a 'multiplier' to arrive at a true figure had first been proposed in the early 1980s by North and a fellow EHO, but only to aid their teaching in courses on hygiene. Their own suggested multiplier was 10, chosen primarily because it made the maths easier. Rowe, for his own purposes, had chosen to magnify this to 100. Subsequent analysis of DH and other statistics has suggested, more realistically, that the true incidence of salmonella poisoning is probably around five times the reported figure.

majored on the point that, compared with the 30 million eggs eaten every day, the number of salmonella outbreaks 'traced back to eggs' was 'very small' (although the figure it gave of 49 outbreaks was up three from the 46 previously cited). Predictably, when Lacey was asked to comment, he repeated his own earlier claim that the real annual figure for the number of people being poisoned by eggs was 146,000.[7]

Then, later that day, came two events that were significantly to shift the terms of the public debate.

The first, just after 1pm, was the startling announcement that Currie had resigned. By early evening, Lacey was on both ITN and Channel Four news, insisting that she had been 'basically right' in claiming that 'most egg production was infected'. On *Newsnight*, deferentially introduced by Jon Snow as 'an independent consumers' expert', Lang said much the same.

Most of the next morning's press coverage was less sympathetic, broadly agreeing with the *Sun*'s view that 'Edwina' had been 'destroyed by the big mouth that made her famous'.

Coinciding with this news, however, came an announcement that MAFF was planning a financial 'rescue package' for the egg industry (as the *Daily Telegraph*'s main front-page headline put it, 'Currie resigns as egg farmers get millions in aid'). When it emerged that this might amount to £19 million (along with reports that egg producers were now showering Currie with writs for compensation), media attitudes towards the egg industry began to change.

No longer were the egg producers seen just as victims of what even the *Guardian* was now calling Currie's 'gaffe'. This promise of compensation, to an industry which was being accused of poisoning the public, was seen as evidence of the power of the 'farming lobby', which, it was now being suggested, acting through its 'friends' in MAFF, had been behind Currie's sacking. As Robin Oakley reported in *The Times*, under the headline 'Farmers ruling the roost', even Tory MPs were now critical of how MAFF had been behaving 'with gun-dog docility these past weeks at the behest of its chief clients'. One MP called her sacking 'a miscarriage of justice', adding 'history will prove her right'.[8] The *Daily Mail*, citing a poll which showed 'public confidence in Britain's egg producers at an all time low', pronounced in an editorial 'Come back Edwina'.[9]

Journalists now began to focus attention on how the rise of

bacterial contamination in poultry might be a consequence of intensive, modern farming methods, such as crowding tens of thousands of chickens into broiler units and battery cages. 'Eggs', wrote Oliver Gillie in the *Independent*, 'are infected with salmonella because hens have been given contaminated food. Chickens are infected because they hatch from contaminated eggs – and so the epidemic spreads.'[10] The same paper next day reported that 25 percent of all the plants processing feed for the poultry industry had been found by MAFF, the previous year, to be infected with salmonella: 'but none of the suppliers was prosecuted, production was never halted and none of the infected food was destroyed'.[11] This was picked up by other journalists, notably the *Guardian*'s Erlichman, a long-time critic of modern farming practices, who suggested that 'hens slaughtered under the government's £19 million rescue package could be sent to protein processing plants and re-enter the food chain as poultry feed'.[12]

Only the *Financial Times* was intelligent enough to ask the relevant question: how much of this contamination in poultry feed had been ascribed to *salmonella enteritidis*, the strain which lay 'at the heart of the health fears surrounding eggs'? The answer came from MAFF's regular testing of the feed supplied by the UK's 94 processing plants. In six years, *enteritidis* had been found on only one occasion.[13] Even if this proved nothing else, it did confirm that the rise in *enteritidis* poisoning, for which eggs were being almost entirely blamed, had not arisen from feed. But to most of the journalists covering this story, carried away by the image of 'contaminated feed', such a detail must have seemed too 'technical' to be worth noting.*

---

* What was also obvious from many of these articles was that their authors found just as offensive the idea that poultry might be fed with animal remains at all, whether 'contaminated' or not. Chickens, like cows, were supposed to be vegetarians. As will be familiar to anyone who has kept free-range poultry, however, in addition to grain they also require proteins, which is why they spend so much time scratching around for insects and worms. This was why, for both poultry and cows, such an important role had come to be played by feeding them with 'bonemeal', or rendered-down animal remains. Attempts to feed battery hens on a solely vegetarian diet proved disastrous, because the birds simply began pecking each other to death in their desperate hunger for protein. The inability of many journalists to grasp this was to become equally relevant to coverage of the BSE story.

Just as dismissible were MAFF's announcements of tests it had carried out on random samples of eggs drawn from across the country. In one, when 4,000 eggs from 150 producers were analysed, salmonella was not found in any. In another, 2,270 eggs drawn from 85 suppliers in the Midlands and the North West were found equally free from infection. Lacey was quoted as saying that 'other studies, including those carried out by the Public Health Laboratory Service, have detected salmonella-contaminated eggs', as if no more needed to be said.[14]

As 1988 drew to its close, most members of the British public, if asked, would probably have accepted, after the media bombardment of the previous few months, that Britain was in the grip of an unprecedented epidemic of food poisoning from which more people were dying than ever before; that the chief cause of this was the contamination of eggs with salmonella; and that the main cause of this in turn lay in the unnatural way in which hens were fed by farmers.

They might therefore have been startled to know what was to emerge when all the official UK figures for salmonella poisoning in 1988 were finally collated a year or two later. It was true that, after a steady rise through the 1980s, the number of individual cases of poisoning had in 1988 shown a nearly 30 percent jump, the largest annual rise ever recorded, from 23,298 in 1987 to 30,241.

But from the figures for deaths attributed to salmonella a rather different picture emerges. Between 1981 and 1982 these had jumped from 43 to 74. Although they had then fallen back a little, the number of deaths recorded in 1988, despite the relentless furore over 'killer eggs', amounted only to 63. In other words, the total was actually 17 percent lower than it had been six years earlier.[15] As for those that could categorically be attributed to 'infected eggs', scientifically the most accurate answer should have been 'probably none'.

Yet the scare, having entered a new phase, was now raging on under its own momentum, in a way which was less connected with reality than ever.

Phase Three: Enter the Politicians – and the Regulators

Once a scare has been launched on its way, it becomes relevant to keep an eye on four groups of players: the public, the media, the politicians and, finally, the regulatory officials.

For the general public, the end of 1988 marked the moment when the great 'egg scare' was all but over. In the six weeks since mid-November, with media hype working up to a crescendo just before and after Currie's statement, egg sales had collapsed by 33 percent. By the end of the year 70 million fewer eggs were being sold each week than a year earlier. But as 1989 began there were the first signs of public confidence returning. Sales began a steady rise, which was to continue until, by the year's end, individual shoppers would be buying as many eggs as before.*

If the 'real world' had started to return to normal, however, the other three groups were now locked into a *danse macabre* that was to continue for a long time to come.

First onto the stage were the MPs of the House of Commons Select Committee on Agriculture, which had decided to stage a full-scale inquiry into salmonella and eggs. On 4 January there was a preliminary flurry of excitement when it was announced that Edwina Currie had refused to appear before her fellow MPs to give evidence.

Next came the media, who, having said almost everything they could about eggs, were now avid for almost anything that could continue to feed their now well-developed appetite for 'food scare' stories. On 8 January, for instance, the *Sunday Times* was able to report on the plight of a 70-year-old CJD victim. Her husband, on seeing a television programme about BSE, had been struck by the similarity between the diseases, and wondered whether BSE-infected meat might have been the cause of his wife's illness.

On 11 January, the Commons Agriculture Committee heard its first oral evidence, from Acheson, the DH's Chief Medical Officer, Rowe of the PHLS and Keith Meldrum, MAFF's Chief Veterinary Officer. A defensive Acheson, according to *The Times*, 'cast serious doubt on whether Mrs Currie had evidence to support her remark

---

* Figures from MAFF. The exception to this would be institutional buyers, such as hospitals and schools, which were to prove much more cautious in returning to buying eggs in their old 'pre-scare' quantities.

that most of the country's egg production was infected with salmonella'. Meldrum told the MPs that MAFF had, the previous year, identified only 33 flocks as infected with salmonella out of 35,000 inspected.

As, by now, the most famous 'food safety expert' of them all, Lacey was, on 12 January, at last given the opportunity to star in a major television programme, to air his views on his original hobby-horse, listeria. He was filmed by ITV's flagship current affairs show *This Week* buying chilled ready-meals in several supermarkets in Leeds, a quarter of which he claimed to have found to be infected with listeria. The DH was quoted as stating that only 23 people had died from listeriosis in 1987, but Lacey suggested that the true figure was '150'. By next morning, when several newspapers picked up on this story, Lacey had raised his figure for listeriosis deaths to '200'.[16]

On Saturday 14 January, under a front-page headline, 'Food alert as baby girl dies', the *Daily Mail* was able to trump them all with the first report of an actual listeriosis death: that of a 'new-born baby' whose mother, unnamed, claimed to have been made ill herself by eating soft cheese and pre-cooked chicken, described as 'the type of food linked to listeria'. The next morning's Sunday papers were at last able to name and depict the attractive young mother who, it turned out, had lost her *unborn* child after 21 weeks of pregnancy, during a holiday in the south of France, when she had eaten goats' cheese. At least this was enough to justify more headline claims from Lacey that 'Contaminated food "kills 200 a year"'.[17]

As this tale continued to obsess journalists for several days, the well-known commentator Paul Johnson wrote in the *Daily Mail*, 'we heard this weekend of the death of a newborn baby from listeria, contracted by her mother from processed food'. The government's refusal to act on 'food processing from modern production methods', he went on, bore all the signs of a 'cover-up which could develop into a major scandal, one which could damage the government more seriously than the Westland affair'. It was not impossible, Johnson suggested, that some 'incident arising from battery-hen farming' could kill people on the scale of the Lockerbie disaster.[18]

In face of this renewed barrage of 'listeria hysteria', it was finally MAFF's turn to lose its nerve. On 18 January, under the headline

'Tougher food hygiene law being planned', the *Daily Telegraph* gave its front-page lead to news that MacGregor, the agriculture minister, had 'unveiled new plans to combat the threat posed by listeria bacteria in pre-cooked meals sold in supermarkets'. What this had to do with a woman suffering a miscarriage from goat's cheese eaten in France was not entirely obvious. The one thing certain was that it represented something of a victory for the campaign launched two years earlier by Professor Lacey.

On 18 January it was the turn of the IEHO's Bob Tanner to come before the Agriculture Committee. Describing it as 'the final piece of the jigsaw', he presented them with the results of a survey of eggs carried out by his members in Bradford, showing that 21 percent of their yolks were found to be contaminated with salmonella. When it then emerged that the eggs had been recovered from eviscerated dead birds in a slaughterhouse, long after cross-contamination could have occurred, the MPs gave him short shrift.

In media terms, nothing better helps to sustain a scare than stories of actual victims, and the press now had a field day with the case of a nine-year-old Dudley boy Zameer Hussain, claimed by his father to have been killed by an 'infected egg'. The boy's body was exhibited in a glass-lidded coffin in the playground of his former school. When the Southwark coroner, Sir Montague Levine, found that 60-year-old Mrs Doris Comber had also died after eating a boiled egg for breakfast, he said 'we might never know where she picked up this particular salmonella. But there is every likelihood that it was caused by an egg or some chicken'. Quoting her daughter, *Today* headlined its version of the story 'Egg farmers' greed killed my mother'.[19]

The *Sunday Times* had now discovered another 'listeria victim'. Joan Ashburn, who had miscarried in 1986 when seven months pregnant, told the paper that she welcomed the warnings from Lacey about listeria in supermarket meals, and that she had 'traced her own case back to French brie only after a friend obtained information about similar cases linked to soft cheese'.[20]

As two more cases came to light of newborn babies having died of listeriosis, the combination of two food-borne diseases making daily headlines was now provoking both politicians and journalists to ever more trenchant condemnation of the state of Britain's food safety. In the Commons, Labour's agriculture spokesman David Clark claimed that 'many of our citizens have died as a result of the government's failure to protect our food adequately'. For the *Sunday Times* it was clear that the blame essentially rested on MAFF's conflict of interest in being keener 'to protect the interests of farmers and the food industry' than on 'policing them to safeguard public health'.[21]

The Agriculture Committee was now ready, on 25 January, to hear the two 'stars' of the salmonella scare, Lacey and Lang. They got a rougher ride from the committee's chairman Jerry Wiggin than they perhaps anticipated, since he sought to establish their authority for making their various allegations in recent months. Lacey had to admit that his written evidence to the committee was based not on his own research work but that of others. When asked how much experience he had of visiting poultry production units, he could only reply 'my family have kept both free-range and battery birds for many years'. In defending his claims, he had frequently to resort to saying merely that it seemed 'the most plausible explanation'.

Essentially his case was that, while the incidence of *enteritidis* had increased and was attributed to poultry and eggs, it had not increased in poultry. Therefore the most plausible explanation must be that it originated in eggs. Lacey still seemed unaware that the *enteritidis* strain was by no means confined to poultry, but even in recent months had also been found in a wide range of other farm animals and pets, not to mention the most significant carrier of all, human beings themselves.

Dr Lang introduced himself as a 'social psychologist' (having done his doctorate in part on social problems related to anorexia), and his LFC as 'a small independent research organization'. When Wiggin suggested that it might be more accurately called 'a propaganda organization', Lang was outraged. Spluttering that he would treat this charge 'with the contempt it deserves', he asked Wiggin to 'read our qualifications'. The suggestion was 'ridiculous'. When he tried to support his claims by citing 'public health laboratories' as having said that '79 percent of frozen chickens have been contaminated', Wiggin cut him short by reminding him that the committee's concern was not with poultry but with eggs.[22]

One significant point which did emerge from all these exchanges was Lacey's call for the setting up of a new food safety agency, independent of any government department, on the model of the US Food and Drugs Administration. It would not be the last that was heard of such a proposal. But by the time the hearing came to be reported in the next day's press, it was completely overshadowed by a letter to Wiggin from Currie.

The originator of the crisis was still adamant that she would not appear before his committee, chiefly, she said, because she would be bound by the rule preventing the disclosure of advice given to ministers by their officials. However she also wished to explain that she had not said, 'as was reported incorrectly in the press', that most of the eggs in Britain were infected. She had merely tried to explain that 'a significant number of the egg-laying hens in the egg-laying flocks in this country are infected with salmonella'. She ended her letter with that time-honoured formula used by ministers or civil servants when they wish to obfuscate an issue, 'I hope this is helpful'.

Currie's explanation was not received kindly by the press, with headlines such as 'Currie admits gaffe over infected eggs' (*Independent*) and 'Eggwina says: I got it wrong' (*Daily Star*). Nor did it go down well with the committee and other MPs, with consequences soon to emerge.

Rather more ominous, however, was an event which took place later that day, Friday 27 January. Not least stung by a series of reports in the *Independent*, tracking down 'infected' farms that had been linked to salmonella outbreaks (prompting Labour's David Clark to call for a mass-culling programme which he said 'could mean killing the majority of chickens in this country'), MAFF had at last taken action.

That evening, without warning, 27 poultry farms were 'raided' by MAFF officials and closed down under the 1975 Zoonoses Order, a legal power never used before (a zoonosis is an animal-borne disease which is transmissible to humans). As the officials drove up in the night, they served each farmer with a 'Prohibition Notice', photocopied from a typed original and faxed to the officials earlier in the day from MAFF's veterinary headquarters in Tolworth, Surrey. This made it a criminal offence to move any birds or eggs from the farm.

The farmers were thus faced with the choice of having either to pay to continue feeding their flocks, without any income, or to destroy them. There was no appeal. One of the farms was that which had supplied eggs to the Ottringham pâté party the previous year, since when the owner, John Biglin, had replaced his flock.

With 100,000 birds, his weekly feed bill was £50,000. Now even his farm shop was shut down, preventing him from selling other farm produce or eggs from elsewhere to survive.[23]

Having finally decided to act, it seemed MAFF was now doing so with a vengeance.

Phase Four: 'Mad Cows' and the 'Westminster Bubble'

In the first week of February it was reported that, despite her refusal to appear before the Agriculture Committee, Currie was to receive £100,000 (including serialization in a Sunday newspaper) for writing a book in which she intended 'to discuss in detail the salmonella in eggs affair'.[24] This provoked political uproar, only made worse when on 7 February she wrote again to the committee, repeating that she could not help them and asking 'Please may I be allowed to get on with the rest of my life'.[25]

When the committee voted nine-to-one to ask the Commons to require her presence, she next day grudgingly agreed to appear. Her performance made front-page headlines. She 'stonewalled every question and acted like a *grande dame*'. She showed 'studied defiance'. She treated the committee with 'barely concealed contempt'.[26]

In the Commons that afternoon Neil Kinnock, the leader of the opposition, asked Mrs Thatcher 'when are you going to clear up this salmonella shambles in your government?' Meanwhile, MAFF followed up its closure of egg farms, by announcing that it was to launch a compulsory slaughter programme for all poultry flocks found infected.

That morning the *Daily Mirror* had also relaunched listeria to the top of the national news agenda by reporting on a 'major three week investigation' into the 'danger bug' which, it suggested, could be 'one of the biggest threats to our families' health this century'. It had found listeria in food sold by six major supermarket chains, as a result of which, it reported, 155 stores had cleared their shelves. 'What the hell is going on with our food?', it asked over two pages in a follow-up the next day.

At the Department of Health, Acheson, the Chief Medical Officer, called a press conference to announce that he was sending a letter to GPs on 'listeriosis and food'. It warned pregnant women and anyone who was 'immuno-compromised' to avoid eating soft or blue cheese, and advised that ready-made cook-chill meals must be reheated until they were 'piping hot'.

This was the government's first formal admission that listeriosis could be food related. It inevitably inspired a flood of headlines, such as 'Cheese can kill your baby' (the *Sun*), and 'Soft cheese can kill babies, women told' (*Yorkshire Post*). The *Mirror* had yet another story headed 'Listeria killed my unborn baby'. To add to the general air of impending doom, the *Guardian*, on the same day, 11 February, accused MAFF of holding back Southwood's final report on BSE because it suggested that BSE could be passed on to humans.

The *Sunday Times*, on 12 February, led its front page with the headline 'Thatcher to ban unsafe food in shops'. The government, it had learned, was to give top priority to a new food safety Bill: 'the Prime Minister has had to step in to sort out a mess that was getting dangerously out of control'.

Elsewhere it was reported that the DH had agreed to a plan by MAFF to ban all unpasteurized milk, and hence unpasteurized cheese ('Maggie bans killer cheese' as the *People* put it). The *Sunday Telegraph* and the *Sunday Times* noticed that this would stoke up huge trouble with the French, because it would have the effect of banning many of France's best-known cheeses (not to mention some of the best cheeses made in Britain itself).

The following day, as Labour accused the government of lurching 'from complacency to panic', it was reported that Mac-Gregor was to hold talks with the French in a bid to avert a 'cheese trade war', while Britain's own specialist cheesemakers, whose products had in recent years enjoyed a notable revival, warned that such a ban could put more than 200 of them out of business. A Devon farmer was quoted as saying 'This is sheer panic. It's been brought about by mismanagement of the egg scare. It's getting to the point where the only acceptable food will be absolutely sterile, but I don't know how you would produce it, or who would want to eat it'.[27]

The confusion only grew worse when it emerged that, just as MacGregor had been in Brussels, reassuring the French that their cheeses were not to be banned, back in England Kenneth Clarke, as health secretary, had been indicating that they were. Kinnock exploited this disarray by publishing a letter to Thatcher accusing her ministers of 'totally inept handling of the food crisis' and of now extending the 'shambles over salmonella' to other foods.

The *Daily Telegraph* that day, 14 February, ran no fewer than six articles on different aspects of the food safety crisis, including one headed 'French defend their cheese on listeria charge'. This revealed that France currently had 600 listeria cases a year, of which 180 proved fatal. In England and Wales in 1988, there had been 291 cases and 63 deaths.*

On 15 February, the *Daily Mail* announced 'Maggie takes charge as the food poisoning scare grows'. The *Telegraph*'s version was 'Thatcher moves to end muddle on food hygiene', as an *ad hoc* Cabinet committee to co-ordinate policy on the crisis was made permanent. But even the *Telegraph* was losing patience, pronouncing in its editorial ('Enough is enough') 'Food hygiene is serious enough ... but the political controversy surrounding this issue has become a farce'. The Germans, it seemed, agreed. 'After salmonella and listeria,' opined their leading business paper *Handelsblatt*, 'all the symptoms point to a third bacillus which hitherto has only affected a small circle of ministers and journalists: the rare – for Britain – hysteria bacillus.'

In answer to this shambles, Labour was now moving towards a new policy proposal, originally put forward by Lacey: the setting up of an independent agency to take charge of all matters relating to Britain's food safety. First to pick up Lacey's suggestion, speaking in the Commons on 16 February, was Labour backbencher Tony Banks. Two days later, thanks to Labour's frontbench health spokesman, Robin Cook, the idea of a food safety agency had become official Labour policy.[28] By 21 February, charging the government, in a heated Commons debate on food safety, with complacency, confusion, contradiction, negligence and an attempted cover-up, Kinnock said that the answer was an 'independent food standards agency with tough regulatory powers to restore public confidence'.

---

* There was no question that the incidence of *Listeria monocytogenes* cases was increasing dramatically, but no one as yet knew why. What was being widely overlooked (not least by Lacey and the media) was that most strains of monocytogenes are harmless and even beneficial (e.g. the bacteria is commonly associated with the ripening process in cheese). It appears that the rise in poisoning incidents might have been due to the emergence of a new 'rogue' strain (or strains). This is covered in more detail in Chapter Four.

Appropriately, that week there appeared in print for the first time a term soon to become famous, when a *Daily Telegraph* article trailing Southwood's final BSE report, expected shortly, was given the headline 'New food storm looms over "mad cow" fears'. A week later another headline, over a story by the same journalist, polished the phrase into its final version: 'Mad cow disease'.[29]

In fact, Southwood's report, published on 27 February, added little to what had been said in his interim version the previous year, other than recommending a new standing committee to advise ministers and to co-ordinate research (originally known as 'the Tyrrell Committee', after its first chairman, this would in April 1990 be re-named the Spongiform Encephalopathy Advisory Committee, or SEAC).

A second report, causing rather more of a stir, was that of the Commons Agriculture Committee on salmonella and eggs, published two days later, on 1 March. At first sight, this seemed to dish out fairly harsh criticism even-handedly in all directions. A 'failure of government' was how Wiggin and his MPs described the affair. 'They all get fried' was the *Guardian*'s headline. 'Guilty, you're all bad eggs' was the *Sun*'s version. The *Daily Telegraph* summed it up as 'MPs castigate ministries, poultry farms and Currie'.

When the report was debated in the Commons the following day, Wiggin went even further. In particular he singled out the television coverage of the crisis for 'pouring oil on the flames', by persistently using Lacey and Lang to stoke up the scare with their more extreme claims.

But, examined more closely, it became clear that the report had carefully avoided any serious analysis of how the scare had arisen, or where and why Currie's statement might have been so mis-leading. The one organization notably escaping criticism was that which had created the scare in the first place, the PHLS. Nowhere did the report attempt to evaluate Rowe's theory that salmonella poisoning could originate from inside the eggs. Nowhere did it look critically at all those investigations which had concluded, on such flawed evidence, that poisoning outbreaks were 'egg asso-ciated', simply because this was the conclusion which was wanted.

The informed verdict from those who had followed the crisis closely was that Wiggin had pulled off precisely what it had always been his intention to produce: a report which, while superficially appearing to criticize almost all those involved, in fact managed to skate around any of the issues which mattered. If such was his intention, he had succeeded. So far as the great 'salmonella in eggs' scare was concerned, with all its potential to embarrass the government, of which he was a supporter, he had achieved some kind of closure.

The Times, on the day following the debate, published a Mori opinion poll, headed 'Concern over food safety "quite low"'. This had shown that 'the level of public concern is much lower than the recent, much publicised scares over salmonella in eggs and listeria in cheese might suggest'.[30]

To anyone not inhabiting the media and Westminster 'bubble', where these scares had been largely played out, such a finding would hardly have come as much of a surprise.

Phase Five: The Scare Winds Down

The report of the Select Committee on Agriculture was a significant turning point. The fever which since December had held journalists and politicians in such a relentless grip was now suddenly on the wane.

Through the rest of 1989, the story split into two parts, almost wholly separate. The first was the way the media, now so attuned to the idea of food scares, would continue to pick away at the subject, sounding one alarm after another without ever recreating the old sense of excitement, scandal and impending doom.

The other story, unfolding largely away from the headlines, was that of the damage MAFF's regulatory response to the salmonella scare was inflicting on the egg industry itself, particularly on the thousands of smaller producers.

On 1 March, the day the committee's report was published, MAFF issued a new Zoonoses Order, giving its officials the power to slaughter any laying or breeding flocks found infected, while paying the owners very modest compensation. This was followed, on 16 March, by another order requiring the owners of all flocks of 25 birds or more to carry out a complex system of testing every two months for salmonella, at a cost of £12.50 for each sample tested. Any proving positive had to be reported to MAFF, which would then act to destroy the flock.

The impact of this new law was much greater on the small egg-producers since, for a flock of only 25 chickens, it required each bird to be tested, whereas, from flocks of 500 birds or more, only 60 samples had to be taken. This highlighted the way in which egg production in Britain was divided into two almost separate industries. The 300 or so large producers (represented by BEIC) sent their eggs to a small number of 'packing stations', from where the eggs were sent on to supermarkets and other large retailers. Because the eggs were all batched together, this made it impossible to track the source of any individual egg. The much larger number of small producers (represented by UKEP, or the United Kingdom Egg Producers and Retailers Association) either sent their eggs direct to shops or sold their own. These smaller flocks accounted for easily the majority of the 50,000 registered by MAFF, and it was on their owners that the new regulations weighed most heavily, since the costs of testing a small flock was in many cases enough to wipe out any profit.

By mid-April 130,000 chickens in 14 flocks had been destroyed. For Lacey, now being described as 'a government adviser', this confirmed as 'soundly based' the belief that salmonella could infect the egg-laying organs of hens. 'It's all been a horrible cover-up,' he added.[31] By the end of June the number of flocks destroyed had risen to 29.

Considering that all registered flocks were now being regularly tested, to have identified salmonella in only 29 out of 50,000 (0.0006 percent) should have suggested that the incidence of infection was infinitely smaller than had been claimed. The real significance of the new regulations lay in their cost in time and money to the small producers. By the summer's end there were the first reports of small egg-farmers going out of business.*

Eventually, thousands more were to follow. But, at least, by October, when John Selwyn Gummer (promoted to be minister of agriculture in a July reshuffle) issued two more statutory orders relating to the testing and registering of laying and breeding flocks, he was able to boast that 'British eggs are protected by the most stringent safety regulations in the world'.

All this remained almost wholly unnoticed by the media. It was

---

* e.g. *Shropshire Star*, 2 September 1989, reporting on a farmer's wife who had reluctantly killed their 75 chickens because she found 'the new salmonella testing rules too much trouble'. 'My customers round the village were disappointed,' she added.

to become a conspicuous feature of scares of all kinds that, although the media would show obsessive interest in publicizing some danger to the public and calling for more regulation, once the regulations followed then their interest evaporated. In general, the media were to be remarkably reluctant to report on the consequences of regulation, even when, as so often, these consequences turned out to be damaging in ways which were unforeseen, and when the regulation itself was serving no useful purpose.

Nevertheless, the media had not lost interest in scares themselves. Through the spring and summer of 1989 scarcely a day went by without some reference to food poisoning. In March, for instance, it was pesticides and mercury in milk, and the danger of dirty glasses in pubs. In April it was Alar, a chemical sprayed on apples and now supposedly linked to cancer; and a PHLS study showing the high incidence of salmonella in cook-chilled airline meals (according to one unnamed expert, 'worse than eggs'). Cow and Gate had to withdraw 100 million jars of baby food from shops, worth £32 million, when they became the victims of a blackmailer who had 'spiked' their products in the hope of extorting a £1 million ransom.

At the Royal College of Nursing's annual conference, however, Jan Maycock, a clinical nursing specialist, accused the PHLS of covering up evidence it had gathered to show that the 'superbug' MRSA, an antibiotic-resistant form of *staphylococcus*, had in 1987 affected 1,891 victims in Britain's hospitals, killing 50. She charged that the PHLS was reluctant to publish these figures about the DH's own hospitals for fear of causing public alarm; in contrast to its willingness to publicize figures which might arouse alarm over eggs.

In May it was a scare over glass in sweets, and also a widely publicized statement by a group of senior pathologists and vets, who accused the government of not doing enough to stop cattle 'infected with an incurable brain disease' from being 'processed for human consumption'. By now more than 4,000 BSE-infected cattle had been slaughtered, with 250 new cases being confirmed every week. One Edinburgh neuropathologist told the BBC's *Face The Facts* that he now always looked in supermarkets for products such as meat pies and pâtés which might contain 'suspect tissues', and that he knew 'several colleagues who are doing the same'.

In June it was botulism in hazelnut yoghurt (22 reported ill);

clostridum in a north London hospital (53 poisoned, two dead); and *campylobacter* in Gateshead (28 ill from a bacterium linked to magpies pecking milk bottle tops). A Commons report on listeria claimed that, had the DH issued its warning to pregnant mothers earlier, the lives of 26 babies might have been saved ('26 Babies Killed By Food Bug Blunder' was one headline).[32]

In July it was the hidden danger of dirty dishcloths; glass found in baked beans and crisps; salmonella in sandwiches; and another scare linking yoghurt to cancer. A routine check by EHOs in Caerphilly discovered listeria in Belgian pâté, setting in train a sizeable scare, which was to lead to several major supermarket chains removing Belgian pâté from their shelves and the suspension of exports from two Belgian production plants. Although there was no specific record of anyone suffering harm from their products, after the Belgian companies took remedial action the recent dramatic rise in the UK incidence of listeriosis came to an end, and figures fell back to their earlier level.

July ended with reports of a major salmonella outbreak in North Wales, which by August had spread to Cheshire, making more than 300 people ill, three of whom died. But this was not 'egg related'. The problem was traced to a butcher's shop where serious hygiene faults had been identified by EHOs several weeks earlier, although the shop had not been informed of this until just before the outbreak. Another serious salmonella outbreak affecting 100 people in Consett, County Durham, was also traced to meat.

Otherwise, August produced a wide crop of scares, ranging from the discovery of listeria in ice cream to botulism in trout, inadequate hygiene checks on imported Thai prawns and two further alarms over listeria in Belgian pâté. Cadbury's withdrew 2.5 million packs of Turkish Delight from shops, after some were found to be contaminated with mould.

In September it was back to listeria in ready-to-eat chilled foods, with new scares over colourants in sweets, and the risk of bacteria in low-salt foodstuffs. A *Daily Telegraph* headline reported '500 percent rise in salmonella over 3 years', even though the actual figures would eventually show a rise amounting to barely a tenth of that figure.[33]

Through all this litany of alarms, one name recurred more than any other. Whenever journalists wanted an 'expert' to talk up a scare, they knew Professor Lacey would be on hand to give them what they wanted. In April, when an earlier *Daily Telegraph* headline had offered 'Cases of salmonella increasing by 37 percent', this turned out to be a claim by Lacey that, although the latest PHLS figures showed only a 17 percent increase on the same period in 1988, adjusting this to take account for the drop in egg sales indicated that the real figure should be 37 percent.

In May, Lacey launched a personal 'food alert hotline' whereby, for up to 38 pence a minute, the public could ring in for 'unbiased food facts on the dangers of anything from doner kebab to the safest way of storing food at home'. When, in June, Lacey gave a quote on botulism in yoghurt, this was quickly used in Parliament by Labour's agriculture spokesman David Clark to accuse the government of having been caught unawares. 'It should not have been,' he went on, 'because the eminent microbiologist Professor Richard Lacey, an official adviser to the Ministry of Agriculture, had predicted it could return unless the catering industry addressed the problem.'

In July, when listeria was in the news, Lacey was again back to his old practice of trawling Leeds shops, this time showing that seven out of seventy samples of pâté were listeria-positive. In September he was calling for 'all sales of non-tinned pâté' to be suspended and for manufacturers to be prosecuted. Invited by the Royal Mail to help launch a new series of stamps featuring microscopes, he warned that the housefly was 'one of the biggest menaces in spreading disease through the food chain ... just as dangerous and far more common than listeria'.[34]

Interestingly, no newspaper reported in the same month on the closure of the staff kitchen at Leeds General Infirmary, after an EHO had found it so riddled with cockroaches that the local Wakefield Health Authority was later prosecuted. The authority's 'control of infection officer', responsible for maintaining good hygiene in its premises, was Professor Lacey.

Even more curious, however, were the methods still being used by official investigators to lay the blame for salmonella poisoning on eggs. One of the most publicized cases in 1989 was a wedding reception at the Savoy Hotel in February, at which 173 guests were made ill, many seriously. The investigators had blamed this on imported eggs used in a champagne sauce. But analysis of 950 eggs left over from the same batch showed no sign of *enteritidis*. There were clear signs that the salmonella poisoning had also been accompanied by staphylococcal poisoning (seven of the guests began vomiting within hours), which almost always originates from a human carrier. One of the staff, employed by contractors, responsible for preparing the sauces was found to be infected with *enteritidis*, which should have been seen as a strong clue to the likely source of the contamination. He was not even interviewed. Because the investigation had begun on the assumption that the poisoning probably originated from eggs, an 'egg-associated' outbreak it remained.

In late July, when 71 guests fell ill of salmonellosis at Keble College, Oxford, it was immediately reported that they had eaten mayonnaise 'containing raw eggs',[35] followed by another report that 'public health officials are confident that infected eggs led to the Keble College salmonella poisoning outbreak'.[36] Yet an independent study showed that five of the guests had not eaten the mayonnaise; no eggs from the same batch had shown any sign of salmonella; there had been previous food poisoning outbreaks at the college; and one of the kitchen staff was an *enteritidis* carrier. But, other than eggs, no alternative sources for the contamination had been considered.*

More remarkable still was a flurry of newspaper stories in August and September on a study carried out by Dr Tom Humphrey of the PHLS showing that 'the salmonella food poisoning bug found in eggs can survive even when the eggs are boiled for 10 minutes'.[37] This was widely reported as confirming the PHLS's belief that even hard-boiling eggs was not enough to kill off any salmonella infection inside them. Only when fuller details of these experiments were published did it emerge that eggs had been injected in the PHLS's Exeter laboratory with massive doses of fresh salmonellae, which had been allowed to grow to as much as 100 million cells, infinitely larger than the 10 to 100 cells which may naturally be found in eggs (and which the natural defence mechanisms of the egg normally prevent from multiplying).[38]

---

* This and the other independent studies of investigations reported here were carried out by one of the authors of this book, Richard North, who had by now volunteered his services as an expert adviser on food poisoning to the small egg-producers' organization, UKEP. This was because he had been so shocked by the way the scare was based on flawed science, and how it had then gone on to pervert professional standards in the methods used to investigate poisoning outbreaks.

Although, when the eggs had then been boiled for ten minutes, some of these colossal concentrations of cells survived, they were still far too few to cause human infection. Scientifically, the experiments were so artificial that they were meaningless. Yet, in media terms, the PHLS myth had been perpetuated. The damage was continuing.

The Daventry Nuns

A bizarre episode in October at last did much to publicize the damage being inflicted on the small egg-producers by MAFF's 'salmonella blitz', helping to swing public sympathy back onto their side.

In July a Warwickshire GP had reported a minor food poisoning case to his local council. Four people had fallen ill after eating a meringue made with raw egg white. *Salmonella typhimurium* had been isolated from the sufferers and the origin of the eggs was traced back to a local convent, the Sisters of Our Lady of the Passion, near Daventry. MAFF was asked to investigate, and two months later, on 21 September, they tested the hens kept by the nuns, claiming to have found one flock infected with an unidentified strain of salmonella. Six days later they served the nuns with an 'Infected Place Notice', prohibiting them from selling eggs, and, using their new legislative powers, fixed 6 October for the birds to be slaughtered.

The nuns, led by Mother Catherine, an indomitable 82-year-old of Canadian extraction, appealed to UKEP for help. Until now, individual small egg-producers had been reluctant to be identified, even though they were suffering severely from the scare, both in lost sales and in the costs of the new regulations (even where a flock was found infected, compensation was only 60 percent of the birds' value, and there was none for the period when farmers were prohibited from selling their eggs).

Mother Catherine, however, was keen to make a public stand. As UKEP's expert adviser, North explained that MAFF had no legal power to force entry to the convent to slaughter the flock. On the appointed date, therefore, the media were invited to observe MAFF officials being refused entry. The ministry vet who arrived to supervise the killing was nonplussed, ringing his office to summon a senior official. Over the next hour, while everyone waited, more than 100 press, television and radio journalists arrived on the scene, joined by animal rights protestors and the police.

That night, after the officials had retreated, the incident received headline coverage on ITN. Next morning, under such headings as 'Nuns in battle to save their flock' (*The Times*) and 'Praise be! Nuns beat off a coop d'etat' (*Daily Express*), the story was on almost every front page.

Over the next few days, while the nuns kept vigilant watch, media coverage continued. Gummer insisted to *BBC News* that the slaughter must go ahead ('the action is to protect the consumer and the producer'). Then a ministry official on site admitted for the first time that the salmonella strain isolated from the flock was *enteritidis*, whereas that found in the food poisoning victims was *typhimurium*.

This discrepancy was looked on as sufficient evidence to mount a High Court challenge to MAFF. The nuns were for the first time given the right to see the ministry's documents, which clearly showed that the laboratory form identifying the strain had been altered. But the judge refused to allow the nuns to arrange for any independent testing. MAFF also warned that any laboratory that agreed to carry out an independent test would lose its licence to carry out such tests in the future. The judge agreed that the law as it stood gave the ministry no explicit power to enter the convent without permission, but ruled that this must be implied if the law was to be enforced. He therefore gave MAFF permission to carry out the slaughter.

Although there seemed little doubt that some type of salmonella had been identified in one of the nuns' flocks, this probably had no connection to the food poisoning that set the whole drama in train. On 20 October a team of vets arrived with ten 'animal health officers', in convoy with two 20-ton trucks and a van pulling a portable toilet. An even greater 'media circus' was now clustered round the entrance, some from as far away as Japan and Canada. The officials took special measures to ensure that, as they rung the necks of 2,500 birds and piled their corpses into boxes, none of this would be visible to any photographers.

The law had taken its course. But in the two months after the original food poisoning incident, the nuns had sold some 12,000 eggs from the supposedly infected flock without a single further case of poisoning being reported. More than anything else, the episode brought home to the public just how draconian were the powers MAFF now had to remove people's livelihoods, while arousing doubt as to whether these were always being exercised fairly or in the public interest.*

End of 'the Year of the Scare'

In the Queen's Speech on 21 November 1989, the government responded to the 'year of scares' by promising a new Food Safety Bill, to be jointly sponsored by MAFF and the Department of Health. To fight Britain's explosion in food poisoning, this would give unprecedented powers to Britain's 8,000 environmental health officers.

Every one of the country's 500,000 food businesses would have to be registered. EHOs would for the first time be able to serve food businesses with 'improvement notices', demanding hygiene improvements which it would be a criminal offence for them not to carry out. They would for the first time be empowered to close down any food business altogether, simply by issuing a 'prohibition notice', which would not require the permission of a magistrate. Fines for any offence would be increased to a maximum of £20,000. The new Act would allow ministers, if they so decided, to make it compulsory for anyone handling food outside the home to be given special hygiene training.

The Bill, which was to be put through Parliament in 1990, promised to grant almost everything for which the EHOs had long been campaigning, not least the possibility that they could raise millions of pounds a year by running all those hygiene courses for anyone working with food.

In the week before Christmas 1989, virtually unnoticed by the media, MAFF announced that it had killed its millionth chicken

---

* Some weeks after the slaughter of their birds, there was to be a further twist to the nuns' tale. In December 'animal rights' activists broke in to release their remaining 2,500 hens, 'going on the rampage and breaking everything they could break'. Said a dismayed Mother Catherine, 'these people who claim to be interested in animals don't appear to be interested in the welfare of the chickens at all. They released the chickens to the mercy of foxes and other predators, and gave them no access to water'.

under the compulsory slaughter programme, with the taxpayers having to foot a compensation bill to date of £756,355.80.

What all this had been in aid of would be revealed when the PHLS and the DH announced their confirmed figures for 'egg-associated' salmonella poisoning outbreaks during the years 1988 and 1989. The final figure for 1988 was 34, rather fewer than the 49 claimed earlier, following Currie's statement. The final 1989 figure would be 42, seemingly showing a 23 percent increase.

But the evidence indicated that, because of all the publicity given to salmonella, there was now a much greater readiness to report cases of salmonella poisoning, and also to find that eggs were to blame, even when this was based on seriously flawed evidence.

The truth was that, compared to the total number of food-poisoning cases, even the official figure still remained relatively tiny. Those which could reliably be ascribed to salmonella originating inside an egg – the PHLS's cardinal article of belief – amounted probably to none. The contribution to food safety made by the new legislation was thus the same.

As 1989 reached its end, no one involved in any part of the food industry could remember a year remotely like it. Scarcely a day had gone by when there had not been news of some crisis or risk to human health, presented by almost every foodstuff under the sun, from beef to baked beans, from apples to Turkish Delight, from pâté to trout. From the relentless way in which it was reported, it seemed almost as if the whole nation's food supply was poisoned.

The real legacy of the food scares of 1988–9 was that politicians, officials and the media – crucially egged on by certain 'scientists' – had all become so much twitchier about hygiene and the possible dangers arising from food than ever before. The full consequences of that departure from common sense and sound science would be seen in the decade that was just about to begin.

A Portent for the Future

The first few months of the 1990s were to see the brief eruption of one more scare – or rather the re-emergence of one which was also an omen for the future.

In November 1989 the West German government had decided to ban any imports of British beef unless it was certified as coming from a BSE-free herd.* Although Britain sold the Germans only 6,315 tons of beef a year, this provoked an international row and put the possible dangers of BSE to human health back on the front pages.

The European Commission told Germany that its move did not appear to be justified on health grounds and might be in breach of the Treaty of Rome. France, for once, supported Britain. 'We think British beef is perfectly safe', said a spokesman, 'and we are satisfied with the measures taken by Britain to deal with BSE.' While continuing to protest at the German move, and to deny any possibility that BSE could infect humans, MAFF announced a ban on any sale of certain offals from British beef, including parts of the animals often used in meat pies.

Then as 1990 began, following a recommendation from the Southwood Committee, the Department of Health set up a national CJD Surveillance Unit in Edinburgh, under Dr Robert Will, to study any changes in the incidence of CJD that might be linked to the BSE epidemic in Britain's cattle. By appearing to acknowledge that there might be some connection between them, this prompted the *Independent* to run the most extensive feature yet on 'mad cow disease', illustrated with a huge picture of BSE-infected cattle burning on a Cornish funeral pyre.[39]

In February 1990 the *Veterinary Record* reported that mice whose brains had been injected with heavy doses of BSE-infected tissue showed signs of developing BSE themselves. Again, this seemed to raise a question mark over MAFF's insistence (confirmed by Southwood) that BSE could not be transmitted from one species to another; and in March this was reinforced when several newspapers reported that five different types of antelopes in zoos had died from spongiform encephalopathies.[40]

In April, Humberside county council became the first education authority to remove British beef from its school menus. Days later, imports of British beef were banned by Mikhail Gorbachev's Soviet Union.

On 10 May media interest exploded when it was reported that a Siamese cat called Max had died of the feline equivalent of BSE (FSE). Three days later the *Sunday Times* led its front page with the

---

* Although this story was to coincide with the toppling of the Berlin Wall, Germany had still to be united.

headline 'Leading food scientist calls for slaughter of 6 million cows'. Professor Lacey had discovered BSE. Curiously described as 'a former government adviser' who had 'resigned from the government's veterinary products committee in protest at Whitehall's failure to heed his early warning of the risk of salmonella in eggs', Lacey was now demanding the slaughter of all cattle from BSE-infected herds and a total ban on British beef exports.[41] The following day his views were heavily promoted by BBC television news.

On 16 May, desperately conscious of the need to avoid any repetition of the salmonella in eggs debacle, the minister for agriculture John Gummer collaborated with the media in staging a stunt. Attending an Ipswich boat show, he was surrounded by cameras while he offered a hamburger to his four-year-old daughter Cordelia. Proclaiming that beef was totally safe, he said 'as you can see my whole family enjoy it, and I have no worries about my children eating it'. Alas for Gummer, his daughter pushed it away because it was too hot. The resulting pictures, blazoned across almost every front page, were long to haunt him.

Two days later Germany called on the European Commission to extend its ban on British beef imports right across the European Community. Lacey announced that he was flying to Brussels to support the German demand. When, on 19 May, it was reported that a second cat had died of FSE, in Belfast, soon followed by a third, this again won saturation coverage.

Beef sales slumped overnight by 25 percent, a fall much steeper than that in the sales of eggs in 1988. When Austria, France, Germany and Italy all in quick succession banned imports of UK beef, a gruelling 22-hour negotiation by EC farm ministers led to a compromise. The various countries would resume imports but only on condition that beef was certified as not coming from one of the 7,000 herds that had now been affected by BSE.

More cats died. In July *The Lancet* published a paper by Dr John Collinge and others, headed 'Human BSE cases more widespread than thought'. Dr Collinge now had a Wellcome Foundation grant to develop a test for CJD, and the paper suggested that, under existing diagnostic criteria, too many cases of CJD were being missed.

Surprisingly quickly, however, the first real BSE scare then died away. A study was later to show that in 1990 national newspapers contained no fewer than 1,092 items relating to BSE, by far the majority in the first half of the year.[42]

The following year, that figure would drop to a mere 93, reflecting the onset of four years when food scares would almost vanish from the news. But during those years, as the price to be paid for the scares of the late 1980s, Britain's 500,000 food businesses would be facing a new and much more damaging threat. It would force many thousands of them to close their doors.

Notes

1. Edwina Currrie, *Life Lines* (Sidgwick and Jackson, 1989).
2. S. A. Hopper and S. Mawer, 'Salmonella enteritidis in a commercial layer flock', *Veterinary Record* (1988), p. 351.
3. *Sunday Times, Mail on Sunday, The People*, 4 December 1988.
4. *Sunday Times, Sunday Express*, 4 December 1988.
5. *Evening Standard*, 5 December 1988.
6. *Sunday Mirror, Mail on Sunday*, 11 December 1988.
7. *Independent*, 16 December 1988.
8. Tim Devlin, MP, quoted in the *Sun*, 21 December 1988.
9. *Daily Mail*, 21 December 1988.
10. *Independent*, 20 December 1988.
11. *Independent*, 21 December 1988.
12. *Guardian*, 21 December 1988.
13. *Financial Times*, 21 December 1988.
14. *Daily Telegraph*, 22 December 1988.
15. All figures were supplied by the Public Health Laboratory Service (for England and Wales) and the Scottish Centre for Infection and Environmental Health and given in answer to a Parliamentary question in 2001 (Hansard, HL, Written Answers, 25 April 2001).
16. *Daily Mirror*, 13 January 1989.
17. *Sunday Times*, 15 January 1989.
18. *Daily Mail*, 16 January 1989.
19. *Today*, 20 January 1989.
20. *Sunday Times*, 22 January 1989.
21. *Ibid*.
22. Personal observation noted by North, present at the hearing.
23. Personal information.
24. *The Times*, 3 February; *Daily Telegraph*, 6 February 1989.
25. *Daily Mail*, 7 February 1989.
26. *Daily Telegraph, Independent*, 9 February 1989.
27. *Guardian*, 1 February 1989.

28. *Daily Telegraph*, *Yorkshire Post*, 18 February 1989.
29. *Daily Telegraph*, 19 February, 26 February 1989.
30. *The Times*, 8 March 1989.
31. *Daily Telegraph*, 14 April 1989.
32. *Today*, 30 June 1989.
33. *Daily Telegraph*, 4 September 1989. The increase in reported salmonella cases between 1986 and 1988 was 56 percent (Hansard, see n.15).
34. *Yorkshire Post*, 4 September 1989.
35. *Oxford Mail*.
36. *Oxford Times*, 18 August 1989.
37. *Yorkshire Post*, 26 August; *Sun* and *Daily Mail*, 27 August; *Mirror*, *Independent* and *The Times*, 1 September; *Today*, 2 September; *New Scientist*, 23 September 1989.
38. *Epidemiology and Infection*, September 1989.
39. 'Mad, sad, bad, story of a British beef', *Independent*, 9 January 1990.
40. *Mail on Sunday*, 11 March; *Daily Telegraph*, *Guardian*, *The Times*, 12 March 1990.
41. *Sunday Times*, 13 May 1990.
42. Jacquie Reilly and David Miller, Media Studies Unit, Glasgow University (from a paper entitled 'Food Scares in the Media', unpublished, but based on a paper presented to the AEGV European Interdisciplinary Meeting, 14–16 October 1993, Potsdam, Germany).

3

Enter the Hygiene Police

Paying the Price, 1990–4

I have the power to close down businesses like this.
First words of young environmental health officer
on entering a Bolton bakery, 1990

On a June day in 1990, a young woman stepped into the family
bakery run by Dorothy Wood in Bolton, Greater Manchester. She
introduced herself with the words 'I have the power to close down
businesses like this', and went on to explain that she was an
environmental health officer from Bolton council. Twice in the
next six months she returned to inspect the bakery but, for over a
year, Mrs Wood heard nothing more. In March 1992, however,
out of the blue, she received summonses to appear before the local
magistrates on ten criminal charges under the food hygiene
regulations.

Naturally Mrs Wood was horrified. But when she read the
charges, she was astonished. One of her alleged criminal offences
consisted of placing a box of butter in the same refrigerator as a
sealed packet of meat. Another charge was that the edge of a table,
used to hold buckets of raw potatoes ready for peeling, had been
'chipped'. A third was that the ceiling of a cellar room, long out of
use, had been 'rough'. Most bizarre of all was the accusation that a
bucket of 'stagnant water' had been found in the shop. This was in
fact a bucket of hot water, being used to scrub the floor when the
EHO had arrived.

The court hearing lasted two days, during which the magistrates
refused to allow expert evidence for the defence from a professional hygiene consultant. They found Mrs Wood guilty on all
charges, and she was fined £2,000. In a state of disbelieving shock,

69

she lodged an appeal against the four charges she had found most outrageous. Shortly before these were due to be heard in the Crown Court, in September 1992, she was told that the council had decided 'not to offer any evidence'. The court quashed all the ten charges on which she had been found guilty, and sent her a cheque for £2,000.[1]

The 'Hygiene Blitz'

One of the more extraordinary dramas unfolding in Britain in the early 1990s was a direct consequence of the food scares of the late 1980s. What made it even more remarkable was that it remained almost entirely unnoticed by the media.

The real damage done by a scare, as this book will show, comes from the response of government, as politicians and officials try to meet the challenge by imposing and enforcing new laws. We have already looked at the first official response to the hysteria over food safety in the late 1980s: the tranche of new regulations targeted at the egg industry. But the impact of the government's second response was to be much wider and more damaging. This was set in train when, in 1990, Parliament approved the new Food Safety Act, granting a wide range of new powers to Britain's 8,000 environmental health officers (EHOs). How they were to use those powers will be the main theme of this chapter.

The profession to which these powers were given had lately been going through a dramatic culture change. Until the 1960s 'public health inspectors' had tended to be older men, recruited to council staff after years of practical experience in other fields. Many were ex-servicemen or former tradesmen, such as plumbers. They saw it as their chief role to give businesses practical advice, falling back on prosecution only as a last resort.

Since their change of title to 'environmental health officer', however, when it also soon became mandatory for them to hold a degree, the profession had developed a very different ethos. The new recruits were much younger, without practical experience, heavily reliant on what they had been taught at college. Many were young women. And their attitude to businesses was now becoming markedly more confrontational, as was reflected in their much greater willingness to bring prosecutions in the courts.

The way had been led on this by the EHOs of one or two inner

London boroughs, notably Westminster and Camden. In the late 1980s Westminster's food safety team had chosen to raise the profile of food hygiene by targeting well-known London restaurants. A widely publicized example was their decision, in 1989, to bring 15 criminal charges against Le Gavroche, run by the master chef Albert Roux and one of only two restaurants in Britain to have been awarded three Michelin stars. When in March 1989 the case came before Wells Street magistrates it lasted for two weeks. Roux was eventually cleared on all charges.

Such was the profession which the Food Safety Act had now armed with draconian new powers. With food poisoning figures soaring, the EHOs saw themselves in the front line of a crusade. As they sallied forth to step up their inspections of food shops, restaurants, pubs, care homes and any business engaged in selling, preparing or handling food, the resulting 'hygiene blitz' was, over the next four years, to inflict significant damage on national life.

For a long time, however, this attracted virtually no attention from the media. The real nature of what was going on only came to light in the closing months of 1992, when we began reporting on it in the *Daily* and *Sunday Telegraphs*.* As hundreds of letters poured in from the owners of food-related businesses all over the country, describing their own experiences at the hands of the EHOs, the picture they conjured up was bizarre.

One of the more striking features of the EHOs' crusade was how little it seemed to be related to genuine hygiene problems and how much it was driven by what we called 'the checklist mentality'. Young, inexperienced EHOs would march into well-run,

---

* The authors of this book first came together following an article by Booker in the *Daily Telegraph* ('Who's That Lurking Behind The Brussels Book of Rules?', 14 September 1992). The article's purpose was to point out how much of the damage then being widely blamed on 'EEC regulations' resulted either from new requirements added on by Whitehall when Brussels directives were translated into British law (what came to be known as 'gold plating'), or from the enforcement of regulations which originated entirely in the UK. Since several of the examples cited related to food hygiene, Booker was contacted by North, then acting as a food safety consultant (and himself an ex-EHO), whose professional expertise provided the original basis of a collaboration which has continued to the present day.

successful food businesses, reeling off all the points they had been told to look for at their colleges or seminars. They would demand that thousands of pounds be spent on 'new walls, floors and ceilings', or order the replacement of anything made of wood, from shelves and chopping blocks to rolling pins and wood-handled brooms. Yet so preoccupied were they with their 'checklists' that, when it came to identifying anything which might pose a real risk, their lack of practical experience might well lead them to overlook it altogether.

Some consequences of this approach might have seemed little more than silly. For years, for instance, the members of Newton Abbot Rotary Club had marked Christmas by serving a turkey dinner to patients on the wards of their local hospital. Just before Christmas 1992, however, they were told by Teignbridge EHOs that, under hygiene regulations, this could no longer be permitted. They had to give the patients orange juice instead. An even older tradition was the Royal Navy's custom of using oars to stir the sailors' Christmas puddings. Again, at Christmas 1992, the authorities in charge of the naval base at Portland were informed by South Dorset EHOs that this was in breach of regulations. Wood was no longer considered hygienic. The sailors would have to use plastic spoons instead.

On many occasions, however, the results were rather more serious. In Basingstoke in 1992 June Vines, the owner of Griffin's, the oldest-established pork butcher in England, was served by her local EHOs with a sheaf of Improvement Notices under the new Food Safety Act. These ordered her to strip away all the traditional patterned tiles from the shop's interior and to replace all her floors, walls and ceilings with 'seamless cladding'. She must either install very expensive new cooling systems, or keep all her meat sealed away in a refrigerated cold store, out of customers' sight.

So prohibitive would be the cost of complying with these notices that, in August 1992, Griffin's closed its doors. 'We are being asked to turn our butcher's shop into an operating theatre,' said Mrs Vines, as she put up the shutters for the last time on the Georgian building, which had housed the business since 1756. In the high streets of Britain, numerous other butchers, fishmongers, bakers and other food businesses were, around this time, being forced to close down for similar reasons.

The closure of Mrs Vines' shop illustrated the power given to the EHOs by the new system of Improvement Notices. When Bognor Regis golf club was in 1991 considering changes to its clubhouse, it was suggested that advice should be sought from the EHOs of Arun council. The officials made an inspection. Shortly afterwards, committee members were astonished each to receive a bulky envelope containing 108 pages (making 2,000 pieces of paper in all). These comprised 36 Improvement Notices, 22 under the Food Safety Act, the rest under the Health and Safety at Work Act. The club was given just two months to carry out the long list of works indicated, or the EHOs would close it down. When their demands were examined, it was highly questionable what most had to do with hygiene or health and safety. But to disobey an Improvement Notice was now a criminal offence in itself, punishable by a fine of up to £20,000 or imprisonment. The members had little option but to pay for largely pointless 'improvements', which cost them £100,000.

Faced with another kind of crisis was the Abbeyfield Society housing association, a Christian organization which ran 1,000 independent homes all over the country where small groups of people, mainly elderly, could live together in a homely setting, sharing domestic chores. In 1991 EHOs began calling on these virtually private houses, announcing that, under the new Food Safety Act, they must now be treated as 'food businesses', subject to all the regulations applying to restaurants and other catering establishments. When an EHO from Salford council walked into the kitchen of a home in Walkden, his first action was to throw a wooden cutting board and rolling pin into the bin, saying 'these aren't allowed', despite protests from their owner that they had been a wedding present many years before.

There followed a battery of Improvement Notices, including a ruling that residents would not be permitted to work in the kitchen without special protective clothing. The Abbeyfield protested that this was not in the spirit of what was essentially a private home, and went to court, where the local magistrates ruled that the requirements should only apply to paid staff. This so incensed the EHOs that they took the case to the High Court in London.

In March 1993 two learned judges spent much of a day arguing over such points as whether a bottle of milk should, within the meaning of the hygiene regulations, be considered as an 'open' or a 'covered' food. Was it still a 'covered' food when the foil cap had been taken off? Their final judgement of Solomon was that the octogenarian residents of the Abbeyfield home might be allowed to peel vegetables or make tea in their everyday clothes, but if they wished to butter scones (butter being an 'open' food), they must put on special overalls. The home's trustees later reported that the residents found all these legal niceties so confusing that, even though they still wanted to help in the kitchen, they were too frightened to do so lest they do something 'against the regulations'.

No record was ever kept of just how many 'food handling operations' were brought to an end by the 'hygiene blitz' of the early 1990s. These included not only food businesses but also the kitchens of offices and village halls, meals-on-wheels services, lunches given by volunteers to groups of pensioners, and countless others. What was particularly startling about this was how often the demands made by the EHOs went way beyond the requirements of the law. A small but typical example was how the people of Tadcaster were shocked in 1992 to lose two of their most popular local businesses: a top-quality cheese stall in their town market, and a van which toured surrounding villages selling fish freshly landed that morning on the Yorkshire coast. It turned out that the owners of both had been forced to close down after being told by Selby EHOs that they must pay for expensive equipment to keep their wares refrigerated. In fact this had nothing to do with the law. There were no regulations to require the refrigeration of either cheese or fresh fish. But such was the general climate of fear and confusion now being promoted by the EHOs throughout the food industry that few dared question it.

In fact, the EHOs were not alone in promoting confusion over the law. In the autumn of 1992 the Department of Health announced that it was about to introduce new regulations under the Food Safety Act imposing a new maximum temperature of $5°$ for the refrigeration of certain foods. All over the country businesses hurried to spend an estimated £100 million on buying new high-performance refrigerators. Reg Gifford, the owner of a well-known country house hotel in the Lake District, had always taken great care to preserve its traditional appearance and ambience. But when he was told about the new regulations, he spent £25,000 on adding a complete new room to the hotel, to house the necessary equipment. In February 1993, only weeks before the new law was due to come into force, the DH announced that it was not to be implemented after all. That £100 million had been spent in vain.

The EHOs themselves did, however, have one particular reason for wishing to blur over the precise nature of what the law did or didn't say. Since 1986 the IEHO had been calling on the government to make it compulsory for all food-handlers to take hygiene courses. These would be administered by the EHOs themselves, for a fee. But although the Food Safety Act had given ministers the power to introduce such a scheme, it was never exercised. This did not prevent the EHOs from somehow conveying to the owners of food businesses, and to thousands of charitable and voluntary bodies, that such training courses were now a legal requirement.

In January 1993, for instance, the authorities in charge of the magnificent mediaeval Bishop's Palace in Wells wrote to local organizations to advertise the popularity of their charity open days as a means of raising funds. They particularly cited the success enjoyed in 1992 by the Somerset Trust for Nature Conservation, which had raised a large sum, not least through the sale of an array of food and drink provided by dozens of members. The letter went on to say, however, that, 'under the Food Safety Act 1990', anyone involved in food handling 'will need to be trained and hold the necessary Institution of Environmental Health Officers Basic Food Hygiene Certificate (the current price for the training is £35 per person)'.

When the trust's organizers read this, they realized they could not afford to send their army of helpers on 'food hygiene' courses at £35 a head, and reluctantly decided they must cancel their plans for another open day. What neither they nor the Palace staff realized was that the Food Safety Act did not require anyone to go on courses. Yet this misunderstanding had certainly served the interests of the IEHO. Since 1991 its members had raised more than £35 million by awarding 'hygiene certificates' to over a million people, providing the IEHO with easily its largest single source of income.

In late 1992 and 1993 we investigated scores of stories about the 'hygiene blitz', from all over the country. Some merely provoked a wry smile, as when EHOs solemnly informed the staff of a Devon hotel that, in making ham and tomato sandwiches, they must always be careful to use one knife for the ham (because it was 'cooked' food) and another for the tomato (because it was 'raw').

The EHOs did not, however, advise which knife should be used to cut the finished sandwich.

Other tales, however, were heartrending, such as the fate of the Green Dragon, just outside Cheltenham, which Bob and Susan Hinton had spent six years building up into one of the most popular country pubs in the Cotswolds. On 16 December 1992, its bars and restaurants were packed with festive pre-Christmas parties, including a group of local teachers. Next day, after a number of customers had fallen ill with food poisoning, EHOs from Cotswold council moved in to investigate, putting out a lurid statement to the local media to the effect that the cause might have been salmonella. This was given headline treatment on local radio and television stations. The Green Dragon's trade, over what should have been its busiest week of the year, fell almost to nothing. Mr and Mrs Hinton received letters from solicitors acting on behalf of the teachers demanding compensation.

Only after a few weeks when the pub had remained virtually empty of customers did the EHOs report back that the cause of the poisoning had not been salmonella but a virus contaminating mushrooms bought from a mushroom farm. This was something the pub would have been powerless to detect or control, and the EHOs decided to carry their investigations no further. But thanks to their reckless mention of salmonella, the damage had been done. In February 1993, while the lawyers were still arguing about thousands of pounds of compensation, Sue Hinton sent out a fax to her many friends and supporters: 'the Dragon is dead. Sadly we have lost our battle against, it seems, the whole world'. The business they had spent six years building up was no more.

Everything described in these past few pages had been set in train by the food scares of the late 1980s. Between 1991 and 1993, the annual number of food inspections carried out by EHOs soared from 150,000 to 419,000. By 1993 the cost to businesses and other organizations of all the changes required by the EHOs was conservatively estimated as having been at least £3 billion. Yet, over the same period, after its dramatic rise in the 1980s, the national incidence of food poisoning remained curiously stable.

In the years before 1990 the annual number of salmonella poisoning cases had virtually tripled, from around 11,000 a year at the start of the decade to around 33,000. Through the first six years of the 1990s, that was where the total remained, neither rising nor falling. The net effect of all that frenzied hyperactivity by the EHOs, it seemed, had been to achieve virtually nothing.*

This was vividly illustrated by a drama that unfolded in Pembrokeshire in the months after June 1992, when 60 people in Haverfordwest fell ill with salmonella poisoning after eating various products from a local health food shop. Although these included a quiche, coleslaw and tuna, the Preseli EHOs focused immediately on just one of the products which had been eaten: egg sandwiches. They discovered that the shop's egg supplier drew on three small free-range egg farms nearby. In two, the flocks tested positive for salmonella. It seemed an open and shut case, and MAFF officials came in to slaughter the flocks.

When the case was independently investigated, however, a rather different picture emerged. A significant number of those poisoned had not eaten the egg sandwiches at all. There was no evidence that the eggs used that day in fact came from the chickens that had been destroyed, as eggs had also been bought from other sources. It was hardly surprising that salmonella had been found in the chickens, because salmonella organisms are as common in the environment as cold germs. There was no evidence that salmonella had been found in the eggs from those two flocks, and even if the eggs had been infected, their hard-boiling to make sandwiches would have been sufficient to kill it. All the evidence, in short, pointed to a case of cross-contamination from some other sources, which had probably poisoned several of the other products eaten that day by those who fell ill, but which the EHOs never bothered to investigate.

This was of little comfort, however, to the two small egg-farmers, Chris Brown and Barry Cheetham, who had not only lost their flocks and their livelihood but also owed considerable sums to their banks. In February 1993, Mr Cheetham was declared bankrupt for owing money he had only borrowed to buy his flock in the first place.

A week later the Advisory Committee on the Microbiological Safety of Food published a report by Professor Heather Dick, an

* In 1980 salmonella poisoning figures for the UK were recorded at 11,221. This rose, by 1990, to 32,829. In 1993, after four years of the 'hygiene blitz', it was 33,749 and in 1996, 32,662 (figures from Hansard, HL, Written Answers, 25 April 2001).

eminent microbiologist. Although the report was carefully worded not to embarrass the government, it concluded that there was insufficient evidence to justify the continuation of MAFF's slaughter policy. That same day, 23 February 1993, Gummer announced that the policy he had introduced in 1989 as MAFF's central defence against salmonella had been scrapped. By now MAFF had destroyed 3.25 million chickens at a cost of £10 million. five thousand smaller egg-producers had been driven out of business, and all to no purpose.

Like the EHOs' 'hygiene blitz', it seemed, the chicken slaughter policy had been doing no more than taking a sledgehammer to miss the nut.

Mr Gummer Closes Down the Slaughterhouses

During these same years of the early 1990s, another even more bizarre disaster was descending on Britain's food industry. But this time it was directed specifically at just one sector.

Again, ostensibly in the name of 'hygiene', Gummer's MAFF officials were busy bringing about an unprecedented revolution in the regulation of Britain's meat industry. So far-reaching was this that within four years more than half the slaughterhouses in Britain would be forced to close their doors. What lay behind it was the need for Britain to comply with two 'meat hygiene' directives imposed by Brussels. But in reality these had very little to do with improving hygiene. Had the food scares of the late 1980s not made food safety such a politically sensitive issue, it is doubtful whether the government could have pushed through such a devastating change with so little questioning or protest.

The story behind this revolution went back nearly 30 years to the early days of the European 'Common Market', when the European Commission had issued a directive imposing common rules on the comparatively tiny number of large abattoirs which wished to export 'red meat', such as beef, lamb and pork, across national frontiers. Based on an old nineteenth-century German model, the new law required the slaughterhouses to make significant structural changes to the way they ran their operations.

This directive, 64/433, did not immediately affect Britain, since she was not yet a member of the Common Market. But soon after joining in 1973 she became obliged to comply with a second directive which extended similar 'hygiene' rules to the production of poultry meat – and this raised for the UK a contentious new problem.[2]

For more than 100 years, Britain and the continent had relied on two wholly different systems for regulating the safety of meat. In Britain, under the system of public health protection originated by nineteenth century reforms, meat inspection in slaughterhouses had been carried out under the supervision of 'sanitary inspectors', now in their new guise as 'environmental health officers'. But on the continent, dating back to the days of Louis Pasteur, this had always been the responsibility of specially trained vets. Now, under the 'poultry hygiene directive', Britain was expected to come into line with the continental system, which for the EHOs was a serious professional rebuff. It meant they would have to hand over supervision of meat inspection to a vet who, without the special training customary on the continent, probably knew much less about meat hygiene than they did.

In the 1980s had come a further step towards integration with the continental system, when Britain's 80 or so large 'industrial abattoirs', producing meat for the export trade and supermarkets, had to comply with all the costly structural requirements of that original 1964 directive: a task so expensive that they were given government grants worth millions of pounds to carry it out.

Finally, with the approach of the European 'Single Market' at the end of 1992, Brussels had decided that the integration of the Community's meat industry must be completed. This meant, firstly, that almost all Britain's smaller red-meat slaughterhouses would also now have to carry out those costly structural changes required by 'EC export rules', although, unlike the big 'industrial abattoirs', they would be given no help from public funds. Secondly, instead of simply replacing the British inspection system with the continental system, MAFF decided that their owners would have to pay for a clumsy combination of both systems. Not only would they have to continue paying for their usual meat inspectors, but also for the services of a vet to supervise them.

One of the oddest features of this revolution was the curiously high-handed and secretive way in which MAFF's officials chose to introduce it. In 1991 they sent out to all the owners of slaughterhouses and other meat businesses a booklet entitled '1992 – Food Sense And You'. When the owners read what would now be required of them to stay in business after the launch of the Single Market on 1 January 1993, they were horrified. They soon calculated that to carry out the elaborate structural changes needed to comply with 'EC export rules' would cost far more than many of them could afford, even though most, sending their meat only to local butchers' shops, had not the slightest intention of joining the export trade.

What MAFF also kept quiet about was that the new directives now being proposed by the EC to bring all this about had not yet even been passed into law. All the Commission was planning to do for the 'red meat' sector was to produce a new version of that original directive, 64/433, now to be renumbered 91/497 (it also proposed a new version of the poultry hygiene directive). But so inadequate and out of date had the methods laid down by 64/433 been, even back in the 1960s, that the Commission had quickly drawn up a second guidance document known as the '*Vade Mecum*'. This did not have the force of law. But it was on this guidance document, without publicly admitting it, that the MAFF officials were now relying in 1991 to impose their revolution on Britain's meat industry. The result was to be a disaster.

An early recipient of MAFF's booklet, '1992 – Food Sense And You', was Andrew Fairweather who, in a series of sheds in the New Forest, ran the second largest quail farm in Britain, selling 200,000 dressed birds a year to wholesalers all over the country. He opened the document without foreboding, only to discover that, although quail had previously been classified as 'game', they were now officially 'poultry' and would therefore come under a proposed new 'EC Poultry Hygiene Directive'. When he read through the 20 pages of requirements, Mr Fairweather gradually realized that his quail farm was now being treated as if it was a large-scale industrial poultry processing plant. To stay in business would involve him in major rebuilding works that would cost far more than his entire annual turnover.

One requirement, for instance, was that he would have to install shower rooms, so that he and his six employees could wash every time they moved from one shed to another, which was many times a day. Mr Fairweather tried to contact MAFF to discuss his problems, but despite months of telephoning he could not find anyone who 'showed signs of understanding my position'. Nevertheless, his customers were now being told by MAFF that, unless he complied with the new regulations, they could no longer be permitted to buy his birds.

Finally he had to accept that there was no way he could afford to stay in business. In December 1991 he closed down the Long Reach Quail Farm, putting six people on the dole. Only later did it emerge that the EEC poultry hygiene directive, in the name of which MAFF had brought all this about, was not even issued until December 1992, a year after his farm closed. The regulations putting this into British law were not published until the middle of 1993. Mr Fairweather had thus been told that it would be illegal for him to stay in business unless he complied with regulations that did not become law until more than 18 months after he closed. When, in 1993, this was raised by his MP with the food minister Nicholas Soames, he merely replied that the closure had been 'made necessary by EEC legislation'. Nevertheless, he added, Mr Fairweather might find it helpful to know that, under a subsequent EEC directive, quail were now no longer classified as 'poultry' but had been reinstated as 'game'.

All over the country in 1991 and 1992 the owners of meat businesses were having similar shocks. Edwin Snell, a Somerset butcher, was told by MAFF in the summer of 1992 that, under their proposed new Fresh Meat (Hygiene and Inspection) Regulations, implementing the proposed directive 91/497, live animals would have to enter his small Chard slaughterhouse by one entrance, while carcasses would have to leave by a different exit. Since his premises had only one access to the nearby road, he would therefore have to spend tens of thousands of pounds building a new roadway.

What puzzled him was why he should spend all this money, supposedly in the name of hygiene, when, within ten yards, the length of his existing access road, the live and dead animals would pass each other on the main road. Even more puzzling, however, might have been the fact that the as-yet unpublished directive contained no reference to any need for separate exits and entrances. Like hundreds of other abattoir owners, Mr Snell was being asked to spend sums he couldn't afford on changes that were not a legal requirement.

In Huntingdonshire, Tom Chamberlain ran a butchery business which had been owned by his family for 100 years. In 1992 he was judged 'Champion Sausage Maker' at the East of England Show.

His business had never been more flourishing. In December, however, he received a letter from a MAFF official informing him that, under the new Fresh Meat (Hygiene and Inspection) Regulations 1992, he must make various structural changes to his premises. If he did not agree by January 1993 he would not receive the new licence required by MAFF and would have to close.

Mr Chamberlain's shop was 20 yards across the yard from his small slaughterhouse but, under the required changes, he would no longer be allowed to carry meat from one to the other. He would have to build a refrigerated tunnel between the two buildings. He would have to build a shower room and rest room for 'visiting lorry drivers', even though most animals brought to his slaughterhouse came from farms within five miles. As he contemplated MAFF's long list of demands over Christmas, Mr Chamberlain concluded that they would cost far more than he could afford. Within a week his family's 100-year-old business had closed forever.

By the end of 1992, nearly half the slaughterhouses in Britain had gone out of business, leaving farmers and butchers over vast tracts of the country without a local abattoir for their animals and their meat. When Mr Gummer, the minister presiding over this disaster, was asked why it had happened, he initially fell back on claiming that it was necessary to improve the quality of Britain's meat, suggesting that many slaughterhouses were filthy, unhygienic and presented a risk to human health. When this was challenged, as being unsupported by the evidence – meat unaffected by cross-contamination was inherently one of the safest of all food products – he and his MAFF officials came up with a new formula. The reason why so many slaughterhouses had gone out of business, he repeatedly explained in letters to MPs, was that their owners 'had taken a commercial decision not to invest in the future of their business'.

As for Gummer's own knowledge of the meat trade, this was, in December 1992, put to the test by one of his constituents. Colin Byford, a Suffolk butcher, bought his meat from a craft slaughterhouse which had been ordered to make changes costing £350,000 to bring it up to 'EC quality standards'. Mr Byford presented Gummer with six samples of pork, beef and lamb. Three were from his own regular supplier, three from a large industrial abattoir which already complied with the standards Gummer was seeking to impose on the whole industry. Asked to choose which samples were in his opinion of the higher quality, Gummer in each case unhesitatingly chose the meat from Byford's preferred slaughterhouse: exactly the type of operation which he and his officials were now determined to drive out of business.

Indeed, the story was far from over. On 1 January 1993 the second stage of the drama began unfolding, when the owners of meat businesses had to begin paying up to £65 an hour for the services of a vet to supervise the inspection of animals and their meat. Near Barnsley, Richard Wartig, for 20 years the owner of a large turkey slaughterhouse, had already been informed by MAFF that, if he wished to get a licence to stay in business, he would have to pay £200 to be instructed by a vet on the correct way to kill a turkey. When he and various colleagues turned up, all with years of experience, they found that their instructor had only been on a two-week course. He knew infinitely less about slaughtering turkeys than any of his 'students'.

In the Farnborough slaughterhouse owned by Bob Newman, during the week when the new regime came into force, nine men were present. Three were experienced slaughtermen. The other six were officials, including the meat inspectors and a vet sent in by MAFF to supervise them. Nearby, a month later, Nigel Batts, chairman of the Reading Abattoir, summoned his 17 employees to tell them that the business had to close. Until recently the business had been doing so well that it was looking to move to new premises. Now the cost of having to pay tens of thousands of pounds a year for supervision by a vet with no experience of slaughterhouses was enough to make the business no longer viable. Mr Batts said afterwards that having to tell his 17 employees that they were out of a job was 'the worst thing I have ever done in my life'.

A few years earlier there had still been more than 1,000 slaughterhouses in Britain. These had ranged from fewer than 100 large industrial-scale plants, mass-producing meat for supermarkets, through hundreds of medium-size slaughterhouses, serving farmers and butchers in their local area, to hundreds more tiny slaughterhouses, usually at the back of a butcher's shop where the meat was sold. Most top-quality meat had come from the medium-size and small 'craft slaughterhouses', where animals could be handled and dealt with individually. Now around 700 of these had either closed down already, or would do so within a few years.

All this was happening in the name of 'hygiene'. But the chief risk of conventional food poisoning from the products of a slaughterhouse lies not in the meat itself, which is intrinsically safe, but from cross-contamination by bacteria such as *E. coli*, which commonly lurks in an animal's gut. Nothing is more likely to promote the escape of *E. coli* onto meat than putting animals under stress, as by forcing them quickly and in large numbers through the killing lines of a large abattoir or subjecting them to long journeys in cattle trucks.

No consequence of the closure of hundreds of smaller slaughterhouses was more obvious than that many more animals were now having to be sent on long journeys of up to 50 or 100 miles, to the nearest abattoir still open. The most serious food poisoning outbreak traced directly to meat in recent years had been in Preston in 1991. It came from *E. coli* in McDonald's beefburgers, made from meat produced by an industrial abattoir which met all MAFF's 'hygiene' requirements and was the proud holder of an 'EC export licence'.

The Plastic Versus Wood Debacle

There was no more vivid illustration of how far the 'hygiene blitz' had gone over the top than the zeal with which the EHOs condemned any use of wood in contact with food as 'unhygienic'. Any implement or surface made of wood was instantly condemned, usually in favour of some plastic substitute. We have already seen several instances, such as the ending of the navy's traditional use of oars to stir Christmas puddings or the EHO who chucked a prized cutting board and rolling pin into the bin.

Another victim was the open-air museum at Beamish in County Durham, attracting hundreds of thousands of visitors a year to its recreation of life in a Victorian mining village. A highlight was to visit the cottage kitchen where a lady dressed as a Victorian miner's wife cooked appetizing pies and cakes on a range. Visitors were then allowed to taste the food, a treat particularly appreciated by large numbers of children. But in 1992 this practice was suddenly brought to an end. When visitors understandably asked what happened to all this delicious food, they were now told 'we have to feed it to the animals on the farm'. This was because Chester-le-Street EHOs had ruled that because the pastry board and other kitchen implements were made of wood this was not legal under hygiene regulations.

In Pembrokeshire Leon Downey, a former viola player with the Hallé Orchestra, had become one of the best-known cheesemakers in the country for the Llangloffan cheese he made with milk from his own Jersey cows. In May 1993 his cheese dairy was inspected by a young EHO from Preseli council. Shortly before this he had passed with flying colours an inspection by an ADAS micro-biologist, under an exacting hygiene scheme set up by the Specialist Cheesemakers' Association. The council EHO, who admitted during her visit that she was unfamiliar with the technicalities of cheese production, was not so pleased. After her visit Mr Downey received a letter from her superior, listing 22 items which required attention, and warning him that unless these were put right within 30 days he would be served with a statutory Improvement Notice.

Expert examination showed that only three of the listed items were required by law (these included a first-aid book to record accidents). But what particularly aroused Mr Downey's ire was a demand that his cheeses should not come into contact with wooden shelves. The wood must be covered with paint or greaseproof paper. The EHOs were clearly not familiar with various expert studies that had showed that these were wholly unsuitable for storing cheeses, because they cause a build-up of slime.

The reason why EHOs in general had become so obsessed with the unhygienic properties of wood in fact originated in a study published more than 20 years earlier, reporting on experiments carried out under the direction of Dr Richard Gilbert of the PHLS (who was now, in 1993, head of the PHLS's food hygiene laboratory). Looking for a task to occupy a young student on work-experience, he had suggested that she seed new wooden and plastic chopping boards with salmonella, then hand-wash them and score them with knives to discover which surface ended up with more bacteria. Her conclusion was that the plastic boards fared better.[3]

When Gilbert's paper was published, its finding that wood was less hygienic than plastic gradually percolated through Britain's public health community to become the prevailing orthodoxy. In vain did other experts over the years point out that his simple laboratory experiments had in no way replicated the conditions to which boards were exposed in normal catering practice; that polyethylene boards could not be properly washed in machines because they warped; that plastic boards tended to become stained with a build-up of rancid fat; and that the teak and other hardwood boards in normal use could be shown to be much less absorbent than plastic.

By the time the 'hygiene blitz' was launched in 1990, it was simply accepted as a scientific fact by most EHOs that wood must be scrapped as unhygienic; which was why, citing a provision of the 1970 hygiene regulations that materials in use with food should be 'smooth and impervious' and 'capable of being readily cleaned', they ordered Britain's food businesses to spend hundreds of millions of pounds replacing wooden shelves, work-tops, spoons, chopping boards, salad bowls and every other kind of equipment and utensil with plastic or other non-wooden equivalents.

In 1993, however, shortly before the young Welsh EHO was trying to prohibit Mr Downey from exposing his cheeses to wooden shelves, two microbiologists at the University of Wisconsin, Dean O. Cliver and Nese O. Ak, published their own findings on a series of experiments originally designed to find ways of reducing the potential of wood to breed bacteria, and to make it as safe as plastic. To their amazement they found that, within three minutes of inoculating wooden boards with cultures of salmonella, listeria and *E. coli*, 99.9 per cent of the bacteria died. Under similar conditions, all the bugs placed on plastic boards survived.

Further experiments confirmed that the woods used for chopping boards and other activities linked to food appeared naturally to have extraordinarily effective bactericidal properties. When plastic, on the other hand, was scored with knives, the bacteria would lurk in the grooves, and despite any amount of washing, would live on to contaminate food brought into contact with it.

With remarkable speed, news of the Wisconsin experiments crossed the Atlantic. As early as June 1993, LACOTS (Local Authorities Co-ordinating Body on Trading Standards), the body then responsible for co-ordinating local government enforcement practice in Britain, was issuing a circular to all EHOs, stating that the use of wood for chopping blocks and other kitchen implements was no longer to be considered an offence against Regulation 7 of the Food Hygiene (General) Regulations after all. Overnight, the belief that plastic was more hygienic than wood had been exposed as a complete myth.*

One of the saddest of many 'plastic versus wood' stories we reported centred on a popular restaurant in Rye, Sussex, run by two Neapolitan brothers, Nello and Giovanni Scardini (the latter, incidentally, a keen member of Sussex County Cricket Club). In August 1991 they had been visited by a young EHO from Rother council who, with the charm and common sense for which her profession was becoming famous, issued a number of peremptory orders. One was that Nello's chopping block, the apple of his eye, made by his craftsman brother-in-law and worth several hundred pounds, was unhygienic and that he must never use it again.

So enraged was Nello by her order that he took an axe to his block, hacked it in pieces and threw it on the fire. When, in obedience to the EHO's instructions, he bought a plastic block, he found it far less efficient and almost impossible to keep clean. In 1993, following the issuing of the new guidelines, the same young lady reappeared, to tell Nello, without a blush, that wood was now back in favour, and that he could resume the use of his old chopping block. As Nello told the story, she little realized how narrowly she had escaped the fate he had already accorded to the block itself.

The startling speed with which this cherished belief of so many EHOs was abandoned was in fact symptomatic of what was happening to the 'hygiene blitz' itself. Thanks not least to our relentless exposure of the follies and illegalities being perpetrated by what we had come to call 'the hygiene police', even mainstream journalists were beginning to take notice that something was seriously amiss.** The case of Mr Downey's shelves, publicized in the

---

* It is only fair to add that a number of more experienced EHOs had long been unhappy about the belief that wood was unhygienic and were delighted when the policy was reversed.
** Although, revealingly, the example of high-handed behaviour by an EHO that drew most attention was not one of the more serious instances of the damage being done countrywide by the 'hygiene blitz'. These had passed most of the media by, although we had been publicizing them for months. In April 1993, however, media attention focused on the Berkshire village of Aldworth, because it happened to be the home of various well-known journalists, including Max Hastings, editor of the *Daily Telegraph*. During a lull in serving lunchtime drinks, the landlord of the village pub had lit up his pipe. He was asked to speak to a man and two women at the other end of the room. The man told him 'we've been watching you –

Sunday Telegraph, attracted attention even from the food minister Nicholas Soames, and the word went out that the EHOs must learn to moderate their zeal.

By the end of 1993, the worst excesses of the great 'blitz' were already beginning to abate. It was not, as we shall see later, that many EHOs had really learned any lesson. But the avalanche of examples of their over-the-top behaviour, which had begun pouring in to us a year earlier, sometimes dozens in a week, noticeably began to decline.

If the EHOs' crusade had been the most conspicuous and damaging official response to the scares of the late 1980s, remarkably little had been achieved by it. Food poisoning figures were to continue at their historically high level for several years to come, and the truth was that no one ever identified a convincing reason why they had risen in this way. Probably much of the increase in salmonella poisoning had resulted from cross-contamination of food while it was being stored and prepared, and possibly the high incidence of salmonella in frozen chickens played a part in this. But certainly the responsibility for it did not lie with 'salmonella-infected eggs'; just as no useful contribution was made to reducing food poisoning by Gummer's imposition of EC 'hygiene directives' on the meat industry.

In 1997 the officially recorded salmonella poisoning figures again shot up from the average of around 33,000 a year, where they had been through the early 1990s, to a new record high of 36,377. But this was the peak, and they then began a dramatic fall, until by 2000 they were back to 16,987, equivalent to where they had last been in the early 1980s. Why they should now have fallen in this way remained just as mysterious as why they had risen in the

---

you've been smoking behind the bar'. The man turned out to be an EHO from Newbury council, who went on to warn the landlord that he was committing a criminal offence. Two days later a letter arrived by special delivery. Headed 'Food Hygiene (General) Regulations 1970', it went on to say 'at midday on 2 April 1993 you were seen smoking behind the bar in The Bell and warned by health manager, Mr John Parfitt, that your conduct was a contravention of the above legislation. It is illegal for a person, engaged as a food handler, to use tobacco in a room in which there is open food'. The landlord was informed that if he were caught smoking in his bar again he would face criminal prosecution. This episode was reported at length by the *Daily Telegraph*, including a major feature by its veteran columnist Bill Deedes.

first place. All that could be said with confidence was that, in bringing this fall about, the heavy-handed interventions of government had been wholly irrelevant.

'Mad Cows' Continued

There was one potential food scare, different from all the rest, which, throughout all these events in the early 1990s, had remained lurking in the background. In 1993 the total number of cattle slaughtered since the BSE epidemic began topped 100,000. But MAFF's chief epidemiologist John Wilesmith predicted that this would be the year when the incidence of the disease would start to decline.[4] Above all, there was still no sign as yet of that elusive precondition needed to turn it into a proper scare, a plausible link between eating beef and CJD.

In fact BSE was following a classic pre-scare pattern. The most obvious 'pushers', Lacey and his microbiologist colleague Dr Stephen Dealler, supported by a few journalists, did not yet have the evidence they were looking for; while the 'blockers', including all the government's senior advisers, were still adamant that there was no risk. When Bob Will, of the CJD Surveillance Unit, reported in March 1993 on a farmer who had died of CJD after exposure to BSE in his cows, he insisted that this was 'most likely to have been a chance finding' and that any link between the two diseases was 'at most conjectural'.[5] Kenneth Calman, the DH's Chief Medical Officer, proclaimed that 'beef can be safely eaten by everyone'. Even when, in July, the Surveillance Unit's annual report showed a rise in the number of CJD deaths from 32 in 1991–2 to 48 in 1992–3, *The Times* headlined its report 'Rise in human brain cases not connected to BSE'.

At New Year in 1994, James Erlichman asked in the *Guardian*, 'Is all well with the food world now that Edwina, salmonella and mad cow disease have dropped out of the headlines?'[6] His answer was that 1994 was likely to be 'the year when we discover whether BSE or mad cow disease is merely a passing misfortune for cattle or a deadly pestilence'. What particularly concerned him was that 'millions of cows have gone, and are still going, to the slaughterhouse incubating the disease, because they were killed before the symptoms were visible'.

Two weeks later the tabloids discovered Vicky Rimmer. Under front-page banner headlines, such as 'Mad Cow Disease: the human link', they claimed that this 16-year-old girl dying from CJD might be the first identifiable victim of BSE-infected beef. 'Mad cow tragedy blamed on hamburger' was how the *Daily Mail* put it.[7]

This provoked Calman into attacking such 'sensational and alarmist' coverage as no more than 'irresponsible scare stories'. CJD was an extremely rare disease, he emphasized, which might be contracted for 'a variety of reasons'; but 'there is no evidence at all that eating meat is one of them'.

The only official response sympathetic to the tabloid line came not from British authorities but from mainland Europe. Prompted by the brief revival of alarm over BSE in Britain, the German government again threatened, as it had in 1990, that, if Brussels did not introduce an EU-wide ban on any exports of British beef not certified as coming from a BSE-free herd, it would impose such a ban unilaterally. This triggered off a political row that was to last for months, leading eventually, on 28 June, to Germany banning any imports of beef from Britain for six months. There was even a report that German tourists were cancelling holidays in Britain, because doctors had advised that they might be exposed to beef and dairy products infected with 'mad cow disease'.[8]

When France threatened to join the German ban, this prompted urgent behind-the-scenes negotiations between EU agriculture ministers. On 18 July they agreed that British beef exports to other member states should be banned, unless they could be certified as coming from herds which had been BSE-free for six years.

Examining the small print of the deal, Britain's beef industry feared that this could threaten the survival of a trade worth £400 million a year, not least since the total number of infected cattle slaughtered had now reached 125,021, on 30,000 farms.

But from then on BSE faded out of the news. Coverage of 'mad cows' became only sporadic and skimpy. Thanks to the continuing unanimity of the authorities that there was no link between BSE and CJD it seemed the 'blockers' had convincingly won the day.*

---

* Just how flimsy was the scientific case at this stage could be seen from an article by Lacey and Dealler in the 1994 summer edition of the journal *Infection*. They took as their starting point a hypothesis of the American biochemist Professor Stanley J. Prusiner that the infectious agent in encephalopathies, such as BSE, scrapie and CJD, was the 'prion', a form of misfolded protein associated with such diseases. They then assumed that this hypothetical 'agent' would of necessity mutate in both humans and

So it was to remain for over a year, during which time a good deal of our own attention was focused elsewhere. We became involved in a comparatively small but significant episode reflecting the damage still being done by a quite different scare: one that had dropped out of the news six years before.

Notes

1. Christopher Booker, 'Spreading Fear and Confusion, Here Come The Hygiene Police!', *Daily Telegraph*, 20 April 1993. Like most of the other examples quoted in this chapter, this story was also included in Christopher Booker and Richard North, *The Mad Officials* (Duckworth, 1994).
2. 71/118/EEC.
3. R. J. Gilbert and Heather M. Watson, 'Some laboratory experiments on various meat preparation surfaces with regard to surface contamination and cleaning', *International Journal of Food Science & Technology*, 6, 2, (1971), 163–70.
4. *The Times*, 23 March 1993.
5. *The Lancet*, 6 March 1993. This first farmer, Peter Warhurst, was followed by another, and over the next year two more.
6. *Guardian*, 1 January 1994.
7. *Today*, 13 January; *Daily Mail*, 25 January 1994.
8. *Sunday Times*, 3 July 1994.

cattle, allowing infection to take place between animals, between animals and humans, and between humans. They then assumed that animal-to-person spread had already occurred, citing the two farmers who had succumbed to CJD (although any connection between this and the fact that they had been in contact with BSE-affected cattle was entirely speculative). They added the case of Vicky Rimmer, pointing out, as if it was significant, that she had been 'a regular consumer of sausages and burgers'. Having piled four or five separate hypotheses (or sweeping assumptions) on top of one another, they concluded that it was therefore inevitable that large numbers of people would eventually die from BSE-induced CJD.

4

'Listeria Hysteria'
The Lanark Blue Case, 1995

I have felt at various points in these lengthy proceedings that it would be so much more satisfactory if the Applicants and the staff of their Environmental Health Department fulfilled their statutory obligations in a less combative and confrontational manner ... Such a dogmatic and unduly rigid 'policing' approach and philosophy ... seems out of place, out of date and unhelpful.

Sheriff Douglas Allen, giving judgement in the
Lanark Blue case, 5 December 1995

Humphrey Errington was hardly the sort of man who might have been expected to feature in the front line of a historic battle with officialdom. His father, Sir Lancelot Errington, had been permanent secretary in the Department of Health and Social Security, he was brought up in the genteel setting of Weybridge, Surrey, and educated at Wellington public school.

Even less would one have expected to find such a man making cheese from sheep's milk, on a windswept farm 1,000 feet up on the hills of Lanarkshire. But in the 1980s, Errington's superb Lanark Blue cheese – hailed as 'the Scottish Roquefort' – established itself at the forefront of the renaissance in British farmhouse cheesemaking. Praised by French cheese experts, it won numerous awards, was said to be enjoyed by the Queen and was sold in the best restaurants and every top cheese shop in London.

In December 1994, however, Errington suddenly found himself plunged into a nightmare. Environmental health officials in Edinburgh had discovered that some of his Lanark Blue contained *Listeria monocytogenes*. It could scarcely have sounded more alarming. Still fresh in the general memory was the great 'listeria hysteria' of 1989, as one of the most celebrated food scares of recent years, originally arising from the deaths caused by listeria in Swiss cheese.

Even though listeria had attracted little publicity since the 1989 scare had faded away, it was perhaps not surprising that, when the Edinburgh discovery was reported to the EHOs of Errington's local council, Clydesdale, they decided to ask the local magistrates to order that all his remaining 1994 Lanark Blue, with a retail value of £54,000, should be destroyed. With it would go his business, on which more than a dozen people relied for their livelihood.

Just before the case was due to be heard, Errington despairingly appealed to us for help. Within a few hours, North was racing up the motorway to Scotland. By the end of the evening, he had been able to make a first assessment of Errington's plight.

The first point on which North was able to reassure Errington was that, despite its lurid reputation, *Listeria monocytogenes* was a much more complex organism than most people were aware. There were scores, possibly thousands of different strains of the bacterium, the vast majority of them quite harmless to human health. They are often found in the rich bacterial flora which is essential to the ripening of blue and soft cheeses. As a leading cheese wholesaler later told us, 'in our routine tests for listeria, counts of 10–20,000 are common. We only get worried when the counts are much higher than that'.

In fact only a tiny handful of strains had been associated with the rare and potentially fatal disease known as listeriosis; and even these were only likely to prove harmful, or pathogenic, to certain 'high risk groups', such as pregnant mothers, babies, the very old and those whose immunity was compromised, such as sufferers from HIV. This was of course why, since the listeria scare of 1989, a wide range of foods had carried a health warning from the Chief Medical Officer, advising those at risk not to eat them.

The only thing which should be relevant in Errington's case, North told him, was whether the listeria in his cheese belonged to one of that handful of strains which had been shown to be pathogenic. They soon established that the strain the EHOs claimed to have found had never been associated with human illness of any kind. Indeed, during the four months it had already been on sale, the equivalent of 63,000 portions of the cheese that the Clydesdale officials wished to destroy had already been sold to the public, without a single report of ill health.

This was not, however, how the officials saw it, as became obvious when the court hearing took place in Lanark, under a local justice, Mrs Wilson. The council's young 'principal environmental health officer', Robert Steenson, made it clear that, in Clydesdale's eyes, all forms of listeria were equally dangerous. What Steenson then revealed was that the EHOs had taken their cue from some forthcoming regulations, implementing an EC directive, 92/46, on 'the hygiene of dairy products'. This ruled, astonishingly, that it would be illegal to sell cheese containing even the tiniest amount of listeria, regardless of its strain.

This was a bombshell. Its implications ran far beyond the immediate case. If these regulations were enforced, it would sooner or later bring an end to the selling of Stilton, Brie or any blue or soft cheeses. When we publicized this in the *Sunday Telegraph*, it provoked uproar. As a spokesman for the National Dairy Council trenchantly put it 'silly, silly Brussels, if we didn't have any listeria in blue cheese, we wouldn't have any blue cheese. It effectively rules out cheese production in this country'.

It was impossible to believe that the French and Italian cheese-makers would allow such absurd 'Euro-nonsense' to halt the production of Camembert and Dolcelatte. Sure enough, a few days after our first article appeared, the *Sunday Telegraph* received a remarkable fax from the MAFF press office. Its officials had discovered a 'derogation' in the directive, under which 'cheese made in a traditional manner' could be given an exemption from the 'listeria standard'. The continental countries had, of course, applied for this exemption. But until that moment MAFF had remained oblivious to the derogation. Only now were they taking steps to ensure that British cheesemakers would in future be able to take advantage of it.

This would be too late, however, to help Mr Errington. Back in Lanark, the Clydesdale EHOs were still locked as firmly as ever into their determination to destroy his cheese. They openly boasted that it was an open-and-shut case which would take only an hour or two to settle. But when Errington's defence team argued that the council had not completed its tests properly, and that anyway the type of listeria found was harmless, the justice Mrs Wilson invited the two sides to hold further discussions, in the hope that the matter could be resolved outside the courtroom.

When the council did complete its tests, their results were startling. These apparently showed every batch of Lanark Blue to be contaminated with levels of listeria so ridiculously high as not to be scientifically credible. A second hearing was inevitable.

Here two new players entered the drama. Errington had been approached by Michael Jones QC, a leading Edinburgh advocate, who offered to lead for the defence. Clydesdale had meanwhile called for help to Dr Jim McLauchlin of the PHLS in London who, since he had published a paper on food-borne listeriosis in 1987, had become regarded as the top official expert on the subject in the country. He was considered so grand a figure in the Scottish courtroom that, by arrangement with Clydesdale's lawyers, Mrs Wilson ruled that, when he had finished his evidence, the defence team would not be allowed to cross-examine him. Questions could only be put to the great man through her. She would then deliver her judgement in writing, promising to give reasons for her decision.

A week later Errington was rung by the local paper. Mrs Wilson, he was told, had issued her verdict. His cheese must be destroyed. She had not given the promised explanation. Fortunately for Errington, her conduct of the case had been so irregular that his lawyers were able to seek leave from the highest civil court in Scotland for a judicial review. In April, at the Edinburgh Court of Sessions, Lord Justice Weir handed down a damning judgement. The refusal to allow Dr McLauchlin to be cross-examined had been 'in breach of natural justice'. He recommended that the case should be heard again by a sheriff, a full-time judge. Clydesdale immediately appealed, but in June Weir's judgement was upheld in even more trenchant terms by the Lord President. The case must be heard again, properly, by a sheriff, he ruled, not by an 'inexperienced lay justice'.

High Noon

By now, as the two sides prepared to resume battle later in the summer, the Lanark Blue case was attracting national attention. Our allies, led by Lord Pearson of Rannoch, had already made it something of a *cause célèbre* in the House of Lords. Media coverage was growing. A well-known Scottish gourmet, Arthur Bell, appeared on television eating what looked like a hunk of Lanark Blue. He immediately received an angry letter from Clydesdale, threatening criminal prosecution unless he revealed where he had obtained the cheese (in fact he had not been eating Lanark Blue but Errington's other blue cheese, Dunsyre Blue).

By August, nine months after the saga began, the two sides had assembled their expert teams. The star witness for Clydesdale was still Dr McLauchlin, retained at a fee of £500 a day, plus lodging in a first-class hotel. But Errington's advocate could now call on a whole array of expert witnesses. These ranged from one of Britain's leading authorities on food safety policy, Professor Verner Wheelock (who had worked previously with North and supervised his PhD on food poisoning), to Mr Jean-Jacques Devoyod, a splendid, moustachioed Frenchman, agreed to be the greatest living expert on the microbiology of Roquefort. When another microbiologist had pulled out, because she was fearful of attracting the ire of MAFF, which sometimes commissioned her for work, North had managed to track down Professor Hugh Pennington of Aberdeen University, then not widely known but a scientist of world standing.

The defence was to be argued under two main heads: firstly, that the strain of listeria found in Lanark Blue presented no risk to public health; and, secondly, that the levels of listeria the council claimed to have found defied all scientific credibility.

With only two days to go to the trial, Clydesdale threw another potentially devastating punch. They handed over the evidence they intended to call, including more than 1,500 pages of technical scientific papers trawled from all over the world. Errington's defence team, working through the night, had just 48 hours to absorb this mountain of documents, even though it became clear that most had been available to the prosecution months before. When these were combed, however, it also seemed that even the prosecution could not have looked at them too carefully. Study after study appeared to confirm the defence's case: that most forms of listeria were not pathogenic and that the strain found had never been associated with human illness.

The hearings began unfolding through three weeks in September, before Sheriff Douglas Allan. For Clydesdale, Dr McLauchlin had not moved an iota from his earlier argument, echoing the EC directive, that all forms of *Listeria monocytogenes* are potentially dangerous. In cross-examination, Jones showed how McLauchlin had contradicted himself and could produce no credible evidence for his case.

Errington's witnesses, including North, pressed home that Clydesdale had avoided the central issue. Did the particular form of listeria found in the Lanark Blue pose a genuine health risk? In the end, with many days of adjournments, it took until November to complete the hearings. Clydesdale made a prolonged effort to blacken North's character, having been given access to MAFF and other official files for any personal evidence which might discredit him (just before North began his evidence they produced another 31 documents relating to his past career, not least as a trenchant critic of MAFF). At another point, the officials asked the sheriff for leave to test Errington's latest 1995 batch of Lanark Blue, which would have cost him another £3,000 in lost cheeses. The sheriff brusquely dismissed this as 'harassment'.

In fact the costs of the case, now rising by thousands of pounds a day, had already become of serious concern to Errington. Because of the technicality that this was an 'administrative hearing', the sheriff had made it clear that, even if Errington won the case, he could not claim his own costs, even though these already amounted to more than £120,000, enough to bankrupt his business. So critical was his plight that a national competition was launched to raise money, under the joint patronage of Lord Tonypandy (formerly, as George Thomas, Speaker of the House of Commons and now an outspoken Eurosceptic) and the well-known cookery writer Sophie Grigson. This was supported by other leading food experts and by an array of well-known cheese shops, hotels, restaurants and food businesses.

For the Clydesdale officials, of course, money was of no concern. Even if they lost the case, they were secure in the knowledge that the taxpayers would foot their own bill, by now estimated at over £250,000.

Finally, in December 1995, after what had become by far the longest food contamination case in British history, Sheriff Allan pronounced a devastating verdict. Showing a remarkable grasp of the technicalities, he agreed that the council's tests were not scientifically credible. He found there was no evidence that the strain of *Listeria monocytogenes* found in the Lanark Blue posed any risk to human health. There was therefore no need for Errington's cheese to be condemned. Furthermore the sheriff described McLauchlin as an 'evasive' and 'less than helpful' witness, who had failed to show the objectivity expected of a scientific expert. He spoke witheringly of the attempt to discredit North, and directed criticism at the Clydesdale officials for the entire way in which they had conducted the case.

Of course the sting in the tail for Errington was that he could not claim costs. Thanks to the officials' relentless war against him, he was now faced with a bill so enormous that even the appeal could not hope to raise more than a fraction. But even here, the terms in which the sheriff had condemned Clydesdale's tactics opened an unexpected door. Errington's QC, Michael Jones, realized that, under an obscure piece of law, if he could show the council to have been 'pugnacious litigants', it might be possible to claim costs after all.

Sheriff Allan accepted his argument and awarded Errington recompense for every penny. Although the laborious process of squeezing the money out of the council was to continue for many months, it had been a historic victory. In the end the only real losers were the taxpayers, left to foot a bill amounting to more than £370,000.

The 'Precautionary Principle'

Inevitably, there was a further twist to the tale. Even though the case had not been brought directly under EC legislation, Brussels cast a long shadow over the whole affair. If it had not been for that directive on dairy hygiene, imposing a complete ban on cheese containing *Listeria monocytogenes* of any kind, the Clydesdale officials might not have been so confident in maintaining that all forms of the organism posed an equal threat to human health.

If there was one lesson which everyone might have learned from the scientific expertise brought to bear on the case, it was that all forms of *Listeria monocytogenes* are not equally pathogenic. Like so much else produced by that peculiar form of bureaucratized science which held sway in Brussels, the EC directive was based on such crude over-simplification as to amount to dangerous nonsense. In the name of bogus science, the insane possibility had been created that many of Europe's finest cheeses might one day be declared illegal.

Yet only six months after the officials' resounding defeat, a letter went out to all UK food authorities from Tony Baldry, the minister of state at MAFF. This coolly stated 'the Government's view remains that all strains (of listeria) are potentially harmful to human health'. His officials were carrying on as if they had learned nothing from the case at all. Echoing the Brussels line, their view was that, wherever it could be imagined that there was the slightest possibility of risk, however improbable, it was vital to follow what had now become known in official circles as 'the precautionary principle'. It was always best to 'play safe', whatever the cost.

Arising at least in part out of the scares of the 1980s, this principle was now coming to exercise an increasingly all-pervasive influence on regulatory legislation of all kinds. Whenever the shibboleths of hygiene, health and safety, or environmental protection were invoked, the 'precautionary principle' was now becoming paramount. The significance of the Lanark Blue case had been that it showed just how far the ranks of officialdom were now prepared to go in elevating the doctrine of 'play safe' above all else, even if it was based on a degree of scientific ignorance which defied reality.

Errington might eventually have won his battle. But in the wider war, as Baldry's letter showed, it was as if the Lanark Blue case had never happened. The 'precautionary principle' had now become the established official dogma of the times. Only three months after the Lanark Blue case was over, it was to play a central part in unleashing the greatest and most damaging food scare of them all.*

---

* Another sequel to the Errington case illustrated the difficulty experienced by many mainstream journalists in grasping the technical complexities of the 'scare phenomenon'. We were commissioned by Alexander Chancellor, the editor of the *Sunday Telegraph Magazine*, to write an article on the Lanark Blue saga. When it was submitted, he said he could not publish it because it was 'too one-sided'. He thought we had not been 'sufficiently fair' to the Clydesdale officials and McLauchlin in giving their side of the story.

It had now become a principle of modern newspapers that 'fair' journalism consists of giving 'both sides of a story', leaving readers to 'make up their own minds'. But this led many journalists into taking at face value the claims made by officials, without doing enough background research to be able to grasp where they might have got it wrong.

Another magazine which decided to run an article on the Lanark Blue affair was the *Reader's Digest*. Again its view was that we were 'too involved' to write the story ourselves. When another journalist Magnus Linklater was recruited to write the article instead, he did so without consulting us. The result was notably thin. By failing to understand the technical arguments which lay at the heart of the case, it missed almost all its real point and drama.

5

Mad Cows and Madder Politicians

The BSE/CJD Scare, 1996–9

There remains no scientific proof that bovine spongiform encephalopathy can be transmitted to man by beef.

Stephen Dorrell, Secretary of State for Health,
House of Commons, 20 March 1996

On 16 June 1995, after months when BSE had virtually dropped out of the news, the former Conservative Cabinet minister Norman Tebbit began an article for the *Sun* with, 'Do you remember the Mad Cows Disease scare?'

That autumn he would have had to eat his words. In October BSE suddenly surged back to the forefront of media interest, for two reasons. Firstly, more CJD 'victims' were appearing, with the first hint that a new pattern might be emerging in the incidence of the disease. Secondly, more scientists were ready to allow that there might be a link between CJD and BSE.

On 6 October, the CJD Surveillance Unit announced that CJD deaths in 1994 had risen to 55, the highest figure yet recorded. But the rate of increase had been similar in other countries; and the unit explained that this might simply have been due to increased awareness of the disease. Kenneth Calman, the Chief Medical Officer, said 'I continue to be satisfied that there is currently no scientific evidence of a link between meat-eating and CJD.'

Two weeks later, however, the *Sunday Times* led its front page with the headline 'Experts fear 1.5 million mad cows eaten – study alleges risk from infected meat'. Lacey's colleague Stephen Dealler was about to publish research suggesting that, since the BSE epidemic began, the average Briton had eaten 80 meals containing beef from infected cattle. The paper was also able to quote Sir

Bernard Tomlinson, 'a distinguished retired neuropathologist' who had changed his mind. 'Initially,' he said, 'I would have said that it was very unlikely that BSE could be transmitted to humans by eating beef. Now I would be far from certain.'[1]

The same edition also ran an article headed 'Human victims of BSE?' This featured Jean Wake, a 38-year-old mother dying of suspected CJD in Sunderland, whose family were sure she had contracted the disease from eating beef or when filling pies in a bakery. Even younger was Stephen Churchill, a Devizes teenager who had died the previous May. Both deaths were notable because CJD was generally associated with much older people. In addition, the number of deaths from CJD of farmers who had worked with BSE-infected cattle was now up to three.

Next day, in its front-page lead, 'New fear over Mad Cow link', the *Daily Mail* reported the death of a fourth farmer, which had prompted 'government experts' to hold a 'secret inquiry'.[2] When the *Daily Telegraph* followed with its own version, it quoted the DH as maintaining that the 'absolute risk', even for cattle farmers, was 'extremely low'.[3] But four days later, following the death of a second teenager, the *Telegraph* reported SEAC's concern that this might mark the emergence of a new trend, with CJD affecting people at ages much younger than had ever been observed before.

In mid-November a spate of press coverage attended an ITV *World In Action* documentary, which centred on Dealler's claim that almost every meat eater in the country had been exposed to infected beef and that 600 cattle with BSE were still being eaten every week. Meldrum, MAFF's chief vet, was so impatient at being repeatedly questioned about this that he put his hand in front of the camera and terminated the interview.[4] Also featured was Tomlinson, who in the next day's *Times* explained that three things had persuaded him to change his mind about beef: the rise in CJD cases, the disproportionate number of dead farmers and the recent deaths of teenagers.[5]

The media were now agog for any new story that could support the growing scare. When the *British Medical Journal* asked six medical professionals their views on a possible link between BSE and CJD, only one went on to be quoted in the national press. This was because Dr Sheila Gore, a Cambridge medical statistician, was the only one of the six who had expressed any concern, suggesting that the recent deaths of farmers and young people must be 'more than chance happenings'.[6]

By 27 November the *Daily Telegraph* had unearthed a 'new victim of "mad cow disease"'. Michelle Bowen, a 29-year-old mother, had died of CJD in Manchester Royal Infirmary three weeks after the premature birth of her third child. The media were quick to note that, as a teenager, she had worked in a butcher's shop, while her husband had once worked in an abattoir.

On cue as always, Professor Lacey on 28 November came out with a book. In *Mad Cow Disease: The History of BSE in Britain*, he claimed that BSE was now endemic, being passed on from cow to calf and into the human food chain; and that ministers had orchestrated a cover-up of its potentially disastrous consequences. On the BBC's *You and Yours*, Tomlinson said that, although he would continue to eat beef and steak, he would no longer eat beefburgers 'under any circumstances'.

This prompted *The Times* to run a picture gallery of academics, doctors and vets giving their views. Several, including Lacey, Tomlinson, Colin Blakemore, Professor of Physiology at Oxford, and Dr Stuttaford, the paper's medical correspondent, claimed that the risks posed by beef were now too great to be ignored. Others, including Sir Richard Doll, doyen of the epidemiological establishment, were still happy to eat beef, believing the risk was insignificant. Also insistent that any risk was 'entirely theoretical' was Dr John Pattison, now chairman of SEAC.[7]

The government tried to steady the ship. The Meat and Livestock Commission took full-page advertisements in every national newspaper, quoting Calman's assurance 'British beef is perfectly safe to eat'. Interviewed on television by Jonathan Dimbleby, Health Secretary Stephen Dorrell reiterated that there was no risk, echoing Gummer from five years earlier by claiming that he was happy for his own children to eat hamburgers.[8]

But public confidence was wobbling. Beef sales had fallen by as much as 15 per cent. Cattle prices were down by £80 an animal. Hundreds of schools across the country had dropped beef from their menus.[9] It scarcely helped that the latest MAFF figures showed that more than half the UK's dairy herds, and 30 per cent of beef herds, had now been affected by BSE (although the number of new cases appearing was now rapidly declining).*

---

* 11,031 new cases had been recorded up to 17 November 1995, compared with 24,288 in 1994, 34,830 in 1993 and 37,057 in 1992.

Through December, as the media continued almost daily to stoke up the scare, government spokesmen continued to offer reassurance. The Prime Minister John Major told the Commons, 'I have both sought and received advice that there is currently no scientific evidence that BSE can be transmitted to humans, or that eating beef causes CJD.' This was echoed by Calman in an article for the *Sunday Times*: 'there is no scientific evidence that BSE can transmit to humans'.[10] At the DH's urging, Pattison and Will put out a joint statement to explain why they believed British beef was safe. 'The government have acted on advice that there still remains a theoretical risk to human health from BSE', but, thanks to all the measures put in place since 1989, SEAC had 'a high degree of confidence that the beef reaching the shops is safe to eat'.

There was even comfort for the government in the latest experiments by Professor Collinge (himself now a member of SEAC). The effect on mice from injecting them with human CJD prions, he announced, was very different from that resulting from injecting them with BSE – leading him to conclude that the transmission of BSE to humans was 'extremely unlikely'.[11]

Despite all the frenzied media pressure of the previous three months, the 'blockers' were still holding the line.[12]

The Dam Gives Way

The tipping point in the unleashing of a full-blown scare is often that moment when a government, having erected against it a dam of denials, then suddenly weakens, implicitly admitting that it had been wrong. What sent the salmonella scare of 1988–9 into orbit was Currie's statement on television. Similarly, the height of the 1989 listeria scare had followed the Chief Medical Officer's announcement that cheeses must carry a health warning. As the dam crumbles, the very fact that the government appears to be disowning its previous assurances ensures that the pent-up energy of the 'pushers' will burst through it with redoubled force. So it was to be with BSE.

During the first two months of 1996, BSE again almost vanished from the news. But during February Bob Will, of the CJD Surveillance Unit, was studying eight cases of CJD so different from anything he had seen before that it seemed to him that they could have arisen from a new strain of the disease. Towards the end of the month, he became so convinced of this that he alerted SEAC. At a specially convened meeting in London on 8 March he presented the committee with his evidence. His colleague Dr Ironside showed a series of slides which the SEAC members watched in stunned silence. As Pattison put it later: 'when he showed us the slides, and before he said anything, we could see what it was. It was dramatically different'.[13]

Will was instructed to contact as many sources as possible to determine whether what they had been looking at was genuinely new. On Saturday 16 March, he and Ironside met with SEAC again to confirm their view that they were looking at 'a previously unrecognized and consistent disease pattern'. Furthermore, they had discovered two more cases.

That evening, Pattison contacted Calman at the DH and Meldrum at MAFF. On Monday morning, 18 March, they broke the news to their respective ministers, Dorrell and Douglas Hogg, the minister of agriculture. When Calman arrived to brief Dorrell in the minister's private office he was improbably dressed in a morning suit. He could not stay long because he was due at Buckingham Palace to be knighted by the Queen.

Dorrell rapidly decided that SEAC's new findings must be put in the public domain as soon as possible. He would make a statement to the House of Commons two days later, on Wednesday 20 March. His press office was instructed to book advertising space in Thursday's national newspapers, to allay any resulting public fears. On Tuesday morning the head of the DH press office met executives of its advertising agency. This was leaked to *Campaign*, the advertising industry's trade paper, which rushed out a report that the agency had been asked to prepare an emergency campaign to calm public fears about 'mad cow disease', following an imminent government announcement.

That same Tuesday morning, SEAC was also back in session. Some members were in Paris, so parts of the conference had to be conducted via telephone. The meeting continued until almost midnight, as members drafted recommendations to be put to the minister the following day. By the time they resumed work on Wednesday morning, the *Daily Mirror* had already picked up the story from *Campaign*. Bannered across its front page was the headline 'Official – Mad Cow can kill you – Govt to admit it today'. Page two was headed, 'we've already eaten 100,000 mad cows'. The splash coverage was accompanied by an article from Lacey headed, 'You're right to be angry'. This accused the government of a seven-year cover-up, and of doing 'its best to vilify all the independent scientists who said there was a danger. But events have proved us right'.[14]

The gaff had been blown. While SEAC members continued to finalize their recommendations, Pattison and Calman were summoned to a meeting of Cabinet ministers chaired by Major, for 'two hours of gruelling questioning'. According to a lobby briefing, several ministers advised strongly against going public. But Dorrell and Hogg insisted that the risk to public health was so great that it called for an immediate statement. Pattison was given less than two hours for SEAC to draft a statement for Dorrell to read to the Commons that afternoon.

At 3.30pm Dorrell rose in front of a packed House. After studying the researches of the CJD Surveillance Unit into ten cases of CJD in people under 42, he told MPs, SEAC had concluded that 'the unit has identified a previously unrecognized and consistent disease pattern'. Reading from SEAC's draft, he went on: 'a review of patients' medical histories, genetic analysis and consideration of other possible causes have failed to explain these cases adequately'. Then came the passage which, like Currie's 20 fateful words in 1988, were to unleash uproar:

> There remains no scientific proof that bovine spongiform encephalopathies can be transmitted to man by beef, but the committee concluded that the most likely explanation at present is that those cases are linked to exposure to BSE before the introduction of the specified offal ban in 1989.

Unsurprisingly, the impression this gave was that the government was in headlong retreat from all its previous soothing assurances. The Opposition benches exploded. In her response, Labour's frontbench spokesman, Harriet Harman at her most strident, scornfully asked, 'Does the Secretary of State acknowledge that public confidence on this issue is hanging by a thread?' 'The public', she went on, 'have to be given the full facts ... there must be no more photocalls of ministers feeding beefburgers to their children.'

Hogg then followed by announcing, also in response to SEAC's advice, that it would now become illegal to sell any meat from cattle over 30 months old (the age after which BSE was likely to show) unless it had first been taken off the bone in specially licensed plants. Incredibly, he told the House that he did not believe the information passed on by Dorrell would 'damage consumer confidence and thus the beef market'.

The statements and the ensuing debate were carried live on television. They continued to lead radio and television news for the rest of the day. That evening when *Newsnight*'s Jeremy Paxman was trying to push Pattison into estimating how many people were likely to die of CJD, he asked whether the eventual figure could rise as high as 500,000. SEAC's chairman said he could not rule it out.

Next morning, the BSE story so dominated the newspapers that one farmer wryly commented that it had taken up more newsprint than the declaration of war in September 1939. For the tabloids the focus was 'the victims'. The *Daily Mirror* gave its first six pages to the story, starting with its front-page headline in white-on-black, 'The Proof', over a picture of Michelle Bowen, terminally ill in hospital with CJD. 'Mad Cow Disease killed mum Michelle Bowen', ran the strap, 'now experts say it could kill 500,000 of you' (a reference to Pattison the previous evening). According to the *Mirror*, Pattison's 'doomsday scenario' echoed the 'bleak predictions' of 'leading scientist Dr Richard Lacey, who first forecast a massive outbreak next century'.

The *Daily Mail*'s preferred front page 'victim' was Vicky Rimmer, followed by many more pages inside.* The *Daily Express* quoted Lacey describing it as 'one of the most disgraceful episodes in the country's history'.

Broadsheet coverage was equally extensive. The *Daily Telegraph* and *The Times* each devoted 12 separate articles to the story (Dr Stuttaford boasting that 'if John Gummer had read *The Times* carefully when he was the Agriculture Minister, he would never have persuaded his daughter to eat a beefburger'). The *Guardian* led its front page with 'Beef warning sparks panic – many millions

---

* Right to the last minute, the *Mail* havered between two articles commissioned for its main feature page. One, by North, argued that SEAC had so far come up with no evidence to alter the perception of risk from BSE. The other, by a consultant in communicable diseases who eight years earlier had attributed a hospital salmonella outbreak to eggs without any evidence, argued that the government had been covering up the true danger of BSE for years and advised readers not to risk eating beef. The editor decided to 'run with the scare'.

in potential danger', while laying the blame on modern agriculture ('farming became too intensive and nature hit back'). The *Independent* ran no fewer than 16 items, leading its front page with a quote from SEAC: 'we considered killing all 11 million cattle – the entire national herd'; and went on to quote Dealler as predicting a major epidemic, which at worst could kill '10 million people' by 2010.

Only here and there did a handful of commentators urge even a hint of scepticism. Andrew Marr in *The Independent*, dismissing the way ministers had hidden behind their scientific advisers, observed that 'on beef, as on many other food issues, politicians should have the courage to admit their ignorance'. He suggested that they 'should simply have noted the scientific news and said something brief, such as: "Use your own instincts about what to eat"'. Simon Jenkins wearily observed in the *Evening Standard*, 'we seem to have lost all ability to judge proportion'. Dr James Le Fanu reminded *Express* readers that 'there have been so many bogus health scares generated by alleged experts that the sensible thing is to shrug one's shoulders and get on with life'.

Meanwhile, in the outside world, the response to Dorrell's statement had been predictable. Every EU country, except Ireland and Denmark, had immediately moved to ban British beef imports; Egypt, Libya and Ghana had gone even further, by banning all imports from the EU. British officials were already on their way to Brussels to explain the new evidence to the Commission, although its first response had been to say 'British beef is perfectly safe as far as we are concerned, unless we receive information to the contrary'.

As beef sales at home collapsed, particularly in the cities,* media coverage over the next two days continued to be intense. Then came Sunday, when the newspapers were either looking for a new angle or sought to push the scare to even greater heights. In the first camp was the *Sunday Telegraph*, leading its front page with '"£12bn bill" for cattle slaughter', as it focused on the possible financial cost of Dorrell's statement. In the second was the *Sunday*

---

* Sales remained markedly more buoyant in country areas. The owner of several butcher's shops in Somerset reported that his sales in the city of Bath were '90 per cent down', whereas in the market town of Wells they remained largely unaffected (personal information).

Times, which led on 'Scientists fear ban must now spread to lamb', as it reported 'fears that BSE may have been passed to sheep'.

Way out in front, however, was the *Observer*, with its full-page feature headed 'A conspiracy to make us all mad', accusing the Tories of a ten-year-long cover-up. 'The more damning the evidence, the more ministers gambled with the nation's health. And in protecting their friends the farmers, they sacrificed the population at large.'

This was the article (quoted in our Prologue to Part One) that painted a picture of Britain as it would be on 20 March 2016, twenty years on from the day when Dorrell had made his fateful statement:

> *Now Britain's National Euthanasia Clinics churn on overtime, struggling to help 500 people a week to a dignified death before brain disease robs them of reason and self-control. This nation, whose leaders spent a decade in denial, is now in quarantine, the world having long since shunned contact with a population in which half a million people a year succumb to CJD spread in the late 20th century through eating beef products. The Channel Tunnel is blocked by five miles of French concrete. The health service is crippled, blood transfusions are impossible because undetectable prions infect most donors and the strain of caring for more than two million CJD victims has overwhelmed support staff.*

Such, said the paper, was the 'vision' of Professor Lacey, 'once reviled by the establishment on the tacit orders of the farm lobby, but now proven right, and whose views last week took on a disturbing new authority'.

The dam erected by the 'blockers' had burst with a vengeance. What was quickly dubbed 'the mother of all scares' had been launched on its way.*

---

* The first person quoted as using this phrase was Anthony Gibson, director of the National Farmers Union in the south-west, although, as we shall see later, it had already been used in America to describe the alarm over global warming.

'No Scientific Proof'

The odd thing about Dorrell's statement, as with Currie's in 1988, was how flimsy was the evidence on which it was based. This was apparent even from the peculiarly tentative wording of the statement itself. SEAC had no 'proof' of any link between BSE and CJD. They could only suggest that this was 'the most likely explanation at present'.

This conclusion derived entirely from Will's puzzlement on finding that the brain tissues of ten people who had died in the three years since 1993 did not share the pattern of the more familiar sporadic form of CJD. Hence his belief, since he personally had never seen it before, that this must represent a 'new variant' form of CJD. But was it genuinely a new form of the disease? Proper data on CJD were in remarkably short supply. A feature of the disease was how little about it was known. Brain biopsies require time and money and are rarely taken from people dying of dementia.

In fact, within a few days of Dorrell's statement it was being reported that Professor Gareth Roberts, a neuropathologist working for SmithKline Beecham, had carried out a study of the most extensive brain bank in the country, the Corsellis Collection. Of 1,000 cases of dementia in the collection, he found that 19 had died of CJD (only 11 had previously been identified as having the disease). He suspected that two of these, much younger than the average, were cases of vCJD. But, significantly, both had died before the start of the BSE epidemic. It already looked as though Will might not be right: vCJD might not be a new disease after all.[15] Worse still, if these examples predated BSE, where then was the link with beef?

Another problem was the lack of any information on the incubation period of the disease. All that was known about the ten cases Will had studied was the date of death, over a period of three years. Nothing was known about their date of onset. Had it been three years? Five years? Ten? All this again would have been highly relevant in trying to determine the possibility of a link with BSE. But nobody knew.

Perhaps the most testing questions of all should have been asked of the epidemiology of the disease. Anecdotal evidence suggested that BSE itself had probably been around for some time even before it was first identified in 1984. If BSE-infected beef eaten at that time had caused vCJD, it would already have had well over a decade for this to show. Indeed, the cases studied by SEAC had already been appearing for three years. If these marked the onset of an epidemic then the incidence curve should now be rising rapidly. But this was not what the evidence indicated. Following Will's original eight cases, only two more had appeared subsequently, suggesting that if anything the curve might be falling rather than rising. On epidemiological grounds, the evidence for any forthcoming epidemic was simply not there. But none of the scientists directly involved had epidemiological training (let alone those outsiders, such as Lacey and Dealler, whose lurid predictions were about to fill the newspapers).

SEAC's conclusions, in short, were based on nothing more than partly informed guesswork. Yet when they were passed on to senior civil servants and ministers, they aroused such alarm that only two days later Dorrell was on his feet in Parliament. Instead of taking charge, weighing the situation with all the care such a potentially explosive issue demanded, he abdicated a significant part of his own ministerial responsibility to SEAC – scientists with no experience in crisis management or how best to handle the press.* He even gave them less than two hours to draft what he was to say. The whole episode bore the marks of collective panic. And the chief reason for this can be seen in the crucial part played in it by the media.

Already the previous autumn, the media had shown how they were itching for a scare over BSE. What created the panic that gripped civil servants and ministers was the fear of being blamed for yet another 'cover-up'. In this context, for Dorrell simply to read out SEAC's statement as written was akin to throwing a lighted match into a pool of petrol. He gave the media just what they wanted. The political, financial and social price to be paid for it would only now begin to emerge.

---

* As Pattison later admitted to the BSE Inquiry: 'I was totally naïve at the time about the interest that the media, the public and the press had in these issues. So the explosive nature of those relationships in March took me rather by surprise' (transcripts of evidence, Phillips Report).

The Disaster Unfolds

As the following week began, cattle markets across Britain stood empty. Meat processing plants began laying off staff in hundreds. Fast food chains such as Burger King and Wimpy announced that they were banning British beef from their restaurants. Within days, Birds Eye, the country's biggest producer of frozen foods, followed suit. Many in the meat industry were describing it as 'the worst week in the history of the trade'.

On Tuesday 29 March the European Commission's Standing Veterinary Committee met in Brussels, comprising the chief vets from each of the EU's 15 member governments. By 14 to 1 they voted to make it illegal for Britain to allow any beef or beef products to move outside its shores. Britain alone voted against the worldwide ban, which covered not only meat and live animals (exports worth £550 million a year) but also any product containing even a trace of an ingredient derived from beef, such as tallow or gelatine. This meant that a vast range of other goods were included in the ban, such as soap, cosmetics, candles, many chocolate products, even wine gums. MPs were outraged to discover that Brussels now had the power to prevent Britain selling beef even to countries still willing to buy it.

David Naish, president of the NFU, visited Hogg to plead on behalf of beef producers, the meat industry and the supermarkets for measures to be taken to 'restore consumer confidence'. Picking up on Hogg's announcement of new restrictions on the sale of beef from animals over 30 months old, Naish suggested that the sale of such beef should now be banned altogether. This went way beyond SEAC's recommendation that, to play ultra-safe, such meat should only be sold after being taken off the bone in licensed 'deboning plants'. But Naish's concern was not with human health. It was to rescue a market in collapse. He proposed that, to restore confidence in beef, meat from animals aged over 30 months should be excluded from the human food chain altogether. Government money should be made available to allow for such animals to be slaughtered and rendered down for burial in landfill sites.

Initially, not least because he could see the practical difficulties and colossal expense this would involve, Hogg rejected the NFU proposal. But he was faced not just with a meltdown of Britain's meat industry at home. The EU's highly damaging export ban was also creating a much wider crisis. What steps could Britain take to get the ban lifted?

When, on 29 March, Major met his fellow heads of government at a European Council in Turin, he was greeted with 'declarations of solidarity'. The ban would be lifted, he was assured, as soon as the British Government came up with a package of BSE-eradication measures which met the approval of the European Commission.

On 2 April, looking somewhat woebegone in a scruffy raincoat and battered fedora hat, Hogg travelled to Luxembourg for a meeting of EU agriculture ministers. In a bid to appease them, he had decided to offer the NFU proposal that all animals over 30 months would be excluded from the food chain. His colleagues accepted this scheme, even agreeing that it could be partly EU-funded. But they made it clear that it had nothing to do with lifting the ban. This could not be considered unless Britain agreed to destroy every cattle herd that had been infected with BSE. This was cloud-cuckoo-land. So many animals would have to be slaughtered – an estimate given at the time of 147,000 was millions below what would have been the true likely total – that there was no way the UK government could agree. Anyway, the necessary records did not exist.

When Hogg returned home empty handed, Major was reported as telling the NFU, at the start of the Easter weekend on 4 April, that the beef scare was 'the greatest crisis to confront the government since the Falklands'. In fact, the following week there were the first signs of beef sales recovering. On 11 April the *Independent*, one of the papers which had done most to hype up the scare, led its front page with the headline 'Where is the CJD epidemic?' 'Official figures', it reported, 'reveal that the number of possible cases of CJD this year do not justify the world-wide panic over beef.'

Three days later, speaking from his home in the Austrian Tyrol, the EU's agriculture commissioner Franz Fischler said, 'I would not hesitate to eat beef in England. I see no medical reason not to.' He admitted that there had been no public safety reasons for imposing the ban. 'We wanted to make sure that the beef market did not collapse as dramatically as was unfortunately the case in Britain. A failure to ban British exports would have meant that no other European country would have been able to export beef either.'

This was such a remarkable admission – that the ban's purpose had been not to protect public health but to protect the farmers of every EU country other than Britain – that the British government immediately served notice that it would challenge the ban's legality in the European Court of Justice. Major was reported as privately describing his EU colleagues as 'a bunch of shits'.[16]

At the same time Hogg announced that £550 million would be made available to finance a 'Cattle Disposal Scheme', whereby farmers would be compensated for all cattle over 30 months old to be withdrawn from the human food chain, slaughtered in dedicated abattoirs and rendered down for disposal as toxic waste, either by landfill or incineration.

Thanks to a MAFF press release, almost every newspaper reported that 70 per cent of the cost of this scheme would be 'funded by the EU'. But this only covered compensation for the animals, not the cost of their destruction. And much of the EU's contribution would anyway be 'clawed back' under the arcane rules governing the UK's EU budget rebate. Only later did it emerge that at least 90 per cent of the bill, eventually running into billions of pounds, would in fact end up being paid by UK taxpayers.

The 'Beef War'

At this point the BSE crisis split into two virtually separate dramas. One centred on the battle to get the EU to lift its export ban; the other on the chaos surrounding the introduction of the government's new scheme to dispose of millions of over-30-month-old cattle.

In the hope of getting his fellow agriculture ministers at least to draw up a timetable for the lifting of the ban, Hogg drew up plans for a 'selective cull' of 42,000 cattle. On 30 April they told him it was nothing like enough. Two weeks later, to the Standing Veterinary Committee in Brussels, Britain offered to double the number, to more than 80,000. When this too was rejected, Major formed a Cabinet committee, dubbed a 'war cabinet', to co-ordinate Britain's battle with Brussels, chaired by Foreign Secretary Malcolm Rifkind. BSE was about to provoke the worst crisis in Britain's relations with her European partners since she joined the Community in 1973.

Through May and early June 1996, as Europhile and Eurosceptic Tory ministers publicly squabbled at home over the wisdom of the policy, in Brussels British ministers and officials launched a policy of 'non co-operation', routinely vetoing almost every legislative proposal where they still had the power to do so. More than 65 measures were brought to a halt, provoking growing anger from other countries and Commission officials.

The fiery Brussels fisheries commissioner, Emma Bonino, took retaliatory action of her own, demanding further drastic cuts in Britain's fishing fleet. She announced that Britain had fallen way short of its EC target for 'decommissioning' fishing vessels, its fleet having 'doubled in size' since 1988 from 116,000 to 239,000 tonnes. In fact the Commission's own figures showed only a marginal increase, from 206,000 to 211,000 tonnes (wholly due to foreign-owned 'flag boats' joining the UK register to claim a share in Britain's fishing quotas). But on the basis of her fictitious figures, Bonino demanded a further 60 per cent cut in the UK fleet. It was a measure of how far tempers had been roused by what was now generally known as the 'beef war'.[17]

By the time of the Florence European Council in June, when he had hoped the EU's heads of government would agree to a timetable, Major knew that his 'war' was lost. He felt he had no option but to give way. He settled for a vague promise that the ban might be gradually relaxed, in return for agreeing to the measure previously ruled as out of the question: a 'selective cull' of 147,000 animals. When he returned to announce this to the House of Commons, Tony Blair, as leader of the Opposition, tore him to shreds. To prolonged Labour cheers, he declared, 'Mr Major is now so desperate to extricate himself from this mess that he will settle for anything. There is humiliation in this deal. There is ignominy in this deal. In fact it is not a deal at all, it is a rout.'[18]

The Danish prime minister Poul Nyrup Rasmussen observed 'it has been very important to me that the Brits got nothing'. Major himself was to call it 'a vintage piece of back-stabbing'. But the misery was not over. On 12 July, the European Court of Justice rejected Britain's plea that the export ban was illegal. In September, when Hogg again asked his fellow agriculture ministers for a reduction in the scale of the cull they were demanding, he was told that either he agree to their demands in full or the ban must remain.

Major accepted defeat. Any plans for a cull were abandoned. Fischler responded that, so long as the British could not meet the EU's conditions, 'an end to the export ban is simply not a possibility'.[19] Klaus Hansch, the president of the European Parliament, tartly observed that, if Britain could not respect joint decisions, it would be better for her to leave the EU altogether.[20] The ban was to remain, indefinitely.

This still, however, left the other part of the price to be paid for the BSE scare. In May MAFF had launched its scheme for the destruction of 1.5 million cattle over 30 months old, now known as the 'Over 30 Month Scheme' (OTMS). Most of these were dairy cows that had reached the end of their useful life, normally sold off to make pies and soups. The vast majority of them were entirely healthy, and hundreds of thousands had been sold off each year to France (yet only in June 1996 was the first ever French case of vCJD recorded). Many more would be cattle of breeds that only reached maturity after 30 months, such as Welsh Blacks, bred to provide meat of the highest quality. Since BSE chiefly affected dairy cows, the disease in such cattle was extraordinarily rare. But the '30 month rule' made no distinction.

The sole declared purpose of the OTMS was not to protect human health but to 'restore consumer confidence'. Ironically, even as it got under way in May, it was reported that beef sales in Britain were already back to 94 per cent of their level of the previous year. The fast-food chains were now putting British beef back on the menu. So far as 'consumer confidence' was concerned, the 'great beef scare' had lasted barely two months.[21]

Indeed, this should have presented the government with a problem. Under the Food Safety Act, it only had the legal power to prohibit food being offered for sale when it posed a risk to human health. The 1981 Animal Health Act only authorized the destruction of animals when this was considered necessary to control disease. Since the purpose of the OTMS was to destroy huge numbers of healthy animals solely as a public relations exercise (and to take beef which could no longer be exported off the market), strictly speaking it was not even legal. But no MPs seemed to notice this. Amid scenes of remarkable chaos and confusion, MAFF's officials gradually assembled an operation to carry out the OTMS. This was, in fact, largely organized for them by the Federation of Fresh Meat Wholesalers, representing the larger abattoirs, the same firms that had earlier given such support to MAFF in its closing down of hundreds of smaller slaughterhouses during the introduction of new 'hygiene' rules under directive 91/497.

The task of slaughtering 25,000 animals a week was thus allocated to just 20 big industrial abattoirs, which were to be paid three times the normal commercial rate for killing them. Although, after protests, 21 smaller firms were later added to the scheme, more than 350 of Britain's slaughterhouses were excluded, at a time when most were struggling to survive because of the loss of business caused by the BSE crisis. When the largest abattoir in Europe, Manchester Meat Market, offered to take part in the scheme at a third of the rate being given to the select few insiders, its offer was ignored. The chosen handful of firms meanwhile enjoyed an unparalleled bonanza, between them earning 'excess profits', courtesy of the taxpayer, at a rate of £2 million a week. Huge quantities of some of the finest and safest meat in the world were going up in smoke, week after week, to serve no purpose at all.

All this had been set in train by Will's reading of the evidence on CJD back in February. By the summer, journalists were still on the lookout for any new stories that might help to keep the scare alive. On 2 June, for instance, the *Sunday Times* reported 'Five more CJD victims', all five of them young. But the response from Professor Pattison was noticeably downbeat. If only five more cases turned up in the next few weeks, was his response, this would suggest that predictions of a widespread epidemic were unfounded. 'I could have envisaged statistics that are a lot more worrying,' he said. It was only three months since, on the night of Dorrell's statement, Pattison had refused to deny the possibility that vCJD caught from eating beef would kill 500,000 people. Already, it seemed, he was severely modifying the views he had expressed when the panic was at its height.

As the months went by, and hardly any new vCJD cases appeared, SEAC's chairman was to modify his views still further. A year later, in May 1997, he told a London conference that the total number of deaths from vCJD might eventually 'end up at around 200'.* By February 1998, shortly after being knighted in the New Years Honours for his 'services to medicine', Pattison was able to

---

* 'We got it badly wrong over BSE admits top scientist', *Sunday Telegraph*, 8 June 1997. The Department of Health's figures at this time showed the incidence of vCJD as seven cases in 1994, seven in 1995, two in 1996 and one in 1997. These were later to be modified to three in 1995, ten in 1996 and ten in 1998.

report to the NFU's annual general meeting that the number of new cases coming to light was now so low that the eventual number of deaths was likely to be 'somewhere between 100 and 1500', although he was reported as believing that 'the final total would be at the lowest end of that scale'.* For Sir John, it seemed, the scare was over.

During the summer of 1996, when the impact of the BSE crisis was at its height, there had been regular press reports of beef farmers committing suicide. A later study, commissioned by the Department of Health from Oxford University, found that suicides at that time had 'averaged two farmers a week', twice the normal rate, usually as a result of hanging or shotgun wounds.[22] This suggests that the number of farmers driven by the stress of the crisis to end their lives probably outnumbered the number of people who had died from vCJD itself.

The Beef Bones Fiasco

History, as Marx wrote, repeats itself, first as tragedy, then as farce. By 1997 the number of new regulations issued by MAFF since 1988 to respond to BSE was around 60. In December that year, now under Tony Blair's Labour government, MAFF's officials produced yet another, the 'Beef Bones Regulations 1997'. Under this new law to sell cuts of beef on the bone, such as prime ribs or T-bone steaks, would be a criminal offence.

The story behind this prohibition, which immediately provoked a storm of outrage in the press, was that a MAFF pathologist, Dr Gerald Wells, had conducted a series of experiments force-feeding cattle with very large quantities of 'neat BSE-positive brain' tissue. In one animal, 39 months old (i.e. nine months older than any now allowed in the food chain), he discovered minute traces of infected material in its dorsal ganglia or spinal nerves. On the basis of this peculiarly contorted evidence, he concluded that there was a one in 1.2 billion chance of one person a year contracting vCJD from

* 'BSE top adviser dismisses fear of CJD epidemic', *Daily Telegraph*, 4 February 1998. In October 1997, reviewing two scientific papers on BSE and CJD in *Nature*, Pattison conceded that, at the time Dorrell made his statement, 'the evidence connecting the two diseases was slight' and that 'SEAC's advice was rightly questioned in both the popular and scientific press' (*Sunday Telegraph*, 5 October 1997).

eating beef still in contact with the bone: in other words, one chance in 20 that a single individual in the entire population might become infected with vCJD in 1998.*

Before this bizarre piece of guesswork could be submitted for the usual peer review by other experts, it was presented on 9 December to Pattison's SEAC, which immediately accepted it. Shortly afterwards, it was reported, Labour's new agriculture minister Jack Cunningham told Blair that, unless he acted on SEAC's advice, he would lose all 'credibility in Brussels'. In other words, if it was revealed that the British government had ignored such a warning, its chances of persuading Brussels one day to lift the ban would be smaller than ever.

Cunningham put out his proposed new law for 'consultation', as official procedures required. But although the list of 'stake-holders to be consulted', on the grounds that they might be pro-fessionally affected by such a ban, included road hauliers, the Association of Circus Proprietors, the British Ceramics Federation, the European Documentation Centre and even the 'Al-Hasaniya Moroccan Women's Group', it did not include a single organiza-tion representing cattle breeders, restaurants or hotels. After five working days, on 16 December the Beef Bones Regulations became part of the law of the land.

In striking contrast to the unquestioning way in which the press had received every other regulation related to BSE, this time almost every columnist was up in arms, pointing out that people would be 120 times more likely to be struck dead by lightning than die from eating a T-bone steak or using ox-tail to make soup. Such ridicule did the ban attract that a number of butchers and restaurant owners let it be known that they intended to defy it.

In a devastating and witty speech in the House of Lords on 27 January 1998, Lord Willoughby de Broke moved that the regula-tions be repealed. He pointed out that, even on the government's own figures, people were 4,800 times more likely to risk choking to death at their lunch table, and 76,000 times more likely to be

---

* For unearthing the origins of the 'T-bone steak ban' we are indebted to Emily Green, formerly of the *Independent*, the only journalist in the British press to resign from her paper in protest against its shamelessly unpro-fessional coverage of the BSE scare. After making this principled stand, she returned to her native America, a sad loss to British journalism (*Sunday Telegraph*, 4 January 1998).

maimed while driving to work. This seemed a curiously flimsy basis, he suggested, on which to threaten pubs and butchers with a £2,000 fine or six months in prison for the crime of serving their customers with a T-bone steak: 'the same penalty as applies, as your Lordships are undoubtedly aware, for keeping a brothel'.

A MAFF junior minister Lord Donoughue fell back on pleading that SEAC's advice had been endorsed by the Chief Medical Officer, and that people would not necessarily be aware of the risk they ran from eating beef on the bone, which was 'why we cannot leave the matter to the consumer'. Willoughby's motion was carried overwhelmingly, by 207 votes to 96. Faced in the Commons with similar criticism, Jeff Rooker, the minister of state for agriculture, blew his top. 'Opposition front-benchers may wish to infect the population', he exploded, 'but the Government will not do so.'

Eventually, despite the universal scorn directed at the new law, one or two brave environmental health officers attempted to prosecute owners of pubs and restaurants for defying it. In April, in a first test case, Jim Sutherland, a farmer and hotelier near Selkirk on the Scottish Borders, faced criminal charges for having staged a 'Prohibition Dinner', serving T-bone steaks at his own expense to 120 guests. Sheriff James Patterson found himself facing a QC, Michael Upton, retained by one of Edinburgh's leading law firms, who submitted a magisterially argued 112-page legal defence.[23]

Upton argued that on four grounds the regulations were invalid. Firstly, ministers had admitted that the purpose of the law was not to protect public health, as the Food Safety Act required, but to persuade the EU to lift its ban on British beef exports. Secondly, the crushing Lords defeat showed that the regulations did not have the full support of Parliament. Thirdly, the claimed benefits of the law were so tiny as to make it wholly 'irrational' and 'disproportionate'. Finally, there were 'serious improprieties' in the way it had been rushed through, not least the farce of allowing only five days for a 'consultation' process that was no more than a charade.

The sheriff knew that if he accepted these arguments, the government would immediately insist on an appeal, prepared to spend any amount of taxpayers' money in trying to ensure that its regulations were upheld. When he nevertheless threw out all the charges, this made headlines across the land. In the Commons, opposition leader William Hague invited Blair to take this opportunity to repeal such a 'ridiculous' law.

Blair replied that the charges had only been thrown out 'on a technicality', and that it would be foolish to ignore advice from the Chief Medical Officer. Before the appeal could be heard, however, the government finally recognized that its position could no longer be defended.

On 9 October 1999, MAFF laid before Parliament its Beef Bones (Amendment) Regulations 1999. These made it once again legal for customers 'to buy beef-on-the-bone, beef bones and foods made using beef bones', so long as this was 'in circumstances where they are able to make an informed choice' (including, for example, by asking in a restaurant if beef has been cooked on the bone).

Two years after it had begun, the 'T-bone farce' was finally over.

A Very Expensive Blunder

Two points were illustrated by this fiasco. One was that this was perhaps the first occasion on record when the only 'pusher' of a scare had been government itself, with the media playing an almost wholly sceptical role as 'blockers'. The other was how twitchy the government had now become over its need to placate Brussels, and how desperate it still was to get that export ban lifted.

By 1999 the incidence of BSE had been hurtling downwards at such a rate since its 1992 peak of 37,000, that confirmed cases in the year were only 2,256. This allowed the European Commission finally to announce on 1 August that it was lifting the ban (although exports of live animals were still prohibited). Britain was now free to resume exporting beef to the world – except that France and Germany responded by announcing their intention to ignore the Commission's ruling.

Four months later the EU's heads of government were due to meet for a European Council in Helsinki. It promised to be highly contentious on a whole range of issues, from the integration of the EU's defence forces to pressure for tax harmonization. Just before the meeting, as a calculated snub to Blair, France's prime minister Lionel Jospin went out of his way to reaffirm his country's refusal to lift the beef ban. At the pre-Council dinner the two men were reported to have been 'barely on speaking terms'. For years afterwards, Blair was to recall the Helsinki Council as the most unpleasant encounter with his EU colleagues of his entire premiership.[24]

Since Major recalled his experience at the 1996 Florence Council in similar light, it could be said that one consequence of the BSE scare was that it had done more than any other single issue to sour Britain's relations with her European 'partners'.

By this time, Blair had already taken one significant step to distance his government from any responsibility for the various disastrous consequences of the scare. On 22 December 1997 Cunningham had announced that there was to be an official inquiry into BSE, under the chairmanship of a senior judge, Lord Justice Phillips of Worth Matravers. The political purpose of this move was betrayed when on 27 December, two days after Christmas, MAFF announced its terms of reference. These were to look into the history of BSE and vCJD from the beginning, but only up to the moment of Dorrell's statement on 20 March 1996. Nothing that took place after that would be its concern.

The Phillips Inquiry opened in February 1998 and lasted well over a year, at an estimated cost of £27 million. It heard hundreds of witnesses and pored in minutest detail over how BSE emerged and how MAFF, the DH and SEAC responded. With a show of transparency, its proceedings were daily reported on the Internet. But, after labouring so mightily, when Phillips finally produced the 16 volumes and 5,000 pages of his report in December 2000, he brought forth only a sadly banal little mouse. His central conclusion was:

> *In the years up to March 1996, most of those responsible for responding to the challenge posed by BSE emerge with credit. However, there were a number of shortcomings in the way things were done.*

Phillips made no attempt to evaluate the scientific judgements that had been arrived at on BSE and vCJD. He accepted SEAC's view that the two diseases were linked without questioning it in any way. He made no attempt to evaluate the crucial part played by the media in creating the context in which Dorrell came to make his statement. The fact that he had been steered away from examining how the story unfolded after 20 March – not least that of the incompetence, corruption and stupendous waste of public money involved in the Over Thirty Month Scheme – meant that his account remained strangely flat and inconsequential.

But at least, as intended, it kept the whole story comfortably remote from anything for which the Blair government could be held responsible. It might have saved a large part of that £27 million if the report could simply have been boiled down to a single sentence: 'Having talked to all the people involved, I conclude that, while nothing in this life is perfect, no one is to blame.'

Gradually the great BSE scare faded into the past. Very considerable sums of public money had gone into various forms of scientific research on both BSE and vCJD, and, not surprisingly, the scientists who received it were reluctant to see their work and funding brought to an end. A characteristic of the years which followed therefore was that, at regular intervals, some new paper would be published, claiming to have established a new link between BSE and vCJD, usually based on the now familiar injection of large quantities of infected tissue into the brains of mice or other animals. These would invariably be accompanied by a press release, dutifully reported by journalists (particularly the BBC) as evidence that the scare might one day be revived.

One particularly bizarre branch of this industry was the tireless attempts that continued to be made to establish a link between BSE in cattle and scrapie in sheep. In September 2001, following the epidemic of foot-and-mouth disease, which had just resulted in the destruction of up to 10 million animals on farms across Britain, the newly formed Department for Environment, Food and Rural Affairs (DEFRA) announced a 'contingency plan' against the possibility that sheep might one day be found infected by BSE.[25]

Under DEFRA's 'worst case scenario', the plan envisaged not just that there would be a complete ban on eating lamb but that Britain's entire national sheep flock of 40 million animals would have to be destroyed. In announcing this, the agriculture minister Elliot Morley said that it was only fair that the public should be made aware of what he and his officials had in mind. 'In the past', he said, 'there is no doubt in my mind that information like this would have been very tightly suppressed because of the fears of food scares.' The trigger for the plan had been Phillips's finding that ministers in the previous government had failed 'to think the unthinkable', that a cattle disease might spread to humans.

What was puzzling about all this was that there had never been a shred of evidence that sheep might be infected with BSE, let alone that such an imaginary occurrence might make it necessary to resort to such a drastic remedy. Not even when the BSE/vCJD scare had been at its height had it been seriously suggested that the entire national cattle herd should be destroyed. But the next month something of an explanation emerged, in the shape of a truly surreal admission from DEFRA.

On Friday 19 October SEAC was due to be presented with some remarkable new evidence by DEFRA's Institute for Animal Health, the results of five years studying the brains of 180 sheep. The IAH was sure its researches showed for the first time that sheep could definitely be infected with BSE. Hence Morley's solemn announcement three weeks earlier. But the day before the SEAC meeting, DEFRA confessed that the IAH scientists had made a mistake. The sheep's brains they had been examining for five long years turned out not to be from sheep at all. They were the brains of cattle. Only now, at the last minute, had this extraordinary blunder come to light.[26]

But the government scientific advisers were not going to give up, as was illustrated by a further bizarre episode the following summer. For 2,000 years, Europe's sausage makers had been casing their sausages in skins made from lamb's intestines. For making an ideal sausage skin, it seems nothing else will do. Much of a European industry worth £2.84 billion a year depended on these skins, and a significant proportion of them were made in Britain by an industry employing 2,000 people and worth £30 million a year. Because they were made from the innards of sheep, these skins had now attracted the attention of the government's new Food Standards Agency, set up in 2000 (for reasons to be explained in Chapter Seven) and first proposed, it may be recalled, by Professor Lacey.

In June 2002 a 'stakeholder subcommittee' of the FSA had proposed that the agency should approach the European Commission to press for an EU-wide ban on the use of lamb's intestines, on the grounds that they might be infected with BSE and therefore a serious danger to human health. This recommendation was put to a meeting of the FSA's main board in Armagh, Northern Ireland, sitting under the agency's chairman Sir John Krebs, an Oxford zoologist, who had also been the chairman of the 'stakeholder committee' that made the proposal in the first place. This was despite a recent report by Dr Eileen Rubery, formerly a senior civil servant with the DH, which had strongly criticized the agency for its failure to take proper account of differing scientific views in reaching its decisions, particularly over issues related to BSE. She had also recommended that Sir John himself should not chair the 'stakeholder committee'.

Two further aspects of this procedure were very odd. One was that only at the last minute did news of the meeting reach the body that represented the sausage skin manufacturers themselves, the Natural Sausage Casings Association. This was headed by Tim Weschenfelder, whose family had been in the trade for over 100 years since his great-grandfather came over from Germany. Although he and his organization should have been the first 'stakeholders' to be consulted, they only learned about the FSA's plans in late May. They were thus given just three weeks to comment on a proposal that could wipe out their entire industry, putting 2,000 people out of work (even though the FSA's constitution required a minimum 10 weeks for such a consultation, which was meant to involve everyone affected).

When Weschenfelder travelled from Middlesbrough to Northern Ireland for the FSA's public board meeting, he was startled to witness Krebs and his fellow board members nodding the proposal through, solely, it appeared, on the basis of an opinion commissioned from Professor Roy Anderson of Imperial College, London. Anderson, a friend and former colleague of Krebs at Oxford, was an epidemiologist specializing in HIV and other human diseases. On Krebs's advice, he had been recruited the previous year to mastermind the government's response to the foot-and-mouth crisis. Although Anderson had no background in animal diseases, it was the computer modelling of his team which had been responsible for the controversial 'pre-emptive cull' policy, whereby more than eight million healthy animals had been destroyed, simply to create a curtain wall round the disease's advance. This policy was widely viewed as illegal, because the Animal Health Act only gave the government powers to slaughter animals that were either infected or had been directly exposed to infection.

Such was the basis on which the FSA was now to press Brussels for an EU-wide ban on natural sausage skins. Fortunately for the manufacturers, there was no sympathy at all for such a dotty proposal from the European Commission (not least because of strong opposition from Germany, where 80 per cent of *wurst* are encased in lamb skin, much of it imported from Britain).

Considering that the scientists still hadn't come up with a scintilla of evidence linking sheep to BSE, it made yet another very odd story. There was only one respect in which the promoters of this particular form of scare did enjoy success. In 2003 they persuaded DEFRA and its Scots and Welsh equivalents to adopt their so-called National Scrapie Plan, designed to eliminate from the nation's sheep flock any rams found genetically more likely to be vulnerable to scrapie. This not only involved sheep farmers in a plethora of expensive paperwork and testing, but also threatened the survival of many of Britain's most-valued rare breeds of sheep.

Bizarrely, these sheep farmers and their stock may well turn out to have been the last victims of the great BSE/CJD scare of the 1990s. By 2006, the incidence of BSE in Britain's cattle had fallen to such a low level (to only little more than 100 individual cases, bringing the total affected to 182,000) that Brussels lifted the last remaining provisions of the export ban. Even France finally agreed to readmit British beef and live animals.

As for the CJD Surveillance Unit's graph showing the incidence of vCJD, this had shown a number of revisions over the years. The latest version showed figures very different from those published earlier, almost certainly due to much increased awareness of the disease and the greater readiness of hospital and medical authorities to look out for it. Thus the peak years were now shown to have been 2000 and 2001, when the number of cases recorded was 28 and 20. But the graph had then fallen sharply to 9 in 2004, 5 in 2005 and only 3 up to October 2006 (bringing the total number of confirmed cases to 106). A question-and-answer sheet on the FSA website rather optimistically predicted: 'the most reliable estimate is that there could be less than one additional vCJD case over the next sixty years. The worst case is that there could be 2.5 additional cases over the next sixty years.'[27]

If the great BSE/CJD scare was over, there were no doubt those who believed that it had been ended by all those control measures imposed by successive governments since 1988, from the ban on feeding cattle with meat and bonemeal to the removal from the food chain of those animals whose age made them most susceptible to BSE. But one of the favourite analogies of epidemiologists is the 'pink banana'. If you paint a banana pink, and you're lucky enough to do so at just the moment when an epidemic starts to decline, you can claim that it only did so because you painted your banana.

The truth is that no one still has any real answer to the main questions raised by this extraordinary story, such as: what really caused BSE in the first place (of several rival theories none can be said to have won the day); what caused it to decline when it did (to ascribe it solely to the ban on feeding cattle with animal remains left far too many questions unanswered, not least why BSE never appeared in those countries which had imported huge quantities of potentially infected British meat and bonemeal); whether vCJD was really a new disease, or simply had not been identified before; and whether there was really any link between vCJD and BSE (eating contaminated beef was much less plausible than the possibility that the disease might have been passed on by contaminated pharmaceutical products).

All that can be said for certain is that Britain had to pay a colossal price for this scare. When in 2006 the 'Over 30 Month Scheme' finally came to an end, with the lifting of the last of the EU's export ban, the total number of animals destroyed had reached 8,074,600.[28] The total cost of this scheme to taxpayers, including compensation to farmers, was shown in 2004 as having been £3.45 billion, or £57 for every man, woman and child in the country.[29] The true total cost, including more than £2.5 billion in lost exports, along with losses sustained by farmers, the meat industry and the rural economy in general, must at least have doubled this figure, to around £7 billion.

Without question it was the most expensive food scare the world has ever seen.

Notes

1. *Sunday Times*, 22 October 1995.
2. *Daily Mail*, 23 October 1995.
3. *Daily Telegraph*, 24 October 1995.
4. The *World In Action* programme was broadcast on 13 November 1995, but it was trailed in that morning's press and reported again the following day.
5. *The Times*, 14 November 1995.
6. 'CJD does not strike by chance', *Daily Telegraph*, 24 November 1995.
7. *The Times*, 2 December 1995.

8. *Jonathan Dimbleby*, BBC TV, 3 December 1995.
9. *Daily Express*, 5 December 1995.
10. *Sunday Times*, 10 December 1995.
11. *Independent*, 18 December; *Meat Trades Journal*, 21 December 1995.
12. *Guardian*, 29 December 1995.
13. Unless otherwise indicated, our source for much of the narrative on the next few pages is the report of 'The Inquiry into BSE and Variant CJD in the United Kingdom', carried out by Lord Justice Phillips and published in 1998. This provides the most comprehensive record available of the events surrounding the BSE crisis and is available online at *http://www.bseinquiry.gov.uk/report/index.htm*.
14. *Daily Mirror*, 20 March 1996.
15. *Daily Telegraph*, 29 March 1996.
16. *Daily Telegraph*, 23 April 1996.
17. Christopher Booker and Richard North, *The Great Deception: Can The European Union Survive?* (London, Continuum, 2005), p. 401.
18. *Daily Telegraph*, 20 June 1996.
19. Reuters, 20 September 1996.
20. *Independent*, 21 September 1996.
21. *The Times*, 13 May 1996.
22. 'Stress and suicide in the country', BBC News website, 14 September 1999.
23. *Sunday Telegraph*, 19 April 1998.
24. Private information. See also Booker and North, *The Great Deception*, p. 447.
25. 'Sheep BSE "worst case" plans outlined', BBC News website, 28 September 2001.
26. 'Sheep BSE research flawed', BBC News website, 18 October 2001.
27. 'OTM Rule – Your Questions Answered', FSA website, posted 18 July 2005. These predictions were credited to the computer modelling team formed by Professor Anderson at Imperial College.
28. Figures from Defra website, posted 23 September 2005.
29. Parliamentary answer, 10 May 2004.

6

Officials Can Kill

Meat, Cheese and E. Coli, *1998*

E. coli, *human version BSE, salmonella, listeria – the food on your plate can be the death of you.*
'Talking Point', *BBC News*, 15 January 1998

Quis custodiet ipsos custodes? (Who guards the guardians themselves?)
Juvenal, *Satires*, Book VI

This chapter tells the story of two tragedies. One involved the deaths of 20 Scottish pensioners, the other that of a well-known English cheesemaker. Both involved the bug known as *E. coli* O157.H7. And both, in their different ways, were caused by very serious failures in the regulatory system set up to respond to the earlier food scares.

Failure At The Bottom

The most famous thing that ever happened in the drab former coal-and-steel town of Wishaw, near Motherwell in the Clyde valley, took place in late November 1996. A group of pensioners gathered in a church hall for lunch, to eat stewed steak and puff pastry supplied by the award-winning local butcher, John Barr and Sons. Afterwards many fell desperately ill, until eventually 21 died. Many more had suffered permanent damage to their health, particularly affecting their kidneys.

The cause of the infection was soon identified as *E. coli* O157.H7, the strain identified since 1982 as potentially lethal and now responsible for the worst *E. coli* outbreak the world had ever experienced. The source of the infection was tracked down to John Barr's shop.

When Barr was told this by Graham Bryceland, the Chief EHO of North Lanarkshire council – until now, Barr claimed, he had never heard of *E. coli* – he agreed to stop selling cooked meats. But Bryceland took no further action and only days later Barr supplied more than 100 guests at an eighteenth birthday party at a nearby bar with 300 slices of turkey, ham and other cooked meats. Again some of the guests soon fell ill. When Bryceland was informed, he summoned Barr out of a service at the local Catholic church for an angry interview at the council offices, but failed to record what was said.

A year later, when in total 200 people around Wishaw had been confirmed as suffering from *E. coli* poisoning, with hundreds more suspected, Barr faced trial, charged with the 'culpable, wilful and reckless supply' of contaminated meat to the birthday party.

Because Bryceland had failed to keep a record of his interviews with Barr, and because there was a dispute about their earlier agreement over cooked meat, a large part of the prosecution case collapsed. Four charges were dropped, and Barr was cleared of any personal blame. On two remaining charges, relating to hygiene and the sale of contaminated meat, his company was, in January 1998, found guilty and fined £2,500.[1]

Three months later, however, a new drama began. Under Scottish law, a Fatal Accident Inquiry had to be held into the first *E. coli* outbreak, because 20 people had died. Its purpose was to establish the cause of death; to determine whether any precautions might have been taken to prevent the deaths; and to identify any system defects that caused or contributed to them.

In April 1998 the inquiry opened, under Sheriff Graham Cox. The Motherwell courtroom was packed with a dozen legal teams, several led by QCs. Seated behind batteries of laptops, most represented public bodies, whose prime concern was to defend their own role in the events surrounding the outbreak. Centre stage were the lawyers for Bryceland and North Lanarkshire district council.[2]

The one exception was a local Wishaw solicitor, Paul Santoni, representing the family of one of the pensioners who died. To act as his chief expert witness, he had called in Dr North, not unknown in the area since the part he had played in the Lanark Blue case three years earlier.

What had particularly caught their attention was the role in the story of the local EHOs, who, after the tragedy occurred, seemed to have found it only too easy to identify 134 serious hygiene faults in Barr's premises and procedures, any one of which might have contributed to the fatal outbreak. But if all these faults were now so obvious, why had North Lanarkshire's health officials not spotted them before the event, during what were meant to be their regular inspections?

Certainly most of the deficiencies were so glaring that an experienced hygiene expert should have picked them up immediately. As one of the most dangerous of the bugs which can damage human health, *E. coli* O157 had in recent years become increasingly common in raw meat, not least because of the stress imposed on animals by the concentration of the slaughterhouse industry into fewer and larger units under the EC's 'hygiene' directive, 91/497.

The design of Barr's premises ensured a high risk that cooked meats might be contaminated by raw meat. No procedures were in place to ensure that they were cooked sufficiently to eliminate *E. coli*. Cleaning procedures were woefully deficient. The catalogue of failings was endless. Yet what came over in the courtroom was a picture of total incompetence, as the various officials sent out to inspect Barr's shop from North Lanarkshire's gleaming council headquarters in the centre of Motherwell limply admitted that they had failed to notice any of these points.

The last full inspection of Barr's premises had been carried out ten months before the disaster took place by a Mr Proctor, a 23-year-old EHO not long out of college. Not only had he failed to identify any of these deficiencies; he had even recommended that Barr no longer need the six-monthly inspections required for 'high risk premises'. The state of the shop was so satisfactory, the young official had advised, that in future it would only need inspecting once a year.

As Santoni and North gradually teased this chilling story out of the increasingly discomfited EHOs, the lessons it conveyed were not lost on Sheriff Cox. When his report appeared in mid-August, they formed the central thread of his conclusions. He identified the council's incompetence as a major system failure which had played a crucial part in bringing the disaster about. He contrasted the inexperience of the young EHOs sent to inspect Barr's shop with the much more experienced inspectors sent in to investigate afterwards, asking why Bryceland had allowed such a risky operation to be inspected by people without appropriate knowledge.

But he went on to point out that, 'having obtained an honours degree in environmental studies, Mr Proctor should have been capable of carrying out an inspection which would have revealed the apparent hazards in Barr's premises'. Even if the shop had remained on a six-monthly inspection rota, the sheriff witheringly argued, this still probably would have made no difference, because of the unprofessional way in which inspections were being carried out.

The real significance of Cox's report was that he did not just confine his findings to underlining the failings of one team of EHOs. His criticisms were much more general, as he emphasized how the whole purpose of arming EHOs with such draconian powers under the Food Safety Act had been to give them prime responsibility for ensuring that food sold to the public was safe.

There had long been a tendency, the sheriff went on, to lay all the blame for breakdowns in hygiene just on businesses, those which produced and sold the food. Certainly, he agreed, Barr should be held liable for his own part in the tragedy. But ultimately, he said, if public officials are to set themselves up as experts in hygiene, then both businesses and the public have the right to expect them to do their job properly. If there was a major failure, as here in Lanarkshire, the inspectors must equally share the blame. Cox said he was far from impressed by the attempts the officials had made throughout the inquiry to shuffle off any responsibility and to place all the blame on an incompetent butcher, who had every right to expect competent advice from those paid to be the official 'experts'.

For the people of Wishaw, the repercussions of this failure would continue to be experienced for a long time to come. In February 1999, more than two years after the tragedy, a *Guardian* reporter visited the town to find that scores of people of all ages were still suffering as a result, chiefly from severely damaged kidneys and abnormal fatigue. Sixteen of those affected were children, many of whom in the future might well need dialysis or kidney transplants to survive.[3]

On behalf of 120 of the most seriously damaged victims, Paul Santoni had been trying to obtain compensation from insurance companies since November 1996. Half had settled, the rest were still fighting, as lawyers continued to argue over who was responsible for the outbreak. Santoni, who had done much of his own work unpaid, was also fighting another battle with the Scottish Legal Aid Board. From more than 50 applications, its officials had so far granted aid to only one applicant.

Altogether, this was not an episode from which the supposed guardians of the public interest had emerged with much glory. In its own way just as chilling, however, was another episode centred on *E. coli* which, during the very months when the Motherwell inquiry was in progress, had been unfolding at the other end of the country.

Failure At The Top

At the end of April 1998, a 12-year-old schoolboy fell seriously ill after eating some Caerphilly cheese bought in Wellington, Somerset. He was diagnosed as suffering from *E. coli* poisoning, which had damaged the functioning of his kidneys. He was rushed to Southmead Hospital, Bristol, to be put on renal dialysis.

The source of the problem was traced back to Duckett's, a small cheesemaking business near the Somerset village of Wedmore, where Sedgemoor council EHOs established that a handful of its Caerphilly soft cheeses were contaminated with *E. coli*.

Only on 8 May, ten days after the boy fell ill and when he was already making a full recovery, did a nationwide food hazard warning go out from the Department of Health in London instructing wholesalers and shops to withdraw Duckett's cheese from sale.

Duckett's biggest single customer was Eastside, a firm in Surrey run by another cheesemaker, one of the most respected in the country, James Aldridge. He had started life as a garage mechanic and scaffolder, and had only come in contact with the world of cheesemaking when a fall kept him at home helping his partner Pat to run her small cheese shop in Southampton. By the 1980s they were running a shop selling British craft cheeses in south London, just when British farmhouse cheesemaking was at the beginning of its spectacular renaissance. It was not long before Aldridge not only knew most of the specialist cheesemakers in the country but also as much about the delicate microbiological processes involved in creating a top class cheese as any of them.

So valuable was his advice that, by 1989 when he decided to become a cheesemaker himself, he was already on the way to becoming a guru for many of his colleagues: as one of them put it, a 'cheesemaker's cheesemaker'. The cheese he created as the centre of his business was Tournegus, washing Caerphilly in brine and Kentish wine, then rubbing it daily for weeks with linen until it emerged with a silky soft texture and a taste so subtle that it soon won acclaim across the trade. By 1998 his customers ranged from Harrods and the House of Commons to top restaurants and every specialist cheese shop in the country.

The cheesemaker from whom Aldridge bought his Caerphilly was Chris Duckett. When the DH issued its hazard warning on 8 May, Aldridge had seven tons of it on his shelves, worth some £50,000. The news of the ban naturally came to him as a devastating blow.

Along with the ban, the PHLS had ordered local EHOs to retain samples of any cheeses originating from Duckett's for analysis. Aldridge's samples proved wholly free of *E. coli*, which was hardly surprising since they had been delivered long before the problem affecting Duckett's cheese arose (in fact tests had shown that only a tiny proportion of Duckett's cheese was affected, 10 out of 200 samples, and it was impossible that any of these could have been delivered to Aldridge). To be absolutely certain, Aldridge had then commissioned an independent analysis of his entire stock, which confirmed that it contained no trace of contamination. Inevitably, since his own cheese posed no risk, he wondered how long his business would be frozen in suspension.

On 19 May, after talking to his local EHOs, they agreed to serve a 'retention order' on him, under Section 9 of the Food Safety Act. The benefit of this was that, since his cheese was proven to be safe, he could then ask magistrates to order compensation for any cheese he was forbidden to sell.

At least it now looked as though Aldridge would be able to make up most of his losses. But next day came the bombshell. Tessa Jowell, minister of state for public health at the DH, took an unprecedented decision. She chose to exercise her power under Section 13 of the Food Safety Act to sign an emergency control order, ordering that all cheeses originating from Duckett's must be destroyed. This was a power that had never been used before, because it had only been intended for use in countering some very serious and widespread threat to public health, calling for urgent action. But the significance of Section 13 was that it withdrew from the food's owners any right to compensation. Furthermore, it imposed on them the responsibility for destroying it at their own expense.

For both Duckett and Aldridge, this created an unimaginable crisis. At least some of Duckett's own cheese had actually been shown to be unsafe. He also had a farming business to provide him with income. But Aldridge was now faced not just with losing £100,000, the income he might have made from the cheese he now had to destroy, but also with the prospect of losing his entire business, itself valued at £200,000. He was ruined. Fourteen other businesses that bought cheese from him would also be seriously affected.

Aldridge's plight was only made even more surreal when, on 5 June, with his solicitor and North, he met a senior official at the Department of Health. She admitted that, even when the order was signed, they were already aware that Duckett's cheese posed no further risk to public health.

The shadow of Wishaw still lay heavy over the Department of Health. It seemed as though the DH officials were anxious to make a statement. They wanted to give the impression that they were prepared to take swift and drastic action to prevent such a tragedy ever happening again. Furthermore, recalling the price to be paid for Clydesdale's abortive bid to destroy Lanark Blue, this time it would not cost the taxpayers a penny.

Two weeks later the issue was raised in a special Commons debate called by the Liberal Democrats' front-bench spokesman Paul Tyler. After setting out the facts of what had happened, he asked Jowell to explain why it had been necessary to use such heavy-handed powers when her own officials admitted they no longer considered there was any threat to public health? How could it be right for businesses to be destroyed in this fashion without any right to compensation?[4]

To those of us who were present what was striking about Jowell's reply was her air of icy self-righteousness. She seemed to have convinced herself that because *E. coli* was 'an organism likely to cause serious illness or even death', this completely justified everything she and her officials had done. She expressed not a jot of sympathy for the two cheesemakers. She ignored Tyler's point that Aldridge's cheese had been repeatedly found to be free of contamination (let alone his citing of the fact that this was known at the time the order was signed). She even claimed that it was only due to the prompt action of her officials that the number of people affected by eating Duckett's cheese was limited to one (although they had taken no action at all for ten days after the boy was admitted to hospital, during which time cheese from Duckett's had probably been eaten by thousands of people). She refused to say any more about Aldridge's case, on the grounds that he was now seeking leave for judicial review of her decision in the High Court.

In a desperate bid to save his business, Aldridge was now pouring all his savings into legal fees. When the case finally came before the High Court in November, Aldridge's QC argued that Jowell's ban had been a 'disproportionate response' to one 'isolated incident', and therefore a violation of his human rights. Mr Justice Moses agreed. The decision to impose the ban, he said, had been 'affected by factors which amounted to no more than fears of administrative inconvenience'. Jowell's ban, he ruled, had been unlawful.

It seemed that Aldridge had won an extraordinary victory. Although he estimated the losses to his business during the time it had been closed at £250,000, in the light of the High Court ruling, he was now free to claim compensation for at least some of what he had lost. Furthermore, he could now plan to resume making his cheese.

But Aldridge had not reckoned with the determination (and bottomless purse) of the Department of Health, which gave notice that it wished to appeal. Seven months later, on 30 June 1999, the Lord Chief Justice, Lord Bingham, ruled in the Appeal Court that Jowell's action had been lawful after all, simply because in his view her department had been faced with an 'imminent threat to the life or health of the public', and that her use of the powers given her by Section 13 was entirely justified. The judge did not question whether it had been 'proportionate' to close down Aldridge's business at such cost, despite the fact that his cheese posed no threat to health. The judge had come to the rescue of the 'system'.

Triumphant in its victory, the Department of Health magnanimously announced that not only would it not pursue Aldridge for its legal costs, amounting to hundreds of thousands of pounds; it would also contribute £300,000 of taxpayers' money towards Aldridge's own costs.

For Aldridge, however, at the age of 59, it was an irrecoverable defeat. Gone were any hopes of claiming compensation for what he had lost, or of providing for his retirement by selling his business to another cheesemaker. He became a haunted man, obsessively talking of the terrible blow that had struck him out of the blue, taking away all he had worked for. He was now virtually penniless. Soon after the legal battle ended, he developed cancer, and on 5 February 2001 he died.

As the Guild of Food Writers put it, in one of many obituaries he was given, the verdict of the Court of Appeal

> *chilled the bones of small producers across the country, and took the life and soul from James Aldridge. Despite the extraordinary support he received from around the world, he could not come to terms with the injustice.*

When, in the BBC's Food and Farming Awards for 2001, he was posthumously given the top honour, the citation ended 'it was a case which many saw as a disgraceful injustice. It nearly bankrupted him and he never recovered from it'.

The food scares that gave rise to the 1990 Food Safety Act had claimed their most celebrated victim.*

* * *

In fact the regulation of food safety in Britain was about to go through a dramatic upheaval. In January 1998, at the time of the Barr trial, the government had announced its long-heralded plans to set up a new Food Standards Agency. This was the idea first put forward by Lacey in 1989, at the height of the salmonella scare, then swiftly picked up to become official Labour policy. But what no one knew in the summer of 1999 was that at the very moment when the new agency was about to be launched months later,

---

* After his death it was announced that Aldridge's contribution to British specialist cheesemaking was to be commemorated by naming a trophy after him in the prestigious annual British Cheese Awards. One early winner was Leon Downey, creator of Llangloffan, referred to in Chapter Three.

supposedly to take supreme charge of all Britain's hygiene regulation, most of its powers would immediately be taken away.
What was to bring this about was arguably the most bizarre food
scare of them all.

Notes

1. *Guardian*, 10 February 1999.
2. For an account of the inquiry and the Sheriff's report, see *Sunday Telegraph*, 23 August 1998.
3. *Guardian*, *op. cit.*
4. Hansard, HC, cols. 338–44 (17 June 1998).

7

The £1 Billion Blunder

The Belgian Dioxins Debacle, 1999

Total havoc. This is a human and economic catastrophe. Our reputation abroad is ruined, the agri-industry threatened, thousands of jobs in danger.

Het Laatste Nieuws, June 1999[1]

The last food scare we describe in this book was in a sense the most dramatic of all, because of the way it blew up seemingly from nowhere. It made headlines all over the world. Millions of people were supposedly at risk. It provoked a major political crisis, bringing down first two Cabinet ministers, then a whole government. Costing more than £1 billion, it dealt a massive blow to the country's economy. It changed the political history of Europe.

Only when the hysteria had died down did it emerge just how absurdly the scare had been inflated out of all proportion. There had been virtually no danger to human health at all.

The country was Belgium. The year was 1999. The problem was the discovery that unknown quantities of poultry feed had been contaminated with potentially carcinogenic dioxins, at levels hundreds of times above the officially recognized 'safe limit'.

Dioxins. Few words could have been calculated to trigger off a more emotive response, because these organic particles were associated with by far the most serious chemical disaster the world had ever known. This was the explosion at a Union Carbide plant making pesticides at Bhopal in India in 1984, causing up to 7,500 people to die instantly and another 16,000 later, with up to half a million said to have suffered long-term health damage.

Bhopal had fixed itself in many people's minds as totemic of all that had become most threatening in modern technological

138

civilization. It was a disaster created by the reckless use of deadly chemicals, inflicted by a vast multi-national corporation on the impoverished people of the Third World. Whenever environmentalist lobby groups wanted to warn against the risks of some large-scale technological process involving chemicals, such as a giant incinerator or a new chemical plant, it might not be long before there was mention of the need to 'avoid a new Bhopal'.

But part of the reason why dioxins provided such an ideal focus for a scare was that, like the bacteria we looked at earlier, these halogenated hydrocarbon particles are so small and mysterious. Most people would be hard put to it to define them at all. In fact dioxins comprise a whole family of chemically related compounds, of which some 419 have been identified but only around 30 of which are considered to be significantly toxic; the most dangerous of all being 2,3,7,8-tetrachlorodibenzo-para-dioxin, known as TCDD.

Dioxins can be found everywhere in the environment, in air, soil, and water, and in the bodies of animals and humans. They are produced naturally by the burning of organic materials, as in forest fires or volcanic eruptions. They are given off by garden bonfires and by a whole range of industrial processes. Their danger to people, deriving mainly from food, is that that they accumulate in fat, persisting for a long time. The more toxic of them can induce skin problems known as chloroacne, damage the immune and nervous system and cause cancer.

Apart from Bhopal, the environmental risk dioxins can pose was never better exemplified than by their association with Agent Orange, the defoliant used by US forces in the Vietnam war, which caused enormous damage to forests, farmland, animals and human beings. But this horror story in itself helped to build up something of a legend about dioxins, and a tendency to magnify the dangers they can pose. Huge alarm, for instance, was caused in 1976 by the accident at a chemical plant in Seveso, Italy, when several kilograms of dioxins were released into the air. Initially it was feared that thousands might die. In the end, although 3,000 animals were found dead around the plant, and some 80,000 farm animals were destroyed to prevent them entering the food chain, there were no human deaths at all. The only obvious human damage was a rash of severe but temporary skin disorders.

A similarly alarming incident made headlines across the United

States in December 1982 when, after a serious flood, the small town of Times Beach, near St Louis, Missouri, was found to be contaminated with dioxins from oil sprayed to keep down dust on its dirt roads. The contractor, it was discovered, had bought the waste oil from a chemical plant manufacturing Agent Orange. In reporting on the disaster it was claimed, based on their effect on guinea pigs, that dioxins were 'the most toxic chemical synthesised by man'. At the town's Christmas party, the 2,400 inhabitants were told that, on a recommendation from Dr Vernon Houk, head of the US Center for Disease Control (CDC), Times Beach was to be evacuated.

President Reagan set up a 'Dioxin Task Force', including the US Corps of Engineers. The entire town was bought by the Environmental Protection Agency and razed to the ground, to be turned into a park. In 1985 *Time* magazine marked the destruction of Times Beach with a famous cover story headed 'The Poisoning of America'. The whole operation cost $138 million.[2]

Four years later Dr Houk told a scientific seminar in Texas that, thanks to more recent researches into dioxins, the CDC now recognized that they probably led to no adverse health effect other than skin rash. 'To put it bluntly,' he said, 'we found that human beings were not nearly as susceptible to dioxins as guinea pigs.'[3] In 1991 he told the *New York Times* that 'given what we now know about the chemical's toxicity, it looks as though the evacuation was unnecessary'.[4]

These admissions, however, attracted very much less publicity than the original scare had done when Times Beach was abandoned and demolished. They were certainly not enough to prevent the crisis which was to engulf Belgium eight years later, which was rapidly to escalate into the biggest 'dioxins scare' of them all.

Stage One: How It All Began

The Belgian dioxins crisis of 1999 unfolded through three stages. We were able to reconstruct the inside story of the all-important first stage – how the problem first came to light – when in 2000 Dr North was invited to a conference at Louvain University to give a paper on 'the dynamics of food scares'.[5] As chance had it, among his audience and listening with particular interest, was Jan van Ginderachter, a nutritionist working for NV De Brabander, an animal feed company, which a year earlier had been at the centre of the crisis.

After the lecture, van Ginderachter explained how it was he who had originally uncovered the Belgian dioxins problem. In February 1999 he had been asked by his company to investigate why some of the poultry firms which bought feed from De Brabander were reporting difficulties with their birds. These were large-scale poultry breeders, producing eggs from which chickens were bred for human consumption. Soon after the feed was delivered, they had noticed reduced laying in their hens. Then hens began to die. Eggs were not hatching. Newborn chicks displayed signs of neural disorder.

Van Ginderachter carried out tests, all of which proved negative, but arranged for the destruction of all chicks at the premises affected. It was not until mid-March that he recalled reading a scientific paper which linked similar ailments with dioxins. Talking next day with a nutritionist employed by another firm which had experienced the same problems, the two men worked out that the one element their products had in common was animal fat supplied by a company called Verkest. This was sufficiently important, thought van Ginderachter, to pass it on to the head of the animal feed section at Belgium's agriculture ministry. He added that, since Belgium did not have a laboratory specializing in dioxin analysis, he was sending samples of the suspect feed from Verkest to one in Holland, Rikilt. The ministry's response was that this was merely 'a commercial matter'.

If it had not been for the diligence of van Ginderachter, as a conscientious food scientist, the dioxins might never have been identified at all, certainly nothing like so soon. Until now, the only official who had shown any interest in his researches was Dr Andre Distickere, the local head of the agency responsible, under the Department of Public Health, for enforcing meat hygiene rules. But the reason for Distickere's interest was that, under another hat, he also worked for De Brabander's insurance company, which had asked him to investigate.

On April 23 Rikilt finally confirmed that van Ginderachter's suspicions were correct. Unbelievably, the poultry feed contained dioxins at 1,500 times the legal limit. There had clearly been a serious system failure, even though van Ginderachter calculated that the dioxins would be so diluted when they passed through breeding birds to chickens in the human food chain that it was extremely unlikely that there could be any risk to human health.

The nutritionist immediately relayed the news of the dioxins find to Distickere, in his role as adviser to the insurance company. But the vet then, in his role as a public official, passed it on to the agriculture ministry, where officials finally began to take notice. They decided to send off their own samples to Rikilt and to trace all Verkest customers who might have received contaminated feed – although they did not start work until 30 April, six weeks after van Ginderachter had first contacted the ministry.

By this time Distickere had also, on 28 April, sent a detailed memo to the public health ministry. This was much more alarmist in tone. He indicated that contaminated fats had not only ended up in laying hens but also in chicks which had been sent to slaughterhouses to be recycled into pig food. These might therefore have introduced dioxins into the human food chain. Although this note was confidential, it was soon to become very public. The 'Note Distickere' was to play a key part in inflating the scare.

Through May the agriculture ministry traced the feed producers supplied by Verkest, ten in all, including one in France and another in Holland. It investigated 417 poultry farms which might have bought the contaminated feed. On 21 and 26 May, when the ministry got back the results of its own samples from Rikilt, these showed alarmingly high levels of dioxins in breeder hens and eggs on several of the farms. It immediately closed down all the farms Verkest had supplied and called a crisis meeting with officials of the health ministry.

It was agreed that the two ministries should share responsibility for tracing contaminated products. But then came a fateful error. A joint press release, already drafted, only mentioned a problem with contaminated chicken feed, and it was this low-key statement which on 27 May was issued to the press. Unsurprisingly, it attracted little attention.

Next day, however, the public health minister Marcel Colla, off his own bat, gave the order for all poultry products to be removed from sale, along with a warning to the public to avoid eating any which had originated in Belgium. The sight of millions of chickens and eggs being cleared from the shelves of shops and supermarkets throughout the country immediately aroused intense suspicion that there might be more to this dioxin story than had been officially admitted.

To make matters worse, the two ministries then put out separate press releases. The health ministry's version assured consumers that banning the sale of poultry products was just a temporary measure and that there was no serious health risk. But that from the agriculture ministry admitted that 'contaminated chicken and eggs have for some months been entering the food chain'. It was a sentence as explosive as those recklessly phrased statements uttered earlier in Britain by Currie and Dorrell.

The media went into orbit. The scare had entered its second stage.

Stage Two: 'Cry Havoc' – the Scare Goes Political

The timing of these events over the last days of May could not have been more damaging. Belgium was now in the midst of an already fraught general election campaign. Jean-Luc Dehaene, in office for eight years at the head of a centre-left coalition, was his country's longest serving prime minister. According to the polls he might well win, but the outcome looked close. His main challenger was Guy Verhofstadt, leader of the centre-right Vlaamse Liberalen en Democratien (VLD) Party.

The last thing Dehaene wanted was the kind of embarrassment by which he was now threatened: a major crisis which laid his government open to charges of a cover-up. He immediately went into full damage limitation mode, cancelling a scheduled EU meeting in Luxembourg and instructing his two ministers to submit a full report to him as soon as possible. As the media were already drawing parallels with BSE in Britain, Dehaene went on television, fighting to defuse the crisis.

The response from abroad was similarly dramatic. By 31 May six countries, including Britain, had imposed an emergency ban on all imports of poultry products from Belgium. One German radio commentator even advised motorists only to travel through Belgium with closed windows.

Then, the same day, came an intervention which was to swamp the election campaign. Dr Distickere, the vet who had been following the affair from the inside since February, was also, it turned out, a member of Verhofstadt's VLD party. He had been indignant at the official press releases which seemed to downplay the dioxin threat and had therefore faxed to Verhofstadt a copy of the 'Note Distickere' he sent to the health ministry more than a month earlier, warning that dioxins could already have got into the human food chain. If ever a politician was given a chance to accuse his rival of a cover-up at the height of an election campaign, this was it.

Verhofstadt planned his ambush carefully. He arranged a meeting with Dehaene and presented him with the note, ensuring that at the same time its text was released to the press. The Prime Minister was stunned. The media could scarcely find headlines big enough to cover the news. The evidence for an official cover-up going right to the top seemed conclusive.

The following day, 1 June, the two ministers resigned. But this only made the situation worse. As the subsequent parliamentary inquiry reported:

> *The resignation of the two ministers had a manifest effect on the later management of the crisis. Their resignation clearly confirmed that there was a serious problem, which had been underestimated in previous months.*[6]

The same day, Socialist members of the European Parliament were demanding an EU-wide ban on a whole range of Belgian foods, including chocolate. The day following, 2 June, the EU's acting agriculture commissioner Franz Fischler castigated the Belgian government for not having notified the Commission about the problem much earlier, while the Commission itself extended Belgium's own ban on poultry products to the whole of the EU.

Countries right round the world were now queuing up to join the ban, and would eventually number more than 30, including Australia, Canada, Russia, South Africa, Egypt, Poland, Switzerland and many more. Some added a range of other products to their bans, from chocolates to pasta. Some banned imports from France, Germany and the Netherlands as well. The USA and Singapore went even further, banning imports of poultry and pork from anywhere in the EU.

From now on the scare seemed to be multiplying in all directions. In Belgium and across Europe newspapers competed with each other to see who could run the most lurid accounts of the dangers dioxins posed to human health.* Brussels' main French-language daily *Le Soir*, observing that the crisis had plunged Belgium 'into a fog', published a long list of foods that were banned or should be treated with caution, including not just chicken, pork, beef but anything containing more than 2 per cent of egg, such as mayonnaise, soups, bakery products, cakes, biscuits and desserts. *Het Laatste Nieuws*, in the words quoted at the head of this chapter, described the country's plight as 'total havoc. This is a human and economic catastrophe'.[7]

On 4 June the European Commission, which was drawing much of its information about the crisis from the Brussels media, extended its restrictions to a whole range of other foodstuffs, including pork, beef and dairy products, on the grounds that the Belgian authorities could not rule out the possibility that contaminated feed had been sold to cattle and pig farmers.

On 8 June the Belgian government produced its final list of farms that might have been supplied with Verkest's feed in January. These included 445 poultry producers, 393 cattle farms and 746 pig breeding farms (40 per cent of all those in the country). But Dehaene was then forced to announce that, although the Belgian authorities had hitherto only regarded as suspect farms supplied by Verkest between 19 and 31 January, the European Commission was now insisting that they must now investigate all farms supplied up to 1 June, a period of nearly five months. This immediately extended the list of 'suspect' poultry farms from 445 to 811.

On 9 June the Commission was able to announce that 426 farms in the Netherlands and 181 in France had also been put under 'quarantine', prohibited from selling any of their products, because of the possibility that they might also have been supplied with suspect feed. On 10 June Belgium's frontier crossings with Germany and the Netherlands were blocked by angry Belgian

---

* A widely quoted preliminary study by Martin van den Berg of the University of Utrecht concluded, based on analysis of two chickens and two eggs taken from hatcheries in April, that people in the areas affected could have consumed 40 times the WHO recommended dioxin limit, which could affect 'neural and cognitive development, the immune system and thyroid and steroid hormones, especially in unborn and young children', although van den Berg conceded that the doses were 'probably too low to cause cancer' (*New Scientist*, 12 June 1999).

farmers protesting at the flood of food imports pouring into their country.

On 11 June the Commission backed down on its ruling that all farms supplied up to 1 June must be investigated, accepting after all that the restrictions should only apply to those supplied in January. It also accepted that further testing need not be for dioxins, because this was complex and expensive, but that it could now be more quickly and cheaply concentrated on PCBs, or polychlorinated biphenyls, because it is from these that dioxins are formed by heat.

On 13 June Belgium went to the polls. Dehaene suffered a crushing defeat, immediately resigning as leader of his party. Verhofstadt became prime minister, thanks more than anything to that critical intervention by his loyal supporter Dr Distickere, and on 18 June he appointed a 'crisis manager' to bring the dioxin crisis 'under control'.

Much of the damage had already been done. Food processors were now filing for bankruptcy. The Federation of Belgian Food Industries (FEVIA) said that 6,000 people were already unemployed, due to the crisis, and that this figure was still rising. On 30 June the new government was able to announce that the cost of the crisis to Belgium's food industry was already $1.54 billion (£1 billion) and still rising.

At least Belgium's prosecution service had now tracked down what was thought to be the original cause of the problem. A small quantity of used vegetable and animal fat collected for recycling by a firm called Fogra and then sold on to Verkest for processing into animal feed had been contaminated with industrial oil from an electrical transformer. Whether this was the result of an accident or a criminal act was never established, any more than was precisely where it had taken place. But on 23 June two Fogra executives were arrested.

On 19 July the EC published its draft proposals for a complete ban on the use of frying oils in animal feed. This in itself would add hundreds of millions of euros a year to the costs of European agriculture, since more expensive substitutes for the recycled oil would have to be found elsewhere (while the food industry would now have to pay for its used oils and fats to be destroyed, instead of being collected for further use).

The scare briefly surged back into the news when two pig farms were found to have high levels of PCBs. This led to 233 more pig farms being placed under quarantine, while all stocks of pork held by meat plants and depots were destroyed. On 29 July a further 175 poultry and pig farms were placed on the restricted list because they were supplied by Verkest and had registered PCB levels above the Belgian 'safe limit' (although they were below the limit recommended by the World Health Organization).

However, the worst of the scare was now over. Seven million chickens had been destroyed and 60,000 pigs. But gradually, through the weeks of August and September, Belgium's food industry crawled back towards some state of normality. Belgian products returned to the shops, as ever more farms were taken off the restricted list. Other countries, one by one, lifted their bans on Belgian imports. And the scientists were at last managing to piece together just how serious the effects of the contamination episode were in fact likely to have been.

An article published in *Nature* on 16 September by Professor Alfred Bernard, head of the industrial toxicology unit in the Faculty of Medicine at the University of Louvain, estimated that the total extent of the contamination was likely to have been just one gram of dioxins and 50 kilograms of PCBs. Given normal consumption habits, he and his team concluded, the quantity of toxins consumed would thus have been much lower than exposure levels recorded in previous industrial accidents. In this case it was unlikely that any harm had been done to the population at large.

The article pointed out that most people's bodies already contain considerable quantities of dioxins and PCBs from other sources, such as contaminated seafood, and that it would have required the consumption of 30–40 meals of highly contaminated chicken or eggs to double that amount. 'Even in such an extreme case,' Bernard suggested, 'levels would be no more than expected in someone regularly eating contaminated seafood.' Yet, ironically, one of the alternative sources of protein recommended to Belgians at the height of the crisis had been fish, very likely caught in the North Sea where dioxin levels are abnormally high.

Such reassuring conclusions were hardly in keeping with the tough line still being taken by the EC which, on 8 September, had reaffirmed its intention to take the Belgian government to the European Court of Justice for breaches of EU hygiene rules, and for having failed to inform it earlier of the seriousness of the crisis.

Only a week later, the Commission's new president Romano

Prodi used the fear which had swept Europe during the dioxins crisis as his cue to propose a startling extension of the Commission's powers, and one which would mark a further significant step forward in the political integration of the European Union.

Stage Three: The 'Beneficial Crisis'

Since the 'European project' had been launched on its way in the 1950s, its central underlying agenda had been to promote ever greater integration, or, as the preamble to the 1957 Treaty of Rome put it, 'ever closer union'. This was to be achieved by a continuous transfer of powers from national governments to the supranational institutions of the Community, so that all the member states could gradually be brought under the same system of laws.

Once the 'competence' to make laws over any particular area of policy had been transferred to the Commission, national governments lost their own right to legislate in that area, except in accordance with laws and policies laid down by the Community. To disguise this process behind a more acceptable front, the Commission was always on the lookout for issues such as hygiene, health and safety, environmental protection or countering discrimination, where extending its field of competence could be justified by showing it as taking the moral high ground, acting to protect the general interests of the 'people of Europe'.

In particular, when some specific problem was hitting the headlines, the Commission was often quick to exploit it as a 'beneficial crisis', which could be exploited to justify a new extension of its powers in the name of promoting the common good. In the early 1970s a succession of monetary crises had been made the excuse to justify 'economic and monetary union'. The Seveso accident had inspired it to introduce new legislation regulating the chemical industry. Damaging oil spills from tankers were used to justify extending the Commission's powers over the regulation of shipping. The international crisis at the time of the 1991 Gulf War had been used to promote the need for a common European foreign and defence policy. Terrorist atrocities, such as 9/11, were to be used to justify further integration not just of anti-terrorism laws but of the EU's police forces and legal procedures.

Never, however, was there a more vivid instance of the 'beneficial crisis' than the way the Commission seized on the Belgian dioxins scare to justify taking over from national governments the power to regulate all forms of food safety. Until this moment, with exceptions, such as the various 'meat hygiene directives', food safety policy had remained a 'competence' of national governments. But in the late summer of 1999 the Commission was in desperate need of some popular initiative which might help to restore its public image, after the embarrassment of the corruption scandals which in March had forced the resignation of the entire team of commissioners, described at the time as the EU's 'biggest crisis in its 42-year history'.[8]

By September, when Romano Prodi, the Commission's new president, appeared for the first time in front of 700 MEPs in the vast, futuristic new European Parliament building in Strasbourg, the Belgian dioxins crisis had for months been a major talking point all over Europe. At the very start of his speech, Prodi was keen to emphasize how vital it was for the EU to win back public confidence by showing how it was looking after the interests of the 'people of Europe' in their everyday lives. Nothing was more important in this respect, argued Prodi, than 'safety of the food we eat'. That was why he was proposing that the Commission should take over from national governments the power to regulate all issues relating to food safety.

No sooner were Prodi and his new team of commissioners settled into Brussels than the planning of this takeover went ahead as a matter of urgency. By 12 January 2000, only four months later, the commissioner appointed to take charge of food safety, an Irishman named David Byrne, was ready to announce his proposals. There was to be a new European Food Safety Authority, in charge of monitoring and regulating food safety throughout the EU. Furthermore, Byrne was already proposing no fewer than 84 new directives, regulations and other legislative measures, to show just how comprehensively the Commission now intended to exercise control over every aspect of food safety law.

To no one was this a more carefully timed snub than the British Labour Party which, at the height of the 1989 salmonella crisis, had adopted as one of its flagship policies the proposal that supreme responsibility for food safety in Britain should be handed over to a new, independent Food Standards Agency. Formal proposals had been published in 1998 and legislation setting up the new agency had been debated and approved by Parliament in 1999.

Never had there been the slightest hint that, by the time the new agency came into being, all its powers would have been taken over by a superior body in Brussels.

On the morning of 12 January 2000 the man chosen to be the first head of the Food Standards Agency, Sir John Krebs, an Oxford professor of zoology, was introduced to the media in London. At almost exactly the same moment in Brussels, Byrne was announcing the launch of his European Food Safety Authority. Instead of assuming control over all food safety issues in the United Kingdom, as intended, Krebs's new agency would merely be acting as one of 15 subordinate branch offices across the EU for this new central organization in Brussels that would exercise all the real power.

Even in the history of the European Community, it was a *coup d'etat* without precedent – and it had all come about thanks to the Belgian dioxins crisis.

At least, later that year, there was a bid by another team of Belgian scientists to paint the dioxins crisis as having posed a genuine threat to the health of many thousands of people. In August 2000 Nik van Larebeke and colleagues from several universities produced a paper predicting that exposure to dioxins and PCBs in 1999 might eventually result in as many as 8,000 deaths from cancer. But the basis on which these academics arrived at their conclusions appeared to be remarkably speculative. Somewhat startlingly they assumed that 'between 10 and 15 kilograms of PCBs and from 200 to 300 milligrams of dioxins were ingested by 10 million Belgians'. 'Estimates of the total number of cancers resulting from this incident', they argued, with curiously imprecise precision, 'range between 44 and 8,316.'

From there on, the paper became vaguer still. Damage to the nervous system was 'also to be expected but cannot be quantified'. The team acknowledged 'huge uncertainties' because of the general lack of information on who might have been affected. Furthermore, they admitted that the PCB analyses had shown up many instances of food contaminated with PCBs that had no connection to the transformer oil incident, including fish and food imported from other countries.[9]

At the same time, a paper produced in the Netherlands by the National Institute of Public Health and the Environment (RIVM) came up with very different findings. 'Considering all available data,' it concluded, 'negative health effects following long-term

average consumption or incidental high consumption of contaminated chicken were unlikely to occur', although they 'could
not fully exclude minor subclinical effects'.[10]

Professor Bernard and a colleague returned to the charge in
September 2002, with a paper not only evaluating everything
published up to that date but also based on 'recent data on the real
scale of the contamination and on the dioxin body burden of the
general population in Belgium'. This included an extensive survey
of dioxin levels in blood conducted at the end of 1999. Their
conclusion was that the number of farms and people affected had
been vastly exaggerated. 'These new data confirm that the incident
was too limited in time and in scale to have increased the PCB/
dioxin burden of the general population at large.' Only 'about 30
farms' had been affected, and the only people whose dioxin levels
might have been significantly increased were any of those farmers
who had 'regularly consumed' their own products. Even so, the
study concluded, it was 'unlikely that these farmers would have
increased their PCB/dioxin body burden above levels prevailing in
the 1980s or now found in communities regularly consuming
seafood'.[11]

It really did seem as if the Belgian dioxins scare had been a case
of much ado about nothing. But its political consequences had been
enormous. At least for the European Union it had turned out to be
a very 'beneficial crisis' indeed. Yet the officials of the body which
had now seized supreme responsibility for regulation of all food
safety in the EU had shown themselves just as susceptible to ill-
informed scaremongering over the dioxins crisis as anyone else.

Notes

1. Quoted in 'Dioxin Scandal Hits Belgium', by Richard Tyler, 8 June
   1999 (World Socialist Website, *www.wsws.org/articles/1999*).
2. 'Times Beach', Wikipedia entry; *Washington Times*, 12 September
   1991.
3. San Antonio seminar on dioxins, June 1989, *Washington Times*, *op.
   cit.*
4. *New York Times*, 15 August 1991.
5. The account of the crisis in this chapter is based on various sources,
   including the inquiry carried out for the Belgian Parliament, published
   on 3 March 2000 (Doc.50 0018/007, Chambre des Représentants

Belgique); Corie Lok and Douglas Powell, 'The Belgian dioxin crisis of the summer of 1999: A case study', Department of Food Health, Guelph University, Ontario (2000); A. Bernard, *et al.*, 'Food contamination by PCBs and dioxins: an isolated incident in Belgium is unlikely to have affected public health', *Nature*, 401 (September 1999); N. van Larebeke, *et al.*, 'The Belgian PCB and dioxin incident of January–June 1999 – exposure data and potential impact on health', *Environmental Health Perspective*, Vol. 109 (March 2001); A. Bernard and S. Fierens, 'The Belgian PCB/Dioxin Incident: A Critical Review of Health Risks Evaluations', *International Journal of Toxicology* (1 September 2002); Richard North, *The Death of Agriculture* (Duckworth, 2001); and personal information.

6. Report of Belgian Parliament, *op. cit.*
7. Tyler, *op. cit.*
8. Christopher Booker and Richard North, *The Great Deception: Can The European Union Survive?* (Continuum, 2005), p. 437.
9. Van Larebeke, *et al.*, *op. cit.*
10. Jan Baars, 'The dioxin incident in Belgium in 1999: trouble or trifle?', National Institute of Public Health and the Environment (Netherlands, September 2000).
11. Bernard and Fierens, *op. cit.*

Epilogue to Part One
The Rise of the 'Health and Safety Culture'

In the autumn of 2006 the broadcaster Terry Wogan reported that an organization responsible for a traditional community bonfire on 5 November was scrapping the idea of burning a straw effigy of Guy Fawkes, the man who 400 years earlier had supposedly conspired to blow up Parliament. They would instead be consigning to the flames the symbolic effigy of someone who, they claimed, had been responsible for 'more pain, suffering misery and damage to the good of the nation' than Fawkes could have dreamed of: 'a health and safety officer'.[1]

Wogan's readers would have needed no explanation as to why by 2006 such a person might be regarded as an appropriate focus for such derision. The 'health and safety officer' represented the rise of what had come to be generally recognized in the previous decade as an obsession with anything which could conceivably be imagined as posing a 'risk', to an extent which often seemed to have lost all contact with reality.

As a typical example, Wogan went on to cite the story of a householder who had been told by his local police to spend more than £1,000 on a safety cover for his swimming pool. This was because, if a burglar should happen to be caught in his property and the police were called, they would not, on 'health and safety' grounds, be permitted to run across his garden in pursuit, unless his swimming pool had been fitted with a cover strong enough to bear the weight of more than two persons.

What had this to do with scares? The answer is a great deal. Having looked at the food scares of the 1990s, we are about to move on to take a much more general look at the scare phenomenon; to see how a similar pattern came to shape some of the more prominent of the 'non-food scares' which were to play such a conspicuous role in Western society in the years that followed.

But first we may note how all the examples we have looked at so far reflected a much wider change that was taking place in the Western world in the 1990s, by no means just in Britain. This derived partly from a fundamental shift in the psychological climate of the time; and partly from a significant change which was taking place in the nature of government.

In 1994 we published a little book called *The Mad Officials*, reporting how almost every kind of business in Britain had in the early 1990s suddenly found itself confronted with a mass of new regulations. The book recorded scores of examples of how this blizzard of 'red tape' had hit farmers and fishermen, hotels and scrap dealers, care homes and playgroups, charity shops, electronics firms and countless others.

There were various reasons for this sudden increase in the bureaucratic pressures affecting businesses. One was the plethora of new directives and regulations flooding out of the European Community, particularly with the approach of its 'Single Market' in 1993. But just as many of these new rules and regulations were the creations of Britain's own officialdom. And their impact, as we saw in the chapter on the 'hygiene police', was only made more oppressive by the newly officious manner in which these laws were now too often being applied by an ever-growing army of officials whose job was to enforce them: health and safety inspectors, environmental health officers, veterinary officials, pollution inspectors, social workers, 'landscape officers' and many more.

The more we investigated this phenomenon, the more it emerged that a kind of mutation was taking place in the way Britain was governed. Far more than had been true until recently, laws and regulations were now being made, not by Acts of Parliament, but by means of 'statutory instruments': administrative fiats proposed, drafted, issued and enforced just by the officials themselves.* To a degree unknown in the past (with the possible

---

* Between 1986 and 2001 the number of statutory instruments issued annually in Britain rose by more than 70 per cent. But the significant change, representing much of the increase, was the amount of major legislation now being introduced not by Act of Parliament but through regulations (many implementing directives from the European Community, on which Parliament could not debate or vote). It was chiefly by this means

exception of wartime), elected politicians had been sidelined in the legislative process. To a great extent, the increasingly complex task of governing a modern society had been handed over to ever-proliferating layers of bureaucracy.

The technocrats of the Commission in Brussels, enjoying the sole right to initiate legislation emerging from the EC, were only one of these layers, as they poured out their hundreds of new directives. A similar culture change had come over the civil servants in Britain's own ministries, as it had the officials in the town halls. The same change of attitude could be seen in the officials employed by a fast-growing number of regulatory 'agencies', the Environment Agency, the Food Standards Agency, the Meat Hygiene Service, the Medicines Control Agency, and many more.

But closely allied to this 'revolution' in government, seeming to provide it with moral justification, was the way so much of the legislation it produced was centred on certain high-minded causes: what we came to call the 'modern shibboleths'.

One of these was 'health and safety', in the name of which everything had to be regulated, checked and double-checked to ensure that no one was ever in any way 'at risk', whether in places of work or on any form of transport or enjoying 'leisure activities', from walking in the countryside to using a children's swing.

Another, strongly reinforced by the various food scares, was 'hygiene': the belief that all food on sale to the public must be strictly regulated to ensure that it was safe for 'consumers' to eat.

A third was 'the environment': by which every measure had to be taken to ensure that air, water and soil were not in any way polluted.

A fourth was what could be called the institutionalized promotion of 'caring' and 'human rights': upholding the interests of women, children, ethnic minorities, 'travellers', the disabled, any group in society which could be portrayed as somehow vulnerable to abuse or discrimination.

Who could object to a form of government which seemed to attach such a priority to promoting such laudable aims? Certainly a large part of the flood of new legislation which poured out of the

that the new regulatory culture was put into place (figures from the website of the Office of Public Sector Information, formerly Her Majesty's Stationery Office).

government machine from the late 1980s onwards was directed towards furthering these socially desirable ends. They were used to justify an ever greater degree of regulatory control by the state, as it intervened in the minutiae of running any kind of business and, increasingly, in the personal lives of citizens themselves.

What this was creating, however, was what came to be known as the 'health and safety culture', centred on the 'precautionary principle', whereby it was always necessary to eliminate the faintest degree of risk, however remote and imaginary that possibility might be.

Allied to this was what came to be known as the 'compensation culture', whereby both the law and the legal profession encouraged people to claim often colossal sums in compensation for any supposed act of negligence by some firm or corporate entity.

This was linked in turn to the newly fashionable ideology of 'political correctness', using the law to promote the 'rights' of anyone who could be portrayed as the victim of any form of discrimination.

As people gradually came to recognize, this impulse to legislate for a safe, fair, unpolluted world tended to erode many valued features of everyday life. One of the most obvious of these, as was constantly observed, was common sense, which the new culture so often seemed to defy. But since the declared purpose of all these new prescriptive controls was so altruistic, a powerful social pressure made it difficult to question them.

This assumption that the ends justified the means built up in those responsible for imposing and enforcing the new culture a strong sense of moral righteousness about what they were doing. The only problem, as we have seen in the preceding chapters, was that it so easily seemed to part company with reality. In practice it so often didn't seem to work. And never was this more obvious than in the way in which it both helped to promote scares in the first place and then to dictate the response to them.

In all the examples we have looked at, the role played by officialdom contributed only to making the effects of the scare worse. If flawed science was on offer, they fell for it. When a scare reached its tipping point, and there was a chance that, with careful management, its effects might be minimized, the officials and politicians panicked, making its effects worse. When it came to making a regulatory response they went way over the top.

In other words, they consistently failed to diagnose correctly the nature of the problem. They then came up with clumsy and often wholly inappropriate bureaucratic remedies. They finally enforced these in the most draconian fashion, wreaking immense damage.

Such was the behaviour pattern we described as 'taking a sledgehammer to miss the nut'. In Part Two of this book we shall see how this pattern was to repeat itself again and again, in scares which were to create havoc on a far greater scale than those we have already looked at.

Notes

1. *Sunday Telegraph*, 29 October 2006.

Part Two
General Scares

Prologue to Part Two

The Millennium Bug

The Millennium Bug is a serious issue. Most people don't realize how serious until they start to deal with it.
                                    Tony Blair, 30 March 1998

We view the dimensions of the year 2000 issue as enormous, with potentially disastrous global consequences to both business and government.
                        Richard Grasso, head of the New York
                             Stock Exchange, 11 June 1998

The Millennium Bug was a saga from Christian, calendar-based myths of comets, Second Comings and Satanic uprisings, not from the Silicon age.
                      Computer expert Duncan Campbell,
                           the *Guardian*, 5 January 2000

No scare of recent times became briefly more famous than 'Y2K': the great panic in the late 1990s over the 'Millennium Bug'.

For more than 20 years computer experts had forecast that when the year 2000 arrived there might be problems. This was because many computer programs, originally to save valuable space, did not include the first two digits when giving the year. On the dot of midnight on 31 December 1999, when the millennium arrived, it was predicted that many date-based programs showing '00' would behave as if time had rolled back a century to 1900.

In the late 1990s the fear of what this might lead to began to

develop into a fully-fledged scare.* Reinforced by growing speculation in the media, predictions as to what might happen could
scarcely have been more apocalyptic. There would be mass-
blackouts as power stations failed. There would be widespread
economic breakdown as millions of computer systems seized up.
Trains and vehicles would become involved *en masse* in fatal collisions. Airliners would crash out of the sky. It was even suggested
that nuclear rockets might inadvertently be unleashed.

Governments and businesses devoted colossal resources to
preparations for the 'Millennium moment'. Computer consultants
had never known such a bonanza, as business corporations queued
up for their services, nowhere more than in the financial hubs of
London and New York.

In December 1997 more than 60 business leaders and academics, including the chairmen of some of Britain's biggest multinational companies, such as Unilever, British Aerospace, GEC,
Lloyds Bank, and Marks and Spencer, wrote to the governments of
Britain, the USA and Canada, to express their 'acute concern'.
They warned that, unless urgent action was taken, there would be
'financial chaos and disruption to health and education'. They
claimed that 'malfunctions in critical areas such as air traffic control and defence may put safety at risk'.[1]

At the same time, an internal report for Britain's National
Health Service predicted that the failure of 10 per cent of the
electronic equipment in Britain's hospitals could cause the deaths
of between 600 and 1,500 people.

No political leader was quicker to take up the new challenge
than Tony Blair, still enjoying the hubris of his first year in office as
Britain's prime minister. On 22 January 1998, he sounded what
was called a '100-week Millennium Bug alarm'. We have 'just one
hundred working weeks', he said, to tackle 'one of the most serious
problems facing British business and the global economy today. Its
impact cannot be overestimated'. Under his government's 'Action
2000' campaign, £370 million would be set aside to tackle problems with computer equipment in Britain's public sector. He

---

* The term 'Millennium Bug' was coined in an e-mail by David Eddy, a
Massachusetts programmer, on 12 June 1995 (see Wikipedia entry on
'Year 2000 Problem').

wanted every branch of the British government to be put on red alert to prepare for the fateful moment.

In March Lord Renwick, chairman of a parliamentary pressure group on the problem, estimated that the cost of remedying the Millennium Bug to the NHS alone might now be as high as £600 million. One of Blair's advisers, Robin Guenier, said 'we are facing an emergency the same magnitude as a war'.

In a further speech, Blair quoted a letter he had received from the chairman of Unilever warning that the bug 'could cause a worldwide recession'.[2] A similar widely quoted prediction was made by one of Wall Street's most respected economists. Edward Yardeni of Deutsche Bank gave odds of 60 per cent that the bug would cause a year-long recession to match that which had followed the fourfold rise in oil prices in 1973–4.

In April, at a seminar at Stanford University, a member of the economics faculty, Michael Boskin, estimated 'the costs of fixing the millennium bug' at 'between $600 billion and $1.6 trillion globally, spread over several years'.

Emeritus professor William Miller, a founder of Stanford's computer science department, told the conference that the total cost of solving the problem in the USA alone might be greater than the entire cost of the Vietnam War.[3] It had certainly by now become widely accepted that the total worldwide cost of Y2K would be between $300 billion and $600 billion.[4]

By June, excitably informing his audience that there were now 'less than 56 million seconds before the year 2000 date change', the BBC's science correspondent warned that it was 'already too late' to fix all the computers that would be affected.[5]

So the predictions of doom were to continue, for 18 months.

Yet when the great moment came, virtually nothing happened. In Japan an alarm sounded at a nuclear power plant two minutes after midnight. In Australia a number of bus ticket machines failed to operate. In the USA 150 slot machines ceased to work at Delaware race tracks. Otherwise, those companies and countries that had done nothing fared no worse than those which had spent an alleged $300,000,000,000 on preparing for the end of civilization.*

---

* Just how much of this astronomic sum was actually spent no one ever reliably calculated. Most governments and other organizations in a

Y2K had turned out to be little more than yet another very expensive scare. But at least it enabled thousands of computer engineers to pay off their mortgages.**

The Seven Basic Attributes of a Scare

From all the examples we have looked at in the first part of this book, we can now set out a rather more detailed version of the pattern by which a scare unfolds. Every scare is manufactured by those 'pushers' who, for whatever reason, wish to promote it. But first it must fulfil the conditions necessary to bring it to that tipping point which unleashes it as a full-blown scare:

1. *A real problem becomes exaggerated, often by extrapolating from it to include something else.*
Usually (if not always) the scare starts off with a genuine problem. What magnifies it into a scare may well come when this becomes erroneously linked to something with which it has little or no connection.

On salmonella poisoning, for instance, there was a real problem over its unexplained rise in the 1980s. The scare developed when this was wrongly attributed to eggs. Equally genuine was the problem of BSE in cattle. The scare only took off when eating beef was linked to CJD. Belgium had a serious but local problem over dioxins in feed supplied to poultry breeders. This was only blown up into a scare when it was widened out to include a range of human food products not affected by it.

2. *The threat must be universal.*
The scare must be centred on something universal, to which anyone might be exposed (e.g. eggs, beef, the mass-malfunctioning of

position to have commissioned such a study were probably too embarrassed by the anti-climax to have wanted to do so.
** To be fair, the remedial programme launched to avert the Millennium Bug had brought to light some genuine problems. The IT director of a leading British company told us, for instance, that he had been informed by his counterpart in a major oil company how, if the 'bug' had not been discovered in time, the computer controlling one of Britain's main pipelines bringing gas from the North Sea to the mainland would have halted the gas flow at midnight on 31 December 1999, causing serious disruption.

computers). It is impossible to generate a full-blown scare around a specific named product, such as a brand of chocolate.

3. *It must contain a strong element of uncertainty.*
The supposed threat must be in some way new and mysterious, providing an opportunity for almost unlimited speculation as to its disastrous consequences (e.g. avian flu, BSE, the Millennium Bug).

4. *The threat must seem scientifically plausible.*
The threat must seem plausible, however ill-founded it later turns out to have been. For this it is necessary that some scientists or 'experts' are seen to endorse it, and to produce seemingly convincing evidence as to why it should be believed. The most significant of these may well be scientists advising the government, as in the cases of 'salmonella in eggs' and BSE. But it is also important that the scare should be endorsed by outsiders who can be portrayed as 'independent experts', even if their scientific background in no way qualifies them to pronounce on the subject matter of the scare (e.g. Professor Lacey, whose expertise was resistance to antibiotics).

5. *The scare must be promoted by the media.*
Crucial to the promotion of any full-blown scare is the role of the media, as they try to raise its profile as 'pushers' in their own right. This provides journalists with an intoxicating sense of self-importance, as they imagine they are exposing some fearful hidden threat to the public good.

But the media also need to be able to quote and project those scientific 'experts' to give their reports 'authority'. As 'pushers' the journalists and the 'experts' thus develop a symbiotic relationship, each needing the other in their efforts to 'imagine the worst' in inflating the scare's potentially disastrous consequences (e.g. the way the BBC and others used Lacey in the salmonella and BSE scares).

None of this on its own, however, is enough to bring the scare to the tipping point. Up to now by far the most effective 'blocker' of any scare is the government. So long as official spokesmen continue to deny a scare, it is virtually impossible for the 'pushers' to carry the day.

6. *The crisis arrives when the threat is acknowledged by government.*
The tipping point comes when the government finally admits that there is a serious problem. For having previously been a 'blocker', the government is thus likely to be accused of a cover-up. But this means that the scare is now out of its control. Ministers and officials therefore wish to be seen to be acting firmly in response to the chaos they have unleashed. This is where the real damage begins, because invariably they overreact. Their regulatory response creates social and economic havoc, at enormous cost. Having misdiagnosed the problem in the first place, they have now been panicked into producing 'remedies' which are irrelevant.

7. *Finally the truth emerges.*
Sooner or later the scare reaches its final stage, when evidence emerges to show how the threat had been wildly exaggerated. But the regulatory response has now become so enshrined in the system that it usually proves very difficult to remove. And by now the media's interest has usually shifted elsewhere.

All this perfectly illustrates the principle of 'taking a sledgehammer to miss the nut'. Throughout the duration of the scare the general public have largely acted as bemused bystanders to a drama played out between the principal actors: scientists, politicians, officials and the media.

In the rest of this book we shall be looking at how some of the more familiar scares of recent years took shape around a similar pattern.

Notes

1. 'Millennium Bug could cripple governments and health services', BBC News website, 30 March 1998.
2. Published on 10 Downing Street website, 30 March 1998.
3. Reported on Stanford News website, 30 April 1998.
4. As can be seen from putting 'Millennium Bug' and '$300 billion' into Google, which produces numerous pages of references.
5. BBC News website, 16 June 1998.

8

A Sledgehammer To Miss the Nut

A Wider Look at the Scare Phenomenon

Banning DDT killed more people than Hitler.
Michael Crichton, *State of Fear*, 2004

We begin this second part of the book by looking at four case studies, each of which helps to shed its own light on the scare phenomenon without, in every respect, fitting the usual pattern.

The first was a classic example of a scare that began with a genuine problem, but then became so distorted and exaggerated, with the backing of government officials, that it created enormous unnecessary damage. A second, also backed by government officials, also did enormous damage, but never attracted many headlines. A third, manufactured by corporate interests for their own commercial purposes, initially won support from government officials, but eventually provoked such protests from the general scientific community that it was defeated. The last was a scare entirely created through a blunder by government officials themselves.

DDT: The Scare that Saved Birds but Killed People

In many ways the first truly modern 'scare' was one that began in America in the 1950s and 1960s, notably associated with a single book.

The runaway concern that developed over the dangers of the chemical insecticide DDT might not seem wholly to qualify as a scare, because in certain respects that concern was fully justified. Only when the threat was exaggerated into posing a risk much wider than was supported by the evidence did it mutate into a genuine scare, with consequences that were to prove catastrophic.

DDT (or dichloro-diphenyl-tricholoroethane), an organochlorine, was first synthesized by a German chemist as long ago as 1874, but its insecticidal properties were discovered by Paul Hermann Müller, a Swiss, in 1939 (for which, in 1948, he won the Nobel Prize for Medicine). It passed into general use with remarkable speed, being widely used by the Allies in World War Two to protect troops and civilian populations from mosquito-borne diseases such as malaria and typhoid. After the war, hailed as a miraculous solution to many of mankind's problems, it became used worldwide, to eradicate malaria and as a general pesticide. In 1955 the World Health Organization used it to launch a global programme to eliminate malaria, reducing mortality rates by more than 95 per cent.[1]

It was soon observed, however, that resistant strains emerged in many insect populations. In North America by the late 1950s naturalists were also noting that DDT inflicted serious damage on wildlife, particularly on birds of prey at the top of the food chain. The accumulation of DDT in their bodies from other creatures further down the chain resulted in a thinning of their egg shells, damaging their ability to reproduce.

It was this which helped inspire the biologist Rachel Carson to write her book *Silent Spring*, published in 1962. Her nightmare vision of a world fallen silent because birds had been wiped out by DDT and other toxic chemicals became a huge instant bestseller, and played a key part in the emergence of the modern environmentalist movement.

No one could dispute that intensive spraying of DDT was deadly not only to insects (which was its purpose) but also to birds, fish and other forms of wildlife. Its toxic effects also persisted in the natural environment for a long time. Even Carson, however, recognized that, used sparingly and selectively, it could play a useful role in eradicating disease. What was to prove much harder to sustain was her claim that DDT could cause cancer in human beings (she herself was to die of cancer two years after the book appeared).

In the late 1960s, US environmental groups campaigned for a complete ban on the use of DDT, and in 1971 William Ruckelshaus, the first head of America's new Environmental Protection

Agency (EPA), was ordered by a court to begin the process for its deregistration, which would force its withdrawal from the market.

After hearing evidence that DDT posed no imminent danger to human health, Ruckelshaus initially rejected a total ban. But this aroused such protests that the EPA held seven months of hearings to weigh evidence from both sides. The examiner, Edmund Swee-ney, finally ruled that there was no scientific evidence to support a ban ('DDT', he said, 'is not a carcinogenic hazard to man').[2] But two months later, under intense pressure from environmental groups (and supposedly without having read Sweeney's evidence) Ruckelshaus claimed that DDT did pose a carcinogenic risk after all. He imposed a complete ban on its use in the USA.

Over the years that followed many other countries across the world followed America's lead. Certainly there was evidence that the ending of indiscriminate use of DDT in agriculture led to marked recoveries in bird populations. But attempts to eliminate the use of DDT altogether continued to remain intensely controversial.

On one hand, no serious evidence was ever produced to support Carson's claim that DDT caused cancer, or indeed that it is sig-nificantly toxic to human beings at all (in not a few cases it was even eaten without causing ill effects). Nevertheless, in 1987, fol-lowing studies on mice, the EPA classified it as a Group B2 carci-nogen (along with coffee and gasoline).

Much more damagingly, however, the loss of DDT as a control on malaria, by spraying the inside of dwellings against mosquitoes, was to prove a huge setback for many of the poorest countries in the world. This disease affects up to half a billion people every year. In parts of Africa and Asia it is the greatest single killer, particularly of young children. Despite resistance problems, the use of DDT had helped to eradicate malaria from large parts of the globe including southern Europe, and undoubtedly saved millions of lives. In Sri Lanka, for instance, where, in 20 years before 1955, 1.5 million cases of malaria had resulted in 80,000 deaths, a DDT control programme reduced incidence of the disease, by 1963, to just 17 cases. Similar evidence was cited for many other countries.

Leading those who, by the early years of the twenty-first cen-tury, were arguing strongly against a worldwide ban was the WHO, which upheld the selective use of DDT indoors as the most effective tool available in the fight against malaria. This was permitted under the worldwide 2001 Stockholm Convention,[3] and the WHO's line was supported by many medical specialists in tropical diseases, and African governments.

However, Western environmental groups, such as Greenpeace and the World Wildlife Fund, continued to press for a total ban. The European Union brought strong economic pressure on African countries to retain the ban, although malaria was now killing more of their people than AIDS. In Uganda alone, the health ministry estimated in 2005 that the death rate from malaria in the country's children ranged between 70,000 and 110,000 a year.[4]

The most damning charge brought by supporters of the selective use of DDT was that the ban had led to millions of deaths: a view echoed by the popular novelist Michael Crichton, one of whose characters in his 'anti-scare' thriller *State of Fear* calls it 'arguably the greatest tragedy of the twentieth century':

> *Since the ban two million people a year have died unnecessarily from malaria, mostly children. All together, the ban has caused more than fifty million needless deaths. Banning DDT killed more people than Hitler.*[5]

In this respect the campaign for a total ban on DDT had taken on all the attributes of a fully-fledged scare. Carson had identified a genuine problem in the damage done to wildlife. But she and others magnified this into a scare over the danger DDT posed to human health, which the evidence did not justify. Ironically, this was to bring about one of the greatest avoidable public health disasters the modern world has seen.

Nitrate: A Government-Sponsored Scare that Cost Billions

The WHO might have been right on DDT. On nitrate, however, it got the science seriously wrong. The supposed danger of nitrate never attracted the kind of attention from the media that might have elevated it into a full-blown scare. Yet the 'nitrate myth' was eventually to cause immense damage. It became a case study in how, once a scare virus becomes established in official thinking, it can be extraordinarily difficult to remove from the system, even when the science on which it is based has been comprehensively discredited.

Nitrogen (N), making up 77 per cent of the atmosphere, is an important natural nutrient. By what is known as the 'nitrogen cycle', between 90 and 140 million tons a year are 'fixed' naturally by plants from the air; another 40 million tons by leguminous plants such as peas and clover; and 80 million tons by agricultural fertilizers (1990 figures). When nitrogen mixes with oxygen, as it does naturally in rainfall, it becomes nitrate (NO_3); at quantities that in temperate areas of the world can measure up to over 60 milligrams per litre. As farmers and gardeners know, few things stimulate growth more obviously than the nitrate-rich rainwater produced by lightning in thunderstorms.

In the early 1960s, when scientific knowledge of the health aspects of nitrate was still relatively rudimentary, the WHO became persuaded by a handful of US studies that its presence in drinking water could cause stomach cancer.[6] In 1962 it therefore set an 'acceptable daily intake' level for human beings, which was accepted the same year by the US government. Only years later did it emerge that the apparent link in certain US states between drinking-water and stomach cancer was due to the fact that water in the study area came almost entirely from wells contaminated with nitrite (NO_2). It was to this rather than nitrate that the cancer might be linked. But it was on this confusion that the official suspicion of nitrate became launched on its way.

In the early 1970s nitrate became blamed for a quite different problem. US studies claimed it could be the cause of a rare condition affecting young children known as methaemoglobinaemia, or 'blue baby syndrome', which had very occasionally proved fatal.[7] By 1977 the US National Academy of Science concluded that 'available evidence on the occurrence of methaemoglobinemia in infants tends to confirm' that the maximum nitrate level below which no adverse health effects were likely to arise could be as little as 10 milligrams per litre. This was far below the level common in drinking water, and even this, said the report, allowed for 'little margin of safety'.[8]

All this alarm from across the Atlantic was picked up in Brussels by environmental officials of the European Commission's DGXI, who were drafting a new directive on standards required for drinking water. In 1980, their directive, 80/778, laid down a maximum permissible standard for nitrates of 50 milligrams per litre, as had originally been proposed by the WHO in 1962 to counter the risk of stomach cancer.

Before this directive was implemented, British doctors and scientists expressed concern as to what evidence could justify such a standard. In response, the Chief Medical Officer commissioned an epidemiological study (CMO 185/13), which found, to general surprise, that in those areas of Britain where nitrate levels in drinking water were higher than average, the incidence of stomach cancer was actually below average. Conversely, where nitrate levels were low, the incidence of cancer was above average.

But the Brussels standards were now set in stone. When, in 1991, Britain's publicly owned water industry was sold off to 29 private companies, one of the first obligations laid on them was to install hugely expensive dentrification equipment, to ensure that drinking water complied with the directive. No overall costs for this were published by the industry, although one company, Anglian Water, cited £80 million as its cost for a single plant, with running costs of £5 million a year. One estimate, extrapolating from this and other information, suggested that the total cost to the industry, including to consumers through higher water bills, might have been as much as £3 billion.*

By the mid-1990s, a series of studies by medical teams in Britain and France produced further evidence to confirm that, rather than nitrate causing stomach cancer, the reverse was the case. High levels of NO_3 seemed to inhibit the disease, whereas low nitrate levels were associated with above-average levels of cancer.[9] Far from being a threat, it seemed, nitrate in water was beneficial. In 1995 even the WHO conceded that NO_3 at or above the natural level was not a cancer risk.

Having lost on cancer, the ranks of officialdom now focused their medical case against nitrate entirely on 'blue baby syndrome'. As the WHO stated in 1993, repeating it in 1996, the purpose of proposing a maximum nitrate level was 'solely to prevent methaemoglobinaemia'. But this 'myth' in turn was comprehensively exposed when various studies (including some of those cited above) showed how this very rare condition (the last case in Britain

---

* Alan Monckton, 'Nitrate Vulnerable Zones: the myths and the facts', *Royal Agricultural Society of England Journal*, 16 December 2002. A government figure, published by MAFF, clearly designed to minimize the financial impact of the directive, put the figure at only £39 million. But this was less than half the cost of one dentrification plant, as cited above.

had been in 1972) had no connection with nitrate but, again, was caused by nitrite from dirty water in wells.

By this time, however, the Brussels legislative juggernaut had already moved on. In 1991 the environmental officials of DGXI, who had no medical qualifications, had produced a new 'nitrate directive', 91/676, designed to curb the amount of nitrate produced by European farmers, to prevent them polluting groundwater, watercourses and rivers. It was proposed that farmland in areas where nitrate levels were high should be designated as 'nitrate vulnerable zones' (NVZs), subject to strict regulation. This would severely limit the times of year when farmers were permitted to manure their fields, and the quantities they could use. And it would require them, at considerable cost, either to provide storage for manure or to have it disposed of by tanker.*

Most European Union governments only attempted to implement this damaging directive in a faint-hearted fashion. The UK government in 1996 designated 1.6 million acres as NVZs, but this represented only 8 per cent of the total area of farmland. Even so, the cost of the scheme to the 8,000 farmers affected was officially estimated at £21 million a year (the National Farmers Union estimated the cost at £50 million, more than twice the MAFF figure).

So discredited by now were the public health reasons for this legislation that the officials had fallen back on a quite different, environmental argument for their opposition to nitrate. They now liked to claim that, as nitrate was washed down rivers to the sea, it caused the 'eutrophication' of estuaries: unattractive algal blooms which, by reducing oxygen in water as they decay, were damaging to fish and other aquatic life (and might also, incidentally, discourage tourism).**

---

* The financial impact of the directive was to fall disproportionately on those types of farming, such as pig breeding, which generate large quantities of manure. In Britain the cost of compliance for a large pig unit might be as much as £100,000.
** It was noticeable at this time how, in much of the general publicity on nitrate put out by the Commission and the UK government, they liked to describe nitrate simply as 'nitrate pollution', without going into detail as to what particular damage it might cause. This indicated that it should now be regarded as an environmental rather than a public health issue and, under the EC's 'polluter must pay' principle, it should therefore be the farmer's responsibility to pay for its removal.

Yet again, however, the scientists were able to show how this thesis was based on misreading the evidence. It was not nitrate which caused algal bloom but phosphate (PO_4). The only contribution made by nitrate to this process was that, once the algae had been established, it helped promote its growth.* Through much of the European Union, particularly in countries such as Britain with fast-flowing rivers, eutrophication was scarcely much of a problem anyway. In the year the nitrate directive was issued, 1991, only two small British estuaries were affected at all.[10]

In the years after 1997, Britain was one of 13 member states (out of 15) taken by the Commission to the European Court of Justice for failing properly to implement the directive. Because it was reluctant to fight the case on scientific grounds (which would have been politically embarrassing, because it would have implied that NVZs were unnecessary), the UK government offered no defence to the charge and was fined £50 million. In response to these 'failures', when the Commission in 2000 introduced its new comprehensive Water Framework Directive, 2000/68, it tightened up the law on nitrate vulnerable zones.

Although the new directive allows for governments to ask for a derogation or opt-out where a case can be made for not imposing NVZ rules on public health grounds, Britain failed to take advantage of this (not least, because, again, this suggested that NVZs had never been necessary in the first place). In 2003 Defra proposed that the area of farmland in England covered by NVZs should be extended to 55 per cent (the percentages for Scotland and Wales were 13 and 8 per cent). Ministers remained remarkably coy about the cost of all this to farmers, although increasing the number of farms affected by 700 per cent suggested that the annual bill might run into hundreds of millions of pounds. Other EU countries, particularly in the pig-breeding states of northern Europe, anticipated similarly substantial costs.

All this was in the name of providing remedies to problems

---

* M. Apfelbaum, *Risques et peurs alimentaires* (Editions Odile Jacob, Paris, 1998), and various Scandinavian papers (cf. Monckton (2002)). Professor Apfelbaum, a noted French nutritionist, also observed in his book: 'It is proved beyond doubt that drinking water which has an unlimited nitrate content, up to and far beyond the level where it tastes foul, has no effect whatever on human health.'

which, as had now been comprehensively demonstrated, had never existed in the first place.

Vitamin B6: A Scare the Lobbyists Wanted

Is it possible to manipulate a government into promoting a scare to serve commercial ends? This was a question inevitably provoked by the curious story of the Labour government's bid in 1997 to prevent thousands of health shops selling dietary supplements containing vitamin B6, a trade worth over the previous ten years some £300–500 million.[11]

Vitamin B6, the commonest form of which is known as pyridoxine, is naturally found in chicken, fish, liver, yeast, wheat germ, bananas and many other meats, fruit and vegetables. It plays a vital role in the human body, working with enzymes to catalyse various chemical reactions. When B6 is deficient as, for instance, it often is in pregnant or pre-menstrual women, this can lead to depression, insomnia, loss of libido, weight loss or gain, and various other disorders. To make up that deficiency, and to relieve other problems such as high blood pressure or asthma, an estimated 3 million people in Britain regularly use B6 to supplement their diet.

On 4 July 1997, shortly after the Blair government came to power, Jeff Rooker, the minister of state at MAFF, issued a surprising press release. On the advice of the Committee on Toxicity (CoT), a supposedly independent body advising the Department of Health, he planned, on health grounds, to introduce drastic restrictions on the sale of products containing B6. Health shops would only be permitted to sell these at very low strength: allowing a maximum daily dose of 10 milligrams. Higher-dose products, by far the majority of those on sale, would only be available from pharmacies and would require a licence from the Medicines Control Agency (MCA). Supplements containing doses above 50 milligrams would only be available on a doctor's prescription.

The effect of this would be to drive scores of popular B6 products off the shelves of health shops, handing a very profitable market to the pharmaceutical companies which alone could afford the hundreds of thousands of pounds needed to get each product licensed, under EC law, by the MCA (which derived its income from these companies).

Rooker's explanation for his proposal was that he had been advised by the CoT that, except in very low doses below 10 milligrams, B6 could damage the nervous system. But further enquiries elicited that the CoT had based its findings solely on one obscure ten-year-old study, by Dr Katharine Dalton, a Harley Street specialist in the problems of women suffering from pre-menstrual syndrome.[12] Based on observation of 172 of her patients, she claimed that those who had taken B6 often displayed 'peripheral sensory neuropathy', causing tingling, numbness, pins and needles and muscle weakness. This she ascribed to B6.

It was immediately observed by doctors and other professionals who read the Dalton paper that these symptoms are often experienced by pre-menstrual women who have not taken B6. Remarkably, the study had not included a control group to establish this point. Even more startling, however, was that the CoT should have based its view of B6 solely on this one paper. No fewer than 10,000 other studies of B6, by scientists all over the world, it was found, had reached very different conclusions.

At a meeting on 23 July, between Rooker and representatives of the health food industry, Professor A. D. Dayan, a member of the CoT, sought to provide confirmation of Dalton's findings by referring to experiments using B6 on dogs. But when these were examined, it turned out that adverse nervous reactions were only reported when the dogs were given doses of 3,000 milligrams, far in excess of the doses recommended in nutritional supplements, usually ranging between 50 and 100 milligrams.

What further attracted attention, however, was the fact that no fewer than nine of the twelve professors and doctors serving on the CoT enjoyed extensive financial links to the pharmaceutical companies which stood to benefit from the new regulations they were recommending. For instance four members, including Dayan, received funding or pensions from GlaxoWellcome, makers of several expensively licensed products in competition with B6, which might anticipate substantially increased sales if the law was changed.[13]

Whether or not this explained the committee's controversial recommendation, over the next few months it helped fire up a remarkable campaign against Rooker's proposal. From thousands of B6 users, the issue drew more letters to the government, as was reported, 'than any issue since BSE'. More tellingly still, the reasoning behind Rooker's decision attracted withering criticism from an ever-growing number of scientists, led by Professor Arnold Beckett, the former president of the Royal Pharmaceutical Society. More than 200 doctors and scientists signed a letter to Rooker urging him to abandon his proposal, on the grounds that the CoT's report was based on 'wholly inadequate consideration of the scientific data'.

In February 1998, a leading American expert on B6, Professor Alan Gaby, reported that a study of his own had shown Dalton's paper to be 'hopelessly flawed'. This found that 70 per cent of women with pre-menstrual syndrome who had not taken B6 displayed the same signs Dalton ascribed solely to B6. Eighty-four per cent of women who displayed these symptoms while taking B6 had already experienced the symptoms before they started taking it.[14]

As the time drew near for Rooker to issue his statutory instrument, MPs and peers of all parties repeatedly raised the issue in Parliament. Ministers remained immovable in their support for the policy, invariably citing the CoT and the Dalton paper, as if they were the last word on the matter.* Rooker himself, who was at the same time having to defend the ban on T-bone steaks, became increasingly tetchy at having to face such criticism.

When a *Channel Five News* interviewer put it to him in February that there had not been a 'single scientifically proven case of toxicity' recorded from B6 at doses of 500 milligrams or below, Rooker exploded: 'so I should wait for a dead body before we take action' (echoing his similar outburst to the Commons on bone-in beef, that 'opposition front benchers may wish to infect the general population, but the government will not do so'). When the interviewer persisted that there was 'no evidence to suggest there is going to be a dead body at a level below 500 milligrams', Rooker angrily retorted, 'No, but you would rather I wait for one before we do anything.'[15]

The row came to a head when, in May 1998, MPs on the

---

* The only outside support given to the CoT's view had come from the MCA, which claimed to have received 42 'yellow card' adverse reaction reports associated with B6 since 1987, including one fatality (Hansard, HL, Written Answers, 30 July 1997). When these were examined, it was found that, in almost every case, other drugs had been administered in conjunction with B6, and that it was these which explained the adverse reactions.

Commons Agriculture Committee held an inquiry into Rooker's decision. One witness was Professor Beckett, who stated that the Dalton study had been 'entirely rejected by the scientific community, including both of the world's leading experts on vitamin B6 neurotoxicity, Dr Herbert Schaumber and Professor Gareth Parry'. It belonged to 'the world of fantasy'. Doses of up to 200 milligrams, said Beckett, had been

> *safely used in the UK for some 40 years. These dosages simply do not give rise to safety concerns, and CoT's contention that they do is as absurd as it is insupportable ... this is an absolutely outrageous situation and I have no hesitation whatsoever in ... stating that CoT has perpetrated one of the worst applications of pseudo-science I have ever encountered.*[16]

Rooker, in giving evidence, tried to open up a new front by claiming that the sale of B6 had to be restricted because medical claims were being made on its behalf. This was significant because medical claims could only legally be made for drugs licensed by the MCA. Rooker did admit that these claims were not being made by the manufacturers and health shops themselves (well aware that the law prohibited them from making such claims). But he argued that the law needed to be changed because claims for the medical value of B6 were sometimes being made by users of dietary supplements in magazines.

When the MPs published their report on 23 June, their verdict on Dalton, the CoT and Rooker's decision could not have been more damning. Objections to the Dalton study were so serious, they concluded, that to use it as the basis for legislation was 'scientifically unjustifiable'. The MPs trusted that:

> *the unfortunate row which has taken place over vitamin B6 will act as a constant reminder to [the committee] of the need to base its recommendations and advice on sound and substantiated scientific knowledge, and adherence to a clear definition of the role and limits of Government intervention in this area as it recommends and Parliament agrees.*[17]

The Committee's findings were so uncompromising that Rooker was forced to find a face-saving way out. His proposed regulation would be abandoned, but the issue of B6's toxicity would be put to a new 'Expert Group on Vitamins and Minerals'. When this reported, five years later, its findings on B6 were a masterpiece of diplomatic ambiguity, carefully avoiding coming off the fence in any direction.[18]

But at least, for the moment, the B6 scare had been seen off. The 'pushers' of the scare had been the government's 'independent' scientific advisers, the CoT; the pharmaceutical companies (which had been actively lobbying for years against any health products not made by themselves); and those gullible ministers who failed to question the validity and provenance of the advice they had been given.* The 'blockers' had been not just the industry most affected, but the entire consensus of independent scientific opinion. The scare had also lacked that ingredient crucial to the successful promotion of any scare: support from the media (most of which remained resolutely sceptical).

By the early years of the twenty-first century, competence to decide on maximum allowable doses of dietary supplements was passing into that twilight zone where it was no longer clear who had the final say: national governments or Brussels. At low doses, vitamins could still be regarded as a food, in which case responsibility lay between Britain's Food Standards Agency and the new European Food Safety Authority. At higher doses, they might be classified as medicines, in which case it lay with the new European Medicines Agency. These battles still had finally to be resolved, but in 2007 the recommendation on the Food Standards Agency's website read as follows:

> *The Agency advises against taking more than 10 mg of vitamin B6 supplements a day.*

This was just what the CoT had been urging on ministers ten years before.

---

* Rooker's predecessor as minister of state for agriculture, Angela Browning MP, told the Commons in 1998 that he had been 'set up' over B6. The CoT had come to her with similar proposals as early as 1995. When she and her officials told them that they did not have sufficient scientific evidence to justify the restrictions, they had waited for the arrival of an untried new minister before trying again. Within two months, on the same evidence, Rooker came out with the same proposals she had rejected (Hansard, HC, 24 June 1998).

Cockles: A Scare Caused by Government Scientists

The Food Standards Agency (FSA) stood at the centre of another curious scare in 2003, when on health and safety grounds it summarily ordered the closure of a profitable British industry, putting many hundreds of people out of work and threatening several firms with bankruptcy.

The sole cause of the scare, it emerged, was a basic error in the scientific method on which the agency relied for its information. For months the FSA defiantly continued to defend its testing procedure, despite expert protests that it was flawed, even from the scientist who had devised it in the first place. Only when the agency surreptitiously modified its procedure did the problem disappear, allowing the industry to resume production.

Despite its archaic associations, Britain's cockle industry, centred on the Thames estuary, South Wales and the Wash, had in recent years spent millions of pounds on new boats and processing facilities to become a remarkable success story, worth £20 million a year and exporting 95 per cent of its products to Europe and the rest of the world.

In 2000 responsibility for monitoring the safety of shellfish was taken over by the new Food Standards Agency, under Sir John Krebs. In 2001, after putting out its laboratory-testing for shellfish to tender, the agency transferred its contract from the National Reference Laboratory in Aberdeen to the Centre for Environmental, Fisheries and Aquaculture Science (CEFAS), an executive agency of Defra, in Weymouth, Dorset.

Immediately, the CEFAS laboratory began coming up with an abnormally high number of 'positive' results, claiming that it was finding an 'atypical' or 'unidentified' toxin in the cockles it was testing. This led the FSA to close one cockle-bed after another. What disturbed scientists such as Dr Peter Hunt of the Shellfish Association of Great Britain was that CEFAS was using a testing procedure known as the 'mouse bioassay', developed in the 1970s by Professor Takeshi Yasumoto of Japan, but since rejected by most other laboratories across the world. This procedure was based on concentrating large quantities of shellfish extract, mixing it with solvents and injecting it directly into the peritoneum of mice. Many promptly went into painful convulsions and died.[19]

So crude was this test that it provided no means of identifying any supposed toxin, let alone whether the cause of death might be the solvent itself. What alarmed the industry and its scientific advisers even more was that CEFAS used no controls to monitor the validity of its testing method. This not only broke all scientific rules but also defied protocols laid down for testing procedures by the European Commission. Yet whenever samples were sent by the industry for independent analysis by other laboratories, both in Britain and abroad, using more modern methods, such as oral testing on rats coupled with an EU-approved system of chemical testing, these consistently came up with negative results.

In January 2003, when the industry had already lost millions of pounds through closures, and when CEFAS had persistently failed to provide convincing answers to questions about its testing method, representatives of the industry met Krebs to put their concerns to him directly. As Dr Hunt reported, 'we had the clear impression he understood the points we were making and that a full investigation would be carried out as a matter of urgency'. Yet, following that meeting, the agency's officials merely concentrated on devising a new protocol in an effort to identify the mysterious toxin their tests seemed to have discovered.

In June the crisis gathering over the industry came to a head. The FSA ordered the National Reference Laboratory, whose findings had repeatedly contradicted those of CEFAS, not to carry out any more independent testing. On 19 June the agency issued a blanket closure order on every cockle-bed in the country. More than 2,000 people were suddenly without livelihood.

What was remarkable about this was that, outside the FSA and CEFAS, no one any longer had the slightest confidence in their testing procedure. Even Professor Yasumoto himself had pronounced that it was now 'time to move on' from his technique. The Irish Food Standards Agency had abandoned the testing procedure used by CEFAS, describing it as 'antiquated and deeply flawed', after discovering that the reason why it consistently came up with false results was that the mice were being killed by the solvents used to bind the cockle meat together. Like many other countries, Ireland had now adopted a much more sophisticated method of chemical analysis.

CEFAS and the agency continued to defend their procedures, claiming that their mouse test was specified under EU law and used by official government laboratories in seven EU countries.[20] They failed to explain that no other country in the world was now using the mouse test in the same way as CEFAS, without ensuring that there was no 'solvent carry over' which was in itself enough to kill the mice.

On 10 July, at a public meeting of the FSA's board in London, Krebs and his officials were confronted by Dr Hunt, flanked by the heads of two of the three largest cockle-producing firms in the country, responsible for 90 per cent of Britain's cockle production and for the livelihoods of well over 2,000 people.* He asked why the FSA was using EC law to close down a large part of the industry, relying on a procedure that had been so comprehensively discredited. Krebs handed over to Dr Wadge, his director of food safety policy, who refused to answer the question directly but merely repeated the claim he had made in the *Sunday Telegraph* that the mouse test was still being used by most other countries in the EU.

That autumn CEFAS, without admitting that its testing procedure was faulty, quietly changed its protocols to allow for the effects of the solvent in killing the mice. The 'unknown toxin' disappeared. The cockle beds of England and Wales were all given clearance. The industry, having lost several million pounds (one firm, Kershaws, had spent £100,000 on scientific advice alone), was back in business.

In February 2004, chaired by the Labour MP Austin Mitchell, the Commons Select Committee held an inquiry into the cockle-bed closures. The MPs reported that the FSA had 'not lived up to its core value of being open and accessible', resulting in 'an atmosphere of distrust and, at times, hostility'. They agreed that the episode had 'highlighted discrepancies in testing across Europe and drawbacks with the animal testing methods used', and recommended that Britain should 'work towards a common European method, which moves away from testing on mice towards primarily chemical testing'.

Although diplomatic in their phrasing, it was clear the MPs had

---

* *Sunday Telegraph*, 13 July 2003. The two industry representatives were Andrew Ratley of Kershaws on the Thames estuary, formerly employing 200, now losing £150,000 a week, and Rory Parsons of Burry Inlet in Wales, who had been forced to lay off most of his workforce of 120. The third firm most affected was John Lake of King's Lynn, whose eight cockle boats supported 1,600 people round the Wash.

got the point. Yet another unnecessary and damaging scare had run its course.*

Notes

1. Much of this account is based on the Wikipedia entry 'DDT'.
2. Sweeney Committee, 25 April 1972, cited by Michael Crichton, *State of Fear* (London, HarperCollins 2004), p. 580.
3. 'Stockholm Convention on persistent organic pollutants' (Geneva, United Nations Environment Programme, 2001).
4. Ugandan Ministry of Health website; *East African*, 4 April 2006; *Sunday Telegraph*, 2 July 2006.
5. Crichton, *State of Fear*.
6. Background information in this section is drawn from Jean L'Hirondel, and Jean-Louis L'Hirondel, *Les nitrates et l'homme: le mythe de leur toxicité* (1996). Professor Jean L'Hirondel was a professor of paediatrics at University College Hospital, Caen, who dedicated his life to researching the health implications of nitrate (an English version, *Nitrate and man: toxic, harmless or beneficial?*, was published in 2002 by CABI Publishing). Also, Alan Monckton, 'Nitrate Vulnerable Zones: the myths and the facts', *Royal Agricultural Society of England Journal*, 16 December 2002.
7. E.g. L. A. Shearer, *et al.*, 'Methemoglobin levels in infants, in an area with high nitrate water supply', *American Journal of Public Health*, 62:1174–80 (1972); H. I. Shuval and N. Gruener, 'Epidemiological and toxicological aspects of nitrate and nitrite in the environment', *American Journal of Public Health*, 62:1045–51 (1972).
8. 'Drinking water and health', National Academy of Sciences, Safe Drinking Water Committee, Washington, DC (1977).
9. See, for instance, N. Benjamin, *et al.*, *Nature*, 363 (1994), p. 502; and also, *Nature Medicine*, 5, (1995) 546–51; R. S. Dykuizen, *et al.*, 'Acidified nitrate is host defence', *Antimicrobial Agents and Chemotherapy*, 40 (6) (1996); this extensive study at Aberdeen Royal Infirmary was part-funded by MAFF; L'Hirondel (1996).
10. Monckton (2002).
11. Briefing paper based on trade sources, published by the Society for the Promotion of Nutritional Therapy (1997).
12. K. Dalton and M. J. T. Dalton, 'Characteristics of pyridoxine overdose neuropathy syndrome', *Acta Neurologica Scandinavica*, 76 (1987), 8–11.

* Commons Select Committee on the Environment, Food and Rural Affairs, Fifth Report, published 11 February 2004. In 2006 Dr Wadge was promoted to become the FSA's Chief Scientist.

13. Declarations of interest by members of Committee on Toxicity of Chemicals in Food, Consumer Products and the Environment, Department of Health (1996).
14. Press release, Consumers for Health Choice, 11 February 1998.
15. *Channel Five News* transcript.
16. A. Beckett, written evidence to Commons Agriculture Committee, 18 May 1998 (report on Inquiry into Vitamin B6, 5th Report of Proceedings, Session 1997–8).
17. Commons Agriculture Committee report (1998).
18. *Safe upper levels for vitamins and minerals: report of the expert group on vitamins and minerals* (Food Standards Agency Publications, 2003).
19. *Sunday Telegraph*, 22 June, 13 July 2003. For fuller background see evidence submitted to Commons Select Committee on the Environment, Food and Rural Affairs, Fifth Report, published 11 February 2004.
20. Letters to *Sunday Telegraph* from Peter Greig-Smith, CEFAS's chief executive (6 July 2003) and Dr Andrew Wadge, the FSA's director of food safety policy (30 June 2003).

9

The Modern Witch Craze
Ritualized Child Abuse, 1987–94

The Police have been astonished at some of the allegations that appear to be accepted by social workers, such as the cooking of babies in microwave ovens (the body, we are told, would explode).

An unshakeable belief system in Satanic ritualistic abuse appears to have developed which could easily lead into a modern day 'witch hunt' . . . all the elements appear to us to be present: rigid preconceived ideas, dubious investigative techniques, the unwillingness to check basic facts, the readiness to believe anything, however bizarre . . . and the unwillingness to accept any challenge to their views.

The Report had warned that if the presentations of ritual abuse information were not stopped there was the likelihood of a 'witch hunt' developing, which would result in grave injustice to children and their abuse by professional staff. Tragically, our prediction proved to be well-founded.

All three quotations from 'The Broxtowe Files'[1]

No account of the modern scare phenomenon would be complete without reference to an example unlike any other described in these pages, although it was arguably the most bizarre 'scare' of them all.

This was the belief, which in the late 1980s swept through the social services departments of many of Britain's local authorities, that the sexual abuse of children was not only very much more frequent than had been generally supposed, but that it was often being organized by groups of adults, with ritualistic or 'Satanic' overtones. Several such cases made national headlines; others received little or no coverage. In 1994 we reported several times on one of these less publicized examples, because it was a drama we were able to follow at fairly close quarters.

Although this 'psychic epidemic' was in some respects very different from the more conventional scares featured in these pages, it did have certain features in common with them: not least in that it centred on a group of public officials who had passed into the grip of a collective obsessional delusion, in a way that became extraordinarily damaging.

Like other scares, this one originated across the Atlantic. In 1980 there appeared in America a best-selling book, *Michelle Remembers*, co-written by a Canadian psychiatrist Dr Lawrence Pazder and an American patient whom he later married, Michelle Smith. The book recounted how, as a child, she had been imprisoned by a satanic cult, who ritually subjected her to various degrading practices. Strongly reminiscent of de Sade's pornographic fantasy novel *Justine*, the book described how she had been raped and sodomized with candles; imprisoned in a cage with snakes; forced to defecate on a crucifix; and made to witness the cutting up of stillborn babies. Her memories of all this, the book claimed, had been repressed for 20 years until brought to light by her relationship with Dr Pazder.[2]

In 1983 a psychotically disturbed mother in California became convinced that her two-year-old son had been anally abused by a male teacher at the McMartin Infant School. Through the local police, she communicated her fears to some 200 other parents at the school. When a social worker, Kee MacFarlaine of the Los Angeles Children's Institute International Child Sexual Abuse Clinic, became involved, she and her assistants subjected the children to a barrage of questioning. Dr Pazder, with his well-publicized belief in satanic cults, was also called in. What emerged from this and other investigations that followed elsewhere, was the charge that the McMartin pre-school was part of a national network of child abusers and 'Satanists', who had focused their attention on infant schools and child care centres.[3]

Thanks to the evangelizing of MacFarlaine and Pazder, this belief rapidly caught on with counsellors, social workers and evangelical Christian groups across North America. In the next two or three years it led to more than 100 trials in the USA and Canada, in which hundreds of defendants were charged.

Almost all these cases had three features in common. One was the nature of the activities alleged to have taken place, centring on the sexual abuse of children by groups of adults in such places as graveyards, cellars, caves and tunnels, often combined with the mutilating, butchering or cooking of babies or children and the drinking of human blood. A second was the way these stories were gradually built up by social workers and counsellors through plying child-witnesses with leading questions. A third was that hardly ever was any physical or verbal evidence produced to support the charges, other than admissions eventually pressured out of children as a result of the relentless interrogations to which they were subjected.[4]

Most of these episodes defied any rational credibility. In Bakersfield, California, for instance, police excavated fields and dragged lakes where child-witnesses had said that the bodies of 23 sacrificially murdered children had been disposed of. They found nothing. In Toledo, Ohio, police bulldozed a field after being told that it was the site where another satanic group had buried 75 children. In Jordan, Minnesota, where 24 adults were prosecuted, all were eventually acquitted but not before they had been financially ruined. People (including the town's deputy sheriff and his wife) were even arrested for saying they believed the accused were innocent.[5]

Few could have guessed that a similar madness was about to spread across the Atlantic to Britain.

The Cleveland Scandal

The first case of mass sexual abuse to attract national attention in Britain was, in important respects, not typical of those which were to follow. It centred on two paediatricians in Middlesbrough General Hospital, in the Teesside county of Cleveland, and a team of social workers working for Cleveland County Council. These were members of a profession which over the previous few years had not enjoyed a favourable press, due to a succession of much-publicized episodes where social workers had failed to notice or to intervene in cases of individual child abuse, such as those involving Maria Colwell, Jasmine Beckford, Tyra Henry and Kimberley Carlisle.

The story began on 9 July 1986 when Linda Wise, a 22-year-old mother, noticed bruises on the arms of her two-year-old daughter Lindsey when she came back from playschool. Puzzled as to what had caused them – only later did she learn that the children had been out bilberry picking – she mentioned them to their health visitor and their GP. To her astonishment, social workers arrived at their home and said that Mrs Wise, her two daughters Lindsey and Paula, aged 18 months, and her husband Barry, also 22, must accompany them to Middlesbrough General Hospital.[6]

There a social worker presented Mr and Mrs Wise, quiet, churchgoing Methodists, with a Place of Safety Order, saying that they would not be allowed to take their girls home. The family would have to be monitored 24 hours a day. If they did not wish to be separated from their children, they must all move to a special family unit at a hospital in Newcastle 30 miles away.

In the Newcastle hospital they were shown into a room, where a young woman doctor told the young parents to take Lindsey's clothes off. She peered at the child's bottom and left the room, saying nothing. Although they did not know it at the time, this was Dr Marietta Higgs, a paediatrician then working at another hospital in the area.

Higgs had recently attended a course in Leeds in which two other doctors, Jane Wynne and Christopher Hobbs, had explained what they claimed was their new scientific technique for diagnosing whether a child had been subjected to sexual abuse. This was based on what they called 'Reflex Anal Dilatation' or 'RAD'. The child was to be made to undress and display its bottom, in such a way that the doctor could squeeze apart its buttocks to examine the anus. If this opened up, it supposedly proved that the child had been subjected to sexual assault.

Lindsey Wise was the first child on whom Higgs tried out this technique. A week later she told Mr and Mrs Wise that she strongly suspected that their daughter had been sexually abused. Two days later she demonstrated her technique to them. Minutes later the couple were arrested by a policeman on a charge of sexually assaulting their daughter. They were taken for interview to Gosforth Police Station. Their last sight of their children was of Lindsey screaming, 'I want to go home', being clung to by her 18-month-old sister.

The two children were taken into foster care. In November

1986 their parents were informed in a letter from the social worker handling their case that the girls were to 'be provided with a permanent alternative family', with the intention that they should be adopted.

In January 1987, Higgs moved to Middlesbrough General Hospital where she instructed a colleague, Dr Geoffrey Wyatt, in the RAD technique. Over the following months, the two paediatricians proceeded to apply it to an ever-larger number of children from the area. Whenever their tests indicated that a child had been abused, they reported this to Cleveland's social workers who, as in the case of the Wise girls, were obliged by law to place the child in foster care.[7]

In April 1987, Higgs saw the two girls again for a medical check-up before they were sent for adoption. Using her RAD technique, she now diagnosed that they were also being sexually abused by their foster parents, whose three children were also taken into care. The children's father, a civil servant, was arrested (20 years later he recalled that 'Marietta Higgs and the others were like religious zealots on a mission').

By May 1987 the number of cases Higgs and Wyatt claimed to have discovered was soaring to scarcely credible levels. Of 165 children they examined, no fewer than 121 were found to have been abused. So many children had been forcibly removed from their homes, often pulled from their beds in midnight or dawn raids, that Cleveland social services had run out of residential or foster homes to put them in. Many were now having to be kept in two wards of the hospital, which were overflowing.

Such startling events were beginning to attract attention from the media. Public concern initially supported Higgs and the social workers, whose interviewing of the children was apparently producing evidence to confirm that a major scandal had been uncovered in Cleveland. In late May, however, a group of parents marched from the hospital to the offices of the local newspaper to give their side of the story. This was at such variance with the version being put out by the doctors and the social workers that sympathy began to swing away from them to the plight of the parents and children.

Among those having serious misgivings as to what was going on were members of the Cleveland social services department itself, but attempts to voice their concerns internally were to no avail.[8]

Equally alarmed were some of Dr Higgs's senior medical colleagues. In July Dr John Forfar, president of the British Paediatric
Association, wrote to her formally pointing out that new diagnostic
techniques, such as that she was using, required 'first to be established within the profession'. This 'takes some time', involving the
presentation of scientific evidence and the need to win acceptance
through 'professional journals or scientific meetings'.[9]

Also highly critical of the conduct of the doctors and social
workers during that summer was Middlesbrough's Labour MP,
Stuart Bell, who, after talking with many of the families involved,
gave his view that an appalling act of injustice was taking place.
But this view was by no means universally shared. To many Higgs
was still an admirable and heroic figure. At that year's Labour
Party conference the MP became the focus of an extraordinary
wave of vituperation, as delegates unanimously passed a motion
applauding the efforts of Cleveland's social services department in
face of the 'hate campaign' mounted against them by Bell and the
media. One female delegate won an ovation by attacking his 'ill-
judged, irrational intervention' for the damage it had done to the
image of social workers.[10]

However, such a furore had by now erupted over the 'Cleveland
scandal' that the government had appointed Britain's most senior
female judge, Elizabeth Butler-Sloss, to hold an inquiry. During
that autumn, as she heard evidence, a rather clearer picture
emerged of just how the doctors and the social workers had played
their part in this remarkable episode. Firstly, children described
how the doctors had carried out their tests on a kind of impersonal
conveyor-belt process. As children were summoned in succession
into the examination room, they were not addressed by name. As
one girl put it, Wyatt was shouting 'nastily'. She was afraid. Higgs
did not say anything nasty, but had a 'nasty face'.[11]

Even more chilling was the evidence of the social workers.
When asked how many children they had taken into care, they
could only answer that, despite the best efforts of ten of their staff
working 'long hours of overtime' on eight computers, they were
unable to say how many of the children were still separated from
their families.[12]

The inquiry saw videos recording how the social workers had
conducted their interviews. They had made routine use of 'anatomically-correct dolls', to assist the children in showing where they

might have been sexually interfered with. They 'were seen to threaten and attempt to bribe children', to pressure them into confirming the unquestioned assumption that they had been abused. The children were repeatedly plied with leading questions, of a type which would never have been allowed in a courtroom.[13]

It was a pattern that was later to become only too familiar. For many of the children, snatched away from their parents for weeks and months on end, for reasons they never understood, it seemed that the only genuine abuse they had suffered was at the hands of the doctors and the social workers themselves.

Butler-Sloss's report, although in many ways pedestrian and anodyne, was highly critical of two of the social workers at the centre of the affair. In particular she was dismissive of their use of leading questions and their 'anatomically-correct dolls'. Higgs had already been suspended from her post, after her 'anal dilatation' method had been discredited by studies showing that more than half of any sample of children who had not been abused would produce the same 'positive' findings she had been claiming.

By this time, the trials of those suspected of child abuse had already begun to take place. In more than 80 per cent of the cases, involving 98 of the 121 children whom Higgs, Wyatt and the social workers alleged had been abused, the courts dismissed the proceedings, on the grounds that the accusations were false. Two defendants hanged themselves in Durham gaol. Only four prosecutions were successful.*

Nevertheless, Higgs and the social workers still had highly vocal defenders, led by the feminist writer Beatrix Campbell.** On 2 March 1989, Stuart Bell raised in a Commons debate a statement to the *Guardian*, allegedly signed by 11 paediatric consultants from Cleveland and Tyneside, insisting that 'in our opinion, the majority (quite possibly 90 per cent) of the children were abused', and

---

* Hansard, HC, col. 501, 2 March 1989. Among the cases which never came to court were those against Barry and Linda Wise who, on a judge's ruling, were reunited with their children.
** B. Campbell, *Unofficial secrets: Child sexual abuse: The Cleveland case* (Virago, 1989). Also seemingly not unsympathetic to Higgs was the BBC's Religious Broadcasting department which in February 1989 invited her to contribute to a series of 'meditations on Christ's Passion'. She chose the text 'They spat in His face and struck Him', to speak about her own sufferings at the hands of the tabloid press.

calling for Higgs's reinstatement. Bell revealed that this document had been organized by one of Higgs's closest allies and sent to the newspaper by Wyatt's wife, under her maiden name.[14]

So shocked was the MP by the madness which had engulfed his town that he had now published a book on the affair, *When Salem Came To The Boro*. This compared events in Middlesbrough to the outbreak of collective psychosis which had gripped the Massachusetts town of Salem in 1692, when children had been terrorized into denouncing their parents and other adults as witches possessed by the devil.

As yet, however, explicit references to 'witches' and 'Satanism' had not yet surfaced in the British version of the story. This was about to change. Cleveland had been merely the scene setter.

Broxtowe

It was Nottinghamshire Social Services Department which imported the concept of satanic ritual abuse from the USA to the UK.

Thus opened a remarkable internal report, jointly produced by members of that department and the local police in 1989 but suppressed for seven years. It is the most revealing single document in reconstructing the collective hysteria which infected many of Britain's social workers between the late 1980s and the mid-1990s.[15]

In October 1987, when the Cleveland scandal was still in the headlines, Nottinghamshire social workers removed seven children of an extended family from their homes in Broxtowe, a suburb of Nottingham, on suspicion that they had been sexually abused by parents and relatives. Sixteen months later, in February 1989, 10 adults of both sexes appeared at Nottingham Crown Court charged with 53 offences of incest, indecent assault and cruelty against 21 children. Long terms of imprisonment were imposed.

It was generally agreed that this was the most serious case of multi-generational sexual abuse within an extended family yet known in Britain. All the children involved had been made wards of court before the trial and placed with foster parents. The social workers and police responsible for bringing the case to a successful conclusion were praised by the judge, local councillors, the media and even the prime minister, Mrs Thatcher.

Much of the evidence for what had happened derived either

from interviews with the children by social workers, or diaries the foster parents were asked to keep, recording what was said by their charges. These recorded how the children had talked of 'witch parties', adults flying on broomsticks, murders of babies, the killing of animals, and of being taken to strange houses and mysterious tunnels to be abused. It was this which had led the social workers to conclude that the children had been the victims of an organized, ritualized satanic or witchcraft cult.

During the investigation, however, it also became clear that a serious rift had arisen between the social workers involved and the police, who had become increasingly sceptical about the evidence the social workers were producing. When the case was over, it was agreed by the Director of Social Services and the Chief Constable that an internal inquiry should be held, conducted by representatives of both sides who had not been involved in the case. The 'joint enquiry team' (JET) began work in July 1989 and five months later produced a damning report. After angry intervention by the social workers responsible for the case, however, this remained locked away. Only seven years later, after many leaks of its contents, was a version of the report published on the internet, as 'the Broxtowe Files'.

The group of children on whom the investigation initially centred came from an extended family, several members of which were educationally sub-normal, living in semi-detached homes on a council estate. Most of the children were very young; one of the key witnesses, 'Craig', having been only three when he was taken into care. Another was less than two. For some months the children spoke only of being abused within the family group. But on 9 February 1989, the foster parents were lectured by an 'expert', under contract to the social workers, referred to in the report as 'Mr W'. He instructed them at length on 'Satanic indicators', taken from an 'American expert', on which they were to quiz the children. These included animal sacrifices, the killing of babies, drinking blood, eating flesh, witches, snakes, monsters, ghosts and being taken to other places, such as 'a mysterious church'.

These were all textbook 'indicators' drawn from the ideology of 'satanic abuse' established in the US since 1983; and from then on the nature of what the foster parents and social workers were able to draw out of the children changed dramatically. The JET report showed how this was done, by repeatedly plying the children and other witnesses with leading questions.

One witness, 17-year-old 'Mary', for instance, was told 'Your father's killed a baby more than once'; 'who told your Dad to kill?' (Mary: 'don't know'); 'we know that your father delivered a foetus and aborted it – he drank the baby's blood' (Mary: 'I didn't know anything about that'); 'you had to eat babies more than once' (Mary: 'I can't remember'); 'we think you did'; 'you killed at least one baby. More than one? Three? 30? How many?' After three months of such interrogation, Mary had been prepared to admit to witnessing 'at least seven child murders and acts of cannibalism'.

As the report explained, the purpose of this relentless questioning seemed to be, firstly, to establish that Mary had been involved in the killing and eating of babies, and liked drinking human blood; then to draw her into naming other adults who might have been involved (had it been associated with a church, were special clothes worn or chants used?); until it appeared to be 'finally established to the social workers' satisfaction that all this has happened because Mary's family was involved in Devil worship'.

Gradually, as diaries and transcripts showed, the social workers built up an extraordinary miasma of allegations, involving numerous murders of babies, some of which were placed in microwaves; the frequent slaughter of sheep; the drinking of blood; many 'witches' parties', some in large houses (which small children were driven around in cars and asked to identify, likewise a church where human sacrifice was alleged to have taken place). All this was intermingled with charges of the sexual abuse of the children by adults, often garbed in weird costumes ('My mum flies on a broomstick,' said one little boy).

The social workers were emphatic that everything witnesses were recorded as having said must be accepted as true. It was a central article of their faith that 'children should be believed', even though almost all the allegations the children were now making had only been fed to them by their interrogators in the first place. Many were in fact physically impossible. As the police tried to point out, babies placed in microwaves would explode. It was inconceivable that slaughtering sheep in the front room of a thin-walled semi on a council estate would not have been audible to neighbours ('sheep are large, noisy, difficult animals' as the report put it, 'and when one was slaughtered by an Indian on a council estate in Leicester it hit the national newspaper headlines the following day'). Children even claimed that they themselves had been 'killed'.

The inquiry team researched the origins of the 'satanic abuse' craze across the Atlantic, and the extent to which the social workers had based their investigative technique on the US model. They even used the offices of the British Embassy in Washington to check on the credentials of the supposed 'American expert' who had briefed 'Mr W' on the 'Satanic indicators' to look for; only to find that 'he had no medical background (despite his claim to be a medical consultant) and that he was a social worker who was unpublished, had no educational pedigree and that he was not taken very seriously by the FBI'.

The social workers had also used a second set of 'Satanic indicators' supplied by another American, when they attended a Reading conference on child abuse and heard him describing how 'children in the US had reported babies being cooked in microwave ovens'. Within days of their returning to Nottingham, several children were coming up with similar lurid stories about microwaves, which had never been mentioned before.

When the inquiry team themselves interviewed some of the adult witnesses, the social workers involved in the case were angry, as they had been when police wanted to check out some of the children's stories before the trial (they 'considered that the Police did not have sufficient knowledge of this type of abuse', and were trying 'to discredit' the witnesses in order 'to disprove and close down the investigation'). One adult, 'Jane', whose child had been taken into care, described how the social workers had badgered her so relentlessly with questions about things she knew not to be true that 'in the end I just got fed up with being asked and said yes'. She had been told by another witness that if she told the social workers what they wanted to hear, 'I could get my daughter back', and that everything she had said was 'lies'. 'The only things I know about witchcraft and magic are the things I've seen on the telly.'

In December 1989 the inquiry team produced its report. They concluded 'there is no evidence of Satanic ritual abuse in the Broxtowe case or its aftermath' and 'no evidence of any other organised abuse'. It was 'doubtful whether the practice of the type of Satanic ritual abuse being promulgated by the Social Services Department actually exists'.

Nevertheless, the report noted that, following the outcome of the trial, 'the staff of our Social Services Department appear to be perceived as experts on Satanic ritualistic abuse'. They had given a presentation to 'a conference in Reading in September 1989 which included 230 representatives from child protection agencies, child psychologists, police and social workers'. They were now giving advice on satanic rituals to other teams of social workers. A tape of their Reading presentation was on sale, and the inquiry was aware that 'many Police forces and Scotland Yard intended to use this as substantiated evidence of Satanic abuse'.

If this 'belief system in ritualistic Satanic abuse' was not checked, warned the report, it could 'lead eventually to grave injustice' and 'a modern "witch hunt"'.

The intention was that the JET report should be submitted to the government and the Social Services Inspectorate, and in April 1990 it was proposed that a shorter version should be made publicly available. But after a mighty row behind the scenes, involving senior members of the social services team involved in the case, the report was suppressed.

The social workers had thus won a victory which freed them to proclaim their message far and wide. According to a new introduction by J. B. Gwatkin, when a version of the JET report was finally published in 1997, they 'ignored the Report's findings, and continued to promulgate the idea of ritual abuse by means of conferences, articles in the social work professional journals, TV appearances and an advisory telephone service'. They helped set up a body called RAINS (Ritual Abuse Information Network and Support) to promote their beliefs across the country.[16]

Among those in the media quick to champion their cause was Beatrix Campbell, who had just published her book supporting the role of Marietta Higgs in the Cleveland affair. She had become closely associated with Judith Dawson, a social worker at the centre of the Nottingham case, and wrote three of the four articles on satanic abuse published by the *New Statesman* in 1990, under such titles as 'Satanic claims vindicated'.

Across the world in California, as it happened, the longest criminal trial in US history had just ended. Seven years after it began, the case centred on the McMartin Infant School had at last concluded. At one point 208 counts of child abuse involving 40 children had been laid against seven adults, including the owners of the school and five teachers. The case had cost local taxpayers more than $13 million (the later O.J. Simpson murder trial cost $8 million) and involved six judges, 17 attorneys and hundreds of witnesses. Finally, in January 1990, the last of the defendants, the teacher originally accused, was acquitted on all charges.

In Britain, however, by a pattern which the McMartin case had originally set in train, the scare over 'Satanic abuse' was now entering on its heyday.

Rochdale

Among the many groups of social workers who had been persuaded by the satanic abuse theory were some employed by the social services department of Rochdale Borough Council in Lancashire. In the spring of 1990, just after the JET report had been completed, this was to initiate a drama in Middleton, a town neighbouring Rochdale, the full story of which could not be publicly told until sixteen years later.

Daniel, a somewhat withdrawn six-year-old boy, one day told his teacher that he was having frightening dreams about a mummy ghost, a daddy ghost and a baby ghost that had died. His teacher reported this to the Rochdale social services department. Daniel was called to the head teacher's office, from where strangers drove him away in a car. Years later, he recalled sitting in a small room where a social worker asked him 'endless questions'. Although he pleaded for his mother, he was taken that night to a children's home. He was not to return home for ten years.[17]

Social workers and police then called at his home on the Langley council estate and took away his two brothers, aged 3 and 4, and his 11-year-old sister. Their clothes were removed and thrown in the bin, including a new coat the girl had just been given for her birthday, which a social worker described as 'filthy'. The children were taken into care, to be subjected to continuous questioning.

Police and social workers then returned to search the children's home, telling their distraught parents, 'you're suspected of black magic and abusing your children'. According to an official transcript, a police officer asked the father about 'black magic', 'devil worship', 'hoods and capes': 'this is the sort of thing we believe to be going on with your children'.[18] The social workers took as 'evidence' a cross the daughter had made from two lollipop sticks, and a wall plaque she had given to her mother showing Jesus on the cross, with the words 'God bless our home'. It contained a small dish for holy water, later alleged to have been used to hold blood.

Some weeks later, on 11 May, Steve Hammond, the editor of the local paper, received a call from the children's father. In a shaking voice he said, 'they say we do black magic on our kids. Our children have been taken away. Please help us, we are innocent'.[19] After the story had been investigated, the paper ran it under the headline 'Couple lose children after "black magic charges"'. The response of Rochdale council was to win a High Court injunction barring the media from making any further reference to the case, and forbidding any contact with anyone involved in it.

The children were meanwhile being quizzed about their friends and anyone they knew on the estate. Early on the morning of 12 June more children from five other families were taken from their beds, subjected to medical examination and interrogation, and placed in care.

Over the next few months, the social workers built up a picture of how the children had been taken to haunted places, been dressed up and put in cages, and seen animals and babies being killed. The officials were sure they had uncovered a massive case of satanic abuse. The police were not convinced. The only support for the social workers' view came from what they had pressured children into telling them. Eventually, in September Manchester's chief constable, James Anderton, issued a statement that 'a lengthy police investigation' had not 'produced evidence to justify the institution of criminal proceedings'.

By now the case was attracting interest from the national media. The *Mail on Sunday* won a change to the High Court injunction, allowing the case to be reported so long as the children were not identified. The day its story was published, the 'Rochdale case' led the national television news, and was reported all around the world.

The social workers were defiant. Their head of department, Gordon Littlemore, issued a statement that 'It is the view of social services and the police that the abuse the children describe is real'. The social workers even forbade parents from sending Christmas cards to their children in care, lest they contain some hidden 'Satanic symbol'.

The 16 children were all still wards of court, and in January

1991 a 47-day hearing began in the High Court to decide whether they should be allowed to return to their parents. On 7 March Mr Justice Douglas Brown ruled that there had been 'a gross breach of good practice' by Rochdale social services. The two social workers chiefly responsible for handling the case, he said, had shown 'an unhealthy degree of single-mindedness'. The judge blamed their superiors for not having kept a closer eye on them. The next day Littlemore resigned.

The judge ordered that 12 of the children should be returned home immediately. Only the original four, including Daniel, for reasons not made clear, remained in care. The two small boys remained in a children's home for seven years. Their sister remained with Daniel in a foster home in Stockport until she was 16, when she was free to leave. She immediately returned home to her parents. When Daniel reached the age of 16, he followed her.

On 11 January 2006 their story was reported for the first time, in a BBC documentary 'The Day Satan Came to Rochdale'. This included videos taken at the time of the social workers interviewing the children. One showed a six-year-old girl crying uncontrollably for 17 minutes while a social worker never ceased to ply her with questions. The two social workers, Julian France and Susan Hammersley, were for the first time named, and the programme reported that both were still working in 'child protection'.

The *Middleton Guardian*, which also reported the story at length, used the Freedom of Information Act to elicit from Rochdale the fact that the council had spent in total £120,000 of taxpayers' money to prevent the media reporting the case: £82,100 in 1990 and 1991, and a further £38,473 in September 2005 simply to prevent the social workers being named. Both bans had now been lifted.[20]

Orkney

So widely across the country had the evangelizing of believers in satanic abuse now spread that the next case to reach the headlines centred on South Ronaldsay, an island of Orkney off the northern tip of Scotland.

Towards the end of 1991, May Willsher, a cheerful, outgoing six-year-old girl, one of a family of eight children, was summoned out of her class by social workers from Orkney Council. She remembered 'running down the school corridors, screaming, being restrained by the arms and bundled into a police car'. A woman social worker in the back of the car said 'you're being taken away because you are being abused by adults on the island'.[21]

She discovered that her brothers and sisters had also been removed, but none could explain what the social worker meant. When they reached the mainland, they were separated, May being taken to a children's home in Glasgow. She was eventually placed with a foster family, then another. She remembers awful car journeys, being driven from place to place, and says she was continually crying and feeling sad. She was no longer cheerful: 'I would sit on my own and just cry, but uncontrollably.'

Initially she was allowed to see her mother once every two weeks, but they were not allowed to touch each other or sit together. 'Social workers would be sitting there, just to watch what we were going to say.' After her move to the second foster home, meetings with her mother were stopped.

The one person May saw constantly, twice a week, was Liz McLean, the social worker who had removed her from school. She would be left alone in the room with McLean for up to two hours. 'I was terrified of her. She was very intimidating, very controlling ... she got very angry. She would want me to agree with what she was saying.' McLean constantly quizzed her about grown-ups interfering with her or her brothers and sisters sexually. One of the rare occasions when McLean seemed pleased with her was when she was asked to draw a circle, then put stick men round it. It might have seemed like a ring of adults engaged in a ritual. 'Very good,' said the social worker.

In the early hours of 27 February 1991, after the children had been interrogated in this way for several weeks, being asked the names of other children and adults they knew – what the social workers called 'disclosure therapy sessions' – police and social workers raided several more homes on South Ronaldsay. Nine more children were pulled from their beds, bundled into a chartered plane and taken to homes on the mainland for further questioning. Like May, several of them later described how McLean was a 'terrifying figure, fixated on finding satanic abuse'.

The social workers were soon convinced they had evidence that the children had all been subjected by adults to organized sexual abuse, made to engage in satanic, ritual sex games in a quarry on the island. When a number of adults were arrested and charged with abusing the children, this was the case presented to Sheriff David Kelbie. After five weeks, the case collapsed. The sheriff ruled that the case was 'fundamentally flawed'. He was 'unclear' what the evidence produced by the social workers proved. They had been 'manipulative' in subjecting the children to cross-examinations intended to make them admit they had been abused; and they had not learned the lessons of the Cleveland and Rochdale cases.

The sheriff ordered that the nine children should be returned to their families immediately. A crowd of parents, relatives and islanders gathered at the airport to welcome them home. A senior judge, Lord Clyde, then conducted a seven-month inquiry into the case, at a cost of £6 million. His 363-page report was highly critical of the way Orkney's social workers had carried out their investigation, rebuking several senior individuals by name, including McLean. He made 192 recommendations as to how such episodes might be avoided in the future. McLean, who was also criticized for her part in a similar case of 'satanic abuse' in Ayr, resigned. In 1992 she disappeared.

May Willsher was eventually allowed to return home, but when she was 17 she left Orkney, still 'terrified' by the memory of her removal and subsequent experiences in foster care. In 2006, now living in England with a partner and their child, she spoke about her experience for the first time.[22]

Pembroke

Cleveland, Nottingham, Rochdale and Orkney had all made national headlines. The episode which followed in Dyfed attracted almost no notice from the national press, although it was certainly as bizarre and tragic as any of them and led to easily the largest and longest sexual abuse trial Britain had known. We were able to report on it in the *Sunday Telegraph* after being approached by someone closely involved who was appalled by what was going on.

In 1989 Dyfed County Council social workers had attended a three-day 'training programme' conducted by the 'Satanic abuse expert' who played such a key role in the Nottingham case in 1988. Although described in the JET report only as 'Mr W', he was later identified as Ray Wyre. Impressed by his briefing on 'Satanic indicators', they returned to Dyfed anxious to look out for any such signs in their area.

In 1990, when a couple with two children living in Pembroke had split up, social workers placed their two children in a foster home. Eight-year-old 'Jason' observed that another child in the home, a girl who had been sexually abused, was given special treatment by the social workers, such as the present of a new bicycle. His female social worker began a long course of 'therapy' with 'Jason', amounting, over more than a year, to 28 interviews, some lasting much of a day. Their sessions included 'sex education' and 'memory work'.

From papers later produced in court, it was possible to see how, during this time, the two of them gradually 'recovered the memory' of how 'Jason' had not only been sexually abused himself, but how this had involved other children and adults, taking place in quarries and barns. 'Jason' was asked for the names of other children and adults he knew.

In 1992 a 14-year-old girl who had run away from home was also interrogated at length by the social workers. She also came up with names of those who could have taken part in a sex ring, eventually claiming that 'around 200 people were involved'.

By mid-1992 social workers and the local police were convinced that 'Jason's' original hints of a sex ring were true. By the end of the year, eleven men and two women had been arrested and charged; eighteen children from nine families were taken into care.

One woman, 'Susan', had been vacuum-cleaning her home at 8 am, with her three small children still in bed, when the doorbell rang. Five people, police and social workers, entered the house, arrested her and took away her children into care. She spent nine months in prison, before being released on bail. As someone accused of child abuse, she was accorded very harsh treatment by some of her fellow-prisoners, such as urinating or putting glass in her food.

After six months of pre-trial reviews, the trial began on 4 October 1993, before Mr Justice Kay and a jury. The courtroom was packed with lawyers, 30 for the defence alone, including a battery of QCs. Until Christmas they were engaged in discussion as to which of the 15,000 pages of evidence presented to the court would be admissible. It was not until the new year that Gerald Elias QC was able to begin putting the prosecution's case. This alone was expected to last until the end of April.

He was to rely on only two adult witnesses, apart from the professionals involved. His other chief witnesses would be a parade of children. Revealingly, since the belief in satanic abuse had now been so widely questioned, explicit reference to this was omitted. But otherwise the story he wished the jury to believe was a classic concoction of the imagery now familiar from such cases, involving sexual and often violent abuse of the children by a group of adults, sometimes wearing wigs and cloaks. This was alleged to have taken place over a long period in places such as caves, barns, a beach, even a playground in the middle of the housing estate where many of the children lived.

On 9 February one child witness, the 12-year-old son of one of the defendants told the court that, although when he was interviewed in 1992, the social workers had 'kept on' at him to say that his father had abused him, this was not true. His father had never abused him.

On 23 February an adult witness, an ex-girlfriend of the man accused of being the leader of 'a paedophile ring which terrorised children in sex orgies', also told the jury that statements she had signed alleging incidents of child abuse by her former boyfriend were untrue. She stated that the social workers had threatened that her children would never be released from care unless she co-operated. She said, 'I was groomed by the social workers. I knew what they wanted me to say – I just added on and added on, but none of it is the truth.' Asked by Elias, 'are you saying that you and the social workers made up things which were a pack of lies?', she replied 'yes'.

On 7 March Elias's other adult witness also said that what she had told the social workers was untrue. They had warned her that, unless she agreed that her husband and other adults were abusing children, she would never see her children again. She described how one social worker, whom she named, had met her at Llanelli police station, before she was due to make a statement to the police, and that he had a notepad listing the names of adults she was to accuse of abusing children. If she co-operated, she would be given immunity from prosecution.[23]

On 11 March the judge ordered that three of the 12 remaining defendants should be acquitted, on the grounds that there was no evidence against them. One was 'Susan', the mother of three young children, who had spent nine months being maltreated in prison.

But although she was now free, she could not apply for permission to be reunited with her children until the case was concluded.

As the case continued over the following three months, the judge discharged two more defendants on the same grounds. Both the prosecution's adult witnesses had retracted their previous testimony, claiming that they had only given it under severe duress from the social workers. The only direct evidence of collective abuse brought against the accused was that of seven children who, having been taken into care, had been interviewed by social workers over periods ranging up to 16 months. Three of these children had now retracted their allegations, denying that any abuse had taken place – as did nine other children called by the defence.

The prosecution was not able to produce a shred of forensic evidence to corroborate that the alleged crimes had taken place. Despite persistent claims that the bizarre scenes had been extensively photographed and filmed on video, prolonged searches by the police had not been able to discover a single picture. None of the medical witnesses for the prosecution could confirm that any of the children had been interfered with. Even though it was alleged that the children had been subjected to serious physical violence on many occasions, no evidence from doctors, teachers or anyone else was produced to confirm this.[24]

Yet, astonishingly, when the jury returned its verdict on 13 June 1994, it found five of the remaining defendants guilty on the charges of running a paedophile ring, and a sixth guilty on other charges of child abuse. Only one was found innocent. On 29 June Mr Justice Kay sentenced them to up to 15 years in prison. Having witnessed events in the courtroom over nine months, having seen all the evidence and the demeanour of those who testified in support of the charges, lawyers for the defence were privately convinced that the case had been an appalling travesty of justice.

Shortly after the jury's verdict, Kay wrote a remarkable letter to the Home Secretary. He wished to complain about the 'prolonged and distressing cross-examination' of the child witnesses by the defence counsel. To save the distress of children at being accused of telling lies, he suggested that in future prosecuting counsel should be allowed to intervene, to reassure them by rephrasing questions in a more 'friendly' fashion.

It was revealing that the judge should have taken this line. The only direct evidence against the accused had come from the seven children. No corroboratory evidence had been produced of any kind. Yet the concern expressed by the judge centred entirely on the way counsel for the defence had interrogated the children in an effort to question their story.

An equally remarkable feature of the case, which did not seem to concern the judge, was the time the social workers had taken in questioning the children during the eighteen months before the trial, including the 28 separate interviews with 'Jason', some taking most of a day, from which the whole story had been concocted in the first place. Following the Butler-Sloss report on Cleveland, the Home Office had issued a Memorandum of Good Practice laying down that, wherever possible, a child should only be interviewed once, and that this should not last more than an hour.

Under the Children Act 1989, which had also followed the Cleveland case, it was laid down that where a child accuses an adult of abuse, the child should be believed, without need for corroborative evidence, unless the adult can prove the accusation unfounded. This contradicted one of the most basic principles of English justice. But, curiously, as the Pembroke case had confirmed, the same presumption that a child should be believed did not seem to apply when the child is protesting an adult's innocence. Some of the most ferocious cross-examination during the Swansea trial had been directed at the 12-year-old son of one of the defendants. For two hours, the boy maintained that he had never been abused by his father, despite Elias repeatedly putting it to him that he was lying. This again did not seem to have concerned the judge.

Those found guilty went off to begin their long prison sentences. Several parents involved in the case embarked on a long and in some cases vain legal battle to be reunited with their children. These included 'Susan' and her husband, who was among those sentenced to a long term of imprisonment. In the autumn of 1994, in a family court reviewing the cases, Mr Justice Connell ruled that not a shred of evidence had been produced against him. On 3 November 1995 the appeal court quashed his conviction. The family was at last reunited.[25]

Some time after the trial was concluded, we learned that 'Jason', the boy whose interviews with his social worker set the whole story in train, had, at the age of eleven, hanged himself.

Epilogue

One of the most vocal champions of Dr Higgs and the social workers of Cleveland, back in 1989, had been an anthropologist, Jean La Fontaine. In 1990 she published a book on the affair, *Child Sexual Abuse*. She was sympathetic to what had come to be known as the 'Californian model' of investigation. She ignored the criticisms made by Butler-Sloss of the technique known as 'disclosure therapy', whereby children might be pressurized by adults into making accusations that were false.[26]

Despite Butler-Sloss's strictures, this was the technique which had lain at the heart of all the subsequent cases: Broxtowe, Rochdale, Orkney and Pembroke. La Fontaine also accepted the theory of 'recovered memory', whereby traumatic memories of sexual abuse could be repressed and subsequently recovered through sympathetic therapy.

Yet, as the belief in satanic ritual abuse became the dominant orthodoxy among so many social workers, La Fontaine's knowledge of witchcraft practices in Africa led her to become highly dubious of this aspect of the belief in organized child abuse. In 1990 she was commissioned to write a report for the Department of Health, which appeared in 1994 as *The Extent and Nature of Organised and Ritual Abuse*. In this she not only dismissed the idea of satanic abuse, but analysed how social workers could gradually draw a child into concocting a story which was essentially an 'adult construction', by means of loaded questions to which the child was anxious to provide answers the interrogator wanted to hear.

The significance of La Fontaine's official report, which appeared in the year of the Pembroke case, was that it reflected the extent to which the satanic abuse scare was now fading away. The very fact that, as one commentator later put it, 'many of the satanic elements had been carefully edited out of the Pembroke trial in order to secure conviction',[27] was itself a measure of how far the scare had now been discredited.

But its memory lingered on, not just for all those countless innocent people whose lives it had ruined, but among some of the social workers themselves, who remained still under the spell of a scare which had given them such a thrilling cause to believe in, and the illusion that they had been given a 'scientific technique' which might enable them to uncover fathomless reserves of evil in their fellow men.

In 2003, in a strange echo of the earlier case in nearby Orkney, eight adults on the Hebridean island of Lewis, including a 75-year-old grandmother, faced trial, charged with having abused children in black magic rituals, involving the sacrifices of cats and chickens and the drinking of blood. A key witness in the social workers' case was Angela Stretton, a woman in her thirties with learning difficulties. After nine months the case was quietly dropped; but not before the accused had become the victims of vigilante attacks and seen their lives turned upside down.

In 2006, Stretton admitted that her story about her own mother and other members of her family being involved in black magic rituals was based on lies. At first, she claimed, she had denied the points being put to her by social workers about the killing of animals and drinking their blood. 'But they kept on and on at me. They said I had to tell the truth for the sake of the children. I felt really under pressure, so I suppose I told them what they wanted to hear. I just agreed with what was being said.'[28]

Her words might have been an epitaph for the entire story of what had been arguably the most chilling scare of them all.

Notes

1. 'The Broxtowe Files', Joint Enquiry Team (JET) Report on the Nottingham child abuse case, 7 June 1990 (as published in 1997, available on www.users.globalnet.co.uk).
2. Michelle Smith and Lawrence Pazder, *Michelle Remembers* (1980).
3. Richard Webster, 'Satanic abuse and McMartin: a global village rumour', *New Statesman*, 27 February 1998; Jean La Fontaine, *Speak of the Devil: tales of satanic abuse in contemporary England* (Cambridge University Press, 1998).
4. 'The Broxtowe Files' (1997).
5. *Ibid.*
6. This account of the Wise family's experience is based on an article by Sue Reid in the *Daily Mail*, 24 February 2007, in which the two girls, now grown-up, spoke publicly for the first time about what had happened to them and their parents in 1986.
7. Charles Pragnell, 'The Cleveland Child Sexual Abuse Scandal: An Abuse and Misuse of Professional Power', available on *www.childrenuk.co.uk*. In 1987 Pragnell was head of research with Cleveland

Social Services. Also, Stuart Bell, *When Salem Came To The Boro* (Pan Books, 1988). Bell was MP for Middlesbrough at the time. Also, Brian Deer, 'Why we must now start listening to the children', *Sunday Times*, 10 July 1988.

8. Pragnell, *op. cit.*
9. *Ibid.*
10. *Daily Telegraph*, 1 October 1987.
11. *Sunday Times, op. cit.*
12. *Daily Telegraph*, 22 October 1987.
13. Pragnell, *op. cit.*
14. Hansard, HC, 2 March 1989.
15. 'Broxtowe Files' (1997).
16. A short version of the JET report was finally made public, via the Internet, in 1997, thanks to three journalists, Nick Anning, David Hebditch and Margaret Jervis, with a new introduction by Gwatkin as the senior member of the original inquiry team.
17. Carol Midgley, 'Our Stolen Childhood', *The Times*, 10 January 2006.
18. *Middleton Guardian*, 12 January 2006.
19. *Ibid.*
20. *Ibid.*
21. Esther Addley, 'I could not stop crying', *Guardian*, 21 October 2006. We are indebted to this article, on which much of the information in this section is based.
22. *Ibid.*
23. *Sunday Telegraph*, 20 March 1994.
24. *Sunday Telegraph*, 19 June 1994.
25. *Sunday Telegraph*, 5 November 1995.
26. Webster, *New Statesman, op. cit.*
27. *Ibid.*
28. 'Satanic abuse key witness says: I lied', *Observer*, 24 September 2006.

10

'Speed Kills'

A Safety Scare That Cost Lives

*Road deaths are a global epidemic on the scale of malaria and
tuberculosis.*
Commission for Global Road Safety, 2006[1]

*Research has shown that speed is a major contributory factor
in about one-third of all road accidents. This means that each
year excessive and inappropriate speed helps to kill around
1,200 people and to injure over 100,000 more. This is far more
than any other single contributor to casualties on our roads.*
Tomorrow's Roads: Safer for Everyone,
Department for Transport, 2000

One of the success stories of modern Britain was the constant fall,
over three decades, in the number of fatal accidents on the country's roads. This gave the UK a road safety record better than that
of almost any other country in the world.

Easily the highest ever figures for road deaths were recorded in
the early years of World War Two, when the night-time blackout
(and masked car headlights) temporarily pushed up the yearly total
to more than 9,000. It then fell back, but, with a three-fold growth
in car ownership in the first 20 years after the war, the annual total
again rose, from around 5,000 to a peak of 7,985 in 1966.

From then on, despite a continuing rise in the number of vehicles on the road, the fatal accident figure steadily dropped, at an
average rate of more than 5 per cent a year. By 1980 it had fallen to
just over 6,000. By 1993 it was below 4,000. Britain's roads were
the safest in Europe. In France and Germany, the annual death toll

was over 9,000. In Portugal the death rate was well over three times as high.

Then the rate of decline suddenly slowed. Over the next decade the total fall was smaller than in any of the years between 1990 and 1993. On five occasions the yearly figure actually rose.

So what had changed?

The most obvious change that took place in the mid-1990s was a radical shift in the government's road safety policy. Ministers and officials had become persuaded that by far the most important single factor in causing accidents was 'speed'. The main focus of police road safety strategy, designed to cut the accident rate still further, now became the rigorous enforcement of speed limits, backed by a growing army of speed cameras.

Yet it was at this very time that the fall in the accident rate markedly slowed. Although millions of motorists were caught by the new 'safety cameras', which were soon costing them more than £100 million a year in fines, the number of people dying on Britain's roads was no longer declining at anything like the same rate as before.

Inevitably, road safety experts connected the two. Had this slowing of the decline in deaths on the roads been caused by the switch in government policy? If the policy had not been changed, they asked, might 7,000 lives have been saved? Had not this new fixation with 'speed', to the exclusion of almost everything else, and supported by highly dubious statistics, taken on many of the familiar characteristics of a scare?

How the Obsession with 'Speed' Developed

Undoubtedly one important factor in the steady fall in the fatal accident rate in earlier decades, despite a doubling in the number of vehicles on Britain's roads – from 12 million in 1966 to 25 million in 1994 – had been the technical advances that made vehicles themselves much safer. But this could not have explained the slowing in the fall of accidents in the1990s, when new regulations had made vehicles safer still.

Another factor in earlier decades had been Britain's policing methods. The efficiency of the UK's traffic police, respected as an elite, had won international recognition. Their regular patrolling enabled them to pick up not just drivers breaking the speed limit, but motorists whose driving or vehicles might need to be checked for many other reasons. Not least of these was a severe clampdown on driving under the influence of alcohol.

By the late 1980s, however, technology had been supplying the traffic police with new tools. Laser guns enabled them to measure the speed of a moving vehicle much more precisely. The emphasis in traffic surveillance began to shift away from human judgement towards the simple act of measuring whether a driver was breaking a speed limit.

In 1991 the government launched its first £1 million television advertising campaign centred on the dangers of speeding ('Kill your speed, not a child'). In 1992 the police were given a new weapon, when the first speed cameras were installed in west London. Their first trials, on the M40 motorway, had shown just how frequently drivers broke the limit, when cameras capable of taking snapshots of 400 cars on each roll of film had used up their quota in as little as 40 minutes.[2]

By September 1994 government spending on TV commercials was running at £2.7 million a year, now centred on the slogan that was to become familiar: 'Speed kills'. In 1997 the yearly advertising budget reached £3.5 million. Speed cameras were now proliferating the length and breadth of the land. Police patrols, except on motorways, were being reduced.* In 1999, as income from penalties for offences recorded by the cameras soared towards £100 million a year, the first 'Safety Camera Partnerships' were formed, allying police forces with local authorities. Yet, in two years out of four, the number of fatal accidents had actually risen.

In March 2000 the government launched a new 'road safety strategy', aimed at reducing by 40 per cent the number of people killed or seriously injured on Britain's roads within a decade. The prime minister Tony Blair told of how he had 'received countless letters from parents, brothers, sisters, friends of those killed and

* Local authorities were also being pressed by the government to introduce other 'traffic calming measures' to curb vehicle speeds, from speed humps and chicanes to a marked increase in the number and severity of highway speed restrictions.

injured on our roads', every one telling of 'a family devastated, lives blighted, of pain, sorrow and anger and the waste of it'.[3]

The government, he promised, would now take action, with a strategy that 'will focus especially on speed'. A government strategy paper claimed, in the words quoted at the head of this chapter, that speed was 'a major contributory factor in about a third of all road accidents'. 'Excessive and inappropriate speed' helped 'to kill around 1,200 people' each year, which was 'far more than any other single contributor to casualties on our roads'.[4]

The source given for this claim, to be repeated as a mantra by ministers and officials for years to come, was a report from the government's Transport Research Laboratory, TRL Report 323, entitled: 'A new system for recording contributory factors in road accidents'.[5]

Not many people would have looked at this report, since it was only available for £45. But some who did were amazed. The evidence the report had cited to support its claim that speed was 'a major contributory factor in about a third of all road accidents' simply wasn't there. Many other factors were named as contributing to road accidents, from driving without due care and attention, to driving under the influence of drink; from poor overtaking, to nodding off at the wheel. But the figure given for accidents in which the main causative factor was 'excessive speed' was way down the list, at only '7.3 per cent'.

So startling seemed the government's exaggeration of the TRL's figures, based on data provided by eight police forces, that it set off an increasingly public and fractious debate. A leading role in this was to be played by Paul Smith, an engineer turned road safety expert, who was so shocked by the government's misuse of its own experts' statistics that in 2001 he set up a website, Safespeed. This was dedicated to exhaustive analysis of why, in his view, the government's misconceived policy, far from making Britain's roads safer, could only make them more dangerous.[6]

Initially, a key part of the debate was focused on how the government could justify its inflation of the report's '7.3 per cent' finding into a claim that speed caused 'a third of all road accidents'. The TRL itself argued, in an attempt to support the government's claim, that speed was also a factor in many accidents listed under other headings, such as careless driving or sudden braking.

Smith and other critics pointed out that this was given the lie by the TRL's own report. Not only did it cite excessive speed as the 'definite' cause in only 4.5 per cent of accidents, but it found that speed was a 'probable' or 'possible contributory factor' in only 8.2 per cent more. Not only was the government itself thus bending the truth; it had brought pressure on the TRL to give a wholly misleading picture of its own researchers' findings.

The more the government's case was examined, the more statistically dubious it became. So determined was it to claim that speed was the chief cause of accidents that it would stop at nothing in misrepresenting the evidence to support its case.

The critics, on the other hand, maintained that, in this single-minded obsession with 'speed', taking their eye off all the other complex causes of accidents, ministers and officials were being dangerously simplistic. Of course speed was a factor in any accident involving a moving vehicle, even if it was moving at only 1 mph. But to anyone seriously interested in why accidents happened, the important thing was to determine what were the real reasons why a driver had made the mistake. Was it lack of attention? Reckless overtaking? Alcohol? Fatigue? Or any one or more of various other causes?

The ministers and officials responsible for the new policy appeared to have convinced themselves that, if only speed itself could be reduced, this would in itself remedy all those other failings in driver behaviour that the TRL itself had identified in its report as the chief cause of the vast majority of accidents.

Even more simplistically, the government also seemed to be defining 'excessive speed' much too narrowly, only in terms of exceeding a speed limit. In fact its own figures showed that only 30 per cent of accidents attributed to excessive speed actually involved breaking a speed limit. The vast majority, 70 per cent, involved vehicles that had been travelling at speeds within the limit. Yet the official effort to improve road safety was now being directed almost entirely at enforcing speed limits, which would do nothing to affect two thirds of the accidents caused by speed.

This was why now, at the very centre of the government's safety strategy, was the nationwide network of safety cameras, which could only be installed where there were official speed limits; and then only where there was evidence that four serious accidents had occurred in the previous three years.

In 2003, to justify this policy, the government produced a report purporting to show that, where cameras had been installed, the accident rate had been reduced by '35 per cent'.[7] But again it was manipulating the figures. Several significant confounding factors had been left out of the calculations; not least the fact that, on many sites, cameras had been installed following an atypical blip in the accident rate. When the rate had then fallen back to its previous average level – what statisticians call 'regression to the mean' – this allowed the researchers, and the government, to claim that the reduction could be ascribed entirely to the arrival of a camera.[8]

So great now was the pressure on ministers, officials and the police to keep on repeating the two key official mantras – 'a third of accidents are caused by speed' and 'speed cameras reduce accidents by 35 per cent' – that few were prepared to challenge them. One exception was Paul Garvin, the chief constable of Durham, whose police area was the only one in Britain that had refused to install speed cameras.

In an interview Garvin explained why. He insisted that, while he believed strongly in 'casualty reduction and trying to make the roads safer', he could not agree with the government that curbing speed was the central answer to the problem. The accident statistics for Durham showed that, of 1,900 collisions in the county each year, only 3 per cent involved cars that were exceeding the speed limit – just 60 accidents a year.

Look more closely at the causes of these 60 accidents, he went on, and, although speed might be 'a factor in the background', the 'actual cause of the accident invariably is drink-driving or drug-driving'. Drug taking was now involved in 40 per cent of Durham's fatal road accidents. Many accidents, he said, were caused by fatigue, although one of the most common causes of crashes was the failure of drivers to watch out for oncoming vehicles when turning right. To none of these could speed cameras offer any remedy. 'The cause of accidents', Garvin concluded, 'is clearly something different than exceeding the speed limit.'*

* *Daily Telegraph*, 7 December 2003. Another feature of official 'anti-speed' policy coming under fire at this time was the government's encouragement of 'traffic calming measures', including the hundreds of thousands of 'speed humps' which could give a serious jolt to the occupants of vehicles driven over them at any speed. The most prominent protests came from the emergency services, led by the London Ambulance Service, which claimed that the need to slow down was costing the lives of

Meanwhile, the senior policeman in charge of speed cameras in England and Wales, Richard Brunstrom, Garvin's fellow chief constable for North Wales, had just sent a remarkable confidential letter to all police forces and local authorities, revealing just how unnerved those running the speed camera campaign had become at charges that their policy had failed in its aim of reducing Britain's road accident figures.

Signing himself as 'Chair of the Association of Chief Police Officers Roads Policing Business Area', Brunstrom instructed all those responsible for operating speed cameras – which in 2003 were raising more than £120 million from two million motorists – that they must on no account respond to any further requests for factual information from Safespeed's Paul Smith.

Smith's offence, according to Brunstrom, was that his 'sole intent seems to be to discredit Government policy'. He had not only 'inundated' the Department for Transport (DfT) and police forces with requests for information, but had also published their replies on the Internet. Brunstrom was also concerned that dozens of serving police officers had contacted Smith to express their personal concern at the way reliance on speed cameras had become a substitute for a road safety policy which, until ten years previously, had been internationally acclaimed as the most successful in the world.[9]

In 2004 Smith was able to reveal even worse news for the government. For some time he had argued that, far from reducing the risk of accidents, speed cameras actually increased it, by distracting drivers and causing them to act unpredictably. This was now confirmed by another report from the Transport Research Laboratory, TRL Report 595, commissioned by the Highways Agency, looking into the effect of speed cameras on motorways.

The TRL had found that, where fixed speed cameras were installed at road works, the risk of accidents giving rise to injury was increased by 55 per cent. Where fixed speed cameras were installed on open motorways the risk of accidents giving rise to

500 patients a year. On 11 December 2003, giving evidence to a Greater London Assembly inquiry into 'The Impact of Speed Humps', the chairman and chief executive of the LAS explained that, for every minute's delay in being rushed to hospital, the life of a cardiac arrest patient could be shortened by 11 minutes, through weakening of the muscles.

injury was increased by 31 per cent. In general, fatal and serious crashes were 32 per cent more likely where speed cameras were being operated. But conventional police patrols reduced the risk of crashes by 27 per cent at road works, and 10 per cent elsewhere.

The report bore out precisely the case Smith had been making. But the DfT had ruled that it was not to be published. If a copy had not been passed to Smith, to be reported on the Safespeed website, it might never have seen the light of day.

Like 'hitting someone over the head with a baseball bat'

In 2005 we were given a personal insight into just how the new road safety policy operated in practice. One of the more active 'Safety Camera Partnerships' in the country was that responsible for Avon and Somerset, with 71 fixed speed cameras and 183 'mobile camera sites', generating penalties of £5 million a year.[10] Somerset in recent years had seen a huge increase in the amount of its roads covered by speed limits, so that roadsides in even the smallest village might now sprout dozens of new speed limit and camera warning signs. The 'Partnership' ran an expensive local advertising campaign, with the slogan 'We're here to save lives'.

In May 2005 one of the authors of this book joined the 11 million motorists in Britain who, in the previous decade, had been caught by a speed camera. On a road with eight changes of speed limit in three miles, a camera sited just past where a 40 mph limit changes to 30 picked him up. As an alternative to three points on his licence, he opted to attend Avon and Somerset's three-hour 'Speed Camera Workshop', necessitating an 80-mile round trip to an industrial estate outside the county town of Taunton. This was just a mile or two from where, in 2000, a police car carrying the then-Home Secretary, Jack Straw, had been caught by a police patrol on the M5 motorway travelling at 103 mph (no action had been taken against the police driver).

Those attending the course had come from as far away as Nottingham and Lincolnshire, involving journeys of hundreds of miles. The three-hour session was conducted on cosy first-name terms by two instructors, 'Ian' and 'Bill'. The aim was to coax those attending from a feeling that they had been unlucky to be caught, through demonstrations of how anti-social it was to 'speed' and how effective cameras were in reducing accidents, to, instead, a deep sense of guilt. They had to understand that breaking a speed limit was as socially unacceptable as 'drink driving', not really any different, as was explained, to 'going out to hit someone over the head with a baseball bat'. By the end, they were meant to have learned to love the camera as Big Brother, as something there to save them from themselves.

All this was supported by a barrage of statistics. The only problem was that every single figure given – although this was hardly the fault of the instructors – was seriously wrong. First, of course, came the familiar claim that 'a third of all accidents' were caused by speeding. Yet a recent study by Avon and Somerset Police themselves had found that in reality only 3 per cent of accidents in their area had been caused by drivers exceeding a speed limit (in only 10 per cent had 'excessive speed' been a factor at all).

Figures were then flashed up to show the horrifying financial cost of accidents. Even a 'slight collision', the audience was told, cost '£17,550'. A 'serious collision' cost '£174,530'. Each 'fatal collision' cost '£1,492,910' (which would make the total yearly cost of UK road deaths £4.2 billion). The hapless instructors were doubtless quite unaware that these highly improbable statistics had originally been compiled by the DfT for a wholly different purpose: to illustrate a study of the comparative benefits of public and private transport (a large part of each sum supposedly represented the cash-value of the 'worry and distress' an accident had caused).

Inevitably, the instructors wheeled on the claim that speed cameras had reduced accidents by '35 per cent'. To illustrate the tragic consequences of breaking the speed limit, they then produced a harrowing video, purporting to show a small child being killed by a car driving down a busy street at 35 mph (what the instructors did not explain was that the average speed at which pedestrians are hit on roads covered by 30 or 40 mph limits is 11 mph, and that, of accidents involving vehicles and pedestrians, only 1.5 per cent are fatal).

Most striking of all was how rigidly 'speed' was defined only in terms of exceeding a speed limit. When the audience was asked what they understood by 'excessive speed', this was the only definition the instructors allowed. A suggestion that it might more realistically be defined as 'driving at a speed inappropriate to the conditions' they impatiently dismissed as wholly unacceptable.

When members of the audience were each asked in turn to describe how they had been driving when caught by a camera, it was evident from the replies that none appeared to have been driving in a way which endangered themselves or anyone else. All had been driving at a speed that seemed to them to be appropriate to the conditions.

But even to think such thoughts was heresy. The overwhelming message of the course – as the government would have wished – was that the audience should be left thinking 'we are all guilty. We must learn to love Big Brother'.[11]

'The anti-social bastards in our midst'

One of the side effects of the government's decision to centre its road safety strategy on speed cameras had been to widen considerably the gulf between many normally law-abiding citizens and the police.

Opinion polls consistently showed, by ratios of two to one, that the cameras were highly unpopular, and were widely regarded as less a road safety measure, and more a lucrative source of income. Other electronic means used to reduce drivers' speed, such as radar-operated 'Slow Down' signs indicating to drivers that they were exceeding a speed limit, met with very significantly more approval, and were welcomed as making a positive contribution to road safety.

The public, and the tabloids, had become noticeably sensitive to the idea that, when it came to observing speed limits, the police now appeared to be operating a marked double standard. Cases where police drivers were not penalized for flagrant breaches of the law were eagerly reported, such as that in 2000 when the Home Secretary's car had been driven at 103 mph.

In December 2003 a police driver was recorded by a patrol car driving at 159 mph on the M54 near Telford, Shropshire, and charged with speeding and dangerous driving. However, when in May 2005 his case came before District Judge Bruce Morgan in Ludlow, he was cleared on all charges, the judge noting that two senior police officers had testified that the defendant's driving was 'not dangerous'.*

* '159 mph speeding charge PC cleared', BBC News website, 18 May 2005. By contrast, Judge Morgan had been quite happy, in April 2001, to

Equally, as a measure of the decline in police driving standards, it was noted that deaths caused by police cars, often travelling in excess of the speed limit, had risen sharply, from 17 in 2000–1 to 36 in 2003–4 and 44 in 2004–5.[12]

In the summer of 2006, the DfT itself published a paper noting the curious discrepancy between the road accident figures as reported by the police and those shown by the records of NHS hospitals. While the police were claiming that the yearly number of people killed or seriously injured had dropped since the mid-1990s by 33 per cent, the hospitals gave a very different picture.

According to the police, the total number of emergency hospital admissions following traffic accidents in 1994–5 had been 38,641, which by 2002–3 had dropped to 31,010. According to the NHS, however, the figure for 1994–5 had been 32,285, and by 2002–3 this had risen to 36,611.[13]

In September 2006 the DfT finally conceded one of the central points which Safespeed's Paul Smith had been arguing for five years: that only 5 per cent of road accidents were caused by drivers who were breaking the speed limit. In the *Daily Telegraph*, Smith was quoted as saying 'the government's case for continuing to install cameras has been destroyed'.[14]

However, the government's determination to reduce accidents by focusing its efforts on speed still had surprising supporters. One of the more conspicuous was the Guardian's star environmental columnist George Monbiot, who had already published a ferocious attack on all those who dared to challenge the government's policy, describing them as the 'road rage lobby'.[15]

Foremost among the targets of his ire was Smith, whom he painted as a member of the 'boy racers' club', and as one of 'the anti-social bastards who believe they should be allowed to do what they want, whenever they want, regardless of the consequences'. 'With the help of some of the most convoluted arguments I've ever read', sneered Monbiot, Safespeed 'even seeks to prove that speed cameras "make our roads more dangerous"'.

Clearly Monbiot could not have read very far into Smith's 'convoluted arguments', or he would have seen that, far from arguing for a free-for-all on the roads, Smith's prime concern was

---

convict a Sunderland market trader, Steve Thoburn, on the criminal charge of selling bananas by the pound instead of in kilograms.

to return to a road safety policy that worked, based not on some abstract dogma but regulated by the methods which had formerly given Britain's traffic police such an enviable reputation and the UK the best road safety record in the world.

In February 2007 the DfT announced that the number of people killed in road accidents in the 12 months to September 2006 had risen to 3,210, compared with 3,177 in the same period a year earlier. As one report put it, these new figures came 'three months after the influential Commons Transport Select Committee said an obsession with cameras was responsible for a "deplorable" drop in the number of officers patrolling Britain's roads'.

Strongly supporting this point was Kevin Delaney, a former head of the Metropolitan Police traffic division, who said, 'any figures that show an increase against a downward trend ought to be ringing alarm bells in Whitehall, in local authorities and in police headquarters'. He went on, 'the deterrent effect on motorists of a police officer enforcing traffic regulations is incalculable, but we are seeing less and less of them'.[16]

Paul Smith would have agreed. George Monbiot would probably have dismissed the former head of the Metropolitan Police traffic division as just a 'boy racer' and an 'anti-social bastard'. Such had been the power of the great 'speed scare'.*

Notes

1. Commission for Global Road Safety press release, 8 June 2006.
2. Private information from the head of a traffic police division, 1992.
3. *Guardian*, 1 March 2000.
4. *Tomorrow's Roads: safer for everyone* (Department for Transport, March 2000).
5. J. Broughton, *et al.*, *A new system for recording contributory factors in road accidents*, TRL Report 323 (Transport Research Laboratory, 1998).

* In June 2007 further figures were announced showing that, while Britain had easily the highest number of speed cameras in Europe (4,875; Germany next highest with 3,108), UK road deaths per million of population (54) now put her well behind several other countries, such as the Netherlands (45) and Sweden (49). In a table comparing the yearly figures for road deaths across the EU25 between 2000 and 2004, the UK had fallen to 18th place. (Figures from European Speed Camera Database and European Transport Safety Council.)

6. *www.safespeed.org.uk*. Many of the arguments summarized below are rehearsed at length on Smith's website, which over the next few years was to establish itself as a leading and much-quoted authority on road safety issues.

7. *Cost recovery system for speed and red-light cameras: two year pilot evaluation*, Department for Transport report, published February 2003; prepared by Adrian Gains and Richard Humble of the PA Consulting Group; supervised by Professor Benjamin Heydecker and Dr Sandy Robertson, University College London.

8. For a full account of these distortions, see the Safespeed website, including an admission by Prof. Heydecker that 'regression to the mean' had not been allowed for, a basic statistical error.

9. *Sunday Telegraph*, 30 November 2003.

10. Avon and Somerset Safety Camera Partnership, *Annual Review*, 2004–5.

11. *Sunday Telegraph*, 25 September 2005.

12. R. Teers and T. Bucke, *Deaths during or following police contact: statistics for England and Wales, 2004/5* (2005).

13. *Road accident casualties: a comparison of STATS19 data with Hospital Episode Statistic* (DfT, June 2006).

14. *Daily Telegraph*, 29 September 2006.

15. *The Guardian*, 20 December 2005.

16. *Evening Standard*, London, 10 February 2007.

11

'We Love Unleaded'

How Confusion Over Lead Cost Billions

The environmental debate has long suffered from too little science. There has been plenty of emotion and politics, but scientific data have not always been prominently featured in environmental efforts and have sometimes been ignored, even when available.

William Reilly, Administrator of the
US Environmental Protection Agency, 1991[1]

February 1989 was, as we have seen, a good time for scares in Britain. Those over salmonella in eggs, and listeria, were still at their height. In Nottingham, as the 'Broxtowe Ten' went on trial, the 'satanic abuse' scare was just getting under way. Meanwhile much excitable media coverage was also now being directed to another, very different concern.

On 13 February, the eve of St Valentine's Day, a surreal scene unfolded at Buckingham Palace in London. Out into the forecourt stepped Her Majesty the Queen, to join a group of 30 school-children. Between them, they released 10,000 helium-filled balloons into the sky, each carrying the slogan 'I Love Unleaded Petrol' (in the case of the Queen, it was noted, her balloons should perhaps have read 'We love unleaded petrol').

It might have seemed a trifle paradoxical, in the name of 'cleaning up the environment', thus to pollute the environment with 10,000 scraps of disintegrating rubber. But this curious publicity stunt was the highpoint of a campaign being waged to highlight the damage done by leaded petrol to human health. Scarcely a day now went by when the fearsome dangers of this menace were not being drummed into the public mind, by the

222

Daily Mail, the *Sunday Times* or the BBC children's programme *Blue Peter*, all of which had taken up the cause with a vengeance.

So generally accepted had it become that lead in any form posed a serious threat to health that it was scarcely taken as odd when one of the nation's most senior policemen, the chief constable of the West Midlands, announced that he had prohibited his force from using lead bullets. But in no way did the sinister effects of lead seem more omnipresent than as an ingredient in the fuel which still powered most of Britain's cars, from the exhausts of which it supposedly poured out into the air to inflict untold damage on people's brains, particularly those of children.

Yet, a keen-eyed observer might have noted that not all the evidence seemed unanimous in supporting this view of the dangers of lead in petrol.

That summer, for instance, considerable coverage was given to a study of lead levels in the blood of local schoolchildren, recently carried out at Edinburgh University. This was because it had confirmed a close relationship between high lead levels and mental impairment, inability to concentrate, even a tendency to aggression. Markedly less notice, however, was paid to its conclusion that the cause of the poisoning appeared to lie almost entirely in lead from water pipes and paint. 'Lead from petrol fumes', the researchers were quoted as finding, 'barely contributed'.[2]

Had rather more attention been paid to a controversy which had already been raging for some years in America, the belief that leaded petrol was destroying the brains of a whole generation of children might not have been so unquestioningly accepted.

Stage One: How a Hazard Became a Scare

The story of lead provides yet another example of how a threat to health that was genuine could gradually become inflated into a major scare, going way beyond what was justified by the facts.

The 'lead scare' developed through three stages. The first, in the 1960s, came when it was suggested that there must be a danger from lead in petrol, before this was supported by proper evidence. As a result of this, in the early 1970s the first steps were taken in the USA to phase out leaded gasoline.

Stage two, in the late 1970s, came with the publication of an influential study which seemed to support this thesis, by showing that children were generally being damaged by exposure to lead at much lower levels than had previously been thought dangerous. Although in the 1980s this study provoked intense controversy when it was charged that the methods used to support it had been highly dubious, it lent powerful impetus to the drive behind phasing out the use of lead in petrol, which was now becoming unstoppable. The study also led to new ultra-cautious safety standards on lead in buildings, which would cost astronomic sums to enforce.

Stage three came when, in the 1990s, further evidence seemed to reveal a new danger from lead, through its leaching out into water supplies. Again, this danger was eventually shown to be baseless (not least by the scientist who had first raised it). But by now it had also inspired a draconian regulatory response, involving further astronomic costs.

The knowledge that lead can be damaging to human health dates back to Roman times. In 14 BC, the architect Vitruvius noted that water carried through lead pipes 'robs the limbs of the virtues of the blood'. Some historians have even suggested that wholesale lead poisoning, induced by the Romans' plumbing methods, was a significant factor in the decay of the Roman empire (our word 'plumbing' derives from *plumbum*, the Latin for lead).[3] But in modern times the nature of clinical lead poisoning has, of course, been much more precisely identified. Acute exposure to lead, chiefly from ingestion, can cause weakness, anaemia, and damage to the brain, inducing hallucinations, blindness and even death.

Over the centuries, the special properties of lead had caused it to be put to an ever-greater array of uses, ranging from cosmetics, and pigments in paint, to the pewter widely used in drinking vessels, plates and cooking implements. By the early twentieth century in America and Europe lead had become all but ubiquitous in the human environment, most significantly in paints, in children's toys, in water tanks and pipes and in the solder used in cans containing tinned food.

Then in 1921 a new use for lead was discovered. Three engineers working for General Motors in Dayton, Ohio, found that tiny amounts of lead added to petrol, in the form of a highly-toxic liquid compound, lead tetraethyl, had a miraculous effect on engine efficiency. By delaying ignition it eliminated the juddering known as 'knock' and allowed higher compression ratios, thus making significant savings on fuel, of 5 per cent or more. It was quickly adopted by oil companies as a routine additive to petrol.

Although in 1925 this practice was temporarily banned, following the deaths from lead poisoning of 19 workers employed in the manufacturing process and serious injuries to 149 more, this problem was soon overcome. Over the next four and a half decades, as car use rose exponentially, the amount of lead added to improve engine efficiency steadily rose, until by 1970 it had reached a worldwide annual peak of 380,000 tons (200,000 tons in America alone).

Long before this, however, around the time of World War Two,* there had already been growing awareness of the dangers posed by lead. In particular, steps began to be taken to address some of the most obvious and serious sources of lead poisoning, such as the ingestion of lead from cans, water supplies and paint.

The results were dramatic. Blood lead levels are measured in micrograms of lead per decilitre of blood; from the mid-1930s on the amount of lead showing up in blood in the USA began steadily dropping at a consistent rate of around 4 per cent a year, from 30 micrograms per decilitre in 1935 to 15 by 1970 (acute toxicity was assessed at 70 or more). The odd thing was that this downward curve remained remarkably constant through the 25 years after the war, during a time when the quantities of lead added to petrol rose by more than eight times.[4]

In the late 1960s, as the modern environmental movement got under way, not least in the USA, one of its chief concerns, alongside DDT, was the noxious smog which built up over American cities – notably Los Angeles – a major contributor to which was fumes from the exhausts of millions of automobiles. This concern, centred on the hydrocarbons and nitrous oxide that combined to form ground-level ozone, prompted the development of catalytic

---

* Leaded petrol had its own influence on the course of World War Two. Before the Battle of Britain in 1940, German fighter planes, such as the ME 109, had a performance edge over their British counterparts, such as the Spitfire, because in 1935 the Germans had bought, under licence from the USA, the right to add tetraethyl to their aviation fuel, considerably boosting its octane rating. Only just in time did the Royal Air Force acquire sufficient supplies of high-octane leaded fuel to give its Spitfires an advantage in terms of speed, which was to play a significant part in the outcome of the battle.

converters. These removed most of the gases but could not work effectively with lead, and it was this, rather than concern over lead itself, which first prompted oil companies to develop unleaded petrol.

In 1966, however, when a US Senate committee was conducting hearings into the proposed Clean Air Act,* its chairman, the Democrat Senator Ed Muskie, particularly focused on the potential dangers of lead in gasoline. Although, as yet, no serious evidence had been produced to indicate that lead from vehicle exhausts might pose a hazard to health (most of it did not pollute the air but dropped as a lead bromide powder onto the ground), Muskie had raised its profile as an alarming possibility.[5]

In 1970 the US Environmental Protection Agency (EPA) came into being, fired with zeal to clean up America's air, soil and water. In January 1971 its first administrator, William D. Ruckelshaus (who was shortly to ban DDT), declared that there was now 'an extensive body of information' to suggest that lead in gasoline posed 'a threat to public health'. This was a considerable over-statement. Virtually no such evidence existed. But the EPA's stance, combined with the growing popularity of catalytic converters, prompted environmentalists, politicians and journalists to join in the chorus for an end to lead in petrol, under the fashionable slogan 'Get the lead out'.

Over the next two years several studies appeared which showed that lead levels in dust in cities were much higher than those in rural areas, suggesting that this could be substantially attributed to deposits from vehicle exhausts.[6] This led the EPA, in November 1973, to insist that such lead-contaminated dust could pose a hazard to children suffering from pica, 'a psychological disorder characterized as an excessive habit of eating material (such as dust and dirt) unsuitable as food'.

It was primarily on this basis that, the following month, the EPA issued regulations demanding a sharp reduction of the lead content in all forms of gasoline. From 1 January 1975, the per-missible amount of lead in petrol was to be reduced over a four-year period by 75 per cent. It was the start of a process which, over the next quarter of a century, was to see leaded petrol completely

---

* Britain's own Clean Air Act, which helped to free London and other cities from smog, had been passed ten years earlier in 1956.

banned in the USA, the EU and many other countries across the world.

Yet so far the evidence on which all this had been set in train was meagre. Although the EPA was also taking steps to reduce further the use of lead in paint and water supply systems, it did not attempt to explain why blood lead levels had been consistently falling, to less than half their 1935 figure, during years when lead emissions from petrol had risen by 700 per cent.

All that had been established was that lead levels in dust were higher in urban areas and near to highways. There was still little evidence to explain just how these tiny quantities of lead might be damaging. The best the EPA itself could offer was that it put at risk those children who put lead-contaminated dust into their mouths.

What was needed was research that could demonstrate some clear connection between even small sub-clinical levels of lead in blood and actual damage to human health. At the end of the decade, it seemed, such a crucial study had at last appeared.

Stage Two: The Strange Affair of Dr Needleman

The lead scare really took off when, in March 1979, the prestigious *New England Journal of Medicine* published a paper by Dr Robert Needleman, a child psychologist from the University of Pittsburgh then working at the Harvard Medical School.

Between 1975 and 1978 Needleman and colleagues had studied lead levels in the teeth of 3,329 children in two Massachusetts communities. After singling out those with the highest and lowest lead counts, he had subjected them and their parents to various psychological tests. Although even the highest lead levels shown were way below the normally accepted threshold of toxicity, the study found that the classroom performance of the children with higher levels was 'significantly poorer' than that of those with a lower lead count. In every way their mental performance seemed inferior, from a three or four point differential in their IQs to their noticeably shorter attention span.

This seemed to provide such devastating evidence that even low lead levels could account for measurable mental impairment that the Needleman study soon attracted notice all over the world. It was the breakthrough that anti-lead campaigners had been waiting for. Even though the study did not ascribe poisoning to any particular cause, the very fact that such low levels of exposure could have such a marked effect was taken to confirm that lead emitted from vehicle exhausts might well be more dangerous than had been supposed, potentially affecting millions of children.

Not everyone, however, was so impressed by the Needleman study. In 1981 the journal *Pediatrics* published an article by another academic child psychologist, Dr Claire Ernhart, who had worked in the same field. Her own researches had suggested that the effects of lead were much too small to be detected by such a crude measure as IQ, except at levels of exposure so high as to be only just below what would be considered toxic.[7] She argued that Needleman's research was based on serious methodological flaws. In particular, she claimed that he had not sufficiently allowed for 'confounding variables' that might have explained the difference in IQ scores, such as poor schools or parental neglect.

In 1982, the EPA began a major review of air-quality standards for lead, and wanted to review all recent data on the health effects of lead exposure. The head of its 'environmental criteria and assessment office' convened an Expert Panel to look into the work of both Needleman and Ernhart.[8] When in 1983 the panel visited Needleman's laboratory to look at his data, he handed over six books of computer printouts, but said that only two panel members could examine them, and for only two hours.

Even during this cursory study, the panel found enough evidence to arouse profound doubts about Needleman's research. Although starting with 3,329 children, he had winnowed out so many, often for apparently arbitrary reasons, that he had ended up basing his conclusions first on 270 subjects, then on just 158. 'Exclusion of large numbers of eligible participants', the panel concluded, 'could have resulted in systematic bias.' In other words, it looked to the panel as though he might have selected his evidence to give the results he wanted.[9]

After levelling further criticisms at Needleman's methods, the Expert Panel concluded that his studies 'neither support nor refute the hypothesis that low or moderate levels of Pb (lead) exposure lead to cognitive or other behavioural impairments in children'. In plain English it found his researches to be valueless.

What happened next said much about the EPA and the growing politicization of science. After Needleman had made angry protests, with a lengthy 'refutation' of each of the panel's findings, he was allowed to present a new analysis of his data. By the time the panel presented its final report, it had, for reasons not properly explained, completely reversed its earlier position. Needleman's findings were now accepted, and formed a large part of the basis on which the EPA drew up its new regulations. These proposed that, from 1986 on, the amount of lead in gasoline would be cut by 91 per cent.

Announcing this in August 1984, the EPA's administrator Ruckelshaus declared: 'the evidence is overwhelming that lead is a threat to human health. This action will greatly reduce the threat, especially for pregnant woman and young children'. Referring to Needleman's research, he went on, 'recent evidence shows that adverse health effects from lead exposure may occur at much lower levels than heretofore considered safe'.[10]

Politically, it seemed, Needleman had won the argument, game, set and match. Scientifically, however, the outcome was rather less certain. In Britain, where steps were also now being taken to reduce the amount of lead in petrol, the Royal Commission on Environmental Pollution, under its chairman Professor Richard Southwood, published a report in April 1983 on 'Lead in the Environment'. After considering various studies of the effects of low-level lead exposure on children, of which Needleman's was easily the most prominent, it concluded, 'while work in this field is interesting, we do not consider that the results represent reliable evidence of the effects of small amounts of lead on the brain function of children'.*

Southwood thus failed to go along with the EPA's endorsement of Needleman. This was notable in that his report generally took as cautious a line as possible on the dangers of lead, based firmly on what would become known as the 'precautionary principle'. It recommended that further steps should be taken to reduce lead exposure from the most obvious sources, such as paint and plumbing. And although it could cite no very obvious reason why lead in petrol might be dangerous, it nevertheless recommended that, to be absolutely on the safe side, this should be phased out.

---

* Royal Commission on Environmental Pollution, ninth report, Cmnd 8852, April 1983. One of the commission members was Donald Acheson who, as Chief Medical Officer, was five years later to appoint Southwood to chair the DH's committee of inquiry into BSE.

Stating that much was still unknown about the effects of lead, Southwood also recommended that all kinds of further research should be carried out. Accordingly, a special study was made of the effects of a further 64 per cent reduction in lead in petrol, which came into force in Britain at the end of 1985. This did find that in 1986 there was a general fall in lead blood levels. But it also found that there had been a similar fall in 1985, before the new limit came into force. In other words, reducing the lead content of petrol had made virtually no difference. Indeed, both falls were in line with the decline in blood lead levels that had been taking place in Britain for years. Limiting lead in petrol – which anyway, according to the report, 'made only a relatively small contribution' to the total amount of lead in people's bodies – appeared to have had no significant effect.[11]

Then, in 1987, three British epidemiologists published their findings on what was the largest study to date comparing lead levels in children's teeth with mental performance. They concluded that by far the most important factor in determining children's IQs was the IQ of their parents. On the Needleman thesis, they uncompromisingly found 'no evidence to support the hypothesis that lead exposure as currently experienced by British children is of any relevance to their intellectual development'.[12]

In 1989 four more epidemiologists published a study based on lead levels in maternal blood samples in South Wales. These had shown a fall of around 20 per cent during a period when there had been no change in petrol sales in the area or in air lead levels. The researchers concluded that 'petrol lead was at most a minor contributor to blood lead'.[13]

Other researchers around the world, in these years, from America and Canada to Australia and New Zealand, were coming up with findings similar to all these studies. Yet none of this had any effect on what had by now become the general political and media consensus. The received view was, firstly, that even the slightest exposure to lead was damaging; and, secondly, that the best way to reduce it was to 'get the lead out' of petrol.

Such was the background to the campaign to which, in February 1989, the Queen was persuaded to lend her authority when she joined those schoolchildren at Buckingham Palace to send 10,000 balloons floating over London declaring their faith in the virtues of 'unleaded'. Needleman, now regarded by the US government as the leading authority in the field and by environmentalists as one of the heroes of the age, had certainly helped to shape history. But the going for his theory was about to become rather rougher.

In 1990 the US federal justice department brought an action against three corporations that had at different times owned a lead smelter in Utah. It was seeking substantial compensation for the hazard posed to local children by 250 acres of lead 'tailings' from the milling process. For its chief expert witness it hired Dr Needleman, who had already played a similar role in a long string of similar cases through the 1980s.

As expert witnesses for the defence, the companies retained two expert child psychologists. One was Dr Ernhart, whose public feuding with Needleman had continued through the decade. The other was Sandra Scarrs of the University of Virginia, who in 1983 had been one of the members of the EPA's Expert Panel that was most critical of Needleman's methodology.

In his affidavit, Needleman promised to allow any scientists wanting to inspect the data on which he had based his 1979 paper to spend as long as they wished at his Pittsburgh laboratory. The two psychologists took him at his word and on 20 September 1990, accompanied by defence lawyers, they arrived at the laboratory, to be greeted by a government attorney. Shown alone into a bare room, they were given six volumes of computer printouts containing Needleman's initial analyses of his data. Although these were not always easy to puzzle out, because they were coded and the investigators had been given only an incomplete key, Needleman refused to see the two women. They left at the end of the day, planning to return next morning.

The following day, on Needleman's instructions, the government attorney asked them to sign an agreement that they must treat everything they had seen in absolute confidence. They could discuss it orally in court, but nowhere else. Faced with what they saw as a gagging order, Ernhart and Scarrs refused. After several hours of negotiations between the lawyers, they also refused an order to hand over all their notes, and left the premises.

As they were later to explain, however, they had already seen enough to confirm all their doubts about Needleman's working methods. According to Scarrs, his first set of analyses had failed to show any relationship between lead levels and the intelligence tests.

'Not one single variable', she wrote, 'came out as statistically different between the top 10 per cent and bottom 10 per cent of the
sample.' Only by repeatedly rerunning the analyses, eliminating all
the variables that might interfere with his thesis, had he eventually
'got the results he wanted'.[14]

Before the psychologists could present their views in court, the
parties agreed to settle, with the defendants paying $63 million for
the contaminated site to be cleaned up. Four days before this
agreement was announced, the government lawyers asked the court
to order that Scarrs and Ernhart must return all their notes and
refrain from ever revealing what they had seen.

The two critics immediately concluded that the government was
trying to protect Needleman, because his research was the back-
bone of its lead policy. A legal battle ensued, with Needleman
claiming that to release his information to the defendants would
give the lead industry the chance 'to manipulate this data as it sees
fit'. On 26 April 1991 a federal district court judge ruled in favour
of the two psychologists on the grounds that there was 'something
inherently distasteful and unseemly in secreting either the fruits or
seeds of scientific endeavours'; particularly when, as here, this had
been paid for with taxpayers' money from the National Institutes
of Health (NIH).[15]

After their victory, Ernhart and Scarrs' first action in May was
to send a 60-page report on the affair to the NIH's Office of Scientific Integrity (OSI), asking for an investigation into whether
Needleman had been guilty of misconduct. They alleged that his
original data had shown 'no significant associations between lead
levels and child IQ', but they had then been treated to 'hundreds of
later analyses in which both control variables and children excluded from the sample were manipulated until "significant" results
were obtained'.[16] But Needleman's media supporters rallied to the
cause, notably with a seven-page feature in *Newsweek* naming lead
as 'the No.1 environmental threat to children'.[17]

That autumn the stakes were again dramatically raised when,
on 8 October, appearing on a television show, Dr James Mason,
assistant secretary for health at the US Department of Health and
Human Services, announced out of the blue that the HHS was
formally lowering the safe limit on blood lead levels from 25
micrograms per decilitre (already the lowest in the world) to just 10
micrograms.

The implications of this were awesome. As was immediately recognized and widely reported, lowering the threshold to this new level meant that the number of children in the USA formally 'at risk' from lead exposure would jump from 400,000 to 4.5 million. As the *Wall Street Journal* put it, in a three-page report in its 'Health and Science' section, 'Four Million Children in the US May be Affected'. This went on to give graphic details of 'How the poison does its damage'.[18]

But, as other reports were quick to point out, not only might this trigger off an avalanche of legal actions, where tenants and employees sued for being exposed to lead above the new 'safe' level. It could also require further remedial works, such as the removal of lead pipes, tanks and paint, in as many as 40 million American homes, along with extensive modifications to most municipal water supply systems. The total cost of all this, it was estimated, might eventually rise as high as $500 billion.[19]

In explaining why his department had come to such an earth-shaking decision, Mason fell back on a formula that had become familiar. 'Extensive studies', he claimed, had shown that exposure to lead, even at low levels, caused 'development deficits in children', lowering their IQ. There was little doubt as to which 'extensive studies' he was referring to. When his officials were formally asked whether the decision had been based on any research other than the Needleman study, they declined to answer.[20] Yet this very study, now again significantly shaping US national policy, was about to face an official investigation into charges that it had no scientific worth.

The investigation into Needleman's study, according to established practice, was handed over to a board appointed by his own University of Pittsburgh. Before it was concluded, Needleman's media supporters were again on the counter-attack, focusing their hostility on Ernhart and Scarrs. A savage feature on the two women by *Newsweek* accused them of being no more than spokespersons for the lead industry, from which one had 'received tens of thousands of dollars in research grants'.[21] Then Needleman himself joined in, suing his own university and the NIH in a legal bid to have the investigation halted.[22]

In fact, when the university board finally completed its deliberations, the result, as so often with official inquiries, found that little had been done wrong. It did find that Needleman had been 'deliberately misleading' in his explanation of how he selected the children on which his study was based. But it completely cleared him of the more serious charge that he done this to 'bias the results' of his study, and he was also acquitted of any 'scientific misconduct'. Indeed, the members of the board agreed, 'the evidence in support of Needleman's hypothesis' was actually 'stronger than reported in the 1979 paper'.[23]

Having successfully fought off this challenge, Needleman's scientific standing as the US government's chief adviser on lead now seemed unassailable. He continued to be given official acclaim for his work. In 1997 he received the Vernon Houk Award from the Society for Occupational and Environmental Health, for playing a 'vital leadership role in advancing national policy to prevent childhood lead poisoning'. In 2000 he was praised for new research purporting to show how '11 to 38 per cent of the nation's delinquency is attributable to high lead exposure'. In 2004 he was given the Rachel Carson Award for Integrity in Science.

Perhaps Needleman's greatest monument, however, came on 29 January 1996, when the EPA's administrator Carol Browner announced that any further use of lead in petrol was now to be banned (except in aircraft, racing cars and certain other off-road engines). 'The elimination of lead from gas', said Browner, 'is one of the great environmental achievements of all time.'[24]

Although the campaign to take lead out of petrol had originated in the USA, its message had long been spread across the world. One of the EPA's allies in the cause had been the World Bank, which made loans to Third World countries, such as Indonesia, conditional on their agreeing to phase out the use of lead in petrol.*

But the EPA had no more faithful disciple in this respect than the European Union. On 16 June, five months after the EPA's announcement, three European Commissioners called a press

---

* One form of pressure applied by the World Bank to client governments was to hold out to them the huge financial savings their countries would make by switching to unleaded petrol. The Bank's estimates included the money they would supposedly save on all those adults who would no longer require hospital treatment for 'hypertension caused by lead poisoning'. Even if this were not fanciful enough, the Bank also vastly inflated the estimated cash savings by basing them on the cost of hospital treatment in the USA. This of course had little relevance to costs in the countries concerned.

conference in Brussels to announce two new directives. One would enforce a 70 per cent reduction in vehicle emissions by 2010. The other would impose a total ban on any further use of lead in petrol by 2000. Even the Commission admitted that such advances would inevitably have their price. The new rules would cost 'consumers' an additional £4.8 billion a year, raise the average cost of a car by up to £600 and force oil companies into £70 billion-worth of new investment.

One cost, however, the Commission failed to include. To make up for the engine efficiency lost by the elimination of lead, Europe's vehicles would now need to consume considerably more fuel (5 per cent or more), significantly increasing their output of CO_2. Unleaded petrol also required greater use of crude oil in the refining process. Studies carried out for the Commission estimated the additional greenhouse gas emissions generated in the EU as a result of the switch to unleaded petrol at 15–17 million tonnes a year.[25] Since the invention of leaded petrol in the 1920s, the total 'savings' this had brought about worldwide were estimated at around 3 billion tonnes.*

For Dr Needleman, of course, this had not been his concern. But as there was already such an alarm among environmentalists over anything that might contribute to rising greenhouse gas emissions, it was interesting how this particular factor never got mentioned.

Stage Three: The Strange Affair of Professor Townsend

The story of lead was far from over. In the closing years of the twentieth century concern began rapidly rising over a new danger from lead in the environment. All over the developed world, and beyond, ownership of electronic goods was exploding. Between 1981 and 2005 global sales of personal computers reached more than one billion.[26] This was in addition to the continued soaring ownership of television sets. Even as early as 1996, the number of TVs and computers in the USA alone was estimated to have topped 300 million.[27] And a vital ingredient in all this electronic

---

* This approximate figure was calculated by Octel (a major supplier of lead additives) on the basis of estimating the additional amount of fuel that would have been needed since 1921 if there had been no savings from leaded petrol.

equipment, because of its uniquely valuable properties, was lead: notably in the solder used in circuit boards, and in the glass used for safety reasons in the cathode ray tubes behind both computer monitor and television screens (the largest of these may contain as much as four pounds of lead, as a protection against harmful X-rays).

In due course, almost all this lead would be disposed of by dumping it into landfill sites as waste. But so negative by now had lead's image become that something of a scare began to develop over what might follow if there was any possibility of it leaching out into the soil and water supplies.

By 1998 there were already discussions on both sides of the Atlantic about a possible need to prohibit the landfilling of electronic equipment altogether. In America, Massachusetts led the way by banning the burial of cathode ray tubes (CRTs). Meanwhile, in Florida Professor Tim Townsend, an environmental engineer, was carrying out a study for the state waste management authority that was to prove something of a landmark.

In December 1998 he gave a preview of the results of his experiments in submitting the glass from 36 cathode ray tubes to a standard test laid down by the EPA, the 'Toxicity Characteristic Leaching Procedure' (TCLP). They were certainly alarming. After mixing the crushed glass with an acid solution designed to simulate the conditions which might be found in a landfill site, Townsend found that most produced a lead leachate far in excess of the EPA's hazardous waste standard of 5 milligrams per litre, with concentrations ranging up to four times that 'safe' level, or more.

As Townsend put it to the media, 'I think the study for the very first time really gives conclusive data that the glass from cathode ray tubes does contain enough lead to be considered hazardous.'[28] When his paper was published in December 1999, it 'triggered a panic among many policy makers and lawmakers calling for a ban of all CRTs from landfills'.[29]

Among those who read it were officials of the European Commission in Brussels who were already discussing a highly ambitious new law, laying down rules for the disposal of electrical and electronic waste (the 'WEEE directive'). This now spawned a separate directive, the consequences of which were to be immense. Known as the 'RoHS directive' from its intention to 'restrict the use of certain hazardous substances in electrical and electronic equipment', it proposed not just to halt the landfilling of equipment containing certain metals, but to prohibit their use altogether. Although the banned metals also included mercury and cadmium, by far the commonest of them was lead.* From the moment the RoHS directive came into force in 2006, it would strictly prohibit the sale anywhere in the EU of any electronic equipment containing lead, whether manufactured in the EU or imported from elsewhere.[30]

Although Townsend's report had been almost universally accepted as a warning of how dangerous these metals might be in landfill sites, not generally noted was a passage making clear that its authors did 'not attempt to draw conclusions' beyond the results of their laboratory experiments. The fact that the EPA's testing method might 'not accurately reflect' what would happen 'under typical landfill conditions', they admitted, was outside the concern of their study.

Someone anxious to put this to the test was Clark Akatiff, a former professional geographer who had become 'landfill manager' for the Californian city of Palo Alto. The Townsend study was particularly relevant to his concerns because, in 2001, it prompted the state of California to ban any further landfilling of television sets and computer monitors. Palo Alto was known as the centre of California's 'Silicon Valley': the headquarters of several famous electronics firms including Hewlett Packard, the world's largest computer manufacturer.

Akatiff therefore carried out his own study, based not on laboratory tests but on what was actually happening on his own landfill site. This was ringed by ten monitoring wells, six of which showed no lead content in the leachate from the site at all. Four showed infinitesimally small amounts of lead, the highest rating being 5.5 parts per billion. This was 1,000 times lower than the EPA's limit of 5 parts per million, and 4,000 times lower than the figures recorded by Townsend in his lab.[31]

The Palo Alto manager hastened to add that he was only offering the findings from one comparatively small landfill site,

---

* A report by the Solid Waste Association of North America (SWANA) in 2004 showed that of the 130,000 tons of heavy metals placed in US landfills in 2000, 98 per cent was lead (mercury and cadmium making up the remaining 2 per cent).

although he observed that, since it had been established 70 years earlier, it probably did not conform to the even more exacting pollution standards applied to newer and larger sites. He went on to explore the economic implications of the California ban, the cost of which had been estimated over ten years at up to $1 billion (multiply that figure across the USA, let alone the rest of the world, and it could have become hundreds of billions of dollars).

Recycling the glass in CRTs was very expensive, as Palo Alto had already found from its own experience. It sent its glass to a lead smelting plant in Missouri, at a cost that was projected to reach $250,000 over the same ten years. But such opportunities for recycling glass in the USA were also strictly limited. Any attempt to assess the real cost of the ban would have to take into account the huge social and environmental price paid for shipping large quantities of CRTs and other electronic equipment overseas to countries such as China, to be 'recycled' in a manner which was 'both dangerous to the workers and results in widespread environmental pollution'.

So influential had Townsend's study become that, faced with the kind of practical questions raised by Akatiff, the Florida professor and his team in 2003 published the results of a further study, this time based on monitoring the leachates from 11 actual landfill sites.[32] The results, as the Palo Alto study had suggested, were startling. Where lab tests had shown lead leachate from computer monitors to average 413 milligrams per litre, the real-life results averaged only 4.1 mg, less than 1 per cent of the lab figure. The results for leachate from the lead solder in computer circuit boards were very similar. The EPA's standard test showed 162 mg, whereas the actual figure was 2.2 mg, nearly 100 times smaller.

Townsend's new figures, in short, not only showed that the genuine hazard from lead leachate was infinitely lower than his earlier study had suggested. They were also well within the EPA's own very conservative 'safe' limit. And this new data came from the very team whose earlier figures had set off such a panic, prompting dozens of lawmaking bodies to take drastic and costly action to avert a danger now shown to be imaginary.

Among those bodies was the European Commission which, in January the same year, had just won approval for its RoHS directive, 2002/95. This not only banned putting electronic equipment containing lead into landfill but went very much further, in outlawing the use of lead and five other metals altogether. 'The most effective way of ensuring the significant reduction of risks to health and the environment', said the directive, would be to replace them with materials that were safer.

The consequences of this new law would of course extend far beyond the EU itself. It meant that, within three years, lead components would have to be removed from all the hundreds of millions of electrical and electronic products imported into the EU each year, from the USA, China and scores of other countries round the world. Furthermore, they and their counterparts within the EU itself would have to spend untold sums having to devise alternative methods of achieving the same purposes, using new and often untried materials.

This problem was also now concerning the EPA, which had done so much to set the whole lead scare in motion in the first place. It commissioned a team from the University of Tennessee to carry out a full study of the likely environmental impact of substitutes for lead in the solder used in almost all electronic products.

When in 2005 the team published its 472-page report, 'Solder in electronics: a life-cycle assessment', its findings gave rise to considerable dismay. The researchers had looked at every stage of the life-cycle of lead-substitute solders, from the initial mining and refining process, through their application in the production of electronic products, to their eventual disposal for recycling. [33]

At every step along the way, the report found, the environmental and health impacts of the materials likely to be used as a substitute compared negatively with those of lead. Because their melting point was invariably much higher than that of lead, they required significantly more energy consumption (giving off more CO_2 emissions). These higher temperatures also raised serious health issues, affecting both the workers who assembled the products and those who would eventually have to recycle them.

But by now the EU legislation forcing the switch from lead solders to those substitutes was irreversible (indeed other countries, led by Japan, were now following suit).

Back in 2003 the UK's Department of Trade and Industry (DTI) had produced a first 'regulatory impact assessment' on the RoHS directive, admitting that it was 'very difficult to quantify the precise costs of the Directive, given its complexity and scope of impact'.

Only 'limited information' was available about 'the extent and cost of substituting the banned substances'.[34]

The industries directly affected, however, had already begun to make their own calculations and were shocked by what they found. Orgalime, a trade association of electronics manufacturers in Europe, had estimated the cost of changes required to switch to lead-free solder alone at £10 billion, to which had to be added higher material and energy costs of around £200 million a year.

By 2005, when it published the regulations needed to implement the new law in the UK, the DTI was admitting that the costs to the UK alone might be as much as £1.3 billion but offered no figure for its supposed benefits. This did not prevent the energy minister Malcolm Wicks putting his signature to the document, declaring, 'I have read the regulatory impact assessment and am satisfied the benefits outweigh the costs.'[35]

By March 2006 only four months remained before the regulations came into force. At this point a bizarre little horror story exploded into British headlines, which reflected just how little Mr Wicks and his colleagues actually knew of how their new law was meant to work in practice.

One of the many industries that would be affected by the lead ban was that responsible for building and repairing musical organs, thousands of which were installed in cathedrals, churches and concert halls across the land. Most use an electric blower to push the air into the organ pipes, which creates the sound. But most of these pipes themselves are made of a lead-tin alloy, for which no workable substitute has ever been found.

As soon as the RoHS directive had first been mentioned back in January 2001, Doug Levey, of the Institute of British Organ Builders (IBO), wrote to the DTI to clarify precisely to which parts of an organ the proposed law, relating to 'electrical and electronic equipment', would apply. Of course he recognized that it would become illegal to use lead in the blower, or in any electronic controls operated from the keyboard. But what he above all needed to confirm was that the pipes themselves would not be regarded as 'electrical equipment' simply because the blower was worked by electricity. This was crucial because, without the ability to install new lead pipes, every organ in Europe would eventually fall silent.

Five years later, long after the directive and regulations had been published, Mr Levey had still never had a reply to his letter. In

February 2006, he therefore wrote to the relevant officials in the European Commission. They merely told him that the onus in determining whether any 'product' was covered by the directive lay with the 'producer', as 'the person best placed to assess the characteristics of his product'.[36] On this basis, the IBO concluded that, although the directive applied to the electrical adjuncts to an organ, it did not apply to the pipes. To describe them as 'electrical equipment' would be like claiming that, just because a building is fitted with air conditioning, the entire structure must count as 'electrical equipment'.

To the astonishment of the organ builders, however, the DTI officials disagreed. They took the view that the organ pipes were covered by the Commission's directive, whatever the Commission itself might say. This seemed so absurd that the issue began to win coverage in the national press. This prompted a statement to the European Parliament by Margot Wallström, who was not only now a commission vice-president but had previously been the environment commissioner responsible for putting the RoHS directive into law. 'You can rest assured', she twice stated, 'that the directive does not cover church organ pipes'.

The following week, the DTI officials again insisted, at a meeting with the IBO, that, whatever Commissioner Wallström might say, in their view the directive did apply to organ pipes. After 1 July organs would be treated as 'electrical equipment'. Although, they conceded, organ-builders could continue to use lead for repairing organs, any use of lead in new organs would be prohibited (even though no organ pipe was ever thrown away, because the lead in it would invariably be melted down for recycling into a new organ pipe).

For weeks the argument very publicly continued, like a pantomime, with one side shouting 'yes it does', the other 'no it doesn't', until eventually the embarrassment this was creating for the DTI ministers became too great for them to bear. A form of words was found to enable them to climb down without admitting they had got it wrong. The organ builders were allowed to know that their craft could continue undisturbed.

As if the DTI officials had learned nothing whatever from this debacle, it then emerged that they were trying exactly the same trick on another, much larger industry. In 2004 the Lighting Association, representing thousands of firms manufacturing and selling every kind of lighting product, had been assured by the DTI that the RoHS directive would apply only to the electrical components in household lighting, such as switches and plugs. In March 2006, however, the Association discovered, almost by chance, that the officials had changed their mind. Now, they had decided, the lead ban would apply to an entire lighting assembly. This included lead in chandeliers, the minute quantities of lead in the glazing on pottery lamps, the lead solder holding the glass in Tiffany-style lamps, everything.

For the industry this threatened catastrophe. Two hundred members of the Lighting Association faced bankruptcy, putting 4,000 people out of work in the UK alone, and untold numbers more in China and the developing world, from which much decorative lighting was now imported.

At the end of May, barely a month before the deadline, the Association asked the officials why their interpretation of the EU law had changed when, for the purposes of the companion WEEE directive, they were still sticking to their previous view that decorative lighting was not included. Having put the entire industry through months of anguish, the DTI officials now said that, having looked at the issue again, they were reverting to their earlier position. Britain's lighting industry was reprieved.[37]

Thus, on 1 July 2006, did the EU's ban on the use of lead in electrical and electronic equipment finally come into effect. Orgalime, the Europe-wide trade association representing the electronics industry, had by now raised its estimate of the overall cost of the switchover to £44 billion. The research and paperwork involved in developing substitute metals alone, it estimated at more than £10 billion. An American study showed the cost of compliance to its exporters at £2 billion.

Apart from their financial cost, it was also generally recognized that the new materials were not as reliable as lead. The electronic equipment using them would probably be less durable and would break down more often (which was why the EU directive exempted military uses from its ban).

Typical of the problems the new law had imposed on vast numbers of small firms were those reported by Lascar Electronics, a specialist manufacturer of digital instruments in Wiltshire. Five of its senior staff had spent much of the previous year sorting out the vast array of technical problems posed by the need to comply with the RoHS directive, at a cost of more than £100,000. What alarmed them as much as anything was to discover how few technical procedures were available to measure whether certain combinations of metals met the directive's exacting technical requirements or not.[38]

In some ways the greatest costs, however, would not arise in Europe at all but in China and other developing countries in the East. The week after the directive came into force, it was reported from China that it was posing huge and in some cases insuperable problems to the 5,000 companies which exported $56 billion-worth of electronic and electrical appliances a year, much of it to the EU. One manufacturer alone, Guangzhou AC Panasonic, announced that a quarter of its 208 suppliers, responsible for making 7,268 assembly parts, would be unable to meet the new standards imposed by the directive.[39]

This was to say nothing of the human price to be paid by those tens of thousands of workers who would have to endure the fumes and much higher temperatures given off by the metal alloys now being used as a substitute for lead. This was a threat to health of which even the EPA itself had warned. Coming from the people who had set the great lead scare on its way in the first place, they must have known what they were talking about.

Notes

1. *Washington Post*, 20 August 1991.
2. G. O. Thompson, *et al.*, 'Blood-lead levels and children's behaviour: results from the Edinburgh Lead Study', study carried out by Department of Education, University of Edinburgh, *Journal of Child Psychology and Psychiatry*, July, 30 (4) (1989), 515–28. An earlier paper by the same team, M. Fulton, *et al.*, 'The influence of blood lead on the ability and attainment of children in Edinburgh', had been published in *The Lancet*, May, 30, 1, 8544 (1987), 1221–6.
3. Jack Lewis, 'Lead Poisoning – A Historical Perspective', *Environmental Protection Agency Journal*, May (1985). See also, Richard Faulk and John Gray, 'Getting the Lead Out – The Misuse of Public Nuisance Litigation by Public Authorities and Private Counsel', Institute for Legal Reform website (2006).
4. See graph, 'Lead in Gasoline – Environmental Issues', International Lead and Zinc Research Organization (1991). Although accurate data for blood lead levels before recent decades are not easy to come by,

when this graph was originally published it was based on figures gathered from a wide range of sources, fully referenced.

5. See Faulk and Gray (2006) for a detailed summary of how lead came to be banned in gasoline in the USA.
6. E.g. 'Airborne Lead in Perspective 30', National Academy of Sciences Committee on Biologic Effects of Airborne Pollutants (1972).
7. *Science*, vol. 253, 23 August 1991.
8. *Ibid.* and 25 November 1983.
9. *AIM Report*, Accuracy in Media, xxi–6, March 1992.
10. 'The EPA wants more lead out', *Time*, 13 August 1984.
11. UK Blood Lead Monitoring Programme, Pollution Report No. 28, Department of the Environment, 1987 (HMSO, London, 1990).
12. S. Pocock, D. Ashby and M. A. Smith, 'Lead Exposure and Children's Intellectual Performance', Department of Clinical Epidemiology, Royal Free Hospital School of Medicine, and Department of Child Psychiatry, Institute of Child Health, London, *International Journal of Epidemiology* (Oxford University Press, 1987).
13. P. Elwood, *et al.*, 'Evidence of a fall in cord blood lead levels in South Wales 1984–5', *Environmental Geochemistry and Health*, Vol. 12–13 (1990).
14. *Science*, 23 August 1991, pp. 843–4.
15. *Ibid.*
16. *Washington Times*, 18 December 1991.
17. *Newsweek*, 15 July 1991.
18. *Wall Street Journal*, 14 October 1991.
19. *Washington Times*, 18 December 1991.
20. *AIM Report* (1992).
21. *Newsweek*, 16 March 1992.
22. *Wall Street Journal*, 2 April 1992.
23. *Journal of NIH Research*, 4 (1992), p. 44.
24. EPA press release, 29 January 1996.
25. See J. M. Dunne, 'A comparison of emission control technology cars and their influence on exhaust emissions and fuel economy', Warren Spring Laboratory, Report LR770 (AP); 'ERGA Air Pollution Summary Report', XI/98/84, European Commission, March 1984; Netherlands Position Paper to Commission Motor Vehicle Emissions Group, 10 January 1991.
26. D. J. Gattuso, 'Mandated Recycling of Electronics', Competitive Enterprise Institute (2005).
27. T. Townsend, *et al.*, 'Characterization of lead leachability from cathode ray tubes using the Toxic Characteristic Leachability Procedure', Florida State University, Florida Center for Solid and Hazardous Waste Management (1999).

28. 'TVs, Computer Monitors Contain High Lead Levels, Study Finds', *University of Florida News*, 3 December 1998.
29. Gattuso (2005).
30. Directive 2002/95/EC on the restriction of the use of certain hazardous substances in electrical and electronic equipment, Official Journal L 037, 13/02/2003 P. 0019–0023.
31. C. Akatiff, 'Is this ban really necessary? A critical investigation of the CRT ban', paper given to a SWANA Western Regional Symposium, May 2002, published on the Internet.
32. Yong-Chul Jang and Timothy G. Townsend, 'Leaching of Lead from Computer Printed Wire Boards and Cathode Ray Tubes by Municipal Solid Waste Landfill Leachates', *Environmental Science & Technology*, Vol. 37, No. 20 (2003).
33. J. Geibig and M. Socolow, 'Solder in electronics; a life-cycle assessment', University of Tennessee for the Environmental Protection Agency, September 2005.
34. *www.dti.gov.uk/files/file29932.pdf*.
35. *Ibid.*
36. *Sunday Telegraph*, 26 March 2006, based on documents supplied by the IBO.
37. *Sunday Telegraph*, 31 May 2006.
38. *Sunday Telegraph*, 11 June 2006.
39. *People's Daily*, 11 July 2006.

12

Smoke and Mirrors

How They Turned 'Passive Smoking' Into a Killer, 1950–2007

A custom loathsome to the eye, hateful to the nose, harmful to the brain, dangerous to the lungs, and in the black stinking fume thereof nearest resembling the horrible stygian smoke of the pit that is bottomless.

King James I, *A Counterblast To Tobacco*, 1604

The effects of other people smoking in my presence is so small it doesn't worry me.

Professor Sir Richard Doll, *Desert Island Discs*, BBC Radio 4, 2001

At the end of World War Two, tobacco smoking in Britain was almost universal. More than four-fifths of adult males were smokers. People were free to smoke at work or at play, in pubs, offices, shops, trains, buses, cinemas, theatres, town halls, village halls, aircraft, ships, almost anywhere except churches, art galleries, concert halls and libraries.

Sixty years later it had become illegal to smoke tobacco in any 'enclosed public space' where people might gather together, apart from private homes or prison cells. In many instances it was even made an offence to smoke in the open air, if it was in proximity to a building where smoking was prohibited, such as an office block, a hospital or on a railway station platform.

This remarkable social transformation, which was paralleled across the western world, came about through three stages. The first began shortly after World War Two when new evidence began to accumulate to show that smokers did serious and often fatal damage to their own health. For several decades this resulted in a steady but dramatic decline in their numbers, gradually dividing the population into three groups: more or less addicted smokers; generally tolerant non-smokers; and those who were so convinced that smoking was a dangerous social evil that they became fiercely intolerant anti-smokers.

The second stage began when these anti-smokers turned their attention on the substantial minority who, despite all the evidence that it was dangerous, had persisted in the habit. No longer was it enough to show that smokers harmed themselves. This horrifying and deadly practice could only be eliminated if it could be shown that they were also harming others, by way of what became known as 'passive smoking'.

For nearly two decades, the battle was fought over a succession of scientific studies, each side enlisting its army of supporters. The anti-smokers seized on a succession of new studies which purported to show that 'environmental tobacco smoke' was doing much more harm to non-smokers than had previously been recognized. But more comprehensive studies then emerged from other scientists who had come to the opposite conclusion, finding no evidence to support this view.

Stage three came with the approach of the twenty-first century. With remarkable speed, the anti-smokers seized the social and political high ground. In just a few short years, all over the world, they managed to impose new laws that banned smoking in almost any 'enclosed public space'. But they did so on the basis of claims about the damage done by passive smoking that had become ever more extreme, parting all company with the scientific facts. In the end, the victory of the anti-smokers in their war on passive smoking had become yet another tribute to the power of the 'scare'.

Stage One: Tobacco is Established as a Killer

The first and still the most famous 'anti-smoker' of them all appeared only a few years after tobacco was first brought to Europe from North America. In his celebrated *Counterblast to Tobacco* of 1604, King James I of England not only launched a ferocious diatribe against what he considered to be a 'vile and stinking' custom. He was in no doubt that this new tobacco was so damaging to health that it was a killer. A man may 'smoke himself to death with it', as he put it, 'and many have done'.

Many references through the next three centuries show that smoking tobacco was widely regarded as offensive to non-smokers. When in 1845 Queen Victoria bought Osborne House on the Isle of Wight as a palatial retreat, she had monograms placed above the doorways of 48 of its 49 rooms showing her initial intertwined with that of her beloved Prince Albert, 'V and A'. Only one doorway carried the letter 'A' alone, to mark the single room in the house where her husband was permitted to smoke. In 1890, the city of New Orleans became the first in the USA to ban smoking on tramcars, to spare non-smoking passengers from exposure to its noxious fumes.

We also find not a few echoes of King James's belief that tobacco was seriously dangerous to smokers' health. In the USA, by 1836, Samuel Green could record how it was well established 'that thousands and tens of thousands die of diseases of the lungs generally brought on by tobacco smoking ... a man will die of an infusion of tobacco as of a shot through the head.'[1]

Despite such caveats, the popularity of smoking continued to grow until, by the middle of the twentieth century, it reached its peak. In no way did it seem odd that world statesmen such as Churchill, Roosevelt and Stalin should all be seen smoking together (Hitler, as a fanatical anti-smoker, was the only exception among the wartime leaders), any more than it did to see the stars light up in almost any Hollywood film. In Britain a nationwide survey in 1948, the first of its kind, showed that no fewer than 82 per cent of adult males could now be classified as smokers.[2] Although the figure for women was only half as high, the rate of female smoking was rising steadily.

The previous year, however, two medical statisticians from the Medical Research Council, Richard Doll and Professor Austin Bradford Hill, had decided to investigate the causes of what they described as 'the phenomenal increase in the number of deaths attributed to cancer of the lung'. In 25 years this had risen fifteen-fold, from 612 deaths in 1922 to 9,287 in 1947.

The basis for the landmark paper they published in 1950 was their study of 649 men and 60 women admitted to a group of London hospitals suffering from carcinoma of the lung.[3] Of the men 647, all but two, turned out to be smokers, as did 41 or two-thirds of the women. The evidence seemed overwhelming that earlier researchers who had suggested that there might be a link between smoking and lung cancer were right. So impressed was Doll by the findings of their researches that, as a smoker himself, he gave up the habit two-thirds of the way through the study.

In October 1951 the two men embarked on a much more ambitious project. They wrote to all male doctors in the UK asking for their co-operation in a long-term study designed to track the connection between smoking and a range of diseases, and assess how much smoking might shorten a human lifespan. 34,439 agreed to participate. When the first results of the study were published in 1956, this confirmed that both lung cancer and heart problems were found significantly more often in long-term smokers than in non-smokers. Further studies carried out at regular intervals over the next 50 years indicated that more than 50 per cent of the subjects who smoked eventually died from diseases known to be smoking-related; and that smoking can decrease expectation of life by up to ten years.

The importance of these researches by Doll and Hill, powerfully endorsed in 1962 by a Royal College of Physicians report on 'Smoking and Health', was that they for the first time established an overwhelming case that tobacco can do serious damage to smokers' health. Gradually the significance of their message percolated into the public consciousness, which was the chief reason why, by the 1960s, the smoking habit in Britain was markedly declining. By 1974, as the first curbs were introduced on tobacco advertising, the number of adult males smoking had already dropped to 51 per cent. For adults as a whole the figure was 45 per cent. By 1982 this had fallen still further, to 35 per cent.[4]

Thus far, almost all the focus of attention had been on the self-inflicted harm tobacco could do to smokers themselves. As early as 1959, however, the American Cancer Society had begun to reflect on whether damage might also be done to those non-smokers who breathed in the smoke of others: what came to be known as 'environmental tobacco smoke' or 'involuntary smoking'. They therefore commissioned a long-term study even more ambitious than the 'Doctors' Study' by Doll and Hill. Its purpose was to 'measure the relation between environmental tobacco smoke, as estimated by smoking in spouses, and long-term mortality from tobacco-related disease'.

This project, which would eventually be associated with the names of the two academics that directed it, James Enstrom and Geoffrey Kabat, both non-smokers, was based on 118,094 adult Californians, whose health was to be carefully monitored over many years. Particular attention was to be paid to the health of 35,561 subjects who had never smoked, married to partners who regularly smoked. The findings of the Enstrom/Kabat study, which was to be the largest ever carried out into the effects of passive smoking, would not be known for several decades.

Stage Two: The Building of a 'Consensus'

Inevitably, as awareness of the dangers of smoking grew, and two out of every three adults were now non-smokers, the thoughts of the anti-smoking lobby turned to the possibility of achieving a ban on tobacco altogether. The rich and powerful tobacco industry was by now very much on the defensive, terrified not just of an eventual complete ban but more immediately of the prospect of an avalanche of legal claims for compensation (hence its persistent refusal to admit publicly that smoking could harm human health at all).

There were, however, distinct political obstacles in the way of making tobacco illegal. One was the fact that a third of adults still smoked, and would fight, as it were, to the death, for their right to continue doing so. Another was the fact that governments continued to derive very substantial revenue from taxing tobacco. Most decisive of all was simply that, to politicians at the end of the 1970s, such a radical step would have seemed unthinkable.

This left the more committed anti-smokers far from happy. In 1980, when legislation proposing mild curbs on smoking was defeated in Maryland, James Repace, later to become well-known as one of America's leading anti-smoking campaigners, was so angry that he said, 'people aren't going to stand for this. Now the facts are clear, you're going to see non-smokers becoming a lot more violent. You're going to see fights breaking out all over'.[5]

Frustrated in their desire for a total ban, the campaigners chose to approach the problem obliquely. They would focus public attention on the risk faced by all those people, particularly children, who, while not smoking themselves, were still being daily exposed to smoke exhaled by others. This would enable the anti-smokers to seize the moral high ground. No longer would they just be trying to defend people from themselves, they would now be defending the majority from being made the helpless victims of a selfish minority. This would eventually tip the whole balance of the debate.

In the 1980s hundreds of millions of dollars began to be invested in studies which might produce unarguable proof that 'environmental tobacco smoke' (ETS) posed a far greater danger to the health of non-smokers than had so far been recognized. Nevertheless, the evidence they needed was to prove elusive. Two early bites at the cherry were the reports produced in 1986 by the US Surgeon General and the US National Research Council.[6] Even the UK's leading anti-smoking lobbying organization ASH (Action on Smoking and Health) later had to concede that these two official surveys were not able to come up with much more in the way of hard evidence than suggesting that 'an association between ETS and coronary heart disease was biologically plausible'.[7] The reports also had to admit that 'the epidemiological evidence was inconclusive'.

In 1989 the US Surgeon General tried a new angle. This time he rested his claim that environmental tobacco smoke must be dangerous on the fact that it contains 'over 4,000 chemicals, some of which have marked irritant properties, and some 60 are known or suspected carcinogens'.[8]

This argument was picked up in 1992 by the Environmental Protection Agency, when it produced its own lengthy review of all the evidence it could find against passive smoking.[9] Noting that recent epidemiological studies had more than doubled 'the size of the database' on passive smoking since 1986, the EPA's headline claim was that '3,000 lung cancer deaths per year' could be 'estimated to be attributable to ETS in the United States'. In the small print, however, it had to concede 'there are statistical and modelling uncertainties in this estimate, and the true number may be higher or lower'.

The EPA's summary of its case again began with the 'biological plausibility' of the belief that inhaling carcinogens must be harmful. This had been demonstrated, it said, by 'lifelong inhalation studies' on hamsters, 'intrapulmonary implantations' in rats and 'skin painting' in mice, all of which showed that the ingredients in tobacco smoke were carcinogenic. The report went on to consider 19 studies of female non-smokers living with husbands who smoked. Of these, 17 had observed higher risks of lung cancer and six of these were 'statistically significant'. It was on 11 of these studies that the EPA based its 'estimate' that ETS was causing '3,000 cancer deaths a year'.

In general the EPA's report almost entirely relied on such 'estimates', based on the claims of other researchers, which it made little attempt to question. This was well illustrated by its section on the increasingly fashionable hypothesis that passive smoking might be responsible for the increase in 'sudden infant death syndrome' (SIDS), or cot death.

The EPA here began by offering yet another 'estimate', without evidence, that ETS exposure contributed '150,000 to 300,000 cases annually of lower respiratory tract illness in infants and children'. It then stated that, in the US, 'more than 5,000 infants die of SIDS annually', adding, again without evidence, that 'the linkage with maternal smoking is well established'. The Surgeon General and the WHO, it went on, 'estimate that more than 700 infant deaths a year from SIDS are attributable to maternal smoking'.

At this point, however, just when the EPA might have been expected to come out with its own endorsement of this claim, the report for once held back from accepting other people's figures. Contradicting its earlier statement that the link with parental smoking was 'well established', it concluded 'there is not enough direct evidence supporting the contribution of ETS exposure to declare it a risk factor'.

In fact the EPA's caution on this issue was more justified than it realized. Repeatedly in the years that followed, on both sides of the Atlantic, attempts would be made to argue that exposure to tobacco smoke had been the key factor in the rise of SIDS. But these claims invariably overlooked one centrally relevant fact. In Britain, the incidence of cot death had risen sharply in the 1970s and 1980s, until it peaked in 1988, after which it began an equally dramatic fall. In 1971, when this cause of death was first officially classified as SIDS, its incidence in the UK had been 0.3 per thousand births. By 1988 this had risen by a startling 500 per cent, to 2 deaths per thousand births.[10] But these were precisely the years when smoking in Britain, by both men and women, had been going through its sharpest decline, from 45 per cent to just over 30 per cent.

The two graphs ran so obviously in opposing directions that, whatever else might have caused the rise of SIDS, it could not have been environmental tobacco smoke. Yet, as can be seen from a glance through the 'literature' on this subject in the 1990s, a minor academic industry was now springing up to prove the exact opposite. So blinkered were these researchers in their determination to pin the blame for cot deaths on smoking that they never took the elementary step of putting these two sets of figures together.*

This self-deluding fixation with SIDS provided a telling insight into just how scientifically undisciplined these attempts to establish the case against passive smoking had become. By now, in the 1990s, new studies designed to highlight its dangers were coming thick and fast. With governments, agencies and well-endowed cancer charities showing ever-greater readiness to provide funding, it was a lucrative field of research. The prize was to come up with the most headline-worthy 'estimate' of the additional risk of disease and death faced by non-smokers exposed to others' smoke.**

Among the projects which attracted most attention were those based on collating a series of papers by other researchers (known as 'meta-analysis'), such as that which in 1997 reviewed 37 epidemiological studies of lung cancer. This enabled the review to claim that living with a smoker gave a non-smoker an additional 24 per cent risk of cancer: a figure which might have seemed alarming until it was recalled that, since non-smokers' chances of contracting lung cancer were so low, even 24 per cent would only have represented a very marginal increase.[11]

The researchers found rather greater scope for this tactic when they turned to the impact of passive smoking on heart disease, since this was the cause of death of nearly 30 per cent of all the 2.4

---

* For years to come, whenever lobby groups repeated this claim, linking ETS and cot death, the BBC and many British journalists would report them parrot-fashion, without bothering to check the facts.
** One of the more imaginative efforts, which made headlines on both sides of the Atlantic in the summer of 1989, was a study by Professor John Relf of Colorado State University that claimed to show that dogs living in the same house as a smoker had a '30 per cent above-average risk of getting lung cancer'. When questioned after publishing his paper, he admitted that cases of lung cancer in dogs were so 'extremely rare' that it was difficult to establish the point one way or another. It later emerged that he had based his findings on only a single animal ('Dog ends', *Daily Telegraph*, 23 August 1989).

million people who died in the USA each year. In 1991 a US study made headlines by claiming that passive smoking now ranked third highest in the list of preventable causes of death in the USA, behind active smoking and alcohol abuse. Non-smokers living with smokers, it found, had an increased risk of heart disease of 'around 30 per cent'.[12]

In 1996 an even larger study for the America Cancer Society, a spin-off of the major ongoing California research project launched in 1959, did not dare go so high, estimating the increased risk at only '20 per cent'. Nevertheless, this was enough to support its headline-winning claim that 'ETS might account for an estimated 35,000 to 40,000 heart disease deaths per year in the United States'.* In 1997 a review of 19 studies raised this additional risk figure to 24 per cent. But what attracted notice here was its claim that the 'immediate risk' caused by 'a single environmental exposure' (just one whiff of tobacco smoke) could be as high as 34 per cent.** In 1999 another review of 18 studies upped the added risk figure to 25 per cent. But here, absurdly, the separate figures given for men (22 per cent) and women (24 per cent) both came out lower than the average.[13]

Nowhere in the world was more interest focused on the dangers of passive smoking than in California, which in 1993 had become the first state to ban smoking not only in workplaces, bars and restaurants, but also within a yard and a half of any public building and on its famous beaches. It was therefore appropriate that, in 1999, the California Environmental Protection Agency should produce the most comprehensive catalogue of the dangers of passive smoking to date. High on the list of 18 separate disorders it now claimed could be ascribed to ETS was SIDS. After continuing

---

* K. Steenland, *et al.*, 'Environmental tobacco smoke and coronary heart disease' in the *America Cancer Society CPS-II Cohort* (1996). This was seized on in Britain by ASH, which extrapolated from the US estimate to claim that 'up to 12,000 non-smokers' a year were at risk of dying from heart disease in the UK (ASH press release, 17 October 1997).

** M. R. Law, *et al.*, 'Environmental tobacco smoke exposure and ischaemic heart disease', *BMJ*, 315 (1997), 973–80. By 2004 ASH was able to assert that a passive smoker's risk of heart disease 'may be as much as about half that of someone smoking 20 cigarettes a day, even though they only inhale about 1 per cent of the smoke' ('Passive smoking: a summary of the evidence', ASH (2004)).

with heart disease, strokes and various forms of cancer, it cited an array of further problems, ranging from spontaneous abortion and learning difficulties to meningitis and cystic fibrosis.[14] It seemed there might soon be no known human ill of which passive smoking could not be presented as the cause.

Indeed, by the end of the decade, although the researchers' claims might differ in detail, the impression was commonly given that there was now near-complete scientific consensus that passive smoking was a huge social problem, causing serious damage to public health. But this was hardly surprising, since almost all those engaged in researching this field were agreed in principle on what they expected to find. Just as relevant, if not more so, was that this was what they were expected to find by those who supplied their funding. Significantly, therefore, there was virtually no proper scientific debate on the issue. The 'consensus' was one that rested on a general unspoken assumption that no one would dare step out of line enough to challenge it.

In reality, however, this meant that the consensus was more fragile than it seemed. It was an artificial construct, created by collective social pressure. And just how ruthless the anti-smoking lobby could be in defending a fiction on which its case so heavily depended was illustrated by a revealing episode that unfolded in 1998.

The one major international public health organization that had so far not given a final verdict on the passive smoking issue was the WHO. This was because, although it had spent large sums on anti-smoking and anti-tobacco campaigns, it had ten years earlier commissioned the largest international study yet conducted into the effects of environmental tobacco smoke. Co-ordinated by its International Agency for Research on Cancer (IARC) in Lyons in France, the project involved teams of researchers from seven countries, based in twelve national centres.

The findings of this mammoth study were eagerly anticipated by the anti-smoking lobby, because they were sure it would finally prompt the WHO to throw all its weight and prestige behind their campaign. But in March 1998 a London newspaper carried a news story which filled them with dismay. The *Sunday Telegraph* reported that, although the IARC's report was complete, the WHO had withheld it from publication. This was because the findings of the study were not what it had expected.[15]

The 27 respected epidemiologists and cancer specialists from across Europe had compared 650 lung cancer patients with 1,650 healthy people. They had looked at non-smokers who were married to smokers or worked with smokers; who both worked with and were married to smokers; and those who had grown up with smokers. Across the board and in all seven countries, their conclusions were consistent. They found no evidence that there was any 'statistically significant' additional risk from passive exposure to smoke, either at home or in the workplace. There was even evidence that, for the children brought up in a smoky atmosphere, this actually seemed to give them some modest degree of protection from the risks of cancer.[16]

If the report itself was embarrassing enough to the WHO, the leaking of its suppression of the report was even more so. It hurriedly issued a press release headed 'Passive Smoking does cause lung cancer – don't let them fool you'.[17] ASH was so outraged by the *Sunday Telegraph* story that it reported the 'false and misleading' article to the Press Complaints Commission, demanding a full retraction and apology.

Faced with continuing criticism, the WHO finally decided to publish the paper, without publicity, in its own journal. Sure enough, when the study finally became available in October, it confirmed everything that had been reported six months earlier. The researchers had in fact found what they considered to be a very small increased risk of cancer from exposure to smoking, both by spouses (1.16, or 16 per cent) and in the workplace (1.17, or 17 per cent). But these odds ratios, the report itself repeatedly insisted, could not be considered 'statistically significant'.

This point was rather more important than might have at first appeared, certainly than was recognized by the anti-smoking lobby, which at once pulled out all the stops to denigrate the IARC report, on the grounds that it was dishonest to claim that these percentages were not 'significant'. But all this demonstrated was how little the anti-smoking lobby knew about the basic rules of epidemiology. The IARC researchers had been acting in accordance with a long-established epidemiological principle: that anything less than a margin of 2.0 (100 per cent) in such cases cannot be regarded as 'statistically significant'.

Furthermore, this principle was set out in the standard textbook on the interpretation of cancer statistics published by the IARC itself. Published in 1980, this stated that 'relative risks of less than 2.0 may readily reflect some unperceived bias or confounding factor, those over 5.0 are unlikely to do so'.[18] More recently this had been endorsed by the National Cancer Institute, part of the US National Institutes of Health, when it emphasized in 1994 that 'relative risks of less than 2 are considered small and are usually difficult to interpret ... Such increases may be due to chance, statistical bias, or effects of confounding factors that are sometimes not evident.' [19]

In other words, it was the IARC's report which had correctly made allowance for bias or other confounding factors, in compliance with the accepted methodology. The only people who had broken the rules were the researchers responsible for those other, much-publicized recent studies, which claimed significance for percentage findings much lower than the scientifically acceptable limit.

Shortly after the publication of the IARC report, the Press Complaints Commission rejected ASH's complaint. ASH's response was to call the PCC's ruling

> *totally unsatisfactory. We continue to believe the* Sunday Telegraph's *article was inaccurate. As far as we are concerned, the matter is not resolved.*[20]

Years later, ASH was still publishing an account of this episode on its website, claiming that the newspaper had only 'misreported' the IARC study because it had 'accepted uncritically' an interpretation of the researchers' findings which it had been fed by a major tobacco company.

This had long since become the ritual response of the anti-smoking lobby to anyone who failed to accept its 'consensus'. No one would dare challenge its collective orthodoxy, the message ran, because their moral and intellectual judgement had been corrupted by the power and money of the tobacco industry. Dissent could no longer be tolerated.*

---

* This was again seen when, in 1998, Covance Laboratories, an independent consultancy, reported on a major study which used personal air-quality monitors carried by more than 1,000 people in cities across Europe to measure precisely, through cotinine levels, the contents of environmental tobacco smoke inhaled by non-smokers. This equated on average to smoking 0.02 cigarettes a day or six cigarettes a year. The Covance

Stage Three: The Silencing of the Dissenters

By the start of the twenty-first century, the campaign against the menace of passive smoking had already come a long way. In the previous decade, on both sides of the Atlantic, smoking had already become markedly less socially acceptable. The majority of work-places had now either restricted smoking only to rooms specially reserved for the purpose, or banned it altogether, so that a familiar urban sight had become that of little knots of smokers huddled in the street outside office doorways.** Restaurants, pubs and bars were increasingly segregating smokers from non-smokers by des-ignating special 'smoking areas', while in many private homes it was no longer allowed at all.

So rapidly had tobacco become socially taboo across the wes-tern world that it was now quite a shock to see old news film of political gatherings, even as recent as the 1980s, showing political leaders, such as Chancellors Schmidt and Kohl of Germany, hap-pily lighting up as they sat at the conference table. By 2000 no politician would have dared smoke so publicly in this way.

Despite all these social pressures, and the prominent health warnings now carried by law on all tobacco products (in the EU this had been made obligatory since 1989 under directive 89/622), around a quarter of the adult population were still smokers. After the steep decline of previous decades, the curve had flattened out in the USA and Britain to around 25 per cent. Those still addicted

---

study, the largest of its kind ever carried out, was subjected to ferocious attacks by ASH and other anti-smoking campaigners, who claimed that it had been commissioned by a body funded by the tobacco industry. The consultants responded that the industry had in no way influenced the nature or findings of its research. In 2004 a much smaller study carried out in Wales, under the supervision of the Department of Epidemiology and Public Health at University College London, confirmed the Covance results, finding that a non-smoker spending 20 hours a week exposed to tobacco smoke in a pub was exposed to the equivalent of smoking 19.4 cigarettes a year (*Wales on Sunday*, 14 November 2004).
** Among the organizations in the forefront of imposing smoking bans were local authorities. In 1998 Welwyn and Hatfield Council became the first in Britain to announce that, as from April 2000, none of its employees, including park keepers and dustmen, would be permitted to smoke while on duty, even in the open air or while driving their own cars (BBC News website, 16 July 1998).

were learning to live with the unacceptability of their habit to non-smokers; and the measures now taken to segregate them from each other were making it much easier than ever before for non-smokers to avoid involuntary exposure.

For the anti-smoking campaigners, however, this was nothing like enough. In 2001 they were furious when Sir Richard Doll, now the most respected epidemiologist in Britain, observed when being interviewed on *Desert Island Discs* that, 'the effects of other people smoking in my presence is so small it doesn't worry me'. So convinced were the campaigners that exposure to smoke in even the smallest quantities posed a deadly risk to health that, in more and more areas of public life, they pressed for smoking to be eliminated altogether. So morally self-evident, they believed, was the case for this, that they became increasingly reckless in their readiness to make claims that were not supported by any evidence.*

In 2002, acting through a variety of organizations which could claim to represent the public interest, they stepped up their campaign to a new level. In April, the London Assembly's 'Smoking in Public Places Committee' produced a survey which, it claimed, had found that 'a thousand Londoners' died each year from heart disease caused by passive smoking. But the committee was not yet prepared to call for a complete ban.[21]

In June, embarrassed by the failure of its earlier study to find any significant link between passive smoking and cancer, the IARC tried to make amends by staging a five-day conference at which '29 experts from 12 countries' examined 'all the major studies looking at smoking and cancer', concluding that non-smokers exposed to 'second-hand smoke' were 'between 20 per cent and 30 per cent

---

* A small illustration of this was the justification offered in 2000 by the first railway company in Britain to impose a total smoking ban on inter-city trains. For well over a century Britain's trains had reserved compartments for non-smokers, and more recently the balance had shifted to the point where smoking was confined to only 12.5 per cent of the coaches. When First Great Western announced that even this concession was to be withdrawn, it claimed it was taking this step to meet the wishes of more than 90 per cent of its passengers and staff. Pressed for details of how it had arrived at this figure, the company was evasive and unable to produce any evidence. Many employees confirmed that their views had never been sought and that the ban was very unpopular even with those responsible for cleaning the carriages. The '90 per cent' claim was just a convenient fiction.

more likely to develop lung cancer'. This much-publicized finding contradicted not only the IARC's own major study of four years before, but also those same methodological rules which it had itself previously upheld as sound science.[22]

In October ASH reported a survey of its own which claimed to show that 85 per cent of Britain's employees considered they should not be 'forced to breathe other people's smoke' (ASH's figure presumably included several million employees who were themselves smokers); and this was linked to a call from the Health and Safety Commission for a new code of practice, under the 1974 Health and Safety at Work Act, to ban smoking in the workplace.[23]

In November the British Medical Association repeated the warning that 1,000 people a year were dying every year in the UK from passive smoking (although the London Assembly had earlier claimed 1,000 deaths each year in London alone), calling for laws to ban smoking in public places to be introduced 'as soon as possible'.[24] Dr Vivienne Nathanson, the BMA's 'Head of Science and Ethics' and a committed anti-smoking campaigner, said that 'by not banning smoking in public places, the government is putting the health of vast numbers of the population at risk and is also placing a huge burden on the NHS'.*

In December came a further landmark, when the EU's Council of Ministers took an important step towards making the whole of the EU a 'smoke-free zone'. It adopted Council Recommendation 2003/54, calling on all member states 'to implement legislation providing suitable protection from the effects of passive smoking at workplaces, in enclosed public places and on public transport'. Although without the force of law, this was to have a significant effect in prompting EU governments to introduce drastic new curbs on smoking across the board.

In April 2003, one of America's most voluble anti-smoking campaigners, James Repace, who had previously carried out research into passive smoking for the California Department of Health, turned his attention to Britain. He claimed to have carried out a study which showed that 'around 900 office workers, 165 bar

---

* For some years a familiar argument in favour of curbs on smoking had been the cost to the NHS of treating smoking-related diseases, originally estimated in the 1990s at £675 million a year. But this compared with the £6 billion a year then received by the Exchequer from taxes on tobacco.

workers and 145 manufacturing workers die each year as a result
of breathing in other people's tobacco smoke at work'. Apportioning estimates of death among different occupations like this
was from now on to become a fashionable tactic for campaigners.[25] Repace also stated that 'more people died in 2002 from
passive smoking in the UK than were killed by the Great London
smog of 1952' (the latest research estimates the total number of
deaths attributable to London's choking fog in those weeks of 1952
at around 12,000).

There then followed an episode that shed light as powerful as
any on just how far the gap had now opened up between the claims
of the campaigners and the evidence produced by more responsible
scientists.

In May 2003 the findings were at last made public of the longest
and most comprehensive scientific study ever carried out into the
effects of passive smoking anywhere in the world. This was the
project launched on its way 40 years earlier, commissioned by the
American Cancer Society, based on a study of 118,094 Californian
adults, including 35,000 couples of which only one partner was a
smoker. As the two researchers, Professor James Enstrom, of the
University of California's School of Public Health, and Geoffrey
Kabat, of New York State University's Department of Preventive
Medicine, neared the end of their gargantuan task, it had become
apparent to their sponsors that the evidence was not producing the
results they had anticipated. The central finding of the study was
embarrassingly stark: there was no 'causal relation between
environmental tobacco smoke and tobacco-related mortality'.

So unexpected and unambiguous was this conclusion that it had
the potential to throw the whole debate over passive smoking back
into the melting pot. What followed was one of the more
remarkable episodes in the history of the politicization of science.

The American Cancer Society tried to abort the project by
withdrawing its funding. Desperate to see the publication of a
study which had absorbed so much of their lives, Enstrom and
Kabat, although both were non-smokers, had no alternative but to
turn to the only source which might now be prepared to finance the
completion of their work: the American tobacco industry. They
knew this was offering a hostage to fortune, but it was the only
way their contribution to scientific knowledge would see the light
of day.

Even when their paper was peer-reviewed and ready for publication, the two researchers ran into another obstacle. Terrified of the implications, no reputable US scientific journal was willing to publish it. This was how, in May 2003, the most important single study ever carried out into passive smoking finally came to be published on the other side of the Atlantic, in the *British Medical Journal*.[26] Although its editor, Dr Richard Smith, was himself strongly opposed to smoking, he argued that his journal's role was to publish science, not polemic. He recognized that the American study was proper, peer-reviewed science and that it would be scandalous for it to be suppressed.[27]

The summary of its conclusions given in the paper's abstract read, in full:

> *The results do not support a causal relation between environmental tobacco smoke and tobacco related mortality, although they do not rule out a small effect. The association between exposure to environmental tobacco smoke and coronary heart disease and lung cancer may be considerably weaker than believed.*

The *BMJ* accompanied its publication with an editorial by the professor of clinical epidemiology at Bristol University, attempting to qualify some of the paper's findings and to downplay its potential impact. Nevertheless, it conceded that the impact of passive smoking on health remained 'under dispute', and suggested that the new paper would 'add to this debate'.[28]

Inevitably the publication provoked a storm, led by the American Cancer Society (which, according to Enstrom, had drafted its complaint 'before they even saw the paper').[29] For weeks the *BMJ* came under fire from all sides, including demands that the paper be withdrawn. Faced with this avalanche of what Enstrom described as 'aggressive, vitriolic hate', Smith himself insisted that, although the *BMJ* was 'passionately anti-tobacco', it was not 'anti-science'.

Four months later, when he gave Enstrom and Kabat space to publish a lengthy reply to their critics, this was accompanied by an editorial statement explaining that, 'owing to the charged atmosphere surrounding the issue of passive smoking', their paper had produced a strong response:

The most disturbing reactions have come from the enforcers of political correctness who pose as disinterested scientists but are willing to use base means to trash a study whose results they dislike. They have no qualms about engaging in personal attacks and unfounded insinuations of dishonesty, rather than judging research on its merits. The resulting confusion has misled many readers and diverted attention from the facts of the study.[30]

Enstrom and Kabat themselves centred their reply on a letter from Michael Thun of the American Cancer Society, 'almost every sentence' of which, they said, was 'misleading'. Methodically they answered point after point, suggesting that 'his attack should be seen for what it is – an attempt to discredit work that is at variance with the position he is committed to'. The evidence for the health effects of passive smoking, they insisted, was 'neither as consistent nor as iron clad as Thun wants to portray it'. The 'widely accepted evidence' which supported the view that passive smoking was harmful was 'the result of selective reporting of data' and 'attempts to suppress divergent data'. The response to their paper, they said, had been 'a prime example of these tactics'.

The two researchers then answered the predictable charges, made by Thun, ASH and others, that they were in the pocket of the tobacco industry. They pointed out that, as epidemiologists of long experience, their integrity had never been questioned before. They had absolutely no connection with the tobacco industry, other than that it had provided the 'final portion of the funding'. 'The tobacco industry never saw any version of the paper before it was published' and had 'never attempted to influence' its contents in any way. Since they themselves were happy to make 'full disclosure' on such issues, they then invited Thun and the American Cancer Society to do the same, by revealing the sources of their own funding.

In reality, however, it did not matter what Enstrom and Kabat said in reply to their critics. In terms of the public debate, their report had no more impact than that produced by the IARC five years earlier. In terms of political influence, that debate was now so dominated by the anti-smoking lobby, armed with its own facts and figures, that these had gelled into an orthodoxy that could not be questioned. Any dissent could be dismissed as no more than propaganda funded by the tobacco industry.

Whenever anyone in a position of influence in the scientific community appeared to be wavering, powerful pressure was applied to bring them back into line. Sir Richard Doll was eventually persuaded to dilute the force of his heretical comment on *Desert Island Discs* by explaining that his lack of concern about passive smoking had been merely a 'personal perspective'. For all his courage in publishing Enstrom and Kabat, Dr Smith of the *BMJ* was also eventually persuaded to disown their findings, saying he was now personally satisfied that passive smoking was a killer after all.[31]

The momentum behind the anti-smoking crusade was gathering force on all sides. On 29 March 2003 New York had joined the growing number of US states which were introducing more or less comprehensive smoking bans in workplaces, restaurants and bars. The anti-smoking lobby claimed that this had boosted their business, but it gradually emerged that hundreds of bars and restaurants in the states affected had suffered such a drop in trade that they were forced to close.

In September 2003, the EU's Irish health commissioner David Byrne, a passionate anti-smoker, said that his officials were looking at the possibility of legislation to ban smoking in public places, and that legal action to ban smoking in bars and restaurants was 'simply a matter of time'.[32] On 1 January 2004 the Netherlands became the first country in the EU to act on its Council Recommendation of a year earlier, banning smoking in many public places such as offices, trains and railway stations. On 29 March Mr Byrne's own country of Ireland followed suit, with a much more comprehensive ban, which also included pubs, bars and restaurants.

As in the USA, the Irish ban was hailed by the anti-smoking lobby as having been so widely welcomed by the Irish people that pubs and bars were enjoying a boom. The reality, revealed two years later by the first detailed study of the effects of the ban on the Irish pub trade, showed that 67 per cent of pubs had in fact lost business, and that for two-thirds of them these losses had been 'significant'. The only pubs bucking the trend, the survey showed, were those that had continued to attract smokers by creating outdoor 'smoking areas', such as heated patios.[33]

In Britain the anti-smoking lobby had found a new champion, Konrad Jamrozik, an Australian academic and fanatical anti-smoker who had come to work at Imperial College. He had been commissioned by 33 London boroughs campaigning for a 'smoke-free London' to produce a study, based on comparing the latest UK death statistics with a survey supplied by ASH showing the percentage of the population exposed to passive smoke at work or at home. In 2004 this enabled him to come up with a finding that the number of Britons dying each year from passive smoking in the workplace was 617. Of these, he claimed, 54, or one a week, had been among the 1.1 million bar staff, waiters and others working in the 'hospitality industry'.[34]

As political ammunition, the seeming precision of these figures caught the imagination of campaigners more than all those previous vague 'estimates' that annual deaths from passive smoking were '1,000', or '3,000', or '12,000'. Particularly effective, following the lead given by Repace, was Jamrozik's focus on all those barmaids and waiters in pubs and restaurants who were forced helplessly to endure toxic smoke at their work. Dying at a rate of one a week, these anonymous victims of the evils of passive smoking now began to feature regularly in the speeches of councillors, MPs and even ministers.

As yet, however, despite the continued pressure, there was still little outward sign of that breakthrough to real political action that the campaigners were after. As late as September 2003, the Department of Health had been quoted as saying that ministers had 'no plans' to introduce any ban on smoking in public places in Britain.[35]

When the end of the story finally came, however, it was to do so with breathtaking speed.

The End Game

Just before the 2005 General Election, when the Labour Party issued its 112-page manifesto, buried away on page 66 was a section which began 'we recognise that many people want smoke-free environments and need regulation to help them get this. We therefore intend to shift the balance significantly in their favour'.

The contents of what followed were certainly dramatic. In line with the EU's Recommendation of 2002, and the lead already given by countries such as Ireland and the Netherlands, the Labour party promised new laws 'to ensure that all enclosed public places and workplaces other than licensed premises will be smoke-free'. This would include all offices, factories and shops, and all restaurants, cafes, pubs and bars that served food. Knowing that the ban would in some quarters be intensely unpopular, the Secretary of State for Health, John Reid, had insisted on one or two important concessions. An exemption from the ban would be given to pubs that did not serve food. The members of clubs, from Pall Mall in London to working men's clubs in the north, from the clubhouses on golf courses to night clubs and casinos requiring membership, would be free to choose whether to allow smoking on their premises or not. The only exception to this, in deference to Mr Jamrozik and his barmaids, was that smoking in any bar area would be strictly prohibited.

Despite the concessions, it seemed as though the 20-year campaign to outlaw passive smoking was on the verge of pulling off a remarkable victory. Within months the Parliamentary Bill was drafted and, on 27 October, presented to the House of Commons for its first reading. An accompanying government statement explained that:

> *public opinion and scientific evidence of the negative health effects of smoking on individuals and those passively exposed to second-hand smoke have increased pressure on the government to act to bring forward smokefree legislation.*

By 29 November the Health Bill had passed its second reading, without a vote. The new Health Secretary Patricia Hewitt claimed that the smoking ban would 'help to reduce' the number of smokers by 'a further 500,000 to 750,000', and the number of 'deaths associated with workplace smoking estimated at some 500 to 600 a year'.

So firmly established by now was the orthodoxy that passive smoking was a mass killer that the time was gone when it might have been possible to question such claims, or to ask for the scientific evidence for them. Any remaining opposition to Hewitt's Bill was centred round a somewhat surprised awareness that it went much further than most people had anticipated, or than many thought reasonable or necessary.

After further discussion in committee, the crucial vote came on 14 February 2006, when MPs packed the House to consider various amendments. The most controversial of these resulted from a belated government decision, led by Hewitt herself, to withdraw the various concessions promised in the manifesto to private clubs and pubs not serving food. What made this even more remarkable was that, in November, no one had argued more strongly for these concessions than Hewitt herself, as a former director of the National Council for Civil Liberties. Most people, she had then insisted, took the view that members of a club should be as free to decide how it was run as if it was their own home.

The atmosphere around Westminster that day was feverish, if not hysterical. MPs radiated a holy glow about the cosmic importance of what they were about to do. Statistics of the number of lives they were all going to save were flung around like confetti. The one exception to the general mood of sanctimonious zeal was a knockabout speech from a Labour backbencher, Stephen Pound, who made what one observer described as 'a witty appeal for tolerance and realism'.[36] Otherwise, so overpowering was the sense of 'consensus' among anti-smokers of all parties that even Tony Blair and Gordon Brown changed their minds, as they prepared to renege on their manifesto commitments of nine months earlier.

The decision to scrap the concession for pubs not serving food was supported by an exceptionally large Commons majority of 328. That imposing the ban on private clubs was carried with a majority of 200. Jubilant officials, it was reported, 'proclaimed the vote a historic triumph', comparing it with the Act setting up the National Health Service in 1948.[37]

By the summer the Health Act 2006 was law. By 1 July 2007, when its anti-smoking provisions came into force, the evil of 'environmental tobacco smoke' would have been eradicated from every building in the land to which members of the public or employees had access. It would now be an offence to smoke tobacco in any pub, restaurant, office, factory or other 'enclosed public space' anywhere in England (a similar law had already come into force in Scotland in March 2006, and Wales introduced the ban three months earlier than England in April 2007).

'Public spaces' to be made 'smokefree' were to include bus shelters and open air platforms on railway stations; any vehicle being used for business purposes, such as a car, van, lorry or farm tractor; ships and hovercraft; tents and marquees; the seating around open-air sports arenas: anywhere where people gathered in close proximity to each other, even if they were all consenting adult smokers. The only exempted 'enclosed spaces' were to be those which people could regard as their permanent or temporary home, including hotel rooms and prison cells.

Anyone caught smoking in a 'smokefree' area was liable to an on-the-spot penalty of £50 (with a fine of £80, under another law, for anyone caught dropping a cigarette end in the street or any other public place). To ensure maximum compliance, much larger fines of up to £2,500 would be imposed on any owner or manager of 'smokefree' premises who knowingly allowed others to smoke illegally (special hotlines were to be opened for employees and members of the public to report anyone they observed breaking the law).

It would become a further offence under the Act, punishable by a fine of up to £1,000, not to put up prominent signs with the statutory wording 'No smoking. It is against the law to smoke in these premises', both inside and outside any building or structure where smoking was now forbidden. This included cathedrals, churches, mosques, synagogues, funeral parlours, operating theatres, stately homes, historic ruins, Buckingham Palace, and any building covered by the Act.* In some parts of England and Wales, councils were already talking of extending the ban to smoking in parks or even the street, and within weeks of the Act being passed Westminster City Council announced that it would be taking on 80 new 'smoking wardens' to ensure that the new law was strictly enforced all across central London.**

The next EU country to follow suit was France. In October 2006, the French prime minister Dominique de Villepin announced that his country was to introduce a complete ban on smoking in public places, including bars and restaurants, in two stages, the first as early as February 2007.[38] Passive smoking, he claimed, killed '5,000 people a year' in France, or 13 a day. Anyone caught

---

* When the Church of England protested in February 2007 that there was no need to put up such signs outside and inside cathedrals and churches, because no one ever smoked in such buildings, it was told by the Department of Health that there could be no exemptions from the law.
** As the day of the Act coming into force approached, the government announced on 15 February 2007 that it was to give councils £29.5 million to pay for 'thousands of officials' to enforce the ban. They would be allowed to work 'undercover', patrolling pubs, restaurants, offices, shops and doorways, and to take photographs and video film as evidence.

smoking in 'smoke free premises' after the law came into force would be fined 75 euros, and the owners of the premises would face a fine of 150 euros. Just before the first part of the ban came into force, it was announced that 175,000 'cigarette police' would be deployed across France to enforce it.[39] This was rather larger than the total number of 136,000 soldiers in the French army.

On 30 January the EU's health commissioner Markos Kyprianou launched a Commission green paper applauding the lead already given by several EU countries, which also now included Malta, Sweden and Italy, and proposing legislation to ban smoking in public places throughout the EU. This was justified, he said, by the fact that the number of deaths caused each year in the EU by passive smoking was '79,000'.[40] This implied that the number killed each year in Britain was over 12,000, twenty times higher than the figure claimed by Mrs Hewitt for the British government itself. But who now was going to quibble over figures, since these were all imaginary anyway?

The scale on which the anti-smoking lobby had, in just a few years, managed to get smoking in public places banned in Europe and many other parts of the world reflected one of the most successful feats of political campaigning in modern times, and the campaigners were the first to congratulate themselves on the importance of what they had achieved.

But what did it actually amount to? Certainly they could claim to have made life more pleasant for all those non-smokers who, like King James I four centuries earlier, found the smell of tobacco smoke offensive. They could certainly be thanked by all those non-smokers who suffered from respiratory disorders, such as bronchitis and asthma, the symptoms of which might be exacerbated by exposure to tobacco smoke. They could even claim that the ban might save the lives of many smokers by encouraging them to abandon the habit.*

What the campaigners against 'second-hand smoke' were not

---

* On the weekend the English ban came into force, the epidemiologist Professor Sir Richard Peto claimed to a press conference that it could save 500,000 lives. His reasoning was that 'half of all smokers are going to be killed by tobacco. If a million people stop smoking who wouldn't otherwise have done so then maybe you'll prevent half a million deaths.' (*Channel Four News* website, 'Smoking ban to save "half a million lives"', 29 June 2007.)

entitled to claim, however, although it was their most constantly repeated boast, was that they were saving thousands of lives which would have been lost through passive smoking itself. Despite their tireless efforts, they had not been able to produce a single, genuinely scientific study that proved beyond doubt that second-hand smoke was actually responsible for killing people. Hundreds of studies had tried to establish this point, at a cost of hundreds of millions of dollars and pounds. But, for all their researchers' ingenuity, not one had produced evidence which in reality was objectively convincing or, under the strict rules of science, 'statistically significant'.

All the most comprehensive studies, carried out in accordance with objective scientific disciplines, had, as Professor Doll himself reflected, come to exactly the opposite conclusion: that the consequences of inhaling other people's tobacco smoke were so negligible that they had little or no effect on health at all.

The triumph of the campaign against passive smoking had provided one of the most dramatic examples in history of how science can be bent and distorted for ideological reasons, to come up with findings that the evidence did not support, and which were in many ways the reverse of the truth. In this respect, it provided one of the most vivid examples in modern times of the psychological power of the scare.

Notes

1. S. Green, *New England Almanack and Farmer's Friend* (1836).
2. N. Wald and A. Nicolaides-Bouman, *UK Smoking Statistics* (Oxford University Press, 1991).
3. R. Doll and A. Bradford Hill, 'Smoking and Carcinoma of the Lung: Preliminary Report', *British Medical Journal*, 30 September 1950 (available on the Internet).
4. 'Health – Cigarette Smoking', Office for National Statistics, January 2007.
5. *Washington Star*, 5 April 1980.
6. 'The health consequences of environmental smoking', Report of the Surgeon General, US Department of Health and Human Services (1989); 'Environmental tobacco smoke: measuring exposures and assessing health effects', US National Research Council (1986).
7. 'Passive Smoking: a summary of the evidence', Action on Smoking and Health (ASH) (London, 2004).

8. 'Reducing the health consequences of smoking: 25 years of progress', Report of the Surgeon General, US Department of Health and Human Services (1989); also, ASH summary (2004).

9. 'Respiratory health effects of passive smoking: lung cancer and other disorders', funded by the Indoor Air Division, Office of Atmosphere and Indoor Air Programs, Office of Health and Environmental Assessment, Office of Research and Development, Environmental Protection Agency (EPA) (1992).

10. Nirupa Dattani and Nicola Cooper, 'Trends in cot deaths, 1971–1998', *Health Statistics Quarterly*, 5 (Office of National Statistics, 2000), 10–16.

11. A. K. Hackshaw, *et al.*, 'The accumulated evidence on lung cancer and environmental tobacco smoke', *BMJ*, 315 (1997), 980–8.

12. S. A. Glantz and W. W. Parmley, 'Passive smoking and heart disease', *Circulation*, 83 (1991).

13. J. He, *et al.*, 'Passive smoking and coronary heart disease – a meta-analysis of epidemiological studies', *New England Journal of Medicine*, 340 (1999), 920–6.

14. 'Health effects of exposure to environmental tobacco smoke', report by California Environmental Protection Agency, Smoking and Tobacco Control Monograph 10 (National Cancer Institute, 1999).

15. 'Passive smoking doesn't cause cancer – official', Victoria Macdonald, *Sunday Telegraph*, 8 March 1998.

16. P. Boffetta, *et al.*, 'Multicenter Case–Control Study of Exposure to Environmental Tobacco Smoke and Lung Cancer in Europe', *Journal of the National Cancer Institute*, 90 (7 October 1998) 19.

17. WHO press release, 9 March 1998.

18. Breslow and Day (1980), *Statistical methods in cancer research. Vol. 1: The analysis of case-control studies*, IARC Scientific Publications 32 (Lyon, 1980), p. 36.

19. National Cancer Institute release, 26 October 1994.

20. *Sunday Telegraph*, 25 October 1998.

21. 'Passive smoking killing thousands', BBC News website, 9 April 2002.

22. 'Second-hand smoke causes cancer', BBC News website, 19 June 2002.

23. 'Workers demand smoke-free offices', BBC News website, 5 October 2002.

24. 'Doctors call for public smoking ban', BBC News website, 6 November 2002.

25. 'Passive smoking killing workers', BBC News website, 7 April 2003.

26. J. Enstrom and G. Kabat, 'Environmental tobacco smoke and tobacco related mortality in a prospective study of Californians, 1960–98', *BMJ*, 17 May 2003.

27. Tim Luckhurst, 'Passive smoking: is there convincing evidence that it's harmful?', *Independent*, 2 May 2006.
28. George Davey Smith, 'Effect of passive smoking on health', Editorial in *BMJ*, 17 May 2003.
29. Robert Matthews, *Sunday Telegraph*, 18 May 2003.
30. 'Passive smoking: authors' reply', *BMJ*, 30 August 2003.
31. Luckhurst, 'Passive smoking' (2006).
32. 'EU public smoking ban considered', BBC News website, 19 September 2003.
33. 'Pubs in Ireland 2006', a study based on 345 pubs by Insight Research, reported in *Sunday Telegraph*, 19 February 2006.
34. 'Passive smoking kills one bar worker a week', *New Scientist*, 17 May 2004.
35. BBC News website, 19 September 2003.
36. Michael White, *Guardian*, 15 February 2006.
37. *Ibid.*
38. 'France to ban smoking in public', BBC News website, 8 October 2006.
39. *Daily Telegraph*, 1 February 2007.
40. 'EU could impose smoking ban across continent', *Guardian*, 27 January 2007.

13

'One Fibre Can Kill'

The Great Asbestos Scam

Asbestos ... the world's most wonderful mineral.
   A. L. Summers, *Asbestos and the Asbestos Industry*, 1919

Asbestos litigation has come to consist, mainly, of non-sick people ... claiming compensation for non-existent injuries, often testifying according to prepared scripts with perjurious contents, and often supported by specious medical evidence ... it is ... a massively fraudulent enterprise that can rightly take its place among the pantheon of ... great American swindles.
   Professor Lester Brickman, 2002[1]

No story in this book is stranger than that of the great asbestos scare that, by the closing years of the twentieth century, had spread across much of the western world.

Like other scares, this one originated in a genuine and serious problem. Asbestos, it had been confirmed beyond doubt in the 1950s and 1960s, was a multiple killer. Breathed in, its sharp fibres had the capacity to inflict horrible damage on human lungs, leading to three fatal diseases, including two forms of cancer.

This naturally aroused acute concern. By this time, asbestos was being put to so many uses – for everything from brake linings and oven gloves to water pipes, guttering, roof slates and many other building materials – that its presence in the human environment was well-nigh universal. Scarcely anyone in the developed world did not in some way have contact with it.

Gradually the impression grew that this fibrous mineral was one of the most dangerous substances known to man. By the 1970s, lawyers in the USA were bringing thousands of compensation claims on behalf of people whose health had been damaged by exposure to asbestos at work. In 1978 a report signed by senior officials of the US government predicted that, within 30 years, asbestos would have killed an additional two million people in the USA alone. Anti-asbestos campaigners began to lobby not just for much tighter controls on its use, but for it to be banned altogether.

By the 1980s and 1990s, the campaigners had been so successful in putting over their message that its use was being prohibited in one part of the world after another, from the USA to the European Union.

By the early years of the twenty-first century, the number of compensation claims posted in the USA had soared above 700,000, worth more than $200 billion. Scores of companies had been forced into bankruptcy, and it was predicted that the total number of claims might eventually top three million. In Britain new laws were passed which would encourage the removal of asbestos from millions of buildings, at a cost to property owners running to many billions of pounds.

But, as alarm over the dangers of asbestos had steadily mounted, the claims made to justify that concern had become increasingly extreme, shrouding the whole issue in an ever-greater fog of misunderstanding. Two misconceptions in particular had allowed that original genuine problem to be exaggerated into a monumental scare.

The first of these was the belief that asbestos in any form was a substance inherently so dangerous that any contact with it might pose a threat to human health. Undoubtedly, reckless exposure to asbestos had led to the deaths of thousands of people. But these had never represented more than a relatively small proportion of the population, and almost all those affected had been exposed to very high levels of asbestos in the course of their work. Despite the prediction of that US report in 1978 that, within 30 years, asbestos would have killed two million Americans, the actual number of deaths attributed to asbestos in those decades turned out to be only a fraction of that figure.

This was because, in order to inflict damage on the human lung, certain conditions must be met. The people most likely to be killed by asbestos have always been those exposed to its fibres in concentrated doses over a long period. Furthermore, it is not enough just to inhale the fibres; the human body has enough natural defences to reject the vast majority of them. To cause serious damage, the fibres must be 'respirable'; of a type, dimensions and quantity sufficient to overwhelm those defences, penetrating the lung tissue in such a way as to trigger off a pathogenic reaction.

Nothing demonstrates this more vividly than the realization that asbestos is, in fact, a substance which naturally occurs so ubiquitously in the earth's atmosphere that each of us breathes in some 14,000 microscopic fibres of it every day.[2] Thanks to microphages and other defence mechanisms of the human body, these are rendered quite harmless. The lungs of anyone over 50 may contain as many as 200 million asbestos fibres. Yet they do not affect our health, because they have not met the conditions needed to cause damage.

This was the first essential point that got lost sight of as the scare over asbestos gathered its momentum. So comprehensively did the campaigners manage to demonize asbestos – not least with their slogan 'one fibre can kill' – that many people were led to believe that the slightest exposure to this 'deadly' substance might be almost as dangerous as contact with anthrax.

The second misconception that played a crucial part in helping to promote the scare centred on a verbal confusion. This arose from the historical accident by which a single word, 'asbestos', had come to be used to describe two quite different types of mineral.

One form of what is generically but loosely called 'asbestos' includes five varieties of iron silicate, known collectively as 'amphiboles'. Of these the most widely used are known as 'blue' and 'brown asbestos'. When breathed in, the longer of their straight, narrow, sharp, acid-resistant fibres can penetrate the lungs and surrounding tissue in such a way that they cannot be dissolved or removed by the body's defences. They are so persistent in the lungs that their 'half-life' is estimated at up to 150 years or more. It is the build-up of such ineradicable fibres which gives rise to potentially fatal disease.*

A much commoner and very different substance is that known as 'chrysotile' or 'white asbestos'. This is a serpentine mineral, a

* The five amphiboles are: crocidolite (known from its colour as 'blue' asbestos) and amosite ('brown' asbestos), both of which were in extensive commercial use; and the much rarer forms tremolite, actinolite and anthophyllite.

form of magnesium silicate, and closely related to talcum powder. It shares some of the physical properties of the amphiboles but in other respects they have nothing in common. Its soft, silky, curved fibres are readily destroyed by acids, so that in even the weakly acid environment of the human lung the fibres will quickly be dissolved, with a half-life of only a few days. Very heavy occupational exposure to the longer fibres of chrysotile can cause lung damage and maybe cancer, but very short fibres are not dangerous.

Furthermore, by far the most extensive use of white asbestos fibres has been as a bonding agent in cement and plaster, as in roof slates and decorative wall coatings. Around 90 per cent of all the asbestos ever used has been to make 'white asbestos cement' products. When chrysotile is mixed with calcium-rich cement in this way the surface of the fibres goes through a chemical change. This helps the cement matrix to bond tightly to the fibre. A consequence is that, even when it is sawn or drilled, the fibres, bonded to the cement, cannot easily escape in a respirable form. Thus, by far the most widely used form of asbestos-containing material on the planet, comprising almost all the asbestos with which most people are ever likely to come in contact, poses no measurable risk to human health.

Yet the blurring of language that allowed this essentially harmless material to be given the same name as the chemically quite different and potentially dangerous amphiboles was used to create one of the most damaging scares the modern world has seen. Not only did this confusion play a central part in inflating the scare in the first place; it opened the door to financial exploitation of the resulting panic, on a scale without precedent.

Top of the list in this respect were the lawyers, particularly in the USA, who specialized in bringing compensation claims on behalf of 'asbestos victims'. Initially, most of the claimants they represented were demonstrably ill. But when it became clear that courts in certain states were prepared to award huge sums in compensation without questioning the evidence, the lawyers began to recruit ever more claimants who could show no damage at all. Eventually the vast majority of the claims being upheld by the courts were exposed as being wholly bogus.

Dubbed the '$200 billion miscarriage of justice' – which played its part in bringing Lloyd's of London to its knees – this fraud would come to be ranked as one of the most notorious scandals in American legal history. This extraordinary story received surprisingly little coverage across the Atlantic although similar practices were copied on a less blatant scale by law firms in Britain.

Almost as high on the list were the contractors who, spotting a highly lucrative new source of business, chose to specialize in removing asbestos from buildings. Many lost no opportunity to exaggerate the dangers of asbestos, even when it posed no risk to health and its removal was not required by law. In both America and Britain, where their dubious practices were actively condoned by the government, they made fortunes from charging hugely inflated sums to homeowners, businesses, local authorities, housing associations, schools, charities, churches and organizations of all kinds, for removing 'deadly' asbestos that in most cases was nothing of the kind.

Also helping to promote the wholesale demonization of asbestos were the multinational companies that became the main manufacturers of the fibrous materials marketed as 'asbestos substitutes'. These substances had often not been subjected to proper safety tests, and turned out in some instances to be potentially as dangerous as asbestos itself.

Other beneficiaries from the scare included all those who fed off it in supporting roles, from trade unions and doctors endorsing bogus compensation claims, to surveyors who earned hefty commissions from passing on work to fraudulent contractors. Between them, unwittingly aided and abetted by politicians, officials and the media, they became parties to one of the greatest scams of the age.

This remarkable saga has unfolded through five main stages.

Stage One: The Emergence of a Tragedy

Naturally occurring in many places across the world, as a by-product of the pressures produced by the shifting of tectonic plates, asbestos is a material like no other. As a rock, it comes in two main forms, massive and fibrous. In this latter form, giving it the properties which made it so useful to mankind, it is made up of a mass of fibres so tiny that, until electron microscopy at last made it possible in the 1960s to count them, no one had any idea how many there were.*

---

* Fibrous asbestos is called 'asbestiform'. In its non-fibrous or 'massive' form it makes up a sixth of the earth's crust (all amphiboles).

So literally microscopic are these threads of rock that one the width of a human hair – say 0.0015 inches thick, or 40 microns – may actually contain 2 million lesser fibres or 'fibrils'. The same number can fit on the head of a pin. If the fibres in a cubic inch of asbestos were placed end to end they might stretch for 15 million miles.[3] It is this which gives asbestos that unique combination of three attributes for which, in the human world, it was valued so highly for so long.

Its best-known property is that it is resistant to fire, hence its name. 'Asbestos' in ancient Greek meant 'unquenchable or 'inextinguishable' (its other Greek name, 'amiantos', meant 'pure, undefiled'). Then, uniquely among rocks, its fibres can be woven into a material, like silk, linen or wool. Lastly its fibres can bind together other substances, such as cement, with a tensile strength greater than that of steel.

The first recorded use of asbestos was in Finland more than four thousand years ago, where a rare amphibole form known as anthophyilite was used to strengthen earthenware pots and cooking utensils.[4]

Probably around the same time in the Mediterranean world, where there are extensive deposits of chrysotile (from the Greek for 'golden hair'), it came to be valued for the way it could be woven into a soft, silky cloth, which was also resistant to fire. It was used for oil lamp wicks, which never burned away, and cremation cloths, which enabled the bodily remains to be gathered up unpolluted by the ashes of the fire.

In later, classical times, it was praised by a succession of Greek and Latin authors, from Herodotus to Strabo and Plutarch. Rich Romans liked to show off how napkins made from white asbestos could be cleaned simply by throwing them into the flames. In a famous passage in his *Natural History*, the Elder Pliny (AD 23–79) wrote that, because asbestos was rare, when any was found it was regarded as equal in value to 'exceptionally fine pearls', and that linen woven from it 'holds the highest rank in the whole of the world'.[5]

In the Middle Ages the miraculous properties of asbestos cloth were known in India and China, and written about by several authors, including Marco Polo who saw it on his visit to the Great Khan. In post-Renaissance times it was increasingly referred to by scholars, such as Sir Thomas Browne. In 1684 a sample, supposedly procured from China and described as 'Salamander's Wool', was presented for examination by the newly founded Royal Society.[6] In 1725 young Benjamin Franklin, visiting London, was paid handsomely by the famous collector of curiosities Sir Hans Sloane for a small purse woven in Massachusetts from chrysotile, which he knew as 'Salamander's Cotton'.*

It was at this same time, however, that asbestos first began to be put to a wider range of more mundane and practical purposes (although in Greece and Turkey it had long been used to strengthen the white plaster or stucco applied to the outside of houses). In the Russian Urals in the eighteenth century chrysotile began to be mined to make fireproof aprons and gloves for local metalworkers. In 1827 an Italian physicist, Giovanni Aldini, used a combination of chrysotile with a metallic gauze developed by Sir Humphrey Davy to create a complete set of protective clothing for firemen which soon caught on across Europe. Over the next 50 years asbestos found a plethora of new uses.

Far outshining them all was the part played by asbestos in the advance of the nineteenth-century industrial revolution. At its heart, in factories, mills, mines, ships and locomotives, was the steam engine. Boilers meant heat, heat needed to be kept in by insulation, and here more than anywhere asbestos earned its newfound reputation as 'the magic mineral'.

In 1871 a small calico-weaving firm in the Lancashire cotton town of Rochdale, Turner Brothers, decided to specialize in supplying cotton seals to prevent steam escaping from engine cylinders. But cotton proved far from ideal for the purpose. In 1879 one of the brothers, Samuel Turner, decided that more effective results would be obtained from using asbestos.[7]

His timing was impeccable. Only the previous year, mining had begun of huge deposits of chrysotile recently discovered in Canada. In 1884 similar large-scale mining began in the Urals. In the same year, in South Africa's Cape Province, the first mine was opened producing 'blue asbestos'. Otherwise known as 'crocidolite' (from the Greek for 'woolly hair') or riebeckite, this was the first

---

* Sloane's collection came to form the original basis of the British Museum (and his name was given to London's Sloane Square).

amphibole form of asbestos to come into large-scale commercial use.*

Turner developed the first power-driven weaving process for asbestos fibres, which enabled him to mass-produce asbestos textiles on a scale never seen before. He was able to take advantage of the cheap asbestos now available from the new overseas sources of supply. So great was the demand for his rapidly expanding variety of products that, by 1900, the firm's workforce of five had grown to 50 working on asbestos alone.

Ten years later this figure was over 300, making everything from protective clothing to brake linings; and asbestos was now finding yet another new use, which would eventually overshadow even its value as a source of insulation against heat. In 1900 an Austrian, Ludwig Hatschek, had discovered how to use asbestos fibres as a binding agent in cement. This was to provide one of the twentieth century's most useful and popular building materials.**
In 1913 Turner opened Britain's first factory mass-producing asbestos cement. The following year, with his firm now completely dominating the British asbestos market, he was, as Mayor of Rochdale, honoured with a knighthood.

But already a shadow had begun to intrude. In 1898, Lucy Deane, one of the first Lady Inspectors of Factories, took part in a study of industries in which workers were so heavily exposed to dust that this might damage their lungs. What particularly caught her notice were 'the evil effects of asbestos dust'. 'Microscopic examination' clearly revealed 'the sharp, glass-like jagged nature of the particles'. Where these were suspended in the air, 'the effects have been found to be injurious'.[8]

---

* Being acid-resistant, unlike chrysotile, blue and brown asbestos, the two main amphibole forms, made a much more effective insulation material for coal-fired boilers, because their steam combined with sulphur from the coal smoke to make sulphuric acid. Herein lay the seeds of a twentieth-century health disaster. No group of workers was to be more damaged than those using amphiboles for insulation purposes, because acids in the human lungs could not dissolve the amphibole fibres. The very property that gave amphiboles their industrial advantage also helped to make them medically much more damaging (letter from Dr Kevin Browne).
** Another very widespread use for asbestos in the twentieth century was to be in the making of seamless cement pipes for water and sewage, a process discovered by an Italian, Adolfo Mazza, in 1911. This became, from the 1920s, the material most commonly used for these purposes.

The following year Dr Montague Murray of Charing Cross Hospital saw a 33-year-old man who was dying of lung disease after working with raw asbestos for 14 years, 10 in the carding room where dust was most intense. In 1906 Murray told a government inquiry that this witness had said, 'of the ten men who worked in the room when he went into it, he was the only survivor'.[9] A French factory inspector the same year reported some 50 deaths among female asbestos textile workers.[10] As with Deane and Murray in Britain, his findings were ignored.

During World War One Sir Samuel Turner's firm continued its rapid expansion, not least thanks to the boom in shipbuilding required by the war effort. In Africa the company opened the first asbestos mines of its own, although it was not involved when, in 1917, mining began in the Transvaal for 'brown asbestos', or grunerite. As another amphibole, known as amosite (from 'Asbestos Mines of South Africa'), this, like crocidolite, was to play its own part in the tragedy that lay ahead.

In 1918 a Turner advertising campaign featured 'Lady Asbestos' as a Greek goddess, defending 'civilization' (shipbuilding, engineering, buildings, electricity) against the perils of fire. A major selling point was the thousands of lives a year now being saved by asbestos in ships, vehicles, skyscrapers, offices, theatres and buildings of every kind. In 1920, following a merger, the firm became known as Turner and Newall. When in August 1924 Sir Samuel Turner died, aged 84, he was given an imposing funeral as one of Rochdale's most successful sons. The firm he had built up virtually from nothing now had a workforce of 5,000.[11]

Six months before Turner was buried, the body of a 33-year-old woman was consigned to an unmarked grave in the same cemetery. Born in 1891, Nellie Kershaw had worked with asbestos much of her life, since 1917 for Turner's. Afflicted by chronic and worsening ill health, she had in 1922 been diagnosed by a local GP, Dr Walter Joss, as suffering from 'asbestos poisoning'. It was a disease with which he had become familiar, from seeing up to a dozen such cases every year.

Unable to work, and destitute, she had appealed, with Dr Joss's support, for help. The response from her employers was to invite Dr Joss to visit the factory to inspect their dust-control measures ('we have been repeatedly congratulated by the Home Office'). They denied that Mrs Kershaw's condition could have any connection with her work. 'We repudiate the term "asbestos poisoning",' they wrote, 'asbestos is not poisonous and no definition or knowledge of such a disease exists.' [12]

When Nellie Kershaw died, the coroner nevertheless found that she had died of 'asbestos poisoning': a verdict which made local headlines and which the company strongly challenged (refusing also to make a contribution to her funeral expenses). The coroner had ordered a microscopic examination of her lungs. The pathologist, Dr William Crookes, saw that they were horribly stiffened and scarred by asbestos fibres: a condition he was to name when he wrote up his findings as 'pulmonary asbestosis'.[13]

It would later be more fully understood how, after years of intense exposure to the fibres, the victims of asbestosis can eventually find breathing so difficult that they may in effect be suffocated to death. Although this was the disease that had already affected many Rochdale textile workers, it had never previously been properly identified. Nellie Kershaw's cruel death had earned her a place in history.

Dr Crookes's publication of his findings helped to prompt an inquiry by two senior factory inspectors, Dr E. R. A. Merewether and C. W. Price. They found that a quarter of all the asbestos workers they studied suffered from asbestosis. None employed for less than four years showed signs of the disease, but among workers employed for 25 years or more the figure was 66 per cent. This led in 1931 to Britain becoming the first country in the world to regulate the asbestos industry. Protection was given to workers entering those 'scheduled zones' where the fibrous dust was most intense. They were to be given regular medical checks and the right to compensation for injury.[14]

None of this, however, hindered the triumphant onward march of Turner and Newall. By the end of the 1930s, thanks to the soaring sales of asbestos-containing building materials, the company, now trading across the globe, controlled 20 per cent of the world asbestos market, employing 10,000 people. Its Rochdale works was the world's largest asbestos factory.

World War Two, like its predecessor, created further boom times for the asbestos industry on both sides of the Atlantic, in everything from the need for thousands of new ships to the demand for tens of millions of gas masks (in the UK, civilian gas masks were made from chrysotile, those for the military used crocidolite).

Apart from Turner and Newall, another prime beneficiary, particularly from the massive use of asbestos in shipyards, was its US opposite number, the giant Johns-Manville Corporation. Only decades later, during the litigation of the 1970s and 1980s, did it emerge how this and other corporations had been aware at the time of the risks to which asbestos exposed tens of thousands of shipyard workers, but had kept quiet about it.

In the post-war building boom, demand for asbestos surged to even more spectacular levels. As Turner and Newall continued to expand its interests across the world, its profits broke all records. In 1953, confident that it had overcome the 'dust problems' which were earlier arousing concern, the firm decided to commission a study of the health of workers in its Rochdale factory. The epidemiologist it chose was Richard Doll, now becoming known for his work showing the connection between smoking and lung cancer. But when Doll revealed his findings, the company was far from pleased.

Doll based his study on 113 Turner and Newall employees, all of whom had been heavily exposed for 20 years or more to what he assumed were exclusively raw chrysotile fibres. Eleven, he found, suffered not only from asbestosis but also from lung cancer. This was an incidence of cancer eleven times higher than would be expected in a non-exposed population. For more than 20 years other observers had been suggesting a possible link between asbestos and lung cancer (not least in Germany in 1943). Here at last it seemed was the proof.

Since they were paying for Doll's study, Turner and Newall tried to suppress it. He arranged for it to be published independently.[15] As yet, however, it was not enough to dent the firm's continued expansion. At the end of the 1950s, as the asbestos industry was enjoying its greatest-ever prosperity, Turner and Newall briefly overtook Johns-Manville as the largest asbestos firm in the world.[16]

Then, in 1960, came a further shock. Dr Christopher Wagner, a South African pathologist, had been studying the abnormally high incidence around the 'blue asbestos' mines in Cape Province of a very rare form of cancer known as mesothelioma. Unlike lung cancer, which affects the inner lining of the lung, this creates tumours on the membranes surrounding the outside of the lungs, the heart and the abdominal cavity. In examining 47 cases of mesothelioma, Wagner found that all but two had followed heavy exposure to crocidolite. Almost all were men who had worked in the mines.[17]

The three potentially fatal diseases associated with asbestos had all now been firmly identified. It was a turning point for the fortunes of what had become one of the most successful industries in the world.

Stage Two: A Tragedy Becomes a Scare

Asbestos now became the focus of considerable scientific attention. Among the researchers who showed particular interest were Dr Muriel Newhouse of London and Dr Irving Selikoff of New York. Following Wagner's paper linking 'blue asbestos' with mesothelioma, Newhouse examined the records of a hospital serving the Barking area in east London, where Cape Asbestos had a factory that processed large amounts of crocidolite. Of 76 recorded mesothelioma cases, she found that two thirds had either worked in the factory, lived with someone who did or lived within half a mile of it.[18]

Selikoff of the Mount Sinai Medical Center was a specialist in lung diseases, who had made his name in the 1950s with researches into tuberculosis. But he had then been struck by the abnormally high incidence of lung diseases, both in asbestos workers and in the former employees of shipyards, particularly Hampton Roads in Virginia, where thousands of workers had been heavily exposed to asbestos while building and repairing ships during World War Two.

Selikoff and his team had difficulty tracking down a sufficient sample of former shipyard workers for study, because their employers refused him access to their records. But eventually, thanks to information provided by their unions, he was able to investigate more than 1,500 shipyard workers, all of whom had been first exposed to asbestos at least 20 years earlier. Almost all the asbestos used in US shipyards for insulation of pipes and boilers had been amosite, as had been made mandatory by the US Navy since 1937.

So significant did Selikoff consider the results that in 1964 he persuaded the UICC (l'Union Internationale Contre le Cancer, or International Union Against Cancer) to set up a working group,

which led to the convening in October of an international symposium under the auspices of the New York Academy of Sciences.
Newhouse, Wagner and many others in the field attended this
event. Selikoff revealed his own findings: that, in the 1,522 cases he
examined, asbestosis was found in 339. The incidence of lung
cancer and mesothelioma were seven times and three times higher
than would normally be expected in the population as a whole.[19]

It was clear from heated exchanges that something of a division
was emerging between those scientists, like Selikoff and Newhouse,
who were convinced they were uncovering a really major public
health disaster, and those, like Wagner, who took a less alarmist
line. Selikoff reportedly made startling predictions of the kind of
sums the insurance industry might be looking at, running into tens
of billions of dollars.[20]

In March 1965, the working group produced a report. This
accepted that exposure to asbestos dust was associated with both
lung cancer and mesothelioma, and that the latency period before
tumours emerged could be so long, up to 60 years, that, even if dust
exposure was reduced, further cases would be occurring for many
years to come. Nevertheless, it also accepted that much was not yet
known. Further research was needed, not least to evaluate the risks
attached to different types of asbestos. Equally important was to
establish the relationship to disease of the scale and duration of
exposure. More information was also required on other factors,
such as how many of those suffering from asbestos-related cancers
were smokers.[21]

The first serious response to this report was a major study set up
in 1966 by John Corbett McDonald of McGill University in
Canada, based on workers in the Canadian chrysotile industry,
which was to last more than 30 years. But in 1971 McDonald and
his team came out with their first preliminary findings. They had
traced 9,981 men who had worked in the Quebec industry between
1891 and 1920. By November 1966 2,413 of these were dead, but
only 97 (4 per cent) had died of lung cancer and three (0.1 per cent)
from mesothelioma.[22]

So different were these results from those reported by Selikoff
and Newhouse that McDonald's findings were greeted with scorn
by the Mount Sinai team, not least when they discovered that
McDonald had accepted a grant towards the cost of his researches
from the Quebec Asbestos Mining Association.[23] Their bitter

personal criticism of McDonald was picked up in a series of crusading articles in *The New Yorker*, later published in a book.[24]

This marked a new stage in the widening gulf between the 'anti-asbestos lobby', led by the Mount Sinai group, and those scientists who they believed were deliberately downplaying the risks of asbestos. But what got lost in this increasingly heated conflict was the fact that McDonald's researches were based on 'white asbestos', while those of Selikoff and Newhouse centred on exposure to 'brown' and 'blue': the amphiboles. This failure to distinguish between two different types of mineral, just because both were called 'asbestos', reflected a fundamental confusion that was to bedevil the debate for decades to come.

By now, the idea that asbestos might have been responsible for a hidden public health disaster was attracting media attention on both sides of the Atlantic. In 1971 a *World In Action* documentary focused on Castle Acre, a Cape Asbestos factory at Hebden Bridge in Yorkshire, opened in 1939 to make 100 million gas masks from crocidolite for the armed forces. The programme's claim that a growing number of former employees were now dying from asbestos-related diseases made it a political cause célèbre.

In the USA the growing notoriety of asbestos was already leading to scores of claims for compensation by former insulation workers. Under existing state and federal law, a claim could only be made against the employer, on a no-fault basis. A successful claim was passed on to the employer's insurer, and awards were fairly limited.

In 1973, however, all this was changed, by a ruling in the case of Borel v. Fiberboard Paper Products, involving a worker who had died from asbestosis. A federal appeal court ruled that a claimant need not sue his employer but could claim instead against the manufacturer who produced the asbestos in the first place. The manufacturer could also be held liable for having failed adequately to warn workers that inhaling asbestos could cause fatal illness. The court further found that the asbestos industry had been aware of these dangers as early as the 1930s, but had suppressed the information. Damages in such cases could thus now be unlimited. The court noted that the number of people in the USA who had been exposed to asbestos could be as high as 21 million.

So dramatically did the Borel judgement widen the opportunities for seeking compensation that some of those at the heart of the insurance industry privately foresaw an apocalypse. One senior underwriter with Lloyd's of London, the world's largest re-insurance group, with which many other insurance companies took out cover against their own liabilities, reportedly warned a colleague, in words later to be widely quoted, 'asbestosis is going to change the wealth of nations'.

Citing Selikoff's 1964 paper, he roughed out on a piece of paper his calculation that, by 1990, claims could reach $66 billion. By 2000 this could have reached $120 billion. In the last resort, he said, 'Lloyd's will probably be bankrupted'.[25]

From the time of the Borel judgement, the number of US compensation claims began to soar, directed particularly at the Johns-Manville Corporation, the world's largest asbestos manufacturer. US asbestos sales also began a rapid decline from their all-time peak in 1973 of 801,000 tons.[26]

In Britain in 1976 the parliamentary ombudsman Sir Alan Marre reported on the Hebden Bridge disaster. Finding that 12 per cent of its workforce of 2,200 had now been affected by asbestos-related diseases, he blamed this on a serious failure of health and safety regulation. The government's Health and Safety Commission (HSC) appointed an advisory committee to review asbestos policy. In 1979 this recommended a complete ban on crocidolite (which the industry itself had already withdrawn in 1970); and that maximum permissible levels of exposure to amosite and chrysotile should be halved to 1 million fibres per cubic metre of air (1 fibre per millilitre).[27]

Meanwhile, across the Atlantic, the 'war' between McDonald and the Mount Sinai team was hotting up still further. In a bid to discredit McDonald's 1971 findings on chrysotile, Selikoff had crossed the Canadian border to carry out a small 'mortality' study on workers who, before their deaths, had worked in the Thetford white asbestos mines. He organized a symposium at which McDonald was invited to read a paper updating his earlier findings. This was followed by the Mount Sinai team revealing their own findings, which appeared to contradict McDonald's. But Selikoff then unveiled his blockbuster: a study of 17,800 insulation workers in the USA and Canada, who had been followed for ten years between 1967 and 1976. Up to that time it was easily the largest asbestos study ever carried out.

The results of Selikoff's latest study appeared to be sensational.

During those ten years, 2,271 of his subjects had died, 612 (or 27 per cent) more than would have been expected on the basis of normal white male death rates in the USA. In fact the number of deaths that could be attributed to asbestos, he claimed, was even higher: 843 or a staggering 37 per cent.[28]

As one expert observer was to comment on Selikoff's figures 20 years later, 'no other studies before or since' had ever come up with a cancer rate 'even approaching such an order'.* Their influence was to spread rapidly across the world.

Yet even Selikoff was about to be outbid by an initiative launched the same year in Washington DC.

Stage Three: The Scare Takes Off

On 11 September 1978 a mimeographed 'paper' was circulated to the US media, in the name of two of the USA's leading health agencies, the National Institute of Environmental Health Sciences (NIESH) and the National Cancer Institute (NIC). It was headed 'Estimates of the Fraction of Cancer Incidence in the United States Attributable to Occupational Factors'.[29]

The paper named nine examples of 'occupational carcinogens', including nickel, PVC, gasoline and asbestos, claiming that in 'forthcoming decades' these might be responsible for as much as 38 per cent of all cancers in the USA. This was certainly shocking, since it was astronomically higher than any normally accepted estimates for cancer attributable to occupational exposure (the Royal Society's figure was 1 per cent). Even more shocking, however, was the paper's projection on exposure to asbestos, which would 'result in over 2 million premature cancer deaths in the next three decades'. This, the paper claimed, would represent 17 per

---

* F. M. K. Liddell, 'Magic, menace, myth and malice', *Annals of Occupational Hygiene*, 41, 1 (British Occupational Hygiene Society, 1997). Professor Liddell, of the Department of Epidemiology and Biostatistics at McGill University (and a colleague of Corbett McDonald) also highlighted Selikoff's claim that the average level of asbestos to which his workers would have been exposed was as small as 4–12 fibres per millilitre. In fact, as Liddell explained, insulation work was one of the 'dustiest' of all occupations, probably involving fibre levels as high as 50 fibres or more per millilitre.

cent of all US cancer deaths between 1978 and 2008: an average of 66,000 deaths a year.

This curious document was clearly part of a carefully planned political initiative, since its release was timed to coincide with the exact moment when the US Secretary of Health, Education and Welfare, Joseph Califano, electrified a major national trade union conference by announcing the same 'alarming facts'. The 'new study', he said, was shortly to be presented to the Occupational Safety and Health Administration (the US equivalent of Britain's HSC and HSE). Four days later a more detailed version of the paper was released to the press and the scientific community, signed by nine top officials of three health agencies, including the directors of the NIESH and the NIC.

Although the paper made headline news, everything about it was odd. It was not clear who had written it. It had not been through any of the normal processes attending a scientific paper. Most striking of all, it produced no new data to support its startling claims.

The document triggered off an explosion of criticism from all corners of the scientific community. Richard Peto of Oxford University called its asbestos figures 'comical', noting that they were 'possibly 1,000 per cent' higher even than those claimed by Selikoff and his Mount Sinai colleague E. C. Hammond. Hammond himself declared himself 'slightly puzzled'. Others described it as 'manifestly silly', 'stupid', a *scandale*. Richard Doll called it 'scientific nonsense', and Califano's speech 'absurd'.

In 1981 Doll and Richard Peto published a detailed attack on what they scornfully called 'the OSHA paper'. Its estimated figures, they wrote, 'were so grossly in error that no arguments based even loosely on them should be taken seriously'. The paper's fundamental error had been to extrapolate from the risks faced by a small minority who had been heavily exposed over many years and to apply this to all workers, however slight their exposure. 'This disregard of both dose and duration of exposure is indefensible.' While the paper 'should not be treated as a serious contribution to scientific thought', it was obvious that those responsible for it had produced it 'for political rather than for scientific purposes'. Doll and Peto feared that it would continue to be used for such purposes in the future, not least by the media.[30]

Their fears were borne out. The paper would be widely quoted for years to come, not least by the trade union movement, which was fast becoming one of the most active champions of the 'anti-asbestos lobby'. One union quick to publicize the paper's predictions was Britain's ASTMS (Association of Scientific, Technical and Management Staff), then, under its general secretary Clive Jenkins, much in evidence.

Ironically, however, if much less publicly, it was earlier work by Doll himself which was now called into question: no less than the basis of the ground-breaking 1955 paper by which he had made his reputation in the epidemiology of asbestos by confirming the link between asbestos and lung cancer. One reason why chrysotile had continued to be seen as potentially so dangerous was that Doll was under the impression that all the cases of lung cancer he studied in Turner and Newall's Rochdale factory 30 years earlier resulted from exposure only to white asbestos.

Since at the time of Doll's study mesothelioma had not been identified as an asbestos disease, in the late 1970s a further study of workers at the factory had been carried out by Julian Peto, Richard's brother. Like Doll, the younger Peto believed that only chrysotile had been used in the factory. When he found several cases of mesothelioma, this significantly changed the perception of chrysotile, which had not hitherto been suspected as a cause of this disease. So unexpected was his finding that it heavily influenced the new 'safe limits' proposed for chrysotile by the Simpson committee in 1979,[31] which in turn helped to shape new asbestos regulations that were to be introduced in the UK in the 1980s.

Peto's paper was included in a book edited by Dr Wagner, who was so struck by this new angle on the disease he had been first to identify that he decided to carry out a further study himself. He and two colleagues, including the future professor Fred Pooley, were able to take full advantage of the advances made in electron microscopy since Doll's study 30 years earlier. When they examined tissue samples from the lungs of 103 men and women who had worked at Turner and Newall's textile factory, and had died between 1964 and 1975, they were surprised to find considerable quantities of crocidolite fibres, at 300 times the UK's average level. It turned out that, far from using only chrysotile, the factory had between 1931 and 1970 processed around 60 tons of crocidolite a year, to assist the weaving process.

This was highly significant, because it was crocidolite, much more than any other type of asbestos, which had been linked to mesothelioma. Tactfully, the team's paper did not suggest that crocidolite was necessarily the cause of the mesothelioma found by Peto. But they suggested that the disease could no longer 'be attributed with any certainty' to chrysotile.[32] What also remained unspoken was the very considerable doubt this discovery cast on the reliability of Doll's 1955 finding that chrysotile was the exclusive cause of the Rochdale lung cancers.*

These revelations prompted Peto himself, with Doll's support, to carry out yet a further study of 3,639 Rochdale workers, which by 1985 had led him drastically, if reluctantly, to revise his earlier findings. He naturally found it impossible to abandon entirely his belief that chrysotile might be a cause of mesothelioma, but in the face of the new evidence he now suggested that 35 years of exposure at 1 fibre per millilitre 'might eventually cause mesothelioma in about one worker in 200'. Although even this prediction, he admitted, was 'of doubtful accuracy'.[33]

Behind the scenes, some of the basic science on asbestos was beginning to look distinctly wobbly. More publicly, however, Doll and Peto in the same year published an extensive general review for the Health and Safety Commission of 'the effects on health of exposure to asbestos'. This acknowledged that the various studies carried out in recent years had sometimes come up with contradictory findings. Nevertheless, they accepted that the 'blue' and 'brown' amphiboles posed a significantly greater risk than chrysotile. While questioning the basis for some of Selikoff's findings in 1979, they indicated that insulation workers exposed to amphiboles were clearly more at risk than any other group in the population.

Right at the bottom of the hierarchy of risks Doll and Peto placed that vast majority of the population who might be 'exposed' to white asbestos cement products in their daily work. Their

---

* Oddly, another factor Doll had failed to take into account in 1955 was the part played in the incidence of lung cancer by smoking. In 1979 Selikoff and Hammond published a paper suggesting that the synergistic effect between asbestos and tobacco was so great that, whereas asbestos exposure alone increased lung cancer risk five-fold and smoking alone increased it ten-fold, the combination of both increased the risk by 50 times (E. C. Hammond, *et al.*, 'Asbestos exposure, cigarette smoking and death rates', *Annals of New York Academy of Sciences*, pp. 473–90).

lifetime risk of death could be estimated at one in 100,000. Even if a fifth of the population were exposed to asbestos cement in the buildings around them for 20 years, this would be unlikely to cause more than 'one death a year' in the whole country. In effect, the risk was so close to zero as to be 'negligible'.[34]

This last claim was greeted with derision by Britain's anti-asbestos campaigners, who regarded all types of asbestos as equally dangerous and who were now becoming increasingly vocal. In 1981 widespread interest had been aroused by a two-hour documentary broadcast by Yorkshire Television, *Alice – a Fight for Life*, presenting in harrowing terms the story of Alice Jefferson, who had died of mesothelioma after only comparatively brief exposure to crocidolite at the Hebden Bridge factory. After the programme, Richard Peto had predicted that Britain would see some 50,000 deaths from asbestos-induced diseases in the next 30 years. He was attacked in the *New Statesman* for grossly underestimating the scale of the impending disaster by two leading campaigners, David Gee, the national health and safety officer for the GMB union, and Nancy Tait, whose husband had died of an asbestos-related disease in 1968.

In response to the recommendations of the advisory committee set up after the ombudsman's report on Hebden Bridge, the government now introduced three new measures, imposing a new regulatory regime over almost every aspect of the use of asbestos in Britain.

For a start, a new profession was called into being: the specialist asbestos removal contractor. From now on almost all work involving the handling or removal of asbestos insulation or sprayed coatings could only be carried out by contractors holding a licence from the HSE.[35] Second, there was to be a complete ban on the importing, supply or use of amphibole asbestos for any purpose (the impact of this was fairly minimal since the industry had already imposed its own ban).[36] Thirdly, the Control of Asbestos at Work Regulations (1987) required employers to ensure that their workforce was not exposed to any risk from asbestos, laying down much stricter limits on the number of fibres per millilitre permissible in any workplace.

All this might have seemed like a measured response to a genuine problem. In this respect, it bore no comparison to what was now happening in the USA, where the anti-asbestos crusade was now carrying all before it. The first sign of this was what was happening in the US courts. Since the Borel judgement, the main target of lawyers for asbestos plaintiffs had been the Johns-Manville Corporation, as the largest asbestos producer in the world. But by 1982, when the number of claimants had reached 16,000, the company foresaw that its liabilities would soon exceed its ability to pay (even though its turnover that year was still more than $2 billion). It therefore filed for what was known as a Chapter 11 bankruptcy, easily the largest and most successful company ever to do so. This meant that it could set aside a trust fund to put a cap on its total liabilities, and also delay paying out for years while a complex litigation process unfolded.

The lawyers thus had to begin looking elsewhere for firms to sue. They began with those, such as construction companies, which had expected their employees to work directly with asbestos. They were aided by a further series of judgements (such as Keene Corp. v. INA, 1981) that allowed defendants to claim even just for exposure to asbestos, without having to prove damage. They were further aided by courts that, particularly in certain states, such as Mississippi, Texas and West Virginia, had been persuaded by the growing alarm over the dangers of asbestos to treat plaintiffs in such cases with particular favour.[37] In 1982, for instance, a young South Carolina attorney, Ron Motley, won $1 million in a Mississippi court for a shipyard worker suffering from mild asbestosis, by arguing that his client should be compensated simply for his fear that this might one day develop into cancer.

By the mid-1980s, as the number of cases continued to soar, the handful of law firms specializing in asbestos injury cases were actively trawling for new clients in all directions. Often with the co-operation of trade unions, they would send out X-ray vans – known as 'examobiles' – to screen hundreds of workers at a time. Each would be asked to sign an agreement promising only to use that law firm. The X-rays would then be sent to the firm's tame radiologist, who would sift them for any sign of an asbestos-related disease that could result in hefty damages.

In 1985 came a further development in this assembly-line justice when, to save time, a federal appeal court allowed the cases of four plaintiffs to be joined together as one, because they had all been part of the same work team. The precedent caught on, to the point where, within two years, a federal judge in Texas was consolidating 3,031 separate plaintiffs into a single case. He said he would hold trials for representative plaintiffs, then extrapolate any compensation awards across the rest.*

Thanks to such strategies, by the end of the 1980s the number of new cases was rising exponentially. This was aided by the growing impression across the nation that asbestos in any form was like an infectious disease, the slightest contact with which could inflict hidden and potentially fatal damage on someone's health. No one did more to foster this than certain US government agencies that had now joined the ranks of the asbestos scare's most active 'pushers'.

In the 1970s, following the publicity given to Selikoff's findings, both the EPA and OSHA had shown a growing interest in regulating use of asbestos, and in 1979, following the release of 'the OSHA paper', the EPA had embarked on a $10 million study of its own, which would eventually run to 100,000 pages.[38] In the early 1980s pressure grew for a total ban on asbestos, but initially this was strongly opposed by the Reagan administration at the behest of the government of Canada, from which 95 per cent of US asbestos was imported.

At least, as a compromise, until this argument was finally resolved, the Reagan administration bowed to the generally mounting alarm over asbestos by accepting, in 1987, Congress's Asbestos Hazard Emergency Response Act (AHERA), the most stringent law on asbestos the USA had yet seen. This required every school in the country to be inspected. Wherever asbestos was found, 'abatement measures' should be taken to eliminate the risk.[39]

The EPA, tasked with enforcing the new Act, estimated that no more than 45,000 schools would be affected, and that the total cost would be $3.1 billion. But until the 1970s asbestos had been so commonly used in school construction, for thermal and pipe insulation, floor and ceiling tiles and fireproofing, that it soon became obvious that the total number of schools affected would be very much higher. In California alone, the state authorities estimated that the cost of abatement in 7,000 schools would be $1

---

* This particular judge was overruled by a federal appeal court, but the practice of what became known as 'jumbo consolidations' became increasingly popular.

billion. The National Schools Board gave a nationwide estimate of $6 billion (towards which the EPA had allocated only $202,000 in federal aid).

Then, in July 1989, the EPA finally got its way over its wish to impose a total ban. It announced that almost any further importing or use of asbestos or asbestos-containing materials would be prohibited. The grounds it gave were that asbestos was 'a human carcinogen' and 'one of the most hazardous substances to which humans are exposed in both occupational and non-occupational settings'.

The EPA ban represented easily the greatest victory the anti-asbestos campaigners had won to date. No other country had gone anything like so far. In effect the ban applied almost exclusively to white asbestos, since imports of blue and brown had already long since been halted (total use of asbestos in the USA had now collapsed to only a tenth of its 1973 figure).

It was notable that the chief reason the EPA gave for its ban was that asbestos was a 'carcinogen'. It was only two years since IARC (the International Agency for Research into Cancer) had put asbestos on its list of 'Class 1 carcinogens'. From then on no argument was to be heard more often from the anti-asbestos campaigners. They would continue to cite the fact that 'asbestos' had been classified as a Class 1 carcinogen as if this was the ultimate irrefutable evidence in support of banning asbestos in all its forms.

What they never mentioned was that the same list of Class 1 carcinogens included nickel compounds, leather, alcohol, chromium, sawdust, oral contraceptives, polyvinyl chloride, solar radiation and a wide range of other substances in universal, everyday use.

None of these substances is banned as unsafe so long as exposure to them remains within safe limits. There is no prohibition on using nickel coins, or drinking a glass of beer, or sawing logs, or walking in the sunshine. What matters is the form in which these substances are presented, determining the nature and intensity of human exposure to them. It is this which can transform a potential hazard into a genuine risk; or, conversely, may turn something that is in itself potentially dangerous into something harmless.

Such was the fundamental principle which the anti-asbestos campaigners had lost sight of, with their constantly reiterated mantras that 'a single asbestos fibre can kill you' or 'one fibre can kill'. Such was the article of faith that the EPA had now enshrined in the law of the land. But before it could become irrevocably established as law, the US Toxic Substances Control Act required that within 60 days it must face legal challenge in any one of the twelve US Courts of Appeals.

Many different industries and environmental groups lined up to mount the necessary challenge, in several courts. But that chosen to give a definitive ruling was the Fifth Circuit Court of Appeals, covering Texas, Louisiana and Mississippi (in which many of the most costly awards had been made in favour of asbestos plaintiffs).[40]

Defending its new law, the EPA itself testified that banning the use of asbestos cement pipes and roofing materials would, over the next three decades, save half a dozen lives. But the agency's own calculations showed that the cost of saving each of those lives, in terms of the expense incurred in replacing those asbestos-containing materials, would amount, in the case of the pipes, to $72 million, and in that of roof shingles to $151 million. The court noted that 'over the next 13 years we can expect more than a dozen deaths from ingested toothpicks'. This was more than twice as many deaths as the EPA was hoping to prevent with its 'quarter billion-dollar bans on asbestos pipe, shingles and roof coatings'.

The EPA conceded that the risks posed by asbestos substitutes, such as PVC and ductile iron pipes, were closely comparable to those posed by asbestos cement pipes themselves. The court concluded that the ban's net saving of human life would probably be zero.

On banning the use of asbestos for brake linings and other friction materials, the court noted that the EPA had failed to take account of either the cancer risk from non-asbestos substitutes or the risk of increased automobile deaths through the use of less efficient braking materials. It feared that banning asbestos brakes would actually do more harm than good.

Overall, the court ruled, on 18 October 1991, that the EPA had 'failed to muster sufficient evidence' to support its ban. Its costs were not justified, in terms either of its claimed benefits or of more productive ways in which such immense sums might be spent. More lives, the court suggested, could be saved by spending part of that money on new hospitals or providing doctors for the poor.

The EPA's ban was thus rejected as unlawful. The only hope of keeping it on the statute book was to appeal to the US Supreme Court. Since much of the evidence on which the ban had been quashed came from the EPA itself, the chances of such an appeal succeeding were considered so slim that the verdict was accepted as final.

Scarcely had the much-vaunted ban been imposed than it was ended. But in no way was the great asbestos scare over. In terms of the damage it was to inflict, the story had scarcely begun.

Stage Four: Counting the Cost (1)

It was one thing to wish to ban the future use of asbestos. Quite another was the cost of dealing with the hundreds of millions of tons of asbestos-containing materials in existing buildings. As early as 1974 the EPA had ruled that no public or commercial building could be renovated unless all 'friable asbestos' had been removed. And so universal now was the fear which had been whipped up over asbestos that millions of property owners and managers were forced to consider the financial risks they faced if they did not 'abate' the asbestos in their buildings.[41]

The trouble was that this was a very costly exercise. In the 1960s asbestos which had been sprayed around vast numbers of buildings as a fire retardant at a cost of 25 cents a foot was now costing $25 dollars a foot, 100 times as much, to remove.

Even the EPA itself had estimated that the cost of 'abatement' in all the country's public and commercial buildings would be as high as $51 billion. Yet in New York, the owners of the World Trade Center and La Guardia airport alone faced a bill of $1 billion. In California, officials estimated the costs of removing asbestos in their state as $20 billion. Industry analysts put the nationwide figure way above that quoted by the EPA: as high as $200 billion. This was hardly surprising since the EPA itself had estimated in 1988 that no fewer than a fifth of the public and commercial buildings in the country, 733,000 in all, contained asbestos in such a potentially dangerous state that, unless it was removed, it could cause 25 deaths every year.

Horror stories abounded, such as the $50 million which had to be knocked off the price of a Los Angeles office building when, just before it was sold to a Japanese buyer, asbestos was discovered which would cost that much to remove. When another Japanese firm wanted to buy the Exxon building in New York, it slashed its offer by $100 million for the same reason.

A long and well-researched exposé of this disaster by Michael Fumento, published in 1989 by the *American Spectator*, opened with the story of a San Francisco high school which had to close for three terms while asbestos was removed, at a cost of $18 million: only for the school authorities to be later expertly advised that the pupils had not after all been exposed to any danger, and that the removal had not been necessary.

So widely had the alarm over asbestos now spread that America was far from alone in facing such massive problems. In 1991 the European Commission discovered that the steel beams of the Ber-laymont, its vast headquarters building in Brussels, had been sprayed with white asbestos as a fire retardant when it was constructed in the 1960s. Its staff of 3,500 officials were evacuated to other premises across the city. It would be 13 years before the building could again be occupied, leaving EU taxpayers with a bill for over £1 billion.[42]

The chief beneficiaries of this particular bonanza were an army of specialist asbestos removal contractors, who had now sprung up in every country affected by the asbestos scare, free to charge their uncomprehending customers almost any sum they wished, for work generally regarded as highly dangerous but desperately necessary. For their owners, the profits for these specialist firms were astronomic. Between 1983 and 1988 the declared turnover of the 4,000 firms registered in the US rose more than thirteen-fold, from $200 million to $2.7 billion, and was still hurtling upwards. But for many of their tens of thousands of employees there might be a distinct downside to this work. If asbestos contained fibres which were potentially dangerous, nothing was more likely to increase that danger than constant exposure to those fibres as they were disturbed by hacking out or stripping off the asbestos to be removed.

Although it was by now customary for operatives handling asbestos to wear full protective clothing (generally known as 'space suits'), OSHA itself estimated that removal work under its own pre-1986 safety standards could still cause 64 lung cancers for every 1,000 men employed. Even under new and stricter protocols introduced that year, it still put the cancer risk at six deaths in every 1,000. And so much money was now involved in asbestos removal work that the pressure to cut corners was intense.

The removal industry itself was notoriously corrupt. In 1988 alone, officials of 23 companies, representing the majority of firms officially registered to carry out the removal and disposal of asbestos in the New York area, were charged with bribing EPA inspectors, usually to persuade them to overlook safety standards. Lower down the scale there flourished hundreds of 'cowboy operations' (known as 'rip and skippers'), which disregarded safety rules even more flagrantly.[43] In New York and other cities, thousands of immigrant workers were prepared to carry out asbestos removal work for $50 an hour, often using no safety precautions at all.

Simply on the basis of estimates published by the official agencies themselves, it seemed that many more lives were being put at risk by removing asbestos than by leaving it in place. One of the odder statistics thrown up by the EPA's attempts to measure the size of the health risk posed by asbestos in buildings was that which showed airborne fibre counts in buildings where asbestos was in good repair at 3.5 nanograms per cubic metre (0.001 fibres per millilitre); whereas those around buildings where asbestos was damaged averaged only 0.25 nanograms (0.0001 fibres per millilitre) or 14 times lower. [44]

Yet asbestos workers in the shipyards of the 1940s had faced exposures at up to a million times these levels. A Harvard University study in 1988 compared the official projection that one person in 100,000 faced a lifetime risk of dying from exposure to asbestos in buildings with the statistical incidence of other types of death. The chances of being run over by a car as a pedestrian were 290 times higher; of dying in an air crash 730 times higher; in a motor accident 1,600 times higher; of being killed by smoking 21,900 times higher.

Naturally few people were calling for the complete banning of motorcars or air travel, or even the right to smoke. But to those now caught up in the general fear over asbestos, egged on by the alarmism of the mass media, such estimates of comparative risk were not of the slightest concern.* It was now a near-universal

---

* Typical of an endless stream of mass-media scare stories at this time (quoted by Fumento) was an article in *Good Housekeeping* headed, 'I

assumption in the public mind that all forms of 'asbestos' posed similar risks.

This had of course been the key to how the whole scare had taken off in the first place. All the most extreme examples of damage to health that had come to light, triggering the original alarm over asbestos, had been caused by massive and prolonged exposure to concentrations as high as 50 fibres per millilitre or more, particularly of amphiboles (as in those shipyard workers of the 1940s or the crocidolite miners of South Africa).

Yet this had become confused with the effects of exposure to a material so different in every way that, if it were not for the historical accident that it was also commonly referred to as 'asbestos', no one would have shown any concern. More than 90 per cent of all the 'asbestos' in America's buildings was high-density white asbestos cement – around 12 per cent chrysotile to 88 per cent cement – the fibre release from which, for all practical purposes, was non-existent (those EPA air samples taken in and around buildings in fact reflected the ambient level of fibres arising from natural causes which can be found anywhere in the world).

Far from seeking to restore some perspective to the debate, however, increasingly frenzied efforts were made in the 1990s to show that chrysotile was far more dangerous than had been supposed. This was vital to the campaigners, since chrysotile was now the only type of asbestos still in serious commercial production. Not only might this enable the EPA to reinstate its total ban on asbestos in the USA, there was now a strong lobbying campaign across the Atlantic to have chrysotile banned by the European Union (which had already banned the importing and use of crocidolite in 1983, followed by amosite in 1991).

In 1991 a meeting at the European Parliament in Strasbourg set up a new European lobby group, Ban Asbestos, with its own secretariat. In 1994, at an international seminar in Sao Paulo,

---

Saved My Family From Asbestos Contamination'. A woman who had found 'death-dealing' asbestos wrapped round some pipes in her home described how this had given her 'many sleepless night wondering if asbestos particles hadn't already escaped into the air and endangered my family'. Only at the end of the article did she admit that tests had eventually shown no fibres being released into the air. Asked where she had first learned of the dangers of asbestos, she said it was from an earlier article in *Good Housekeeping*.

Brazil, this was expanded into a global organization to campaign for a completely 'asbestos-free world'. Its support came from trade unions, 'progressive' politicians, 'concerned scientists', environmental pressure groups, such as Greenpeace, and 'asbestos victim support groups'.

The campaign also, however, found an unlikely ally in two multinational companies: Eternit based in Belgium and St Gobain in France. These two corporate giants had long been major asbestos producers themselves. But they supported the campaign for a ban because they were now hoping to dominate the fast-emerging world market in the materials being promoted as substitutes for asbestos, from cement made with synthetic or glass fibres to rockwool.*

A number of scientists lent support to the campaign with studies purporting to show that chrysotile was much more dangerous than had hitherto been supposed, particularly in causing mesothelioma. A team led by John Dement reported on a group of textile workers in South Carolina, concluding in 1994 that 'chrysotile asbestos is by far the main contributor to pleural mesothelioma causation in the US'.[45] In 1996 another paper (Smith and Wright) was actually given the title 'Chrysotile asbestos is the main cause of pleural mesothelioma'.[46]

These studies were eagerly publicized by the anti-asbestos campaigners, and in 1999 helped inspire a paper by Julian Peto, now a professor at the London School of Hygiene and Tropical

* The prime mover in this, by his own account, was the late Eric Menghem, the managing director of Eternit (UK) and a director of the group, Eternit Belgium. Eternit was having problems with the prices charged by its Canadian suppliers of chrysotile. Menghem's plan was for Eternit to get out of white asbestos production and to concentrate instead on manufacturing cement made from asbestos substitutes. A good way to further this aim, he calculated, was to give support to the campaign for a ban on chrysotile. His chief concern was that, if Eternit backed the ban by supporting claims that chrysotile was harmful to health, this would be used as evidence by US lawyers to claim compensation against his company. At a meeting in Chicago he reached an agreement with a group of top US claims lawyers that, if he supported the ban (which would help their cause), they in return would not bring any claims against Eternit in respect of asbestos products the company had supplied in the past. Both sides kept their word, and Eternit remained immune to compensation claims (based on testimony from Menghem to a business colleague).

Medicine, predicting that asbestos-related cancer cases in western Europe would soar over the next 35 years, causing half a million deaths. Half these would be from mesothelioma. These were figures far higher than any previous projections.[47]

All this helped bring about another landmark victory for the 'Ban Asbestos' lobby. Several EU countries had already banned chrysotile in the 1990s, including Germany, Italy and the Netherlands. But now, in its directive 1999/77, the EU ruled that 'no threshold level of exposure has yet been identified below which chrysotile asbestos does not pose carcinogenic risks'. In effect this was enshrining in law that central article of the campaigners' faith that just one fibre was enough to kill. The directive accordingly imposed a ban on the importing, manufacture or sale of any products containing white asbestos, to be made absolute throughout the EU by 2005.

In Britain, the environment minister John Prescott rushed to implement the EU ban almost immediately. It would be enforced by the Health and Safety Executive, which in 1996 had commissioned its own in-house 'review of fibre toxicology' from Maureen Meldrum. After setting out the basic fact that the 'degree of hazard' posed by asbestos depended on the type of fibre ('greater with amphiboles than with chrysotile') and the size and length of the fibres (long fibres more hazardous than short), she went on to state that 'the balance of toxicological evidence does not support the no-threshold model for asbestos-induced lung cancer. A practical threshold is likely'.

In other words, Meldrum accepted on behalf of the HSE that there was a threshold level of exposure below which asbestos was not dangerous. She went on to assert that

> *very few cases of mesothelioma can be reliably attributed to chrysotile, despite the many thousands of workers who have had massive and prolonged exposure to this type of asbestos. In contrast, mesotheliomas have been observed among some workers who experienced only brief exposures to amphiboles. These differences are most likely explained by the limited durability of chrysotile in the lungs.*

Each of her statements ran directly counter to the central claims of the anti-asbestos lobby, that one type of asbestos was as dangerous as another; that 'one fibre can kill'; and that chrysotile was a major cause of mesothelioma.[48]

Four years later, the HSE published a much more comprehensive paper by two of its leading statisticians, John Hodgson and Andrew Darnton. This was based on a comprehensive review of all the major studies carried out on different types of asbestos over the previous 20 years that had included data on exposure levels: more than 70 in all. Their conclusions were considerably more detailed than Meldrum's. So slight was the risk of incurring mesothelioma from chrysotile, their consensus of researches showed, that crocidolite was 500 times more dangerous than white asbestos; the risk from amosite 300 times greater. Although they suggested that it was not so easy to reach firm conclusions on the risk ratios for lung cancer, their survey indicated that the risk posed by crocidolite was at least 50 times greater than that from chrysotile, and that by amosite 10 times greater.[49]

However, these figures were chiefly drawn from studies based on highly exposed groups, such as insulation workers, textile workers and miners. When it came to assessing the risks from exposure at much lower levels, such as those faced by the vast majority of the population from contact with asbestos in the average home or workplace, the levels of danger fell very dramatically. Hodgson and Darnton's 'best estimate' for the risk of contracting mesothelioma from the kind of exposure caused by contact with asbestos cement was that this was so low as to be 'probably insignificant'. As for the risk of contracting lung cancer it was 'strongly arguable' that this was 'zero'. Yet this represented the scientific consensus on the risk to health posed by more than 90 per cent of all the asbestos-containing materials in existence.

The significance of these conclusions was not just that they contradicted almost every article of faith on which the anti-asbestos campaigners based their case. It was that they now represented the considered official view of the HSE. Yet this was the body now charged with enforcing in Britain legislation based on precisely those beliefs that the HSE's own researches had so comprehensively refuted.

Over the next few years this contradiction, between its own science-based assessment and the EU-derived law it was now bound to enforce, was to place the HSE in a very anomalous position. But before we consider the consequences of this we must recap on another drama that had been unfolding in the same years: one so remarkable that it merits a section to itself.

Counting the Cost (2): 'the largest fraud in history'

Since the early 1970s, the growing panic over asbestos had been leading to two immense financial disasters which for many years had been developing largely away from public view. The first was the explosion in compensation claims in the US courts, which by the 1990s were annually doubling in number.

The other arose from the matter of who was to pay these astronomic bills, now rising at billions of dollars a year. The firms against whom claims were successful were suffering damage enough. But much of the compensation awarded against them was covered by insurance; and this rendered no organization more vulnerable than Lloyd's of London, the ancient and unique institution which much of the international insurance industry used to provide reinsurance cover for its own liabilities.

To pay its own bills, Lloyd's could ultimately make unlimited call on the assets of its 6,000 members, known as 'Names'. But with the Borel case in 1973 greatly magnifying the potential scale of compensation claims, a few senior members of Lloyd's had been quick to appreciate that the implications for their own business were catastrophic. As one had predicted, in words eventually to become famous, 'it will bankrupt Lloyd's of London and there is nothing we can do to stop it'.[50]

Those senior insiders did, however, take steps to minimize their own liability. While concealing how serious the losses threatened to become, they drastically relaxed the financial conditions needed to qualify as a 'Name' and actively trawled for new members, not least in the USA itself, thus vastly expanding the number of people liable to cover those losses. They then, in the early 1980s, unloaded their own personal potential losses from asbestos claims, and those of syndicates of which they were members, by reinsuring them with other syndicates from whom the scale of the approaching disaster had been concealed. Among the documents they withheld was a new report from Selikoff in 1982, now estimating that the total number of Americans exposed to asbestos was 27 million.[51]

By 1988, when the number of Names had risen more than five-fold to 34,000, Lloyd's for the first time made a brief public admission that it was faced by an 'asbestos problem'. Over the next twelve months, the coincidence of the growing weight of asbestos claims with a succession of other disasters, such as the sinking of the tanker *Exxon Valdez* and an earthquake in San Francisco, began to bring the crisis out into the open.

Lloyd's deficits for 1988, 1989 and 1990 totalled £4.5 billion. For the new Names in particular, whose liabilities were more than twice those of existing members, the losses were devastating. Scores were bankrupted, an estimated 30 committed suicide, ancient estates had to be sold up. It sent a wave of shock through the upper reaches of society, on both sides of the Atlantic. In four years the number of Names almost halved.

In 1995 the New York State Insurance Department reported that the Lloyd's American Trust Fund alone was showing a deficit of $18 billion. In 1996 the Lloyd's chief executive Peter Middleton resigned, admitting that there had been fraud at the top of the organization.

Faced with a deluge of legal claims from its own members, Lloyd's launched a 'Reconstruction and Renewal' plan, setting aside £12 billion for a new company, Equitas, to take responsibility for all its pre-1993 asbestos obligations. Names were offered a reduction in their own liabilities, so long as they paid up immediately and waived their claims.

Sir William Jaffray, one of many former Names who persisted in his demands for legal redress, said of the prolonged cover-up, 'we were the victims of a massive swindle'. Another called it, 'one of the greatest commercial and political crimes of the twentieth century'. Thomas Seifert, a New York lawyer representing a group of US Names, claimed in a letter to Tony Blair on 7 October 1997, 'Lloyd's has committed the largest, most extensive and pervasive fraud in history'.[52]

How had the most respected insurance institution in the world been thus brought to the edge of ruin? Much of the answer lay in the extraordinary drama which had been unfolding in the US court system in the 1990s, the truth of which did not receive the full glare of publicity until 2002.

In March 2002 the leading US business magazine *Fortune* ran a long cover story by Roger Parloff headed, 'The $200 Billion Miscarriage of Justice'.[53] It opened with the story of a case heard the previous October in a small rural courthouse in Mississippi. The jury had awarded damages to six plaintiffs. Their lawyers had only been able to produce the flimsiest of evidence that any of the six men had been damaged by exposure to asbestos in their work. None had ever needed to visit a doctor or lost a day off work. Four doctors for the defence, after examining them, testified that they showed no sign of lung damage whatever.

Yet the jury awarded the men damages of $150 million; $25 million for each plaintiff. Sixty per cent of the damages were awarded against a tiny Pennsylvania insulation company which had never had offices in Mississippi, never carried out contracts on any of the sites where the plaintiffs worked and had sold few products containing asbestos. The $83 million damages awarded against the firm were more than all its earnings in the 43 years since it was founded. The bill was to be picked up by the insurers.

As Parloff went on to explain, this case was only too typical of what had recently been happening in the US court system, turning asbestos litigation into 'the ultimate mass farce'. The relatively small number of law firms specializing in compensation claims had created a major industry, one of the most lucrative in America.

The lawyers had been able to expand their business for two chief reasons. Firstly, as many of the firms which had been the original focus of most compensation claims went bankrupt, such as big asbestos producers, the lawyers gradually widened out the nature of the firms and industries they targeted to extract money. Eventually more than 1,000 corporations were being sued, covering such a wide range of industries that they included 44 of the 82 sectors into which the US economy was officially divided.

'The concept is picking low-hanging fruit', as it was put by one of the country's leading plaintiffs' lawyers, Steven Kazan of Oakland, California. 'In the early days of the litigation, you had Manville, Manville goes away. Next in line are the regional distributors. If they go away, next in line are the contractors who bought from them. If these guys disappear, there are cases where we very legitimately are suing the neighbourhood hardware store, because that's where the guy bought asbestos joint compound; or the lumberyard where he bought asbestos shingles; or the floor company where he bought floor tiles. They say, "all of a sudden, why me?" One answer is "consider yourselves lucky you were left alone for 20 years". We're now higher in the tree.'

The second reason for the explosion in claims was that judges and juries, carried away by the publicity given to the dangers of asbestos, became increasingly relaxed about the standards of proof they needed to show that a plaintiff had suffered genuine damage.

Through mass X-ray sessions, advertisements and trawling union records, the law firms recruited tens of thousands of clients from whom often the only evidence required was an indication that, sometime in the past, they might have worked in the vicinity of some form of asbestos. The plaintiffs were carefully coached in how to respond to questions. A memo from one leading law firm, which inadvertently fell into the hands of defence lawyers in 1997, included such instructions as 'have a family member quiz you until you know ALL the products listed on your Work Sheet by heart'. These were merely asbestos-containing products which the lawyers planned to allege had been used in the plaintiff's place of work.

In 1990, when independent researchers checked the lung X-rays of 439 former tyre workers who had brought claims against a now bankrupt defendant, they found that 'possibly 16, but more realistically 11 of the 439' might have had 'a condition consistent with exposure to asbestiform minerals'.* A Kansas judge called this 'a mockery of the practices of law and medicine'. It was later to be established that as many as 90 per cent or more of all compensation claims were at best dubious and at worst downright fraudulent.

Claims filed against just one defendant rose from 31,000 in 1999 to 91,000 in 2001, almost all alleging mild and non-malignant 'asbestos-related conditions'. As ever more defendant companies went bankrupt, the lawyers were having to draw their net ever wider for firms to sue, although any connection they had with asbestos might have been very slight. Cases brought against firms in the textile industry jumped by 721 per cent in 2000 and

---

* R. B. Reger, *et al.*, 'Cases of alleged asbestos-related diseases: a radiologic re-evaluation', *Journal of Occupational Medicine*, 32 (1990), 1088–90. Another study of 114 power workers who had been subject to 'significant exposure to asbestos' over many years found that only seven showed impaired lung function, six of these being heavy smokers and the seventh an ex-smoker (Dr Joseph Miller, 'Benign exposure to asbestos among power plant workers' (1990), cited by Brickman, see note 1).

2001; in the paper industry by 296 per cent; against food and drink companies by 284 per cent. A defence lawyer called this 'the search for the solvent bystander'.

The law firms had long since discovered, however, that, if they brought their claims in certain jurisdictions across the USA, they had every chance of winning. By the start of 2002, the cases of 49,000 plaintiffs were awaiting trial in Mississippi alone, few having any connection with a state in some counties of which there were now more asbestos-claims before the courts than they had inhabitants. This was the state in which, in October 2001, six plaintiffs had been awarded $25 million each, not one of whom could produce convincing evidence that he had suffered any damage to his health.

In June 2001 the worldwide business consultancy Towers Perrin estimated that the total corporate liability to US asbestos plaintiffs was likely to rise to $200 billion. Sixty per cent of this bill would be paid by the insurance industry, to be passed on to the public at large in higher premiums. It was forecast that the total number of claims might eventually rise as high as 3.1 million, of which only 570,000 had yet been filed.

By now the corporations filing for bankruptcy included some of the bigger names in US business, including the glass makers Pittsburgh Corning, the boiler makers Babcock and Wilcox, the chemicals giant W.R. Grace and the auto-parts conglomerate Federal-Mogul. What finally brought down this last, ironically enough, was not so much its own activities but the fact that it had recently bought what remained of Turner and Newall, once the largest asbestos firm in the world. At the time Federal-Mogul entered on Chapter 11 bankruptcy proceedings in October 2001, it had been inundated with 360,000 asbestos claims, most of them since acquiring the British company in 1998.

The significance of Parloff's article was that it at last brought to public attention what many observers, including not a few lawyers, had come to see as one of the greatest scandals in America's legal history. One of these who had long been expressing outrage at the practices of his fellow lawyers was a New York law professor, Lester Brickman, who summed up what had happened, in the words quoted at the head of this chapter, as 'a massively fraudulent enterprise that can rightfully take its place among the pantheon of great American swindles'.[54]

The story had begun all those years before with a genuine tragedy, and with a shocking and systematic cover-up by certain companies of the damage they were knowingly inflicting on their workers. But this had then been used to promote a scare that parted all company with reality, ending in wholesale fraud on a scale for which it was hard to recall a precedent.

There had been three chief beneficiaries of the scare, whom it had enriched beyond their wildest dreams. The first was those plaintiffs awarded huge sums in compensation for damage to their health that was imaginary (known in the trade as 'unimpaireds'). The second was their lawyers, who were estimated to retain between 30 and 40 per cent of the damages they succeeded in winning.[55] The third were the specialist contractors who also made billions by talking up the scare to encourage the removal of very much more asbestos than for legal or safety reasons was necessary.

So far we have looked at this largely in the context of what was happening in the USA. But it was also happening in Britain, as we ourselves were about to discover.

Stage Five: The Scare Is Challenged (1)

A few weeks before *Fortune* published Parloff's article in March 2002, we were contacted by a senior member of the Federation of Small Businesses. He wanted to put us in touch with someone he thought had a remarkable story to tell.

John Bridle had been working in the asbestos industry for 40 years. His practical knowledge of asbestos products was second to none. Until the mid-1990s, when he sold his companies, he had been one of the biggest importers of white-asbestos cement-products in the country. But he had continued to follow with amazement the campaign by the anti-asbestos lobby to portray white asbestos as a mass killer. He had been in contact with many of the leading independent academic experts on asbestos, who shared his dismay at how the science was being distorted.*

---

* These included Professor Fred Pooley of Cardiff University; toxicologist Dr John Hoskins; pathologist Dr Alan Gibbs; Dr Kevin Browne, who had worked with Wagner; and Dr David Bernstein, an international consultant based in Geneva.

What was particularly alarming Bridle in January 2002 was a set of new regulations proposed by the HSE, after close consultation with the Asbestos Removal Contractors Association (ARCA). This was the body that represented most of the 800 specialist firms licensed by the HSE who had the exclusive right to handle or remove most forms of asbestos. Even on the HSE's own original estimate, the cost of its new Control of Asbestos at Work (CAW) regulations would be £8 billion. This would make them one of the two most expensive laws ever introduced in Britain.*

In theory, the purpose of these regulations, nominally implementing a series of EU directives, might have seemed entirely reasonable. This was to require everyone owning or managing Britain's five million commercial or public buildings, including blocks of flats, to identify any asbestos in their properties, and to ensure that it posed no risk.

In practice, however, so great was the general fear and confusion now surrounding everything to do with asbestos that most property owners would wish to call in the supposed official 'experts': the asbestos removal firms. What Bridle feared, with good reason, was that this would repeat what had already happened in America. The contractors (or surveyors working for them on hefty commissions) would have every incentive to talk up the dangers of any asbestos they found, even to invent its presence. They would then insist that it needed to be removed, demanding vastly inflated sums which their customers would find it hard to question.

Bridle showed us considerable evidence that this was already happening, even before the new law came into force. In his role as a consultant, he had been called in to advise on a whole series of cases where contractors had grossly exaggerated the dangers of real or imaginary asbestos in a building; and then demanded anything up to £100,000 or more, for work which could in fact have been carried out, safely and legally, for a fraction of that figure. In many instances they were charging for work that was not necessary at all.

So widespread were such practices that Bridle had tried to raise them with senior officials of the HSE. Not once had any action

---

* Their only possible competitor was the Working Time Regulations 1998, also introduced to implement an EU directive, which the government estimated would cost £2.1 billion every year.

been taken to call these rogue contractors to account. Indeed, in certain parts of the country, it was only too obvious that local HSE inspectors were working hand in glove with contractors to uphold their fraudulent claims.

In every way, it appeared, the system set up by the HSE in consultation with the contractors, was designed to maximize their profits at the expense of the public. To work with asbestos, the HSE, based on information supplied by the removal industry, had drawn up a 'protocol', MDHS100, which was heavily skewed in favour of removal, even when this was not necessary. It was widely promoted to the industry that, to qualify to carry out the work, it was now necessary to have a certificate called a P402. This required no expertise in asbestos other than familiarity with the procedures laid down in MDHS100. The P402 was administered by the British Institute of Occupational Hygienists (BIOH), which sounded like an official body but was in fact a private charitable organization closely linked to the contractors and other anti-asbestos campaigners. There was in fact no legal requirement to hold one of its certificates.

Whenever samples of asbestos needed testing these had to be sent to a laboratory approved by the 'UK Accreditation Service' (UKAS). Again this sounded like an official body but was in fact a private company closely linked to the contractors, who owned many of its 'approved' laboratories. Even the HSE's own 'asbestos helpline', to advise members of the public, was run by one of the largest of the contractors.

Such was the potentially fraudulent system which was about to be greatly reinforced by the new CAW regulations, drawing millions more property owners into the net. What would make the new rules particularly damaging was the opportunity they would give to contractors to treat white asbestos products on the same basis as the dangerous amphiboles, since these comprised well over 90 per cent of all the asbestos-containing materials in the country.

Nothing better illustrated the influence of the contractors over the drafting of the new law than its inclusion of 'decorative textured coatings', such as Artex, used in the walls and ceilings of millions of homes built between the 1950s and the 1970s. These coatings were made of plaster mixed with amounts of white asbestos so small that they posed no conceivable threat to health. The chairman of ARCA told a conference in 2000 how, when the

HSE originally proposed that Artex should be listed in the regulations as a 'high risk material', he had expressed surprise, pointing out that Artex posed virtually no risk. The HSE had nevertheless asked him whether ARCA would still like to see Artex retained on the list. The chairman's reply was that, since it was potentially a very lucrative source of income, they would be very grateful.[56]

In January 2002 we began reporting all this in a long series of articles in the *Sunday Telegraph*.[57] When we gave Bridle's contact details, the response from readers was startling. First hundreds, eventually thousands of emails poured in from members of the public, describing their shock at the exorbitant sums demanded of them by asbestos contractors. Particularly interesting was how many of these were private homeowners, who were not supposed to be affected by the HSE's proposed regulations. But already, it was clear, they were falling foul of the system, often at the behest of surveyors, estate agents and building societies, telling them that, unless all asbestos was removed (even if it was only an asbestos cement roof on their garage), their homes would be devalued by up to £50,000.

So committed was Bridle to his role as 'whistleblower' that, in many instances, he was happy to give the practical advice needed to resolve such problems for nothing (most cases involved white asbestos cement, which householders, unlike businesses, were still legally entitled to remove themselves). In more serious cases, requiring an inspection, Bridle would charge for his time; but invariably this still resulted in huge savings for the customer over the sums demanded by contractors.

It was not long before we calculated that he had saved readers of the *Sunday Telegraph* several million pounds. One, a London businessman, who had been saved over £1 million on work needed to his properties in Mayfair and Birmingham, was so impressed that he agreed to set up Asbestos Watchdog, a company dedicated to saving members of the public from the wholesale frauds being practised under the officially approved system.

Inevitably our campaign to expose the inadequacies of the HSE's proposed regulations (and the misinformation being put about over the dangers of white asbestos cement) provoked a storm of protest from the anti-asbestos lobby. This provided a curious picture of the coalition of interests it represented. On one hand were the asbestos contractors, supported by the HSE (which dismissed our campaign as 'irresponsible'). On the other were Labour MPs, such as Michael Clapham, who had long been a strident champion of the 'ban asbestos' campaign; trade unions, such as the GMB (which published a glossy booklet attacking our campaign); 'asbestos victim support groups'; and, in the background, the International Ban Asbestos Secretariat, now being run from London by Laurie Kazan-Allen, whose brother Stephen Kazan was one of the most prominent asbestos plaintiffs' lawyers in the USA.

It might have seemed odd, thus, to see left-wing politicians and trade unions lining up in support of a lobby whose real purpose was to enrich various commercial interests: first, the asbestos removal industry; second, the lawyers who, increasingly in Britain as in America, were making a fortune from often dubious compensation claims; and thirdly the multinational companies which only supported the cause because they thought it would help them to sell 'asbestos substitutes'.

What angered these critics even more was when our campaign won the support of the Conservative Party, then under the leadership of Iain Duncan Smith. In August 2002, when it emerged that the HSE was hoping to sneak through Parliament the statutory instrument which would put its CAW regulations into law before the end of the summer holiday, Duncan Smith wrote to Nick Brown, the minister responsible for the HSE, demanding that this should not happen until MPs had been given a chance to debate the regulations.

The government had already reduced its estimate of the cost of the CAW regulations from £8 billion, first to £5.1 billion, then to £3.4 billion. Now, faced with this demand from the leader of the opposition, it gave way. In October the Tories' front-bench spokesman John Bercow moved, in a trenchant speech, that the regulations should be withdrawn for redrafting, on the grounds that in their existing form they would merely act as a 'cowboys' charter'.[58] He cited several examples of how the public was already being ripped off by the very people to whom the new law would give even more opportunity to exploit public ignorance. The Minister promised to look at Bercow's examples. But he then claimed, without explanation, that the cost of the regulations had now miraculously come down even further, to only £1.5 billion.

No sooner was the debate over than he left the Commons chamber to sign the regulations, unamended, into law.*

Two months later a further lengthy debate was initiated in the House of Lords by a Conservative peer, Lord Onslow. He again emphasized how the dangers of white-asbestos cement had been wildly exaggerated and that this could lead to the public being defrauded on a colossal scale.[59]

By now the anti-asbestos lobby was becoming so irked by Bridle's attempts to expose what they were up to that they concocted a strange little plot to discredit him. Three years earlier, after a meeting at the HSE when Bridle had revealed in confidence to those present some commercial details about a large overseas company he was acting for, these had immediately been leaked to Eternit. So embarrassed by this breach of confidentiality was the head of the HSE, Tim Walker, that, by way of making up to Bridle he said he could help him obtain one of the new P402 certificates, which the HSE itself had advised Bridle was to become a legal requirement for working with asbestos. Bridle went on a course, to be taught about the HSE's MDHS100 protocol by someone who turned out to have virtually no knowledge of asbestos science. When he was told he had qualified, he ran off two sample letterheads, including a reference to P402, sending one to the BIOH to inform them that he had passed.

He was then informed, however, that he was not qualified after all, because he regarded the MDHS100 as so flawed that he would not use it. He never used the BIOH's qualification again. But two years later, after his whistleblowing campaign had attracted such attention, the BIOH brought pressure on his local trading standards office to prosecute him for fraudulent use of its certificate

---

* Bercow's successor as Tory spokesman supplied Brown with the details of six typical cases of fraudulent behaviour by HSE-licensed contractors. These included, for instance, a public library in Wales where two small white asbestos ceiling panels had been damaged. An ARCA contractor had said that it would be necessary to remove the entire roof, at a cost of £100,000. The panels were legally replaced for less than £100. In west London HSE-licensed contractors had claimed that a block of flats was riddled with 'dangerous asbestos' that would cost more than £60,000 to remove. When the building was inspected the alleged 'asbestos' turned out to be horsehair. After these case studies were presented to the Minister, no more was heard.

under the Trade Descriptions Act. Out of the blue, Bridle was faced with five criminal charges, all relating to his innocuous use of the P402 qualification on the letterhead he had sent to the BIOH.

This seemed so surreal he assumed the court would throw it out. But the story then became ever murkier. The HSE claimed to have lost its notes on the meeting at which Walker had suggested to Bridle that he should obtain a P402 qualification. In Bridle's absence, while he was lecturing in America, his solicitor, without authorization, pleaded guilty on his behalf to all charges (the solicitor was later struck off). In 2004 the case was reheard, in front of a judge who found its arcane details so confusing that he settled on what he thought was a compromise fair to both sides. He accepted that Bridle was 'honest', of 'impeccable character' and had not 'attempted to deceive', striking out four of the charges. But on the two remaining counts he found Bridle technically guilty.

Bridle's enemies were overjoyed. A lurid version of his conviction was immediately given wide circulation round the industry and the trade press. From then on, whenever he was involved in any asbestos-related battle, details of his 'criminal record' were anonymously sent to everyone involved, from judges to the local papers.

Undeterred, Bridle carried on as before. His opponents therefore now tried a different tack. The chairman of ARCA privately said he now wished to support the campaign to 'clean up the industry', providing Asbestos Watchdog with offices and funding. Bridle was also suddenly treated by the HSE with much more respect. In November 2004 it appointed him as an official 'stakeholder', to be consulted by the HSE on future asbestos policy.*

In his now regular meetings with senior HSE officials, Bridle lost no opportunity to report some of the more flagrant cases of fraud and overcharging that he and Asbestos Watchdog were continuing to come across. The victims ranged from private homeowners, churches and charities to businesses so big that they were household names. On just one large factory in the Midlands, thanks to the intervention of Asbestos Watchdog, the makers of JCB earthmoving equipment were able to save nearly £6 million

---

* The proposal that Bridle should become a 'stakeholder' was made by Bill McDonald, the HSE's Head of Asbestos Policy, and confirmed in a letter from their legal department dated 27 November 2004.

over the price quoted by contractors. One of Britain's largest housebuilders was quoted £8 million as the cost of clearing a prospective building site in the east of England. When a Watchdog inspection revealed only a scattering of asbestos cement fragments, these were removed by an honest contractor for less than £10,000.

It was clear that, for many of the firms and organizations that could see no alternative to dealing with licensed contractors, the cost of dealing with asbestos had become precisely the disaster Bridle had predicted. It was reported, for instance, that the Royal Albert Hall alone had faced a bill of £70 million for the removal of asbestos, much of it probably quite unnecessary. According to another report, the bill faced by the Royal Palaces was £10 million, most of which, with proper advice, could again probably have been saved.

Among the organizations falling foul of this disaster were local authorities and housing associations, which between them owned and managed millions of properties. One of their most serious problems was that presented by Artex, which, under the CAW regulations, only licensed contractors were now permitted to handle. It also had to be sent for expensive analysis to a UKAS-approved laboratory. For this alone the housing associations estimated that their bill could end up at more than £1.3 billion. Asbestos Watchdog inspected a typical block of council flats in Hammersmith, where each flat contained small quantities of Artex below the windows. The cost of removing this from the flats had been quoted at £700,000. The council owned dozens of similar blocks across the borough.[60]

The HSE's senior officials still refused to take any action on the specific examples of fraud with which they were presented. But so huge and unnecessary was 'the Artex problem' that they eventually agreed to review the requirement that it could only be handled by licensed contractors.

This would be a devastating blow to ARCA, for whose members Artex work contributed as much as a third of their income. They therefore lobbied the HSE relentlessly for it to be retained in the regulations. In June 2005, when Bridle was due to meet senior ARCA members at a London hotel, they boasted to him that they had just had a successful private meeting upstairs with the current HSE minister, Lord Hunt of Kings Heath, unaccompanied by his officials. They were now confident that they would get their way.[61]

Over the following year, however, the HSE's own laboratory, the Health and Safety Laboratory (HSL) carried out exhaustive tests on Artex that confirmed research carried out for Asbestos Watchdog showing that it posed no measurable risk to health. In July 2006 the HSC issued a press release announcing that, to implement EC directive 2003/18, it would shortly be introducing a new, amended version of the CAW regulations.

On one hand, as a concession to the campaigners, the maximum permissible exposure limit for all forms of asbestos was reduced to one fibre per millilitre. This was a change for which the campaigners had long been lobbying Brussels, because it rated chrysotile as just as dangerous as amphiboles. On the other hand, Artex was to be 'removed from the licensing regime as research shows that the levels of exposure to asbestos fibres from such work are low'.[62]

For at least part of Bridle's campaign, this was a considerable victory. He had enjoyed a good year. In November 2005, his international work on behalf of a better understanding of chrysotile had been recognized with the award of an honorary professorship from the prestigious Russian Academy of Medical Science (Russia and Canada being the largest producers of white asbestos in the world).

In June 2006 he had enjoyed another victory, after being invited by Thailand's health minister to speak at a conference in Bangkok. A fellow speaker was to be Dr David Bernstein, an internationally respected, independent toxicologist based in Geneva, whose work on asbestos was recognized all over the world (he had been used as a consultant by, among others, the European Commission).

It then turned out that the conference was organized by Laurie Kazan-Allen's International Ban Asbestos Secretariat, to lobby the Thai government into banning white asbestos. When she heard that the Thai government had invited Bernstein and Bridle to put an alternative point of view, she insisted there was no way they could be allowed to attend.

When Kazan-Allen spoke, she flashed up large pictures of Bridle and Bernstein, attacking them both as spokesmen for the Canadian chrysotile industry and describing Bridle as a charlatan. The following day, Bernstein and Bridle had a long meeting with the minister, who was sufficiently impressed by their evidence to announce that his country would now be reconsidering its decision to ban white asbestos.

To the anti-asbestos campaigners, this made Bridle more of a hate-figure than ever. A concerted effort must be made, it was decided, to destroy his reputation so effectively that he could inflict no more damage on the cause.

A first puzzling sign came when the senior officials of the HSE suddenly broke off the friendly relations he had enjoyed with them for two years, without explanation. But he only discovered what was really afoot when friends in two of the more honest removal companies warned him that a researcher for a BBC radio consumer affairs programme, *You and Yours*, had been trawling around the industry for anything damning about him she could dig up. It seemed she was being advised by a particularly zealous anti-asbestos activist, an ally of Kazan-Allen, who had himself worked for a firm of lawyers specializing in compensation claims.

When Bridle contacted her to find out what she was up to, it became obvious that nothing he said was going to influence the slant of the planned programme. Even when he invited her to look at documentary evidence that would disprove some of her wilder charges, her response was that this would not be necessary.

When *You and Yours* went out on 18 October, it was one of the most bizarrely partisan programmes the BBC can ever have broadcast. Echoing the points made by Kazan-Allen in Bangkok, Bridle was attacked as a charlatan, a liar and a fraud. Every point ever made against him by his enemies was presented again in the most distorted fashion. Inevitably, full play was made of his conviction in 2004, to portray him as a crooked 'businessman' with a criminal record. Spokesmen for every group opposed to his campaign were wheeled on to say their piece, including two asbestos-removal contractors, two senior HSE officials and the veteran anti-asbestos lobbyist MP Michael Clapham.

The programme was full of factual errors. One HSE official denied that Bridle had ever been appointed a HSE 'stakeholder' (the letter officially confirming this had been among the evidence the researcher had refused to look at). But the most damaging allegation was that he routinely broke the law by 'testing' asbestos himself, instead of sending it off to be analysed by a UKAS-approved laboratory.

Had the programme bothered to check the hearsay evidence it

was given by Bridle's enemies, it would soon have discovered that there was not a shred of truth in this charge. If asbestos could be accurately identified on sight, the law did not require it to be analysed. So experienced was Bridle in recognizing almost every type of asbestos product that in most instances he did not need to 'test' it. Wherever there was any doubt, however, he sent it to be analysed by one of the greatest experts in the country, Professor Fred Pooley of Cardiff University (whose laboratory was accredited by UKAS).

What was particularly odd about this farrago of make-believe was not just that it should be broadcast by the supposedly impartial BBC, but that it should appear on a programme which claimed to champion 'the consumer'. Bridle's sole crime was that for four years he had been trying to expose a major commercial racket. Instead of investigating the facts and supporting the man who was trying to save 'consumers' from this scam, *You and Yours* had allowed itself to be used as a mouthpiece by the very interests which were defrauding the public to the tune of hundreds of millions of pounds a year.

By all those who stood to lose from Bridle's campaign, this carefully planned operation to discredit him was regarded as a major coup. Transcripts and CDs of the programme were instantly distributed throughout the trade, publicized on the internet and, as on the previous occasion, sent to anyone who had professional dealings with Bridle: from companies for which he had acted, to the judge in a case in which he was an expert witness.

Bridle was legally advised that, although the programme was blatantly defamatory, to sue the BBC for libel would be a gamble. With a bottomless purse of licence-payers' money, its lawyers could afford to run up the costs to such an astronomical level that, on a limited budget, he would find it hard to stay in the game. More effective, he was advised, would be first to mount a complaint to the broadcasting regulator Ofcom, on the grounds that the BBC had broken pretty well every professional rule in the book. An official rebuke would force the BBC to withdraw.

A formal complaint was duly lodged. For months, the BBC continued to spin out the resulting exchanges. By the time this book went to press, Ofcom had not yet given its verdict. Meanwhile Bridle's campaign continued. He received dozens of messages from people and companies he had helped, shocked at how the

BBC had been used to discredit him. In the weeks following the broadcast, enquiries to Asbestos Watchdog rose by a third.

Challenging the Scare (2)

With the exception of the *Sunday Telegraph*, the media in Britain had been almost wholly gullible in falling for the misinformation put out by the promoters of the scare. Typical of many examples had been a shock-horror story run over three pages by the *Sunday Express* in April 2006, under a huge front-page headline 'Asbestos kills 147 teachers'. This claimed that, between 1991 and 2000, 147 British teachers had died of mesothelioma, because they worked in 'death-trap classrooms' that were 'riddled with asbestos'.[63] This 'death toll', the paper reported, had been 'discovered by the Government's Health and Safety Executive', after it had been prodded into a study by Michael Lees, whose wife, a teacher, had died of mesothelioma.

What the paper could have learned from a quick look at the HSE's website, was that, on investigating Mr Lees's claim, the HSE found that his belief that 'the number of deaths of primary school teachers from mesothelioma was disproportionately high' was 'not borne out by the facts'. The mortality rate for female teachers was 'in line with the average for the whole of the female working population'.[64]

In the USA, however, where the standards of investigative journalism were rather more rigorous, Roger Parloff's famous *Fortune* article in 2002 had been followed by a succession of other exposés. In August 2004, for instance, the professional journal of US radiologists published a devastating study led by Professor Joseph Gitlin of the Johns Hopkins School of Medicine. Four hundred and ninety-two chest X-rays used by plaintiffs' lawyers in support of compensation claims were submitted for re-evaluation to a group of six independent radiologists. The lawyers' 'B readers' had found that 96 per cent of the radiographs showed signs of damage compatible with exposure to asbestos. The independent team found that only 4.5 per cent showed any 'abnormalities', and these were mostly non-malignant scarring which probably had little connection with asbestos.*

* Gitlin, *et al.*, 'Comparison of B Readers' Interpretations of Chest Radiographs for Asbestos Related Changes', *Academic Radiology*, August

The following month the *St Louis Post-Dispatch* shone the spotlight on how, in just one small county in Missouri, a single local law firm, headed by Randall Bono, had since 2000 earned hundreds of millions of dollars bringing claims on behalf of supposed asbestos victims. In 2003 alone more than $1 billion-worth of new claims had been filed in Madison County, where the courts were run by elected Democrat judges, whose campaigns were lavishly funded by Democrat plaintiff lawyers. Of 1,500 mesothelioma suits filed in the whole of the USA in 2003, 457 had been filed in Madison County, 375 by Bono's firm.[65]

In the same month, Parloff himself returned to the charge with another major investigation in *Fortune*, updating on his earlier exposé in 2002. He focused on another law firm, Motley Rice, which had made billions of dollars out of both asbestos and tobacco compensation cases. Ron Motley had first sprung to prominence as a young asbestos lawyer in the early 1980s when he had won $1 million to compensate a client just for the fear that he might one day get cancer. In 1998, he and his partner Joe Rice negotiated a settlement with the tobacco industry that would ultimately cost $246 billion, earning $2–3 billion in fees for Motley Rice. In 1999 Motley was glowingly portrayed for his role in fighting the tobacco barons in a Hollywood film, *The Insider*.

Since Parloff's first article, the legal asbestos scam had become even more fanciful. Not only were the vast majority of claims now being made on behalf of the 'unimpaireds'. Having bankrupted more than 70 major firms, the lawyers had extended their targets to include corporations whose connection with asbestos was vestigial or non-existent, such as the mail-order giant Sears Roebuck, sued because it had sold asbestos-containing products. 3M was sued for selling dust masks which allegedly failed to protect workers from asbestos, even though the masks were never designed for this purpose.

The consequences for the insurance industry, which had to pick up most of the bills, were proving catastrophic. Typical of the continuing disaster was an announcement in 2002 by just one insurance firm, Royal Sun Alliance, that, 'due to asbestos claims',

2004. A 'B reader' held a certificate from the Institute of Occupational Safety and Health (IOSH) entitling the holder to testify on the basis of interpreting radiographic evidence.

its six-monthly profit figure had fallen from £459 million to zero.[66]

Even some of the lawyers themselves had become alarmed by the implications of what was happening. In 2000, Laurie Kazan-Allen's brother Steven Kazan had set up a committee to campaign against the way so many billions of dollars were being siphoned off by the firms who filed mass-claims on behalf of the unimpaireds. This, Kazan argued, meant that there was very much less money available to compensate those, such as his own clients, who were genuinely damaged.[67]

In a desperate bid to provide some final resolution to this unending nightmare Senator Orrin Hatch, Chairman of the Senate Judiciary Committee, in 2003 introduced a bill known as the Fairness in Asbestos Injury Resolution Act (FAIR). Funded by industry, this would set up a $140 billion trust fund to pay off all present and future asbestos claims. It was resolutely opposed by a caucus of Democrat senators who had each received huge sums in campaign funding from law firms, and in 2004 they prevented the bill from coming to a vote.*

This prompted President George W. Bush, in his State of the Union speech in January 2005, to deplore the way 'justice is distorted and our economy is held back' by 'frivolous asbestos claims'.

Not until June 2005 was the scandal finally brought to a head when, in a court in Corpus Christi, Texas, Judge Janis Graham Jack delivered a trenchant 249-page judgement in a case involving 20,000 compensation claims against 250 companies for silicosis. As a former nurse, Jack could not understand how a disease that officially caused fewer than 200 deaths annually in the entire country could result in so many claims. Her suspicions were further aroused by the fact that 99 per cent of the diagnoses of silicosis had been carried out on behalf of the law firms involved by just nine doctors. She had become even more suspicious when she learned from the defence that 60 per cent of the plaintiffs had already claimed, through the same law firms, for lung-damage caused by

---

* Among those senators who worked to defeat the FAIR Act, with the funding registered as having been contributed to their campaigns by law firms, were Joe Biden (Delaware, $873,116), Edward Kennedy (Massachusetts, $654,000), John Kerry (Massachusetts, $1.4 million), Hillary Clinton (New York, $2 million) and John Edwards (North Carolina, $4.66 million): *www.asbestoscrisis.com*.

asbestosis, since she was aware that it was clinically all but impossible to differentiate between the two diseases.[68]

Even as early as February, Jack had characterized the evidence being laid before her as raising 'great red flags of fraud'. Of the 8,179 'silicosis victims' whose X-ray details had been put to the court, 78 per cent had been diagnosed by a single doctor, who had also been responsible for diagnosis in 52,600 asbestos claims against the Manville Trust. He charged a minimum of $10,000 a day to take part in screenings, and it was estimated that his diagnoses had probably over the years cost asbestos defendants more than $3 billion.*

In her judgement, Jack noted that statistics alone should have shown that the case before her defied 'all medical knowledge and logic'. She was withering about the conduct of the doctors, one of whom openly admitted that he did not even know the criteria for diagnosing silicosis but had merely inserted in each of his reports a paragraph dictated by the screening company acting for the lawyers. 'These diagnoses', she said, 'were driven by neither health nor justice: they were manufactured for money.'[69]

But Jack reserved her most damning criticism for the law firms themselves. In showing 'reckless disregard of the duty owed to the court', their 'clear motivation' had been 'to inflate the number of plaintiffs and overwhelm the defendants and the judicial system'.

Although the case before Jack centred on silicosis, she left no doubt that its implications extended to the infinitely larger number of cases brought in relation to asbestos. Within months grand Juries had been empanelled in Texas and New York to investigate the conduct of law firms and medical witnesses involved in asbestos claims.

Whatever serious or lasting effect this might have on the scandal that had been corrupting America's legal system for three decades, the fact remained that, for the first time, a diligent judge, aided by the skilful researches of the defence team, had called the bluff of what had become the greatest single collective fraud in legal history. In that respect, her judgement recalled the trenchancy of that

---

* R. Parloff, 'Diagnosing for dollars', *Fortune*, 13 June 2005. Parloff described how certain law firms had moved on to silicosis cases when, around 2001, the future of the asbestos claims industry became shadowed by the possibility of Congressional action to halt the scam.

ruling by the federal appeal court in 1991 which had thrown out the EPA's bid to ban almost all forms of asbestos, on the grounds, *inter alia*, that this would lead to spending $250 million just to avert a risk considerably less than that of dying from swallowing toothpicks.

The Most Expensive Word in History

No one can ever know the true overall cost of the great asbestos scare, except that it will certainly amount to hundreds of billions of pounds. So many different groups of people have been affected by it in so many ways, ranging from the giant corporations brought to their knees by what President Bush called 'frivolous asbestos claims', to householders told by mortgage companies that their homes are unsaleable because they have asbestos cement on their roof. Ultimately almost everyone in the western world will have been financially affected, through higher premiums from the insurance industry, which has had to foot so much of the bill.

The key to the scare was that confusion between the different minerals passing under the same name. In earlier times, possibly tens of thousands of people suffered often-fatal damage to their health through prolonged workplace exposure to very high doses of amphiboles. But by the twenty-first century amphiboles had so long been withdrawn from common use that very few people born after 1940 would be affected.

The greatest trick of the scaremongers had been to ascribe those same dangers to white asbestos: in particular to the cement products which formed 90 per cent of all asbestos-containing materials. For years there had been confusion even among the scientists themselves as to how the risks posed by the different types of 'asbestos' were actually caused. But in the early twenty-first century a series of studies by a small number of independent scientists established this very much more clearly.

In 2005, for instance, Dr Bernstein and others showed by a series of experiments using electron microscopy that even longer chrysotile fibres were cleared so soon from the lung that their half-life was only 11.4 days.[70] In a further study, they found that chrysotile fibres showed no significant pathological response even at exposure concentrations 5,000 times greater than the USA's maximum permissible limit.[71]

A separate study by Dr Bernstein and Dr John Hoskins showed how chrysotile fibres rapidly break up in the human lung into fibrils so small that their effect is similar to that of dust particles. This was why 'heavy and prolonged exposure to chrysotile can produce lung cancer'. Proper scientific understanding had been confused by animal experiments, which had 'unfortunately been performed at very high fibre concentrations resulting in lung overload'. The relevance of these to human exposures was thus 'extremely limited'. They concluded that 'low exposures to chrysotile', of the type likely to be experienced by anyone not working industrially with huge quantities of raw chrysotile (such as those factory workers a century ago), present no 'detectable risk to health'.[72]

In 2007 Bernstein, Hoskins, Professor Pooley and four other respected scientists published a further magisterial paper on 'misconceptions' arising from the classification of white asbestos by the IARC as a Class 1 carcinogen. They criticized the IARC for drawing insufficient distinction between a 'hazard' and a 'risk', leading 'governments and pressure groups' to misrepresent 'hazard data' as 'risk data'. They particularly blamed the IARC for failing to distinguish between chrysotile and amphiboles, when 'the overwhelming weight of evidence available indicates that chrysotile can be used safely with low risk'. They emphasized the damage that any further bans on white asbestos could do to the developing world, where 'cement products such as water pipes and boards for housing' have proved invaluable. If these were no longer available, this would 'cost rather than save lives'.[73]

What had been lost, as much as anything else, in all the years when the scare swept all before it, was the chief reason why asbestos had originally been hailed as the 'magic mineral'. This was because, thanks to its fire-resistant properties, it saved human lives. It had then become a life-saver in a quite different fashion, on an even greater scale, by providing the cheapest and most efficient means to supply water to those billions of people across the world for whom this is one of the biggest problems they face.

Even now there is no scientific evidence that the fibres from the synthetic materials advertised as 'asbestos substitutes' are in fact any safer than the asbestos they are intended to replace.* Not only

---

* A report in 1998 on 'Health effects of asbestos substitute fibres' by INSERM, France's leading institute for medical research, stated that

is there overwhelming evidence that cement made from white asbestos is safe. It is probably very much safer than many of its substitutes.

Thus, in every possible way, thanks to the linguistic confusion which allowed the same term to be used for two quite different minerals, did the scare make 'asbestos' arguably the single most expensive word in history.

Notes

1. Lester Brickman, 'Asbestos litigation: malignancy in the courts', *Civil Justice Forum*, 40, August 2002.
2. 'Asbestos and other natural mineral fibres', *Environmental Health Criteria*, 53 (WHO, Geneva, 1986).
3. Geoffrey Tweedale, *Magic Mineral to Killer Dust: Turner and Newall and the Asbestos Hazard* (Oxford University Press, 2001), to which this section is particularly indebted.
4. Malcom Ross and Robert P. Nolan, 'History of asbestos discovery and use and asbestos-related diseases in context with the occurrence of asbestos within ophiolite complexes', Geological Society of America, special paper 373 (2003).
5. Pliny, *Natural History*, Book XIX, 4. Anti-asbestos campaigners have tried to claim that Pliny described the dangers of asbestos to those who mined it (Bk.33.122), but this was based on a misreading. Pliny was describing those who worked with cinnabar or mercury ore (K. Browne and R. Murray, 'Asbestos and the Romans', *The Lancet*, 336, p. 445). For a history of asbestos textiles from the ancient world to modern times, see Clare Browne, 'Salamander's Wool: the historical evidence for textiles woven with asbestos fibre', *Textile History*, 34, (1), 64–73 (2003) (drawing also on the extensive knowledge of her father Dr Kevin Browne, a leading medical expert on asbestos).
6. Browne, 'Salamander's Wool' (2003).
7. We are particularly indebted in this section to Tweedale, *Magic Mineral to Killer Dust* (2001).
8. Lucy Deane, 'Report on the health of workers in asbestos and other

'because the fibre structure of asbestos is a major pathogenic factor, any new fibre proposed as an asbestos substitute (or for any other use) should automatically be suspected as being pathogenic because of its structure'. It is remarkable how little research has been carried out into the risks posed by these materials, which it is safe to predict will one day be the subject of a major 'scare'.

dusty trades', *Annual Report for 1898*, HM Chief Inspector of Factories and Workshops.

9. Montague Murray, *Minutes of Evidence*, HM Departmental Committee on Compensation for Industrial Diseases (1907), p. 127.

10. M. Auribault, 'Sur l'hygiene et la sécurité des ouvriers dans la filature et tissage d'amiante', *Annual Report of the French Labour Inspectorate, 1906.*

11. Tweedale (2001).

12. *Ibid.*

13. W. E. Cooke, 'Fibrosis of the lungs due to the inhalation of asbestos dust', *British Medical Journal*, 26 July 1924, ii, 147; and *BMJ*, 3 December 1927, ii, 1024–5.

14. David Gee and Morris Greenberg 'Asbestos: from "magic" to malevolent mineral', in *Late Lessons from Early Warnings: the Precautionary Principle 1896–2000* (European Environment Agency, 2001).

15. R. Doll, 'Mortality from lung cancer in asbestos workers', *British Journal of Independent Medicine*, 12, (1955), 81–6.

16. 'UK asbestos: the definitive guide', compiled by a Working Group of Actuaries and presented to GIRO Convention, Killarney, 2004 (available on *www.actuaries.org.uk*).

17. J. C. Wagner, *et al.*, 'Diffuse pleural mesothelioma and asbestos exposure in the North Western Cape Province', *British Journal of Industrial Medicine*, Vol. 17 (1960), pp. 260–71.

18. M. Newhouse and H. Thompson, 'Mesothelioma of pleura and peritoneum following exposure to asbestos in the London area', *British Journal of Industrial Medicine* (1965). See also, D. Gee and M. Greenberg (2001).

19. I. J. Selikoff, *et al.*, 'The occurrence of asbestosis among insulation workers in the United States', *Annals of the New York Academy of Science*, 132 (1965) 139–55.

20. Witness statement by Roger Bradley, in Utah v. Lloyd's of London, 19 July 1996 (*www.truthaboutlloyds.com/litigation*).

21. 'Working Group on Asbestos and Cancer: Report and recommendations of the working group convened under the auspices of the International Union Against Cancer', *Annals of the New York Academy of Sciences*, 132 (1965), 706–21.

22. J. C. McDonald, *et al.*, 'Mortality in the chrysotile asbestos mines and mills of Quebec', *Archives of Environmental Health*, 22 (1971), 677–86.

23. F. M. K. Liddell, 'Magic, menace, myth and malice', *Annals of Occupational Hygiene*, 41, 1 (British Occupational Hygiene Society, 1997), pp. 3–17.

24. Paul Brodeur, *Outrageous Misconduct: the asbestos industry on trial* (Pantheon Books, 1985).
25. Bradley, witness statement, *op. cit.* Bradley was reporting on a conversation with Ralph Rokeby-Johnson, a leading underwriter, while they were playing golf in October 1973 (see also 'The decline and fall of Lloyd's of London', *Time Europe*, special report, 21 February 2000, Vol. 155, no. 7).
26. Working Group of Actuaries (2004).
27. D. Gee and M. Greenberg (2001).
28. Selikoff, *et al.*, 'Mortality experience of insulation workers in the United States and Canada 1943–1976', *Annals New York Academy of Sciences*, 330, 91–116.
29. Detailed sources for this episode can be found in Edith Efron, *The Apocalyptics: How Environmental Politics Controls What We Know About Cancer* (Simon and Schuster, 1984), pp. 437–49.
30. R. Doll and R. Peto, 'Avoidable risks of cancer in the United States', *Journal of the National Cancer Institute*, 66 (1981).
31. J. Peto, 'The incidence of pleural mesotheliomas in chrysotile asbestos workers', in J. C. Wagner (ed.), *Biological effects of mineral fibres*, International Agency for Research into Cancer, Scientific Publications No. 30 (1980); J. Peto, 'The hygiene standard for chrysotile asbestos', *The Lancet*, 4 March (1978), pp. 484–9.
32. J. C. Wagner, *et al.*, 'Mesotheliomas and asbestos type in asbestos textile workers', *BMJ*, 285 (1982).
33. J. Peto and R. Doll, *et al.*, 'Relationship of mortality to measures of environmental asbestos pollution in an asbestos textile factory', *Annals of Occupational Hygiene*, 29 (1985), 305–55.
34. J. Peto and R. Doll, 'Asbestos: effects on health of exposure to asbestos', (HMSO, 1985).
35. The Asbestos (Licensing) Regulations 1983.
36. The Asbestos (Prohibition) Regulations 1985.
37. Two main sources for this section are Roger Parloff, 'The $200 Billion Miscarriage of Justice', *Fortune*, 4 March 2002; Brickman, 'Asbestos litigation' (2002).
38. Environmental Working Group: 'The Asbestos Epidemic in America', *www.ewg.org/reports*.
39. Michael Fumento, 'The Asbestos Rip-Off', *The American Spectator*, October 1989.
40. Corrosion Proof Fittings v. EPA, 947 F2d 1201 (5th Circuit) 1991.
41. For figures in this passage, see Fumento, 'The Asbestos Rip-Off'.
42. *Sunday Telegraph*, 8 August 2004.
43. Fumento, 'The Asbestos Rip-Off'.
44. *Ibid.*

45. J. M. Dement, 'Chrysotile Asbestos Exposure: Cancer and Lung Disease Risks', *New Solutions*, Vol. 5, No. 4 (1994); and 'Lung cancer mortality among asbestos textile workers', *Annals of Occupational Hygiene*, 38.

46. A. Smith and C. Wright, 'Chrysotile Asbestos is the Main Cause of Pleural Mesothelioma', *American Journal of Industrial Medicine*, 30 (1996) 252–66.

47. J. Peto, *et al.*, 'The European mesothelioma epidemic', *British Journal of Cancer*, 79 (1999).

48. M. Meldrum, 'Review of fibre toxicology' (HSE Publications, 1996).

49. J. Hodgson and A. Darnton, 'The quantitative risks of mesothelioma and lung cancer in relation to asbestos exposure', *Annals of Occupational Hygiene*, 44, 8 (2000).

50. Bradley, witness statement, *op. cit.*

51. I. J. Selikoff, 'Disability compensation for asbestos-related disease in the United States'. For a summary of this story see 'Timeline of fraud at Lloyd's of London' on *truthaboutlloyds*, the website of the American Names Association.

52. *Time Europe*, special report (2000).

53. Parloff (2002).

54. Brickman, 'Asbestos litigation' (2002).

55. R. Parloff, 'Welcome to the new asbestos scandal', *Fortune*, 6 September 2004.

56. ARCA's chairman Terry Jago speaking at a conference at Aston University, Birmingham, 1 November 2000 (eyewitness report). See also *Sunday Telegraph*, 20 July 2003.

57. *Sunday Telegraph*, 13 January 2002.

58. Hansard, HC, 24 October 2002; *Sunday Telegraph*, 27 October 2002.

59. Hansard, HL, 5 December 2002.

60. *Sunday Telegraph*, 20 July 2003.

61. *Sunday Telegraph*, 6 August 2006.

62. Health and Safety Commission press release, 27 July 2006.

63. *Sunday Express*, 2 April 2006.

64. *Sunday Telegraph*, 9 April 2006.

65. *St Louis Post-Dispatch*, 18 September 2004.

66. *Sunday Telegraph*, 10 February 2002.

67. Parloff (2002 and 2004).

68. *Wall Street Journal*, 14 July 2005.

69. P. Banyard, 'The domino effect: how asbestosis is hitting US Inc.', *Credit Management*, November 2006.

70. D. Bernstein, *et al.*, 'The Biopersistence of Canadian Chrysotile Asbestos Following Inhalation', *Inhalation Toxicology*, 17 (2005), 1–14.

71. D. Bernstein, *et al.*, 'The Toxicological Response of Brazilian Chrysotile Asbestos', *Inhalation Toxicology*, 18 (2006), 313–32.
72. D. Bernstein and J. Hoskins, 'The health effects of chrysotile: current perspective based upon recent data', *Regulatory Toxicology and Pharmacology*, 45 (2006), 252–64.
73. D. Bernstein, A. Gibbs, F. Pooley, *et al.*, 'Misconceptions and Misuse of International Agency for Research on Cancer "Classification of Carcinogenic Substances": the case of asbestos', *Indoor and Built Environment*, 16, 2 (2007).

14

Saving the Planet

Global Warming: The New Secular Religion

A secret report, suppressed by US defence chiefs and obtained by The Observer, *warns that major European cities will be sunk beneath rising seas as Britain is plunged into a 'Siberian' climate by 2020. Nuclear conflict, mega-droughts, famine and widespread rioting will spread across the world ... deaths from war and famine run into the millions, until the planet's population is reduced by such an extent the Earth can cope. Access to water becomes a major battleground ... Rich areas like the US and Europe would become 'virtual fortresses', to prevent millions of migrants from entering, after being forced from land drowned by sea-level rise or no longer able to grow crops.*

The *Observer*, 2004[1]

This disaster is not set to happen in some science fiction future many years ahead, but in our lifetime. Unless we act now ... these consequences, disastrous as they are, will be irreversible.
Prime Minister Tony Blair, 29 October 2006[2]

It is irresponsible, reckless and deeply amoral to question the seriousness of the situation. The time for diagnosis is over. The time to act is now.
Gro Harlem Brundtland, 9 May 2007[3]

Almost everywhere, climate change denial now looks as stupid and as unacceptable as Holocaust denial.
George Monbiot, the *Guardian*, 21 September 2006

Some say the world will end in fire, some say in ice ...
Robert Frost, 'Fire and Ice'

It was as early as 1991 that Aaron Wildavsky, a respected professor of political science at the University of California, Berkeley, described global warming as 'the mother of all environmental scares'.[4]

In a way it had all started some 20 years earlier, when a number of scientists and environmentalists, followed by the media, first began to predict that Planet Earth could be facing a disastrous change in its climate.

In December 1972, following a conference of academic scientists at one of the USA's leading universities, its two organizers wrote to warn President Nixon of the strong possibility that the world's climate might be about to go through a change for the worse, by an 'order of magnitude larger than any hitherto experienced by civilised mankind'.[5]

'There are ominous signs', reported *Newsweek* some time later, 'that the earth's weather patterns have begun to change dramatically, and that these changes may portend a dramatic decline in food production – with serious implications for just about every nation on earth.'[6]

Newsweek quoted a report by the US National Academy of Sciences that 'a major climactic change would force economic and social adjustments on a worldwide scale'. The evidence cited for such a change ranged from a two-week shortening since 1950 of the English grain-growing season to 'the most devastating outbreak of tornadoes ever recorded' in the USA, where, in 1974, '148 twisters killed more than 300 people'.

The science section of *Time* had already reported on how 'a growing number of scientists', reviewing 'the bizarre and unpredictable weather pattern of the past several years' were beginning to suspect that 'a global climactic upheaval' might be under way.[7] The article opened:

> In Africa drought continues for the sixth consecutive year, adding terribly to the toll of famine victims. During 1972 record rains in parts of the US, Pakistan and Japan caused some of the worst flooding in centuries. In Canada's wheat belt a particularly chilly and rainy spring has delayed planting ... rainy Britain, on the other hand, has suffered from uncharacteristic dry spells ... a series of unusually cold winters has gripped the American Far West, while New England and

northern Europe have recently experienced the mildest winters within anyone's recollection.

The fear they were all expressing, of course, was not that the earth was warming but that it was dangerously cooling. It had been noted that, for more than three decades, average temperatures across the globe had been dropping. As a *New York Times* headline put it, 'Scientists ponder why world's climate is changing: a major cooling widely considered to be inevitable'.[8] *Time* reported how 'telltale signs are everywhere – from the unexpected thickness of pack ice in the waters around Iceland to the southward migration of a warmth-loving creature like the armadillo'.

In 1973 *Science Digest* had run an article headed, 'Brace yourself for another ice age'. This described how, as the earth gradually cooled and the icecaps of Greenland and Antarctica grew, winter would eventually last the year round, cities would be 'buried in snow and an immense sheet of ice could cover North America as far south as Cincinnati'.[9]

For several years the fear of global cooling continued to inspire a spate of articles and books, such as Stephen Schneider's *The Genesis Strategy* and *Climate Change and World Affairs* by a British diplomat, Crispin Tickell. *The Cooling* (1976) by the US science writer Lowell Ponte claimed that 'the cooling has already killed hundreds of thousands of people in poor nations'. In 1975 Nigel Calder, a former editor of the *New Scientist*, wrote that 'the threat of a new ice age must now stand alongside nuclear war as a likely source of wholesale death and misery for mankind'.[10]

But then, quite suddenly, around 1978, global temperatures began to rise again. The panic over global cooling subsided faster than it had arisen.

Cooling and Warming

There was a simple explanation for this temporary hysteria over cooling in the 1970s. In imagining the future, as we know from the history of science fiction, human beings like to project onto it an exaggerated version of some tendency already evident in their own time. And what scientists were noticing in the 1970s was that, for more than 30 years, the average temperature of the earth had been in decline.

After many decades of rising temperatures in the earlier twentieth century, particularly between 1920 and 1940, the earth had suddenly begun to cool again. In Britain, for 30 years we became used to harsher winters, like those of 1946/7 and 1962/3, when snow remained on the ground for nearly three months between December and March. This phase was to become known to climate scientists as 'the Little Cooling', to distinguish it from the generally higher temperatures in the decades before and after it.

The one thing certain about climate is that it is always changing. And in our own time we now have so many ways of measuring the changes in climate and temperature of the past, from the width of tree rings and organic residues in marine sediments to ice cores dating back hundreds of thousands of years, that we can get a pretty accurate picture of how the earth's temperature has fallen and risen, stretching back to the start of the Ice Age a million years ago and even way beyond.

We have become accustomed, for instance, to the idea that we are still living in the period known as 'the Ice Age'. At least four times in the last million years, since the start of the Pleistocene, the world has gone through long periods of freezing so intense that up to 30 per cent of its land surface has been covered in ice, drastically lowering sea levels and reducing much of the remaining land to cold, dry deserts.* But these have been punctuated by warmer, interglacial periods, lasting up to 20,000 years before the ice returns. It is in one of these 'interglacial warmings', that which began around 18,000 years ago, that we are living today.**

By 15,000 years ago the earth had warmed sufficiently for glaciers to be in retreat and for sea levels to begin rising. Since the end of the last glaciation, the average temperature of the earth has risen by around 8.8 degrees Celsius, and the sea by 300 feet

---

* Although it has long been recognized that there were four major stages of glaciation in the Pleistocene period, these between them contained up to 14 individual glaciations.

** For a general account of temperature and climate changes over the past 10,000 years, based on a wide range of sources, see *Unstoppable Global Warming: Every 1,500 Years* (2007) by Fred Singer and Dennis Avery. Chapter Seven, citing 62 sources, is based on human recorded evidence. Chapter Nine, citing 121 sources, shows how this has been confirmed by a mass of recent physical studies, covering every continent and ocean, using data ranging from pollen and stalagmites to boreholes and tree lines.

(separating Asia from Alaska 8,000 years ago and Britain from mainland Europe 6,000 years ago).

But this rise in temperature has been far from consistent. Within the general overall rise, there have been marked fluctuations between warmer and cooler times. During the warmest period of man's time on earth, known as the Holocene Maximum or Climate Optimum, roughly between 7000 and 3000 BC, the evidence shows that the world was on average hotter than it is today.

Average temperatures then declined slowly, dropping even more sharply in the three centuries around 700–400 BC, to create what is known as the 'pre-Roman Cold' phase. But this was followed by another rapid rise. Between around 200 BC and the sixth century AD, coinciding with the pre-eminence of Rome, the world enjoyed what is called 'the Roman Warming'. Vine-growing for the first time spread up through Italy into northern Europe, as far as Britain. By the fourth century AD the climate in many parts of the globe was warmer than it is now.[11]

The Roman Warming came to an abrupt end in the sixth century, coinciding with dramatic meteorological events around AD 540, which were followed by a sharp cooling. This ushered in the cold period of the Dark Ages, lasting more than three centuries. But around AD 900 temperatures again began to rise, leading to the 400-year-long period known as 'the Mediaeval Warming'. The Vikings colonized Greenland. Vines returned to Britain. The European civilization of the High Middle Ages flowered, as a new prosperity and spiritual and artistic confidence gave rise to the great Gothic cathedrals. Physical evidence from across the world again indicates that temperatures at the height of the Mediaeval Warming were generally higher than those of the present day.[12]

Around 1300, shortly before the Black Death reached Europe in 1347/8, temperatures again began to drop significantly, leading to the four centuries of what is called 'the Little Ice Age'. This became particularly severe after 1550, when average temperatures dropped to their lowest level since the end of the last glaciation.

As usual, there were temporary reversals of the trend. The 1730s in central England, for instance, recorded seven of the eight hottest years since accurate records began to be kept in 1659.[13] But in general the Little Ice Age was to last until the early nineteenth century. In human terms we associate the chilling winters of those centuries with the snowscapes of Pieter Brueghel, images of ice fairs on the River Thames and records of the sea freezing for miles around the coasts of Europe and Iceland. Glaciers all over the world advanced dramatically. Greenland became uninhabitable. All this reflected an exceptional period of cooling which has again been confirmed by physical data from all over the world.

The last recorded freezing-over of the Thames was in the winter of 1813/14, a year after much of Napoleon's Grande Armée froze to death in the snows of Russia. Slowly, average temperatures again began to rise through the nineteenth century, giving rise to what is known as 'the Modern Warming'.

As always, however, there have been anomalies. A temporary advance of glaciers across the world at the end of the nineteenth century first prompted speculation about the approach of a new ice age, which was to continue on and off for several decades. In 1923, under the front-page headline 'Scientist says Arctic ice will wipe out Canada', the *Chicago Tribune* quoted Professor Gregory of Yale University warning that North America would disappear as far south as the Great Lakes and that huge parts of Asia and Europe would be 'wiped out'.[14]

In fact already, as we have seen, temperatures in those decades between the two world wars were rising rapidly, faster than in any other phase of the Modern Warming. By the end of the 1920s this too was attracting attention. A US government meteorologist in 1933 noted that 18 of the previous 21 winters in Washington DC had been warmer than normal. In light of this 'widespread and persistent tendency towards warmer weather', he asked, 'is our climate changing?'[15]

Within a decade he had an answer: that sharp drop in temperatures which was to lead to nearly four decades of the Little Cooling. But no sooner had this given rise, by the 1970s, to those widespread predictions that the world was fast heading for a new ice age than 'climate-change' again went into reverse. By the 1980s it was obvious that surface temperatures were again quite rapidly rising. Increasingly we began to hear two hitherto generally unfamiliar phrases: 'global warming' and 'the greenhouse effect'.

The 'Greenhouse Effect'

As early as 1827, the French mathematician and engineer Josephe Fourier had theorized that the earth's atmosphere plays a crucial part in determining surface temperatures by trapping heat radiated by the sun, thus preventing it from escaping back into space. This 'greenhouse effect' was crucial to the survival of life on earth because, without it, the global average temperature of around 15°C would drop to minus 18°C, creating an intense, worldwide ice age.[16]

In 1860 John Tyndall, the Irish physicist, reported that only certain gases in the atmosphere had this invaluable property. As the earth is heated by the sun, the commonest gases, nitrogen and oxygen, do not prevent this heat, in the form of infrared radiation, escaping back into space. But the 'greenhouse gases' do, thus retaining the sun's heat. By far the most important of these greenhouse gases is water vapour, contributing around 95 per cent of the 'greenhouse effect'. This is followed by carbon dioxide (CO_2) (3.62 per cent); nitrous oxide (0.95 per cent); methane (0.36 per cent) and others, including CFCs, or chlorofluorocarbons, (0.07 per cent).[17]

In 1896 the Swedish chemist Svante Arrhenius attempted to calculate what might be the consequences of mankind continuing to burn vast amounts of fossil fuels, thus adding to the natural quantity of CO_2 in the atmosphere. If CO_2 was to double, he suggested, this would increase the average temperature by 5°C, equivalent to more than half the warming which had carried the earth from the depths of the last ice age to its present state.

In 1938, inspired by the rapidly rising temperatures of the 1920s and 1930s, a British meteorologist, Guy Callendar, suggested that the cause of this rise might be the marked increase in the burning of coal and oil in the age of mass industrialization, electricity and the motorcar. Far from seeing this as an unqualified disaster, however, he saw it as likely in several ways 'to prove beneficial to mankind'; not least in allowing for greater agricultural production. It might even hold off the return of a new ice age 'indefinitely'.[18]

What Callendar was recognizing, of course, was that although CO_2 makes up only a minuscule proportion of all the gases in the earth's atmosphere – compared with nitrogen, oxygen and the rest it represents a mere 0.04 per cent of the total – it plays an absolutely vital role in the survival of life. Of the estimated 186 billion tons of CO_2 that enter our atmosphere each year from all sources, only 3.3 per cent comes from human activity. More than 100 billion tons (57 per cent) is given off by the oceans. Seventy-one billion tons (38 per cent) is breathed out by animals, including ourselves. And on that supply of CO_2 depends the survival of the entire plant kingdom, without which the rest of life could not exist.

Trees and all other plants absorb CO_2 from the atmosphere, transforming it by photosynthesis into the oxygen essential to all animal life. And, as Callendar was aware, an increase in CO_2 serves to promote plant growth, which was why he foresaw a higher CO_2 level as likely to boost human food production.

Scarcely had Callendar made his prediction, however, than the Little Cooling arrived. As temperatures began dropping again, there now seemed little immediate cause for concern over global warming. But the essence of what he and Arrhenius had been saying was not forgotten. This was particularly true when the 1960s saw the rise of the modern environmentalist movement, rooted in a conviction that man's reckless greed in despoiling the planet was threatening to disturb the balance of nature to such an extent that the very survival of life was in doubt.

Even at the height of that 1970s panic over a new ice age, the article cited earlier from the *Science Digest* ended by quoting two geologists that 'man's tampering with the environment' might lead to the opposite effect: a 'global heatwave' caused by an excess of carbon dioxide emissions. Through 'the so-called "greenhouse effect"', they said, this could lead to such a rise in temperatures that the 'nine million cubic miles of ice covering Greenland and the Antarctic' would melt. The world's sea levels would be raised to such an extent that every coastal city would be flooded.

When, shortly afterwards, measurements showed surface temperatures sharply rising again, all might have seemed set for a revival of the belief that the ever-increasing emissions of CO_2 resulting from human exploitation of the planet's resources were about to lead to a wholly unnatural and potentially catastrophic degree of global warming. This belief was reinforced by the findings of a team of American scientists who, for more than 20 years, had been systematically recording the amount of CO_2 in the atmosphere from a weather station on top of a Hawaiian volcano, Mauna Loa.

Dr Roger Revelle of the University of California's Scripps Institution of Oceanography was an outstanding scientist in his field. He and his colleagues were well aware that, as part of the earth's climatic regulatory system, the oceans not only give out a huge amount of carbon dioxide but also absorb it from the air above them. At the time of the International Geophysical Year in 1957 they had surmised that so much carbon dioxide was now being pumped out by the burning of fossil fuels that there might be too much for the oceans to absorb it all. Might this excess be leading to a gradual build-up of the CO_2 in the atmosphere?

To test this theory, Revelle commissioned Dr Charles Keeling and a Scripps team to begin taking detailed readings at Mauna Loa. In 1959, the first year of their study, they measured the amount of CO_2 in the atmosphere at 316 parts per million (316 ppm). By 1980 this had risen to nearly 340 ppm, an increase of more than 7 per cent in just 20 years. Since even this represented less than one 3,000th of all the gases making up the atmosphere, it might still have seemed insignificant – had not readings based on ice cores taken by the Vostok research station in East Antarctica begun to show that CO_2 levels stretching 650,000 years back into the Pleistocene age had been as low as 180 ppm during glaciations, only rising occasionally as high as 300 during interglacial warmings.

Furthermore, it seemed widely accepted that, until the late eighteenth century, CO_2 levels had for 10,000 years not been higher than around 280 ppm. Only with the coming of the Industrial Revolution and the ever-increased burning of fossil fuels had this level begun to increase. Now, according to Keeling's researches, it was rising at such a rate that, within a few decades, it might be above 400 ppm.*

Here, it seemed, was the 'smoking gun'. The obvious explanation for why CO_2 was rising to record levels was the reinforcing of the 'greenhouse effect' by man's unprecedented burning of coal, oil and other fossil fuels. This created too much CO_2 for oceans and plants to absorb the excess. The earth's natural regulatory system was breaking down. The result, as Arrhenius and others had long indicated, was the rise in global temperatures.

---

* For long periods of geological time, covering some 250 million of the last 600 million years, isotope readings and other evidence indicate that CO_2 levels in the atmosphere were far higher than in more recent times, rising as high as 3,000ppm. The last such epoch was in the Jurassic, the 'age of the dinosaurs', between 150 million and 200 million years ago.

Unless urgent and drastic action was taken to curb CO_2 emissions, the temperature rise would soon be so great as to unleash catastrophic consequences. The ice caps would melt. Sea levels would rise. Deserts would expand. The world's climate systems would be thrown into chaos. Thus was the fear of 'global warming' born.

IPCC 1: The Forging of a 'Consensus'

There were two striking features of the alarm over global warming which emerged to such prominence around 1988 and 1989. One was the speed with which it became the prevailing orthodoxy of the time. The other was the conviction of its adherents that their case was so self-evident that scientifically it was no longer open to question. To emphasize the transcendent importance of their cause they felt the need to insist repeatedly that it was supported by an overwhelming 'consensus' of scientists.

There was no more dramatic indication of both these points than what followed when, in 1988, responsibility for the collective response of the human race to global warming was assumed by the United Nations. Under the auspices of its World Meteorological Organization and the United Nations Environment Programme, the UN set up an 'Intergovernmental Panel on Climate Change' (IPCC). The purpose of this was threefold: to assess (a) the scientific evidence for climate change; (b) the likely environmental, social and economic impacts of such change; and (c) what should be the political response.

An active lobbyist for the planned IPCC had been the UK's permanent representative at the UN, Sir Crispin Tickell, now an evangelist on global warming (although a decade earlier his book *Climate Change And World Affairs* had warned of the dangers of global cooling). He had briefed Britain's prime minister Mrs Thatcher on the overriding importance of global warming, although, as a former scientist herself, she was insistent that any political response must be based on 'good science to establish cause and effect'.[19] The man chosen to be the first chairman of the IPCC's Working Group was Sir John Houghton, director of the UK's Meteorological Office.

The summer of that year 1988 was unusually hot in the USA. As the topic of the moment, climate change was being discussed in

Washington by the Senate Committee on Science, Technology and Space, under its chairman Senator Al Gore of Tennessee.

Gore had first been introduced to global warming at Harvard in the late 1960s, when he attended classes given by Dr Roger Revelle. It was here he first heard of the findings by Revelle's Mauna Loa team that CO_2 levels in the atmosphere were sharply rising. One of the witnesses before his committee was James Hansen, director of the Goddard Institute for Space Studies, who said he was virtually certain that world temperatures were rising and that his computer model provided evidence of a man-made 'greenhouse effect'.[20]

Inconclusive though Hansen's evidence was, his testimony was warmly welcomed by Gore and widely publicized; unlike that of Lester Lave, a professor of economics, who received short shrift for his suggestion that the issue of global warming was still 'controversial'; i.e. that not all scientists were agreed on it. Lave was so surprised to be thus dismissed by Gore's committee that he wrote to one of America's leading climate scientists, Richard Lindzen, professor of meteorology at the Massachusetts Institute of Technology, to check that he was right. Lindzen confirmed that the case for global warming was not only 'controversial' but also, in his own view, implausible.[21]

In 1992 Lindzen was to write an informal paper recalling the extraordinary pressure which had built up in the late 1980s to convey the idea that there was 'scientific consensus' on global warming. He described how fervently the cause had been taken up at that time by environmental lobby groups, such as Greenpeace, Friends of the Earth and the Environmental Defence Fund, with 'budgets of several hundred million dollars' and whose support was 'highly valued by many political figures', such as Gore.

In 1989 a group known as the 'Union of Concerned Scientists', originally formed to campaign for nuclear disarmament and now campaigning against nuclear power, organized a petition urging for the recognition of global warming as potentially the greatest danger faced by mankind. Of the eventual 700 signatories, including Nobel laureates and many members of the National Academy of Sciences, 'only about three or four' were climatologists (at the 1990 meeting of the National Academy, the president went out of his way to warn members against 'lending their credibility to issues about which they had no special knowledge').

The cause became equally fashionable among leading figures in

Hollywood and show business. In the summer of 1989 Robert Redford hosted a much-publicized seminar on global warming at his Sundance Ranch in Utah, proclaiming that it was time to 'stop researching and begin acting' (as Lindzen commented, this might have seemed a 'reasonable suggestion for an actor to make'). Barbra Streisand pledged financial support to the work of the Environmental Defence Fund. Meryl Streep appealed on television for global warming to be halted.

Although, with such interest from the UN and politicians, there was suddenly a great deal of public money available for research into climate change, it soon became clear that projects that cast any doubt on global warming were not popular. Lindzen recalled how, in the winter of 1989, the National Science Foundation had withdrawn funding from one of his MIT colleagues, Professor Reginald Newell, when his data analyses failed to show that the previous century had seen a net warming ('reviewers suggested that his results were dangerous to humanity').*

Lindzen himself submitted a critique of the global warming thesis to *Science*, the journal of the American Association for the Advancement of Science. His article was rejected as being of 'no interest' to its readership, although *Science* then proceeded to attack his unpublished paper in print. Although it was eventually published by the *Bulletin of the American Meteorological Society*, the editor made 'a determined effort to solicit rebuttals', including an attack by Stephen Schneider (another prominent global warming campaigner who ten years earlier had been warning of global cooling).

Letters from the *Bulletin*'s readers, however, were predominantly sceptical of the case being made for 'anthropogenic' or man-made global warming. Indeed a subsequent Gallup poll of climate scientists belonging to the American Meteorological Society and the American Physical Union showed that no fewer than 49 per cent rejected anthropogenic warming. Only 18 per cent

---

* At the same time Lindzen was surprised, when invited to a seminar on global warming at another university, to find he was the only scientist on a panel of 'environmentalists'. 'There were strident calls for immediate action and ample expressions of impatience with science.' A Congresswoman from Rhode Island acknowledged that 'scientists may disagree, but we can hear Mother Earth, and she is crying'.

thought that some warming was caused by man, and 33 per cent didn't know.

As one of the world's most distinguished climatologists, Lindzen's own doubts about the global warming thesis were profound. He did not deny that limited warming had taken place in the twentieth century, or that CO_2 in the atmosphere had risen. But he believed that the computer models used by the global warming advocates to make their case were much too crude. By failing to appreciate the subtle complexities and interactions of the earth's climatic system, their findings were demonstrably misleading.

In particular, by concentrating their attention on CO_2 and other man-made contributions to greenhouse gas, they had tended to overlook or to misjudge the part played by water vapour, by far the most important greenhouse gas of all, comprising all but a tiny fraction of the total. They had also failed to allow for the 'negative feedback' effect of cloud-cover.[22] In both these respects, the computer models had 'neither the physics nor the numerical accuracy' to come up with findings which were not 'disturbingly arbitrary'. Put these two factors properly into the equation, argued Lindzen, and it could be seen that the 'greenhouse effect' caused by rising CO_2 levels had been wildly overstated. What was more, this could be demonstrated by running those same computer models retrospectively, to 'predict' where temperatures should have been throughout the twentieth century.

It became glaringly obvious that these over-simplified programmes failed to explain the actual variations, which had taken place in twentieth-century temperature levels. In the 1920s and 1930s, when greenhouse gas emissions were comparatively low, temperatures had sharply risen. But in the very years when emissions were rising most steeply, during the Little Cooling between the 1940s and the 1970s, temperatures were in decline.

In fact, the assumptions on which the models were based would have led them to predict a twentieth-century warming four times greater than the rise that had been actually recorded (with most of that rise taking place before atmospheric CO_2 had reached anything like its present level). On this basis, how could any trust now be placed in their attempts to estimate future rises?

Clearly some significant factors were getting missed out by the modellers as they made their extravagant predictions of future warming. But the campaigners were already becoming distinctly impatient with 'climate sceptics', such as Lindzen, who dared question their thesis. They were attacked in books and in a long article in the *New York Times* by Senator Gore, who compared 'true believers' such as himself to Galileo, bravely standing for the truth against the blind orthodoxy of his time. And in 1990 the global warming advocates won their most powerful support of all when the UN's Intergovernmental Panel on Climate Change produced its 'First Assessment Report' (FAR).

Over the years ahead the IPCC, through a succession of such reports, was to become the central player in the debate. As this initial report exemplified, these emerged from an elaborate two-stage process. The first involved compiling a three-part scientific report, under the main headings of the IPCC's agenda: assessment of climate change, assessment of its impact, and recommendations for action. This technical report was compiled by three working groups, made up of many different scientists, economists and experts of every kind. These 'authors' contributed to a series of 'chapters', under the guidance of 'lead authors' and a 'lead chapter author'. The resulting draft was then circulated to hundreds of 'expert reviewers' throughout the world for comment.

The second stage was the drafting of a 'Summary for Policymakers', under the direction of the IPCC working group's chairman Sir John Houghton. This began with the submission of the technical report to governments, each of which could insist on changes. The result, as soon became apparent, was that the 'Summary for Policymakers' often became significantly different in key respects from the main technical report itself, although it was the Summary which would be most widely read, publicized and quoted.

The way this was to work in practice was illustrated by the IPCC's first report. The Summary for Policymakers began by saying virtually everything the advocates of global warming could have hoped for. The IPCC was 'certain' that there was a 'greenhouse effect', enhanced by 'emissions from human activities'. It was 'confident' that the increase in CO_2 alone had been 'responsible for over half the enhanced greenhouse effect', and that this would 'require immediate reductions in emissions from human activities of over 60 percent to stabilise their concentrations at today's levels'.

'Based on current models', the Summary predicted that, unless action was taken, global mean temperatures would increase through the twenty-first century by between 0.2° and 0.5°C per decade. This was an increase greater than any 'seen in the past 10,000 years'. Over the previous 100 years, it found, surface temperatures had increased by between 0.3° and 0.6°. It was thus now predicting a roughly similar increase every ten years. Hence the need for such drastic action.

The Summary did go on to admit, however, that this twentieth-century increase could have been 'largely due to natural variability'. This appeared to contradict its earlier claim that increased CO_2 was responsible for half the increase in greenhouse warming. To make the picture still more confused, the Summary hastened to add that natural and 'other human factors could have offset a still larger human-induced greenhouse warming'. Finally the Summary conceded that to reach an 'unequivocal' view of the 'enhanced greenhouse effect' would not be possible for 'a decade or more'.

These ambiguities were at least in part explained by comparing the Summary with the hundreds of pages of the main report. Here the findings of the technical experts were often much more cautious and even contradictory, supporting nothing like so straightforward a set of conclusions as the Summary tried to suggest.

As Lindzen was to comment:

> *The report as such has both positive and negative features. Methodologically, the report is deeply committed to reliance on large models, and within the report models are largely verified by comparison with other models. Given that models are known to agree more with each other than with nature (even after 'tuning'), that approach does not seem promising. In addition a number of the participants have testified to the pressure put on them to emphasise results supportive of the current scenario and to suppress other results. That pressure has frequently been effective, and a survey of participants reveals substantial disagreement with the final report.*

Lindzen went on to underline the startling contrast between the scientific report and the Policymakers Summary, written, as he said, 'by the editor Sir John Houghton':

His summary largely ignores the uncertainty in the report and attempts to present the expectation of substantial warming as firmly based science.[23]

Another academic critic similarly observed how 'comments that were not welcomed by the main authors stood little chance of being considered seriously'.[24] He went on to quote Houghton himself confirming this, in admitting that:

whilst every attempt was made by the lead authors to incorporate their comments, in some cases these formed a minority opinion which could not be reconciled with the larger consensus.[25]

Genuine consensus or no, the IPCC's report had given the global warming campaign tremendous momentum. Its most dramatic consequence came two years later in 1992, with a proposal that the world's governments should meet in Rio de Janeiro for an 'Earth Summit'.

Frenzied lobbying by environmental groups, such as Greenpeace and Friends of the Earth, ensured that 20,000 activists from all over the world were destined to meet in Rio at the same time. This evidence of remarkable popular support ensured that politicians from 170 countries arrived in Rio, including no fewer than 108 prime ministers and presidents.

While most of the activists staged a giant rally nearby, known as the 'Non-governmental Organization Forum', 2,400 of them were invited to the main conference itself, to cheer on the politicians as they signed a 'Framework Convention on Climate Change'. This was a voluntary agreement that CO_2 emissions by the year 2000 would be no higher than they had been in 1990. The intention was that this should soon be replaced by a series of 'protocols', setting mandatory targets for curbing emissions of all greenhouse gases (the first was to be agreed at Kyoto five years later).[26]

For the campaigners on global warming this was a heady moment. No one was more eager to exploit it than Al Gore, as he stepped down from the US Senate to become the Democratic Party's vice-presidential candidate alongside Bill Clinton.

Gore had now made his stand on climate change the defining issue of his political career. In his bid to become the Democrats' nominee, he had published a book, *Earth In The Balance*. Like much of his environmental writing, this was interspersed with personal reminiscences. One of the more important moments in his life, he recalled, was how he had been introduced to the cosmic significance of climate change at Harvard by Dr Revelle, father of the research project which had given the world those epoch-making figures on the rise in carbon emissions.

Gore seemed unaware that Revelle had for some time been taking a rather more cautious line on the panic over global warming than fitted in with his own agenda. In that summer of 1988 when Gore was conducting his Senate hearings on climate change, Revelle had written to several members of Congress urging that any action on global warming should be delayed, since not enough was yet known about the workings of the climate.[27]

In 1990, at a conference of the American Association for the Advancement of Science in New Orleans, Revelle presented a paper on the theory that seeding the world's oceans with nutrients such as iron filings would stimulate the growth of plankton, thus increasing marine absorption of CO_2. After the lecture he was approached by an old friend, Fred Singer, professor of environmental science at the University of Virginia and formerly the first director of the US National Satellite Weather Service. Next day the two men met to discuss writing an informal paper together on global warming, later inviting Dr Chauncey Starr, an expert on energy, to join them.

Singer drafted the paper, which, after discussion, was submitted to a new, small-circulation journal, *Cosmos*. When he and Revelle met to discuss the proofs, Revelle expressed scepticism about computer climate models (Singer tried to assure him that within ten years they would be greatly improved). After they had agreed several amendments, the article was published in April 1991, entitled 'What to Do About Greenhouse Warming: Look Before You Leap'. The article's main conclusion, echoing the views that Revelle had expressed earlier in his letters to Congressmen, was that

> *the scientific base for a greenhouse warming is too uncertain to justify drastic action at this time. There is little risk in delaying policy responses.*

The article attracted little attention at the time. Three months later, professionally active to the end of his life, Revelle died aged 82.

Later that year Singer was invited to contribute to a book on global warming and, being busy, suggested that the article be republished.

The following summer, when Gore was running hard for the vice-presidential nomination, an article in *Newsweek* contrasted his reference to Revelle in his new book with the conclusion of the article Revelle had co-authored in *Cosmos*. This was picked up elsewhere in the media and even later raised in a televised election debate. Gore angrily protested that Revelle's views had been 'taken completely out of context'.

In the middle of this embarrassing coverage, Singer was called by one of Gore's associates, Dr Justin Lancaster of Harvard University, insisting that Revelle's name be removed from the article. When told this would not be possible, Lancaster persisted in his request, suggesting that Revelle had not really co-authored the article and that his name had only been included 'over his objections'. He claimed that Singer had pressured an old man when he was sick, with his mental capacities failing.

Similar accusations were made by a member of Gore's staff to the publishers of the book in which the article was shortly to be reprinted, with a demand that it be dropped. When these allegations were repeated, in April 1993, by which time Gore had become US vice-president, Singer sued Lancaster for libel. In the course of legal discovery, Lancaster revealed that he had been rung by Gore after the *Newsweek* article appeared, asking about Revelle's mental capacity at the end of his life. He now agreed that Revelle had in fact been 'mentally sharp to the end'. He also admitted that Revelle had shown him the article before it was published, observing that there did not seem to be anything in it that 'was not true', and that 'it was honest to admit the uncertainties about greenhouse warming'.*

This was not the first occasion on which Gore had been associated with attempts to distort or suppress the views of those who disagreed with him. In one of the last of the hearings of the Senate committee he chaired, Professor Lindzen had appeared as a witness. In the course of arcane exchanges about the role of water vapour in the upper troposphere, Lindzen admitted he had now had to revise a point he had argued two years earlier about the

---

* These last details emerged from a computer disk containing a draft letter sent by Lancaster to Gore (Singer, 'The Revelle-Gore Story' (2003)).

effect of water vapour from clouds. Subsequent research had shown that another process, probably ice crystals from the clouds, must also be involved (even though this did not alter the overall effect).

Gore picked up Lindzen's admission that he had changed his mind, asking whether he was now rejecting what he had said two years earlier. When Lindzen agreed, Gore called for the recording secretary to note that Professor Lindzen had 'retracted his objections to global warming'.[28]

Others present assured Gore that Lindzen had done nothing of the kind and that he was confusing matters. But soon afterwards, in the *New York Times*, Tom Wicker, a prominent journalistic ally of Gore's, repeated the charge that Lindzen had retracted his opposition to global warming. Lindzen tried to correct this with a letter, which was eventually, more than a month later, published. But this did not prevent Gore from repeating the claim yet again in his book, despite Lindzen's attempt to set the record straight.*

In February 1994, an ABC News presenter, Ted Koppel, revealed on his *Nightline* programme that Vice-President Gore had rung him to suggest that he expose the political and economic forces behind the 'anti-environmental movement'. Gore had urged him to expose the fact that several US scientists who had voiced sceptical views about global warming were receiving money from the coal industry and other dubious interests.

Such charges were to become an only too familiar feature of the debate. Any prominent scientist who dared to challenge the global warming orthodoxy would be likely to face accusations that he was funded by energy firms, 'Big Oil' or even the tobacco industry.**

---

* This was not the first time Wicker had been involved in similarly rewriting history. A year earlier Robert White, former head of the US Weather Bureau, had written an article for the *Scientific American* suggesting that the scientific basis for global warming predictions was totally inadequate to justify any costly actions. The only actions that should be taken were those which would be justified even if there was no warming threat. Wicker reported this in the *New York Times* as a call by White for immediate action on global warming (Lindzen, 'Global Warming' (1992)).
** Singer himself would be vilified in this way for having participated with Fred Seitz, a distinguished former president of the National Academy of Sciences, in a report criticizing the EPA's efforts to demonize passive smoking. The report's authors were described as 'corrupt' for having 'received funding through ideological partners of the tobacco companies'

Not only did Koppel call Gore's bluff by reporting their conversation on air, he observed that there was

> some irony in the fact that Vice President Gore – one of the
> most scientifically literate men to sit in the White House in this
> century – (is) resorting to political means to achieve what
> should ultimately be resolved on a purely scientific basis. The
> measure of good science is neither the politics of the scientists
> nor the people with whom the scientist associates. It is the
> immersion of hypotheses into the acid of truth. That's the hard
> way to do it, but it's the only way that works.

Gore's attempt to use a leading news programme to denigrate his
opponents in this way provoked such political embarrassment that,
shortly afterwards, Lancaster settled his case with Singer by issuing
a full retraction and apology.***

One bid to promote the illusion of 'consensus' had failed. But it
was now to be followed by another, very much more public, and
conceived on an altogether grander scale.

IPCC 2: The 'Fingerprinting' Fraud and Kyoto

By the mid-1990s, the Clinton–Gore administration had become
closely involved in pushing America's energy interests across the
world. In particular it was close to the new Texas-based energy
giant, Enron, a significant contributor to Democratic Party funds.
Washington supported Enron with $4 billion of federal loans, and
supported the company's bids for a series of huge contracts to open
up new oil and gas fields and to build power stations and pipelines
in India, Russia, China, the Philippines, South America and Africa.

Gore took a close interest in some of these projects. In particular, in December 1995, he was reported as visiting South Africa

---

(see the *ecosyn.us* website, which also accused President George W. Bush's
family of having supported genocide and financed Hitler).
*** Twelve years later, in 2004, Lancaster issued a full 'retraction' of his
'retraction' on a website ('The Cosmos Myth', *http://home.att.net/~espi/
Cosmos_myth.html*). He omitted, however, any reference to the evidence
that had come to light during the discovery process of the legal action. This
included his admission that Revelle had told him that he agreed with the
main point the article sought to make: that the science on global warming
was not yet sufficiently settled to justify drastic action.

to lobby the country's new president, Nelson Mandela, on behalf of Enron's bid to develop a large new gas field in Mozambique.*

The Vice-President had not, however, lost his interest in the battle against global warming, and his visit to South Africa coincided with final political agreement being given to the next report of the Intergovernmental Panel on Climate Change, due to be launched in May the following year.

The second IPCC report (SAR) went rather further than the first in endorsing an anthropogenic explanation for global warming. The biggest headlines were reserved for its claim that 'the balance of evidence suggests that there is a discernible human influence on global climate'. These words were to be quoted more often than any others in the report. But the story behind how they came to be included in the Summary for Policy Makers was curious.[29]

The source of this sentence was given as Chapter Eight of the technical report, the 'lead author' of which was Ben Santer, a relatively junior scientist working for the US government's Lawrence Livermore National Laboratory. This included much the same wording: that 'the body of statistical evidence' now 'points to a discernible human influence on the global climate'.

When the report containing these sentences was published, however, the scientific reviewers who had signed off the technical chapters the previous year were dismayed. These words had not appeared in the draft they had formally approved. It seemed they had been added subsequently, by the 'lead author' himself. Santer had also, it emerged, deleted a number of key statements from the agreed text, all of which reflected serious scientific doubt over the human contribution to global warming. They included these passages:

- None of the studies cited above has shown clear evidence that we can attribute the observed changes to the specific cause of increases in greenhouse gases.

---

* See 'Enrongate', *www.craigslist.org*. Gore's personal and family links with the oil industry went back a long way. His father Senator Albert Gore Sr had been a close friend and protégé of Armand Hammer, the head of Occidental Oil, who helped to set him up in the businesses that were the basis for the Gore family fortune. Hammer, who died in 1994, had been a friend of Lenin, and throughout the Cold War was under official suspicion for his exceptionally close ties to the Soviet Union.

- No study to date has positively attributed all or part (of the climate change observed) to (man-made) causes.
- Any claims of positive detection and attribution of significant climate change are likely to remain controversial until uncertainties in the total natural variability of the climate system are reduced.
- When will an anthropogenic effect on climate be identified? It is not surprising that the best answer to this question is 'We do not know'.

All these sentences had been deleted from the original version. What was particularly odd about the new additions to the text was that the only source cited in support of them appeared to be two papers co-authored by Santer himself, which had not yet been published. That much-cited claim about 'discernible human influence on climate change' was based on what were known as 'fingerprinting studies'. These compared the patterns of climate change predicted by computer models with changes actually observed in the real world. Where these coincided (or displayed the same 'fingerprint'), this was taken as evidence that the computer model was correct.[30]

However, when Santer and several colleagues published their first, all-important paper, two other scientists, Dr Patrick Michaels and a colleague, examined their evidence. They were surprised to discover that its conclusions in favour of global warming had been based only on part of the data. The supposed 'fingerprinting' parallel between the computer models and observed data applied only to the years between 1943 and 1970. When the full set of data was used, showing earlier years going back to 1905 and later years after 1970, the warming trend claimed by Santer and his colleagues disappeared.[31]

This was surprising enough, in view of the significance attached to Santer's revised wording of Chapter Eight by the Summary for Policymakers and in all the publicity which followed. The realization that a comparatively junior contributor could have been allowed to make such a crucial change after the scientific text had been formally approved, gave rise to quite an uproar.

Even *Nature*, which published the Santer paper, was not happy about the rewriting of Chapter Eight to 'ensure that it conformed' with the Summary. The *Wall Street Journal* expressed outrage, both in an editorial ('Cover-up in the Greenhouse'),[32] and in an excoriatory article by Frederick Seitz, the much-respected former president of the National Academy of Sciences, headed 'Major Deception on Global Warming'.[33]

Just as surprising, however, was the sequence of events that, it seemed, had preceded these changes to the text. Just before the wording of the report was finalized in December 1995, there had been a 'plenary' gathering in Madrid, attended by politicians and officials from 96 nations and representatives of 14 non-governmental organizations. Their task had been to go through the 'accepted' text line by line.

Shortly before this, as later emerged, the IPCC working group's chairman, and lead editor Sir John Houghton, had received a letter from the State Department in Washington, dated 15 November. This read:

> *It is essential that the chapters not be finalized prior to the completion of the discussions at the IPCC Working Group I Plenary in Madrid, and that chapter authors be prevailed upon to modify their text in an appropriate manner following the discussion in Madrid.[34]*

The senior official who gave this instruction, that chapter authors should be 'prevailed upon to modify their text', worked with Timothy Wirth, the Under-Secretary of State for Global Affairs. Not only was Wirth an ardent advocate of global warming. He was a close political ally of Vice-President Gore.[35]

The chief purpose of the second IPCC report was to provide the underpinning for a major international conference, to be held the following year in Japan. Its purpose, based on the Rio Framework Convention on Climate Change, was to agree the first 'Protocol' which would lay the practical foundations for humanity's response to the global warming crisis.

The most obvious feature of the long and complex discussions which preceded this treaty, involving 160 countries, was a split between the industrialized countries, mainly in the northern hemisphere, held to have been responsible for most 'greenhouse forcing' up to this time, and the still-developing countries of the Third World. These were adamant that they could not be made to accept restrictions on their economic growth which would prevent them catching up with the developed world.

In these fraught negotiations Gore played a very active role. But he had something of a setback in the summer of 1997 when, on 21 July, the US Senate voted by 95 to 0 for a resolution opposing the proposed Protocol. This was precisely on the grounds that it was to be so damagingly one-sided. For it was now proposed that the already developed countries, led by the USA, would have to accept very severe restrictions on their greenhouse gas emissions, while still developing countries, such as China and India, would be excluded, even though their economies were now growing so fast that they would soon be major CO_2 contributors.

If such a treaty left out the Third World, the Senate observed, the reductions required of the industrialized world would be so great that this would 'result in serious harm to the US economy, including significant job loss, trade disadvantages, increased energy and consumer costs'.

Despite the likelihood that the world's leading economic power would not participate, the planned treaty remained on course. On 8 December 1997, representatives of 160 countries gathered in Japan to agree the 'Kyoto Protocol'. They were addressed at the start of the conference by Vice-President Gore. He told his vast audience:

> *Since we gathered at the Rio Conference in 1992, both scientific consensus and political will have come a long way. If we pause for a moment and look around us, we can see how extraordinary this gathering really is. We have reached a fundamentally new stage in the development of human civilization, in which it is necessary to take responsibility for a recent but profound alteration in the relationship between our species and our planet.*

'The most vulnerable part of the Earth's environment', Gore went on:

> *is the very thin layer of air clinging near to the surface of the planet, that we are now so carelessly filling with gaseous wastes that we are actually altering the relationship between the Earth and the Sun – by trapping more solar radiation under this growing blanket of pollution that envelops the entire world ... Last week we learned from scientists that this year, 1997, with only three weeks remaining, will be the hottest year*

since records have been kept. Indeed, nine of the ten hottest
years since the measurements began have come in the last ten
years. The trend is clear. The human consequences – and the
economic costs – of failing to act are unthinkable. More record
floods and droughts. Diseases and pests spreading to new
areas. Crop failures and famines. Melting glaciers, stronger
storms, and rising seas.

Inspired by Gore's vision, delegates proceeded to agree the Protocol
that had been hammered out through those months of hard
negotiation. Signatories could begin ratifying the treaty from
March the following year.

The Kyoto Protocol applied to all those industrialized countries
listed in its Annex I (including Russia and its former satellites).
These countries agreed, by 2008–12, to reduce their collective
emissions of greenhouse gases by 5.2 per cent of their 1990 levels.
Because their emissions levels would otherwise have increased, the
true effect of these restrictions was estimated as equivalent to a cut
by 2010 of 29 per cent.

Still developing countries, such as China and India, would not
be bound by the agreement, however rapidly their own CO_2
emissions might be increasing. Some industrialized countries would
be permitted to increase their emissions (Australia, for instance, by
8 per cent). The substantial emissions from international aviation
and shipping were excluded from the agreement. And the Protocol
would come into force only when it had been ratified by enough
developed countries to have accounted in 1990 for 55 per cent of
the world's CO_2 emissions.

Just how these targets were to be achieved, no one as yet had any
real idea. It would be up to each country to work out its own way to
meet them. But Kyoto also introduced the idea of 'emissions trading',
whereby countries or firms that were failing to meet their reduction
targets could buy 'carbon credits' from those which had already
more than met them, thus offsetting 'failures' against 'successes'.

One of the most obvious intended consequences of Kyoto was
to discourage the use of fossil fuels, such as coal, oil and gas, and to
promote a switch to those energy sources which do not emit
greenhouse gases, such as 'renewables' (wind, wave, solar and
hydro). Nuclear power also offered a much more effective source
of large-scale 'carbon free' energy than any of them. But most of

the proponents of Kyoto were strongly opposed to it, since they viewed it as potentially 'polluting the planet' in a different way, by creating dangerous wastes.

Revealingly, no official attempt was made to put a figure on just how much all this was going to cost the economies of the developed world. But in a study funded by the National Science Foundation and the Department of Energy, William Nordhaus, a Yale University economics professor, estimated the cost of the first phase of Kyoto emissions reductions at $716 billion. Two thirds of that would fall on the USA, as the world's leading CO_2 'polluter'. But this would only be the case if the USA agreed to participate, which, in light of that Senate vote, seemed highly unlikely.[36]

In terms of 'saving the planet', what would all this achieve? It was generally agreed, even by supporters of the Kyoto Protocol, that, even if all its targets for emissions reductions were met, the resulting reduction in global temperatures by 2050 would be equivalent only to 0.05°C, or one twentieth of a degree.[37] By the year 2100, it was estimated, Kyoto in full would have delayed the process of warming by a mere six years.

Recognizing this, global warming campaigners expressed disappointment that the targets had not been tougher. But they rested their hopes on the prospect of very much more drastic emissions reductions being agreed in a new 'Kyoto Two' protocol after 2012.

For Gore's 'consensus', it had overall been quite an achievement. To up the ante still further, however, what was to follow was one of the most bizarre examples of the politicization of science in history.

IPCC 3: The Great 'Hockey Stick' Fiasco

Although it had long seemed peculiarly important to the global warming lobbyists to insist that their beliefs were supported by that 'scientific consensus', it was not always easy to see the evidence for this.

In 1996, for instance, the *UN Climate Change Bulletin* had reported on a survey of 400 American, Canadian and German climate researchers. When asked whether it was 'certain that global warming is a process already underway', only 10 per cent were prepared to express 'strong' agreement. Nearly half those surveyed, 48 per cent, said they didn't have faith in the forecasts of the global climate models.[38] In 1997, a survey of climatologists employed by the 50 states of the USA found 90 per cent agreeing that 'scientific evidence indicates variations in global temperature are likely to be naturally occurring and cyclical over very long periods of time'.[39]

One of the most awkward problems confronting those who wanted to link human activity with a sudden dramatic rise in global temperatures was how to explain that mass of evidence from every kind of historical and scientific source that there had been similarly dramatic fluctuations in temperature in the past, before man began adding to greenhouse gases. Particularly hard to explain was why temperatures during the Mediaeval Warming should have been higher than they now were at the end of the twentieth century.

Even the first two IPCC scientific reports had accepted this as not open to question, each showing a graph which reflected the received scientific view of how the world's climate had changed over the past 1,000 years. This showed temperatures during the Mediaeval Warming higher than those of the 1990s; falling steeply during the Little Ice Age; rising again in the nineteenth century with the Modern Warming; then falling during the Little Cooling between 1940 and 1975, just when CO_2 levels had been rising sharply.

The warming enthusiasts, anxious to emphasize the influence of human activity on climate, tried to explain this last point by arguing that the warming effect of rising CO_2 emissions had been masked during the Little Cooling by the 'dimming' effect of tiny aerosol particles produced by sulphur dioxide emissions from power stations burning coal and oil. These, they claimed, had shut out enough sunlight to counteract the effect of the increase in greenhouse gases. But, as even the IPCC was to accept in its next report, most of these aerosols were emitted in the northern hemisphere, which should have meant that, while its temperatures fell, the southern hemisphere continued to warm. Yet the Little Cooling had been experienced worldwide, showing no distinction between north and south.*

---

* The third IPCC report accepted that between 1900 and 1940 the world had warmed by 0.4°C, that between 1940 and 1975 it had cooled by 0.2°C (the Little Cooling), and that from 1975 onwards it had warmed again by 0.4°C, thus giving an overall warming trend for the twentieth century of 0.6°C.

A much larger problem to explain away were those fluctuations in temperature which had occurred in earlier times. And here in 1998 the whole debate was suddenly, dramatically transformed by a new scientific study. Its chief author was Michael Mann, a young physicist-turned-climate scientist at the University of Massachusetts, who had only just completed his PhD.

Mann published in *Nature* a paper on temperature changes over the previous 600 years.[40] In 1999 he and his colleagues published a further paper, extending their original findings to over 1,000 years.[41] These had enabled them to produce a new temperature graph quite unlike anything seen before. Instead of the rises and falls shown in previous graphs, this one showed the average temperature having scarcely fluctuated at all through nine centuries. But it then suddenly shot up at the end, to by far its highest level ever recorded.

In Mann's graph such familiar features as the Mediaeval Warming and the Little Ice Age had simply disappeared. All those awkward anomalies were shown as having been illusory. The only real fluctuation that emerged from their studies was that sudden exponential rise appearing in the twentieth century, culminating in the 'warmest year of the millennium', 1998.

There were several very odd features about Mann's new graph, soon to be known as the 'hockey stick' because of its shape, a long straightish line curving up sharply at the end.[42] But none was odder than the speed with which this, on the face of it, very obscure study by an unknown young scientist came to be adopted as the new 'orthodoxy'.

Within twelve months Mann's complete rewriting of climate science had become the major talking point of the global warming debate. In 2000, it was featured at the top of a major new report published by the US government, the *US National Assessment of the Potential Consequences of Climate Variability and Change*.

In the following year, 2001, when the IPCC's 'Working Group I' (still chaired by Houghton) published its 'Third Assessment Report' (TAR), Mann's 'hockey stick' was promoted even more dramatically. Not only was it printed at the top of page one of the Summary for Policymakers; elsewhere in the report, it was printed four more times, sometimes occupying half a page. The old graphs included in the IPCC's previous 1990 and 1996 reports, showing the Mediaeval Warming and the Little Ice Age, had vanished. Like those articles in *The Times* rewritten by Winston Smith in *Nineteen Eighty-Four*, they had been blotted out of the record.

Mann was the hero of the moment. He had been made an IPCC 'lead author' and an editor of the prestigious *Journal of Climate Change*. He was besieged by the media. But then some rather serious questions began to be asked about the basis for his study.

For a start, although he cited other evidence for his computer modelling of historical temperatures, it became apparent that he had leaned particularly heavily on data provided by a study five years earlier of tree rings in ancient bristlecone pine trees growing on the slopes of California's Sierra Nevada mountains. According to the 1993 paper, these had shown significantly accelerated growth in the years after 1900. But the purpose of this original study had not been to research into past temperatures. As its title made clear, it had been to measure the effect of increased CO_2 levels in the twentieth century on the trees' growth rate.[43]

As the authors had specifically pointed out, temperature changes could not account for the faster growth of these long-established trees. It must have been due to the fertilizing effect of the increase in CO_2. The pine trees had been chosen for study because their position, high up on the mountains, made it likely that they would exhibit an unusually marked response to CO_2 enrichment.

Tree rings are a notoriously unreliable reflector of temperature changes, because they are chiefly formed during only one short period of the year, and cannot therefore give a full picture. This 1993 study of one group of trees in one untypical corner of the USA seemed a remarkably flimsy basis on which to base an estimate of global temperatures going back 1,000 years.*

Then there was Mann's unqualified acceptance of the recent temperature readings given by hundreds of weather stations across the earth's surface, which helped confirm the widely received view that temperatures in the closing years of the twentieth century were soaring to unprecedented levels, culminating in the record year 1998.

But this picture was already being questioned by many expert

---

* Mann and his colleagues did at least seem in small part to acknowledge this when, in the title of their second paper, the phrase 'Global-scale temperature patterns' was changed to 'Northern hemisphere temperatures'.

scientists who pointed to evidence that readings from surface stations were becoming seriously distorted by the 'heat island effect'. The majority of such stations were in the proximity of large and increasingly built-up population centres. It was well established that these heated up the atmosphere around them to a significantly higher level than in more isolated locations.

Nowhere was this better illustrated than by contrasting the temperature readings taken on the earth's surface with those which, since 1979, had been taken by NASA satellites and weather balloons, using a method developed by Dr Roy Spencer, responsible for climate studies at NASA's Marshall Space Center, and Dr John Christie of the University of Alabama. Surprisingly, the readings showed that, far from warming in the last two decades of the twentieth century, global temperatures had in fact slightly cooled.[44] As Spencer was at pains to point out, these avoided the distortions created in surface readings by the heat island effect. The reluctance of the IPCC to take proper account of this, he observed, confirmed the suspicion of 'many scientists involved in the process' that the IPCC's stance on global warming was 'guided more by policymakers and politicians than by scientists'.[45]

There was nothing the IPCC welcomed more in Mann's 'hockey stick' than the way it showed the line hurtling upwards at the end, to portray 1998 as having been 'the hottest year in history'. But, as many scientists had predicted at the time, 1998 was likely to be exceptionally warm because of the unusually strong 'El Niño' of that year: the result of air currents in the Pacific failing to replace warm surface water off the western coast of America with colder water, which invariably results in warming over a large area of the earth's surface.

What was also remarkable about the 'hockey stick', as was again widely observed, was how it contradicted all that mountain of evidence which supported the generally accepted picture of temperature fluctuations in past centuries. As was pointed out, tree rings are not the most reliable guide to assessing past temperatures. There were scores of more direct sources of evidence from Africa, South America, Australia, Pakistan, Antarctica – almost every continent and ocean of the world.*

---

* One of the first attempts to summarize this, in response to the 'hockey stick' thesis, was a paper by Willie Soon and Sallie Baliunas, published in

Whether evidence was taken from lake sediments or ice cores, glaciers in the Andes or boreholes in Greenland, the results had been remarkably consistent in confirming that the familiar view was right. There had been a Little Ice Age, all across the world. There had similarly been a Mediaeval Warming. Furthermore, a mass of data confirmed that the world had been even warmer in the early Middle Ages than it was in 1998.[46]

If Mann and his colleagues had got it hopelessly wrong, nothing did more to ram this home than a study carried out in 2003 by two Canadian outsiders: Stephen McIntyre, a financial consultant on minerals, and Ross McKitrick, an academic economist. They might not have been climate scientists but they knew something about using computers to play around with statistics. They were also wearily familiar with people using hockey stick-like curves, showing an exaggerated upward rise at the end, to sell a business prospect or to 'prove' some tendentious point.

McIntyre and McKitrick approached Mann and his colleagues to ask for their original study data. This was eventually, with some difficulty, provided, but 'without most of the computer code used to produce their results', suggesting that no one else had previously asked to examine it, as should have been required both by peer-reviewers for their paper published in *Nature* and, above all, by the IPCC itself.[47]

Feeding the data into their own computer, they found that it simply did not produce the claimed results. This was 'due to collation errors, unjustifiable truncation or extrapolation of source data, obsolete data, geographical location errors, incorrect calculation of principal components, and other quality control defects'.[48] 'Had the IPCC actually done the kind of rigorous review that they boast of', McKitrick was to tell the House of Lords committee in 2005,

the journal *Climate Research* in January 2003. After reviewing 240 different studies, they reported that, according to the balance of evidence, the twentieth century had not been the warmest period of the last millennium. This enraged the global warming lobby, provoking a major internal row that resulted in half the journal's ten editors resigning. An account by one of them, Clare Goodess of the Climatic Research Unit, University of East Anglia, is published on the website of SGR (Scientists for Global Responsibility).

*they would have discovered that there was an error in a routine
calculation step (principal component analysis) that falsely
identified a hockey stick shape as the dominant pattern in the
data. The flawed computer program can even pull out spurious
hockey stick shapes from lists of trendless random numbers.*

Using Mann's algorithm, the two men fed a pile of random and
meaningless data into the computer thousands of times. Every time
the graph which emerged bore a 'hockey stick' shape. Even the
telephone directory would have come out like a hockey stick. They
found that their replication of Mann's method failed 'all basic tests
of statistical significance'.

When they ran the program again properly, keeping Mann's
data but removing the bristlecone pine figures on which he had so
heavily relied, they found that the Mediaeval Warming once again
emerged, large as life. Indeed their 'major finding' was that Mann's
own data confirmed that warming in the Middle Ages exceeded
anything in the twentieth century.

But McIntyre and McKitrick reserved their most withering
condemnation for the IPCC itself. Not only had it failed to subject
Mann's methods to any proper professional checking, but it had
then given extraordinary prominence to

*the hockey stick data as the canonical representation of the
earth's climate history. Due to a combination of mathematical
error and a dysfunctional review process, they ended up promoting the exact wrong conclusion. How did they make such a
blunder?*[49]

So embarrassing was this analysis that in 2004 Mann and his
colleagues published a grudging 'Corrigendum'. They conceded
that their proxy data had included errors, but insisted that 'none of
these errors affect our previously published results'.

No admission of error came from the IPCC, for which the
'hockey stick' remained the single most prominent underpinning of
its entire case on global warming. Although the graph had been as
comprehensively discredited as any hypothesis in the history of
science, the IPCC seemed determined to stand by it.*

* When the IPCC's Fourth Assessment Report came to be published in
2007 the 'hockey stick' graph was notably omitted. But the 'hockey stick'
continued to have fanatical supporters among the scientific community,

As Orwell had written in *Nineteen Eighty-Four*:

Everything faded into mist. The past was erased, the erasure was forgotten, the lie became the truth.

A Close-up of the IPCC at Work

Although the 'hockey stick' debate should have raised fundamental questions about the IPCC's scientific credibility, it was by no means the only issue over which its conduct attracted criticism. One example is worth a brief further note because it gave a unique inside picture of just how the IPCC was able to arrive at the conclusions that those in charge of it wanted.

Paul Reiter, a British-born professor at the Institut Pasteur in Paris and a senior adviser to the World Health Organization, was arguably the world's leading expert on mosquito-borne diseases. Giving evidence to members of the House of Lords in 2005, he explained how, before the 1996 report, he had been invited to join the IPCC's Working Group II, to act as a 'contributory author' to Chapter 18, assessing the impact of global warming on human health.[50]

Among his fellow 'contributing authors' he had been surprised to find one whose 'principal interest was the effectiveness of motorcycle helmets (plus a paper on the health effect of cell phones)'. Not one of the chapter's 'lead authors' had ever written a research paper on mosquito-borne diseases. Two were full-time 'environmental activists', one of whom had written articles on topics ranging from mercury poisoning to land mines.

It soon became clear that the preoccupation of the lead authors was to demonstrate that global warming would increase the range and intensity of 'vector-borne' diseases (those spread by insects and other carriers), as 'predicted' by a 'highly simplistic' computer model. Reiter tried to explain that malaria was not a disease confined to hot countries, as was familiar to anyone versed in the history of the disease, but this appeared to fall on deaf ears.

environmentalists and the media. An account of that time recalled how Mann's defenders 'united in organised efforts' to rebuke and discredit anyone who dared criticize the 'hockey stick', often 'resorting to personal attacks against the critical party' ('Hockey Stick, 1998–2005, R.I.P.', *www.worldclimatereport.com.*)

When he saw the resulting chapter, he was shocked at how 'the amateurish text' reflected the 'limited knowledge' of the '21 authors'. Almost the only texts cited were 'relatively obscure' articles, almost all suggesting that disease became more prevalent in a warm climate. The text was riddled with 'glaring indicators of the ignorance of the authors', such as a claim that 'mosquito species that transmit malaria do not usually survive where the mean winter temperature drops below 16°–18°C' (some species, Reiter pointed out, can survive temperatures of 25° below zero).

In their determination to prove that greater warming was already causing malaria to move to higher altitudes, the authors quoted claims that 'had repeatedly been made by environmental activists', but which had been 'roundly denounced in the scientific literature'.

'In summary,' Reiter went on, 'the treatment of this issue by the IPCC was ill-informed, biassed and scientifically unacceptable.' Yet the Summary for Policymakers, drafted at political level, was able to use this chapter to support a claim that 'climate change is likely to have wide-ranging and mostly adverse impacts on human health, with significant loss of life'. It went on to predict that climate change at the upper end of the IPCC's predicted range would increase the proportion of the world's population vulnerable to malaria to 60 per cent, leading to 50–80 million additional cases every year.

Following the publication of the report, Reiter was shocked to see how

> *these confident pronouncements, untrammelled by details of the complexity of their subject and the limitations of these models, were widely quoted as 'the consensus of 1,500 of the world's top scientists' (occasionally the number quoted was 2,500). This clearly did not apply to the chapter on human health, yet, at the time, eight out of nine major websites that I checked placed these diseases at the top of the list of adverse impacts of climate change, quoting the IPCC.*

Reiter went on to describe how, when he was invited back to take part in preparing the third, 2001 report, he and a colleague, who were the only authors with any knowledge of vector-borne diseases, repeatedly found themselves 'at loggerheads with persons who insisted on making authoritative pronouncements, although they had little or no knowledge of our speciality'. Reiter eventually resigned, although when he saw a first draft of the report he was shocked to see his name still listed as a contributor. Only with great difficulty did he eventually succeed in having it removed.

For the IPCC's fourth report, due to be published in 2007, Reiter was nominated by the US government as a 'lead author'. He was rejected by the 'IPPC Working Group II Bureau' in favour of two 'lead authors', a hygienist and a specialist in fossil faeces. Neither had any knowledge of tropical diseases but they had both co-written articles with 'environmental activists'. When Professor Reiter questioned this with a relevant IPCC official (who worked for the UK Meteorological Office in Exeter), she thanked him for his 'continued interest in the IPCC' and told him that selection was decided by governments: 'it is the governments of the world who make up the IPCC, define its remit and direction' according to 'the IPCC Principles and Procedures which have been agreed by governments'. To his question as to why the 'lead authors' chosen appeared to have no expertise in the chapter's subject matter, he got no answer.

Faced with such evidence, Reiter went on to muse how:

> *the issue of consensus is key to understanding the limitations of IPCC pronouncements. Consensus is the stuff of politics, not of science ... in the age of information, popular knowledge of scientific issues – particularly issues of health and the environment – is awash in the tide of misinformation, much of it presented in the 'big talk' of professional scientists. Alarmist activists operating in well-funded advocacy groups have a lead role in creating this misinformation. In many cases they manipulate public perceptions with emotive and fiercely judgmental 'scientific' pronouncements, adding a tone of danger and urgency to attract media coverage ... these notions are often reinforced by drawing attention to peer-reviewed scientific articles that appear to support their pronouncements, regardless of whether these articles are widely endorsed by the scientific community. Scientists who challenge these alarmists are rarely given priority by the media, and are often presented as 'sceptics'.*

> *The democratic process requires elected representatives to respond to the concerns and fears generated in this process.*

Denial is rarely an effective strategy, even in the face of pre-
posterous claims. The pragmatic option is to express concern,
create new regulations and increase funding for research …

In reality a genuine concern for mankind and the environ-
ment demands the inquiry, accuracy and scepticism that are
intrinsic to authentic science. A public that is not aware of this
is vulnerable to abuse.

It was an admirably acute analysis of the essence of the scare
phenomenon – from an 'authentic' scientist, puzzled by how mad
the world had grown.

The Great Wind Power Fantasy

If the IPCC's 'consensus' had made clear with just what a crisis
global warming was facing the world – not least thanks to that
terrifying exponential upward flick at the end of the 'hockey stick'
– what was the world going to do about it?

Nearly seven years after its signing, the Kyoto Protocol still
hadn't come into force. This could not happen until it had been
ratified by countries representing 55 per cent of all the world's
human CO_2 emissions in 1990. The only real hope of this happening was that it would be ratified by either the USA or Russia.
The USA had so far been ruled out by that unanimous Senate veto
in 1997. As for Russia, in December 2003 President Vladimir Putin
reiterated that it had no intention of ratifying, because the treaty
was 'scientifically flawed' and 'even 100 per cent compliance with
the Kyoto Protocol won't reverse climate change'.[51]

In fact this continuing delay had not prevented various richer
countries, led by those making up the European Union, from
already taking steps towards meeting those Kyoto targets on limiting carbon emissions. But even if Kyoto did one day come into
force, there were limits to what these nations could hope on their
own to achieve.

One problem was that, because it only applied to developed
countries, there were so many sources of carbon emissions the
developed world could do little or nothing about. The second
largest human cause of CO_2 emissions, for instance, accounting for
some 18 per cent or nearly a fifth of the world total, was deforestation. But this was mainly centred in countries not affected by

Kyoto, such as Indonesia and Brazil, where the destruction of their rainforests contributed 85 and 70 per cent of their total carbon output.

Just behind this, contributing around 14 per cent each, were agriculture, industry and transport. Again a significant part of agricultural emissions, as in those from rice growing which is particularly 'carbon-intensive', came from countries which would be unaffected by Kyoto. Some of the world's most polluting industries were in China and India, which would also be unaffected. Marginal steps were already being taken in industrialized countries to reduce carbon emissions from cars and lorries, but aviation (contributing around 3 per cent) and shipping (slightly more) were again not covered by Kyoto.

By far the biggest single contributor to carbon emissions, however, responsible for around 40 per cent or two-fifths of the total, was the use of fossil fuels for generating electricity. Inevitably it was here that the attention of those countries that wished to show their determination to 'fight global warming' had to be focused.

The most effective way to generate 'carbon-free' electricity would have been to revive the use of nuclear power, which for 20 years, after the scare over a relatively minor nuclear incident at Three Mile Island in 1979 and the rather more serious emergency at Chernobyl in 1986, had become distinctly unpopular. The most nuclear-dependent country in the world was France, which, after its scare over future sources of energy in the 1970s, following the Yom Kippur war, had built the 58 new nuclear power plants which now supplied 83 per cent of its electricity. But from the environmentalists, so much in the ascendant, any talk of a return to nuclear power provoked howls of outrage, even though it offered by far the most practical solution to the problem they claimed to care about more than any other: the rise in greenhouse gases.

This left those 'renewable' energy sources, solar, wave and tidal power and, above all, wind, which had now seized the imagination of the environmentalists as being the answer to all their dreams. Everything about 'green' energy seemed appealing. It relied directly on the beneficence of nature itself, on such elemental forces as the sun, water and wind. It was pure, it was clean, it gave off no 'polluting' greenhouse gases, and, bar a little initial investment, it was free.

Thus it was that, from the early 1990s onwards, many of the countries of the western world had embarked on a love affair with the idea of 'renewable' energy as something which governments should do all in their power to encourage. As early as 1989, the British government introduced a 'non-fossil fuel obligation' (NFFO), whereby its newly privatized electricity supply companies were obliged to buy a percentage of their power from 'renewable' sources.

In 1997, no one was more enthusiastic for the Kyoto Protocol than the EU, which was soon aiming to set its own 'Kyoto targets' whereby, within 13 years, 10 per cent of all the EU's energy would be 'renewable'. In 2001 the member states committed themselves to an even more ambitious target, issuing a directive which laid down that, by 2010, 'of the total electricity consumption of the Community', no less than 22.1 per cent, more than a fifth, must be derived from renewable energy sources.[52] In 2002 this prompted the British government to introduce a Renewable Obligations Order, replacing the NFFO with a new system whereby electricity suppliers were obliged to buy an annually increasing percentage of their electricity from renewable sources. For this they would have to pay an inflated price, designed to encourage further investment in 'renewables', which would then be paid for by their customers through their electricity bills.

The most obvious source of additional renewable energy in Europe was wind.* The three EU countries that led the way in building thousands of wind turbines were Denmark, Germany and Spain. By 2002 little Denmark was claiming to be generating nearly 20 per cent of its power from the giant turbines which now dominated vast tracts of its flat countryside and coastline.

But it was around this time the penny began to drop that wind power was not all it been imagined to be. Its most serious failing was the simple fact that wind does not blow at a consistent speed, and often not at all. The wind companies invariably liked to talk of their turbines in terms of 'installed capacity': as, for instance, 'two megawatts'. The politicians and the media almost invariably fell

---

* Apart from in the handful of countries, such as Switzerland, that had mountains large enough to allow extensive use of hydro-electric power. In the UK, according to the DTI's 2006 Departmental UK Energy Statistics (DUKES 7.4), hydro-electricity in 2005 provided 29 per cent of total renewable energy, mainly from schemes built in the Scottish Highlands in the 1950s. Biofuels contributed 53 per cent, wind power only 17 per cent.

for this, imagining that such a turbine was capable of producing two megawatts (2 MW) of electricity.

Because wind speeds were so inconsistent, however, this in fact meant that the average output of a turbine in the UK was only a quarter of its capacity (known as the 'load factor'). Indeed all too often, notably on cold days in winter when electricity demand was at its highest, there was not enough wind to keep the turbines turning.

In short, wind turbines were extraordinarily unreliable. Furthermore, thanks to the vagaries of the wind, they were also unpredictable. This meant that, in order to guarantee a continuous supply of electricity to the customers, alternative sources of power had to be kept permanently on standby or 'spinning reserve', ready to step in at a moment's notice to make up for the lack of supply from the windfarms. Even when the wind was blowing, these back-up power stations, usually coal-fired, would have to be kept running, using fuel, generating steam, emitting CO_2, ready to ramp up their turbines the moment the supply from the wind machines stopped coming.

This remained one of the best-kept secrets of the wind power lobby, because what it meant was that the wind turbines were not saving anything like the amount of CO_2 they liked to claim. Some 'spinning reserve' was unavoidable, to provide back-up for conventional power sources. But the greater the number of windfarms, the more it would be necessary to keep conventional plants running just to provide them with round-the-clock cover. When seeking planning permission to build a new windfarm, developers would invariably boast that it was going to help combating global warming by saving 'X thousand tonnes of CO_2' from being emitted to the atmosphere. In fact it was going to save very much less.

In reality the contribution made by wind power, in terms of both the electricity it generated and its 'carbon savings', was derisory. By 2005 Britain was priding itself on having built 1,200 turbines, covering hundreds of square miles of countryside. But the amount of electricity they produced was less than half that generated by one 1,200 MW nuclear power station; and barely an eighth of that supplied by the huge 4,700 MW coal-fired plant at Drax in Yorkshire.

When it was proposed that the largest windfarm in England should be built at Whinash in Cumbria, 27 huge turbines, each

two-thirds the height of Blackpool Tower, the developers boasted
that this would save '178,000 tons of carbon emissions a year'. Yet
even the *Guardian*'s George Monbiot, the most prominent global
warming crusader in Britain's media, had to admit that 'a single
jumbo jet, flying from London to Miami and back every day,
releases the climate-change equivalent of 520,000 tonnes of carbon
dioxide a year'. One Boeing 747 thus cancelled out three giant
wind farms.[53]

Another illusion about wind power was that it was cheap. In
fact generating electricity by wind turbines was significantly more
expensive than conventional power sources. A study carried out for
the Royal Academy of Engineering in 2004 showed that the cost of
a kilowatt hour of electricity produced by an onshore wind turbine,
including the cost of standby generation, was 5.4p; more than
double that of power from gas (2.2p), nuclear (2.3p) or the more
efficient coal-fired plants (2.5p). From an offshore windfarm, the
7.2p cost made it well over three times more expensive.[54]

One reason why this was not more widely recognized was the
ingenious way the government had managed to conceal the massive
subsidy given to the owners of wind turbines. Under the Renewables Obligation, the electricity supply companies were required to
buy an ever-higher percentage of their electricity from turbine
owners, rising from 3 per cent in 2002 to 15 per cent and more in
future years. In addition, they had to pay a Climate Change Levy
on every MW-hour of electricity produced from conventional
sources, from which renewables were exempted.

The net effect of all this was that the electricity supply companies were forced to pay twice as much for wind-generated electricity as they did for conventional power. In 2005 this amounted
to around £90 per MW-hour compared with the normal price of
£45. But this was hidden from the public because the additional
cost, now approaching £1 billion a year, was merely added,
without explanation, to their electricity bills.[55]

For the turbine developers themselves this created an extraordinary bonanza. Each 2 MW turbine, although on average it
produced only 500 kilowatts of electricity, earned its owners
around £400,000 a year, of which £200,000 was the value of the
electricity and £200,000 the hidden subsidy. A big windfarm might
have dozens of such turbines, like the 140 2.3 MW giants being
erected in 2006 at Whitelee, south of Glasgow, the largest on-shore

windfarm in Europe. Covering 30 square miles of moorland, with an installed capacity of 322 MW, this was due to earn its developers £32 million a year in subsidies alone. Yet its total output would be only 7 per cent of that of a nuclear power plant occupying less than a 30th of the same amount of land.*

In many people's eyes, of course, wind turbines had another serious failing. It seemed ironic that, in the name of some claimed 'environmental benefit', these vast industrial structures were all too often being erected in particularly beautiful stretches of countryside, such as the Scottish Highlands or the mountains of mid-Wales, severely intruding on their natural environment. Rising as much as 400 feet into the air, the height of a tall city office block or the spire of Salisbury Cathedral, these incongruous towers of steel, with their blades giving off a dull, low-frequency 'whump' each time they revolved, dominated the once unspoiled landscape for miles around.

To others these towers seemed beautiful, not least because they symbolized man's belated attempt to 'save the planet' from his own folly. But even the greatest enthusiasts for wind power might have had pause for thought had they bothered to discover just how little, in practice, it was solving the problem that so concerned them. And a further huge practical drawback to turbines only became really apparent as ever more thousands of them came to be built.

The European countries which led the way in building wind turbines were Denmark and Germany. In 2002, Denmark announced that its dash for wind was so unbalancing its electricity supply that it was not going to build any more. In 2004, although turbines nominally represented 20 per cent of Denmark's electricity production, the wind blew so inconsistently that it in fact provided only 6 per cent of the power the country consumed. Because at any given time it either had too little wind or too much, Denmark either had to import power at considerable cost from other countries, or, worse, it had to export its surplus wind-generated electricity at a loss to Norway (because there was no means of storing it). In 2004

---

* In 2005 Sir Donald Miller, the former head of Scottish Power, announced that to meet the EU's target of 20 per cent of the UK's power from renewable sources by 2020 would cost £30 billion in subsidies through higher electricity bills.

this represented a staggering 84 per cent of all the power Danish turbines produced.[56]

The more dependent a country became on wind power, the more likely it was that this would create serious instabilities in its electricity grid, as conventional power stations switched on and off to compensate for the unpredictable vagaries of the wind. This was why Ireland in 2003 decided to follow Denmark by putting a moratorium on any more turbines.

The prospect of renewable energy in itself being able to make any significant contribution to the battle against global warming was beginning to look increasingly dubious. Rather more seriously for the climate change crusaders, however, the Kyoto Protocol itself, seven years after it was agreed, still remained unratified.

'Planet Savers' versus 'Holocaust Deniers'

At this point, in 2004, the temperature over global warming visibly rose. It was not that the earth's temperature itself continued to rise. The El Niño year of 1998 was still regarded as the hottest on record.* But as climate change had increasingly come to dominate the thinking and utterances of politicians, so were critics of the official orthodoxy becoming more vocal and better informed as to what the debate was about.

The real political prize was to get Kyoto ratified, and here the British government now tried to take the initiative. In January 2004, Sir David King, the British government's Chief Scientist and a close adviser to Tony Blair, published an article in *Science* warning that climate change was now 'the most severe problem we are facing today' and 'a far greater threat to the world than international terrorism'.[57]

In Britain alone, said King, the number of people at high risk of flooding was expected to more than double, to nearly 3.5 million by 2080. Damage to property could run to tens of billions of pounds every year. But, asserting that the USA was responsible for more than 20 per cent of the world's greenhouse gas emissions (compared with only 2 per cent from the UK), King then attacked

---

* This was according to the World Meteorological Organization and the Climate Research Unit in the UK. James Hansen's Goddard Institute for Space Studies claimed that 2005 was even hotter.

the Bush administration for failing to play its proper role in tackling the crisis by refusing to sign up to Kyoto (he did not mention that it was the Senate, under the previous Clinton–Gore administration, which had voted against Kyoto).

In April 2004, Blair himself joined the assault, warning that the situation facing mankind was 'very, very critical indeed'. In May, launching 'a new alliance of governments, businesses and pressure groups' to tackle global warming, he said he could not think of 'any bigger long-term question facing the world community'.[58]

Speaking on the same occasion, King claimed that the earth's temperatures had risen to their highest level for 60 million years, and that by the end of the twenty-first century Antarctica was likely to be the only habitable continent left on earth. Sixty million years ago, he claimed, CO_2 levels had risen to 1,000 parts per million, causing 'a massive reduction of life'.

With full backing from the Blair government, King then led a determined bid to pressure the Russian government to change its mind on Kyoto. In July 2004 he took a team of British scientists to Moscow, to take part in an international seminar on climate change staged under the auspices of the Russian Academy of Sciences. Mounting a ferocious attack on Russia's position, King repeatedly insisted that scientists critical of Kyoto were 'undesirable' and should not be allowed to speak. He gave an ultimatum that two-thirds of the scientific contributors invited by the Academy should be excluded. Frequently members of his team interrupted other speakers, or spoke themselves for much longer than their allotted time. On four occasions proceedings broke up in disorder. At one point, King, unable to answer Professor Reiter's evidence that the melting ice on Kilimanjaro had been shown to be caused by factors other than global warming, stormed out.

At the end of the conference Putin's chief economic adviser, Alexander Illarionov, was withering about the behaviour of King and his followers, which had shocked many of those present.[59] He declared that 'European Union pressure on Russia to ratify the Kyoto Protocol was equivalent to a war on truth, science and human welfare'.[60] He spelled out even more emphatically than Putin the previous December why Russia was not prepared to ratify Kyoto. The Russian government and its scientific advisers simply could not accept that rising temperatures were caused by rising CO_2 levels. The Roman and Mediaeval Warmings had both seen higher temperatures when CO_2 levels were significantly lower. There were no correlations between warming and higher sea levels, the spread of diseases or extreme weather events. Furthermore, global temperature changes correlated better with the patterns of solar radiation than with the rise in CO_2 emissions.

Four months later, however, despite such vehemence from his own experts, Putin made a complete U-turn. He had struck a political deal with the EU which had no connection with climate change. Russia wished to enter the World Trade Organization on favourable terms, by being classified as a 'developing country'. In return for the EU agreeing to support him, Putin agreed to ratify Kyoto. He had also been made aware that, because Russia had closed down large parts of its most polluting industries since the collapse of the Soviet Union, its carbon emissions had already dropped drastically since the cut-off year of 1990. This meant that Russia would be able to make billions of dollars a year selling those 'carbon credits' which were a key part of the Kyoto system.

By this curious deal, the 55 per cent threshold had at last been reached. The Protocol could come into force. The Kyoto band-wagon could start rolling in earnest. And so keen now were the politicians and their advisers to talk up the threat of global warming there was scarcely need any longer for the environmental activists to egg them on.

In 2005 Blair made tackling climate change the keynote policy of his six months in the chair of the G8 nations (alongside 'making poverty history' in Africa). In announcing this he said 'the science is well established and the dangers clear. For example, the number of people worldwide at risk of flooding has increased twenty-fold since the 1960s'.[61]

When, later that year, the opposition Conservative Party elected David Cameron as its new leader, he at once announced that the fight against climate change would be at the top of his party's agenda. To highlight his environmental credentials, he was photographed bicycling to work at the House of Commons (his chauffeur driving discreetly behind with a clean shirt and shoes). He flew off to Spitzbergen, to be filmed watching glaciers melting and driving a team of huskies across the fast-disappearing Arctic ice. He applied for permission to erect a mini-wind turbine on the chimney of his Notting Hill home. It seemed as if the need to tackle global warming was virtually his only policy.

Of all the world's politicians trying to identify themselves with the fight to 'save the planet', however, none was more prominent than the man who had been at the centre of this battle for nearly 20 years; who now liked to introduce himself to audiences all over the world with the words 'I used to be the next President of America'.

In the summer of 2006, with the backing of the Hollywood publicity machine, Al Gore launched an unprecedented bid to project the threat of global warming to a worldwide mass audience. His screen version of *An Inconvenient Truth* raced up the charts to become the highest-earning documentary-film in history (going on in February 2007 to win two Oscars). The book version became a runaway bestseller.

The publicity-release for *An Inconvenient Truth* began:

> *humanity is sitting on a ticking time bomb. If the vast majority of the world's scientists are right, we have just ten years to avert a major catastrophe that could send our entire planet into a tail-spin of epic destruction involving extreme weather, floods, droughts, epidemics and killer heat waves beyond anything we have ever experienced.*

As with everything Gore did, his presentation was heavily larded with very personal autobiography, packed with pictures of his wife, children, parents and sister (who, he wanted to emphasize, had died of smoking-related cancer because she believed the lies told by tobacco companies). He recounted how he had first come to see global warming as by far the greatest threat mankind had ever faced when he attended those classes given by his hero Roger Revelle in the 1960s; the man who had first alerted mankind to the soaring levels of CO_2.

With the aid of powerful imagery and dramatic graphs, Gore pulled out all the emotional stops. Beginning with shots of fragile Planet Earth from space, vanishing glaciers and those fast-disappearing snows of Kilimanjaro, he moved on to a cleverly redrawn version of the Mann 'hockey stick', allowing for the 'Mediaeval Warm Period' as a tiny 'blip', then showing temperatures suddenly shooting up at the end to levels never before known. He took a sideswipe at the 'global warming sceptics', a group 'diminishing almost as fast as those mountain glaciers', who had 'launched a fierce attack on the "hockey stick"'. But, fortunately, other scientists had since confirmed Mann's 'basic conclusions in multiple ways'.[62]

Nothing was missing from Gore's recital: poignant images of polar bears struggling to survive, even drowning as the Arctic ice melted; penguin populations plummeting by 70 per cent as their Antarctic ice shelves crumbled; chilling shots of the tragedy which had engulfed New Orleans only a few months earlier when it was devastated by Hurricane Katrina.

The horrors he used to illustrate his points fell into three main categories. The first was that the melting of all that ice, at the Poles, in Greenland, on the world's glaciers, would produce too much water. Sea levels would rise by 20 feet, inundating many of the most populous places on the planet. Computer-enhanced satellite images showed how part or all of many of its most famous cities would disappear, from Shanghai and Beijing to New York and San Francisco. Sixty million people would be displaced in Calcutta and Bangladesh alone; another 20 million in China. As the world's climate systems were thrown into chaos, there was already evidence of cyclones, tornadoes and floods arriving with an intensity never recorded before (cue for shots of New Orleans under water).

Elsewhere the problem would be too little water. The melting of the Himalayan ice sheet, on which seven major river systems depended, would eventually rob 40 per cent of the world's population of their water supplies. Lake Chad in Africa, once the world's sixth largest lake, had already, thanks to global warming, all but dried up: a significant factor in the tragedy wracking that whole region of Africa, from famine to the genocide in Darfur.

The third problem would be the massive disruption of nature wrought by the changing climate. This would lead to a mass extinction of species, already 1,000 times higher than the normal rate; and to an explosion in 'vector-borne' diseases, as mosquitoes and other carriers rapidly extended their range into once-cooler parts of the world where people and forests were already dying as a result.

This apocalyptic vision, claimed Gore, was now endorsed by every climate scientist in the world (apart from that tiny handful of 'sceptics', who were vanishing as fast as the glaciers). Citing a recent study by Naomi Oreskes, he presented a graphic showing that the 'number of peer-reviewed articles dealing with "climate change" published in scientific journals in the previous 10 years' was '928'. 'Percentage of articles in doubt as to the cause of global warming', it went on, was 'zero'.

But all was not lost. What was called for was an unprecedented human effort to avert this catastrophe. Greenhouse gas emissions must be cut back by 60 per cent. And on all sides there was evidence of how this could be done: from the tens of thousands of wind turbines appearing in America and Europe to carbon emission trading schemes ('the European Union has adopted this US innovation and is making it work effectively').

Everyone, Gore exhorted, could make a contribution to this cosmic battle, by such means (he listed them) as using energy-efficient light bulbs; insulating homes; walking or using a bicycle instead of a car; eating less meat; composting food waste; unplugging the TV and computers instead of leaving them on standby.

Urged on by such a call to arms, it was not surprising that, for those who shared Gore's view, their impatience with anyone still daring to question it reached new heights. For a long time, like Gore himself, they had liked to claim that the only scientists who 'denied' global warming were those who were in some way funded by energy companies or 'Big Oil'. But in April 2006, they had been given a new term of abuse for all these 'deniers', when a long-time media crusader in the cause, Scott Pelley of CBS, was asked why his two latest reports on global warming on *60 Minutes* had not featured a single contribution from a scientist who was sceptical.[63] 'If I do an interview with Elie Wiesel,' replied Pelley (referring to the concentration camp survivor who won the Nobel Peace prize in 1986), 'am I required as a journalist to find a holocaust denier?'

This attempt to draw a parallel between global warming sceptics and those who denied the historical facts of Hitler's murder of six million Jews quickly caught on. By September, the *Guardian*'s George Monbiot (in the words quoted at the head of this chapter) was writing that 'climate change denial now looks as stupid and as unacceptable as Holocaust denial'. He may well have been inspired by the contributor, two days earlier, to an American 'green' blog, praising Monbiot's latest book, who had carried this even further, exclaiming (in words that were themselves to win wide currency):

When we've finally gotten serious about global warming, when the impacts are really hitting us and we're in a full worldwide

> *scramble to minimize the damage, we should have war crimes*
> *trials for these bastards – some sort of climate Nuremberg6.*[64]

'Holocaust deniers' or not, the chorus of media acclaim given to
Gore's film had already begun to arouse some very different
responses, from scientists such as Professor Bob Carter, an outspoken Australian expert in palaeoclimatology. So shocked was
Carter by Gore's cavalier approach to the facts that, shortly after
the film's launch, he exploded to a journalist that Gore's 'propaganda crusade is mostly based on junk science'. 'His arguments are
so weak that they are pathetic. It is incredible that they and his film
are commanding public attention.'[65]

Inconvenient truths

Over the following months, other academics began to subject the
claims in Gore's film to rather more measured analysis. In general
they agreed that he had produced nothing but a caricature of the
familiar case for global warming. He had picked over the literature
for almost every extreme projection he could find, then exaggerated
them still further. But it was when each of his claims came to be
tested in detail against the latest scientific knowledge that the real
flaws in his argument began to be exposed.

For a start there was his unabashed reliance on Mann's 'hockey
stick'. As a nod to the fact that it had been so comprehensively
discredited, he did have it carefully redrawn to include three tiny
warming 'blips' between 1100 and 1400. But even of these, only
one was allowed to represent the 'Mediaeval Warm Period', by the
trick of showing the Middle Ages as having begun in 1200, rather
than two centuries earlier as is common usage.

Then there were those iconic 'snows of Kilimanjaro', cited in
the US Senate by Hillary Clinton and John McCain as evidence for
global warming which could 'not be refuted by any scientist'.[66] In
fact observers had first noted the receding of the ice cap on the
summit of Africa's highest mountain shortly after it was first
climbed in 1889. Detailed recent studies by an international team
had shown that this was due not to global warming but to a drier
climate recorded in the area from 1880 on, the effects of which
were probably reinforced by local deforestation.[67]

Few images in Gore's film were made to seem more shocking

than those of retreating glaciers in the Andes, the Alps and the USA, implying that glaciers were sharply receding all over the world. But the film ignored a number of recent studies reflecting a much more complex picture.[68] Glaciers have been perpetually retreating and advancing for millennia, not in response to changes in CO_2 but synchronous with changing patterns of solar radiation.[69] They were thus generally in retreat during the Mediaeval Warming but advanced dramatically during the Little Ice Age, between the fifteenth and nineteenth centuries. The current retreat began with the start of the Modern Warming, long before any marked rise in CO_2. But there were significant exceptions to this pattern, not least in Greenland and the Antarctic, which between them contain 99.4 per cent of all the ice on the planet. In each case, although there was melting on the periphery of the landmass, the overall ice mass in the interior was increasing, and many of their glaciers were advancing.[70]

The Polar regions inevitably played a central part in Gore's thesis: partly because they provided emotive imagery in themselves (polar bears drowning, vast ice shelves collapsing into the sea); and partly because all that melting ice would provide the mass of water needed to raise the world's seas to unprecedented levels. But, again, almost every detail of his scenario was contradicted by expert evidence.

A series of studies, for instance, had shown that the Arctic was, in general, warmer at the end of the 1920–40 warming phase than it was 60 years later.[71] After a drop in temperatures during the decades of the Little Cooling, they had risen again from the 1980s onwards, without yet reaching their levels of the 1930s. Far from heading rapidly for extinction, polar bears across most of the region were in fact flourishing. Of 13 main polar bear groups in eastern Canada, 11 were growing in numbers or stable, only two were declining (it was on one of these, in west Hudson Bay, that environmentalists liked to focus attention).[72] An extensive study published in 2007 by the US National Biological Service similarly found that polar bear populations in western Canada and Alaska were so thriving that some had reached optimum sustainable levels.[73]

The myth of those 'drowning polar bears', it emerged, was based on a single incident when four bears had been found drowned following a violent Alaskan storm.[74]

Similarly in Greenland, home to 9.9 per cent of the world's ice, the evidence again showed that temperatures had been higher in the 1930s than in the 1990s.[75] Gore's computerized graphics showed a dramatic melting of the ice around the periphery of the world's largest island, particularly in the south, where there had been significant warming. This was based on a much-publicized paper which had claimed that in 2005 alone the ice had been melting at more than 200 cubic kilometres a year.[76]

Although this sounded immense, it in fact amounted to only eight-thousandths of one per cent of the total mass of the Greenland ice sheet (and very much more than this would have melted before Greenland could first be extensively inhabited during the Mediaeval Warming). But what both this paper and Gore's film ignored was a study published the previous year in the same journal showing that the peripheral loss was also being accompanied by a sizeable increase in the size of the ice-cap in Greenland's interior.[77]

Even more remarkable was the skewing of the evidence for what was happening at the other end of the world. The audiences for Gore's film were treated to more of those already familiar images of colossal chunks of ice calving off into the sea from the edge of the Antarctic, holding 89.5 per cent of all the world's ice. But almost all the studies of the effects of global warming on the world's fifth largest continent, larger than Europe, had focused on just one tiny corner of that immense frozen landmass, the Antarctic Peninsula, stretching up towards South America.

Here there had indeed been dramatic evidence of warming, caused by a 0.3°C temperature rise in the surrounding Southern Ocean. But a table of recorded temperatures across the rest of Antarctica showed that, almost everywhere else, the preceding decades had seen a distinct cooling. This, combined with increased precipitation as the surrounding ocean warmed, had led, as in Greenland, to a thickening of the continent's vast ice-sheet and a lengthening of many of its glaciers.[78]

Gore's misrepresentation of the amount of water being released by melting of ice at the Poles then led him on to absurdly exaggerating the projected rise in sea levels. Those computer graphics purporting to show the drowning of many of the world's major cities were based on his prediction that by the end of the century sea levels would rise by as much as 20 feet. But even the IPCC, scarcely known for its understatement, forecast a rise only between 4 and 17 inches.*

When Gore blamed global warming for the fact that London's Thames Flood Barrier had already had to be raised far more frequently in recent years than ever before, he omitted to explain that the decision to build the barrier had been taken in the 1970s, when the fear was of global cooling. The reason for this was that London had long been sinking by inches every year, thanks to abstraction of water from subterranean aquifers and the general slow subsidence of Britain's east coast. To reinforce his point, Gore also took his graph back to 1930, to show that there had been virtually no flood alerts in those earlier decades. His cut-off point was significant. Had he taken it back just two more years, to 1928, he would have had to include the worst Thames flood on record.**

Gore did, however, take the fullest possible advantage of the recent flooding of New Orleans in the wake of Hurricane Katrina, using it to support his claim that global warming had produced a huge increase in the frequency of hurricanes and other 'extreme weather events'. This flatly contradicted the historical evidence, which showed that Atlantic 'Category 3–5' hurricane activity after 2000 was actually lower than it had been in the 1950s, a decade into the Little Cooling. It had fallen off between the 1960s and the 1990s, before rising again. Whatever caused these oscillations, it was not global warming.***

---

* The third IPCC report (2001) found that the average sea-level rise in the twentieth century had been around 1.5mm a year (B4, 'observed changes in sea-level'), and that 'no significant acceleration in the rate of sea level rise during the 20th century has been detected'. This gave a total rise of 6 inches. The IPCC's predicted rise in the twenty-first century was between '11 and 43 centimetres' (4.3–16.9 inches). Predictions that Pacific coral islands such as Tuvalu would soon disappear had already been generally discounted, not least since coral growth would more than make up for any minimal rise in sea levels.

** The truth about the increased number of closures was even more complicated. In recent times, particularly in two 'freak' years between 2000 and 2003, the barrier had much more often been closed to retain river water rather than to shut out the sea (Hansard, HC, Written Questions, col. 1251W, 18 January 2007; and see also, *www.ecn.ac.uk/iccuk//indicators/10.htm*).

*** Graph showing hurricane activity 1900–2005 from the National Oceanic and Atmospheric Administration (NOAA) and National Hurricane Center (NHC). Oceanographers and climate scientists had long

Virtually every point in Gore's case was based on similarly misrepresenting, distorting or even inverting the scientific evidence. According to researchers using data from NASA, for instance, the chief reason for the shrinking of Lake Chad (only a very shallow lake at the best of times, which had dried up completely more than once in the past) was over-abstraction for human and animal use, following a succession of local droughts unconnected to global warming.[79]

The predicted 'mass-extinction' of species caused by global warming was another popular myth which Gore had then vastly exaggerated. This had been largely inspired by local studies in the USA and Central America shown to have been based on seriously misinterpreting the data (if anything, warming encouraged many species to extend their geographical range).[80] As for Gore's excitable claim that warming was already leading to a spread of 30 diseases, including malaria, this was based not least on further exaggerating those basic errors by the IPCC which had already been magisterially dismissed by Professor Reiter.[81]

Just as worrying as Gore's wholesale abuse of the science, however, were his recommended prescriptions as to how humanity should respond to this unprecedented threat. Having conjured up the prospect of a fast-approaching apocalypse, drowning cities, raging hurricanes, billions of people deprived of water and threatened with diseases running out of control, he ended in thudding anti-climax, with those suggestions that the human race might somehow avert catastrophe by using low-energy light bulbs and not leaving television sets and computers on standby.

But he also suggested two further ways in which global warming might be tackled on a more collective scale. One was that the power for these gadgets could be provided from renewable sources, such as wind turbines. The other was that the world should cut back its output of CO_2 by adopting 'carbon emissions trading schemes', of the kind in which he claimed the EU had so

pointed out that the effect of climate change, which warmed the Polar regions more than the Equator, would be to level out disparities in sea temperature, thus reducing rather than increasing the likelihood of hurricanes and cyclones. Gore's film similarly exaggerated the recent US incidence of tornadoes. For discussion of how data on extreme weather events had been distorted to promote the global warming thesis, see Michaels (2006) (note 70 above).

'effectively' led the way. And it was here as much as anywhere that Gore and his allies showed how completely their vision had parted company with reality.

Paying the price

Until this time, all the increasingly frenzied talk about the threat of global warming had been little more than that: just talk. But, as with any scare, the tipping point had now come, when the politicians wanted action.

In October 2006, only months after Gore's film hit the cinema screens, Tony Blair launched a huge 570-page report by a former Treasury economist Sir Nicholas Stern. Blair claimed that this was 'the most important report on the future ever published by this government'.[82] It showed how the scientific evidence of global warming was now 'overwhelming' and that the consequences of failing to take action would be 'literally disastrous'.

Stern went even further than Gore's film. His report predicted that up to 200 million people could become refugees as their homes were hit by drought. Floods from rising sea levels could displace up to 100 million more. Melting glaciers could cause water shortages for one in six of the world's population. Wildlife could be so devastated that up to 40 per cent of the world's species might become extinct. Climate change would be so damaging to the world's economies that it could reduce global GDP by up to 20 per cent.

But all was not lost. If drastic action was taken immediately, advised Stern – which need cost no more than 1 per cent of GDP – the worst of this apocalypse could be averted.

One means of doing this would be to give a huge boost to renewable energy. Shortly after Stern's report appeared came an episode which illustrated one rather serious flaw in this strategy. No country in the world had gone more overboard for wind turbines than Germany. Despite the Danish lesson, it had continued to build wind machines so quickly that by 2006 it had no less than 31 per cent of the world's entire wind capacity.[83] But power experts were keenly aware that, although this represented more than 20,000 MW of installed capacity, in reality Germany's thousands of giant turbines were generating only 2,000 MW of usable electricity, less than that produced by a single medium-sized fossil-fuel power station.

To produce this derisory amount of power, the Germans were already becoming worried about the amount of their country they needed to cover not just with the turbines themselves but with costly high-voltage transmission lines to move the power to where it was needed. They were now having to plan another 2,700 kilometres just to cope with new windfarms.[84]

In addition to this, thanks to the wind's unpredictability, there was the threat of growing instability to the grid. On the evening of Saturday, 4 November 2006 a huge area of Western Europe suddenly blacked out. Because of high winds and a surge of power into the 'pan-European grid' from German wind turbines, power from conventional generators had hurriedly to be closed off, causing repeated failures when they had to be reconnected. From France to Italy, it was reported that 'a real catastrophe' had been only narrowly averted. Heinz Kaupa, director of Austria's Power Grid, bluntly explained that his own country's system was becoming so unbalanced by the 'excessive' building of wind turbines that within two years the whole of Europe would be 'confronted with massive connector problems'.[85]

Despite these dire practical warnings, the blind faith of Europe's politicians in wind power seemed unshakeable. In the 2007 election campaign for the Scottish Parliament, the governing Labour Party promised that by 2020 Scotland would be producing no less than 40 per cent of its energy from renewable sources. At the time, Scotland was producing only 12 per cent from 'renewables', almost all of it from hydroelectric schemes built 50 years earlier. Only a fraction was coming from the country's 640 turbines.

To achieve this new target would require building at least 8,000 more turbines, covering 7 per cent of Scotland's entire land area. But even these would generate only 3,300 MW of electricity, equal to the output of the coal-fired power station at Didcot in Oxfordshire.[86]

The infatuation with wind power had become as much of a fantasy as those windmills which Don Quixote took for giants. Yet, on 9 March 2007, amid a fanfare of publicity, the European Union's 27 heads of government meeting in Brussels pledged themselves to a new 'mandatory target'. By 2020, they announced, no less than 20 per cent of the EU's energy must be derived from renewable sources (they must have forgotten that they had already issued a directive to that effect six years earlier).

It was clear from the woolliness of their communiqué that not one of them had the faintest practical idea how such a target could be achieved. But this was meant to show, in the words of José Manuel Barroso, the President of the European Commission, that 'Europe is now able to lead the way on climate change'.*

As Gore had pronounced in his film, the EU was also already leading the way in the other main strategy devised to cut back on carbon emissions. On 1 January 2005, as recommended by the Kyoto Protocol, it had launched the world's largest 'Emissions Trading Scheme' (ETS). Each country had agreed to 'cap' its CO_2 emissions at a certain figure, and individual enterprises within that country had then been allocated their own 'carbon allowances'. If they exceeded their allowance, they could continue to 'pollute', but only so long as they bought 'carbon credits' from those firms or countries which were emitting less than they were allowed.

A major flaw in this scheme was that each EU country was allowed to nominate its own national allowance, fixed for the first three years the scheme was in operation. Some, notably Britain, playing by the spirit of Kyoto, nominated figures substantially

---

* 'Europe agrees renewable energy target', BBC News website, 9 March 2007. It was this same meeting of the European Council which arbitrarily decided that, as from 2009, it would become illegal to sell or manufacture standard incandescent light bulbs in the European Union and that only 'long-life low-energy' Compact Fluorescent Lamps (CFLs) would be permitted. Clearly the heads of government had not been properly briefed on this proposal, since its practical drawbacks would be immense. Since, to maximize their life, CFLs need to operate continuously, the energy savings would be minimal. For many purposes they cannot be used (e.g. in microwaves, ovens, freezers or enclosed spaces). A study carried out for Defra in 2005 ('Energy scenarios in the lighting sector') had found that 'less than 50 per cent of the fittings installed in UK homes can currently take CFLs'. Replacing hundreds of millions of fittings in UK homes alone would thus cost upwards of £3 billion. Many people dislike the harsher light given off by CFLs, which are larger and heavier than normal light bulbs, and when used for reading their rapid flicker can produce eye-strain. The Council's decision was yet another quixotic gesture prompted by the warming scare and would almost certainly prove impossible to implement by 2009 (even Philips, a giant EU lighting firm which had been lobbying for the change because it had invested heavily in CFLs, had not suggested that the transition could be made in less than 10 years).

lower than their existing emissions level. Others, notably Germany, chose figures higher than their existing level. The total allowable emissions in the EU of 1,829 million tons a year were thus larger than its existing emissions of 1,785 million tons.[87]

A year later the first results of this lop-sided scheme became apparent. Several countries, including Poland, had not participated at all. Only four countries had been forced to buy carbon credits to remain within the allowances they had set themselves. By far the worst hit country was Britain, which had paid out £470 million. Germany, on the other hand, had been able to make a profit of £300 million selling carbon credits to the losers. Over the first three years of the scheme, it appeared that British firms would be transferring nearly £1.5 billion to their competitors.

An even greater anomaly was revealed by comparing those organizations in Britain that were forced to pay out for credits with those that made a profit from selling them. NHS hospitals, for instance, had been obliged to spend £1.3 million on buying credits, while giant oil and energy firms had enjoyed a bonanza from selling them. BP had sold '1.4 million tons' of emissions credits across the EU, thus earning £17.9 million for doing nothing. Shell's first-year profit was £20.7 million. Even these sums were dwarfed by comparison with the profits enjoyed by the electricity generating companies, which, according to UK government figures, had enjoyed a windfall of up to £1.3 billion.*

The business pages were soon full of articles reporting on how the new 'carbon trading market' had become either the best new investment going or a scandalous racket, according to taste. Unwittingly, the biggest contributors were electricity consumers who had seen their bills rise by between 7 and 12 per cent to pay for the scheme, without their being told why.

But the most telling comment on the ETS, which had been praised by Gore as being so effective, was the revelation that, in its first two years of operation, the EU's total carbon emissions, far from falling, had risen by up to 1.5 per cent.[88] At the same time, it

---

* 'Carbon trade scheme is failing', BBC News website, 5 June 2007. Most of the 'carbon permits' on which the generating companies made these immense profits were given to them free. Across the EU as a whole the windfall profits enjoyed by the electricity supply industry under the Emissions Trading Scheme were estimated at £13.6 billion a year (*Financial Times*, 18 June 2007).

was announced that emissions in the USA, now universally reviled for its continuing refusal to sign up to Kyoto, had in 2006 fallen by 1.6 per cent.[89]

In face of figures like these, it was salutary to recall that the EU's leaders, led by Germany's Angela Merkel, were calling for a worldwide reduction in carbon emissions of 60 per cent by 2050.[90] A McKinsey study in March 2007 had estimated that for the EU alone to reach its target of a 20 per cent cut by 2020 would cost up to €1.1 trillion (£747 billion).[91] Yet, in 2004, EU countries had spent €5.6 billion subsidizing the production of coal, and in 2006 Germany opened a giant new mine in the Ruhr producing brown coal, the most polluting fossil-fuel of them all.

It was equally salutary to recall just what a huge percentage of all the worldwide sources of CO_2 emissions was not covered by the Kyoto Protocol at all. These included aviation, shipping, and deforestation, the second largest contributor, and, of course, the two fastest-growing and potentially most polluting economies on the planet, China and India.

In face of such myriad contradictions, it seemed only appropriate that in the very week of February 2007 when Gore was being fêted by Hollywood for his efforts to save the planet, it was revealed that his own 20-room home in Nashville, Tennessee, used 221,000 kilowatt-hours of electricity a year, 20 times the US national average.[92]

Having exhorted each of his fellow-American citizens to reduce their personal 'carbon footprint', Gore's only defence was that, as a multi-millionaire, he had bought 'renewable energy credits' to 'offset' his own carbon use. But it then emerged that he bought them from a London-based company called Generation Investment Management, run by one of his former staffers and of which he himself was chairman, which had been set up specifically to cash in on the multi-billion-dollar 'carbon offsets' boom.[93]

It was hard to recall any historical precedent for the outpouring of hypocrisy that had come to shroud the issue of global warming. So overwhelming now was the collective pressure to subscribe to the prevailing orthodoxy that scarcely a single politician in the western world dared challenge it.

Particularly in the EU, it was being used to justify almost any action governments might wish to take, from raising new taxes to requiring building-owners to pay for expensive 'energy efficiency certificates', or overriding established planning laws to force through the building of new windfarms against the democratic wishes of local communities. Yet the EU's emissions were still rising, and somehow this craze to impose new laws and costs in all directions did not seem to affect plans to increase the capacity of Europe's airports to handle millions more passenger-flights per year.

Governments were now annually pouring billions of dollars, pounds and euros into every kind of research related to global warming. But almost all these funds were conditional on that research coming up with results that the governments wanted to hear. Since few grants were available to those scientists who might challenge the official orthodoxy, the only surprise was how many were still prepared to express a sceptical view.[94]

So rare had it become for the mainstream media, led by organizations such as the BBC, CBS and NBC, to voice anything but that orthodoxy that when one broadcaster dared put forward a dissenting view, as did Britain's Channel Four in March 2007, with a 90-minute documentary *The Great Global Warming Swindle*, featuring many of the leading academic dissidents on both sides of the Atlantic, this made headline news for days.*

Yet at the heart of this supposedly overwhelming political, scientific and media 'consensus' remained a glaring contradiction. On one hand, upholders of the orthodoxy were only too happy to proclaim that, unless the most drastic steps were taken to combat the threat of global warming caused by fast-rising greenhouse gas emissions, Planet Earth faced unprecedented catastrophe. On the other, surveying the range of measures that were actually being taken to avert this apocalypse, it was quite clear that, even on their own terms, they were still at this stage astonishingly trivial. Not all

---

* So unquestioningly had most of the media now assimilated the global warming thesis that whenever there was any kind of unusual weather event, heatwaves, storms, droughts or floods, some broadcaster could be relied on to describe it as 'further confirmation of climate change'. This became particularly comical when, unthinkingly, they described some event as the 'hottest/coldest/wettest' since some specific date in the past, unaware of how this implied that weather might have been just as extreme before 'global warming' began. In 2007, for instance, they had no hesitation in ascribing to climate change Britain's 'warmest April since 1865', and then Britain's 'wettest summer since 1912'.

of them combined would have the slightest effect on the world's climate. Even if the aspirations of Kyoto were met in their entirety, this would only supposedly delay the global temperature rise predicted for 2100 by six years. On the evidence of what had actually been achieved so far, it was obvious that even this was only wishful thinking.

The politicians of the developed world might well exhort the less developed nations to join them in a crusade which would deprive the vast majority of mankind of any hope of ever catching up with the rich minority; asking the peoples of rural Africa, for instance, to remain in the kind of abject poverty which would continue to kill them in tens of millions a year. But there was not the slightest chance that fast-developing nations such as China and India would agree to halt their drive to greater material prosperity, necessitating an explosion in carbon emissions which might before long put them even ahead of America as the world's leading 'polluters'.

Nothing more vividly brought home the unreality of all this than the fact that in 2006 alone China increased its electrical generating capacity by 25 per cent. The 102 GW (gigawatts) of capacity it added to its existing 400 GW in twelve months was almost equivalent to the entire 112 GW generating capacity of France. Furthermore, 88.5 per cent of this came from new, heavily CO_2-emitting coal-fired power plants. By mid-2007 China was building a new coal-fired generating station every four days. It was on course to exceed the 978 GW capacity of the USA within four years, and probably to become the world's leading CO_2-emitting nation even sooner.[95]

The rich Western nations themselves might be prepared to cover their countryside with wind turbines, impose new taxes on airline passengers, introduce regulations to curb emissions from the vehicles on their roads and play around with their 'carbon trading schemes'. But just as those wind turbines did nothing whatever to reduce carbon emissions, so in reality did their airline traffic continue growing and their numbers of vehicles continue to increase. Measured against the scale of the forthcoming disaster about which they so liked to fantasize, none of these amounted to anything more than sentimental gestures.*

---

* A startling exception in 2007 was the EU's decree that by 2020 'biofuels' must account for 10 per cent of all transport fuels. A major source of this

When the leaders of the G8 countries met at Heiligendamm in Germany in June 2007, they were invited to talk grandly of limiting the world's future temperature rise to just 2°C.** How heady it must have felt to imagine they might between them have the power to determine the future climate of the planet with such fine-tuned precision. England's King Canute might have smiled to know of it, as he sat enthroned on his beach to demonstrate to his courtiers that even a great ruler like himself could not order a halt to the advance of the incoming tide.

So what hope was left that Planet Earth could be saved? There was perhaps just one ground for hope: that in conjuring up their vision of that future apocalypse and blaming it all on *homo sapiens* for allowing CO_2 to soar to 383 parts per million of the atmosphere, those scientists who set the whole fear of global warming in motion might in fact have been looking in completely the wrong direction.

The Missing Piece of the Jigsaw

That the earth had warmed in the twentieth century no one could sensibly deny, according to the IPCC by 0.6°C. Equally generally accepted was that the level of CO_2 in the atmosphere had risen in 200 years from around 280 ppm to more than 380.

According to the orthodox global warming thesis, the second of these two facts provided a full and sufficient explanation for the first. The only possible explanation for the rise in temperatures was the rise in levels of CO_2 and other greenhouse gases. The only

---

would be wheat (BP, in June 2007, announced plans to build a £200 million plant in Hull to process a million tons of wheat a year into fuel). To meet the EU's target from wheat alone, Britain would need to grow 14 million tons a year, against its total harvest for food production in 2006 of 11 million tons. By 2020 she would thus need to import 13 million tons of wheat annually. But this target was laid down just when a world wheat shortage had already led to a doubling of prices in two years. Even if other crops, such as sugar beet, were used to meet the 10 per cent biofuel target, this would still take up a similar area of farmland (*Sunday Telegraph*, 22 July 2007).
** This was a proposal put forward to her fellow G8 members by the German Chancellor, Angela Merkel, in her role as G8 president. Although supported by several other heads of government present, the proposal was not accepted.

explanation for the rise in CO_2 was the activity of man. This in turn led inexorably to the conclusion that, if only some way could be found to reduce those levels, then the rise in global temperatures might be halted.

One particularly worrying feature of this thesis was how much of the story of the earth's climate its supporters seemed to need to distort or suppress in order to make their case. The most glaring instance of this was the lengths to which they had gone to strike out of the record all the evidence for temperature fluctuations in the past, notably the Mediaeval Warming, the Little Ice Age and the twentieth-century Little Cooling. This was because these events appeared to contradict the simplicity of their theory: not least in that the Mediaeval Warming had long preceded any rise in CO_2 levels and that the Little Cooling had coincided with a time when CO_2 levels were sharply rising.

Was there then any other explanation that might more plausibly fit the facts? One of the most interesting features of the debate as it developed in the early years of the twenty-first century had been the increasing number of scientists from many countries coming round to the view that one hugely important factor had been overlooked. This was the link between what were far and away the two most conspicuous determinants of the earth's climate.

Whenever we talk of climate, even just of today's weather, two considerations dominate everything else. One is the sun. The other is cloud cover. It is this which determines the extent to which the earth is exposed directly to the sun's heat.

All attention in the public debate over global warming had been focused on the contribution man might be making to shaping the climate by producing gases which make it harder for heat from the earth to escape back into space. But nothing like enough attention had been paid to the source of all that heat in the first place: the great radiant ball of fire in the heavens without which no life could exist, and which is far and away the most powerful determinant of all the variations in climate on earth.

One of the first scientists to note an apparent connection between the state of the weather and that of the sun itself was the astronomer William Herschel, who in 1801 suggested that there seemed to be a correlation between the price of wheat and the number of sunspots. These are the seemingly dark patches which appear on the sun's disc, associated with intense magnetic activity.

The regularity of their appearance is generally governed by various overlapping cycles, of which the shortest is every 11 years.*

Later in the nineteenth century, a German astronomer Gustav Spörer and then Edward Maunder, in charge of keeping sunspot records at the Greenwich Royal Observatory, noted the remarkable decline in sunspot activity between 1645 and 1715. In one 30-year period barely 50 sunspots had been recorded, instead of the usual 40,000–50,000. The particular significance of what is now known as the 'Maunder Minimum' is that it coincided with the coldest period of the Little Ice Age.

For a long time no one was aware of quite what mechanism might allow sunspot activity to influence the earth's climate, although scientists from many different disciplines contributed what would eventually be seen as vital pieces of the jigsaw. One was Victor Hess, an Austrian physicist, who was to win a Nobel prize in 1936 for having discovered the constant bombardment of the earth by what he called 'cosmic rays'. These are fast moving, highly charged atomic particles originating from astronomical events in many parts of the universe, such as exploding stars. Some of these particles manage to penetrate the earth's lower atmosphere (indeed the earth itself), taking the form of secondary particles known as muons, or 'heavy electrons'.

Two pieces of the jigsaw were particularly important. One was the discovery that sunspot activity, creating what is known as the solar wind, stretching out throughout the solar system, determines how many of these cosmic particles reach the earth. When the magnetic force from the sunspots is high, cosmic rays are deflected from the earth. When sunspot activity is low, the quantity reaching the earth increases.**

The other more recent discovery has been how these cosmic particles are related to the cloud-cover in the lower atmosphere, which plays such a crucial part in shaping the earth's climate.

---

* The economist William Stanley Jevons (1835–82), who had some scientific background, also suggested that there appeared to be a link between the rises and falls of sunspot activity and business cycles.
** As early as 1962, a landmark paper by Minze Stuiver, a University of Washington biophysicist, correlating tree-ring records with solar activity over the past 1,000 years, showed that whenever the sun was active, creating more solar wind to deflect cosmic rays, less carbon-14 was available to be absorbed by the trees.

Many scientists have played a part in this story, one of the most remarkable in modern science.[96]

In 1991 two Danish scientists, Knud Lassen and Eigil Friis-Christensen of the Danish Meteorological Institute, published a paper noting a striking correlation between quickening of sunspot activity and the rise in temperatures in the Northern Hemisphere in the twentieth century.[97] At the end of 1995 their colleague Henrik Svensmark, a physicist, began studying data compiled by NASA's Goddard Institute for the International Cloud Climatology Satellite Project. Drawn from satellites all over the world, this charted changes in cloud-cover between 1983 and 1990. It showed a remarkable correlation between the extent of cloud and the relative intensity of cosmic rays.

In 1996 Svensmark and Friis-Christensen decided that their findings were so striking that they should be published.[98] It was not until 1997 that they appeared, because they diverged so far from the generally received view, which wanted to see CO_2 as the only driver of climate change. In 1992, when a Danish delegation had suggested to the IPCC that the influence of the sun on climate should be added to the list of topics worthy of further research, the proposal was rejected out of hand. In 1996, when the IPCC's overall chairman Professor Bert Bolin was asked to comment on the two men's findings, after they had been previewed at a conference of the Royal Astronomical Society in Birmingham, he angrily dismissed them as 'scientifically extremely naïve and irresponsible'.[99]

Threatened with loss of funding, the two men continued to receive derisive comments from fellow scientists, not least at a conference of Nordic scientists addressed by Svensmark later that same year; although when Markku Kumala, the Finnish chairman of the International Commission on Clouds and Precipitation, was invited to join in the general scorn he surprised everyone present by observing that Svensmark's idea 'could be right'.

At the end of 1997 Friis-Christensen became director of what was to become the Danish National Space Centre. In 1998 he asked Svensmark and an English colleague Nigel Marsh to join him, giving them the opportunity for a much more systematic review of the data linking solar radiation with cloud cover round the globe. By 2000, they had reached their conclusions. The link between 'solar variability' and 'low clouds' was inescapable.

By this time other studies were beginning to lend credibility to the theory that variations in global temperature had been influenced by fluctuations in cosmic rays, not just in recent times but far back into prehistory.

In 2001 a team led by a Columbia University geologist, Gerard Bond, came up with remarkable confirmation of this point, correlating evidence of past cosmic ray levels from beryllium-10 isotopes in sediment cores with the pattern of climate shifts shown by fragments dropped by 'armadas' of icebergs in the North Atlantic during different Ice Age glaciations.[100] Although Bond and his Swiss colleague Jurg Beer could not accept Svensmark's view that the final explanation lay in cloud-cover (they were not cloud experts), their overall findings significantly reinforced the thesis that climate change over the past 10,000 years had been much more plausibly driven by solar radiation and cosmic rays rather than by CO_2. Their rises and falls simply coincided much better with the evidence, including that for all the major climate shifts up to the present day.

Other studies were following thick and fast. When Charles Perry, of the US Geological Service, and Kenneth Hsu looked at the correlation between solar radiation and carbon-14 in tree rings over 90,000 years, they found the matches so exact that any idea of modern global warming being 'caused solely by an increase in CO_2 concentrations' must be regarded as 'questionable'.[101]

A cross-disciplinary study published in 2003 by Nir Shaviv, an astrophysicist at the University of Jerusalem, and Jan Veizer, a University of Ottawa geologist, analysed data showing world temperature levels going back 500 million years. They found little correlation between the earth's climate and CO_2 levels (at times CO_2 levels had been as much as 18 times higher than today's and were 10 times higher even during the intense Ordovician glaciation).[102]

The more evidence that became available, the more the correlation with solar activity and cosmic rays seemed to explain all those past fluctuations in temperature that had previously been such a puzzle, from the Mediaeval Warming and the Little Ice Age (coinciding with the Maunder Minimum) to the Little Cooling (when solar magnetic activity again fell) and the resumed warming of recent decades.[103]

Such coincidences were all very well, but the one thing missing was a proper explanation of how the 'stardust' particles of cosmic rays could in themselves have a part in forming those clouds, which are such an important factor in shaping the world's climate. Building on all that was known about the processes behind cloud formation, going back to researches carried out in the nineteenth century by a British engineer John Aitken, a final clue was provided by a series of experiments begun by Svensmark in Copenhagen in 2004.

It had long been established that the molecules of water vapour that form clouds require an initial 'seed' to begin forming up together. Most often this consists of minute droplets of sulphuric acid in the atmosphere. But a question that had never been answered was how such 'seeds' themselves are formed. Do they in turn require some even smaller speck of matter to begin the process?

Svensmark and his colleagues created a large box, full of artificial pure air, together with traces of sulphur dioxide and ozone as are found in unpolluted air in the atmosphere. For months they subjected it to rigorous experiments, designed to replicate conditions in which sulphuric-acid droplets form in the air to set the process of cloud-forming in train. By the summer of 2005, after checking and cross-checking every detail, they had their cloud formation. The results were even more conclusive than they had anticipated.

The SKY project had shown that the seeding which initiated the process leading to cloud vapour could only have originated from the electrons liberated by cosmic-ray muons passing through the box. It looked as though those muon particles did indeed play a key part in cloud formation. The more cosmic rays enter the earth's atmosphere, the more clouds are likely to form and thus the more the climate is likely to cool. The more solar radiation deflects the cosmic rays, the fewer the clouds that can form and the more the temperature will rise.[104]

So challenging were the findings of Svensmark's experiment to the prevailing scientific orthodoxy that one scientific journal after another refused to publish them. Eventually they were accepted by the Royal Society of London for publication in 2007, under the title 'Experimental evidence for the role of ions in particle nucleation under atmospheric conditions'. In October 2006, the society released an advance draft of the paper online. A press notice went out from the Danish National Space Centre, accompanied by a comment from its director Professor Friis-Christensen:

> *Many climate scientists have considered the linkages from cosmic rays to clouds to climate as unproven. Some said there was no conceivable way in which cosmic rays could influence cloud cover. The SKY experiment now shows how they do so, and should help put the cosmic ray connection firmly onto the agenda of international climate research.*[105]

By the early months of 2007, so much attention was being drawn to Svensmark's theory (not least by Channel Four's *The Great Global Warming Swindle*) that some riposte from the upholders of climate change orthodoxy was inevitable. On 11 July it came. Bearing all the signs of a carefully planned operation, the media, led by the BBC and *Nature* (both long-time champions of the orthodoxy), suddenly came out with a rash of news items trailing a new study which, it was claimed, had completely demolished the 'solar warming' thesis.[106]

The paper, published online by the Royal Society, was by Professor Mike Lockwood, a physicist at the Rutherford Appleton laboratory, and Claus Frölich of the World Radiation Center in Davos, Switzerland.[107] They claimed that a fresh look at the data for the previous 100 years showed that Svensmark's solar data were seriously wrong. Although they admitted that the sun's magnetic activity had been higher in the twentieth century than in previous centuries, and that in earlier years this had significantly influenced global temperatures, in 1985 it had peaked and started to decline. Yet global surface temperatures had continued to rise. This proved, they claimed, that solar activity could not be the cause of recent warming.

Supporters of the official dogma were exultant at their coup. 'This paper is the final nail in the coffin for people who would like to make the Sun responsible for present global warming,' one German climate scientist told *Nature*.[108] 'This should settle the debate,' said Lockwood himself, expressing particular anger at the Channel Four programme, which he described as 'so bad it was almost fraudulent'.[109]

Yet the Royal Society's paper had a number of odd features. One was that its seven pages of text were written so opaquely, citing so many sources, that it looked as though the authors' chief purpose was just to put across their central headline message.

They were at pains, for instance, not to argue with the mass of research showing that, up to recent times, solar effects had played a significant part in influencing global temperatures ('it is becoming feasible', they conceded, 'to detect genuine solar forcing in climate records'). The focus of their concern was the period since 1985, in assessing whether 'solar variations could have played any role in observed present-day global warming'. Here, having established that solar activity had weakened, they could put across their central message: that, because surface temperatures had continued to rise, there could be no connection between current warming and the sun.

But here was an even odder feature of their argument. Why had they only included a graph of recent surface temperatures, and not one showing satellite data? The latest NOAA satellite record of lower air temperatures since 1979 showed that, following the El Niño year 1998, levels had fallen markedly, even, in 2000, by as much as a full degree. In May 2007 the temperature level was 0.6° lower than it had been in 1998. Indeed it was slightly lower than the level it had first reached in 1983.[110]

Not to include this was suspect enough. But even the record of surface temperatures on which Lockwood and Frölich hung their case was curiously selective. Looked at more closely, the latest data from the Climate Research Unit of East Anglia gave a very different picture from the averaged graph shown in their paper. The data showed that, in the six years between 2000 and 2006, even surface temperatures had not continued to rise, flattening out around an average level more than 0.2° lower than in 1998.

Why did the authors prefer long-term averages to the simpler message of year-by-year data? The latter would have exposed a crucial flaw in their argument. If rising CO_2 levels were the main driver of global warming, then temperatures should also have continued to rise. If temperatures were flattening out at a time when CO_2 levels were still increasing, this raised a fundamental question mark over the entire case for man-made global warming.

There were now two quite different theories as to why global temperatures had risen in the twentieth century. Each, according to its supporters, would account for all of the observed temperature rise of 0.6°. The explanation could not lie in both equally.

Which one more closely fitted the evidence? The next few years would provide powerful clues as to which was nearer the truth.

A New Marxism or the New Secular Religion?

In the early years of the twenty-first century, the world's astronomers were observing something very odd going on in different parts of the solar system.

It had first been noticed in 1998, when researchers at the Massachusetts Institute of Technology reported that, according to observations by the Hubble telescope, Triton, the largest moon of the planet Neptune, seemed to have heated up significantly since it was visited by the Explorer space probe in 1989. Frozen nitrogen on the moon's surface appeared to be melting into gas.[111]

In 2002 there were reports that the atmospheric pressure on Pluto had tripled in 14 years, indicating a 2°C rise in temperature.[112] In 2006 this was confirmed by astronomers in Tasmania, who said that if anything Pluto's atmosphere had got even denser.[113]

In 2003 the project manager for NASA's Odyssey mission, orbiting Mars, reported that there was also evidence of global warming on Mars.[114] In 2005 NASA confirmed that the CO_2 'ice caps' near Mars's South Pole had been diminishing three summers in a row.[115] Habibullo Abdussamatov, head of the Pulkovo Observatory in St Petersburg, described this as evidence that the current global warming on earth was being caused by changes in the sun. 'Man-made greenhouse warming', he said, 'has made a small contribution to the warming seen on Earth in recent years, but it cannot compete with the increase in solar irradiance.'

In 2006, scientists from Berkeley reported that Hubble was now providing evidence, from the emergence of a new red 'storm spot' on Jupiter, that temperatures on that planet too seemed to be rising, in places by as much as 10°.[116]

In other words, there seemed surprising evidence that warming was taking place throughout the solar system. Even though the mechanism for this might not yet be clear, it implied that some common cause was at work which was not limited just to events on Planet Earth. And how many other bodies orbiting round the sun were suffering from a sharp rise in man-made greenhouse gas emissions?

If man-made global warming does turn out to have been no more than a colossal 'scare', it will certainly be by far the greatest the world has ever seen. The practical implications of this are so immense that they can scarcely be measured.

One distinguished scientist prepared to contemplate this was Nigel Weiss, emeritus professor of applied mathematics and theoretical physics at the University of Cambridge, a past president of the Royal Astronomical Society and known for several major contributions to physics including the theory of 'flux expulsion', which explained the process whereby magnetic flux is expelled from the sun and other stars.

In January 2007, Weiss observed in an interview that, throughout the earth's history, its climate had been driven by factors other than man. 'Variable behaviour of the sun is an obvious explanation', he said, 'and there is increasing evidence that Earth's climate responds to changing patterns of solar magnetic activity.'

While insisting that the science was far from settled, he maintained that there was one virtual certainty. The world was about to enter a period of cooling. 'We live', he explained, 'in a period of abnormally high solar activity.' Such hyperactive periods do not last long, he went on, 'perhaps 50 to 100 years, then you get a crash. It's a boom-bust system, and I would expect a crash soon.' The sun's polar field, he noted, was now at its weakest since measurements began in the early 1950s.[117]

For well over a decade observers had noted that the peculiar passion with which many enthusiasts for the man-made global warming thesis argued their case fitted a very recognizable ideological pattern. They firmly laid the blame for the catastrophe they were sure was now hanging over the world on the greed and materialism of the richer Western nations in general, and on the USA and the giant corporations in particular.

Never did this show more obviously than in their visceral hatred for President George W. Bush for 'his' refusal to sign up to the Kyoto Protocol: a hostility equally shared by environmentalists and political 'progressives' in the USA itself and by the political class of Europe, for whom it helped feed their general resentment of America and its political, financial and cultural 'hegemony' in the world.

Any scientist who dared question the global warming orthodoxy was immediately anathematized as being in the pay of 'Big Oil' or other capitalist vultures determined to exploit the world's resources, and the vast majority of mankind, to their own advantage at any cost.

In the name of their 'green' ideology, the environmentalists and their allies might dream of returning to a purer, simpler, more natural way of life, in which people would reduce their 'carbon footprint' by using bicycles for transport and drawing their electricity only from wind, waves and sun. But what seemed to fire them more than anything was their wish to see the 'rich' deprived of their luxurious lifestyle: their 'gas-guzzling' vehicles, their 'polluting' air travel, electronic gadgetry and all the other trappings of a self-indulgent existence lived at the expense of the planet (even if it was not unknown for the 'environmentalists' themselves, exemplified by Al Gore, to enjoy their share of the same collective Western materialism).

Indeed it was equally noticeable how such sentiments were very much less evident outside the developed, Western world itself. The fast-developing nations, led by China and India, had shown how reluctant they were to accept the restrictions on their economic growth implicit in the measures being urged on them by the developed world in the name of saving the planet. They could not see why they should voluntarily renounce the chance to emulate the kind of material prosperity the societies of the West already enjoyed, even if some of those societies, led by the European Union, were now talking of restrictions on their own economic growth (such as were implicit in a 60 per cent cut in carbon emissions within a few decades), which might bring about a drastic cut in their own material standard of living.

Even more anomalous was the plight of the peoples in those undeveloped regions of the world, such as Africa, who saw the West exhorting them to renounce any chance to struggle out of the material deprivation which condemned countless millions of them to premature deaths. A telling vignette of this was included at the end of Channel Four's *The Great Global Warming Swindle*.

A doctor in charge of a clinic in rural Kenya showed how his surgery had been permitted to derive its electricity only from solar panels. So small and unreliable was the amount of power these produced that he had to choose between running a light to examine his patients or running the refrigerator in which he kept his medical supplies. He could not do both. Yet at the same time, not far away in an air-conditioned conference centre in Nairobi, we saw a UN-sponsored gathering of 6,000 officials and 'environmentalists' from scores of governments and non-governmental organizations, driving up in SUVs to discuss the need to combat global warming.*

It was inescapable that parallels should be drawn between the high-minded idealism of the modern environmental movement and that of the Marxist ideology of the previous century. Each had its 'narrative' to explain why the human world was in such a corrupt state, dominated by a greedy capitalist system centred on America, which ruthlessly exploited the planet for its own ends. A powerful part of the appeal of the global warming thesis was that it provided a truly moral cause, dividing the world into the 'goodies' who had seen the light and the 'baddies' whose power needed to be overthrown. And the prize was inestimable: nothing less than that the planet itself and all life that was on it should be saved.

In that sense, as we shall discuss in the Epilogue, it was perhaps not irrelevant that the rise of the modern environmentalist movement, from its beginnings in the 1960s, should have finally come into its own in the years around 1990, with the fading away of the Cold War nuclear threat, as the one truly global cause left for progressive idealists to fight for.

Few, by the turn of the twenty-first century, could dispute that man had created all sorts of horrendous problems and was courting some ultimate disaster by the reckless speed and scale on which he was exploiting the resources of the planet to his own material ends. Few could dispute that it would be wise to husband those resources more carefully or that it would be morally desirable to see them

---

* This was a point that had been powerfully argued by the Danish political scientist Bjørn Lomborg, not least in his book *The Skeptical Environmentalist: Measuring the Real State of the World*, originally published in Danish in 1998. Although he accepted a measure of man-made contribution to global warming, he regarded the measures proposed to tackle it as being both unrealistic and likely to inflict disproportionate damage on the undeveloped world. In 2004 he convened a meeting of eight leading international economists, who agreed what was known as the 'Copenhagen Consensus'. This listed what they believed should be the top 20 economic priorities confronting mankind. Top of the list was HIV/AIDS. This was followed by the need to tackle malnourishment in the Third World, barriers to trade, and malaria. Bottom of their list were measures to halt global warming, such as Kyoto.

being shared out more equally. Many might even agree that, in reshaping the world to his own advantage, man had committed offences against the rest of creation beyond all measure. *Homo sapiens* had become the ultimate cuckoo in the nest, capable of destroying the world.

But in projecting so much of that idealism into just that one cosmic cause, the need to save the planet from global warming, all those who had become caught up in it evoked an even older parallel from collective human experience down the ages. One of the more obvious characteristics of the believers in man-made global warming was just that: that they were 'believers'. They had committed themselves to a supreme act of faith: that global warming existed, the great sin of mankind, dooming the planet to a world-ending apocalypse unless in the nick of time humanity repented and changed its ways.

Beside that act of faith all else was secondary. The purpose of assembling all those mountains of 'evidence', exemplified in the successive portentous reports of the IPCC, was not to explore objective scientific truth but simply, like so many theological treatises, to provide support for the act of faith. That was why anyone who dared to question the faith was to be branded as a 'denier', a heretic, heaped with personal vilification, consigned to outer darkness, fit only to be hailed before some Nuremberg-style court of judgement as a criminal against mankind and revealed truth.

Students of the perversion of mankind's religious instinct down the ages were particularly struck by the hypocrisy of the 'carbon trading' scheme enshrined in the Kyoto Protocol, when it was issued in 1997 like some mediaeval papal bull. As with the system of papal indulgences introduced in the late Middle Ages, this made it possible for anyone with enough money to buy their freedom from damnation by purchasing enough 'credits'. This gave them an official licence to continue sinning, by emitting excessive amounts of CO_2, regardless of what a corrupt sham the whole system had become.

In many respects, however, the alarm over global warming was only the most extreme example of all the scares described in this book. Yet again it had followed the same familiar pattern: the conjuring up of some great threat to human welfare, which had then been exaggerated far beyond the scientific evidence; the collaboration of the media in egging on the scare; the tipping point when the politicians marshalled all the machinery of government in support of the scare; and finally the wholly disproportionate regulatory response, inflicting immense economic and social damage for a highly questionable benefit.

In that sense the time has come to look at this extraordinary phenomenon of our modern world from a wider perspective. This we shall do in the Epilogue. But before that, as a final chapter in our narrative, we shall consider just one more story, that of the 'scare that never was': what, in terms of trying to understand the scare phenomenon, might be called the exception which proves the rule.

Stop Press

August 2007, as this book went to press, brought three significant new developments in the global warming saga.

Stephen McIntyre demolisher of the 'hockey stick', identified a serious flaw in the programme on which the Goddard Institute of Space Studies, run by Gore's ally James Hansen, based its influential record of US surface temperatures since 1880. The error was so glaring that GISS immediately had to post a revised graph. This showed that the hottest year of the twentieth century was not 1998 but 1934. Of the ten warmest years since 1880, it turned out, four had been in the 1930s, only three in the most recent decade.

Secondly a leaked briefing to ministers by DTI officials on the cost of complying with the European Council decision in March 2007 that by 2020 the EU must derive 20 per cent of its energy from renewables estimated that this could cost UK electricity users alone an additional £22 billion a year, 2 per cent of GDP (double Stern's estimate for the entire cost for halting global warming). In practice, the officials predicted, this was not remotely achievable anyway.

Thirdly, new calculations by Yale's Professor Nordhaus showed that Gore's proposed cuts in greenhouse gas emissions might possibly save $12 trillion (£12,000 billion) – but only at a global cost of $34 trillion, nearly three times as much.

Notes

1. 'Now the Pentagon tells Bush: Climate change will destroy us', *Observer*, 11 November 2004.
2. The *Independent*, 30 October 2006.
3. Associated Press, 9 May 2007.
4. Quoted by Richard Lindzen in 'Global warming: the origin and nature of the alleged scientific consensus' (1992). Wildavsky, known

as an expert on 'risk', was echoing Saddam Hussein's boast in January 1991 that the allied attack on Iraq in the first Gulf War would lead to 'the mother of all battles'.

5. Robert W. Reeves, *et al.*, 'Global Cooling and the Cold War', US National and Atmospheric Administration, National Weather Service, *www.meteohistory.org/2004polling_preprints/docs* (2004). The conference was organized by two senior geologists at Brown University, Rhode Island, in January 1972 and reported in *Science* in October 1972.

6. *Newsweek*, 28 April 1975.

7. *Time*, 24 June 1974.

8. *New York Times*, 21 May 1975.

9. *Science Digest*, February 1973.

10. *International Wildlife Magazine*, July/August 1975.

11. This was originally suggested by Hubert Lamb, founder of the Climate Research Centre at the University of East Anglia, a pioneer in documenting climate changes over the past 2,000 years (H. Lamb, *Climate, History and the Future* (1977)) but has since been confirmed by physical data.

12. Fred Singer and Dennis Avery, *Unstoppable Global Warming: Every 1,500 Years* (2007).

13. Data from Meteorological Office, cited in evidence given to House of Lords Select Committee on Economic Affairs, *The Economics of Climate Change, Vol. II: Evidence* (2005), pp. 229–31.

14. *Chicago Tribune*, 9 August 1923. This is quoted in an entertaining and well-researched anthology of climate-change predictions reported in the American press between 1895 and the present day, by R. Warren Anderson and Dan Gaynor, published by the Business and Media Institute on *www.businessandmedia.org*.

15. J. B. Kincer, *Monthly Weather Review*, September 1933.

16. Sir David King, evidence given to House of Lords Select Committee on Economic Affairs, *The Economics of Climate Change, Vol. II: Evidence* (2005).

17. 'Global warming: a closer look at the numbers' (2003), *www.geocraft.com*. These figures do not represent quantities, but allow for the different heat-retention properties of the various greenhouse gases.

18. G. S. Callendar, 'The Artificial Production of Carbon Dioxide and Its Influence on Climate', *Royal Meteorological Society Quarterly J.*, 64 (1938), 223–40.

19. Margaret Thatcher, speech to the Royal Society, Fishmongers' Hall, 27 September 1988.

20. Richard S. Lindzen, 'Global Warming: The Origin and Nature of the

Alleged Scientific Consensus', Proceedings of the OPEC Seminar on the Environment, 13–15 April 1992 (republished on the website of the Cato Institute).

21. *Ibid.*
22. *Ibid.*
23. *Ibid.*
24. C. R. de Freitas, 'Are observed changes in the concentration of carbon dioxide in the atmosphere really dangerous', *Bulletin of Canadian Petroleum Geology*, 50, 2 (June 2002) (available on *www.friendsofscience.org*).
25. J. T. Houghton, *et al.*, *Climate Change: The IPCC Scientific Assessment* (Cambridge University Press, 1990).
26. Singer and Avery (2007).
27. Fred Singer, 'The Revelle-Gore Story: attempted political suppression of science' (Hoover Press, 2003), also available on *media. hoover.org*. The following account has been based largely on Singer's version, although inevitably this has been savagely attacked by global warming campaigners.
28. Lindzen, 'Global Warming' (1992).
29. Reconstructed from de Freitas (2002), and Singer and Avery (2007).
30. Santer, *et al.*, 'A search for human influences on the thermal structure of the atmosphere', *Nature*, 382 (1996), 39–46.
31. P. J. Michaels and P. C. Knappenburger, 'Human effects on global climate', *Nature*, 384 (1996), 522–3.
32. *Wall Street Journal*, 11 June 1996.
33. *Wall Street Journal*, 12 June 1996.
34. Quoted in Singer and Avery (2007).
35. Singer and Avery (2007). Some of this political background to the IPCC's 1996 report emerged in evidence given to the US House Committee on Small Business, chaired by Congressman James Talent, in August 1998.
36. W. D. Nordhaus and J. G. Boyer, 'Requiem for Kyoto: An Economic Analysis of the Kyoto Protocol', abstract (Yale University, 1999).
37. M. Parry, *et al.*, 'Adapting to the inevitable', *Nature*, 395 (1998). See also, Nordhaus and Boyer, 'Requiem for Kyoto' (1999).
38. Dennis Bray and Hans von Storch, '1996 survey of climate scientists on attitudes towards global warming and related matters', *Bulletin of the American Meteorological Society*, 80 (March 1999).
39. 'Survey of State experts casts doubt on link between human activity and global warming', Citizens for a Sound Economy, Washington, DC, press release (1997).
40. M. E. Mann, *et al.*, 'Global-scale temperature patterns and climate forcing over the past six centuries', *Nature*, 392 (1998), 779–87.

41. M. E. Mann, *et al.*, 'Northern hemisphere temperatures during the last millennium: inferences, uncertainties and limitations', *Geophysical Research Letters*, 26 (1999).

42. The term 'hockey stick' was given to Mann's graph by Jerry Mahlman, head of a laboratory at the US government's National Oceanic and Atmospheric Administration.

43. D. A. Graybill and S. B. Idso, 'Detecting the aerial fertilization effect of atmospheric CO_2 enrichment in tree-ring chronologies', *Global Biochemical Cycles*, 7 (1993). See also Singer and Avery (2007), Chapter 5.

44. National Research Council, 'Reconciling observations of global temperature change' (National Academy Press, 2000).

45. Roy Spencer, 'When science meets politics on global warming', *Washington Times*, 3 September 1998.

46. For a representative summary of this evidence, with sources, see Singer and Avery (2007), Chapter 9; John Daly, 'The "Hockey Stick": a new low in climate science', *www.john-daly.com*; 'Hockey Stick, 1998–2005, R.I.P.', *www.worldclimatereport.com*.

47. R. McKitrick, evidence given to House of Lords Select Committee on Economic Affairs, *The Economics of Climate Change, Vol. II: Evidence* (2005).

48. S. McIntyre and R. McKitrick, 'Corrections to the Mann *et al.* "Proxy data base and northern hemisphere average temperature series, 1998"', *Energy and Environment*, 14 (2003). Their paper was refereed by the World Data Center for Paleoclimatology.

49. McKitrick, evidence to House of Lords (2005).

50. Written evidence given by Professor Paul Reiter to the House of Lords Select Committee on Economic Affairs, *The Economics of Climate Change: Vol. II, Evidence* (2005) pp. 284–8.

51. *New York Times*, 2 December 2003.

52. Directive 2001/77/EC of the European Parliament and of the Council of 27 September 2001, 'on the promotion of electricity from renewable energy sources in the internal electricity market' (*Official Journal L 283* of 27.10.2001).

53. George Monbiot, 'An ugly face of ecology', *Guardian*, 26 April 2006.

54. 'The Cost of Generating Electricity', Royal Academy of Engineering, 2004.

55. Figures supplied by Dr John Etherington, technical adviser to *Country Guardian*.

56. ABS Energy Research Wind Power Report 2006, quoting the chief executive of Eltra.

57. *Science*, 9 January 2004.

58. *Independent*, 2 May 2004.
59. 'Bad manners at the Moscow Kyoto Protocol Seminar', *Financial Post*, 13 July 2004.
60. 'EU pressure described as war on truth, science', *Environment News*, 1 September 2004.
61. *G8 2005* website.
62. This summary is based on the book version of *An Inconvenient Truth* (Bloomsbury, London 2006).
63. *60 Minutes*, CBS, 19 March 2006. See also, 'Public Eye', CBS News website, 23 March 2006.
64. 'Gristmill, the environmental news blog', *http://gristmill.grist.org*, 19 September 2006.
65. *Canadian Free Press*, 12 June 2006. Carter was a senior research professor working for the Marine Geophysical Laboratory at James Cook University, Queensland, and Adelaide University.
66. Center for the Study of Carbon Dioxide and Global Change, *www.co2science.org*, 10 March 2004.
67. T. Molg, D. R. Hardy, and G. Kaser, 'Solar-radiation-maintained glacier recession on Kilimanjaro drawn from combined ice-radiation geometry modeling', *Journal of Geophysical Research*, 108 (2003); G. Kaser, *et al.*, 'Modern glacier retreat on Kilimanjaro as evidence of climate change: Observations and facts', *International Journal of Climatology*, 24 (2004).
68. For sources see for instance, Singer and Avery (2007), Chapter 9.
69. See, for instance, P. J. Polissar, *et al.*, 'Solar modulation of Little Ice Age climate in the tropical Andes', *Proceedings of National Academy of Sciences*, 103, 13 June 2006, 24.
70. Patrick J. Michaels, 'Is the sky really falling? A review of recent global warming scare stories', *Policy Analysis* No. 576, Cato Institute, 23 August 2006. Michaels was formerly president of the American Association of State Climatologists.
71. E.g. Igor V. Polyakov, *et al.*, 'Variability and trends of air temperature and pressure in the maritime Arctic, 1875–2000', *Journal of Climate*, 16 (2003).
72. Dr Mitchell Taylor, research director for Nunavut Wildlife Service, in a report to US Fish and Wildlife Service, dated 6 April 2006, arguing against a petition by Greenpeace and other environmental lobbyists to have polar bears put on the 'endangered species' list.
73. Steven Amstrup, *et al.*, 'Polar bears in Alaska', Alaska Science Centre (2007).
74. Announced to conference in San Diego, as reported in *Sunday Times*, 18 December 2005.

75. W. Krabill, *et al.*, 'Greenland ice-sheet: high elevation balance and peripheral thinning', *Science*, 289 (2000).

76. E. Rignor and P. Kanagratnam, 'Changes in the velocity structure of the Greenland ice-sheet', *Science*, 311 (2006).

77. Ola M. Johannessen, *et al.*, 'Recent ice-sheet growth in the interior of Greenland', *Science*, 310 (2005). This study was based on direct measurement of the interior ice-sheet, whereas the later paper used a computer model to estimate this, by extrapolating from data of what was happening on the coast.

78. For table of temperatures and an analysis of the various competing and contradictory versions, with sources, see Michaels (2006).

79. J. A. Foley and M. T. Coe, 'Decline of Lake Chad', *Journal of Geophysical Research (Atmospheres)*, 106 (2001).

80. For detailed discussion of these erroneous studies, see Michaels (2006).

81. For an interesting analysis of this passage by a lay critic, see Mary Ellen Tiffany Gilder, 'Good news, Mr Gore, the apocalypse has been postponed', *www.sitewave.net*.

82. 'Running the rule over Stern's numbers', BBC News website, 26 January 2007.

83. European Wind Energy Association press release, 1 February 2007.

84. ABS Energy Research, *op. cit.* (2006).

85. News report from *www.financial.de/newsroom*, 5 November 2006.

86. *Sunday Telegraph*, 8 April 2007.

87. Figures in this passage are taken from 'The high price of hot air: why the EU Emissions Trading Scheme is an environmental and economic failure', *Open Europe* report, 2006.

88. BBC News website, 5 June 2007.

89. US Energy Department figures, released May 2007.

90. 'Germany wants 60 per cent cut in CO_2 by 2050', *EU Observer*, 5 March 2007.

91. *Guardian*, 28 March 2007.

92. *Daily Telegraph*, 28 February 2007.

93. 'Gore's carbon offsets paid to firm he owns', *WorldNetDaily*, 2 March 2007.

94. For one account of the pressure on scientists to follow the orthodox line, see Richard Lindzen, 'Climate of fear: global warming alarmists intimidate dissenting scientists into silence', *Wall Street Journal*, 12 April 2006.

95. 'IEA revises China's 2Q demand', *Energy Tribune*, 26 April 2007; 'China to become top CO_2 emitter in 2007 or '08 – IEA', Reuters, 19 April 2007.

96. Much of the story below has been based on Henrik Svensmark and

Nigel Calder, *The Chilling Stars: A New Theory of Climate Change*, (Icon Books, 2007).

97. E. Friis-Christensen and K. Lassen, 'Length of the solar cycle: an indicator of solar activity closely associated with climate', *Science*, 254 (1991), 698–700.

98. H. Svensmark and E. Friis-Christensen, 'Variation of cosmic ray flux and global cloud coverage – a missing link in solar-climate relationships', *Journal of Atmosphere and Solar-Terrestrial Physics*, 58 (1997), 1225–32.

99. Svensmark and Calder, *The Chilling Stars* (2007).

100. G. Bond, *et al.*, 'Persistent solar influence on North Atlantic climate during the Holocene', *Science*, 294 (2001), 2130–6.

101. C. Perry and K. Hsu, 'Geophysical, archaeological and historical evidence support a solar-output model for climate change', *Proceedings of the National Academy of Sciences*, 97 (2000).

102. N. Shaviv and J. Veizer, 'Celestial driver of phanerozoic climate?', *Geological Society of America*, 13 (2003).

103. 'NASA study finds increasing solar trend that can change climate', Goddard Space Flight Center press release, 20 March 2003.

104. The SKY experiment is described in full in Svensmark and Calder, *The Chilling Stars* (2007).

105. *Ibid.*

106. '"No Sun link" to climate change', BBC News website, 11 July 2007; 'No solar hiding place for greenhouse sceptics', *Nature*, 11 July 2007; 'Sun's activity not to blame for climate change', *The Register*, 11 July 2007, and many more.

107. M. Lockwood and C. Frölich, 'Recently opposite directed trends in climate forcings and the global mean surface air temperature', *Proceedings of the Royal Society A*, published online, 13 July 2007.

108. *Nature*, 11 July 2007.

109. *The Register*, 11 July 2007.

110. *http://vortex.nsstc.uah.edu/public/msu/t2lt/tltglhmam_5.2.*

111. MIT News Office, 24 June 1998.

112. 'Global warming on Pluto puzzles scientists', *www.space.com*, 9 October 2002.

113. *ABC News*, 26 July 2006.

114. NASA's Jet Propulsion Laboratory, Pasadena, *http://mars.jpl.nasa. gov/odyssey/newsroom*, 8 December 2003.

115. *National Geographic News*, 27 February 2007.

116. *USA Today*, 4 May 2006.

117. 'Will the sun cool us?', interview with Lawrence Solomon, *Financial Post*, 12 January 2007.

15

Licensed to Kill

OPs: The 'Scare That Never Was'

The Countess of Mar: My Lords, I am grateful to the noble Lord for that reply. Is he aware that it is some 13 years since I started asking questions about organophosphates? ... Can he explain, if organophosphates are safe and they have been tested for their safety, efficacy and their quality, why farmers have been required since that time to wear space suits when they are dipping and to have a proficiency certificate to allow them to buy sheep dips? Why are all those precautions taken if they are safe?

Hansard, House of Lords, 9 March 2005

At first sight, the story we tell in this last chapter might seem wholly out of place in these pages, because it is not describing a scare. But the very way in which it was the reverse of every other example we have looked at helps to put the scare phenomenon into a rather wider perspective.

The essence of a scare, as we have seen, is that it is based on some threat to human wellbeing that either becomes exaggerated out of all proportion or turns out to have been wholly imaginary. The tipping point comes when a government endorses the scare and launches its response.

The story set out in this chapter was the opposite. It began with the coming to light of a public health disaster that was genuine, inflicting serious harm on thousands of people. It not only ruined their health and their lives in a peculiarly horrible way; it may well have ended up by killing as many people as all the diseases which set off those earlier food scares put together.

In normal circumstances, such an event might have been

expected to excite headline coverage by the media. Pictures of sick 'victims' would have been blazoned across the front pages. The government machine would have been cranked up to carry out an urgent investigation into why so many people were falling ill. Since, for many of them, the cause of the disaster was the misuse of highly toxic chemicals in their place of work, it would certainly have attracted fierce attention from the Health and Safety Executive, responsible for regulating safety in the workplace. Regulations would have been rushed out to ensure that people were never exposed to such dangerous substances again.

In this case, however, none of these things happened. The media showed remarkably little interest in the plight of the victims, even when their cause was taken up by well-informed campaigners, including expert doctors and scientists, pleading with the government to take action. But the government remained strangely silent, refusing to acknowledge even that any disaster had taken place.

For this there was one reason. Ministers and officials were acutely aware that responsibility for bringing about this tragedy lay with the government itself. If they admitted that its true cause was a serious regulatory system failure, the consequences would have been horrendous. Not only would it have been a major political embarrassment. It would have laid the government and the manufacturers of the chemicals open to vast compensation claims. Not only did they therefore deny that the disaster had taken place; they did all they could to stifle every attempt made to investigate its causes. In this they were almost wholly successful.

The story of the disaster caused by organophosphorus chemicals (familiarly known as 'OPs') showed just how effectively a determined government can prevent a supposed threat to health from blowing up into a 'scare'. This was because, in this instance, the threat was not only, for once, entirely real; the blame for it rested firmly at the government's own door.

A Tragedy Is Set In Train

This strange saga began back in the 1930s, when Gerhard Schrader, a chemist working for the German chemical company IG Farben, began to develop insecticides based on combining phosphorus with carbon. These OPs killed insects by interfering with their nervous system. They block the production of cholinesterase,

the enzyme that controls the flow of chemical signals round the body on which any animal's nervous and immune system relies.*
Such deadly potential led IG Farben's scientists to develop OP compounds such as TEPP, sarin and tabun for use in chemical warfare, experimenting with them on prisoners in Auschwitz.

Although the years after World War Two were the heyday of DDT and the other pesticides based on organo-chlorines, OPs began to be increasingly widely used at the same time, as a means to destroy insect pests and weeds. It was also recognized, however, that, wrongly used, they could pose a considerably more serious danger to human health.

In 1951 a working group under Sir Solly Zuckerman, the British government's leading scientific adviser, produced a report for the Ministry of Agriculture and Fisheries on 'Toxic Chemicals in Agriculture'. While recognizing their value in raising agricultural production, he noted the evidence that certain OP compounds could be extremely dangerous to humans. They could be absorbed into the body in many different ways: through ingestion, through breathing and through the skin. In particular he noted that, although even a single exposure could result in death from acute OP poisoning, repeated exposure at lower level could result in cumulative poisoning, causing serious chronic damage to the nervous system.[1]

Zuckerman noted that workers using OP compounds often showed 'an astonishing level of carelessness about their own safety'. He recommended that farmers, contractors and others should be trained in elaborate safety procedures including the need to wear adequate protective clothing, such as 'rubber gloves,

---

* Much of the efficient working of the body depends on the transmission of nerve impulses that control muscles and other organs. Each time these cross a synapse or junction the transmission relies on the release of a chemical agent, acetylcholine. This must then be cleared or inactivated, at up to 1,000 times a second, so that the flow of neural impulses does not get confused and can be repeated. This is achieved by an enzyme, cholinesterase, produced by the liver and carried in the blood stream. The effect of organo-phosphorus is to inhibit the operation of cholinesterase. This, either suddenly or cumulatively, impairs the working of the nervous and immune system, thus reducing control of muscles (including the heart and the lungs) and causing the body's systems to malfunction: hence the efficacy of OPs both as 'pesticides' and as chemical weapons (see, for instance, the entry for 'Cholinesterase' on Cornell University website).

rubber boots, an eye shield, white cotton overalls with a hood and, in confined spaces, a respirator'. Despite the force of Zuckerman's warnings, it was to become remarkable in hindsight just how many of his recommendations, over the years ahead, would remain ignored.

Only in the late 1960s, when the post-*Silent Spring* alarm over the risks of DDT took hold, did OPs finally enter into their own. Because the persistence of their residues in soil and water was much lower than that of the organo-chlorines they were now replacing, they were widely welcomed by environmentalists as a major advance.[2] Within a decade they would become the most widely used group of pesticides in the world. But somehow the earlier concerns of Zuckerman and others as to the dangers OPs posed to human health had been allowed to slip below the horizon.

One of the more conspicuous uses to which OPs were put was to destroy the parasites which cause damage to farm animals. In 1976, faced with a fast-rising incidence of such parasites in Britain's sheep flock (scab and blowfly), the Ministry of Agriculture, Fisheries and Food (MAFF) ordered that every one of the 37 million sheep in the country must be dipped in toxic chemicals every year. Farmers had the choice between organo-chlorine dips or proprietary brands of OPs, manufactured by rich and powerful pharmaceutical companies. In 1984, when the organo-chlorine dips were withdrawn from the market, farmers were ordered to dip twice a year. Effectively, their only remaining choice was now to use products based on OPs.

For most farmers this involved running their sheep through a dipping bath, containing an OP solution. The process of marshalling animals into line to be manhandled through the dip was so awkward that it was difficult for the farmer and his assistants, often including members of his family, to avoid getting splashed. The dip cans supplied by the manufacturers carried only minimal safety information, often stating no more than that the liquid they contained was 'inflammable' and 'corrosive', with no mention of toxicity. Some dippers wore gloves, boots and overalls, many did not. Yet they were exposing themselves to a substance which might damage their health in any of several ways. They could be affected not only if it got into their mouths or touched their skin, but even if they breathed in the aerosol coming off the tank or the sheep themselves.

Initially, few farmers had any suspicion that the chemicals in the dips could harm them. There was nothing on the packaging to warn that they might pose any danger. The farmers had been ordered to dip their sheep by the government, which they trusted to look after their safety. Most importantly, every dip product had been licensed as safe to use by the Veterinary Medicines Directorate, following its approval by MAFF's Veterinary Products Committee. The packs round the cans carried the words 'MAFF Approved'.

Some officials in government, however, were undoubtedly aware of the hazards posed by OPs. This was shown when, in 1981, the Health and Safety Executive (HSE), responsible for regulating safety in the workplace, produced a leaflet, MS17, entitled 'Biological Monitoring of Workers Exposed To Organophosphorus Pesticides'. This warned that 'any job which involves contact with OP pesticides either directly or indirectly constitutes a potential source of absorption'. Talking of 'cumulative toxicity', it explained that the effect of repeated exposure to OPs, even in small doses, built up steadily and became progressively more damaging. It admitted that OP formulations, such as sheep dip, which included organic solvents, could even penetrate protective clothing. It described the cumulative damage done to the nervous system in this way as being 'irreversible'.

Strangely, however, no farmer saw this leaflet until years later. It was never made available to those using OPs, or to vets, GPs, hospitals or anyone to whom it might have been professionally useful. Indeed almost everything about how and why MS17 came to be produced was a mystery. The HSE did not advertise its existence and made it so difficult to buy a copy (although other safety leaflets were free and widely distributed) that it clearly had been decided that this document should be all-but suppressed. Yet, somewhere in the HSE, those responsible for the leaflet had known the truth about OPs and thought it should be passed on to others.

As the 1980s progressed, with tens of thousands of farmers compulsorily dipping their sheep twice a year, stray stories began to appear in local newspapers about 'farmer's' or 'dipper's flu'. Many had begun to notice that, every time they dipped with OPs, they felt ill. Most soon seemed to recover. But as the years went by, ever more of them were becoming seriously ill, in a way which often made it difficult for them to continue working. They felt acutely tired, weak and nauseous. Their joints and muscles were agonizingly painful. They sweated or salivated, and experienced chronic breathing difficulties. Their memories, speech and vision became blurred. They became incontinent, losing muscular control, so that their hands and legs might twitch uncontrollably. Their teeth began to rot. Some developed severe heart problems. They fell prey to extreme mood swings, plunging some into violent rages, others into suicidal depressions, which in not a few cases led to actual suicides.

Few farmers at that stage, if any, were aware that these were all well-attested signs of chronic OP poisoning: the result of repeated low-dose exposures which had been gradually attacking the power of the nervous system to control the functioning of their bodies. Such symptoms had been known and written up for years in specialist scientific and medical journals. But so unfamiliar were they to most members of the medical profession, who had very little training in toxicology, that, when sufferers consulted their GPs, they met with scant understanding or sympathy. Some were diagnosed as suffering from an unidentified 'virus'. Others were told that their problem was psychological, or even that they must have a hidden 'drink problem'.

As years went by, however, and the health of farmers worsened, it became ever harder to hide the fact that something serious was going on.

In 1991 the National Farmers Union carried out a systematic survey through its branches in the south-west of England. Of 300 sheep farmers questioned on a random sample basis, more than a third reported ill effects from dipping. A survey in Cumbria found 40 per cent affected. The farmers reported adverse reactions ranging from 'flu-like symptoms' that might force them to take a day or two in bed to much more serious physical and mental disabilities, comparable to those experienced by victims of multiple sclerosis or ME (myalgic encephalopathy).[3]

Also by now aware of the problem was the HSE, which in 1990 had commissioned two of its officials to carry out a confidential internal study. When they circulated their report, 'Sheep Dip Field Study', to 16 of their colleagues in May 1991, its findings must have seemed chilling.

The HSE, it seemed, had known of problems caused by OP sheep dips since 1987. The report confirmed this. The health of farmers, it found, was being seriously damaged (the report described how even the HSE's own observers had experienced adverse reactions, simply from watching farmers dipping their sheep).* They found that the dips had been made much more dangerous by highly toxic phenols and solvents, added to OP products since the early 1980s to maximize their effect. They found that farmers were not being properly informed of these dangers. They were particularly withering about the inadequacy of safety measures recommended by manufacturers, asking 'if, with all the resources available to them, a major chemical company proves unable to select appropriate protective equipment, what hope is there for an end-user?' The report found that 'the repeated absorption of low doses have a cumulative effect and can result in progressive inhibition of nervous system cholinesterase'. Furthermore, they found that OP residues in fleeces remained at dangerous levels for a long time after dipping, and that farmers could thus be re-exposed every time they handled their sheep.

So shocked were the officials by what they had discovered that, mindful of their statutory duties under the 1968 Medicines Act, they arranged a meeting with the manufacturers, on 12 March 1991, to inform them of their findings. A copy of their report was given to the Veterinary Products Committee, on whose advice the Veterinary Medicines Directorate (VMD) had licensed the products as safe to use. The report was soon arousing urgent concern in all the government departments involved, including MAFF, the Department of Health and the VMD itself.

The issue uppermost in their minds was that, if the OP sheep dips were as dangerous as the HSE had found, they had a disaster on their hands, and one for which they had direct responsibility. But if they were now publicly to admit that the OP products were as dangerous as the HSE had found them to be, this would trigger off a major scandal. The government and manufacturers might well face an avalanche of compensation claims. It was clearly vital that no such admission should be made. The shocking details contained in the HSE report must be kept out of the public domain.

---

* We were told more than once that rather more serious adverse reactions had been reported by inspectors attending dipping operations on MAFF's behalf to ensure that farmers were complying with the law, and that this was arousing considerable concern.

Thus did the great 'OPs cover-up' begin.

The Government Cover-Up

The first step taken by the officials was to ensure that the HSE report remained tightly under wraps. An anodyne 'summary' of the document was prepared for eventual publication, with all its damning findings removed. The original version was to be kept firmly under lock and key.*

A second step came in October 1991, when the VMD ordered the manufacturers to restrict the use of phenols and other additives that had made their dips so much more dangerous.** This was followed early in 1992 by a bland announcement from MAFF, the government department which had made sheep dipping compulsory since 1976, that it was carrying out 'a review' of OP dip products, with special reference to 'the toxicity of other ingredients and solvents in the product formulations'.***

The third step came on 8 June 1992 when Nicholas Soames, the most junior MAFF minister, issued a surprise announcement, again without proper explanation, that sheep dipping would no longer be compulsory. The government, he said, had 'decided that responsibility for action to deal with sheep scab should rest with farmers'.[4]

Thus emerged the official strategy for ensuring that the OPs disaster did not blow up into a fully-fledged 'scare'. Without giving the real reason, everything was to be done (short of banning OP

* The very existence of the HSE's original report remained a secret until we reported it in the *Sunday Telegraph* on 10 March 2002 ('Ministers hushed up report on dangers of sheep dip'). Even though we now had a copy of the full original report, which had been brought to light by the Countess of Mar, the HSE still tried to give the impression that its sanitized 'summary' was the only version that existed.

** Letter from Dr K Woodward of the VMD, dated 5 October 1991. This began by warning the manufacturers that 'the safety aspects of this product group, both to operator and consumer, are of particular concern' and that some of these might have been 'overlooked'. It also ordered the firms to carry out extensive tests to measure the effect of their dips on users.

*** MAFF News Release 28/92. The OP compound that featured most commonly in the cases which came up over the next few years was Diazinon. This was often mixed with Sulfotepp, itself an even more dangerous OP.

dips altogether) to lessen the risks to which farmers were exposed. First, the ingredients which made OP dips most dangerous would be removed. Secondly, dipping would be voluntary, in an attempt to shift responsibility from the government to farmers themselves.

In 1993 came further moves in the government's stealthy tactical retreat. The front line of its defence was MAFF's Veterinary Products Committee, the VPC, which approved sheep dip products as safe to use. No fewer than 11 of its 17 members had financial or other links with companies which manufactured OP dips, and they relied for their safety information almost exclusively on data provided by the firms themselves.

The VPC had been entrusted with carrying out the review of the safety of OP sheep dip products promised by MAFF the previous year. It now advised agriculture minister John Gummer that the sale of dips should continue, but only on new conditions. 'Because of evidence that a significant proportion of farmers were failing to take the necessary precautions, the supply of sheep dips should be restricted to qualified persons.' A new system would be introduced whereby farmers could only use OP dips after being given a certificate to show that they had been trained in how to use them. In addition, 'since all sheep dips were likely to present some degree of hazard if label recommendations were not observed', steps should be taken to encourage 'a reduction in potential exposure to OP dips', and 'the knowledge of potential toxicity should be enhanced'.[5]

Furthermore, the VPC proposed to set up a Medical and Scientific Panel to evaluate the products 'in relation to possible human exposure'; and that a 'carefully targeted' epidemiological study should be carried out by the Institute of Occupational Medicine in Edinburgh, jointly funded by the VMD, the Department of Health and the HSE.

All this was part of the strategy designed to conceal the fact that there had been a catastrophic failure in the government's regulatory system. Publicly, the line to be held at all costs was that OPs did not cause chronic long-term damage. In the summer of 1993, the Chief Medical Officer, Sir Donald Acheson, issued a new leaflet on OPs in sheep dip, admitting that these could give rise to acute poisoning. He was careful, however, to make no reference to the risk of chronic poisoning.

Above all, it was seen as vital that no one in government should ever admit that users had not been properly warned of the dangers of OPs, by either government or manufacturers. If health problems did arise, the official line ran, this could only be the fault of the farmers themselves, for their failure to take sensible precautions.

Finally the government tried to give the impression that it was quite prepared to commission further scientific research; but, noticeably, only so long as this was kept firmly under its own control. There were two areas in which the OPs crisis called for thorough investigation. One was the need for clinical and epide-miological studies to demonstrate the nature and scale of the problem; the other the need to develop a diagnostic test which could identify OPs as the specific cause of a patient's symptoms. In neither respect could government or manufacturers afford to see findings emerging which might prove embarrassing to them.

The 'cover-up' was in full swing. By now, however, the victims were gathering enough support from influential allies to ensure that the government would have a fight on its hands.

Challenging the Cover-Up

By this point in the story we ourselves had become involved when, in the spring of 1993, we were contacted by Mrs Elizabeth Sig-mund, a remarkable woman in her early 60s living in a Cornish farmhouse. For some years she had been researching into Britain's secret experiments in chemical warfare at Porton Down, many of which, in the 1950s, had involved exposing hundreds of unwitting servicemen to sarin and other OP compounds. Hundreds, much later, blamed this for their long-term chronic health problems.*

Living in sheep country, Mrs Sigmund had picked up on the growing problem of ill health among farmers and was assembling a record of hundreds of individual cases. She also set up what was to become the OP Information Network, bringing together a network of experts professionally concerned by what was happening, to

---

* Between 1945 and 1989 Porton Down carried out chemical weapons tests on 3,400 human 'guinea pigs', the largest such programme in the world. This only emerged many years later, when in the early twenty-first century it became the subject of a four-year police investigation. In 2004 an inquest on Airman Ronald Maddison, who died in 1953 after exposure to sarin, found that his death had been 'unlawful'.

exchange information and co-ordinate pressure for official action to be taken.

One of her allies, at the South Glasgow General Hospital, was a Kurdish-born neurologist, Dr Goran Jamal, who was working with scores of sheep dip victims to establish a reliable method of diagnosing its long-term effect, based on cholinesterase levels. It might have seemed appropriate that a Kurd should become involved in this work because the best known occasion on which OPs had made headlines was when Saddam Hussein used sarin and tuban, mixed with mustard gas, to kill thousands of Kurds at Halabja in northern Iraq on 16 March 1988.

Another ally was Paul Tyler, the Liberal Democrat MP for North Cornwall, who in 1992 had set up an all-party parliamentary group on OPs to give political voice to the campaign. Alongside him, from the House of Lords, was the Countess of Mar, 31st holder of the oldest title in the UK peerage. She herself was not only a sheep farmer but also an OP victim.

When we first met Lady Mar in the House of Lords in May 1993, introduced by Mrs Sigmund, she described how just 'one splash of dip' getting into her boot in 1989 had left her with all the classic symptoms of chronic OP poisoning.[6] For two years she had been mystified by all the pains and difficulties she had faced, as had a succession of doctors, who ascribed it variously to 'the menopause', 'shingles' or 'ME'. One even suggested that it was 'all in the mind' and that she should see a psychiatrist. Only in 1991, when by chance she came across a paper on the symptoms of OP poisoning, did she finally begin to understand what the cause of her problems might be. When she consulted Dr Jamal, she was horrified to learn that the sheep dip had inflicted 'permanent, irreversible and untreatable damage' to her nervous system. But at least she would now be able to put this to some purpose. Over the years which followed, constantly battling with her disabilities, she was to become a continual thorn in the side of successive governments, as the most authoritative OPs campaigner in the country.

By the time we met the Countess, for the first of what was to become a long series of reports on this drama, it was already crystallizing round one central issue. How long could the government, as 'blocker', manage to hold the line in its determination to cover up the tragedy? What could be done to force it to admit the truth?

There were two separate but related strategies whereby campaigners would fight to break that stranglehold. One was the hope
that scientific evidence could be assembled to make the case for the
long-term damage wrought by OPs unarguable. The other was that
the cover-up could be broken open by use of the law and the
courts.

Over the next few years we met or came in contact with many
OP victims. Almost invariably their stories were similar: how, after
dipping, they had gradually or suddenly found their health sharply
deteriorating, in remarkably similar ways. So familiar did their
catalogue of symptoms become that when, occasionally, we were
approached by someone whose illness did not fit the pattern, it was
quite easy to explain sympathetically that, whatever its cause, it
was unlikely to be exposure to OPs. Conversely, however, we
encountered people who were seriously ill, for reasons they did not
understand, but with symptoms which appeared compatible with
those of OP poisoning. Only when they were questioned did it
emerge that they had been exposed to OPs without being in any
way aware that this might be the cause of their illness.*

Every case we came across was harrowing, but some more than
most. David Layton, a Radnorshire farmer, became so disabled
after dipping in 1989, he could no longer walk properly. Over the
next five years his three young sons were all similarly struck down
in turn. When their mother checked back in her diary, she could see
how in each case their symptoms had first appeared shortly after
dipping.

In South Wales, the Rees family was struck twice from different
directions. The father, Tom, a fit and active farmer in his forties,
noticed how, after dipping, he suffered terrible tiredness, twitching
and depression. In 1992 his health markedly deteriorated, to the
point where he spent much of his time slumped in a chair, suffering
from 'agitated depressions' which drove him near the point of

---

* A striking example was that of a well known journalist, who described
in an article how, after collapsing on a London underground station, she
had been diagnosed with ME. So familiar were the symptoms she described
that we contacted her. She knew nothing about OP poisoning, but it turned
out that some years before she had married a farmer, and had often taken
part in sheep dipping. In one small area of Somerset we knew of four
different people who had fallen sick after exposure to dip, two of whom
died comparatively young from their disabilities.

suicide. His 19-year-old daughter then went to work at a hunt kennels in Kent, where she was asked to clean animal skins with a solution containing OPs. So severely did this damage her health that she was forced to return home, scarcely able to leave the house for months.

Indeed it soon became clear that problems caused by OPs were far from being limited just to sheep dip. We reported a string of cases where people had suffered severe damage to their health in now only too familiar ways, after being exposed to OPs used for other purposes: as a herbicidal spray on council playing fields; as an insecticide in a children's hospital; as a general crop spray, from where it drifted across fields into people's homes; as a treatment for head lice in children; as a treatment for eye problems;* even in collars for household pets, on sale in any supermarket.

One thing almost all these victims had in common was the consistent failure of the medical profession to recognize their condition as chemical poisoning. Many OP victims, as advised by the Department of Health, were referred by GPs to the National Poisons Unit, a curious little organization run, under the Department's auspices, at Guy's Hospital in London.

Tom Rees, like many others, was puzzled on arrival at being asked to fill in a lengthy psychological questionnaire, which appeared to have no relevance to chemical poisoning. It had apparently been designed (in the USA) merely to establish whether or not the respondent was mentally unstable. The NPU seemed markedly reluctant to find that any patient's illness had resulted from long-term exposure to OPs. The fact that doctors all over the country were instructed by the DH to refer patients displaying the symptoms of chemical poisoning to a unit that only rarely seemed prepared to identify this as the cause of their problem certainly conformed to the government's policy of denying that such a problem existed.

Just occasionally, however, an OP victim did find a doctor who

---

* One case we reported was that of a pensioner in Bedfordshire who kept a small flock of pedigree sheep as a hobby. After being ordered by the government to use dip, he continued to fondle his animals, having been given no warning that their fleeces could remain dangerous for months. When this damaged the functioning of his eyes, the medication he was given turned out to be itself an OP product, making his condition considerably worse.

recognized the pattern of his symptoms as compatible with OP exposure. One such was Gary Coomber, a Kent farmer in his mid-30s, who in 1992 was rushed into Maidstone hospital with a heart problem so severe that he suffered a cardiac arrest and almost died. Coomber had previously had milder heart problems, always after dipping sheep, and his GP, Dr Richard Bernhardt, became convinced that OPs were the cause. He referred his patient to one of the world's leading heart specialists, Professor William McKenna at St George's Hospital, London, who in March 1995 recorded that the cause of Coomber's illness was 'organophosphorus myocarditis'. Armed with this, Coomber's lawyers served writs on the pharmaceutical companies which had produced and distributed the dips, seeking compensation for permanent damage to his heart.

Another victim who sought a legal remedy was Brian Anderson, a Christian minister who, after serving as a policeman in Africa, had run a small religious community in Perthshire. An active sportsman and market gardener, he had in 1989 been suddenly struck down, after sheep dip, poured away by a neighbouring farmer, leached into the well from which the community drew its water. Among his symptoms were not only the usual acute tiredness and muscular pains but violent hallucinations, such as waking up at night imagining that he was about to be run down by an InterCity train. By 1993 he was so ill that he was completely unable to work.

Anderson lodged an official complaint with the European Commission in Brussels that the British government was allowing the disposal of dangerous chemicals in clear breach of two Community directives on water quality. In May 1993 the Commission served notice that it was embarking on legal proceedings which could end in the UK government being taken before the European Court of Justice. Privately, officials of DG-XI in Brussels said they were 'amazed and horrified' that the British government had permitted the use of such 'dangerous neurotoxins' at all.[7]

Still lacking more than anything else, for those who wished to challenge the government, was the scientific evidence needed to confirm that exposure to OPs in sheep dip could result in long-term chronic damage. In May 1995 *The Lancet* published an epidemiological study specifically designed to address this issue. A team of scientists from the Birmingham Institute of Occupational Health tested 146 sheep farmers who had been exposed to sheep dip, comparing them with a control group of 143 non-exposed quarry workers.

'The farmers', they found, 'performed significantly worse' in tests designed 'to assess sustained attention and speed of information processing'. They 'also showed greater vulnerability to psychiatric disorder'. 'Repeated exposure to organophosphate-based pesticides', the paper concluded, 'appears to be associated with subtle changes in the nervous system.' It recommended that 'measures should be taken to reduce exposure to organophosphates as far as possible during agricultural operations'.[8]

Although relatively limited in their scope, these findings seemed to threaten exactly the challenge the government feared. They confirmed that exposure to sheep dip did cause significant long-term damage. The VPC promptly went into full denial mode, producing a report in July that dismissed the IOH's findings as worthless. 'The study', it pronounced, 'did not provide sufficient scientific evidence to support the hypothesis that chronic health effects were associated with long-term low level exposure to OP sheep dips.' Without attempting to argue, the VPC merely used its official authority to brush aside the very point the IOH's study had confirmed.[9]

It might have seemed contradictory that the VPC should at the same time try to cover itself, by emphasizing that farmers needed to follow the advice given in a new safety leaflet on dipping put out by the HSE. It became painfully obvious, however, that this leaflet, AS29, fell far short of the advice the HSE itself had previously set out in MS17. It omitted all its own earlier warnings about the inadequacies of protective clothing, cumulative toxicity and chronic OP poisoning. It even omitted any reference to the damage OPs could inflict on the nervous system. In other words, it deliberately set out to conceal much of the information included 14 years earlier.

The fact that the VPC could so comprehensively dismiss the first serious challenge to its position from independent researchers reflected the lengths to which it was now prepared to go to hold the line. This showed how hard it is, when a government is sufficiently single minded in its determination to act as 'blocker' in denying a threat, for anyone to counter it.

The Battle Continues

The two sides now settled in for a war of attrition. Evidence continued to accumulate that not only had a large number of people suffered horrifying damage to their health after exposure to OPs, but that in a number of cases this had proved fatal, notably through suicides arising from the extreme states of clinical depression caused by the way OPs reduced serotonin levels.

A number of observers, including Dr Bob Davies, a Somerset hospital psychiatrist who studied more than 200 OP victims, suggested that sheep dip probably played a significant part in the recent sharp rise in the number of farmers killing themselves, which had moved them into second place (after vets) in the list of occupations most prone to suicide.

One tragic instance was that of a young Oxfordshire farmer who, after suffering serious damage from OPs, had been confined to a psychiatric hospital. Here he threw himself through a plate glass window, his body being found days later floating in the nearby Thames.[10] A three-year-old boy was reported as having been taken to hospital in a state of collapse, after suffering permanent damage to his lungs. He had fallen into a tank of sheep dip, abandoned the previous year following the suicide of the farmer's daughter, who had used it for contract dipping.[11]

Yet, to all this the government remained studiously oblivious. Indeed, two small further episodes revealed just how extensively its determination to hold the line now reached. For many years, in its classification of those entitled to claim industrial injury benefit, the Department for Social Security had reserved a specific category, C3, for those disabled through OP exposure in their work.

A number of people had lately applied for C3 benefit. Annette Griffin was one of a group of nurses at a Cheshire hospital unable to work since 1992, after their wards were heavily sprayed with OP insecticides. Several doctors were prepared to diagnose OPs as the cause of her symptoms, and in May 1993 the Department confirmed her claim, subject to a medical assessment. For well over a year, however, it proved impossible to arrange her examination. She was then told that this might no longer be possible because so many medical records had 'gone missing'.

Robert Shepherd, a Durham farmer, was certified by Dr Jamal and two other doctors as suffering from severe disabilities caused by OP poisoning. He appeared before a medical tribunal, for a short hearing, when he was 'made to feel like a criminal on trial'. His case was adjourned indefinitely. A Devon couple, sheep farmers whose health had been so badly damaged that they could no longer work, applied for benefit in 1992. Two years later they were told that, because there was 'no way of measuring the degree of disablement of OP sufferers', their disability could only be assessed at '5 per cent'. The minimum needed to qualify for benefit was 14 per cent. When in September 1994 we asked the Department how many claimants had been allowed benefit under the C3 classification, it replied 'none'.[12]

Then, on 1 July 1995, we reported, it became legally impossible to buy any new protective clothing for use when sheep dipping. This was because new regulations had come into force implementing the EC's Personal Protective Equipment directive, 89/686. These ruled that it was now a criminal offence to sell such equipment unless it carried a 'CE mark', to certify that it had been specifically tested as safe to use with OPs by 'an independent inspection body'. No such equipment, we had confirmed, was currently on sale in the UK.

In the House of Lords, the minister responsible for the HSE, Lord Inglewood, described our article as inaccurate, claiming that it had 'caused considerable concern and distress'.[13] We therefore challenged him to produce the data sheets showing we were wrong. The HSE officials supplied data for two products that they claimed met the new legal requirements. One, it turned out, made no pretence at having been tested for use with OPs at all. Although the other, supplied by Kimberley Clark, carried a CE mark and was specifically advertised 'for use with Sheep Dip', the data sheet showed it had been subjected to only the most perfunctory testing, lasting a minute. The firm's technical manager confirmed to us that this had been carried out 'in house', not by an independent testing body. To sell either of these products was thus a criminal offence.[14]

In other words, Lord Inglewood had seriously misled Parliament. No doubt this was because he had been deliberately misled by the HSE officials, who now claimed that it was not their job 'to enforce a directive'. The CE mark, they said, was 'merely a marketing issue'. Yet this was the same HSE normally so zealous in enforcing regulations that, only a short time before, when a Leicestershire potato farmer had been almost killed by one of his own machines, it waited until he was out of hospital, then brought a criminal prosecution against him. This had led to the now permanently disabled farmer being fined £5,000.[15]

The Countess of Mar, meanwhile, had widened the range of her relentlessly well informed questioning of ministers in the Lords to a new area of concern. It emerged that 3,000 British servicemen who took part in the first Gulf War had developed serious, often crippling disabilities. Part of the problem lay in their adverse reaction to an untested concentration of vaccines. But many suffered from a classic range of symptoms associated with OPs, which they maintained had been indiscriminately used as insecticidal sprays on their clothes and in their living quarters.

When Lady Mar and others pursued defence ministers on this, they were repeatedly assured that OPs had never been used in the Gulf. But in August 1996 she was given documents supplied to Dr Jamal by a former Gulf NCO, Sergeant Worthington, an environmental health technician, which showed beyond doubt that OPs, including Diazinon, had been used, widely and with reckless disregard for troops' safety. So incontrovertible was this evidence that, in October 1996, Nicholas Soames, now a junior defence minister, was forced to admit to the Commons that

> *organophosphate insecticides were used more widely in the Gulf than we had been led to believe. I regret that the information given to the Defence Select Committee and to other hon. Members in the past few years has proved to be incorrect.*[16]

It was highly unusual for a minister to make such a frank admission that earlier statements made by himself and his colleagues were untrue.[17] Nevertheless, two months later, in a startling break with parliamentary convention, Soames tried to excuse himself by explaining that he had been misled by his officials. From the minister who, at MAFF five years earlier, had himself played a central part in initiating the OP cover-up, this complaint that he himself had been misled was richly ironic.[18]

False Dawn

In the summer of 1997, from across the world, came news of an event that promised to change the balance of the debate. Kristan

Phillips was an American musician who, ten years earlier, had been playing the timpani with the Hong Kong Philharmonic Orchestra. A Sunday morning rehearsal had coincided with insecticidal spraying of the building with diazinon by a team of men wearing full protective clothing, including facemasks. Many members of the orchestra felt so ill after the spraying that their rehearsal was suspended. Phillips, then in his late 30s, was so seriously affected that he was rushed to hospital with suspected acute OP poisoning.

Over the following months his health deteriorated to the point where he was forced to abandon his career, eventually retiring to Wyoming with symptoms typical of chronic OP poisoning, including severe heart problems and a general 'shrivelling' of his muscular system. After lonely years without work or help, he was put in touch with a British lawyer, Peter Lunning, working in Hong Kong, and with Dr Jamal. With the aid of a leading British QC, Daniel Brennan, they mounted a case for compensation against all those responsible for the spraying episode, including the Diazinon's manufacturers, Ciba-Geigy, one of the largest pharmaceutical companies in the world.

The court hearings lasted six months, with Dr Jamal acting as chief expert witness for Phillips. The lawyers for the defendants, including the Swiss-based multinational chemical firm, were keenly aware that this was a test case that could have worldwide implications. They tried everything to discredit Jamal, who, over eight days, was subjected to gruelling cross-examination by five teams of lawyers, each led by a QC.

Finally, on 31 July, Judge Conrad Seagroatt delivered his 211-page judgement. He went out of his way to dismiss the 'full-frontal attack' on Jamal as 'spurious', 'ill-informed', 'unconvincing' and 'highly unsatisfactory'. Repeatedly praising the 'authority' of Jamal's evidence, he said it had been crucial in establishing that Phillips had sustained irreversible chronic damage from just a single exposure to the OPs. He awarded Phillips £1.9 million in damages, after a case that had itself cost an estimated £40 million.[19]

To everyone involved in the OPs debate across the world, this seemed a landmark moment. Only four days before the judgement, a retired senior MAFF official, in a letter to the *Sunday Telegraph*, had accused us of whipping up 'hysteria' over the OPs issue. This was the day before it was announced that a Labour MP, Graham

McMaster, had committed suicide. As his GP confirmed, he had become a typical OP victim, after being regularly exposed to OPs by his work as a council gardener in the 1980s.[20]

Soon afterwards, from Australia, came a second judgement, in another case in which Dr Jamal was the key expert witness. This involved three men irreparably damaged by diazinon in the fleeces of sheep they had been shearing. Ruling in their favour, the New South Wales Supreme Court in October awarded them £300,000 in damages.

On 1 November, in the London High Court, a third judge found in favour of a plaintiff seeking compensation for health damage by OPs, this time a farm worker, James Hill, who had been exposed to a pesticidal spray used in a grain store. Again the case turned on evidence from Jamal as the chief expert witness. On this occasion, the judge, Mrs Justice Smith, seemed to find it hard to grasp some of the technical points he had raised, criticizing him in her judgement for 'faulty technique' and 'lack of objectivity'. Nevertheless she accepted the force of his arguments, awarding Hill £50,000 in damages. But the key role played by Jamal in all three cases had now marked him down in the eyes of those supporting the OPs cover-up as a man who needed to be stopped.

Over the following weeks, Smith's judicial criticisms of Jamal were widely circulated, by those who had an interest in seeing him discredited (including government officials). This was reflected in the curious response of the *British Medical Journal*, which customarily gave full coverage to important medico-legal judgements. In this instance, however, it had failed to report the earlier Hong Kong and Australian judgements at all. But, after the Hill case, it quoted the judge's criticisms of Jamal at length. When this strangely one-sided reporting attracted letters of protest from an array of medical, scientific and legal experts familiar with all three cases, including two professors and Daniel Brennan, the QC who had won the Hong Kong case (soon to become chairman of the Bar Council), the *BMJ* declined to print them.[21]

By this time, however, Britain had been through a political watershed, with the arrival of the new Labour government. Along with the series of court judgements, this held out the promise that policy on OPs might at last see a fundamental change. In October 1996, Labour's shadow environment minister Michael Meacher had published an official party document entitled 'Dangerous Dips

– the truth about organophosphates'. He made no bones about where he stood on the central issue. His recommendations closely echoed many of those for which the campaigners had long been calling.

There should be a moratorium, proposed Meacher, on any further use of OP products in sheep dips. The government should commission an urgent study of cases where farmers and others had been damaged by OPs. The HSE and DH should begin 'an urgent programme of public education on the potential dangers of OP use', and should ensure that health professionals were properly briefed on symptoms and treatments. The licensing system should be reformed, to reduce its dependence on manufacturers' toxicity data, and products containing OPs should only be sold to the public when accompanied by proper advice about their health risks and safety precautions.

From a man who only seven months later would be minister of state in charge of environmental protection in Blair's government, this might have seemed to promise that a significant shift in government policy was on the way. This was reinforced by the fact that other senior Labour ministers had expressed similar views. Nevertheless, when the moment came, an early statement from the new minister for agriculture, Dr Cunningham, (whose PhD thesis had been on OPs), was rather less hopeful, although he did offer a revealing clue as to why that might be. At a meeting with the OP Information Network on 14 July 1997 he said he could not ban OPs 'because of advice from Government lawyers'.

Since 1993, Tyler's parliamentary group had several times met privately with ministers, more than one of whom had expressed concern at what they were told, promising action. But in each case, following 'advice from Government lawyers', those promises had dwindled to nothing. With the new Labour government, it was to be just the same, Meacher's brave resolve, once he arrived in office, faded like the Cheshire Cat, leaving behind only a wistful smile of sympathetic concern.

There continued to unfold that elaborate strategy, set in train five years earlier, whereby new reports commissioned by the government would each pretend to take account of public concern over OPs, while being studiously careful not to yield an inch on the central issues.

First, in November 1998, came a report by a working party of the Royal College of Physicians and Psychiatrists, commissioned the previous year by the Chief Medical Officer. This went so far as conceding that people exposed to OP sheep dips could display 'genuine and often very severe symptoms', and recommended that they should be treated sympathetically by doctors. Curiously, however, the report could not accept that there was yet sufficient evidence to confirm that OPs were necessarily the cause of those symptoms. It also recommended that the National Poisons Unit be asked to advise on whether specialist advice should be made more widely available.

Next, in July 1999, came a report by the Institute of Occupational Medicine in Edinburgh on the epidemiological study which had been commissioned four years earlier on the advice of the VPC. Again, this found that almost a fifth of the farmers studied reported symptoms of nerve damage; even conceding that some of these might be due to OPs. But further than this the study was not prepared to go (as might have been expected from a project jointly funded by the VMD, MAFF and the DH). The MAFF minister, Jeff Rooker, solemnly promised that these findings would be studied by an OPs working group of the Committee on Toxicity (CoT), due to report that autumn.

Since the CoT included many members with links to the pharmaceutical industry,[22] it was hardly surprising that when it published its findings, in October 1999, these merely reiterated the official line that there was insufficient evidence to show that long-term, low-dose exposure could cause chronic ill-health. Having deliberately excluded from its own study any farmers whose health had been damaged sufficiently to force them to give up work, the CoT concluded that the risk of serious health effects from low-dose exposure was insignificant.

Two months later came a further exercise in damage limitation, when MAFF announced that all OP sheep dips were to be temporarily withdrawn from sale until the manufacturers had designed new containers that could minimize the chance of users being splashed by dip when pouring it. The minister who announced this, Baroness Hayman, was one who, more than any, had privately expressed genuine concern when she met with campaigners. Soon after this she resigned from office.

This episode again reflected the curiously ambivalent policy whereby the government remained determined to insist that OPs posed no risk of long-term damage to health, while at the same time constantly taking new steps to reduce that damage by demanding additional safety measures. In less than ten years, the safety advice given to farmers had changed out of all recognition. In the early years, as the HSE's secret report of 1991 admitted, they had been given so little warning of the dangers of OPs that many had dipped virtually without any protective clothing at all. Now, step by step, the point had been reached where they were being advised to dress up in full 'space suits', complete with respirators. Yet all this had been achieved without the authorities ever having to come clean about the full extent of the damage OPs could cause.[23]

Meanwhile, across the country, thousands of farmers, their families and many others were having to live with the consequences of this tragedy. For many their ordeal was now only made worse by the long drawn-out fiasco of an attempt that had been made, since 1997, to mount a legal claim for compensation against various branches of government and the manufacturers of sheep dips.

At one time more than 1,000 potential claimants were signed up to this group action, supported by what would eventually become £2 million in legal aid.* Much of this money would end up in the hands of the various teams of lawyers that at different times represented the plaintiffs (while even greater sums were being spent on legal costs by the array of defendants).

So tortuously chaotic was the handling of the case that following all its twists and turns became painful, particularly for the victims themselves as they increasingly wondered where, if anywhere, their legal representatives might be taking them. One fateful decision by the lawyers was that all the different individual cases should be merged into one action, regardless of how different those cases might be. Another was that the case should only focus on the OPs themselves, and that the highly significant effects of other additives, such as phenols, should be ignored. This was eventually to prove a fatal weakness in the overall case.

---

* The terms on which the legal aid was granted required all compensation claims involving sheep dip (such as the case brought by Gary Coomber referred to earlier) to be combined into a single action. This was convenient for the government, since it meant that if the group action failed, all individual cases would fail with it.

At one point, after their case had been switched from one firm to another, then to a third, the Legal Aid Commission put a halt to any further public funding. But, even when this was renewed and the number of plaintiffs had been drastically reduced, the judges involved clearly took the view that the case, poorly argued and unsupported by any significant new medical or scientific evidence, was a forlorn enterprise.

On 29 January 2002, in the High Court, Mr Justice Morland finally ruled that the case must be abandoned. Only weeks later did a copy emerge of that 1991 HSE report, revealing just how much the government had been aware all those years before that it had a serious public health problem on its hands.

It was this report that, as much as anything, had led to the official cover-up policy, a central part of the purpose of which had been to head off compensation claims. With the collapse of the group action, it now seemed that this policy had been brilliantly successful. Had the HSE's report come to light earlier (and been put into the hands of lawyers as capable as those who won the Hong Kong case), one may speculate that the only serious attempt made to call the British government legally to account for the sheep dip tragedy might have had a rather different outcome.

Constructive Ignorance and Intellectual Corruption

Tragic though the story of the sheep farmers was, this particular disaster obviously affected only one comparatively small group of the population as a whole. But it was already coming to light that the damage done to human health by organophosphates might stretch very much wider than this. To so many different uses had these nerve-gas-related chemicals been put that there were countless other ways in which people could be exposed to OPs: from garden weed killers to kitchen fly-papers, from head lice treatment to pet collars, from spraydrift off fields and orchards to pesticide residues in fruit and vegetables. A British Medical Association report in 1990 cited a study that had established the surprising extent to which the residues of OPs used to protect grain in storage remained in flour used for baking bread.[24]

It was observed how similar were the symptoms of OP poisoning to other mysterious ailments which had been markedly on the increase in recent years, such as ME, asthma and many types of allergy. As early as 1993 we were contacted by Professor Peter Behan, a neurologist at Glasgow University, who had for some years been working on a very extensive study of ME, estimated to be affecting more than 150,000 people in Britain. He and his team had been struck by how many of the ME victims they examined turned out to have been exposed, through their occupation, to OPs.[25]

In 1999, Dr Bob Davies and two others published a paper based on surveys comparing neuropsychiatric symptoms in three groups: farmers who had used sheep dip; people who had been exposed to OPs in other ways; and farmers who had not been exposed to OPs. The two groups that had been exposed showed remarkably similar symptoms. This contrasted dramatically with the absence of such signs in the non-exposed group. Davies and his colleagues suggested that exposure raised the chances of finding these symptoms by as much as 10,000 times; concluding that their research provided strong evidence of 'a causal relationship between organophosphate exposure and significant neuropsychiatric disorder'.[26]

Yet none of the studies commissioned by the government came to remotely similar conclusions. They invariably confirmed the official line that high-dose exposure to OPs could cause acute damage to the nervous system, but that cumulative low-dose exposure could not cause chronic damage. The array of official bodies involved were never going to accept anything else (even though the HSE back in 1981, when it produced MS17, and in 1991 when it produced its secret report, had thought so differently).

This was the technique we came to describe, on the model of the legal principle known as 'constructive dismissal', as 'constructive ignorance'. Publicly the government went out of its way to ignore or dismiss any evidence that did not support the official line, and to discourage any research that threatened to come up with such evidence. The reason for this was simple. Every toxic chemical product on the market had been licensed as safe to use by one of the government's own regulatory agencies: either the Veterinary Medicines Directorate, as advised by the Veterinary Products Committee and the Committee on Toxicity; or the Pesticides Safety Directorate, responsible for licensing non-veterinary products. If such a product was in practice found not to be safe, this would indicate that the regulatory system had failed. Responsibility for that failure would therefore lie ultimately with the regulators themselves, who thus came to share a common interest with the manufacturers in suppressing any evidence that exposed the system's failure.

In this sense, they had entered into a conspiracy against the public. This was reinforced by the other close links that had been established between the manufacturers and the regulators. Many members of the VPC, like those of the CoT, had financial or other links with the pharmaceutical companies that manufactured OPs. The VPC, in judging whether these products were safe, relied almost exclusively on data supplied by the companies themselves. Furthermore, the main income of the licensing authority itself, the VMD, was derived from the fees it charged to the companies for granting them licences. So intimate had become the relationship between the regulators and the firms they were regulating that this provided a classic instance of what is known as 'regulatory capture'; the process whereby the regulation of an industry comes in effect to be dictated by the convenience of the larger, more powerful firms running that industry.*

This was further reinforced by the fact that there was no independent body to monitor whether or not the system worked effectively. This job was also given to the same regulators, whose task was, therefore, to check on the results of their own work. In the case of sheep dip, those who thought that it had damaged their health were invited to make what was called a 'suspect adverse reaction report' (SARR), recording the details of their exposure and the adverse reactions this had led to. But the report then had to be submitted to the VMD, which proved predictably reluctant to find that products it had itself licensed as safe were in fact nothing of the kind.

A similar situation, we noted, had arisen in the 1960s, when the Cairns Committee was investigating aviation safety.[27] Cairns strongly criticized the arrangement whereby the Civil Aviation Authority was responsible both for certifying aircraft as airworthy and also for investigating the causes of aircraft accidents. This

---

* Although this phrase was popularized by the right-wing economist Milton Friedman, he took it, ironically, from a Marxist historian Gabriel Kolko (*Railroads and Regulation, 1877–1916*, (Princeton University Press, 1965)).

made it impossible, Cairns suggested, for the CAA to be fully objective in apportioning blame when evidence indicated that an aircraft should never have been certified as safe to fly in the first place.

In 1962 Cairns had described this conflict of interest as leading to 'intellectual corruption'. Three decades later his term was recalled in the House of Lords by Lady Mar, when she suggested that it could now be equally aptly used of the VMD in the case of sheep dips. The VMD had a similar vested interest in not being prepared to recognize any damage done by products that the VMD itself had certified as safe.[28]

Her point was vividly illustrated by the peculiar system the VMD used to monitor the incidence of adverse reactions to sheep dip. The procedure for making a 'SARR' was so complex that it deterred many would-be complainants from submitting their forms at all. Despite this, in the early 1990s, the number of SARRs rose dramatically. Between 1991 and 1992 the number of reports submitted to the VMD almost quadrupled, from 63 to 227, of which 154 related to OPs. But with remarkable consistency the VMD found reasons to explain why these reports could be disregarded. Three years later, when MPs on the Commons Agriculture Committee were reviewing the workings of the VMD, a senior agency official privately admitted to their chairman that the VMD didn't really know what to do with the SARRs reports. 'We just put them away in a file', he was reported as saying.[29]

There was still a faint possibility, however, that, sooner or later, some outside inquiry or court might wish to examine the SARRS forms, with potentially embarrassing results. In 2003 the VPC was asked to review the workings of the SARRs system. Its chief finding was that, in future, SARR forms should be sent, not to the VMD, but to the holders of 'market authorisations': in other words, to the pharmaceutical companies themselves. The government was now to be excused from playing any part in the transaction. Those wishing to report that they had been damaged by OPs could now report only to those who had manufactured them: the very people who had the strongest interest in ensuring that their complaint was ignored. It was a perfect closed loop. For both government and manufacturers, this must have seemed like game, set and match.

A New Disaster: the Airline Pilots

Just as the legal battle over sheep dip had been winding to its conclusion, evidence was coming to light of an immense new problem caused by OPs, which few could have predicted. Organizations representing the staff of airline companies, including the British Airline Pilots Association and the US Association of Flight Attendants, were becoming alarmed by the number of pilots and aircrew being forced to give up work after being struck down by mystery illnesses.

The cause of this epidemic of sickness, it emerged, lay in the air circulating round the cockpits and cabins of airliners. The air, 'bled off' from the aircraft's engines, was becoming routinely contaminated with various chemicals, including an OP compound, tricresyl phosphate (TCP), used in the engine oil as an anti-wear additive. As pilots and aircrews were continually exposed to small amounts of neuro-toxic chemicals, many had begun to develop a range of mental and physical disorders that were all too familiar.[30]

The ramifications of this were clearly very serious. Not only did the possibility that pilots might themselves become incapacitated without warning raise obvious safety concerns. If contaminated air was causing sickness in aircrew, what might also be its effect on millions of passengers?

This problem had in fact first been identified as early as 1977, following a potentially fatal incident when the flight personnel of an airliner were 'acutely incapacitated' while attempting to land at Minneapolis-St Paul in the USA. A full medical examination of one crew member at the time had concluded that the cause of his 'mental and neuromuscular' dysfunction was almost certainly contamination of the air by synthetic engine oils containing a form of TCP, triorthocresylphosphate.[31]

By the late 1980s, without any knowledge of this incident, many pilots and aircrew in Britain and other countries were beginning to experience 'flu-like symptoms, nausea, severe fatigue, blurred vision, confusion of memory and speech, even temporary blackouts. They came particularly to associate these with the smoke and unpleasant smells which filled an aircraft following the switching on of its internal air supply. Among them was Susan Michaelis, who piloted BA146s in Australia.

In 1997, after three years experiencing short-term health problems, which she came to associate with switching on the cockpit
air supply, Michaelis suffered such a severe adverse reaction following such an incident that she was no longer able to continue
flying. After losing her pilot's licence, she began researching into
why she had been incapacitated.

An Australian aircrew union supplied her with voluminous data
showing that scores of other pilots and aircrew had been similarly
affected. It had already been clearly established that their illness
was related to oil fume contamination of the air bled off from
aircraft engines. She sent her evidence to the Australian transport
ministry and 50 politicians. The only one who responded positively
was an independent-minded Senator, John Woodley, who in 1999
organized a Senate committee to investigate.[32]

Woodley's committee did a very thorough job. It heard from a
wide range of witnesses, including Mobil, manufacturers of much
of the oil used in airline engines. Their technical evidence confirmed
the chemical make-up of the TCP used in its product, which had
been identified as long ago as the 1920s as a dangerous neurotoxin.

Mobil's data revealed that TCP contained a bundle of isomers,
of which three were particularly relevant. Triorthocresylphosphate
(TOCP) had been identified as among the chemicals causing the
collapse of two pilots which had nearly caused that airliner to crash
near Minneapolis in 1977. But in 1958 a German chemist, Dietrich
Henschler, had established that two associated isomers were very
much more dangerous: Diorthocresylphosphate (DOCP) was more
toxic by five times, Monorthocresylphosphate (MOCP) by ten
times. Furthermore, since engine oil contained very much more
MOCP than TOCP, its toxic effect was 6 million times greater.[33]

Such was the beginning of a saga that was eventually to provide
strikingly close parallels to that of the cover-up over sheep dip. The
properties of the different isomers in TCP would become highly
relevant to the methods later used to promote the cover-up of what
became known as 'aerotoxic syndrome', because government
bodies and the two industries involved, the aircraft manufacturers
and the airlines, soon learned to refer only to TOCP, the least toxic
of the isomers, carefully suppressing any reference to the others.

At this early stage, however, the Australian Senate inquiry had
caught them off-guard. When it reported in October 2000, it found
unequivocally that the 'cabin air problem' experienced on the

BA146 was due to contamination from 'the burning of lubricating oil' used in the aircraft's engines. It made eight recommendations as to how the problem should be remedied (almost all of which were ignored).

Very different was the response that same year of another inquiry, held in the UK by the Science and Technology Committee of the House of Lords, into the general safety of airline passengers. Although the British Airline Pilots Association (BALPA) presented evidence to show that aircrews in Britain were experiencing similar air quality problems, this made little impression on the committee. It preferred to accept the evidence given by the industry and other witnesses, including the National Poisons Unit, that this could not be ascribed to contaminated air. In only a brief reference to air quality, the report concluded that 'concerns about significant risk to the health of airline passengers and crew are not substantiated'.[34]

Over the next few years, evidence accumulated that adverse reactions in pilots and aircrew following exposure to contaminated air were much more widespread than had been supposed. These were particularly associated with certain types of aircraft, such as the BA146, Boeing 757 and A320.

What was potentially at stake here for the international airline industry was obviously very much greater than anything that might have arisen from the sheep dip disaster. Not only might hundreds of pilots and aircrew be in a position to claim compensation for the loss of their health and livelihood, putting both airline companies and aircraft manufacturers at huge financial risk. Also to be taken into account was the possible response of millions of passengers if it became publicly known that they too were being exposed to contaminated air.

A recognition of the manufacturers' awareness of the problem was that, when in 2004 Boeing launched its new 787 Dreamliner, this incorporated a wholly different air supply system. No longer was the air ducted to the cabin bled off from the engines, it was drawn by compressor fans from outside the plane. But any public admission that cabin air was creating a health problem would be disastrous for the industry. It was vital to continue denying that the problem existed.

In 2004, following two serious incidents relating to pilots who had been taken sick after exposure to contaminated air, the Civil

Aviation Authority (CAA), responsible for regulating airline safety, held its own inquiry. Its report closed ranks by finding that, although the incidents had been caused by contaminated air, this was merely due to 'irritants' in the engine oil. They could not have been due to TCP, the report claimed, because this was unlikely to have been 'present in sufficient concentration to have significant effect'. In a pattern which was to become only too familiar, the report also referred only to the least toxic of the three isomers, TOCP.[35]

Among those dismayed by the evasiveness of the CAA report was a senior British pilot Captain Tristan Loraine, who had himself experienced a succession of chemical incidents while piloting 757 jumbo jets. As a former member of BALPA's national executive, he was now collecting data on 'aerotoxic syndrome' on its behalf, assisted by the research already carried out by Michaelis in Australia. Having already recorded details of several hundred significant 'air contamination incidents' (the number would later top 1,000), he was aware that the problem was being severely 'under-reported'.

In April 2005 BALPA staged a 'Contaminated Cabin Air Conference' at Imperial College, London, attended by more than 200 delegates from all over the world. They included an array of scientists and doctors who were by now studying the problem from many angles.

Professor Chris van Netten, an epidemiologist from the University of British Columbia, told the conference, for instance, how he had been analysing swabs taken from the interiors of hundreds of airliners. Traces of TCP had shown up in more than 80 per cent. Another contributor was Dr Sarah Mackenzie-Ross, a clinical neuro-psychologist from University College, London, who in 2003 had been given funding by Defra to carry out an extensive study of the clinical effects of OP exposure on sheep farmers. But she had now widened her investigation to include a separate study on the effects of OPs and other chemicals on airline pilots. Her preliminary findings were alarming. So consistently were people being exposed that, based on the CAA's database for 2004, she estimated that, in that year alone, as many as 197,000 passengers on British airliners might have been exposed to toxic fumes.[36]

The overwhelming weight of the evidence presented to the conference suggested that many airliners were being operated in breach of the international regulatory requirements that an aircraft could not be considered airworthy unless its internal air supply was 'free from harmful or hazardous concentrations of gases or vapors', and that crew members were supplied with 'a sufficient amount of uncontaminated air' to enable them 'to perform their duties without undue discomfort or fatigue'.[37]

Faced with such pressure, the Department for Transport and the Department of Health now played another card familiar to those who had followed the government's tactics in covering up the sheep dip disaster. They called in the CoT to carry out a review of BALPA's claims concerning 'the cabin air environment, ill-health in aircraft crews and the possible relationship to smoke/fume effects in aircraft'.

While this inquiry was getting under way in the summer of 2005, Loraine had a personal shock. He had such a devastating attack of ill health in a 757 that he had to stop flying. When he was examined by a succession of specialists, including Jamal and Professor Mohamed Abou-Donia, an internationally recognized authority on OPs at Duke University, North Carolina, they all found evidence of brain-cell death, cognitive problems and exposure to TCP and other carcinogens and immuno-depressants.

Abou-Donia had coined the term OPIND (organophosphate delayed neuropathy disorder) to describe the long-term chronic nerve damage caused by exposure to OPs. Jamal's own version was COPIND (chronic organophosphate induced neuropsychiatric disorder).* Both were agreed that Loraine's immune system and cognitive abilities were seriously impaired. But his company's doctors assured him there was nothing seriously wrong and that he could soon resume flying.

In April 2006, after continuing to pilot 757s for several more months, Loraine suffered another adverse reaction so severe that the CAA now grounded him for good. When he went back to the

---

* In 2002 Jamal, now working at the neurosciences department of Imperial College, London, published the most comprehensive review to date of studies of the neurological effects of long-term, low-level exposure to OPs (COPIND). Of 30 studies, 26 had found a positive link to neurotoxicity. His paper concluded that 'the weight of current evidence' overwhelmingly supported the view that OP exposure damaged the nervous system (G. A. Jamal, *et al.*, *Toxicology*, 27 December 2002, 181–2, 223–33).

specialists, their tests showed that, since the previous year, his condition had markedly worsened. The very condition on which he had been campaigning on behalf of his fellow-pilots had now cost him his own health and livelihood.

At least Loraine had long been familiar with the cause of his problem. Thanks to the refusal of the airline companies and regulators such as the CAA to admit that the problem existed, the majority of pilots affected were still not aware of why they were ill. Typical in this respect was Captain John Hoyte who, while piloting BA146s since the 1980s, had frequently experienced short-term adverse effects from 'cabin smoke', some of which had left him unable to speak or think coherently. In 2004, however, he was knocked out by an attack so serious, while on a scheduled flight to Salzburg, that on his return he was temporarily grounded by CAA doctors. He was diagnosed by a CAA psychiatrist, Professor Turnbull, as suffering from 'operational stress'. In 2005, after a further incident, he voluntarily decided not to fly again.[38]

Hoyte was quite unaware at this stage of any link between his breakdown and TCP (although his next-door neighbour in Warwickshire turned out to be a former cabin crew employee of British Airways, forced to retire from working on 757s after being struck down with similar symptoms).

In January 2006, however, Hoyte was contacted by Loraine and asked to take part in Mackenzie-Ross's project at UCL. In May 2006, the month after Loraine himself had been finally grounded, tests showed that Hoyte had cognitive deficiencies and other abnormalities consistent with OP and chemical exposure, similar to those that had shown up in the other pilots in the UCL study. For the first time he had clear evidence that the breakdown in his health was not due to 'psychiatric problems' or 'stress' but was due to the contaminated air he had been breathing for nearly 20 years in his work as a pilot.

Another pilot, Captain Julian Soddy, also had no idea why he suffered repeated adverse effects while flying 146s, until one incident proved so serious that he was temporarily grounded. He discussed it with his company and with the CAA's chief medical officer, a personal friend. Neither could see any reason why he should not resume flying. He then had another attack that left him, by his own account, in 'a vegetable state'. He went to his doctor, whose father had been a Welsh sheep farmer damaged by sheep dip. The GP was struck by the similarity of their symptoms. When Soddy was then referred to Jamal, the cause of his problem was confirmed. The CAA itself accepted this as evidence for failing his pilot's medical certificate, agreeing that his symptoms 'would indicate that you may be suffering from some sort of chemical exposure in the BAe 146'. Soddy was now grounded for good, having lost a job that paid him £100,000 a year.[39]

When the CoT had begun its inquiry in 2005, the pilots were initially delighted. Unaware of how the CoT had been used by the government to support its cover-up over sheep dip, they imagined that it would be genuinely concerned to dig out the truth. But as a succession of meetings took place, spun out over the next two years, they began to wonder what the committee was up to.

Typical was the meeting between BALPA and the CoT secretariat held at the DH in February 2006.[40] BALPA was represented by several internationally respected scientists, such as Professor Abou-Donia from North Carolina and Professor Clem Furlong, a geneticist from the University of Washington, Seattle. But the CoT seemed remarkably uninterested in anything these distinguished experts had to say, trying to steer the discussion away from TCP and OPs as much as possible. They tightly controlled what was allowed to appear in the minutes, and promised a paper which more than a year later had still failed to materialize.

In June 2006 the government took a further step to close down the debate, when Mackenzie-Ross was informed by Defra that her project, now well advanced, was to be closed down. This, she was told, was because the VMD had questioned her research protocol, in particular her selection of a control group to the sheep farmers. She submitted twelve more options for the make-up of a suitable control group, all of which the VMD turned down without explaining what sort of control group it might find acceptable. After suggestions that this looked like yet another attempt to sabotage research which threatened to come up with results the government would find embarrassing, Defra in December 2006 announced that funding for the project might continue after all, but only under severe new constraints.[41]

So successful, it seemed, were these efforts to suppress the dangers posed by OPs that, on 18 June 2007, three of the most vocal campaigners on behalf of pilots, aircrews and passengers, the former captains Michaelis, Loraine and Hoyte, joined forces.

Backed by 110 MPs and peers, including such veteran OP campaigners as the Countess of Mar and Lord (Paul) Tyler, they and
some 20 damaged fellow-pilots met in Westminster to launch the
Aerotoxic Association, a new campaigning group designed to
promote their cause.*

That same week the CoT produced the minutes of yet another
of its meetings, held the previous March. As an example of official
obfuscation these were almost a self-parody. Although they began
by referring to BALPA having submitted 'data relating to organophosphates', this was the only reference to OPs in the entire
document. From the remaining twenty-odd pages, dealing with
anything from carbon monoxide to the need to review pilot
training procedures, it was clear that the committee had not the
slightest interest in discussing whether cabin air was being contaminated by TCP in engine oil. It was clear that its sole purpose
was to find any conceivable way of sidestepping the very issue that
had led to it being set up in the first place.[42]

Once again, it seemed, the 'blockers' were winning hands down.

The Wider Picture

So far in this chapter we have concentrated almost entirely on the
story of how the government and its industry allies managed to
suppress the evidence of how just one type of chemical was
damaging the health of untold numbers of people. The regulatory
system supposedly designed to protect the public against these
dangers was so corrupted that it did the very reverse.

As we have seen, however, OPs represented only one of the
countless ways in which anyone may be exposed to toxic chemicals
in the modern world. To a far greater degree than most people are
aware, they may risk such exposure every day. Yet the system on
which the public is expected to rely for protection against these
poisons is essentially the same as that which created the sheep dip
disaster. Once any toxic chemical product has been licensed as safe
to use, the regulators and manufacturers have a very strong vested

---

* The MPs had signed an Early Day Motion calling on the industry to fit
filtration systems to all the aircraft types affected, and that passengers
should be informed whenever they had been exposed to contaminated air.

interest in dismissing any evidence which shows that it may nevertheless still be a danger.

To illustrate this we end with just two more examples of the official response to attempts by determined campaigners to expose fundamental flaws in this regulatory system.

The first relates to a quite different toxic compound sold for a wide variety of purposes, known as tributyltin or TBT. This was licensed as safe for use in many commercial products, from wood preservatives, commonly used to protect the beams and floors of people's homes, to anti-fouling paint used by sailors to keep the hulls of their yachts and motor-boats free of barnacles.

In 1988 Margaret Reichlin, the retired head of a London school art department, suffered severe health problems after a cocktail of toxic chemicals, including TBT and lindane, had been sprayed on the timbers of her Hampshire cottage. To have her home and its contents decontaminated cost her £25,000. Furthermore, she discovered that this intense exposure had sensitized her not just to the slightest contact with TBT but to other chemicals as well, which meant she now had to be extremely careful which products she came near. Otherwise, as she found from experience, her health problems might well recur.

When she raised this with the HSE, which had licensed TBT as safe, it dismissed her concerns as groundless, insisting that TBT was 'not harmful to humans'. In a 1990 safety leaflet issued to the public, the HSE stated that TBT posed 'no risk to human health'. But a list of 'substances hazardous to health' published by Croner's, based on information supplied by the HSE for use by hospitals, the police, firemen and other professionals, classified TBT as 'immunotoxic, neurotoxic, skin and lung irritant', and as having 'an extremely high mortality rate'.

At a meeting arranged by her MP at the HSE's headquarters in 1990, with officials of the HSE and the Advisory Committee on Pesticides, Miss Reichlin asked them to explain the discrepancy between these two statements. Dr Robin Foster of the HSE told her, 'we tailor our information to our audience'.[43]

She then discovered that widespread scientific concern was now being expressed at the damage being done to dolphins, fish and other marine life by the use of TBT on ships (which would soon lead to severe restrictions on its use).

At least Miss Reichlin had been able to identify TBT as the

chemical used on her property from the data sheets which manufacturers were obliged to supply under the HSE's 1988 Control of Substances Hazardous to Health Regulations (COSHH), implementing an EC directive. So when, in 1995, she wanted to paint her cottage's external walls, she again asked her supplier what chemicals the paint contained. The manufacturers, ICI, provided 22 pages of small print, but nowhere did these answer her question.

When she asked the HSE why she could no longer obtain the information she needed, she was told that what she had been given were 'the new CHIP data sheets', introduced under the 1994 Chemicals Hazard Information and Packaging Regulations (implementing three more EC directives). Miss Reichlin was startled to hear that these, unlike the old COSHH sheets, did 'not have to list dangerous substances'. She was therefore even more puzzled to read in two glossy booklets from the HSE, *Chip 2 For Everyone* and *The Complete Idiot's Guide to Chip*, that 'the objective of Chip 2 is to help protect people and the environment from the ill-effects of chemicals'.[44]

In other words, the effect of the new system was precisely the opposite of what it was claimed to be. The public had been deprived of the right to know to which toxic chemicals they were being exposed. Furthermore, Miss Reichlin then discovered that TBT was also being marketed under a series of innocuous sounding tradenames such as Ultrafresh, used as a 'biocide' in a whole range of common domestic products, from shower curtains and duvets to shoe soles and carpets. Thus anyone sensitized to this chemical might now suffer an adverse reaction to such products without having any right to know what had caused it.

Another glaring flaw in the system the regulators had erected to protect themselves was brought to light some years later by another remarkable campaigner, Georgina Downs, who had moved with her parents in 1983 to a home in Sussex, adjoining open farmland. Before long, Miss Downs and her family all began to suffer serious health problems. It was not until some years later, however, when she was admitted to hospital with severe muscle wastage and other chronic effects, that she began to wonder what might be their cause. It was only then that she noticed that many of the symptoms became particularly acute whenever the field next to their garden was sprayed with chemicals designed to kill insects and weeds.

Wanting to find out more about the regulatory system governing pesticide use, Miss Downs approached the HSE and the Pesticides Safety Directorate, responsible for licensing the 31,000 tons of chemicals sprayed on Britain's farmland each year. She was struck by how suspiciously quick they seemed to be to dismiss her concerns. She was then amazed to discover that there was no legal bar to spraying toxic chemicals right next to people's gardens and the open windows of their homes; and equally that a farmer was under no legal obligation to reveal which chemicals he was using on his land or to warn his neighbours of when he was going to shower his fields with poison.

Being an unusually determined young woman, she then in 2002 began a relentless campaign to expose these curious anomalies in the law. She first, at a public meeting in York in 2002, staged a famous confrontation with the chairman of the Advisory Committee on Pesticides (a body equivalent to the VPC, with similarly close links to the chemical industry). She compiled a database of reports of clusters of illnesses and diseases in rural communities all over the UK, including various cancers, including leukaemia, non-Hodgkins lymphoma, and neurological conditions such as ME and Parkinson's among others. She then set her sights on a succession of ministers, including Michael Meacher, then in charge of the environment, continually putting them on the back foot by her mastery of the legal and scientific facts and by her skilful use of publicity.

Both ministers and officials repeatedly tried to fob her off with claims that the law provided the public with perfectly adequate protection. But repeatedly she was able to demonstrate the hollowness of such claims, as when she showed that the official tests carried out to assess the risks of crop sprays to members of the public were based only on fleeting exposures lasting barely five minutes. Nothing at all had been done to measure the risks of the prolonged and repeated exposures suffered by those who, like herself and her family, lived in immediate proximity to farmland that was sprayed many times in a year.

Miss Downs won extensive media coverage and an array of awards for her campaign. She was even in 2005 given significant support by an inquiry carried out by the Royal Commission on Environmental Pollution. But what was yet again only too obvious was the ease with which, however powerful the evidence she mustered, the ranks of officialdom were able simply to slam the door in her face. The one fixed point on which no minister, department or government agency was ever going to give an inch was in conceding that any chemical licensed by the government as safe could damage human health. It was the one 'scare' no government could allow. The implications if they admitted the truth, it seemed, were too horrendous to contemplate.

Even now, however, there was to be a twist to the tale that no one could have predicted.

The Twist to the Tale

In the second half of 1998 Britain had held the rotating presidency of the European Union. One of the duties of each government that takes on this six-monthly presidency is to put forward new proposals for EU legislation. Every Whitehall department was therefore asked to come up with its own suggestions. High on the agenda was one from Michael Meacher, as minister of state for the environment, who two years earlier had published his pamphlet calling for much stricter regulation on the use of OPs in sheep dip.

Frustrated at not having been able to put his proposals into effect when he came into office, when Britain chaired the council of EU environment ministers at Chester in December 1998 Meacher proposed that a new EU-wide system should be set up for the regulation of chemicals. By 2003 the Brussels officials had come up with what was known as the Registration, Evaluation and Authorization of Chemicals directive (REACH).

Not only would every one of the 30,000 chemicals manufactured in the EU have to be tested and authorized, to ensure that they were not harmful to human health or the environment. So would 140,000 separate compounds and formulations containing those chemicals, used for every imaginable industrial purpose, from colouring plastics to treating luxury leather goods. Each application of chemicals would thus have to be separately tested and authorized as safe, under a set of procedures to be supervised by a new EU Chemicals Agency.

So complex were the Commission's proposals that negotiations on them had involved a record 12,000 pages of documents. The initial response from industry, in particular from Germany, France and Britain, three of the countries that made Europe a world leader in chemical manufacturing, was one of horror. It would take at least 100 years, they predicted, to test 170,000 chemical products. The cost would be astronomic. In Britain alone, it was estimated, REACH would cost £6 billion a year, more than the UK chemicals industry made from exporting its products all over the world. And because these rules would not apply to imports from outside the EU, it was claimed, the directive would merely result in exporting vast numbers of jobs to countries such as China, which would continue to manufacture chemical products without the need to comply with the new testing procedures.[45]

After three years of fierce argument behind the scenes, in December 2006 a version of the REACH directive was finally approved as a regulation by the European Parliament. Although it had been modified from its original form, it would still be one of the most expensive pieces of legislation the European Commission had ever proposed, imposing huge costs on the EU's economies. And this might never have come about had it not been for the tragedy inflicted by organophosphorus sheep dips on thousands of British farmers and their families.

A first irony, however, was that the REACH regulation excluded all pesticides and biocides. These were supposedly covered by other legislation. A second was that the system whereby tens of thousands of other chemical products were now to be regulated by the EU, in the name of preventing them causing any further damage to human health, was essentially no different in principle from the system whereby those OP sheep dips and other toxic chemicals had been authorized for use in years gone by.

The theory behind the new system was still that, if a chemical was licensed by a government agency as safe, then safe it must be. In practice, however, as we have seen, it was precisely that principle which had been a major factor in bringing about the sheep dip tragedy in the first place.

The real lesson of the 'intellectual corruption' implicit in such a system had not been learned. Simply calling into being a new form of licensing offered no guarantee that the regulatory agencies responsible for authorizing chemicals as safe would not become just as compromised as their predecessors. No agency in Britain had been more compromised by its role during the sheep dip affair than the Health and Safety Executive. Yet when a British minister was asked in May 2006 which authority would be responsible for administering the REACH directive in the UK, he replied that *the chosen competent authority will need to demonstrate an ability to work closely with the Health and Safety Executive who have overall policy and enforcement responsibility for occupational health legislation.*[46]

In all the examples we looked at earlier, the real damage done by a scare came when the government moved in to launch its regulatory response. In the case of toxic chemicals, the government had done all it could to prevent the threat they posed turning into a 'scare'. Even so, the 'scare that never was' still ended up by producing an absurdly disproportionate regulatory response, which would in itself add even more damage to that already inflicted by the chemicals themselves.

In light of the genuine tragedies the government had already set in train, it was likely to become yet another example of taking a colossal sledgehammer to miss the nut.

Notes

1. *Toxic Chemicals in Agriculture*, a report of a working group chaired by Solly Zuckerman, was presented to the Minister of Agriculture and Fisheries in January 1951.
2. See, for instance, Kenneth Mellanby, *Pesticides and Pollution* (1967), which spoke in glowing terms of the environmental benefits of OPs, as opposed to the now discredited organo-chlorines.
3. 'Organophosphate Insecticides – Their Use By The Farming Community', report by Standing Committee D (Agriculture and Fisheries Issues) of the Northern Ireland Forum for Political Dialogue, presented to the Northern Ireland Assembly, 3 April 1998.
4. Hansard, HC, 8 June 1992.
5. MAFF press release, 112/93, 1 April 1993.
6. Christopher Booker and Richard North, *The Mad Officials* (Duckworth, 1994).
7. Booker and North, *The Mad Officials*, p. 209.
8. R. Stephens, *et.al.*, 'The neuropsychological effects of long-term exposure to organophosphates in sheep dip', *The Lancet*, 345, 8958 (6 May 1995) 1135–9.
9. 'Report on Organophosphorus Sheep Dips', Veterinary Products Committee, 1999.
10. *Sunday Telegraph*, 27 July 1997.
11. *Farming News*, 5 September 1995.
12. *Sunday Telegraph*, 11 September 1994.

13. Hansard, HL, col. 271, 21 June 1995.
14. *Sunday Telegraph*, 20 August 1995.
15. *Sunday Telegraph*, 20 August 1995.
16. Hansard, HC, 4 October 1996.
17. Hansard, HC, col. 67, 15 October 1996.
18. Hansard, HC. Also, *Sunday Telegraph*, 2 March 1997.
19. *Sunday Telegraph*, 3 August, 14 December, 1997.
20. Letter from Geoffrey Hollis, *Sunday Telegraph*, 3 August 1997.
21. *Sunday Telegraph*, 14 December 1997.
22. See Chapter Eight. The CoT was the body at whose urging Rooker had recently been fighting to restrict the sale of vitamin B6.
23. Cf. Countess of Mar, Hansard, HL, 9 March 2005.
24. *Pesticides, Chemicals and Health*, British Medical Association (1991).
25. Personal communication.
26. D. R. Davies, *et al.*, 'Chronic Organophosphate Induced Neuropsychiatric Disorder (COPIND)', *Journal of Nutritional and Environmental Medicine*, 9, 123–34.
27. Cairns Committee on Civil Aircraft Accident Investigation and Licence Control, report (cmnd. 1695) (1962).
28. Hansard, HL, col. 1559, 24 June 1997.
29. *Sunday Telegraph*, 27 August 1995.
30. For further background on this section, see the website set up by some of the aircrew affected, *www.aerotoxic.org*.
31. Mark R. Montgomery, *et al.*, 'Human intoxication following inhalation exposure to synthetic jet lubricating oil', *Clinical Toxicology*, 11, 4 (1977), pp. 423–6.
32. 'Air safety and cabin air quality in the BA146 aircraft', report by Senate Rural Affairs and Transport References Committee, October 2000.
33. D. Henschler, 'Tricresyl phosphate poisoning', *Klinische Wochenscrift*, 36, 14 (1958).
34. Air Travel and Health, House of Lords Science and Technology Committee, Fifth Report, 2000.
35. CAA Paper 2004/04, Cabin Air Quality, *www.caa.co.uk*.
36. S. J. Mackenzie-Ross, *et al.*, 'Ill health following exposure to contaminated air on commercial aircraft: psychosomatic disorder or neurological injury?' *Journal of Occupational Health and Safety, Australia and New Zealand*, 22, 521–6. One passenger who was vocal about being affected was Gary Coomber, mentioned earlier in this chapter as a sheep dip victim. See Paul Tyler website, *www.paultyler.libdems.org*.

37. Federal Aviation Regulations, FAR 25/831 (and its international equivalents).
38. John Hoyte, written evidence to House of Lords Science and Technology Committee, June 2007.
39. *www.paultyler.libdems.org*, 15 July 2005.
40. Meeting between CoT Secretariat and BALPA at DH, Skipton House, 22 February 2006 (Annex 3 to TOX/2006/21).
41. *Chemistry World*, November 2006, January 2007.
42. CoT update discussion paper, TOX/2007/10.
43. Taken from a recording of the discussion.
44. Christopher Booker and Richard North, *The Castle of Lies: Why Britain Must Get Out of Europe* (Duckworth, 1997), pp. 15–16.
45. Christopher Booker and Richard North, *The Great Deception: Can The European Union Survive?* (Continuum, London, 2005), p. 610.
46. Hansard, HC, 25 May 2006, written answer from Ian Pearson, Minister of State for Defra.

Epilogue

A New Age Of Superstition

Beneath the surface of an ever more sophisticated society, what dark passions and inflammable credulities do we find, sometimes accidentally released, sometimes deliberately mobilised!
Hugh Trevor-Roper, *The European Witch-Craze of the Sixteenth and Seventeenth Centuries.*[1]

For 200 years in the sixteenth and seventeenth centuries, Europe's Christian civilization became haunted by a great fear. Many leading figures of the age had become convinced that society faced a terrifying threat. Huge numbers of women, they believed, had been drawn into a vast, shadowy conspiracy. They had entered into a pact with the Devil. They were branded as 'witches'.

Backed by voluminous and detailed evidence, supported by Popes and secular rulers, lawyers, theologians and learned men of all kinds, the regulatory authorities went into action. Countless thousands of witches and their supposed male accomplices were tortured, imprisoned, burned, hanged, drowned or otherwise hounded to their deaths.

Only by the end of the seventeenth century did it finally become clear that witches did not exist. The great 'witch panic' had been based on no more than an immense collective fantasy.

Few things about previous ages arouse in us such puzzled scorn as those bouts of collective hysteria to which our ancestors so often fell victim, as they responded to some supposed threat to society, which eventually turned out to have been imaginary. History is littered with examples, large and small: the 'Catholic conspiracy' with which Titus Oates whipped up hysteria in the England of the 1670s; the conspiracy of 'Communists in high places' with which

Senator McCarthy chilled the hearts of patriotic Americans in the 1950s; most deadly of all, the fear of a 'Zionist conspiracy', which appeared in Europe at the end of the nineteenth century, coming to its dreadful climax in the Nazi death camps.

How could the people of past ages, we ask, have been so credulous, so easily carried away by mass-delusions? Yet it is a remarkable fact that no period in history has been more ready to give credence to imaginary 'scares' than our own.

It is true that their nature has changed. No longer, on the whole, is the shadowy threat to society seen to be coming from other groups of human beings (although some of the more fanciful claims inspired by the menace of terrorism have been a conspicuous exception).

Today the danger is seen as more intangible. The true modern equivalent of those witches of old has been a whole succession of supposed threats to human health and wellbeing: from mysterious and deadly new viruses and bacteria in our food, or floating about in the environment, to toxic substances in our homes and work-places; all culminating in the ultimate apocalyptic visions conjured up by the fear of global warming.

In this epilogue we address two issues. First, in light of the evidence we have looked at, we take a final look at the role of each of the main groups in society that are crucial to the promotion of any successful scare.

We then move on to explore some of the deeper reasons why this particular form of irrationality should have become so characteristic of our time. What weakness in the psychological make-up of our modern society has made us so peculiarly susceptible to the kind of scares this book has described?

The Power of the Nyktomorph

The first precondition of any scare is that it is based on a lack of certainty. At the beginning of the book we quoted those words from Shakespeare:

> *in the night, imagining some fear,*
> *how easy is a bush supposed a bear.*

What Shakespeare was pointing out is a fundamental feature of the way we perceive the world. What can lead us into imagining that some shape glimpsed indistinctly in the darkness might be a bear (or a burglar, a ghost or whatever), is that our brain is not being given enough information to resolve the image correctly. The very fact that we cannot see it clearly teases our imagination into seeing it as something much more significant than it is.

We see this trick of perception in many different contexts. It is centred on what we may call a 'nyktomorph' or 'night shape' (from the Greek words *nyktos*, night, and *morph-*, form or shape). All the scares analysed in this book derived their force from a nykto-morphic effect. Because initially not enough is known about the true nature of the supposed threat, it plays on people's fears, becoming inflated out of all proportion to its reality. Only as more information becomes available does it become possible to see that it was only a harmless bush all along.

As we have seen, for any fully-fledged scare to take off, it requires the participation of particular groups of 'pushers'. These include scientists, the media, politicians and officials. Also influential in egging on the scare may be non-governmental organizations and lobby groups, such as Friends of the Earth and Greenpeace, cancer charities or anti-asbestos campaigners.

The precise part played by each of these groups in creating the momentum that can bring a scare to its tipping point may vary. But one contribution that is invariably crucial is that of the scientists. One factor any scare needs to be successful is plausibility – something which in our modern world only scientists have the authority to provide.

The Role of the Scientists

At the heart of every scare we have looked at has been a group of scientists or technical experts making a wrong or exaggerated guess on the basis of what eventually turned out to be inadequate data. Usually they have put two things together, and then guessed wrongly that one was the cause of the other.

When Bernard Rowe and his colleagues at the PHLS were confronted with a rise in salmonella poisoning in humans and a rise in salmonella contamination in poultry, they jumped to the conclusion that the two must be linked and that hens must be laying eggs that were already internally contaminated. When John Patti-son and his colleagues at SEAC, charged with investigating BSE, were confronted with what they imagined to be a new form of human brain disease, they guessed that the first might be the cause of the second.

When scientists such as Irving Selikoff discovered that the amphibole forms of asbestos were responsible for a large number of deaths, they concluded that a mineral with quite different properties, just because it also happened to pass under the same general name, must be equally dangerous. When various scientists discovered that CO_2 and global temperatures had both been rising, they became convinced that one must have been the cause of the other, despite the fact that earlier, while CO_2 levels had for several decades been rising, temperatures had fallen.

Once this initial false step has been made comes the second stage, when those persuaded by the thesis develop such an obsessive interest in pursuing it that this blinkers their vision, leading them to overlook any evidence that might contradict it.

So convinced became the PHLS that contaminated eggs must be the origin of the rise in salmonella poisoning that its investigators failed to look for any other cause. So convinced were the Cleveland paediatricians that their 'anal dilatation' system for diagnosing child abuse was scientifically reliable that they pursued it to the exclusion of anything else; just as did the social workers who had fallen for 'expert evidence' that remarkable numbers of adults were becoming involved in groups practising satanic ritual abuse.

Researchers looking for evidence that non-smokers were being harmed by 'environmental tobacco smoke' became so possessed by the idea that adult smoking must have been responsible for the rise in cot deaths that they quite overlooked the fact that, during the very years when cot death figures had been hurtling upwards, the incidence of smoking had been rapidly falling.

This is how, within the scientific community, a scare develops a powerful momentum of its own. Researchers not only become fixated on one particular thesis to the exclusion of anything else; but this in itself gives them a heady sense that they are on the track of something extremely important to society.

This leads on to a third stage in the scientific evolution of a scare when those promoting it become so carried away by the rightness of their cause that they are prepared actively to suppress any evidence which contradicts it. When Dr Needleman was studying the effect of lead on children's brains, as Ernhart and Scarrs pointed out, he repeatedly reduced the size of the group he was studying to exclude any data which failed to support his thesis. When the WHO and the American Cancer Society found that the major inquiries they had commissioned into passive smoking were not coming up with the results they wanted, they attempted to prevent the results from being published.

The most notorious example of such manipulation was the IPCC's promotion of the 'hockey stick' graph as proof of its chosen 'scenario' on global warming. Only by using one very unrepresentative set of data, out of context, and excluding all the overwhelming weight of data from other sources, was the IPCC provided with the re-written version of history that it wanted.*

By the time a scare has reached this stage we may see how the science behind it is being further manipulated by its 'politicization'. So great by now is the momentum behind the scare that, in the academic, corporate and official bureaucracies it has become the established orthodoxy. The most obvious way we see this at work is in how the funding vital to most scientific research is directed by governments, university departments and big business only towards projects designed to corroborate the new orthodoxy.

When British government officials took it into their heads that sheep could be infected with BSE, millions of pounds were spent trying vainly to prove the point. Hundreds of millions of dollars were poured into research trying to prove that passive smoking was harmful to non-smokers. When it came to the greatest scare of them all, global warming, it was estimated that by 2007 more than $100 billion had already been devoted to thousands of different projects based on the official orthodoxy that climate change was due to human activity and that human action could halt it.

---

* In 2007, Dr Michael Griffin, the head of NASA, provoked an international furore by saying in a US radio interview that he was not sure global warming was a problem mankind was right to try to 'wrestle with'. Among those who publicly attacked him was Michael Rowan-Robinson, president of the Royal Astronomical Society, who called on Griffin to withdraw his views on the grounds that they were 'counter to the strong advice of the world's climate scientists, expressed through the UN Intergovernmental Panel on Climate Change' ('Nasa chief attacked over climate stance', *LabnewsOnline*, 6 July 2007).

Indeed, once such an orthodoxy has taken hold and become part of what may be called the ruling consciousness, it becomes very difficult to win financial support for any research project likely to challenge it. This was again conspicuous in the field of climate change, as when Henrik Svensmark and his Danish colleagues found it impossible to get funding for their researches until they were saved by a generous contribution from a private foundation set up by Carlsberg. Other examples of censorship through denial of funding have abounded, such as the various attempts made to stifle independent researches into the damage inflicted on human health by OPs. But most such cases, by definition, go unreported.

Perhaps the most notorious example of funding being refused, in an effort to stifle research that had come up with results unacceptable to its sponsors, was the American Cancer Society's last-minute withdrawal of support from the mammoth Enstrom and Kabat study into passive smoking. As in this case, the only organizations prepared to fund independent researchers may be those industries that see their interests being threatened. This in itself, of course, plays further into the hands of the lobbyists for the scare, because it provides them with an immediate propaganda weapon in arguing why such research can be dismissed.

Even though Enstrom and Kabat had all-but completed their study while the American Cancer Society was still footing the bill, the fact that they could only in the end get it published with financial help from the tobacco industry meant that this was used to discredit all their work over the previous 40 years. So enraged was the passive-smoking lobby by their findings that systematic attempts to discredit the two men continued for years. The American Cancer Society itself reported Enstrom to his university, UCLA, for 'scientific misconduct', posting its accusations against him on 1,000 Internet sites. In the spring of 2007 he was finally cleared on all charges, describing the relentless campaign to discredit him as 'four years of the most brutal assault you have ever seen'. He claimed that the world of academic science had now been taken over by a 'climate of "McCarthyism"'.[2]

Enstrom's experience had become only too typical. Rather than honestly debate the science, examples abounded of how the upholders of any scare orthodoxy would routinely use similar *ad hominem* tactics to discredit any expert who disagreed with them. When Ernhart and Scarrs questioned the methodology of

Needleman's lead study, they were immediately vilified as being 'in the pay of the lead industry'. When various independent scientists tried to challenge the travesty of science that was being used to demonize white asbestos, almost the only people willing to fund them were the chrysotile industries of Canada and Russia. This was at once used to discredit their findings by the anti-asbestos lobby, even though this was itself funded by law firms, trade unions and other commercial interests for whom the scare was providing such a lucrative source of income.

For the scientific profession as a whole, our modern age of scares has scarcely shown it in a very creditable light. Rarely since Trofim Lysenko became Stalin's favourite scientist for promising to double the Soviet Union's grain harvests has the energy of so many scientists been harnessed to such dubious political ends. But, again and again, in fields ranging from global warming to OPs, from lead to asbestos, there were shining exceptions: those still principled, independent-minded scientists who could not accept the officially approved line and battled on to establish a more objective under-standing of the evidence.

Many had to face every kind of professional difficulty as a result, from loss of funding to sustained personal abuse. Their claim to our respect was that they upheld the traditional disciplines of true science. They refused to be pressured into compliance with the official orthodoxy, or panicked by those shadowy and beguiling nyktomorphs.

The Role of the Media

A second group of people who make an essential contribution to promoting any successful scare are the journalists. As we have seen, the only instance in this book of a scare in which the media were willing to act predominantly as 'blockers' was when they almost unanimously poured scorn on the government's ban on T-bone steaks. In a sense this was ironic because the scare over BSE, from which this ban arose, was the one more than any which the media themselves had helped to create. If it had not been for the hysteria worked up over BSE by the media, the government would not have been panicked into unleashing the scare in the disastrously incompetent way it did in March 1996.

In general, scares are meat and drink to the media because they are sensational. In journalistic terms, bad news will almost always make better copy than good. Few things are more likely to set editors' pulses racing than the chance to chill the blood of their readers and viewers by warning of the approach of some terrifying and mysterious new threat to their health and wellbeing. It has all the psychological appeal of a real-life disaster movie. Even better if it can be associated with charges of a 'government cover-up', so that journalists can 'exclusively reveal' some alarming detail the authorities have tried to conceal from the public.

We have seen this kind of apocalyptic sensationalism reflected in the coverage of almost every scare described in these pages: from the way the arrival of avian flu in Europe was tracked night after night by television in the autumn of 2005, to the hidden menace of lead in petrol, which made daily headlines in the late 1980s; from the threat of 'killer' asbestos cement in our garage roofs to the hidden bug that in 2000 was going to immobilize half the world's computers and bring airliners crashing from the sky; from the BSE that by 2016 we were promised would have killed millions, to the drowning of half the world's cities and the death of billions in the ultimate global catastrophe, to be brought about by climate change.

Few newspapers or broadcasting stations remained immune to the temptation to jump on the scare bandwagon, but some sections of the media were even more eager to promote scares than others. In America, for instance, the counterparts of British newspapers such as the *Observer*, the *Sunday Times* and the *Daily Mail* were *Time* and *Newsweek*, always looking for scares on which they could run scarifying cover stories, from dioxins to lead, from global cooling to global warming.

Notably to the forefront in this respect was the BBC. It was a measure of the profound culture-change which had come over the BBC in recent years that, although once known for the sober and balanced authority of its reporting, there was not a single scare described in these pages it did not go out of its way to promote. A famous early instance was the time when Jeremy Paxman egged on the head of SEAC to predict that by 2005 half a million people in Britain might be dead from CJD. But no example was more blatant than the BBC's shamelessly one-sided promotion of 'LiveEarth', the series of rock concerts organized by Al Gore on 8 July 2007 in seven cities across the world to publicize his views on the 'climate crisis'.*

In the food scares of the late 1980s and 1990s, a particularly active part was played by the new breed of 'consumer affairs' and 'environmental' correspondents, for whom filing headline-worthy 'scare stories' was the easiest way to raise their own profile and win themselves more space.

To lend plausibility to their stories, of course, the journalists needed the collaboration of 'scientific experts', particularly those who could be relied on to provide some suitably extreme prediction or alarmist quote. Such figures thus played a vital role by providing the journalists with 'scientific authority'. When Professor Lacey was filmed for television, he liked to reinforce this impression by appearing in a white coat in his laboratory. But it was also noticeable how often the scientists who provided the media with their choicest comments in fact had no scientific background in the subject of the scare they were discussing.

Lacey's own work, as we saw, had been in resistance to anti-biotics, which gave him no qualification to pronounce on food-poisoning; just as the specialism of Professor Sir David King, who was later to provide many a media soundbite on global warming, was 'surface chemistry', as far removed from climatology as could be imagined. But to most of the media, so long as they had some 'man in a white coat' to lend credibility to their stories, such considerations were immaterial.

What more than anything bore out the one-sided way in which the media exploited scares was their almost universal reluctance to question the scientific claims on which any scare rested. In every instance described in this book, there were reputable experts in the field all too conscious of the fallacies in the arguments on which the scare relied. But these could be ignored because their views

---

* The BBC devoted no less than 15 hours to this event, centred on the concert staged at Wembley, in which music from an array of rock bands and celebrity pop singers was interspersed with propaganda videos for the Gore thesis. This extravaganza failed to attract anything like the 'two billion viewers' predicted by its advance publicity. In Britain the average TV audience was well under two million, and the bad language used by many of the performers led to the event being dismissed by the tabloid press as 'a foul-mouthed flop'.

contradicted the 'narrative' that the media collectively wished to promote.*

Never was this more obvious than in the years after 2004 when global warming soared to the top of the scare agenda. So unquestioning was general acceptance of the orthodoxy on climate change, particularly by the broadcast media, that when, in 2007, Channel Four for once put out a documentary critical of the orthodoxy, featuring such leading 'climate sceptics' as Professors Lindzen, Singer and Seitz, this was regarded as so unusual that the broadcast itself, as we saw, made headline news.

Equally revealing was the media's reluctance to give critical coverage to the practical consequences of any scare, even though these often created such financial, social and moral havoc. They showed, for instance, remarkably little interest in the regulatory disaster being inflicted on every kind of food business in the wake of the food scares of the late 1980s. They showed no interest in the bizarre scheme to send eight million healthy cattle up in smoke in the wake of the BSE/CJD scare, even though this had no scientific justification and cost taxpayers £3 billion.

At least in America, as we saw, one or two diligent journalists were prepared to carry out detailed investigations into the costly and corrupt scandals unleashed by the asbestos scare. But in Britain the media simply accepted at face value the claims made by those who had similarly exploited the scare to create a series of massive scams. Again led by the BBC, they showed themselves similarly gullible over the overblown claims made on behalf of wind power, when this was likewise allowed to mushroom into a commercial racket by the fear of global warming.**

---

* As exceptions to this, there were of course newspaper articles and comments expressing scepticism about any particular scare, but these were invariably presented as personal views dissenting from the generally accepted orthodoxy.

** In tirelessly promoting wind power, it was noticeable how the BBC never explained that most basic technical facts about wind turbines: their inefficiency and unreliability: the hidden subsidy system which disguised their true cost; how little electricity they generated relative to other power sources. The BBC invariably echoed the propaganda put out by the wind industry, wildly exaggerating the benefits of turbines and caricaturing opposition to them as coming only from 'nimbys' who did not want them 'spoiling the view'. Only in 2007 did Radio Four finally respond to

There was a time long ago when the British press liked to think of itself as 'the fourth estate', worthy to stand alongside the two Houses of Parliament and the Church as one of the pillars of a mature democratic society. But the media only deserve that title when they can show themselves capable of speaking with their own independent authority. This means developing sufficient expertise in a subject to be able to see it in proper perspective.

Far too often in their reporting on scares, the media failed that test. They saw their role as simply to become scaremongers themselves, publicizing and even exaggerating the claims of those promoting the scares, without subjecting them to the rigorous questioning which might have assisted their audiences and readers to arrive at a more balanced understanding. In this sense, the media had abdicated their role as serious contributors to the debate. They had preferred merely to remain part of the entertainment industry. In doing so they did more than anyone to promote the unthinking credulity that made our modern 'age of scares' possible, with all the untold damage that has set in train.

The Role of the Politicians

The part played by politicians in any scare is obviously crucial, because no scare can properly take off until the politicians in power accept the evidence for it and decide to act. This has marked the tipping point of every scare we have looked at, from the time when Currie and Dorrell unleashed the scares over salmonella and BSE, to the day in 1997 when, by agreeing the Kyoto Protocol, the governments of the world put global warming firmly onto the international agenda.

In this respect, however, the politicians are not so much acting as 'pushers' of the scare as giving way to pressure put on them by others. There are, of course, times when politicians do act as 'pushers', the most obvious example being the role played by Al Gore. As most scares develop, politicians will join the bandwagon. But, in the initial stages of a scare, the most conspicuous role we are likely to see them playing is that of 'blockers'. Part of the reason for including an account of the pesticides story in these pages was

criticism of its one-sided stance with a brief documentary admitting some of the drawbacks of wind power ('Costing the Earth', August 30 2007).

to show just how effective a government can be in blocking any attempts to bring some matter of public concern into the open when it has a strong enough vested interest in doing so.

In other examples we have looked at, governments began by trying to block a scare, but then gave in to it, thus laying themselves open to the charge of having covered it up. A classic instance was the Belgian dioxins crisis. This was the only example in this book of a scare that exploded into the middle of a general election campaign. The opposition leader, as 'pusher', was able to exploit the hysteria so effectively that he was able to oust a prime minister from office.

A real problem politicians have with scares is one they share with journalists. Much of the business of modern government has become so technical that it is often very difficult for politicians (or journalists) to get their heads round its complexities. They cannot develop an informed view of their own. Ministers under all the pressure of a scare are thus very much in the hands of their officials and advisers. If the advisers themselves have fallen under the scare's spell, it would take a minister of unusual intelligence and strength of character to be able to identify the flaws in their advice and overrule it.

Consider the examples we have looked at. Currie was a youngish junior minister, eager to make a reputation. When confronted by one of her most senior official experts on food poisoning with his fixation that the cause of the rise in salmonellosis was eggs, she had neither the intelligence nor judgement to question it. She fell for his message without even understanding it properly, making her bid for the headlines in a way that guaranteed disaster.

When Dorrell was suddenly presented by his expert advisers on BSE with their supposedly shocking new information about vCJD, he did not have the personal qualities that might have allowed him to take charge of the situation and restore a calmer perspective. He was so panicked by the hysteria raging in the media that, in effect, he abdicated his proper role, handing over responsibility for what he was to do and say to the officials.

When Tessa Jowell, again as a junior minister, was confronted by her officials with a very minor incident of *E. Coli* poisoning, they had been rendered so twitchy by the earlier *E. Coli* disaster in Scotland that they wildly over-reacted. When they suggested using emergency powers that were wholly inappropriate to the situation, she did not have sufficient strength or judgement to question it. The result was that the department got locked into its over-reaction in a way that eventually led to a tragic outcome.

The Belgian dioxins crisis was essentially manufactured out of nothing by the incompetence of two groups of officials who gave their respective ministers conflicting advice. This triggered off the panic which, by the time it hit the prime minister Dehaene in the middle of his election campaign, was so intense that the crisis was way beyond his control.

The scare over the 'Millennium Bug' was already developing momentum when in 1998 Tony Blair decided to join in, by talking it up and announcing that he was to take 'personal charge'. He saw it as a modish, 'modern' cause with which he wanted to identify himself. But since he knew nothing about computers, there was no way he could have asked enough of the right questions to avoid making a fool of himself.

When transport ministers were presented by their officials with the idea that the focus of Britain's road safety policy should be switched to the enforcing of speed limits with the aid of speed cameras, they did not seek enough alternative advice to establish whether the policy proposed by the officials might in fact have serious flaws. This left them for years afterwards helplessly trying to defend the policy, continuing to fall back on the same bogus arguments and statistics supplied by the officials who had proposed it, long after the evidence suggested that it had failed.

The decisions to ban lead in petrol and electrical products evolved so completely within the recesses of various US and European bureaucracies that by the time the politicians were called on to approve and defend them there was little they could do but parrot the justifications with which their officials had provided them. This was exemplified by the British minister who claimed, as he signed into law the regulations implementing the EU's ban on the use of lead in electronic goods, that, having 'read the regulatory impact assessment', he was satisfied that 'the benefits outweigh the costs'. Even if he had genuinely read the document, he wouldn't have had the faintest idea whether it was accurate or not (it wasn't). And, since it was EU law, he had no choice but to sign the words put in front of him anyway.

By the time the English smoking ban came to be voted through by the House of Commons, both ministers and MPs had become so carried away by the hysteria over passive smoking that scarcely anyone in the House would have known or cared that almost every statistic being quoted in support of the ban was fictitious.

Again, the legislation generated by the asbestos scare in both America and Britain was supposedly so technical that, by the time it emerged from the various technical and advisory committees to be passed into law, there was probably not a single politician on either side of the Atlantic who could have given an informed or coherent account of the science behind the new laws. The few politicians who took any interest in the subject were almost entirely propagandists for the anti-asbestos lobby. When, in Britain, Opposition spokesmen did belatedly present the government with evidence of some of the flagrant abuses that were arising from the legislation, the ministers made not the slightest attempt to investigate them. They merely handed the evidence on to the officials who had already been conniving in these abuses and who naturally therefore ignored it.

Tellingly, the only really effective and properly informed challenges to any of the scares described in this book came not from politicians but from a handful of judges sitting in courtrooms. In America there was the Appeal Court judgement that in 1991 threw out the EPA's asbestos ban, based on a meticulously argued appraisal of its costs and benefits. In 2005 there was the trenchant ruling whereby a Texas judge exposed the racket being operated by various law firms in bringing bogus compensation claims.

In Britain it was interesting that almost all cases we described where an effective challenge was made to the follies of officialdom were conducted under Scottish law by Scottish sheriffs. In the Orkney child abuse case, Sheriff Kelbie dismissed the case brought by the social workers as not credible. In the Lanark Blue case, Sheriff Allan showed a remarkable grasp of the technical issues in dismissing the scare-driven arguments put by the government's top listeria expert. In the Lanark *E. coli* inquiry, Sheriff Cox comprehensively exposed the flaws in the official system for preventing food poisoning. In Selkirk, Sheriff Patterson, again showing a grasp of the issues that few politicians could have equalled, in effect overturned the government's ban on T-bone steaks.

South of the border, where the judiciary was markedly more reluctant to challenge the official system, it is unlikely that these cases would have had a similar outcome; as was demonstrated by the Pembroke ritual abuse case, or the judgement upholding Jowell's misuse of her powers to ruin the cheesemaker James Aldridge.

The same general pattern of politicians handing responsibility to officialdom was seen over global warming. The turning point in the launching of this scare was the setting up in 1988 of the International Panel on Climate Change. This in effect allowed a small coterie of officials to play a dominant role in running the scare (albeit with input from influential political 'pushers', led, while he was US vice-president, by Gore).

Yet again the politicians had abdicated their responsibility to arrive at an informed, independent judgement of their own to a group of highly partisan technocrats, on the grounds that they were the 'experts'. As the IPCC produced its successive reports, the politicians increasingly became little more than its puppets. Their role was simply to act as cheerleaders for the scare, relying on the heavily spun data provided them by the IPCC.

In our final story, that of 'the scare that never was', the position of the politicians was similar, even though the purpose of the officials here was not to arouse public alarm but to allay it. Whenever a minister became personally concerned about the disaster being created by toxic chemicals (as several did), the officials were there to make clear to them how vital it was never to admit that the disaster had occurred. Once again, confronted with the mysterious complexities of modern government, the politicians showed how powerless they were to arrive at any independent judgement of their own. They felt they had no choice but to do their officials' bidding.

The Role of the Officials

We have seen how important was the part played by the officials even in those scares where politicians nominally appeared to be at the centre of the stage. The crises over salmonella and BSE/CJD may have been publicly associated with the names of two ministers, Currie and Dorrell. But in reality we can see how the two politicians were merely acting as 'front men'. They were being carried along by a sequence of events initiated behind the scenes by their official advisers, which neither was strong enough to question or resist.

Other scares, however, were so completely driven by the officials that the politicians did not even have a walk-on part. One
example was the 'Satanic abuse' scare. Politicians had no role in
this craze, which swept through so many social services departments in the late 1980s and early 1990s. It was the social workers
acting entirely off their own bat who initiated the mass-arrests, the
seizures of scores of children from their parents, the interrogation
techniques by which they managed to fabricate their fantastic tales
of ritual abuse and the slaughtering of babies. One of the odder
features of these episodes was how they could take place without
politicians having any control over them at all. Having handed
over to the social workers the power to act, the politicians now no
longer had the power to intervene.

This has been a common pattern in recent years. One of the
more pronounced tendencies of modern government, not just in
Britain but in the USA and the European Union in general, has been
for elected politicians to hand over regulatory powers to agencies
or other bodies of officials which are then free to operate almost
autonomously. The officials then naturally look for ways to exercise and extend their powers. This has particular relevance to the
scare dynamic, because the supposed public concern behind a scare
provides them with an ideal opportunity to justify a further
extension of their power by issuing new regulations.

We have seen a whole string of scares brought to the tipping
point in this way, with elected politicians playing virtually no part
(except subsequently to defend what the officials had done). In
several of them, for instance, a key role was played by one of the
first such autonomous bodies of officials to be set up, the US
Environmental Protection Agency.

It was the EPA, shortly after it was called into being in 1971,
which responded to the clamour from environmental campaigners
by banning the use of DDT, even though its own seven-month-long
expert inquiry had recommended against a total ban. It was the
EPA which, through the 1970s and 1980s, was looking for a way
to respond to the mounting clamour for a ban on all use of
asbestos; although, when it finally thought it had enough evidence
to justify such a ban in 1989, this was two years later overturned
by the courts on the grounds that its evidence didn't stack up.

It was the EPA which, in the 1990s, led the way, not very
successfully, in the search for evidence to justify a ban on

'environmental tobacco smoke'. It was the EPA which, in the 1970s, was quick to fasten on concern over lead in petrol and then used Needleman's evidence to justify proposing a complete ban, even though its own expert panel had found this evidence to be so flawed as to be worthless. And it was the EPA which later led the way in wanting to ban all use of lead in electronic equipment, even though a 472-page report by its own experts found that substitutes for lead would be significantly more damaging to both the environment and human health.

Another scare almost entirely manufactured by officials in this way was that over the supposed dangers of nitrate, even to the point where they had to change the scientific justification for their itch to regulate no fewer than three times.

Once some fixation has entered the collective mind of a bureaucracy, it becomes hard to eliminate. There will be officials whose status and careers have become identified with that issue. Even though their proposals may initially be rejected, they will keep on placing it on the agenda. Once the issue has entered the system like a virus, it will remain there, not least because of the inbuilt tendency of bureaucrats to protect their own backs. If ever a question has been raised over the possibility that something might represent a risk, much better to play safe by ensuring that it should be regulated or even banned altogether.

Thus does the 'precautionary principle' become elevated to such a central place in the mindset of modern government. It is this which makes officialdom such a natural potential ally to all those wishing to promote a scare. It opens up another opportunity for them to busy themselves with regulation, all of course in the cause of serving the public good, even if the problem turns out to have been imaginary.

Where a problem is real, however, but is found to have been caused by a flaw in the bureaucratic system itself, as in the case of toxic chemicals, then the precautionary principle flies out of the window. When it comes to the crunch, the prime concern of the official system is to protect its own interests, at almost any cost to truth or the interests of others.

The Role of the Lobby Groups

One of the oddest features of all the scares we have looked at was how little they directly involved the general public. Each scare was a largely self-contained drama played out between the four main groups of participants, scientists, the media, politicians and officials.

The public were merely bemused bystanders, involved only in the sense that they were treated to such obsessive coverage of scares by the media. On this basis, they might well discuss a particular scare and take a view on it. Sometimes they might be convinced that it seemed serious, as something that should concern them. But just as often people viewed scares with a considerable degree of scepticism. By and large, regardless of how much the importance and urgency of a scare was talked up by the media, it seemed fairly remote from their own lives. As we saw with the major food scares over eggs and beef, although in each case consumers initially shied away from them it was only a matter of months before sales returned more or less to normal.*

There was, however, a fifth group of participants involved in these dramas, who very much saw their role as that of representing the public interest. These were the lobby groups and 'non-governmental organizations' which played such an active part in promoting many scares. They may have done so out of a passionate sense of commitment. But they also had a strong financial interest in pushing a scare agenda, because they needed to sustain a climate of fear to attract the public donations and support on which they depended for their survival.

Never far away from the food scares, for instance, were the animal rights groups, such as Compassion in World Farming, using salmonella and BSE to highlight their opposition to factory-farming and the dehumanized methods of modern agri-business. Hundreds of millions of dollars were poured into the campaign to demonize passive smoking by rich cancer charities, supported by

---

* Despite the best efforts of the politicians and the media, a UK-wide Ipsos Mori poll in July 2007 showed that 56 per cent of the population still did not accept that there was scientific consensus on global warming. Fifty-nine per cent said they were doing nothing about it, and most of those who said they were doing something thought that recycling their rubbish was enough.

highly vocal anti-tobacco campaigning groups such as ASH. The 'anti-speed' policy, along with all its meretricious statistics, was tirelessly promoted by 'safety groups', such as BRAKE and ROSPA, the Royal Society for the Prevention of Accidents.

Few campaigning groups were more influential behind the scenes than the Ban Asbestos Secretariat, lobbying governments all round the world to make the manufacture and sale of white asbestos illegal. Their mission was supported by that strange coalition of commercial interests, including law firms and trade unions, removal contractors and the manufacturers of substitutes for asbestos, all of which stood to benefit financially from maximizing public fear and confusion over asbestos, by equating chrysotile with the amphiboles which had long since been banned.

The most influential campaigning groups of all, however, were those that originally emerged from the environmentalist movement of the 1960s and 1970s, led by the Friends of the Earth and Greenpeace. Three decades later these had become so rich and powerful as worldwide bodies that, although known as 'non-governmental organizations', they in many ways enjoyed almost official status, deferred to and even paid by governments for their advice.

The environmental lobby, of which the first heroine had been Rachel Carson, had won its first serious victory as long ago as the early 1970s, when it was largely responsible for pressuring the EPA into reversing the verdict of its own experts by banning DDT. Its most significant achievement of all, however, had been the campaign in the late 1980s to push global warming to the forefront of political attention. This culminated in those extraordinary scenes in Rio in 1992 when 20,000 'environmentalists' gathered from all over the world to cheer on the representatives of 160 governments as they signed the Framework Convention on Climate Change.

All these campaigning groups had two things in common. The first was that they were naturally convinced of the supreme importance and rightness of their cause. In this they were the modern successors to some of the 'single issue pressure groups' of earlier times, such as the Campaign for Nuclear Disarmament or the various pacifist movements which flourished between the wars.

Of course there are many different types of 'single issue pressure group', and many have played a valuable role in Western society, back to the days of the campaign to abolish slavery in the nineteenth century. In our own time, such pressure groups have continued to play an admirable part in trying to raise awareness of social wrongs or political injustices. Amnesty International in its early days was one example, or more recently Survival International, fighting on behalf of the world's oppressed indigenous peoples, such as the Amazonian Indians or the Kalahari Bushmen.

What marked out those who were in the grip of a scare, however, was the peculiarly extreme nature of their conviction not just that they were right but that anyone who disagreed with them was morally wrong. Again and again in this book we have seen the self-righteous vehemence with which they argued their case, their reckless disregard for the facts and the angry intolerance they showed towards those who failed to share their mindset.

Early in our story we saw the fanatical zeal of those young environmental health officials as they visited their 'hygiene blitz' on Britain's food businesses, closing thousands of them down for no good reason. Carried away by the idea that they were serving the holy cause of hygiene, they were quite unaware that most of them were singularly ill equipped to do anything of the kind.

We saw the way the promoters of the BSE scare liked to parade the dying victims of CJD across newspaper front pages, implying that anyone who doubted the link with eating beef must wish to see millions more reduced to the same piteous state. Frequently this was linked to charges that BSE had been caused by the unnatural practices of modern farming, such as 'feeding cattle to cattle', with the implication that CJD was the inevitable price.

We saw the petulant outbursts of the food minister Jeff Rooker, as he suggested that anyone who dared oppose his proposed bans on health shops selling B6 tablets or restaurants serving beef on the bone could only be wanting to see 'dead bodies'.

We saw the fanaticism of the anti-smoking campaigners, as they waged their holy war on the evil of 'second-hand tobacco smoke'. No words of abuse were too strong for them in castigating those still addicted to this 'filthy', 'noxious', 'disgusting', 'repulsive' habit. Fired up with the belief that they were saving the lives of millions, they were happy to quote any fictitious figures which supported their belief; but ruthless in their determination to discredit any facts which contradicted it – these could only have been put forward as propaganda by the tobacco industry, lurking in the shadows as the real villains of the piece.

We saw the fanaticism of the 'one fibre can kill' anti-asbestos campaigners, originally fired up by their desire to wreak vengeance on the powerful asbestos companies which had so shamelessly profited from knowingly exposing tens of thousands of workers to dangerous amphiboles. But over the decades this had gradually turned into something very different, where the main financial beneficiaries were those supporting the campaigners themselves. They were still eager to promote the cause by parading hapless victims, although these might now have to be carefully coached to convey the desired message: that even the slightest exposure to any form of asbestos could reduce anyone to the same tragic state, even if it was only a notice board in a classroom or a sheet of asbestos cement on their roof.

Finally we saw the fanaticism of those 'true believers' in the most cosmic cause of all: the need to save the entire planet from the evil of global warming. Again we saw how that faith could only be upheld by reckless manipulation of the scientific facts. Again we saw the vituperation that was directed at all those 'deniers' who dared question the faith, who could only be doing so because they were puppets of the corporations that profited from oil and coal.

Yet here more than in any other scare we also saw the doublethink of those who exhorted others to tread the path to salvation but only in the spirit of Shakespeare's preacher who 'reck'd not his own rede'.

At least when Noah predicted the end of the world as a punishment for human wickedness, he was consistent with his preaching in building an ark, to fill with all the creatures he hoped to save. When the prophet Gore had finished criss-crossing the world in a CO_2-emitting jet to preach the need for repentance, he then flew back to his Nashville mansion to carry on using more electricity monthly than his average fellow-American consumed in a year. But he was able to excuse himself by explaining that he would atone for his sins by buying more shares in the company he had set up to profit from the trade in 'carbon offsets'.

When it came to pious humbug, the leaders of the European Union were not far behind.

The New Puritanism

What was it about the collective psychology of modern Western society which in the closing decades of the twentieth century made it susceptible to such a rash of 'moral panics'?

This was a phrase originally coined in 1972 by the criminologist Stanley Cohen to describe the way in which the media could become censoriously obsessed by some social group whose members deviated from the norm in the way they behaved, thought and dressed. It was later widened out to include all those historical examples referred to earlier, such as the great post-Reformation witch craze or the rabid anti-Semitism of the early twentieth century, where some minority group in society became the focus of extreme fear and hostility.[3]

There is no reason why the term 'moral panic' should not be widened further to include our modern scare phenomenon, where the same combination of panic and censorious moralizing is directed not so much at social groups but at those nyktomorphic threats to society's wellbeing that become the focus of scares.

By looking at each of the scares in this book individually, we have not so far focused on how they fit together chronologically. We have seen how the modern scare phenomenon began to emerge in the 1960s, at the time of the great 'environmental awakening', when people all across the West first began to become aware in a new way of the reckless damage that humanity was inflicting on the natural world with all the arsenal of modern technology, not least through the damage to wildlife caused by toxic chemicals. In the 1970s concern began to spread to those substances that could cause damage to human health: lead and asbestos.

It was not until the late 1980s, however, that the scare phenomenon at last really took off. Suddenly, in 1987 and 1988, scares began proliferating in all directions. AIDS, salmonella and BSE, 'Satanic abuse', passive smoking, lead, asbestos, climate change: all were up and running and filling the headlines within the space of little more than twelve months.

By the late 1990s some of these scares, such as salmonella, BSE/ CJD and 'Satanic abuse', seemed to have run their course. Others, such as lead and asbestos, continued their steady advance, joined from time to time by comparatively short-lived new recruits, such as the Millennium Bug and avian flu. But eventually, by 2007, the field was dominated by the one scare that had come to overshadow them all, global warming.

What else was happening to Western society in those decades which might help to explain the sudden emergence of this susceptibility to scares, particularly at the end of the 1980s?

The first and most obvious change that had taken place, from the late 1950s onwards, was that the West had entered on a quite unprecedented period of peace and economic prosperity. In what came to be known as 'the consumer society', the majority of people were materially more comfortable than they had ever been in history. They were also more secure than they had ever been from many of the risks and dangers of the past, such as the scourge of epidemic disease.

If there was one great underlying fear which still haunted them in these years, it was one which had been with them since World War Two: the knowledge that the world was politically divided between two rival systems, each armed with weapons capable of destroying all life a hundred times over. However remote for much of the time it may have seemed, there was always the possibility that one day peace might end in the nuclear Armageddon of World War Three.

It was this fear that had given rise in the late 1950s to the nuclear disarmament movement, which continued to wax and wane for the next 30 years. In the USA, the rivalry with Communism had been brought home by the trauma of the Vietnam war, which among many Americans aroused a new distrust of their own government. Then in the late 1980s the Communist empire began to disintegrate with startling speed. Suddenly the world was no longer divided into two mighty armed camps. The greatest nightmare threat most people had ever known was no longer there.

It was not irrelevant that when, around 1988 and 1989, there was that sudden explosion of interest by campaigning groups in the new threat of global warming, many of those most actively involved, such as Friends of the Earth and Greenpeace, had previously been focused on the cause of nuclear disarmament, along with opposition to nuclear power and the dangers of nuclear waste.

Friends of the Earth was originally founded in the USA in 1969 to protest against nuclear power stations. When Greenpeace was launched by a group of US anti-war protestors two years later, their first act had been to try to halt US nuclear weapons testing on an island off Alaska. Its most famous action had been a bid to halt French nuclear tests in the Pacific in 1985, which ended in the sinking of its ship the *Rainbow Warrior* in Auckland Harbour by France's secret service.

Now that nuclear war was suddenly no longer top of the global threat list, for many idealistic campaigners the threat of climate change appeared with remarkably apt timing to take its place. The causes might be very different, but their prize was the same: the saving of the planet from the deadly follies of mankind. Look at the early years of Friends of the Earth and Greenpeace and their obsession was all with the nuclear threat. Thirty years later their websites were entirely dominated by global warming.

A third change which had come over Western society in the closing decades of the twentieth century was the gradual emergence of a new, informal but extremely powerful kind of 'progressive' consensus. As old-fashioned Socialism slipped into history, this amorphous and unlabelled new ideology had many different aspects.

The new set of values and attitudes had first begun to take shape in the student and anti-Vietnam war protests of the late 1960s and the rise of militant feminism in the 1970s. One of its key principles was 'gender equality' and all the moral strictures associated with what came to be known as 'political correctness'. It laid heavy emphasis on 'rights', particularly of those who could in any way be viewed as the targets of racial or sexual prejudice, as underdogs or as in any way 'victims', whether they were people or animals.

The adherents of the new ideology prided themselves on their concern for 'ecological issues' (even if they often didn't know very much about nature). They generally displayed hostility to big business (exemplified by the 'power of the multinationals' or 'the power of the supermarkets'). They feared the power of America (particularly when it was under a Republican president). They despised the countryside (which they identified with cruelty to animals, such as battery-chickens, cows fed on the remains of other cattle, or foxes). In general they were opposed to any beliefs, values or institutions which could be regarded as in any way 'conservative'.

A marked feature of this new mindset was the pressure it created to conform with its own values. It saw the world in rigidly moralistic terms. Although claiming to believe in toleration, it was contemptuous of anyone who did not share its own values and attitudes. Although it claimed to distrust governments, it believed strongly in the need to regulate for a fairer, safer, less polluted world. In this sense its show of concern for the general welfare played a significant part in the rise in the 1980s and 1990s of the priggish 'health and safety culture', supported by an avalanche of new regulations, which sought to create a world in which no one should be exposed to any kind of risk.

Certain sections of the media in Britain came perfectly to exemplify the attitudes of this new culture: newspapers such as the *Guardian*, the *Independent*, the *Observer*; and, as much as anyone, the BBC. It was no accident that it was these same organizations which were at the forefront of promoting every scare described in this book; because each scare in its own way, from BSE to passive smoking, from lead in petrol to global warming, could provide them with a 'narrative' which reflected their world view.

Above all, a scare could give them another emotive cause to champion, another claim to be speaking for the welfare of society as a whole against those powerful, selfish interests which simply wanted to exploit the world and turn everyone into 'victims'. It gave them yet another chance to moralize, to glory in high-minded, righteous intolerance. It gave their lives a sense of significance.

Where have we come across all this before?

The New Apocalypse

For thousands of years men and women drew the ultimate sense of purpose and significance in their lives from religion. It explained to them who they were and why they were on this earth. It taught them the difference between good and evil. It told them that evil lay in the capacity of all human beings to behave selfishly, separating them from the totality of life and existence of which we are all but fleeting expressions.

It told them that we are all divided beings. We have a material, physical existence that is only, by definition, temporary. But we have another deeper part of ourselves, which connects us with other people, with nature and with all that totality of existence of which we are part. On this selfless, spiritual level of our being we are part of eternity. But if we ignore that part of ourselves, religion told us, if we live only for ourselves on a physical plane, if we defy nature and our deeper instinctive selves, this must lead ultimately to destruction.

As many people in our secular, post-religious age have been quick to point out, religion itself led to many evils and to some of the darkest chapters in the human record. But the examples they like to cite have invariably resulted from a disintegration of the religious instinct, whereby men have projected the propensity for evil outside themselves and onto other people or groups.

In the Middle Ages it was such a projection which led the Catholic Inquisition to seek out and burn heretics. If only those 'others', possessed by the Devil, could be hunted down and slain, Christian society would be restored to wholeness. At the end of the Middle Ages, in the age of the Reformation and the Renaissance, it was an even greater collective projection that led both the Inquisition and many Protestant rulers to imagine the threat being posed to the health of their societies by witches.

When the first Protestants defied the authority of the Pope, to create their new 'reformed' churches, they did so in the belief that they were returning to the original spirit of Christianity. But, by claiming that they themselves now had the individual authority to interpret the meaning of that spirit, many of them became inflated with self-righteousness, confusing their own personal judgement with that sense of the whole they claimed to be serving.

In Britain this led in the seventeenth century to the brief rule of the Puritans, many of whom were quick to project their sense of evil onto others. Possessed by an urge to moralize, they sought to impose their own rigid, oppressive system of values on the whole of society. It was no accident that the Puritans were among the last people in England who were convinced that there were witches, seeking them out to destroy them.

When the more aggressively secular thinkers of our own time look back on all the evils committed in past ages in the name of religion, they like to believe that this was all that religion was about. If only it could be eradicated from the world, they argue, we should be finally freed from the curse of such cruel and infantile superstitions forever.

What they do not realize is that the need for religion is an instinct, programmed into the human unconscious. If it is not given its proper, selfless archetypal expression, it does not just go away and vanish. It remains buried in the deeper reaches of the psyche,

ready to shape human thinking and behaviour in all sorts of per-
verse, inferior ways.

When religion itself begins to lose its hold, its patterns of
thinking begin to reappear in secular form. G. K. Chesterton may
never have actually said 'when men cease to believe in God, they
believe not in nothing but in anything'. But the very fact that these
words have been quoted so often indicates that they are pointing to
some truth which people recognize. It is not so much that men
without religion believe in anything, as that their religious instinct
unconsciously continues to express itself in ways that echo many of
the patterns of religion, but in a secular, material context.

The most obvious example of this was what happened to Russia
when that deeply religious country was taken over by the believers
in Marx's dialectical materialism. Although Lenin's Bolsheviks
were aggressively atheist, they promptly set about creating a form
of society that in many ways was like an exact dark inversion of the
religiously ordered society it replaced.

The creed and ideology of Communism replaced those of Christianity, explaining everything from how the world began to how
individuals should lead their lives. Russia had its bearded prophets,
Marx and Lenin, whose writings were regarded as holy writ, and
whose images were displayed all over the country like secular icons.
The purpose of life was no longer to live according to the precepts of
the Church in order one day to reach some heavenly paradise. It was
to live according to the precepts of the Party, in order one day to
achieve the paradise of a Communist society on earth.

No characteristic of Communism, however, was more conspicuous than its need constantly to explain why that secular
paradise had not yet arrived, by pointing to all those enemies of the
people and the Party who were working to subvert it. Not only
were there all those capitalist enemies seeking to destroy the
Socialist world from outside, there were an endless succession of
saboteurs, wreckers and deviationists within.

Stalin's tyranny lived on inventing a constant supply of imaginary threats to the safety of the state. He and the Party institutionalized the creation of scares; all to provide the comforting
certainty that there was something out there to fear, someone to
hate and to blame, some terrifying threat which could chill the
blood of all good Communists but at the same time reinforce their
sense of moral superiority.

Communism eventually died on its feet. But so long as it and Socialism lasted, there were always pale shadows of the same ideological faith on offer in the West, ready to lend significance to the lives of their followers and co-believers with versions of the same dreams and nightmares, the same imaginary threats, the same targets for hate and blame.

The most obvious reason why these faiths faded away was that the world had moved on. In particular the Western world had moved on. It had discovered that unprecedented state of material prosperity that came about in the second half of the twentieth century. No longer did the old ideological divisions of the past seem relevant enough to generate passion. Compared with all the struggles and difficulties faced by previous generations, life in the West seemed comfortable, easy and safe, without challenges.

But those old archetypal instincts to see the world in moral terms, as a battle between good and evil, that desire for selfless causes to champion and threats to face, had not just vanished away. There was a spiritual and psychological vacuum in the life of the West. One of the ways in which that vacuum was filled was through the conjuring up of scares.

By the closing decades of the twentieth century, the prevailing values of the West were as completely secularized as those of any society the world had known. Human life was seen in almost entirely physical and material terms. No longer was the most important thing in life to preserve one's immortal soul for eternity. Society's highest value now related to bodily existence, using all the resources of science and medicine to preserve it for as long as possible.

It was no accident, therefore, that when these mysterious threats emerged in the shape of scares they took the form of threats to people's physical wellbeing. The food they ate might conceal horrific diseases. The buildings they lived and worked in might contain invisible fibres, causing long-term cancers. The air they breathed might contain toxic particles of lead or carcinogens from other people's tobacco smoke. Other mysterious diseases might be approaching from distant continents, carried by migrating birds. The computers on which the whole of Western civilization now depended might suddenly crash because of some hidden bug, causing trains to collide and airliners to fall out of the sky.

All this was enough to provide regular frissons of fear and to keep the media supplied with that succession of disaster-movie scenarios on which their journalists thrived. But none of it triggered off those deeper archetypal responses that in another, purer form had once been at the heart of the religious life of mankind.

What was quite different from all the rest was the fear of global warming. Here at last was a cosmic scenario that had found expression in almost all the religions of the world, from the Jewish legend of Noah and the Christian vision of the Apocalypse to the world-ending Ragnarok of the Norse sagas and the Teutonic *Götterdämmerung*, the twilight of the gods.

The appeal of the fear of global warming was that it fitted so neatly into the plot of a story with which everyone is familiar. Man in his selfish and reckless exploitation of the planet has committed a great and unpardonable sin, if not against God then certainly against Nature. Unless he repents and learns to mend his ways, he and all life on the planet will face unthinkable punishment. The seas will rise and flood the cities of the earth. Great storms will rage, on a scale never before known. Vast tracts of fertile land will be reduced to barren deserts. Nature itself will lie stricken before the onslaught. Billions of human beings will die.

And all this will happen very soon. The end of the world is nigh. The Last Judgement is upon us – unless we repent and mend our ways by acting on the Kyoto Protocol.

Put it like that, and at once we see opening out before us the almost unfathomable abyss of unreality into which our readiness to believe in scares has been leading us. Even within its own terms of reference, and if the predictions of the effects of global warming were all true, it is already clear that the response has shown a quite breathtaking degree of self-deception. Even if the terms of the Kyoto Protocol were all met to the letter, its most fervent advocates have been unable to deny that its effect on global temperatures would be totally insignificant.

Yet in the name of this holy cause, one part of mankind, led by the European Union, is prepared to contemplate measures (such as a reduction of CO_2 emissions by 60 per cent by 2050) which could only lead to a massive reduction in its material standards of living. Meanwhile another part of mankind, led by China, is engaged in such a headlong rush to raise its people's standards of living that this is already making the assumptions behind Kyoto look utterly nonsensical. In other words, those nations whose leaders are possessed by the scare are preparing to commit economic suicide, leaving the others to inherit the earth.*

This in itself must constitute the most bizarre collective flight from reality by any group of political leaders in history. But one has only to examine any aspect of the politicians' adoption of global warming as the greatest crisis facing mankind to see how skin-deep it is; how little they understand the implications of what they are saying; and how far they are only indulging in a series of empty gestures.

Certainly it must give those politicians a sense of extraordinary self-importance to think that they can pronounce on nothing less than the future of all life on earth and that they are the ones who can save it, sitting round a table, as did those EU heads of government in 2007, imagining that they might somehow have the power to determine that global temperatures should not be permitted to rise by more than an exact 2 degrees.

But it is these same politicians who, on other occasions, see no contradiction in boasting about how they will be taking steps to encourage their economies to grow. Like their patron saint Al Gore, as the lights blaze away in his air-conditioned mansion, they present perfect examples of those two age-old human weaknesses familiar to all religions: overweening pride and unwitting hypocrisy.

Even all this political charade, however, is dependent on the extraordinary act of collective will which was required to elevate a belief in man-made global warming into the orthodoxy of the time in the first place. We have seen something of that reign of terror that was imposed on the community of science to provide the necessary theological underpinning for this belief; how shamelessly

---

* Just coming to the fore as this book was going to press were the astonishing implications of the EU's decision, in January 2007, that by 2020 10 per cent of its transport fuel must be derived from 'biofuels'. The major source of this would be wheat. For the UK alone to meet this target would require it to grow 14 million tonnes of wheat a year. Its current production (2006) was 11 million tonnes. Not only would its entire existing production therefore have to be diverted to biofuels, it would have to import an additional 3 million tonnes for fuel, leaving it with no wheat for food use. Since there was already in 2006/7 a global wheat deficit, the additional demand on wheat for biofuels would predictably send prices through the roof. This was economic madness of the highest order.

the evidence had to be manipulated; how ruthlessly the non-believers had to be anathematized as heretics; all to maintain the illusion that the orthodoxy was now supported by a 'scientific consensus'.

This in itself recalls not just the enforcement of earlier scientific 'orthodoxies' by the totalitarian regimes of the twentieth century, but also the efforts of the Church to enforce its own orthodoxy over Galileo, when at the dawn of the modern age, he came up with a view of the relationship of the earth to the sun so heretical that it had to be suppressed at all cost.

There is, however, one enormous difference between a religion of the spirit and those quasi-religious belief systems that seek only to explain the secular world. Sooner or later, the claims of the secular religions can always be put to the test of hard evidence. Communism in the end collapsed not least because history proved it wrong. All its vainglorious claims over the decades could eventually be seen to have been based on lies.

The same is the case with scares. However plausible they may seem for a time, eventually the evidence piles up to show that they have been based on some fundamental misreading of the facts. This has already proved true of most of the scares described earlier in this book; and if some of the later ones still exercise their spell and remain widely accepted, the scientific evidence on which they were based now looks increasingly shaky.

Of none is this truer than the predictions of global warming. Despite all the frenzied insistence that the scientific evidence on which it is based is unassailable, that evidence itself, however flawed much of it can already be seen to be, will have to remain consistent. There were already scientists in 2007 predicting the possibility that the warming of the late twentieth century on which the whole panic was based is likely in due course to go into reverse, and that we might return to a period of global cooling. If, sometime in the next few years, we find that temperatures are not rising nor even staying flat, but falling, the whole belief-system on which the fear of global warming is based will begin to come crumbling down.

So much political and economic capital is now being invested in the conviction that this act of faith is true that it would take years before the politicians, scientists and businessmen were prepared to acknowledge that fact. But a collective act of faith is what they rest on, and, unlike a belief in God, it is one which the evidence can ultimately refute. If it does so, we can at least take comfort from knowing that this was by far the greatest scare of all, and that with it one of the more extraordinary chapters in the psychological evolution of mankind has come to an end.

The likelihood is that the century just begun will sooner or later confront the human race with many other genuine challenges, some probably as great as any it has ever faced before. Some of these will result from the pressures created by over-population and man's over-exploitation of the resources of the planet. Others will result simply from his continuing inability to resolve conflicts between one group of human beings and another, based on irreconcilable differences of race and religion.

Almost certainly some of the most fearful crises that lie ahead will arise from that moment when, after many decades of uneasy peace enforced by the shadow of the hydrogen bomb, the world finally sees the stupendous power of nuclear weapons beginning to escape out of the political control that since 1945 has held it in check.

When those real crises come upon us, people will look back on the closing decades of the twentieth century, and the early years of the twenty-first, as a time of unnatural peace, prosperity, security and ease. They may even see it as a time when Western society grew so comfortable and soft that it had to invent a whole succession of imaginary scares to feed its need for sensation and a sense of significance.

When the real crises come, there will be little time for imaginary scares. We shall be back living, very uncomfortably, in the real world.

Notes

1. H. Trevor-Roper, *The European Witch-Craze of the Sixteenth and Seventeenth Centuries* (Penguin Books, 1969).
2. Taken from an unpublished article written for the *Observer* by John Dodd, based on an interview with Professor Enstrom, July 2007.
3. S. Cohen, *Folk Devils and Moral Panics* (MacGibbon and Kee, 1972).

Index